YOUTH CRIMINAL
JUSTICE LAW

ESSENTIALS OF
CANADIAN LAW

YOUTH CRIMINAL JUSTICE LAW

NICHOLAS BALA

Professor of Law
Queen's University

YOUTH CRIMINAL JUSTICE LAW
© Irwin Law Inc., 2003

Published in 2003 by

Irwin Law
14 Duncan Street
Suite 206
Toronto, Ontario
M5H 3G8

ISBN 1-55221-057-X

National Library of Canada Cataloguing in Publication Data

Bala, Nicholas, 1952–
 Youth criminal justice law / Nicholas Bala.

(Essentials of Canadian law)
Includes index.
ISBN 1-55221-057-X

 1. Canada. Youth Criminal Justice Act. 2. Juvenile justice, Administration of — Canada. I. Title. II. Series.

KE9445.A323B34 2002 345.71'08 C2002-904750-1
KF9780.ZA2B34 2002

The Publisher acknowledges the financial support of the Government of Canada through the Book Publishing Industry Development Program (BPIDP) for our publishing activities.

Printed and bound in Canada

 2 3 4 5 07 06

SUMMARY
TABLE OF CONTENTS

DETAILED
TABLE OF CONTENTS

FOREWORD

Professor Bala's *Youth Criminal Justice Law* will be an invaluable addition to the library of anyone working or studying in the youth justice field. It is a timely publication, focusing on Canada's new *Youth Criminal Justice Act*, which replaces the *Young Offenders Act*. The new legislation is more complex than its predecessor, and introduces new principles and policies that will significantly alter practice and procedure in Canada's youth justice system. This book identifies and explains the significant changes to the laws governing procedure, evidence, and sentencing. Abundant references to recent court cases, relevant articles — including many from related disciplines — and critical commentary can be found in every chapter. As a result, it will be indispensable to lawyers and judges, but also to probation officers, youth workers, and other youth justice professionals.

A leading authority with an international reputation in children's law and youth justice, Professor Bala is the author of a number of books and many articles in journals of law, sociology, psychology, and medicine. All levels of court in Canada frequently cite his work. And as his experience and expertise extend beyond law, he is able to explain adolescent offending behaviour, children's evidence, and other aspects of the *Youth Criminal Justice Act* from a broader social and psychological perspective.

Youth Criminal Justice Law, as a professional text, is exceptional. Professor Bala draws on his skill as an award-winning educator and effective communicator to translate complex legislation and difficult issues into language that is easy to read and understand.

Heino Lilles
Chief Judge
Territorial Court of Yukon

PREFACE

The way in which the justice system responds to young persons who violate the criminal law is profoundly significant, not only for those who are directly involved in the process but also for society as a whole. A society's response to young offenders conveys important messages about its attitudes to youth and has significant implications for its future. This book is intended to give lawyers, judges, probation officers, and other justice system professionals an introduction to the law governing young people who come into conflict with the law, with a particular focus on Canada's new *Youth Criminal Justice Act*. The book is also written for students in law schools, criminology programs, and other related disciplines.

The field of youth justice law is an important, controversial area that is undergoing major reform with the enactment of the new *Youth Criminal Justice Act*, which is to come into force on 1 April 2003, replacing the *Young Offenders Act* of 1984. The new statute is a complex piece of legislation that changes many of the principles and specific rules that govern youth justice issues. Although the new Act has a significantly different philosophy from that of the *Young Offenders Act* and many different provisions, some portions of the old Act have been incorporated into the *Youth Criminal Justice Act*.

This book focuses on the new Act, although many issues can best be understood by considering how the former statute was applied and interpreted. In significant measure the new Act is a response to some of the failings of the old one, and the *Youth Criminal Justice Act* can best be understood as a response to problems that arose under the *Young Offenders Act*.

While the primary focus of this book is on the legal issues that arise in the youth justice system, the book is premised on the belief that youth justice issues must be understood in a broader context. This book includes some discussion of constitutional, evidentiary, and procedural issues that are relevant to youth justice, and explores some of the ethical and practical issues that confront lawyers and other professionals working in the youth justice system. The book also considers

the broader social and political context for issues of adolescent offending and youth justice.

While law students and those with legal training comprise a primary audience for this book, this work should also be a useful text for
probation officers, social workers, mental-health professionals, and
teachers who work with young offenders, as well as for university and
college students and others with an interest in youth justice issues.

Chapters 1 to 3 of this book serve to introduce essential background. Chapter 1 introduces the youth justice system and discusses
the rationale and history for the system. The chapter considers the context in which the new *Youth Criminal Justice Act* was introduced and
offers an introduction to the problem of youth crime in Canada.
Chapter 2 discusses the principles that guide responses to youth crime;
the main focus is on the explicit Declaration of Principle found in
Canada's youth justice legislation. Some consideration is also given to
the *United Nations Convention on the Rights of the Child* and to the principles that apply in other countries, so that readers can appreciate the
choices that have been made in this country. Chapter 3 explains the
jurisdiction of the youth justice court, including the controversial
issues related to age jurisdiction.

Chapters 4 to 9 provide a more detailed discussion of the salient
issues that arise in the course of the youth justice process in Canada.
Chapter 4 considers the arrest, police questioning, pre-trial detention,
and other issues related to the apprehension of a young person and the
first appearance in court. This chapter includes a discussion of how the
police and court system relate to school authorities, as this is a setting
in which many young persons are apprehended. Chapter 5 describes
the range of alternatives for the diversion of young persons, especially
those facing less serious charges, from the formal youth justice court
process, to be dealt with informally or by various forms of extrajudicial
programs. These alternatives to the youth court system have received
increased emphasis in the *Youth Criminal Justice Act*. Chapter 6 deals
with access of young persons to legal services and the controversies
around the role of lawyers in the youth justice system. Chapter 7 discusses youth justice court trials, including the restrictions on disclosure of information and on the publication of identifying information
about youths involved in the justice system. Chapter 8 deals with the
sentencing of young offenders, including issues related to custodial
placements and the judicial control over youths in the corrections system. Chapter 9 discusses how the most serious cases are dealt with,
those where there may be an adult sentence.

While law reform is not a major theme of this book, an effort is made to offer some suggestions on how to improve Canada's responses to youth crime, in particular in Chapter 10, in the context of a discussion that recognizes the limits of the law as a solution to the universal human problem of adolescent deviance and delinquency.

This book provides an introduction to a set of complex, interdisciplinary topics that can be the subject of lifelong study. While there are many references to jurisprudence and secondary legal literature, this book does not purport to be a comprehensive legal research tool. Those who may be dealing with some of the complex legal issues that may arise in the interpretation of the *Youth Criminal Justice Act*, including lawyers, judges, and law students, may find a useful introduction in this text, but will also want to consult the case law and specialized legal texts or data bases. Non-lawyers with specific legal problems should get appropriate legal advice. Readers are also encouraged to study the growing body of non-legal literature that deals with youth crime and the youth justice system. Some of the important literature in this area is written by criminologists and psychologists; there is also an increasing amount of research by scholars and practitioners taking a critical perspective, including works by feminists, Aboriginal writers, and by those who have had personal experiences with the youth justice system.

This book is being written prior to the new *Youth Criminal Justice Act* coming into force, with the aim of assisting professionals in dealing with a very complex piece of new legislation, as well as providing students with an understanding of the youth justice system. Some of the discussion has a speculative aspect as the actual implementation of the new law will depend on how judges and governments deal with it, but I hope that the book will be useful during the first few years that the new Act is in force. Readers are cautioned that the introduction of the new law will make this a dynamic field, and case law and legislation are always subject to change. However, the principles and fundamental issues related to responding to youth crime in Canada are unlikely to change dramatically in the next few years. Those with specific legal problems should check for recent legal developments.

The book focuses on matters which make the youth justice system distinctive from the adult system. Readers looking for a detailed discussion of the principles of substantive, procedural, and evidentiary criminal law that are applicable to both adult and youth proceedings will have to consult other books in the Irwin *Essentials of Canadian Law* series or to other sources.

I want to acknowledge those who helped me complete this book. I especially wish to thank law students Rebecca Jaremko Bromwich

(Queen's LL.M. 2002) and Annelise Saunders (Queen's LL.B. 2003), for their research and editorial assistance, and Chief Judge Heino Lilles of the Yukon Territorial Court for writing the Foreword to the book. I am also very grateful to Professor Sanjeev Anand of the University of Alberta who reviewed the entire manuscript and co-authored Chapter 10. I also want to acknowledge that I learned much about the new Act from listening to the discussion and debates at the Youth Justice Education Committee of the National Judicial Institute, and I wish to thank all of the members of that Committee, especially Dick Barnhorst, who faithfully answered my queries about the Act. I also wish to acknowledge the support and advice throughout this project of Professor Don Stuart, my colleague at Queen's University, and of Jeff Miller, Publisher of Irwin Law Inc. Finally, I would like to thank Emily Bala for her careful proofreading and editing of the final page proofs of this book

Some parts of my 1997 text for Irwin Law Inc. on *Young Offenders Law* have been incorporated into this new book. The preparation of the manuscript for this book was assisted by a grant from the Social Sciences and Humanities Research Council of Canada.

Nicholas Bala
September 2002

CHAPTER 1

RESPONDING TO YOUTH CRIME IN CANADA

A. ADOLESCENCE AND THE RATIONALES FOR A YOUTH JUSTICE SYSTEM

Every legal system recognizes that children and youths are different from adults and should not be held accountable for violations of the criminal law in the same fashion as adults. There are, though, very substantial differences in how countries give effect to this principle and in how they define such concepts as "youth" and "child." In Canada, the nature of the special legal treatment for youth has dramatically evolved over the course of history and remains controversial today. But there is widespread recognition that children and adolescents — having special needs and limited capacities — require distinctive, or at least separate, treatment from adults.

When children are born, they have no physical, moral, or social capacities. Although newborns have legal rights (for example, to inherit property) and are entitled to the protection of the law, these legal rights can be exercised only through a legal guardian or other adult. As children mature, they gradually gain physical strength, intellectual judgment, and social maturity, and can begin to exercise legal rights and assume legal obligations on their own. By the time legal adulthood is reached (currently at the age of eighteen in most provinces in Canada), a person generally has a full range of legal rights and obligations.

By the beginning of adolescence, about the age of twelve, youths display a growing social, intellectual, moral, and sexual awareness, as well as increasing physical size and strength. While for many youths, physical growth ends at about the age of fifteen, adolescents continue to mature intellectually, neurologically, psychologically, and socially until adulthood. Indeed, attitudes, values, and behaviour change over the course of adult life as well. Adolescence is a time of great change and development, as parents, teachers, and youth themselves know. Sometimes adolescents seem quite childish, while at other times they act like adults or at least want to be treated like adults. Adolescence is a period of growing self-awareness and increasing autonomy. It is a period of life when challenging authority figures and testing limits become very important. Adolescents tend to want new challenges and excitement, to be more concerned about immediate consequences rather than with their long-term well-being. They are also more susceptible to peer pressure than adults. While adolescents are accumulating knowledge of the world around them, they often lack judgment and maturity. Frequently, they feel as though they are "invulnerable," and act in an impulsive and irresponsible fashion.

In far greater numbers than adults, adolescents engage in high-risk activities, such as unsafe sex, drunken driving, substance abuse, and violent behaviour.[1] Adolescence is often characterized by feelings of alienation from parents, teachers, and society as a whole, with a greater willingness to test social norms and conventions, as well as a greater propensity to engage in offending behaviour. Adolescence is also a time when, for some individuals, feelings of depression may peak, when there is a high risk of suicide and self-destructive behaviour. While there are very substantial differences among countries in types and levels of crime and deviant behaviour, in all modern societies the rates of violent and antisocial behaviour peak in late adolescence and early adulthood — between the ages of fifteen and twenty-one — reflecting

---

1   On the relatively high rate of depression, smoking, drug use, and engaging in unsafe sex practices by Canadian adolescents, see Health Canada, *Toward a Healthy Future: Second Report on the Health of Canadians* (Ottawa: Ministry of Supply and Services, 1999) available online at time of publishing at <www.hc-sc.gc.ca>. The American psychologist William Damon points out that, "even more than in the past, peer groups are highly significant for today's adolescents: as a group, they lead lives that are more adult-free than those of previous generations. This generation has spent more time on their own than any other in recent history. . . . Teens are isolated to an extent that has never been possible before" ("A World of their Own," *Newsweek*, April 30, 2000).

the immaturity and lack of judgment of this period, as well as its energy and search for excitement.

Canadian law recognizes three distinct stages of criminal accountability. Childhood, lasting to the age of twelve, is without criminal liability. Youth, from twelve through seventeen years of age — a period corresponding roughly to adolescence — is a stage of life with limited accountability under the *Youth Criminal Justice Act*.[2] Legal adulthood, starting at eighteen years, requires full legal accountability as well as providing a full set of adult rights. The rationale for this distinctive age-based treatment can be found in the basic premises of criminal law and in the nature of childhood and adolescence as distinct periods of life.[3] The fundamental criminal law concept of moral accountability and the policy objectives of achieving social protection through deterrence of crime and rehabilitation apply differently to children and youth than to adults, because children and youth are different from adults.

A central premise of criminal law is that individuals are held accountable for their acts only if they have a requisite degree of moral culpability or responsibility, often known as *mens rea* (the guilty mind). Therefore, a person who kills another by accident, such as the driver who runs over someone darting in front of her vehicle, may have no criminal accountability. A person who commits a wrongful act while sleepwalking — even a very serious offence such as killing another person[4] — must be acquitted because of the lack of intent to do harm. Those who commit criminal acts while suffering from a mental disorder that renders them "incapable of appreciating the nature and quality" of their acts are not criminally responsible for their acts, although they may be confined to protect the public or themselves.[5] Because of the lack of capacity at the time of the offence, they are not criminally accountable; if they later recover their mental capacity, they must be released, even if they have committed very serious wrongful acts.

Similarly, the *Youth Criminal Justice Act* is premised on a recognition that to be a youth is to be in a state of "diminished responsibility" in a

---

2   *Youth Criminal Justice Act*, S.C. 2002, c. 1 (royal assent February 19, 2002, to come into force April 1, 2003), often referred to in this book as the *YCJA*. The *YCJA* repeals and replaces the *Young Offenders Act* (*YOA*), below note 23, which also had an age jurisdiction of twelve through to the eighteenth birthday.

3   Some commentators and politicians argue that adolescence is not sufficiently different from adulthood to justify distinct legal treatment: see, for example, S.J. Morse, "Immaturity and Irresponsibility" (1998) 88 J. of Criminal Law and Criminology 15.

4   *R. v. Parks*, [1992] 2 S.C.R. 871.

5   *Criminal Code*, R.S.C. 1985, c. C-46, s. 16.

moral and intellectual sense. Adolescents, and even more so children, lack a fully developed adult sense of moral judgment. Adolescents also lack the intellectual capacity to appreciate fully the consequences of their acts. In many contexts, youths will act without foresight or self-awareness, and they may lack empathy for those who may be the victims of their wrongful acts.[6] Youths who are apprehended and asked why they committed a crime most frequently respond: "I don't know." Because of their lack of judgment and foresight,[7] youths also tend to be poor criminals and, at least in comparison to adults, are relatively easy to apprehend. Youths who commit horrible murders often boast of their misdeeds to their friends, even taking their friends to see the body of the victim, making their arrest virtually inevitable. This is not to argue that adolescent offenders should not be morally or legally accountable for their criminal acts, but only that their accountability should, in general, be more limited than is the case for adults.

An important function of the criminal justice system is the protection of society through deterrence of potential offenders: young people may resist the impulse to commit crimes for fear of being caught and punished. Because youth, especially those who are prone to committing offences, generally have less foresight and judgment than adults, the deterrent effect of the youth justice system is much weaker than that of the criminal justice system for adults. Although improved policing, thereby increasing the chances of catching offenders, can have a deterrent effect on youth crime, increasing the severity of sanctions — that is, increasing the consequences of getting caught — appears to have no impact on youth crime.[8] This is not to argue that there should be no consequences for youths who commit criminal offences, but that there should be no expectation that social protection can be increased by imposing more severe punishments on young offenders.

---

6   See, for example, E. Cauffman and L. Steinberg, "(Im)maturity of Judgement in Adolescence: Why Adolescents May Be Less Culpable than Adults" (2000) 18 Behavioural Sciences and the Law 731–60.

7   Courts dealing with tort cases (civil actions for monetary damages as a result of negligence) have also ruled that teenagers should not be held to an adult standard of care, with the reasonableness of their conduct assessed in light of their age and experience: *Nespolon v. Alford* (1998), 40 O.R. (3d) 355 (Ont. C.A.)

8   See, for example, A.N. Doob, V. Marinos, and K.N. Varma, *Youth Crime and the Youth Justice System in Canada: A Research Perspective* (Toronto: University of Toronto, Centre of Criminology, 1995) at 56–71.

A further rationale for having a separate youth justice system is that adolescents generally lack the judgment and knowledge to participate effectively in the court process and may be more vulnerable than adults. This justifies having a special court with legal rules and procedures that protect the rights of youth and attempt to ensure their meaningful participation in the legal process.

Historically, the prime rationale for establishing a youth justice system that was separate from the adult system was the belief that youths are more vulnerable than adults as well as more amenable to rehabilitation. Long-term social protection can best be achieved by concentrating resources on their rehabilitation and by protecting them from the full glare of public accountability. At the very least, concerns about the corruption or abuse of children and youth placed in correctional facilities with adult offenders offer justification for their separate confinement. However, concerns about the special needs and rehabilitation of youth do not necessarily translate into more lenient treatment. At times in Canada's legal history, a desire to promote rehabilitation formed the basis for a more intrusive approach or longer periods in a custody facility than an adult might receive for the same offence, albeit the youth custody facility was separate from those used for adults with more emphasis on the provision of rehabilitative and educational services. The rationale for a longer sentence was that the youth needed the benefit of a longer period in a rehabilitative environment or a longer period away from a corrupting situation at home.

The *Youth Criminal Justice Act*, however, provides that a youth should not receive a greater punishment than an adult convicted of the same offence in similar circumstances;[9] in most cases a concern with rehabilitation and the principle of limited youth accountability will result in a less serious sanction.[10] The *Youth Criminal Justice Act* makes clear that youth court sentences are not to be a vehicle for imposing mental health or other treatment services if this type of response is more intrusive than warranted by the offence and the record of the youth. While one must not imagine that all young offenders want to be or can be rehabilitated, the rehabilitative ideal remains an important rationale for having a distinct youth justice system.

---

9 *YCJA*, above note 2, s. 38(2)(a).

10 Principles of youth justice court sentencing, found in the *YCJA*, above note 2, ss. 3 and 38, are discussed in Chapters 2 and 8.

B. THE HISTORY OF CANADA'S YOUTH JUSTICE SYSTEM

Prior to the nineteenth century there was little legal recognition of the special needs of children and youth. Children might be subjected to harsh discipline by parents and employers. Except among the upper classes, by the age of seven, children were expected to work along with adults on farms, in mines, and in trade shops. Only upper-class children would receive any schooling, with an emphasis on the education of boys. While youths had few civil or property rights until the age of twenty-one, criminal liability started at the age of seven, and children convicted of criminal offences were subjected to the same punishments as adults, including hanging for such offences as theft. Children under seven were considered to be "under the age of discretion" and were not criminally accountable under the English common law, which also came to be applied in Canada. By the seventeenth century it was established that a child between the ages of seven and fourteen could raise a defence of *doli incapax* (incapacity to do wrong) and would have criminal immunity, if it were not proven that the child had the capacity to understand the "nature and consequences of his acts and to appreciate that it was wrong."[11]

The nineteenth century saw a growing understanding of the nature and significance of childhood, with the beginnings of the modern disciplines of psychology and psychiatry. In England, the United States, and Canada, social reform movements aimed at improving the lives of children were loosely linked to the movements to abolish slavery and, later, to gain the vote for women. Legislation was enacted to prohibit child labour in mines and factories. Publicly funded education was introduced and child-welfare agencies were established to care for homeless and orphaned children. In the latter part of the nineteenth century the positivist approach to criminology came into prominence, premised on the belief that children and adolescents engage in criminal behaviour as a result of such external influences as poverty, family breakdown, and lack of education, and that with appropriate social intervention, these youthful offenders could be saved from a life of crime. In 1857 the first Canadian legislation was enacted to separate child and adolescent offenders from adults, placing them in training schools or reformatories rather than adult penitentiaries. Initial steps

---

11   See S.S. Anand, "Catalyst for Change: The History of Canadian Juvenile Justice Reform" (1998) 24 Queen's L.J. 515.

were taken for community-based alternatives to incarceration for youthful offenders, and the first probation officers specifically for juveniles began to work with them. In 1899 the first court to deal with youthful offenders in a special judicial setting separate from adults was established in Chicago.

1) The *Juvenile Delinquents Act*

In Canada, reformers persuaded Parliament to enact the *Juvenile Delinquents Act* in 1908.[12] This Act created a juvenile justice and corrections system with a welfare-oriented philosophy based on positivist criminology and a distinct *parens patriae* (parent of the country) philosophy. This approach reflected the belief that there was little need to distinguish between juveniles who were offenders and those who were abandoned or neglected by parents. One of the principal drafters of the *Juvenile Delinquents Act*, W.L. Scott, explained the philosophy of the Act:

> There should be no hard and fast distinction between neglected and delinquent children. All should be recognized as in the same class and should be dealt with a view to serving the best interests of the child. . . . The spirit of the court is always that of a wise and kind, though firm and stern, father. The question is not "What has this child done?" but "How can this child be saved?"[13]

Under the *Juvenile Delinquents Act*, children could be subjected to "delinquency proceedings" for violating any federal, provincial, or municipal law, or for the status offence of "sexual immorality or any similar form of vice." Although "sexual immorality" was not an offence for adults, it was felt that the well-being of children who engaged in this type of behaviour could be promoted, if they were subjected to the jurisdiction of a juvenile court and thereby obtained apparently appropriate treatment.

The philosophy that society should promote the welfare of youth was reflected in provisions of the *Juvenile Delinquents Act* and in provincial laws that dealt in similar ways with both delinquents and children in need of protection. Generally, youths were processed through the same courts and often placed in the same facilities whether they were delinquent or in need of protection. Most provinces allowed children to

---

12 *Juvenile Delinquents Act*, enacted as S.C. 1908, c. 40; subject to minor amendments over the years, finally as *Juvenile Delinquents Act*, R.S.C. 1970, c. J–3.

13 Scott, quoted in O. Archambault, "*Young Offenders Act*: Philosophy and Principles" (1983) 7:2 Prov. Judges J. 1 at 2–3.

be committed to training school for truancy and such vague offences as "unmanageability." The original courts for juveniles operated very informally with the intention to ensure that "unnecessary technicalities" would not interfere with or delay the treatment considered to be in each child's best interests.

The *Juvenile Delinquents Act* specified that no action of a juvenile court was to be set aside because of any "informality or irregularity where it [appeared] that the disposition of the case was in the best interests of the child." Even though most of the judges in the original juvenile courts had no legal training and lawyers rarely appeared, the *Juvenile Delinquents Act* restricted rights of appeal to courts presided over by legally trained judges.[14] The Act required judges to treat a delinquent "as far as practicable . . . not as criminal, but as a misdirected and misguided child . . . needing aid, encouragement, help and assistance."[15] This philosophy was reflected in indeterminate custodial sentencing. If a delinquent was ordered by a juvenile court judge to be confined in a training school, the youth would be released only when correctional officials for juveniles determined that this was consistent with the "best interests" of the youth. There were broad powers to return a youth who was released back to training school until the juvenile became an adult, at that time the age of twenty-one.

The *Juvenile Delinquents Act* and the justice system for youths that it created were an enormous improvement over the harsh treatment inflicted on children and adolescents in the nineteenth century. Even today that Act's child-oriented philosophy has appealing aspects. Yet it must also be recognized that the Act was often applied in an arbitrary or discriminatory fashion. Youths from "good families" who committed quite serious offences might be returned to the care of their middle-class parents, while children from lower-income, Aboriginal, or immigrant families could serve long periods in training school for quite minor offences. These decisions would have been considered to be in the "best interests" of the youths by judges, most of whom were white, male, and middle class. Female adolescents were often sent to training school for the vaguely worded status offence of "sexual immorality." In practice, this offence was used almost exclusively against girls, typically those from socially disadvantaged backgrounds and racial minority groups.[16]

---

14   *Juvenile Delinquents Act*, above note 12, ss. 7 and 37.

15   *Juvenile Delinquents Act*, above note 12, s. 38.

16   S. Barnhorst, "Female Delinquency and the Role of Women" (1978) 1 Can J. Fam. L. 254; and C. Strange, *Toronto's Girl Problem: The Perils and Pleasures of the City, 1880–1930* (Toronto: University of Toronto Press, 1995).

While training schools in theory promoted the "best interests" of their residents, these often harsh environments subjected many youths to physical and sexual abuse by staff.[17] Tragically, this reality did not begin to become publicly known until the 1980s when former inmates of juvenile facilities — many of them emotionally scarred adults — started to come forward to disclose the abuse they had experienced decades earlier as adolescents in the care of the state. Today, abuse in youth corrections facilities continues to be a serious concern, although increased government supervision and improved access to advocates for young inmates have resulted in less abuse by correctional staff. In contrast to the high level of political and media attention to youth justice issues at present, the original enactment of the *Juvenile Delinquents Act* in 1908 received scant public attention and only ten minutes of Parliamentary debate.

For the first half of the twentieth century there was relatively little public concern about the legal responses to youth crime.[18] By the 1960s the *Juvenile Delinquents Act* was coming under growing scrutiny and attack. More legally trained judges and an increasing number of lawyers were appearing in juvenile courts. The informality and lack of legal rights for youths were being challenged, especially since the *Juvenile Delinquents Act* created a highly discretionary regime which gave judges, police, and juvenile correctional officials broad powers to deal with individual youths in accordance with their own perceptions about each child's "best interests." Too often, and perhaps inevitably, the discretionary "best interests" standard seemed to reflect the values and biases of individual officials. A further concern was expressed that the *Juvenile Delinquents Act* allowed for substantial interprovincial variation in how juveniles were treated. This was most obvious in regard to age jurisdiction: the minimum age of juvenile court jurisdiction by province varied from seven to fourteen years of age, and the maximum age ranged from fifteen to seventeen years. There were also substantial disparities in access to legal services, in the degree of respect for legal rights, in the use of diversion from juvenile court, and in the use of custodial sentences for juveniles.

By the 1960s fundamental questions were being raised about the welfare-oriented philosophy underlying the *Juvenile Delinquents Act*.

---

17   There have recently been public inquiries, as well as civil suits and criminal prosecutions against staff at many of the juvenile institutions as a result of abuse in the period from 1940 to 1980: see R. Bessner, *Institutional Child Abuse in Canada* (Ottawa: Law Commission of Canada, 1998).

18   S.S. Anand, "Catalyst for Change: The History of Canadian Juvenile Justice Reform" (1999) 24 Queen's L.J. 515.

While there was acceptance of the importance of promoting the well-being of juveniles, there was a growing controversy about whether this should be the *only* principle guiding the societal response to juvenile offenders. A number of critics challenged the rehabilitative ideal, pointing out that many delinquents were not being rehabilitated by the juvenile justice system. In addition to problems of abuse by staff in some juvenile correctional institutions, many youths, even in well-run facilities, were not being rehabilitated and reoffended after their release.[19]

Critics of the *Juvenile Delinquents Act* argued that the protection of the public and the accountability of offenders are as important as rehabilitation — perhaps even more important. Indeed, it was apparent that, while the Act, as it was written, focused on the best interests of juveniles, in practice judges were not focusing exclusively on the interests of children. In fact, concerns about social protection and accountability were often reflected in sentencing decisions under the Act; this was most apparent in decisions about transfer to adult court, which was to occur only if both the "*good of the child* and the interest of the community *demand* it" [emphasis added].[20] On its face, this standard for transfer would seem to be almost impossible to meet, especially in murder cases where a juvenile might face capital punishment after transfer. Judges nevertheless regularly persuaded themselves that the "good of the child" demanded the possibility of facing hanging rather than the much more lenient juvenile sentence.[21] While these transfer decisions may have been socially justifiable, it was appropriate to rewrite the law to acknowledge frankly that the interests of the youth was not the dominant factor considered in making a decision about transfer.

2) The *Young Offenders Act*

The deficiencies of the *Juvenile Delinquents Act* were becoming clear by the mid-1960s. Youth justice reform, however, was not a priority of the federal government, especially in the face of controversy among different provincial governments and various advocacy groups about the best approaches. The release of the federally commissioned report, *Juvenile*

---

19   See, for example, S. Shamsie, "Anti-Social Adolescents: Our Treatments Do Not Work — Where Do We Go From Here?" (1981) 26 Can. J. Psychiatry 357.

20   *Juvenile Delinquents Act*, above note 12, s. 9(1).

21   See, for example, *R. v. Truscott*, [1959] O.W.N. 320 (H.C.J.): "it would be for the good of the child to have his position in respect of such a serious charge established by a jury which would remove any possible criticism of having such a serious matter determined by a single [Juvenile Court] judge in *in camera* proceedings" (at 321).

Delinquency in Canada,[22] in 1965 began a lengthy period of debate and gradual reform. By the 1970s some provinces, most notably Quebec, took steps to change their juvenile justice system by, for example, ensuring that youths had access to lawyers. Other provinces continued to maintain informal juvenile courts with little recognition of legal rights. At the federal level, discussion papers and draft legislation were released and commented on; it was not until February 1981 that the bill which would finally be enacted as the *Young Offenders Act* was tabled in Parliament.[23]

A strong impetus to federal action was the constitutional entrenchment of the *Canadian Charter of Rights and Freedoms* in 1982. The informality and lack of legal rights for youths in the *Juvenile Delinquents Act* were inconsistent with the legal protections recognized in the *Charter*, while the interprovincial variation allowed by the *Juvenile Delinquents Act* appeared inconsistent with the equal protection of the law guaranteed by section 15 of the *Charter*,[24] a provision that came into effect in 1985. The *YOA* was enacted in 1982 with the support of all members of Parliament and came into force on April 1, 1984.

The *YOA* provided much more recognition of legal rights than the *Juvenile Delinquents Act*, as well as establishing a uniform national age jurisdiction, developments consistent with the emphasis in the *Charter* on due process of law and equal treatment under the law.[25] The *YOA* tried

---

22 Canada, Department of Justice, Report of the Committee on Juvenile Delinquency, *Juvenile Delinquency in Canada* (Ottawa: Queen's Printer, 1965).

23 *Young Offenders Act*, R.S.C 1985, c. Y-1, enacted as S.C. 1980–81–82–83, c. 110.

24 *Canadian Charter of Rights and Freedoms*, enacted as Part I of the *Constitution Act, 1982*, being Schedule B to the *Canada Act, 1982* (U.K.), 1982, c. 11 (subsequently referred to as the *Charter*). Policy makers in 1982 feared that the differences in age jurisdiction under the *Juvenile Delinquents Act*, above note 12, would violate s. 15 of the *Charter* and acted to prevent a court challenge. No court ever ruled on this issue. There is also an argument that such variations might be constitutionally justifiable in a federal state; see *R. v. S.(S)*, [1990] 2 S.C.R. 254.

25 Some critics have decried the increased emphasis on due process and legal rights. See, for example, J. Hackler, "An Impressionistic View of Canadian Juvenile Justice: 1965 to 1999" (2001) 20 Can J. Comm. Mental Health 17, who writes that the enactment of the *YOA*, above note 23, represented: "a basic change . . . a transfer of influence from social workers to lawyers. Juveniles got certain legal protections, but we did not foresee that the juveniles and their families would become victims of the legal process. . . . The vast increase in the number of judges, prosecutors, defence lawyers and closed-custody institutions is the result of one profession, law, expanding into an area previously dominated by another, social work . . . but it is too late to go back. Lawyers have replaced social workers as the main players in juvenile justice. We must work with them" (at 17–21).

to balance a concern for the special needs of youth with the protection of the public. It abolished the indeterminate sentences of the *Juvenile Delinquents Act*, providing for determinate (fixed) custodial dispositions, subject to judicially controlled early release. The *YOA* was a much more detailed piece of legislation than the *Juvenile Delinquents Act*, regulating every stage of the youth justice process, including arrest and police questioning, diversion to alternatives to youth court, access to legal counsel, public disclosure of information, and the sentencing process, as well as the possibility of transfer to adult court for youths charged with the most serious offences. The *YOA* moved away from the child-welfare philosophy of the previous Act, abolishing the vague status offence of "sexual immorality" and focusing on federal criminal offences.

At the same time the *YOA* came into force in 1984, several provinces transferred some or all of the responsibility for young offenders from their social services ministry to the adult corrections ministry, although this was not required by the new federal Act. Quebec, however, maintained a youth justice and corrections system that was closely linked to its child-welfare system.

In 1986 minor amendments were made to respond to some concerns raised by police and provincial governments about difficulties implementing the *YOA* and to toughen the Act slightly. Provisions were added to facilitate charges for breach of probation orders and to allow publication in a community of information about the identity of dangerous young persons at large.[26]

By the late 1980s the *YOA* was subject to public criticism. Concerns were being raised about the perceived inadequacy of the maximum three-year sentence for violent young offenders, especially those convicted of murder, and the difficulty in transferring youths to the adult court where they might face much longer sentences in adult prisons. In 1992, the Progressive Conservative federal government responded by enacting further amendments to the Act, lengthening the maximum sentence for murder in youth court to five years less a day, and amending the transfer provisions to stipulate that the "protection of the public" was to be the paramount consideration.[27]

In 1995 the Liberal federal government enacted another set of amendments to the Act, again primarily intended to demonstrate to the

---

26 *An Act to amend the Young Offenders Act, the Criminal Code, the Penitentiary Act and the Prisons and Reformatories Act*, R.S.C. 1985 (2d Supp.), c. 24, in force September 1, 1986 and November 1, 1986.

27 *An Act to amend the Young Offenders Act and the Criminal Code*, S.C. 1992, c. 11. See N. Bala, "Dealing with Violent Young Offenders: Transfer to Adult Court and Bill C-58" (1990) 9 Can. J. Fam. L. 11; see also Chapter 9 of this book.

public that it was getting tougher, in particular for the most violent offenders. These amendments lengthened to ten years the maximum youth court sentence for murder, created a presumption that sixteen- and seventeen-year-olds charged with the most serious offences would be transferred to adult court where longer sentences could be imposed, and promoted information-sharing with such professionals in the community as teachers.[28] Other amendments were also introduced to attempt to emphasize the rehabilitative themes of the *YOA* and, in particular, to increase the use of community-based dispositions for youths who did not pose a risk of serious harm to the community.

3) Canadian Politics and Youth Crime

When enacted by Parliament in 1982, the *YOA* was supported by all federal political parties and was hailed as ushering in a new era in juvenile justice. Ironically, after unanimous Parliamentary support when it was enacted, the Act became the focus of enormous public controversy and was ultimately attacked by federal and provincial politicians across a broad political spectrum for being too lenient with young offenders and failing to protect society adequately. In 1993, for the first time in Canadian history, federal politicians made juvenile justice an election issue with all parties taking a stand concerning — typically against — the *YOA*. The four national parties played to growing public fears of youth crime and pledged to toughen the Act again.[29] The Bloc Québécois, prepared to "speak out against law-and-order rhetoric," supported the Act, taking an approach consistent with the provincial policies more oriented to child welfare in Quebec.[30] These attacks on the Act continued in the 1997 and 2000 federal election campaigns, as well as in some provincial elections, even though criminal law is an area of federal responsibility.

Since 1984, although it is not clear that youth crime has actually become an increasingly serious problem, the political concern about youth crime and media reporting about this issue have greatly increased.

---

28 *An Act to amend the Young Offenders Act and the Criminal Code*, S.C. 1995, c. 19. See N. Bala, "The 1995 *Young Offenders Act* Amendments: Compromise or Confusion?" (1994) 26 Ottawa L.Rev. 643. See also Chapter 9 of this book. For a critical commentary on the 1995 reforms, see K. Campbell, M. Dufresne, and R. MacLure, "Amending Youth Justice Policy in Canada: Discourse, Mediation, and Ambiguity" (2001) 40 Howard J. 272.

29 The Liberal, Reform, Progressive Conservative, and the New Democratic parties. See Bala, above note 28 at 652.

30 See L. Gagnon, "Quebec's Soft-Love Approach to Young Offenders," *Globe and Mail*, March 13, 1999: D3.

While *police reports* of youth crime in Canada increased in the late 1980s, the reported rate of youth crime peaked in the early 1990s. The rise in police reports about youth crime in the late 1980s and early 1990s reflected, at least in part, changes in police charging patterns and in reporting practices; for example, school officials were required by policies of zero tolerance of violence to report minor assaults that previously would have been resolved informally.[31] Certain key indicators of serious youthful criminality, such as the youth homicide rate, have remained relatively constant for years, as have measures of youth offending based on self-reports by adolescents.[32] Further, as media reports about youth crime and political concerns about the *YOA* were increasing in the 1990s, the actual rate of youth crime reported by police was slowly falling for much of the decade. Although youth crime may not have been increasing in the 1990s, media reports of youth violence and public anxiety about the problem of youth crime have escalated dramatically in Canada.[33]

There was a public misperception that the *YOA* contributed to, or at least was associated with, a substantial increase in youth crime. Ironically there was even a vague sense among the public that the old legal regime under the *Juvenile Delinquents Act* afforded the public greater protection than the *YOA*, although in reality the former Act actually had more of a welfare-oriented philosophy. While the actual youth crime rate may not have increased substantially after the *YOA* came into force, that Act resulted in a more punitive regime than under the *Juvenile Delinquents Act*, with much higher rates of custody use for adolescent offenders.

Public perceptions about the inadequacy of police and court responses to crime are affected more by the fear of crime than by actual experience as a victim.[34] The media, by focusing on relatively rare

---

31   P.J. Carrington, "Trends in Youth Crime in Canada 1977–1996" (1999) 41 Can J. Crim. 1.

32   M. LeBlanc and S. Girard, "The Generality of Deviance: Replication over Two Decades with a Canadian Sample of Adjudicated Boys" (1997) 37 Can J. Crim. 171.

33   J.B. Sprott, "Understanding Public Views of Youth Crime and the Youth Justice System" (1996) 38 Can J. Crim. 271. See F. Estrada, "Juvenile Violence as a Social Problem: Trends, Media Attention, and Social Response" (2001) 41 Brit J. Crim. 639–55 analyzing the sharp increase in media coverage and police reports of youth crime in western Europe despite other evidence that youth crime rates are quite stable.

34   J.B. Sprott and A.N. Doob, "Fear, Victimization and Attitudes to Sentencing, the Courts and Police" (1997) 39 Can. J. Crim. 275.

instances of serious youth violence, may contribute to a distorted public perception of youth crime. Fears about youth crime may also be
fuelled by the ageing demographic make-up of the population, and by
the insecurity felt by many Canadians in the face of accelerating social
and economic change. Owing to differences in birth rates in various
ethnic communities, Canada's population has a relatively high proportion of youth from visible minority and Aboriginal backgrounds. As a
result, some of the public fear about youth crime may derive from
unarticulated elements of racism, as reflected in certain expressions of
concern about crimes committed by youths who are immigrants or
from visible minorities.[35]

Political and public criticisms of the YOA also held an element of
anti-youth sentiment. The perception of many adults that youth are
more rebellious and less respectful than when they were young is as old
as human history. But the level of anti-youth rhetoric may be more
intense today, as reflected in the 1999 Ontario election campaign;
Progressive Conservative premier Mike Harris argued in favour of lowering the maximum age of youth court jurisdiction to fifteen and complained that the YOA was "too soft . . . too lenient, it does not teach
respect and responsibility and it's got to be toughened up." At the same
time, the Premier suggested that teenagers' "lack of respect" might be
improved by introducing a province-wide common code for schools of
student behaviour and dress.[36] This campaign rhetoric clearly plays to
the sentiments of many older members of the public that young people
are increasingly out of control.

Adult sensitivity to antisocial adolescent attitudes may be heightened by certain aspects of popular culture, reflected in music, movies,
videos, and computer games. Over the decade of the 1990s, some
aspects of youth culture became increasingly alienated from adult culture. The dress, language, and demeanour of many young people con-
form less to adult expectations than in the past. Many youth now have
more of an aggressive attitude and are less respectful of adults than
teenagers of a few decades ago. But it must be appreciated that adult
society has also changed dramatically: interactions take place on an

---

35 During the 1999 Ontario election campaign, the Toronto Police Association
    sponsored a controversial advertisement urging voters to support "law and
    order" candidates. The ad pictured five obviously Latino young men, who were
    actually in Los Angeles when the picture was taken: "Group Wants Apology for
    Police Poster," Globe and Mail, June 1, 1999: A13.
36 Canadian Press, "Teenagers Still a Hot Topic: Premier Renews Call for Tougher
    Young Offenders Act," March 2, 1999.

increasingly informal basis and adults do not display the same defer-
ence to authority figures that they once did. There is generally greater
social tolerance of profanity, and sexual matters have become a frequent topic of public commentary. This greater adult informality — a
broadening of the scope of acceptable social behaviour — has important repercussions for youth. To test social limits — a normal step in
attaining autonomy as one matures — adolescents have to go further.
A generation ago, mild but visible adolescent rebellion might have
been signalled by wearing blue jeans, for females not wearing a
brassiere, and for males growing their hair long. Now this type of
appearance would be considered normal for adults. Youths and some
young adults search for other forms of distinctiveness, through bright-
ly coloured hair, tattooing, and body piercing.

Adolescents today treat adults in a less deferential manner; previous
generations would not have dreamed of behaving toward that way their
elders. This behaviour, which is easily perceived as disrespectful, can be
shocking for older people. However, less deferential adolescent behaviour mirrors a generally less deferential society. Young people face a
more uncertain and competitive economic future than did previous
post-World War II generations. Does some of the political rhetoric
about youth crime reflect adult fears that young people seem increasingly out of control and perhaps less likely than the youth of earlier
generations to assume future roles as productive tax-paying citizens?

In Canada, a vital element of the political and administrative concerns
about youth justice issues relates to the division of responsibilities
between the federal and provincial governments.[37] Under the *Constitution
Act, 1867*, section 91(27), the federal government has jurisdiction over
"Criminal Law . . . [and] Procedure," while the provinces have jurisdiction under section 92(14) for the "Administration of Justice," as well as
responsibility for such important related services as education, health,
and child well-being. The federal legislative power in this area has been
interpreted by the courts "in its widest sense," to permit the federal
Parliament to enact laws "intended to prevent . . . juveniles [from
becoming] prospective criminals and to assist them to be law-abiding
citizens."[38] The courts consistently rejected challenges under the

---

37 Territorial governments have essentially the same responsibilities as provincial
governments with regard to youth justice, although their jurisdiction derives
from federal statutes. For the sake of simplicity, most references in this text are
only to provincial governments.

38 *B.C. (A.G.) v. S.*, [1967] S.C.R. 702 at 710.

Constitution Act, 1867 to the *Juvenile Delinquents Act*[39] and the *YOA*, accepting that the federal government could enact laws to deal with prevention of youth crime, the control of youth corrections facilities, and diversion from the court system. The courts have also rejected most *Charter* challenges to the *YOA*, accepting that some restrictions on the rights of young persons are justifiable in light of the more limited sanctions that they face.[40]

The federal government has a broad power to enact legislation dealing with young offenders, and may enact laws to deal with such issues as protection of the privacy of proceedings[41] and the establishment of non-court alternative measures.[42] Provincial governments are obliged to implement these laws, including paying for the legal, judicial, correctional, and social services required for youths. The federal government transfers money to the provinces for some of the expenses associated with the administration of juvenile justice, but after the *YOA* came into force in 1984, as a result of efforts to reduce the federal deficit, the level of federal financial support for such services declined. For financial and philosophical reasons, some provincial governments disagreed with various provisions of the *YOA*. For example, when the Act was enacted in 1982, provinces such as Ontario, which had a minimum age of sixteen under the *Juvenile Delinquents Act*, opposed establishing eighteen as the minimum age of adult jurisdiction. Quebec, which already used eighteen as the adult minimum under the *Juvenile Delinquents Act*, supported the higher age. The opposition of Ontario reflected financial concerns about the increased cost of their youth court jurisdiction, as well as a belief that sixteen- and seventeen-year-olds are mature enough to be treated like adults.

In a federal system, it is understandable that provincial politicians will criticize federal politicians for imposing costs and obligations on provincial governments. The federal government consults extensively with provincial governments about law reform in the youth justice field, and the provinces played a significant role in the development of

---

39 Some of the provisions of the *Juvenile Delinquents Act*, which failed to adequately recognize legal rights, were successfully challenged in the period after the *Charter* came into effect in 1982 and before the *YOA* came into force in 1984. See N. Bala, "Constitutional Challenges Mark Demise of *Juvenile Delinquents Act*" (1983), 30 C.R. (3d) 245.

40 See, for example, *R. v. L.(R.)* (1986), 52 C.R. (3d) 209 (Ont. C.A.), upholding denial of right to a jury trial.

41 *Southam Inc. v. R.* (1984), 48 O.R. (2d) 678 (H.C.J.), aff'd. (1986), 53 O.R. (2d) 663 (C.A.).

42 *R. v. S.(S.)*, above note 24.

the *Youth Criminal Justice Act*. However, the provinces do not always agree among themselves about the directions that they would like the federal government to take. Further, in regard to some issues the federal government was not prepared to adopt the consensus position of the provinces, although the *YCJA* gives the provinces significantly more flexibility to shape youth justice policies than they had under the *YOA*. While the increasing provincial control over juvenile justice policy has given the new law a degree of provincial support, it has also increased concerns that youths in different provinces may receive very different legal treatment.

By the end of the 1990s the decline in the level of federal financial support for provincial spending on youth justice ended. The *YCJA* is part of a federal strategy that includes some additional federal support for provincial spending on youth justice, although the federal government is imposing conditions on how this increased funding is to be spent, with an emphasis on community-based programs and alternatives to custody. The decrease in federal financial support in the early 1990s was bound to cause political tension in this area. While somewhat increased federal funding may help to reduce tensions, the provinces are concerned about burgeoning federal controls on their spending.

There was another dimension to some of the provincial critiques of the youth justice system, given increasing public concern over youth crime. The *YOA* was an easy target for provincial politicians responsible for many of the expensive services that most directly affect public safety, such as policing, social services, and child welfare. It may, for example, be easier for provincial politicians to attack the federal legislation for not being tough enough than to take responsibility for improving police services to increase community protection, or to make the changes to the health, education, and social service systems that may in the long term produce a less violent society.

C. THE ENACTMENT OF THE *YOUTH CRIMINAL JUSTICE ACT*

Demands for politicians to get tough with youth crime grew louder in the late 1990s as Canada became more conservative. The Reform (now Canadian Alliance) Party with its law-and-order agenda pressed for major changes in many criminal laws, including those governing the youth justice system. This included demands from some Reform Party members for the total repeal of the *YOA*, although even the advocates of this position recognized the value of both separate correctional facilities for most young offenders and special treatment for less serious offences committed by adolescents.[43] Especially when elections are close, politicians seem to focus on getting tough with young offenders, although in their more reflective moments most politicians and many members of the public appreciate the limitations of this approach as a way of reducing youth crime and of increasing the protection of society.

While making demands for getting tough on youth crime, politicians have become increasingly aware of the costs of an approach to youth crime that emphasizes use of expensive custody facilities. Although the numbers of youth in custody rose sharply after the YOA came into force, more than three-quarters of youth receiving custodial sentences under that Act had not committed violent offences. Compared to other countries, Canada relied very heavily on court and custody responses to non-violent youth crime that are relatively expensive and ineffective. Other countries divert most of their less serious adolescent offenders from the court system, and make greater use of community-based dispositions for those who are sent to court. For example, the United States has a much more serious youth crime problem than Canada — a youth homicide rate that is six times higher than that in Canada. But under the YOA, Canada was sending youth into custody at twice the rate of American courts.[44]

1) Reform of the *Young Offenders Act* in 1995

Government publicity surrounding the 1995 reforms to the YOA focused on facilitating transfer to adult court for a relatively small number of the most violent offenders. Some of the less publicized provisions of those reforms, however, were intended to increase the use of community-based dispositions for youths not committing offences

---

43   See, for example, R. Howard, "Reform's Grassroots Dig in on Tough Ground: Party Would Scrap *Young Offenders Act*, New Gun-Control Law," *Globe and Mail*, June 8, 1996: A4.

44   Department of Justice Canada, *A Strategy for Youth Justice Renewal* (Ottawa, May 1998) at 20, and J. Hornick, N. Bala, and J. Hudson, *The Response to Juvenile Crime in the United States: A Canadian Perspective* (Calgary, AB: Canadian Research Institute for Law and the Family, 1995). It is interesting to observe that, in the United States in the 1990s, politicians and the public demanded a get-tough approach to youth crime, even though youth crime rates were actually falling: see Barry Glassner, "School Violence: The Fears, the Facts," *New York Times*, August 13, 1999.

involving serious personal injury. There was also in 1995 a specific addition to the *YOA*'s Declaration of Principle to recognize that crime prevention and the protection of society are best achieved by addressing the causes of crime and rehabilitating youth.[45] Although less publicized than the demands to toughen the *YOA*, there are many examples of Canadian politicians recognizing the need to address the root causes of youthful criminality. Indeed many politicians and members of the public who in some contexts appear to support "get-tough" policies also recognize the importance of crime prevention, rehabilitation of young offenders, and the application of principles of restorative justice for young offenders.[46]

In introducing the 1995 *YOA* amendments, which increased sentences for murder in youth court, the Justice Minister at the time observed: "If the answer to crime was simply harsher laws, longer penalties and bigger prisons, then the United States would be nirvana today. . . . We are only going to be able to have long term and effective results if we create a society in which we minimize the conditions which breed crime."[47] Even Ontario's Progressive Conservatives, who campaigned in the 1995 elections on a law-and-order platform — including a promise of boot camps for young offenders — recognized, once in office, that there is no quick fix for youth crime. The government's pilot program for strict-discipline custody emphasizes competent staffing, counselling, education, and employment skills, while accepting that discipline as a punishment will not prevent youths from reoffending but must be part of a program to change the attitudes and values of young offenders and to instil self-discipline. Following a period in secure custody, youths in the new Ontario strict-discipline program have significant community-placement participation involving their families and,

---

45   *Young Offenders Act, 1995*, above note 28, s. 15(i) (enacting *YOA*, s. 24 (1.1)). *Young Offenders Act, 1995*, *ibid.*, s. 1 (enacting *YOA*, s. 3(i)(a) and (c. 1)). Even the Reform Party, which sought to "replace the *Young Offenders Act* with measures that hold young criminals accountable for their actions," also pledged to "[p]ursue crime prevention through social policies that strengthen families and communities." See the Reform Party of Canada's 1997 election platform, *A Fresh Start for Canadians*.

46   See "Canadians Prefer Prevention," *Southam News*, March 12, 2001 reporting on a public opinion poll in which a majority of Canadians recognized that poverty, inadequate social programs, and difficult family situations caused most crime, not a "lenient criminal justice system." A further 68 percent said that preventive programs are the most effective deterrent against youth crime.

47   Then Justice Canada Minister Allan Rock, quoted in R. Howard, "Longer Terms for Young Killers Expected in Legislation Today," *Globe and Mail*, June 2, 1994: A6.

where appropriate, help to secure employment.[48] In early 1999 Ontario's Conservative government even announced that it would be expanding community-based diversion programs for minor first offenders. A few months later in a provincial election campaign, Ontario's Conservatives loudly denounced the federal Liberal government for its weak responses to youth crime and attacked the leader of the provincial Liberals for being soft on crime on the grounds that he had previously worked as a lawyer representing youths charged with offences.

2) Federal–Provincial/Territorial Consultations on Youth Justice

In response to public and political pressures to deal with youth crime, the federal, provincial, and territorial governments established a task force of senior bureaucrats to review the *YOA* and propose amendments. In 1996 this task force delivered its report.[49] The federal government then had a Commons Committee hold hearings across Canada to gather responses to youth crime and propose amendments to the *YOA*. The final report of this Committee, released in the spring of 1997, reflected the political tensions over youth justice issues.[50] The Liberal majority on the Committee wrote a report that tried to place greater emphasis on crime prevention and rehabilitation, while toughening some of the provisions of the *YOA*. The report, for example, recommended increased federal spending on crime prevention and greater use of such alternatives to youth court as family-group conferencing. It recommended explicit recognition of the principle that the protection of society is the main goal of criminal law, but also advocated that, for young offenders, the protection of society, crime prevention, and rehabilitation are mutually reinforcing strategies. Recommendations in this report included lowering the minimum age of youth court jurisdiction

---

48 Ontario, Solicitor General and Minister of Correctional Services, *Recommendations from Task Force on Strict Discipline for Young Offenders* (Toronto: Queen's Printer, 1996); see also Canada, House of Commons, *Twelfth Report of the Standing Committee on Justice and the Solicitor General: Crime Prevention in Canada: Toward a National Strategy* (Ottawa: Ministry of Supply and Services, 1993).

49 Canada, Federal–Provincial/Territorial Task Force on Youth Justice, *Review of the Young Offenders Act and the Youth Justice System in Canada* (Ottawa: Ministry of Supply and Services, 1996).

50 Canada, House of Commons, *Thirteenth Report of the Standing Committee on Justice and Legal Affairs: Renewing Youth Justice* (Ottawa: Ministry of Supply and Services, 1997).

for serious offences from twelve years of age to ten, facilitating transfer of serious offenders to the adult system, and publishing the names of young offenders believed to pose a risk of serious harm to the community after their release.

The Bloc Québécois members of the Parliamentary Committee criticized the majority report for its lack of understanding of the problem of youth crime and opposed any amendments to the YOA. The Bloc also opposed any efforts by the federal government to change provincial spending priorities for youth justice, arguing that provincial jurisdiction must be respected. The Reform Party also criticized the Liberal majority for its recommendations about spending on crime prevention, as an area of primarily provincial jurisdiction. But the Reform members advocated sweeping changes to the YOA, including establishing an age jurisdiction from the tenth to the sixteenth birthdays, providing automatic transfer to adult court for fourteen- and fifteen-year-olds charged with violent offences, imposing longer sentences in youth court, and allowing publication of identifying information about any violent young offenders.

After the Parliamentary Committee report was released in 1997, the federal government again consulted with the provinces, convening a meeting of Cabinet ministers with the hope of achieving a consensus about reforming the youth justice system. The discussions included financial and philosophical, as well as detailed law and policy, issues. As the discussions proceeded and public pressure for a response to the Parliamentary Committee report increased, the federal government developed a strategy for reform that included but was not limited to legislative reform. The May 1988 document, entitled *Strategy for the Renewal of Youth Justice*, set out the general themes the federal government was adopting.[51] After further consultation, mostly with provincial officials, the Liberal government introduced Bill C-68, called the *Youth Criminal Justice Act* in March 1999, setting out the new law.[52]

The original Bill was the subject of lengthy committee hearings during which it was criticized by the Canadian Alliance and Conservative parties for being too soft on young offenders, while the Bloc Québécois continued to argue that no changes were needed in the YOA, expressing concern that the new law would result in more youths being treated as adult offenders. The Bloc had strong support from youth advocates in Quebec, and delayed the progress of the original

---

51   Department of Justice Canada, *A Strategy for Youth Justice Renewal* (Ottawa: 1998). (Available online at time of writing at <http://canada.justice.gc.ca>.)

52   Bill C-68, First session, 36th Parliament, First reading March 11, 1999; reintroduced as Bill C-3, 2nd Session, 36th Parliament, October 14, 1999.

Bill through Parliament. When the federal election was called in the fall of 2000, the *YCJA* had not yet been enacted. Youth crime was again an issue in that election, the Liberals pledging to act on their youth justice strategy, the conservative opposition parties again raising such issues as lowering the age of youth court jurisdiction, and the Bloc Québécois criticizing the federal plans as interference with provincial responsibility over youth justice.

3) The New Act

When the Liberals were re-elected in 2000, they reintroduced the *Youth Criminal Justice Act* (Bill C-7), making a few relatively minor changes to the previous version of the new law.[53] To try to ensure relatively swift passage of the Bill through Parliament, only federal and provincial government officials were called as witnesses to the Commons committee hearings held in the spring of 2001. The Ontario government made public calls for amendments that would "finally get tough on youth crime," for example by allowing publication of names of any youth charged with serious offences, having mandatory custody terms for youth convicted of weapons offences, and imposing longer sentences for youths dealt with as adults.[54] In June 2001, however, the *YCJA* was passed by the House of Commons without further amendment.

In the fall of 2001, the Senate Committee[55] held hearings on the *YCJA*, with strong representations from Quebec to give that province

---

53 *YCJA*, above note 2. The relatively minor changes responded to some of the concerns expressed during prior hearings, and tended to "soften" the new law a little, for example restricting the scope for admission of youth statements that police obtained in situations where youth were not fully apprised of their legal rights.

54 Ontario Ministry of the Attorney General, "No More Free Ride for the Young Offenders Act," June 12, 2001. (Available online at time of writing at <www.attorneygeneral.jus.gov.on.ca>.)

55 Canada's Parliament is made up of two chambers, the elected House of Commons and the appointed Senate. Technically the Senate has considerable power but, since all of its members are appointed by the prime minister and serve to age seventy-five, it has little legitimacy. There is near-unanimous public agreement that the Senate should be radically reformed or abolished but, because of a lack of consensus about how to do this, it continues as an unreformed reminder of Canada's history as a colony run by appointees of the British government. For a discussion of the role of the Senate in Canadian government, and the challenges of reforming that body, see Michael Lusztig, "Federalism and Institutional Design: The Perils and Politics of a Triple-E Senate in Canada" (1995) 25 Publius 35–50.

more flexibility and to give the Act more focus on rehabilitation, while the Ontario government again advocated more of a get-tough approach. The Senate Committee, slowed in its hearings when the government gave priority to anti-terrorism legislation, then recommended more than a dozen changes to the Act, mainly aimed at addressing some of the concerns raised by witnesses from Quebec. A few days before voting on the YCJA, the Senate had been pressured by the Liberal government into accepting anti-terrorism legislation without amendment.

The full Senate adopted only two relatively minor amendments to the YCJA that gave more explicit recognition to the need to consider all alternatives to custody in the sentencing of young offenders, with particular attention to the circumstances of Aboriginal youth. These amendments were not significant, as section 39 of the Act already made clear that youth justice court judges are to consider all alternatives to custody and the Declaration of Principle stated that those responding to youth offending should respect the needs of Aboriginal offenders.[56] While greater clarity on the need for special consideration of the circumstances of Aboriginal offenders may have been desirable, the Senate amendments were more of a political statement: the message was that Senate approval of legislation should not be seen as a formality.

The more substantial amendments to the Act that had been proposed by the Senate Committee were not adopted by the full Senate. On February 4, 2002, the Senate amendments to the YCJA were approved by the House of Commons and the Act received royal assent on February 19, 2002. The federal government, in response to pressure from the provinces, announced that the law would not be proclaimed into force until April 1, 2003, to allow time for provincial governments to introduce the new programs and policies required by the new Act.

The federal youth justice reform strategy was intended to respond to the belief that there had been a "disturbing decline in public confidence in the youth justice system" in Canada. The most prominently publicized aspect of the strategy, accordingly, was the stated intention "to respond more firmly and effectively to the small number of the most serious, violent young offenders."[57] But there was also an important recognition by the federal government that Canada has made too much use of expensive and often ineffective court-based responses and custody for the majority of young offenders who are not committing serious violent offences. The federal strategy also calls for more use of

---

56   YCJA, above note 2, s. 3(1)(c)(iv).
57   Remarks in Ottawa, May 12, 1999, by (then) federal Justice Minister, Anne McLellan.

community-based alternatives to court and custody, and for more resources for crime prevention. The strategy aimed to achieve these objectives by changing the law, and working with the provincial governments and various professional groups to change the way in which the youth justice and corrections systems operate.

The main area of federal authority in this area under the *Constitution Act, 1867*, is statutory, and this is where much of the government's efforts have focused. The federal government also committed over $200 million to provincial governments, principally to increase community-based alternatives and over $30 million to initiatives to prevent youth crime, mainly directed to local groups. One of the significant developments in youth justice has been the federal initiative to give provincial governments greater flexibility in how they deal with youth justice and youth corrections. While greater provincial flexibility increases the support of provincial governments for the strategy, it also tends to increase disparities in the ways in which different provinces deal with youth offenders.

Initial federal government planning in 1997 had called for the amendment of the *YOA* rather than enactment of an entirely new statute. Significant changes were contemplated to the *YOA* but not the type of radical reforms that the *YOA* had produced when it replaced the *Juvenile Delinquents Act* in 1984. However, as discussions with the provinces about changes to the Act continued, the changes grew in number and complexity. It also became apparent that an entirely new statute would be easier to understand and use than adding a large number of amendments. Politically, the repeal of the *YOA* and its replacement by a new statute enabled the federal government to claim that it had put "a new youth justice regime in place."[58] Institutionally, the enactment of a new statute signals police, prosecutors, judges, probation officers, and others that some fundamental changes are expected in the administration of youth justice.

The new *YCJA* is a complex piece of legislation, a detailed consideration of which is the prime focus of this book. Despite the complexity of the Act, its salient features in comparison to the *YOA* can be summarized as:

- a Declaration of Principle that places a clearer emphasis on the long-term protection of the public, meaningful consequences for offenders, and reparation to victims, while continuing to recognize that,

---

58   *Ibid.*

compared to adults, there should be a lesser degree of accountability and more emphasis on rehabilitation;

- making "fair and proportionate accountability" a central sentencing principle, and making clear that custodial sentences are not justified solely for achieving rehabilitative objectives;
- introducing statements of principle and specific provisions intended to encourage police and prosecutors to divert more young persons from the court process, and to encourage more use by judges of non-custodial sentences for youths not convicted of serious violent offences;
- encouraging involvement of victims, parents, and members of the community in the youth court process, for example through conferences that may advise the court or meet to deal with youth outside the court system;
- facilitation of the imposition of adult sentences on the relatively small number of young offenders fourteen years and older who commit the most serious violent offences;
- permitting the publication of the names of young offenders convicted of the most serious violent offences in specified circumstances;
- giving courts limited authority to admit statements made to police even if there has been a technical irregularity in the way in which a youth has been fully advised of his/her legal rights;
- allowing provinces to require parents with financial means to repay governments for legal counsel provided to their children;
- giving provinces greater authority to establish youth justice policies, for example by allowing provincial correctional officials rather than courts to determine the level of custody for young persons, and by permitting provinces to select a higher age than 14 for the very serious charges for which there is a presumption of an adult sentence being imposed;
- requiring that young offenders receiving custodial sentences ordinarily serve the last third of their sentence on community supervision, thereby promoting a planned reintegration of the youth into the community;
- introducing new sentencing options such as "intensive rehabilitative custody" and "attendance centres."

The new legislation in many respects represents a political compromise. It is an attempt to find a better, or at least a more politically popular, balance on youth justice issues.

To appease the large vocal law-and-order lobby, a number of provisions of the *YCJA* appear to get tough on youth crime by increasing accountability, especially for serious violent offenders, and addressing some concerns of victims. These provisions are likely to result in a relatively small number of the most serious offenders serving longer sentences, sometimes in adult prisons, and in the publication of identifying information about young offenders who have committed very serious offences. While the new statute continues to recognize that young persons have the right to due process of law, there is a weakening compared to the *YOA* in the protection of legal rights — a further reflection of the law-and-order agenda. Especially troubling is the provision in the *YCJA* that allows provinces to require parents to reimburse their governments for the cost of legal services provided to their children. This may result in many youths feeling parental pressure to waive the right to counsel, which will in turn may make it much less likely that youths will be able to enforce their legal rights.

For child-advocacy groups and politicians who wanted a more supportive and preventive approach to youth offending, the *YCJA* offers the prospect of increased rehabilitative services in the youth corrections system, although it will be up to each province to determine whether these services will be more available. The new Act is also intended to move youths charged with less serious offences out of custody facilities and the youth courts, and to have more effective community-based responses to youth offending. The overall strategy adopted by the federal government includes a recognition of the social context of youth crime and attempts to address crime prevention issues. One can also see the *YCJA* as placing a greater and clearer emphasis on some of the salient themes of 1995 amendments to the *YOA*: more of an effort to divert many youthful offenders from court and make use of community-based responses to youth crime, and, for a small minority of the most violent youth offenders, increased possibilities for adult sentences and publication of identifying information.

The *YCJA* substantially changes how the justice system responds to youth offending and will significantly affect both youths and professionals. However, the legislation does not provide for the type of sweeping change that occurred in 1984 when Canada repealed the *Juvenile Delinquents Act* and adopted the *YOA*.[59] Rather, the *YCJA* has a large number of relatively small changes, which cumulatively should result in significant change in the youth justice system.

---

59   The title of one of the books that was written a few years after the *YOA* came into force reflects the profound change that Act was intended to effect: A.W. Leschied, P. Jaffe, and W. Willis, eds., *The Young Offenders Act: A Revolution in Canadian Youth Justice* (Toronto: University of Toronto Press, 1991).

D. THE NATURE AND CAUSES OF YOUTH CRIME IN CANADA

While a detailed discussion of the nature and causes of youth crime is beyond the scope of this book, some appreciation of these issues provides a necessary context for understanding the youth justice system. To work effectively in that system, professionals must have sensitivity to the complexities and variation in youth crime. In 2000–2001, under the *YOA*, youth courts processed just over 99 000 cases involving young persons charged under the *Criminal Code* and other federal criminal statutes. This represented about 21 percent of all criminal cases in Canada, even though youths aged twelve to seventeen represent only about 8 percent of the total Canadian population.[60] About 60 percent of these cases resulted in convictions. These 99,000 cases involved about 60,000 youths, as some were charged on more than one occasion; that is roughly 3 percent of the population aged twelve through seventeen.

Charge rates are low for twelve-year-olds but increase rapidly for each age group until sixteen-year-olds, when they start to level off; just over half all charges under the *YOA* involved sixteen- and seventeen-year-olds. Males represent just under 80 percent of youths charged, although the proportion of female adolescents charged has been slowly increasing in recent years. By the time a generation of youths reaches the age of eighteen, about 12 percent of the male population and 3 percent of the female population were charged under the *YOA* at least once with a violation of the *Criminal Code* or another federal statute.

1) Recent Patterns in Youth Crime

The majority of Canadian youths are charged with such property-related offences as break and enter or theft. Under the *YOA*, about one-quarter of all charges against young persons arose out of breach of probation terms, or a failure to attend court or to obey a court order. In other words, a substantial number of youths were charged not because of any immediate risk to the public but because of their failure to respond appropriately to earlier judicial intervention. One of the aims of the *YCJA* is to reduce the tendency of an initial minor offence resulting in

---

60   Canada, Canadian Centre for Justice Statistics, *Youth Court Statistics 2000–2001* (Ottawa: Statistics Canada, March 2002) and Statistics Canada, *Youth Court Statistics 2000–2001* (2002) 22: 3 Juristat. Some of the cases involved more than one charge against a young person.

a series of more intrusive involvements with the youth justice system, by focusing more on prevention and diversion of cases from the court system. About one-fifth of youth charges involved violence, with minor assaults being by far the most common offence. While youth homicide (murder, manslaughter, and infanticide) has been the focus of media attention, such offences represent a tiny fraction of all charges: an average of about 50 youth homicide charges a year. The rate of youth homicide in Canada has remained relatively constant over the past few decades at about 2 per 100,000 youths. While youth charges represent over 20 percent of all criminal charges, adolescents commit only about 10 percent of all homicides in Canada. Although Canada's rate of youth homicide is less than one-sixth that of the United States, it is still one of the highest in the world.[61]

The number of charges under the YOA increased dramatically from the time that Act came into force in 1984 until 1991. While the rate fell slowly after 1991 — with the greatest decline for property-related offences — by 2001 the officially reported level of youth offending was still significantly higher than when that Act came into force in 1984. Official police and youth court statistics, however, tell only part of the story. Criminologists engage in serious debate about whether the level of youth crime in Canada actually increased under the YOA.[62] Most offences involving youth are not reported to the police or other authorities and, even for those cases that are reported, the police have a significant discretion about whether to lay a charge and take a youth to court or deal with the matter informally (for example, by simply warning the youth and speaking to the parents). Some criminologists argue that, at least in part, increased reporting to the police and increased charging by the police resulted in the increase in youth crime statistics. For example, as noted earlier, some time after the enactment of the YOA in 1984, many school boards and provincial governments adopted a policy of zero tolerance for violence; school officials were required to report to the police relatively minor assaults that previously might have been dealt with informally by a teacher or principal in the school.

In contrast, other criminologists and some police officers and teachers who work with youth argue that there have actually been increases in youth crime since the early 1980s. While recognizing that

---

61 W. Meloff and R.A. Silverman, "Canadian Kids Who Kill" (1992) 34 Can. J. Crim. 15; and T. Harper, "The Truth is Kids Aren't Getting away with Murder," Toronto Star, September 7, 1996: C1.

62 Contrast Carrington, above note 31, and A. Markwart and R.R. Corrado, "A Response to Carrington" (1995) 37 Can J. Crim. 74.

some of the increase in official youth crime statistics may reflect changes in reporting and charging practices, they argue that changes in the family, social, and cultural structure of Canadian society are producing youth who are more prone to violence and offending.[63] Family structures and behaviour have changed profoundly over the past few decades, with divorce and single-parent families becoming increasingly common. Even in two-parent families, both parents may work long hours, leaving less time and energy for parental involvement with children. Computers and the Internet may also have an impact on youth crime, allowing some disaffected youth, for example, to find it easier to communicate with one another and plan criminal activities. Through such electronic links, youths anywhere can acquire greater exposure to violent images, hate propaganda, or even information about how to make bombs. Some commentators argue that there is an international trend, with the combined effects of violence in movies, on television, and in video and computer games as well as changes in social and familial structure, resulting in a culture of violence. Thus, vulnerable youths today may be less empathetic and more prone to violence.[64]

In all societies and throughout history, adolescence has at least for some youth been a period of alienation from adult values and attitudes. Some commentators, though, are arguing that changes in family structure and technology have broadened the gulf between youths and adults. Some types of behaviour have clearly changed, such as, for example, more teenagers being sexually active at an earlier age than were adolescents a decade ago.[65] Youth unemployment is at high levels and the economic future for many youth, especially those with difficulties in the school system, seems uncertain. While among the wealthier nations of the world, Canada nevertheless has increasingly serious child poverty; a sizeable group of have-not youth have limited education and bleak employment prospects in our knowledge-based society.

---

63   See, for example, Reginald W. Bibby, *Canada's Teens: Today, Yesterday, and Tomorrow* (Toronto, ON: Stoddart, 2001); and D. Owen Carrigan, *Juvenile Delinquency in Canada: A History* (Concord ON: Irwin Publishing, 1998).

64   See, for example, David Grossman, *Stop Teaching Our Kids to Kill* (New York: Random House, 1999).

65   See Bibby, above note 63; and Patricia Hersch, *A Tribe Apart: A Journey into the Heart of American Adolescence* (New York: Ballantine Books, 1998). See also "Teens Have Sex Early, Often, and Unprotected," *Ottawa Citizen*, October 23, 1999, reporting on an international survey indicating that North American youth lose their virginity on average at the age of fifteen, and that the average age of loss of virginity has been falling over the past half-decade.

All of these factors may be affecting youth crime rates in Canada. Ultimately, it may not be possible to establish with certainty the extent to which the increase in reported youth crime in the period after the enactment of the YOA reflected actual changes in behaviour as opposed to changes in reporting. It seems certain that some of the increase in reported youth crime simply reflected changes in reporting practices. It also seems likely, however, that over the past half century the nature and amount of youth crime have changed as a result of profound societal changes. D. Owen Carrigan, a social historian, is among those who argue that social and cultural changes have resulted in "an increasing number of young people who are angry and disdainful of authority" and, as a result, there is more youth violence and crime than was the case a few decades earlier.[66]

2) Risk Factors for Youth Involvement in Crime

Even if the total national level of youth crime has not increased substantially since the YOA came into force, patterns of youth crime are not constant. As society and communities change, so do patterns of youth crime. Economic, social, and demographic changes as well as population migration affects crime patterns and rates in individual communities. Studies based on interviews and anonymous surveys of adolescents indicate that almost all youth commit some offences — primarily property-related crimes or offences involving drugs or alcohol — but that most of these offences are not reported. Indeed, widespread offending by young people occurs in all societies, although its nature and extent vary in different societies.

Typically, youths commit relatively few, minor offences and are likely not be apprehended; if arrested and charged, most do not reoffend. Some adolescents, however, have a more serious history of illegal behaviour, committing a greater number and broader range of offences and, if apprehended, reoffending even if charged and sent into custody. A relatively small portion of all adolescents are in the latter group of more serious, repeat offenders, who are responsible for a disproportionately large amount of violent offences and cause the youth justice system the greatest difficulty. A Montreal study, for example, found that 6 percent of youths account for 20 percent of all adolescent offenders brought before youth courts and for 50 percent of the charges.[67]

---

66   D. Owen Carrigan, above note 63 at 163–212.
67   National Crime Prevention Council, *Offender Profiles* (Ottawa: 1995) at 5.

Research suggests that children who have early contact with the police as a result of offending behaviour under the age of twelve are more likely to have significant and repeat involvement in the youth court system later in adolescence.[68]

No single theory can explain why adolescents commit crimes, nor why some youths commit more violent offences or repeatedly offend. No model can predict with certainty whether a particular youth will or will not offend. Perhaps more crucially, from the perspective of the youth justice system, there can be never be certainty about which of the youths who appear in court will reoffend despite intervention. There are cases of youths — seemingly ordinary and from an advantaged background without any prior history of offending — who commit the most brutal crimes with no apparent warning or explanation. Cases in which offending behaviour appears unpredictable or inexplicable, however, are relatively rare. More commonly, certain social and personal risk factors can strongly predict which adolescents are likely to be involved in the youth justice system on a recurrent basis. The Commission on Youth Violence of the American Psychological Association observed:

> Although no definitive answer yet exists that would make it possible to predict exactly which individuals will become violent, many factors have been identified as contributing to a child's risk profile. Biological factors, child rearing conditions, ineffective parenting, emotional or cognitive development, gender differences, sex role socialization, relation to peers, cultural milieu, social factors such as economic inequality and lack of opportunity, and media influences among others, all are thought to be factors that contribute to violent behaviour. Psychologists continue to search for a unified theoretical model that can account for these factors and assign them appropriate weight as risk factors for a child's or adolescent's involvement as a perpetrator, victim, bystander or witness.[69]

Among the factors that researchers associate with a high risk of serious or repeat offending are:

---

68   D. Day, "Risk for Court Contact and Predictors of an Early Age for Court Contact among a Sample of High-Risk Youth" (1998) 40 Can J. Crim. 421. See also B.B. Potter, *et al.*, *Youth Violence: A Report of the Surgeon General* (Washington D.C.: Surgeon General, 2001).

69   American Psychological Association, Commission on Youth Violence, *Violence and Youth: Psychology's Response* (Washington, D.C.: American Psychological Association, 1993) at 17. See also Statistics Canada, "Problem Behaviour and Delinquency in Children and Youth" (2001) 21:4 Juristat.

- poor parenting behaviour, which includes such home factors as child abuse, poor supervision or neglect, and erratic or excessive discipline;
- high levels of parental conflict[70] and living in a family where there is spousal abuse or battering even without direct abuse of the children;
- parental drug or alcohol addiction;
- a parental record of criminal activity;
- difficulties in school, which may be the result of a learning disability[71] or a condition such as fetal alcohol syndrome (FAS) or fetal alcohol effect (FAE): a child who has trouble learning in school will often have difficulty in learning societal rules, and delinquent behaviour is associated with truancy and dropping out of school;
- drug and alcohol abuse in adolescence or even in childhood: a risk factor in itself, many crimes are committed when drugs or alcohol have reduced inhibitions.

Poverty by itself is not a significant risk factor for delinquency, but economic deprivation when associated with family disruption or poor parenting exacerbates other risk factors. While poverty in childhood is related to poor educational achievement and to low income as an adult, it does not in itself seem to correlate significantly with delinquency.

Street youth who have left home are prone to engage in offending behaviour. These youth, who have left their families and have no permanent residence, are likely to be neither attending school nor working. They may sleep in shelters, parks, or abandoned buildings, or stay with diverse friends in rotation for short periods at each place. Such youth may commit various offences, including prostitution and drug offences, as well as violent and property offences. Some of this offending doubtless relates to their economic difficulties, as youths under eighteen have difficulty finding employment or getting welfare, as well as to the lack of supervision that characterizes life on the street. Parental abuse and neglect often contribute to adolescents leaving

---

70 Interestingly, it would appear that living in a single-parent family does not in itself correlate with a higher rate of criminal behaviour, but children who grow up in a family where there is a high level of parental conflict, whether or not the parents ultimately divorce, is related to higher levels of offending behaviour: H. Juby and D. Farrington, "Disentangling the Link between Disrupted Families and Delinquency" (2001) 41 Brit J. Crim. 22.

71 Research indicates that as many as three-quarters of young offenders in custody have some form of learning disability; assessment and treatment of young offenders should take this into account. See Learning Disabilities Association of Canada, *Position Paper on the Proposed Amendments to the Young Offenders Act* (Ottawa: 1996).

home and engaging in offending behaviour;[72] not all street youths are from neglectful or abusive families and sometimes anguished parents turn to the police and various social agencies to try to get their children off the street.

Research suggests that, while no single factor determines how an adolescent will behave, the more risk factors a youth has the more likely it is that the youth will engage in criminal or self-destructive behaviour.[73] While most serious or repeat offenders have at least one of these risk factors, and often more than one, not all of them do. Many youths from apparently deprived backgrounds do not become involved with the justice system. The lack of a single clear explanation for youthful criminality suggests that this social problem can never be wholly solved. The fact that virtually all young people engage in some criminal activity also indicates that, at least at some level, youthful offending should probably be viewed as a normal societal occurrence. Further, even youth who commit quite serious offences may simply be going through a "phase," and will "outgrow" their anti-social behaviour.

3) Prediction and Prevention

In relatively rare but highly publicized cases, young people without a significant history of offending and without apparent risk factors commit very violent acts. This has occurred recently, for example, in tragic shootings at schools, more often in the United States, although it has also happened in Canada. The youths who commit these offences invariably felt alienated from their families and socially isolated from their classmates, and have been suffering psychological disturbance. In some cases, hindsight has suggested that there were warning signs to which parents or others might have reacted, which might have prevented the tragedies — but some seem almost impossible to have predicted.[74] Some acts of this nature might have been prevented through community or school-based programs, or through better school security, but increased sanctions in the justice system would have had no effect. The youths committing some of these school shootings were

---

72   M. Webber, *Street Kids: The Tragedy of Canada's Runaways* (Toronto: University of Toronto Press, 1991); and B. Schissel and K. Fedec, "The Selling of Innocence: The Gestalt of Danger in the Lives of Youth Prostitutes" (1999) 41 Can J. Crim. 33.

73   James Gabarino, *Raising Children in a Socially Toxic Environment* (San Francisco, CA: Jossey-Bass, 1995) at 149–64.

74   E.P. Mulve and E. Cauffman, "The Inherent Limits of Predicting School Violence," [2001 October] *American Psychologist* 797–802.

clearly not concerned about possible apprehension, and were usually suicidal as well as homicidal.

Social and legal policies may contribute to a reduction in offending behaviour but cannot eliminate all youth crime. This does not mean that youth crime should not be the subject of legal responses. It is important, though, to assess the appropriateness of societal responses to youth crime in context. There are steps that society can take in terms of prevention, policing, and intervention that can reduce (but not eliminate) youth offending. A simplistic approach to youth offending that focuses on longer custody and more adult sentences is not likely to have a significant impact.

It should also be recognized that certain social policies and conditions can contribute to an increase in the youth crime rate. A comparison with American circumstances should make Canadians who are concerned about youth crime very cautious about wanting changes to gun-control laws or further fraying of our social safety net. While there is no single explanation, commentators have suggested factors that, in combination, have created a much higher rate of serious youth violence in the United States than in Canada: relatively poor public health and education systems, relatively great income disparities, lax gun-control laws, and a history of institutionalized racism. The fact that the American juvenile justice system has much more severe sanctions, including in some states capital punishment for juveniles who commit murder, clearly shows that a get-tough approach is not an effective approach to creating a safer society. While youthful offending in Canada is not as serious as in the United States and may not have significantly increased in recent years, youth crime in Canada — especially violence — is a serious social problem.

E. GROUP AND GANG OFFENCES

The most frequent victims of youth crime are other adolescents. There is significant evidence that many Canadian youth are afraid of acts of violence and extortion perpetrated by other youths in their schools and elsewhere.[75] One of the realities of youth crime is that most offences involve more than one adolescent perpetrator; in many cases, a few

---

75   See, for example, C. Ryan, F. Matthews, and J. Banner, *Student Perceptions of Violence* (Toronto: Central Toronto Youth Services, 1993); and S. Trevethan, "Teenage Victims of Violence" (1992) 12:6 Juristat 1. See also "Shakedowns in the Schoolyard," *Globe and Mail*, October 4, 1997: A1.

youths form an informal group that becomes involved in committing criminal acts, perhaps with one or more youths taking a leadership role and others feeling pressured to participate. Youths who are generally law abiding may become involved in criminal activities when with their peers. This has resulted, for example, in incidents of swarming (a group taunting or attacking an individual) and groups of adolescents committing robberies or acts of violence, sometimes against lone individuals. The infamous beating death of teenaged Reena Verk in Victoria, B.C., by a group of youths, many of whom barely knew her, is a troubling example of how adolescents in a group may behave in a more callous and brutal fashion than any member of the group might do alone. Interaction with peers who seem untroubled by an initial assault can result in an escalation of violence by members of the group.

The term "gang" does not have a precise legal or sociological definition, but is generally used to describe a group of adolescents or young adults who regularly engage in criminal activity, often together. There is great diversity in the composition and activities of youth gangs.[76] Some gangs are just loose groups of friends who only occasionally engage in criminal acts, usually without much planning.

Some gangs can have a quite stable membership and leadership structure, perhaps with some unifying form of behaviour or dress code, such as distinctive colours. These more formal gangs engage in criminal acts with much more deliberation and a clearer monetary objective, for example, drug dealing and extortion. In more criminally oriented gangs, violence within and between gangs is common, and innocent individuals are frequently victimized.[77] While some of these criminal gangs are ethnically mixed, others — to which the media now give prominent attention — form along ethnic lines: these include Aboriginal gangs in prairie cities, Chinese and South-Asian gangs in Vancouver, and Vietnamese gangs in Toronto.[78] Although criminal

---

76   See, for example, Esbensen, et al., "Youth Gangs and Definitional Issues: When is a Gang a Gang, and Why Does it Matter?" (2001) 47 Crime & Delinquency 105–30.

77   See, for example, R. Weiler, T. Caputo, and K. Kelly, *Youth Violence and Youth Gangs: Responding to Community Concerns* (Ottawa: Solicitor General Canada, 1994); I.A. Spergel, *The Youth Gang Problem: A Community Approach* (New York, NY: Oxford University Press, 1995); and L.W. Sherman, *et al.*, *Preventing Youth Crime: What Works, What Doesn't, What's Promising* (Washington D.C.,: Office of Justice Programs, U.S. Department of Justice, 1997).

78   See, for example, "Teen Gangs: Fear in our Schools", *Toronto Star*, October 24, 1998; and "Gangs Recruiting in Schools: Police," *National Post*, September 6, 2001.

gangs have conventionally been more of a concern for low-income youth, there is some evidence that disaffected middle-class youths also form gangs that engage in criminal and violent acts.[79] Some gangs may avow a political, religious-cult, or social philosophy that might be described as anarchist or racist (i.e., skinheads and white-power groups); such thinking may be used to justify violence or other criminal acts. Some youths belong to groups that engage in occult practices, or participate in secretive recreational, religious, or cultural practices. Abuse of drugs and alcohol is common among criminal gangs.

Parents or other adults may be concerned about the involvement of youth in groups whose members have antisocial attitudes or a distinctive youth-culture appearance, even if they do not engage in criminal behaviour. For youths who have weak relationships with parents, teachers, or other adults, gang membership may take on a special importance: indeed, many youths who are members of gangs may find their primary sources of social interaction and values among other members of their gang. Gang membership may also be vital for social support or physical protection inside of custody facilities, although this is a more widespread concern in adult rather than youth custody facilities.

Some public discourse about gangs appears to be based on an assumption that youth gangs are a recent phenomenon, a reflection of societal disintegration, or even related to the existence of a legal regime that is perceived by critics to be ineffective. However, there have long been concerns about youth gangs, the existence of which is a phenomenon of concern to a greater or lesser extent in many modern societies. The public of seventy-five or a hundred years ago in Canada was also very concerned about gangs formed by youths from disadvantaged immigrant groups, at that time Irish and Jewish gangs. While the identity of the socially disadvantaged groups forming gangs may have changed, the problem of youths from disadvantaged groups forming gangs is not new. The situation today, however, may be worse than the one a hundred years ago, owing to changes in societal values and social structures. Popular culture may tend to glorify gangs more than was once the case, and the breakdown of family units may make gangs a more significant source of emotional support and protection for greater numbers of adolescents than in the past. Canada is now a much more urban society. Youth gangs engaging in criminal activities tend to be a more serious problem in cities, although youth gangs are becoming a concern in suburban areas as well as in some rural and remote Aboriginal communities.

---

79 Dan Korem, *Suburban Gangs: The Affluent Rebels* (Richardson, TX: International Focus Press, 1994).

While the media may exaggerate, there is no doubt that youth gangs are a serious social problem. In particular, students in schools may be intimidated by the presence of even loosely organized groups whose members are prepared to use threats and violence to extort money or gain other advantages; students from certain ethnic communities may be especially vulnerable to extortion and intimidation. Effective policing in schools and elsewhere in the community can play a substantial role in dealing with youth gangs. Improved recreational programs, community-based mentoring, and violence-prevention programs in schools may also be useful in reducing levels of gang-related offending. Numerous communities are also trying to have social (or street) workers meet with gang members and redirect them away from criminal activities.[80]

Participation in a group offence may be legally significant in that members may be charged as parties to an offence pursuant to section 21 of the *Criminal Code*. If youths have formed a common intention to commit a criminal act and provided assistance in doing the act, they are "parties" to an offence — that is, technically equally guilty to the principal perpetrator. However, youth courts tend to be more lenient in making decisions about sentencing a youth who was only a party to an offence with a relatively minor role, as opposed to being a principal perpetrator or ring-leader. If a situation involves a very serious offence, such as a homicide, the court may assess the degree of participation in the violence and character of each youth before passing sentence and deciding whether to impose an adult or a youth sentence. A judge in a case under the *YOA* deciding whether a youth should be tried in adult court observed that it "is self-evident that a young person who delivers the death blows to a victim is more likely to be a threat to the safety of the public than one who is an aider or abetter, and perhaps a somewhat reluctant one, to a murder."[81]

In 1997 Parliament made participation in a criminal organization a criminal offence under section 467.1 of the *Criminal Code*. A "criminal organization" is defined as: "any group . . . consisting of five or more persons, whether formally or informally organized, having as *one* of its *primary* activities the commission of an . . . offence [punishable for an adult by a sentence of five years or more] and any . . . members of which . . . engage in . . . the commission of a series of such

---

80   See "Youth Input Urged in War on Teen Gangs," *Toronto Star*, January 19, 1999; and S.S. Anand, "Preventing Youth Crime: What Works, What Doesn't, and What it All Means for Canadian Juvenile Justice Policy" (1999) 25 Queen's L.J. 177.

81   *R. v. S.(G.)* (1991), 5 O.R. (3d) 97 at 108 (C.A.), Goodman J.A.

offences."[82] A criminal organization may have members who are young persons as well as adults. Under section 467.1(2), if an adult, or a young person who is to be sentenced as an adult, is found to be member of a criminal organization in the context of the commission of any offence, a sentence consecutive to any other sentence is to be imposed for membership in the organization. While the mandatory sentencing provisions of section 467.1 do not have direct application to youths sentenced under the YCJA, youth courts may take gang membership into account as an aggravating circumstance in sentencing or in deciding whether to deal with a youth as an adult.

Sometimes a youth court judge will decide that a particularly severe response to an offence is necessary because it was committed by a gang member and a message must be sent to other gang members in the community — that is, a sentencing decision may be intended to have a deterrent effect. For example, a sentence of twenty-four months' secure custody was imposed under the YOA on a seventeen-year-old member of a street gang who injured another youth while the gang was stealing skateboards; in upholding the sentence, the Manitoba Court of Appeal stated: "Although deterrence to others is less of a goal in the case of a young offender, it remains a factor in a group crime such as this. Extremely violent behaviour by groups of youth simply cannot be tolerated. A lengthy term of secure custody is therefore in order."[83]

The principles that govern adult sentencing set out in section 718.2 of the Criminal Code require that a court should consider as an aggravating factor that an offence was committed "for the benefit of, at the direction of or in association with a criminal organization." While this provision is not directly applicable to youths sentenced under the YCJA, youth justice court judges, prosecutors, and police will likely be

---

82 Criminal Code, s. 2 (enacted as S.C. 1997, c. 23). This legislation was enacted in response to the growing concern about some of the very sophisticated organized criminal gangs that engage in a range of illegal activities including drug dealing, prostitution, money laundering and extortion, gangs that use violence and murder as a part of their ordinary operations. These criminal gangs often have international affiliations. The more sophisticated, stable criminal gangs do recruit younger members, though they tend to have largely adult membership. They tend to regard adolescents as too inexperienced, unreliable or unpredictable to have regular membership or central roles, although some of these criminal gangs do have affiliated members or "wannabes" who are under eighteen years of age. In some cases, criminal gangs may exploit these younger members to engage in criminal activities with the assurance (not always reflecting the reality) that they will receive more lenient treatment in the courts if they are apprehended.

83 R. v. E.(R.K.) (1996), 107 Man. R. (2d) 200 at 204 (C.A.), per Twaddle J.A.

influenced by the principles articulated by judges under the *YOA* and, accordingly, treat gang participation or involvement as an aggravating factor in sentencing and other decisions, such as whether to divert a youth from the court system.

F. YOUTH OFFENDERS FROM VISIBLE MINORITY AND ABORIGINAL COMMUNITIES

While offences are committed by youths from all economic and ethnic backgrounds, some special issues relate to youth offenders from visible minorities and Aboriginal communities in Canada, as in other countries. Nationwide data on the ethnicity of young offenders are not kept in Canada since this type of information can be difficult to obtain reliably, and governments have been reluctant to collect it for fear that it may be misused. Some national data, however, are available about Aboriginal youth in the justice system: while they comprise only about 5 percent of the adolescent population of Canada, based on 1998–99 data, Aboriginal youth accounted for 18 percent of youth court probation orders and 24 percent of the youth custody admissions, with the greatest proportion of Aboriginal youth in custody in Canada's western provinces and northern territories.[84] Further, several local studies have been done, and some police forces and corrections departments collect some youth data based on ethnicity. These data clearly reveal that the majority of young offenders in Canada are Caucasian; they also reveal that youths from certain backgrounds — including black (i.e., of African, Caribbean, and other ancestry), East Asian (i.e., of Pakistani, Indian, or other ancestry), and Aboriginal — are over-represented in the youth justice system by comparison with their proportional representation in the total Canadian population.[85]

84   Statistics Canada, "Youth Custody and Community Service 1998–99" (2000) 20:8 Juristat 9; Quebec and New Brunswick did not provide data. Aboriginal peoples, under the *Constitution Act, 1982*, above note 24, s. 35(2), are Inuit, Métis, and "Indians" (now mostly known as First Nation members).

85   See, for example, Ontario, *Report of the Commission on Systemic Racism in the Ontario Criminal Justice System* (Toronto: Queen's Printer, 1995) at 85; L.D. Bertrand, *et al.*, *The Experiences of Minority Youth in the Canadian Justice System* (Calgary: Canadian Research Institute for Law and the Family, 1996), and S. Moyer, "Race, Gender, and Homicide: Comparisons between Aboriginal and Other Canadians," in Ruth M. Mann, ed., *Juvenile Crime and Delinquency: A Turn-of-the-Century Reader* (Toronto: Canadian Scholars Press, 2000).

Although the causes for higher representation of youths from social minorities in the justice system are debated, two basic explanations are accepted. First, the social and economic conditions faced by many youths with racial minority backgrounds affect relative rates of offending behaviour. Secondly, systemic discrimination on the part of police, justice, and corrections officials — most of whom are not themselves from social minorities — affects how Aboriginal youths and youths from visible minorities are dealt with by the justice system. While some try to argue that differences in reported offence rates are exclusively a product of discrimination, or exclusively a reflection of the differential offending patterns which in turn are a product of social and economic conditions,[86] it is apparent that both are operative concerns.[87]

From all that is known about the causes of delinquent behaviour, one would expect that youths who are members of minority groups that are socially and economically disadvantaged would have high rates of youth crime. While some media reports express — in purely racial terms — concerns about Aboriginal and immigrant youth gangs or violence in urban Canada, more detailed news reports acknowledge that "[p]olice, sociologists and outreach workers agree the street-gang phenomenon is the consequence of an endemic and unrelenting cycle of poverty, racism, family breakdown and unemployment."[88] Adolescents from some disadvantaged immigrant groups have high youth crime rates; the relative poverty, social dislocation, family stresses, and cultural upheaval often associated with immigration may all play a role. Children who have grown up in brutal war-torn environments or refugee camps and then move to Canada may face special risks.[89]

---

86   There are also a few "biological determinists" — such as psychologist Philippe Rushton of the University of Western Ontario — who seek genetic explanations for differential rates of criminal behaviour, but there is no evidence from biologists or geneticists to support these extreme and widely discredited views.

87   Since Canadian researchers are only starting to address this type of issue, it is difficult to draw conclusions about the weighting of the factors. The Canadian Race Relations Foundation collects research of this nature: see <www.crrf.ca>. An American scholar writing about his assessment of the experience in the United States concluded: "Racial disparities, especially affecting Blacks, have long bedeviled the criminal justice system. . . . Racial bias and stereotyping no doubt play some role, but they are not the major cause. In the longer term, disparities in jail . . . are mainly the result of racial differences in offending patterns" (M. Tonry, "Racial Politics, Racial Disparities, and the War on Crime" (1994) 40 Crime & Delinquency 475 at 479–80).

88   D. Roberts, "The Street Gangs of Winnipeg," *Globe and Mail*, May 18, 1996: D5.

89   See, for example, T. Appleby, "Battle-Scarring Tied to Violence," *Globe and Mail*, June 13, 1990: A8; and M. Valpy, "When Jamaican Children Come to Canada," *Globe and Mail*, March 5, 1996: A17

Canada is a culturally and racially diverse society. While some commentators remark on the relative racial tolerance of today's youth, many of whom are attending schools with multiethnic populations,[90] racial conflict is a problem in some Canadian schools.[91] Adolescents from a visible minority or immigrant background are sometimes the victims of racially motivated bullying in schools and violence in their communities, which in turn may provoke a violent response by minority youth.[92] Some youth offending reflects racist, sexist, or homophobic attitudes at their crudest and most overt. Over-representation of Aboriginal and minority youth in police charge statistics may represent subtler, covert forms of the same sentiments within the justice system.

Unemployment and a host of social problems also affect Aboriginal communities and have an impact on the criminal behaviour of adolescents. Some Canadian research suggests that the risk of offending behaviour may be very similar for Aboriginal and non-Aboriginal populations *provided* that account is taken of such factors as relative rates of unemployment, family background, academic difficulties, and alcohol or drug abuse.[93] Aboriginal youth also face enormous challenges, whether they live on a reserve or in a city. They often grow up in communities that are culturally and economically marginalized by the dominant society and where parenting skills have been damaged by inter-generational cycles of abuse and violence traceable to victimization in Aboriginal residential schools. Great social, economic, and cultural dislocation and inter-generational tensions arose when Aboriginal parents and Elders were forced to give up their nomadic existence and settle into communities where their children could attend school and learn a language and culture with which parents were not familiar .[94]

Aboriginal leaders are concerned about the effects of poverty, systemic racism, and the loss of identity and self-esteem, and the "cultural genocide" that has led to cycles of abuse, family dysfunction, high

---

90   See, for example, Bibby, above note 63 at 321.

91   See, for example, "Racial Violence Grips B.C. High School," *National Post*, October 12, 1999.

92   For a particularly gruesome example, see "Suspect Confessed to 'Racist, Nazi Beliefs'," *National Post*, May 29, 2001, describing the racially motivated murder by a sixteen-year-old youth of a fifteen-year-old girl who immigrated from Cuba when an infant.

93   J. Bonta, et al., "Risk Prediction and Reoffending: Aboriginal and Non-Aboriginal Offenders" (1997) 39 Can. J. Crim. 127.

94   See, for example, R. Ross, *Dancing with a Ghost: Exploring Indian Reality* (Markham, ON: Octopus, 1992) and *Returning to the Teachings: Exploring Aboriginal Justice* (Toronto: Penguin, 1996).

youth suicide rates, and drug and alcohol abuse.[95] These circumstances in turn have contributed to a relatively high prevalence of fetal alcohol syndrome or FAS. (FAS is a condition manifested by neurological brain damage and sometimes physical appearance that is caused by a mother's ingestion of alcohol during pregnancy. A related but less severe condition is known as fetal alcohol effect or FAE.) Adolescents (and adults) with FAS or FAE have significant learning disabilities and have greater difficulty in comprehending the difference between right and wrong. In some Aboriginal communities there are also very significant problems with children and adolescents sniffing gasoline and other solvents, which can cause serious and permanent neurological damage. Rehabilitation and reducing offending behaviour among those who suffer from fetal alcohol syndrome or the effects of solvent sniffing is much more challenging than with other offenders, although adolescents with this condition can learn to control their behaviour through appropriate treatment.[96]

1) Systemic Discrimination in the Justice System

When considering issues relating to ethnicity and culture in adolescent crime, it is important to address both relative offending rates and the effects of systemic discrimination. Studies have long documented the problem of racism in the American justice system.[97] There is now a growing body of evidence that racism affects how Canadian youth are dealt with by the justice system, including effects on police arrest practices; decisions in the courts by judges, lawyers, and probation officers; and the actions of corrections officials.[98] Canadian judges are demonstrating

---

95 See, e.g., Canada, Royal Commission on Aboriginal Peoples, *Bridging the Divide: A Report on Aboriginal People and the Criminal Justice System in Canada* (Ottawa: Ministry of Supply and Services, 1996).

96 See "Native Murder Rate in Manitoba Alarming, Study Shows," *Globe and Mail*, November 2, 1998.

97 See, for example, L. LeFlore, "Minority Youth in the Juvenile Justice System: A Judicial Response" (1990) 41 Juv. & Fam. Ct. J. 1.

98 See, for example, Ontario report on systemic racism, above note 85 at 86; and Bertrand, *et al.*, above note 85. Others include: John Boyko, *Last Steps to Freedom: The Evolution of Canadian Racism* (Toronto: J. Gordon Schillingford Publishing, 1995); Frances Henry, Carol Tator, Mattis Winston, and Tim Rees, *The Colour of Democracy: Racism in Canadian Society* (Toronto: Harcourt Brace, 1995); Sherene H. Razack, *Looking White People in the Eye: Gender, Race, and Culture in Courtrooms and Classrooms* (Toronto: University of Toronto Press, 1998); and R. James, "Why I fear for my sons," *Toronto Star*, October 21, 2002, A1; part of a series on "racial profiling" in the *Toronto Star*.

greater awareness of issues of systemic and societal discrimination. For example, it is now a regular practice for potential jurors in trials involving non-Caucasian accused persons to be asked whether they have racial prejudices that might prevent them from fairly deciding a case.[99] While this reflects a recognition that the biased attitudes of some members of the community may influence their judgments and actions, screening jurors by asking whether they perceive themselves as biased does not assure that all who may be influenced by race are excluded from serving on a jury. While many who work in the youth justice system in Canada are becoming more sensitive to discrimination, and are trying to ensure that their decisions and actions are not tainted by bias, there continue to be concerns, for example, about the high incidence of police arrests and of police shooting of visible-minority youths and young adults.

In recent years, at least in the courts, incidents of overt racism have been relatively rare, since professionals are generally cautious about what they say in such a public forum. However, outside the courtroom there are many documented cases of police and correctional workers using racial epithets and stereotyping, and some lawyers and judges may do so as well. Judicial bias may be barely disguised even in the courtroom, as in a 1990 Toronto case where the sentencing judge stated:

> Sometimes I send young men from Vietnam to jail rather severely. They've been in Canada a short time . . . and I have to work out a sentence that appears to have no bias. We're supposed to treat everyone in front of us the same way . . . but often I have to lay out sentences to make it clear that in the circumstances of recent immigrants' arrival into Canada. . . . I lay out some severe sentences that perhaps wouldn't apply in the same set of facts with someone who'd been in Canada [longer].[100]

This judge, while stating that there is a need to treat everyone fairly, was in fact suggesting that recent immigrants from Vietnam should be punished more severely. Beyond the more obvious discriminatory attitudes and acts, there is a concern that subtle, often unconscious, discriminatory attitudes and acts have a cumulative effect over a range of decisions, including those involving police charging and arrest, prosecutorial failure to use non-court diversion, judicial decisions about pre-trial detention, adjudication and sentencing, and decisions of correctional workers and probation officers about access to programs and

---

99 *R. v. Williams*, [1998] 1 S.C.R. 1128; *R. v. Koh* (1998), 42 O.R. (3d) 668 (C.A.).
100 *R. v. Butcher* (September 4, 1990) (Ont. Prov. Div.) (unreported), quoted in the Ontario report on systemic racism, above note 85.

release from custody.[101] While decision makers may be unaware that their judgments may be influenced by cultural factors or communication difficulties, youth likely to be targets of systemic discrimination clearly perceive that they are less likely to get "the benefit of the doubt," for example, when a police officer is deciding whether to caution a youth rather than lay charges.[102] Crucial decisions about a youth and assessments of credibility may be affected by perceptions of police, prosecutors, and judges about the attitude and demeanour of such youths or their parents.

The complex task of identifying and responding to systemic discrimination is illustrated by *R. v. S.(R.D.)*, a youth court case from Nova Scotia that ended up in the Supreme Court of Canada. A fifteen-year-old black-skinned youth had been charged with interfering with an arrest and with assault on a police officer, arising out of an incident that had occurred when a police officer was arresting the youth's cousin. The officer alleged that the youth came onto the scene of the arrest, yelled at the officer, and then pushed into him. The youth acknowledged that he was at the scene of his cousin's arrest but said that he was only speaking to his cousin, who was already in a police car, to ask if he should call the cousin's mother. The youth denied that he had pushed into the officer but testified that the officer had told him: "Shut up, shut up, or you'll be under arrest too."[103] The youth testified that, when he had kept talking to his cousin, the officer had put him in a choke hold and arrested him. The case was tried before the only black female judge in Nova Scotia, Judge Sparks, who concluded:

> The Crown says, well, why would the officer say that events occurred in the way in which he has recalled them to the Court this morning.

---

101 See, for example, P. J. Carrington, S. Moyer, and F. Kopelman, "Factors Affecting Pre-Dispositional Detention and Release in Canadian Juvenile Courts" (1988) 16 J. Crim. Just. 463.

102 J. Warner, *et al.*, "Marijuana, Juveniles, and the Police: What High-School Students Believe about Detection and Enforcement" (1998) 40 Can J Crim. 401. See also G.S. Bridges and S. Steen, "Racial Disparities in Official Assessments of Juvenile Offenders: Attributional Stereotypes as Mediating Mechanisms" (1998) 63 Am. Sociological Rev. 554, who suggest that it may not be overt racism that results in probation officers being more likely to recommend a more severe sentence. Rather, it is the assessment of "character" that is influenced by race: "In so far as [probation] officials recommend more severe sentences for black youths than white, they do so because they recommend more severe sentences for youths whose crimes they attribute to more negative personality traits and who they perceive as more dangerous than others" (at 567).

103 *R. v. S.(R.D.)*, [1997] 3 S.C.R. 484 at para. 67.

I am not saying that the Constable has misled the court, although police officers have been known to do that in the past. I am not saying that the officer overreacted, but certainly police officers do overreact, particularly when they are dealing with non-white groups. That to me indicates a state of mind right there that is questionable. I believe that probably the situation in this particular case is the case of a young police officer who overreacted. I do accept the evidence of [R.D.S.] that he was told to shut up or he would be under arrest. It seems to be in keeping with the prevalent attitude of the day.

At any rate, based upon my comments and based upon all the evidence before the court, I have no other choice but to acquit.[104]

The Crown appealed the acquittal, arguing that there was a reasonable apprehension that the black judge was biased against the Caucasian police officer.

The Supreme Court was badly split on how to deal with the case, although the majority upheld the acquittal.[105] In writing the plurality opinion, Justice Cory acknowledged the problem of system discrimination in the Canadian justice system: "[T]here is a realistic possibility that the actions taken by the police in their relations with visible minorities demonstrate both prejudice and discrimination . . . racial tension exists at least to some degree between police officers and visible minorities. Further, in some cases, racism may have been exhibited by police officers in arresting young black males."[106] But Cory J. went on to suggest that the comments by Judge Sparks were troubling since "there was no evidence . . . that would suggest that anti-black bias influenced this particular police officer's reactions." Cory J. concluded that, considering the judge's reasons in their entirety, the Crown had not demonstrated that there was a reasonable apprehension of bias, although her remarks were "close to the line."[107]

Justices L'Heureux-Dubé and McLachlin agreed in the result but went further than Cory J., arguing that Judge Sparks was "alive to the well-known racial dynamics that may exist in interactions between police officers and visible minorities" and concluding that her

oral reasons show that she approached the case with an open mind, used her experience and knowledge of the community to achieve an understanding of the reality of the case, and applied the fundamental

---

104 *Ibid.* at para 4.
105 *Ibid.*
106 *Ibid.* at para. 149.
107 *Ibid.* at paras. 150–152.

principle of proof beyond a reasonable doubt. . . . In alerting herself to the racial dynamic in the case, she was simply engaging in the process of contextualized judging which, in our view, was entirely proper and conducive to a fair and just resolution of the case before her.[108]

In a dissenting judgment, Major J. argued that, in the absence of evidence of specific racist attitudes or behaviour by this particular officer, the trial judge herself was displaying bias: "It can hardly be seen as progress to stereotype police officer witnesses as likely to lie when dealing with non-whites. This would return us to a time in the history of the Canadian justice system that many thought had passed. This reasoning, with respect to police officers, is no more legitimate than the stereotyping of women, children or minorities."[109] Although the Supreme Court was split on the question of how trial judges should take account of the possibility that systemic discrimination has affected the conduct or testimony of police officers in a particular case, all of the judges recognized that it is a serious concern in the administration of justice in Canada, including the youth justice system.

While it may never be possible to determine fully the effects of systemic discrimination on the administration of youth justice in Canada, many members of Aboriginal and visible-minority communities believe that there is bias in the justice system, and there is substantial evidence to justify their perception that they are victims of discrimination.[110] Everyone working in the justice system needs to be aware of problems of subtle racism and cultural bias. Lawyers need sensitivity and training for representing youths from diverse backgrounds. Programs for young offenders need to take account of the needs of youths from a range of cultural backgrounds and ethnic ancestries. There should be appropriate mechanisms for dealing with complaints about bias.

---

108 *Ibid.* at para. 59.

109 *Ibid.* at para. 18.

110 See also *R.* v. *Brown* (2002), 57 O.R.(3d) 615 (Sup. Ct.), where a young black-skinned adult male driving an expensive car in Toronto was stopped by a police officer and ultimately charged with impaired driving. He made an application for dismissal of the charges based on a violation of the *Charter*, above note 24, arguing that this arrest was "arbitrary as he was stopped based on 'racial profiling,' rather than due to any erratic driving or excessive speed. "The trial judge refused the application, saying that he had "distaste for the matters raised." The appeal court found that there was a "reasonable apprehension of bias" on the part of the trial judge, and ordered a new trial, with Trafford J. commenting: "It is helpful to emphasize that racism, whether it be conscious or unconscious, will rarely, if ever, be proven directly. If it be proven in court, it will be proven most often through circumstantial evidence" (at para. 17).

2) Aboriginal Youth Justice Issues

Issues relating to Aboriginal youth reflect both the unique constitutional and political position of Aboriginal peoples within Canada, and the relatively large numbers and concentration of Aboriginal offenders in Canadian youth courts and custodial facilities. In some parts of the country, Aboriginal youths form a majority of the population in custody, and in some youth courts — those sitting in Aboriginal communities — all of those who appear are Aboriginal youth.

Because Aboriginal communities in Canada tend to have a relatively large youth population, there is a profound concern that these communities will suffer long-term consequences if its young members grow into adult offenders rather than productive, contributing adults. Aboriginal communities are also anxious about youth crime issues because members of their communities are the most frequent victims of this offending and bear the immediate costs of it.

The treatment of Aboriginal peoples in Canada's justice system is a long and well-documented tragedy, reflecting at best insensitivity and at worst blatant racism.[111] Problems in the courts may be compounded by cultural and language difficulties. For example, as some Aboriginal youth may lack comprehension of such legal concepts as "not guilty," they may plead guilty in circumstances where other youth might not. Or their cultural background may make them reluctant to engage in an adversarial trial process.[112] The significant cultural variations among Aboriginal communities have produced diverse traditions and philosophies for dealing with offending behaviour, which differ from those found in the Canadian justice system. A member of the Oji-Cree Sandy Lake First Nation in Ontario stated in a presentation that: "Probably one of the most serious gaps . . . is the different perceptions of wrongdoing and how to best treat it. In the non-Indian community, committing a crime seems to mean that the individual is a bad person and therefore must be punished . . . the Indian communities view a wrongdoing as a misbehaviour which requires teaching or an illness that

---

111 See, for example, Manitoba, *Report of the Aboriginal Justice Inquiry of Manitoba* (Winnipeg, MN: Queen's Printer, 1991), ch. 15; Canada, Royal Commission on Aboriginal Peoples, *Bridging the Divide: A Report on Aboriginal People and Criminal Justice in Canada* (Ottawa, ON: Ministry of Supply and Services, 1996); Ross 1992, above note 94; and D. Bercuson and B. Cooper, "Justice System is No Friend to Indians," *Globe and Mail*, February 8, 1997: D2.

112 See, for example, T.T. Daley, "Where Cultures Clash: Native Peoples and a Fair Trial" (1992) 8 Can. Fam. L.Q. 301; and C.C. Brant, "Native Ethics and Rules of Behaviour" (1990) 35 Can. J. Psychiatry 534.

requires healing."[113] Although the restorative philosophy of the *YCJA* may be closer to traditional Aboriginal philosophies than those principles found in the *Criminal Code* for dealing with adult offenders, the challenges of dealing effectively with Aboriginal youth who offend have no easy solution. Some Aboriginal communities are working toward establishing Aboriginal control over police forces and justice programs, with a special emphasis on dealing with young persons.

The Canadian justice system is being modified to deal more fairly and effectively with Aboriginal youth and adult offenders, with some judges using "sentencing circles" — composed of community members, the victim, and the offender as well as the police, prosecutor, and defence counsel — to try to reach a consensus about an appropriate disposition. While in theory the judge is not bound by the outcome of such a sentencing process, in practice it is rare for a judge not to adopt a restorative justice solution proposed by this process. Sections 19 and 41 of the *YCJA* expressly allow for conferences involving family and community members to advise the courts, police, and youth probation officers. These provisions are especially relevant for Aboriginal youth and should encourage various forms of both community-based and court-based "sentencing circles" to provide advice and support for the appropriate response to youth who are engaging in offending behaviour. (Conferences and sentencing circles are discussed more fully in Chapters 5 and 8.)

Some Aboriginal communities — on reserves and in urban settings where there are significant Aboriginal populations, especially in western Canada — are also establishing innovative treatment programs for Aboriginal young offenders, often involving community Elders, an Aboriginal philosophy, and healing principles. A long-term objective of many Aboriginal communities is the establishment of autonomous Aboriginal justice systems: pilot projects have been set up to deal with certain less serious offences in some Aboriginal communities. To ensure that adequate attention is paid to the interests of the offender, the victim, the Aboriginal community, and Canadian society, many political, practical, and philosophical questions are to be addressed in undertaking this type of project.[114]

---

113 From the justice proposal made to the Ontario government, quoted in Ross, 1992, above note 94 at 123.

114 C. LaPrairie, "Community Justice or Just Communities? Aboriginal Communities in Search of Justice," (1995) 37 Can. J. Crim. 521. For a good discussion about the idea of Aboriginal justice, see Ross 1992 and 1996, above note 94.

In 1996 Parliament added section 718.2(e) to the *Criminal Code* to require a court sentencing an adult offender "to consider all available sanctions other than imprisonment that are reasonable in the circumstances . . . with particular attention to the circumstances of Aboriginal offenders."[115] In *R. v. Gladue*, the Supreme Court of Canada recognized that this provision was a response to the "acute problem of the disproportionate incarceration of Aboriginal peoples," and the failure of incarceration to reduce levels of offending.[116] The Court recognized that support for the Aboriginal ideal of restorative justice — which involves "some form of restitution and reintegration into the community . . . [and] for offenders to take some responsibility for their actions" — means that an "aboriginal offender's community will frequently understand the nature of a just sanction in a manner significantly different from that of many non-aboriginal communities."[117]

The Supreme Court emphasized that section 718.2(e) does not necessarily require a less severe sanction for all Aboriginal offenders. Concerns about deterrence, accountability, and protection of the public, especially from the most serious violent offenders, may require similar treatment for Aboriginal and other offenders. However, for Aboriginal offenders who commit less serious offences, there should be special judicial consideration of alternatives to incarceration, such as holding the offender accountable through a community-based sanction, even if the individual has a significant record of prior offending. Justices Cory and Iacobucci further emphasized that these principles apply to the sentencing of Aboriginal offenders in urban centres as well as those who live on reserves, stating:

> the different conceptions of sentencing held by many aboriginal people share a common underlying principle: that is, the importance of community-based sanctions. Sentencing judges should not conclude that the absence of alternatives specific to an aboriginal community eliminates their ability to impose a sanction that takes into account principles of restorative justice and the needs of the parties involved. Rather, the point is that one of the unique circumstances of aboriginal offenders is that community-based sanctions coincide with the aboriginal concept of sentencing and the needs of aboriginal people and communities. It is often the case that neither aboriginal offenders nor their communities are well served by incarcerating offenders,

---

115 *Criminal Code*, above note 5, s. 718.2(e).
116 *R. v. Gladue*, [1999] 1 S.C.R. 688.
117 *Ibid.* at para. 77.

particularly for less serious or non-violent offences. Where these sanctions are reasonable in the circumstances, they should be implemented. In all instances, it is appropriate to attempt to craft the sentencing process and the sanctions imposed in accordance with the aboriginal perspective.[118]

While most of the sentencing principles and provisions of the YCJA differ from those sections of the Criminal Code that govern the sentencing of adults, section 718.2(e) of the Criminal Code has been specifically incorporated into the new Act to apply to the sentencing of Aboriginal youth.[119] Further, section 3(1)(c)(iv) of the Declaration of Principle of the YCJA has a general statement that young persons who commit offences should be treated in a manner that "respect[s] gender, ethnic, cultural, and linguistic differences and respond[s] to the needs of Aboriginal young persons." It is therefore clear that the approach of the Supreme Court in Gladue is relevant to the sentencing of Aboriginal youth.[120] The Court's sensitivity to the unique circumstances of Aboriginal offenders is also relevant for the types of decisions made by police, probation officers, Crown prosecutors, and community members about how to deal with Aboriginal youth. Even if they are not first offenders, consideration should be given to community-based responses rather than making use of court and custody.

The recognition of special provisions to deal with the sentencing of Aboriginal youth is not uncontroversial. The conservative Canadian Alliance Party has been opposed to this type of special treatment of Aboriginal offenders, arguing that it is racist. That party was especially critical of section 38(2)(d) of the YCJA, which was added in 2002, as a result of the action of the Senate, and provides that "all available sanctions other than custody that are reasonable in the circumstances . . . with particular attention to the circumstances of Aboriginal offenders." In arguing against the enactment of this provision, Chuck Cadman, the leading Canadian Alliance spokesman on youth justice issues, said:

> Gail Sparrow, former Chief of the Musqueam Band, has been very critical of this type of legislation. The majority of crimes by Aboriginals [sic] are committed against other Aboriginals [sic]. The

---

118 Ibid. at para. 74.
119 YCJA, above note 2, s. 50; see also s. 38(2)(d).
120 See, for example, R. v. Bero, [1998] O.J. 4882 (Prov. Div.), per Renaud Prov. J., which held s. 718.2(e) should be applied when an Aboriginal youth was sentenced under the Young Offenders Act.

legislation would diminish the suffering and recognition the victims deserve. Sufficient guidelines already exist for judges to consider all mitigating factors for all offenders irrespective of race. The declaration of principles already sets out respect for ethnic, cultural and linguistic differences.

Why is it necessary to introduce an element of race into the legislation? Why should any victim receive a lesser degree of justice based solely on the racial origin of his or her victimizer?[121]

While these views are shared by many conservative commentators and even some academics,[122] Parliament has recognized the unique constitutional status and great social disadvantages of Aboriginal youth by requiring youth justice court judges to take special account of their circumstances. The approach adopted by Parliament reflects the recognition that conventional Canadian judicial responses to youth crime based on custody have generally proven ineffective in dealing with Aboriginal young offenders, who have had high rates of recidivism.

The YCJA encourages use of community-based responses to youth crime, such as police cautioning, diversion from the court system for extrajudicial measures, conferencing, and youth justice committees. These types of programs are especially important for Aboriginal communities, giving them some control for responding to their youthful offenders, while allowing Elders, victims, and family members of the youth to be involved in decisions that invoke Aboriginal concepts of restorative justice.

---

121 Canada, *Hansard*, No. 138, House of Commons, Thirty-Seventh Parliament, First Session, February 4, 2002 (12:50). Chuck Cadman's son, Jessie, was killed by a young offender (not Aboriginal) who at the time had been released on bail and was supposed to be under parental supervision. The young offender was in breach of his curfew at the time of the killing, which was an unprovoked stabbing in the course of the robbery of Jessie Cadman. Prior to this tragic killing, Chuck Cadman had had little interest in politics, but after that he became involved in the victim's rights movement and was then elected to Parliament as a member of the Reform — now the Canadian Alliance — Party.

122 P. Stenning and J. Roberts, "Empty Promises: Parliament, The Supreme Court, and the Sentencing of Aboriginal Offenders" (2001) 64 Sask. L Rev. 137 and S.S. Anand, "The Sentencing of Aboriginal Offenders: Continued Confusion and Persisting Problems: A Comment on the Decision in R. v. *Gladue*" (2000) 42 Can. J.Crim. 412.

G. FEMALE YOUNG OFFENDERS

Only about one-fifth of charges against youths involve females, but concerns about the incidence and treatment of female young offenders are growing. Under the *Juvenile Delinquents Act*, relatively few females were charged, although girls were far more frequently charged with the vague status offences of "sexual immorality" and "unmanageability" than boys. Some girls were charged with these delinquent acts for prostitution-related activities, and it was quite common for parents to have this type of charge brought when their daughters were perceived as being "out of control" or merely sexually active. Girls charged with "sexual immorality" or "unmanageability" could serve long periods in training schools; it is now tragically clear that many of these girls were sexually exploited by training school staff with long-term emotional harm.[123] The *YOA*, with its offence-oriented approach and emphasis on legal rights, reduced the possibility of the juvenile justice system being used in this highly discriminatory and destructive fashion. It did not, however, eliminate concerns related to gender bias.

In 2000–01 about 21 percent of charges involving youths were against females; in 1988 the rate was only 16 percent.[124] The increase in relative offending rates, as well as the opinions of professionals in the field, suggest that female adolescents are engaging in more offending behaviour, including more violent offences, although they are clearly not as violent as males.[125] Female children and adolescents can be as emotionally aggressive and callous toward their peers as males, but they are more likely to engage in manipulation and verbal aggression, for example, by spreading false rumours, and less likely to engage in criminal acts of violence towards their peers.[126] While female adolescents rarely commit the most serious offences (i.e., homicide or sexual assault), they are charged with a greater proportion of ordinary assaults (about 30 percent) than property offences (about 20 percent). In the category of property offences, girls make up a relatively small

---

123 See, for example, Bessner, above note 17.
124 Statistics Canada, *A Profile of Youth Justice in Canada* (Ottawa: 1998); Statistics Canada, *Youth Court Statistics, 2000–2001* (2002) 22:3 Juristat.
125 See, for example, I. Vincent, "Girl-Gang Violence Alarms Experts," *Globe and Mail*, September 12, 1995: A10.
126 See, for example, "Experts Report Girls as Aggressive as Boys But in Verbal Ways," *Globe and Mail*, October 23, 1999 at A3; and A. Cummings and A.W. Leschied, "Understanding Aggression with Adolescent Girls: Implications for Policy and Practice" (2001) 20 Can J. Comm. Mental Health 43.

proportion of those charged with the more serious offence of break and enter (under 10 percent) in comparison to those charged with theft under $5000, mainly shoplifting (about 25 percent). Female adolescents are much more likely than males to be charged with prostitution-related offences.

Many of the characteristics of persistent female adolescent offenders are similar to males, such as having learning disabilities and mental health problems, and coming from homes where there is a history of abuse or family violence. However, female adolescent offenders may be somewhat more likely to have emotional and psychological disturbances, and to have been victims of sexual abuse.[127] Research also shows that male offending increases with age throughout adolescence and peaks between the ages of seventeen and twenty-one, while female offending peaks at the age of fifteen, and declines in the sixteen- and seventeen-year-old population.[128] This is consistent with the fact that girls tend to reach physical and psychological maturity earlier than boys.

Youth courts are apparently more lenient with female young offenders than with males. Taking into account the seriousness of the offence and the prior record, an adolescent female is less likely to receive a custodial sentence for any given offence than a male youth.[129] While this lenient treatment may seem to be advantageous to females, and may reflect judicial biases about females, it may also reflect a judicial recognition that females have lower rates of recidivism. Available Canadian research indicates that females have substantially lower recidivism rates following probation or a custodial sentence than male young offenders.[130] Further, despite the relative leniency in sentencing, research also suggests that under the *YOA* there was still a tendency for judges to impose custodial sentences on female adolescent offenders to

---

127 R. Corrado, C. Odgers, and I. Cohen, "The Incarceration of Female Young Offenders: Protection for Whom?" (2000) 42 Can. J. Crim. 189–207.

128 P.J. Carrington, *Age and Youth Crime in Canada* (Ottawa: Department of Justice, 1995).

129 See, for example, Statistics Canada, "Sentencing of Young Offenders in Canada, 1998–99" (2000) 20:7 Juristat; S.M. Kowalski and T. Caputo, "Recidivism in Youth Court: An Examination of the Impact of Age, Gender, and Prior Record" (1999) 41 Can. J. Crim. 57; M. Reitsma-Street, "A Review of Female Delinquency" in A.W. Leschied, P.G. Jaffe, and W. Willis, eds., *The Young Offenders Act: A Revolution in Canadian Juvenile Justice* (Toronto: University of Toronto Press, 1991) 248; and P. Pearson, *When She Was Bad: Violent Women and the Myth of Innocence* (Toronto: Random House Canada, 1997).

130 Statistics Canada 1998, above note 124; S. Moyer, "A Profile of the Juvenile Justice System in Canada," *Federal–Provincial/Territorial Task Force on Youth Justice* (Ottawa: Ministry of Supply and Services, 1996) at 182.

"protect them" from engaging in such high-risk activities as prostitution and drug use, rather than because of concerns about accountability or the protection of the public.[131]

Because females constitute a relatively small proportion of the young offender population, they have difficulty getting access to appropriate programs and services. In particular, a disproportionate number of female offenders have been victims of physical and sexual abuse but do not have access to adequate treatment in custody for the emotional and behavioural problems that often result from such abuse. Although many open-custody facilities have both males and females, programming tends to be geared to the males, who are the majority of residents. While some secure-custody facilities are co-educational, there is a tendency to segregate older and more serious offenders by sex, resulting in fewer facilities for the relatively small number of female offenders and a greater likelihood that they will be sent farther away from home or even placed in adult facilities.

A 1999 Alberta case under the *YOA*, *R. v. K.L.M.*, illustrates some of the issues that can arise for female young offenders.[132] A girl who had committed a number of offences received a sentence of ninety days of open custody, and was placed in the female offender unit of a "prison for youth" (as it was characterized by the judge in the case). The centre had several units for males with different levels of security and freedom, but since there were few female offenders, there was only one unit for them, designated by the government as both open and secure custody. The girl was the only female youth on open custody, and her living conditions and daily routine were identical to that of the girls in secure custody. The girl challenged the legality of her continued confinement. The province argued that the small number of female offenders did not warrant creation of a separate unit for open-custody female offenders, and that there was no suitable place for this girl at the small number of open custody facilities for girls in the community. The girl was eighteen years old by the time she was sentenced, and correctional officials had considered placing her in a correctional facility for female adults — which would have required court approval — but they could not justify such

---

131 Corrado, Odgen, and Cohen, above note 127. See also J.M. MacDonald and M. Chesney-Lind, "Gender Bias and Juvenile Justice Revisited: A Multi-Year Analysis" (2001) 47 Crime and Delinquency 173–95.

132 *R. v. K.L.M.*, [1999] A.J. 943 (Q.B.). This case was decided on an application for *habeus corpus* [Latin for produce the body] to a superior court to review the legality of detention.

a request. The court ruled that, under these circumstances, the girl had to be placed in a truly open custody facility or be released.

Section 3 of the *YCJA* recognizes that young persons who commit offences should be treated in a manner that "respect[s] gender . . . differences" as much as possible; accordingly, there should be programs and facilities that meet the distinctive needs of female offenders. In cases involving female youths being sentenced under the *YCJA*, it may be appropriate for a court to consider the lack of suitable available custody facilities in reasonable proximity to a youth's residence as a factor in favour of imposing a non-custodial sentence. There may also be an argument, in some cases, that unequal access to suitable programs or facilities for girls may violate section 15 of the *Charter*, the guarantee against discrimination based on gender.

H. OVERVIEW OF THE YOUTH JUSTICE COURT PROCESS

Before beginning the detailed study of the principles and provisions of the *YCJA* — the focus of the rest of this book — it is useful to have an overview of the youth court process and of salient issues that typically arise in these cases. (See Figure 1.)

A significant proportion of offences committed by youths, especially minor ones, are resolved informally by victims or are not detected. Many offences, however, are reported to the police by witnesses or victims. A police investigation will involve the questioning of the victim and any witnesses, and possibly some forensic work (i.e., the taking of fingerprints from a crime scene, or, in a sexual assault case, having a medical exam performed on the victim). If the police are not able to discover who committed an offence, no further action can be taken. Assuming that the investigation identifies a suspect, the police will usually attempt to interview the suspected perpetrator of the offence. All the protections of the *Charter* apply to youths who are suspects of criminal offences, and the *YCJA* requires that the police must take special measures to protect the rights of young persons who are being questioned by police about offences they are suspected of having committed.

In some cases involving less serious offences, the police may decide not to take any official action against a youth whom they believe committed an offence. The *YCJA* encourages the police to consider an informal response to less serious offences, by cautioning a youth. The police may warn the youth about not committing any further offences,

Figure 1: YOUTH JUSTICE COURT PROCESS

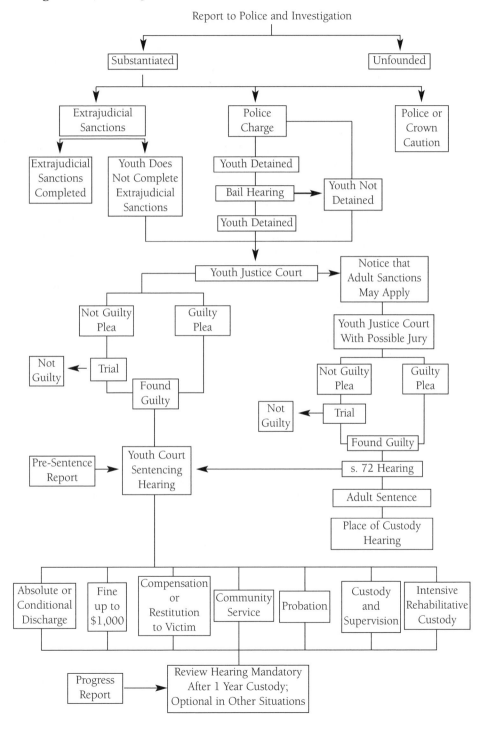

perhaps speaking to the parents as well. The youth, and possibly the parents, may also be referred to a social agency or some other source for assistance on a voluntary basis. If, however, the police have reasonable grounds to believe that a youth has committed an offence, the police may lay charges and commence the youth justice court process. Before or after a charge is laid, a youth may be diverted to a program of "extrajudicial sanctions" instead of proceeding through court. These programs are intended to provide a relatively expeditious, informal resolution for less serious cases and may, for example, involve restitution, an apology to a victim, or community service. In more serious cases that are proceeding through the court system, the Crown prosecutor, in consultation with the police, may decide to seek detention of the youth in a custody facility pending trial. The decision about whether to detain a youth is made by a judge at a pre-trial detention (bail) hearing. A youth should not be detained before trial if an adult in a similar situation would be released, or if the youth would not receive a custodial sentence if convicted. The judge may decide not to detain the youth but may impose conditions on release. It is not uncommon for youths to be released into the care of their parents, provided that the parents are willing and able to supervise their child.

As soon as a youth is arrested, the police must inform the youth of the right to consult a lawyer. In proceedings under the *YCJA*, if a youth wants to have legal assistance and is unable to afford a lawyer, there is a right to have a government-paid lawyer, though if parents have the means to pay for a lawyer, the provincial government has the option of seeking reimbursement from the parents after the conclusion of the court proceedings. The lawyer may provide assistance at the time of pre-trial questioning by the police, at a pre-trial bail hearing, at trial, and at a sentencing or review hearing. After an initial appearance before a judge, a youth, often acting with the advice of a lawyer, will decide whether to plead guilty or not guilty. In practice, most youths decide to plead guilty, sometimes in the context of a plea bargain with the Crown prosecutor. Trials in youth justice court are generally resolved by a judge sitting without a jury, with special rules to limit the public disclosure of information about the youth before the court. After a trial a youth may be found not guilty and be acquitted, or found guilty of the offence.

If there is a finding of guilt, the youth court judge will impose a sentence on the youth. In some cases, a sentence will be imposed immediately after the finding of guilt. In more serious situations, the case is likely to be adjourned so that a pre-sentence report may be prepared, or a medical or psychological assessment may be carried out for the sentencing hearing. The *YCJA* gives judges a range of sentencing alternatives, from a verbal reprimand to three years in youth custody, except that for a conviction of murder in youth justice court, the maximum sentence is ten years. There is not a direct equivalent to parole for young offenders. However, if a youth justice court imposes a custodial sentence, normally the last third of the total sentence is to be served under community supervision. The period of community supervision is intended to allow for the reintegration of the young offender into the community under supervision. There is a narrow discretion for a youth justice court to decide later that, if the youth is too likely to reoffend, the youth will not be released for the last third of the custodial sentence. The youth justice court retains jurisdiction to review the sentence of a youth, that is, to lessen its severity. For example, a young offender may be released from custody by a youth justice court judge at a review hearing even before two-thirds of the sentence have been served, if there has been sufficient progress toward rehabilitation. Unless a youth is in breach of a term of an original order, a more severe sentence cannot be imposed as part of the review process.

Several provisions of the *YCJA* are intended to protect the privacy of young offenders. These provisions reflect notions of the limited accountability of youth and are intended to promote their rehabilitation and reintegration into society. There are restrictions on the disclosure of information from the records of police and the courts about young offenders. There is a prohibition on the publication of information that might identify a young person involved in the youth justice court process. The only exception is a narrow judicial discretion to allow publication when a youth has been convicted of a very serious offence, or where a youth at large poses a serious risk to the public. Youth justice court proceedings are presumptively open to the public, though the judge has the discretion to exclude specific witnesses or members of the public.

The *YCJA* provides that young persons aged fourteen and older may receive adult sentences for the most serious offences. In these cases, before the youth decides how to plead, the youth must be informed of the possibility that an adult sentence may be sought. The youth then has the right to have a jury trial, although even if there is a jury trial the provisions of the *YCJA* concerning issues such as pre-trial detention, admissibility of statements, and prohibitions on public disclosure of identifying information apply to the proceedings until the completion of the trial. If the youth is found guilty, the court proceeds to hold a hearing to determine whether the sentencing options of the *YCJA* are adequate to hold the youth accountable for the offence. If the

Act is considered adequate, the youth is sentenced under it. If the provisions of the Act are not considered adequate to hold the youth accountable, the youth will receive an adult-length sentence and may be identified in the media. The court may determine that part of an adult sentence be served in youth custody facilities. In most situations a youth receiving an adult sentence will be eligible for parole under the adult rules, although, in the case of murder, youths may be eligible for earlier parole.

FURTHER READINGS

ANAND, S.S., "Catalyst for Change: The History of Canadian Juvenile Justice Reform" (1999) 24 Queen's L.J. 515

BALA, NICHOLAS, J.P. HORNICK, M.L. McCALL, & M.E. CLARKE, *State Responses to Youth Crime: A Consideration of Principles* (Ottawa, ON: Department of Justice, 1994)

BIBBY, REGINALD W., *Canada's Teens: Today, Yesterday, and Tomorrow* (Toronto, ON: Stoddart Press, 2001)

CANADA, DEPARTMENT OF JUSTICE, *A Strategy for Youth Justice Renewal* (Ottawa, ON: Ministry of Supply and Services, 1998)

CANADA, FEDERAL–PROVINCIAL/TERRITORIAL TASK FORCE ON YOUTH JUSTICE, *A Review of the Young Offenders Act and the Youth Justice System in Canada* (Ottawa, ON: Ministry of Supply and Services, 1996) cc. 2, 12

CANADA, HOUSE OF COMMONS, *Thirteenth Report of the Standing Committee on Justice and Legal Affairs: Renewing Youth Justice* (Ottawa, ON: Ministry of Supply and Services, 1997)

CORRADO, R., *et al.* eds., *Juvenile Justice in Canada: A Theoretical and Analytical Assessment* (Toronto, ON: Butterworths, 1992)

DOOB, A.N., V. MARINOS, & K.N. VARMA, *Youth Crime and the Youth Justice System in Canada: A Research Perspective* (Toronto, ON: University of Toronto, Centre of Criminology, 1995)

GROSSMAN, DAVID, *Stop Teaching Our Kids to Kill* (New York, NY: Random House, 1999)

KOREM, DAN, *Suburban Gangs: The Affluent Rebels* (Richardson, TX: International Focus Press, 1994)

LESCHIED, A.W., P.G. JAFFE, & W. WILLIS, eds., *The Young Offenders Act: A Revolution in Canadian Juvenile Justice* (Toronto, ON: University of Toronto Press, 1991)

MANN, RUTH M., ed., *Juvenile Crime and Delinquency: A Turn-of-the-Century Reader* (Toronto, ON: Canadian Scholars Press, 2000)

ROSS, R., *Returning to the Teachings: Exploring Aboriginal Justice* (Toronto, ON: Penguin, 1996)

SCOTT, E., & T. GRISSO, "The Evolution of Adolescence: A Developmental Perspective on Juvenile Justice Reform" (1998) 88 J. L. and Criminology 137

UNITED STATES, *Youth Violence: A Report of the Surgeon General* (Washington DC: Surgeon General, 2001)

CHAPTER 2

PRINCIPLES FOR RESPONDING TO YOUTH OFFENDING

A. PRINCIPLES OF YOUTH JUSTICE LAW

What principles should be applied when responding to adolescent offending and administering the youth justice system? This is an important, contentious question to which different societies have different answers. Almost all societies now recognize that adolescence is a distinct stage of life, with youth having less maturity than adults but distinctive needs and vulnerabilities. Even so, there is controversy over how to respond to youth crime. Within Canada, there have been dramatic changes over the past one hundred years in the fundamental principles that Parliament has articulated for responding to youth crime. Deciding which principles should govern the youth justice system remains highly controversial.

The *Juvenile Delinquents Act* of 1908, which established Canada's first juvenile justice system, had a *parens patriae* (parent of the country) or child-welfare orientation. The *Juvenile Delinquents Act* stated that a delinquent was not to be treated "as a criminal, but as a misdirected and misguided child, and one needing aid, encouragement, help and assistance."[1] While this philosophy was not always reflected in how juveniles were treated in the courts and juvenile corrections system, the stated objective of the *Juvenile Delinquents Act* was the promotion of

---

1   The *Juvenile Delinquents Act*, S.C. 1908, c. 40, s. 31; later R.S.C. 1970, c. J-3, s. 38(1).

the welfare of juvenile offenders, with limited concern about punishment for specific offences.

The introduction of the *Young Offenders Act* in 1984[2] signaled a marked change in philosophical approach. Although continuing to recognize the limited maturity of adolescents, it placed greater emphasis on the protection of society, accountability for specific offences and respect for legal rights. Under the *Youth Criminal Justice Act*,[3] which replaces the *YOA*, Canada continues to have a separate criminal justice system for youth predicated on the idea that youths are to be treated differently from both children and adults. The Preamble and Declaration of Principles of the *YCJA* are intended to give direction to the judges, police, prosecutors, and youth correctional staff responsible for the implementation and interpretation of the Act. The enactment of the *YCJA* reflects a change in legislative emphasis; the new Act has a more coherent set of principles than the *YOA*. However, the change from that Act to the *YCJA* is less dramatic than the change that occurred in 1984, when the *YOA* replaced the *Juvenile Delinquents Act*.

In recognition of the vulnerability of adolescents, the *YCJA*, like the *YOA*, extends legal protections to youth which are more extensive than those afforded to adults. The *YCJA* continues the legal recognition that youth, because of their immaturity, have special needs and circumstances that mandate special treatment. It also continues the philosophy of the *YOA* that in comparison to adults young offenders are to have *limited* accountability, and accordingly it emphasizes the value of diversion of youth from the formal court system. Despite continuing central aspects of the former law, the *YCJA* makes some important changes to general principles and a large number of changes to the specific rules that govern youth justice issues in Canada. The *YCJA* places a greater emphasis than did the *YOA* on using accountability as a principle of sentencing. This is an attempt to ensure that the youth justice system is not used to impose sanctions intended to meet the needs of troubled adolescents that are a disproportionate legal reaction to the offence. Child welfare or other social services are expected to meet needs of youth who commit less serious offences.

The *YCJA* provides a more explicit recognition of the role of the youth justice system in protecting society than did the *YOA*. It also makes more explicit reference to the importance of the justice system

---

2   *Young Offenders Act*, R.S.C 1985, c. Y-1, enacted as S.C.1980–81–82–83, c. 110.
3   *Youth Criminal Justice Act*, S.C.2002, c. 1 (royal assent February 19, 2002, to come into force April 1, 2003), usually referred to in this book as the *YCJA*. The *YCJA* repeals and replaces the *Young Offenders Act*, above note 2.

respecting the needs of victims. It has a clearer set of provisions and principles for dealing with serious violent offenders, for whom there is an increased emphasis on accountability and a greater prospect for the imposition of an adult sanction. In a broad sense, the *YCJA* continues the shift begun with the enactment of the *YOA*. It moves away from a welfare model and toward a more clearly criminal model of youth justice law without becoming simply a *Criminal Code* for youth.

Some ideas have continued to be important throughout the evolution of Canadian youth justice over the past century. Principles of limited accountability, rehabilitation, and the need to address the underlying causes of youth crime remain central to society's response to offending behaviour by adolescents. There continues to be a recognition that, for many adolescent offenders, an informal community-based response is preferable to a formal court process.

This chapter discusses the principles that have guided responses to youth crime with a specific focus on the principles in Canada's new legislation. The chapter begins with a consideration of the historical evolution of approaches to youth justice in Canada. The chapter concludes with a discussion of the significance of the United Nations *Convention on the Rights of the Child* for Canada's youth justice system and a brief comparison of the principles of the *YCJA* with the principles that govern youth justice systems in some other countries.

B. THE EVOLUTION OF PRINCIPLES GOVERNING YOUTH JUSTICE

As discussed in Chapter 1, Canadian youth justice law changed dramatically over the course of the twentieth century. An understanding of the historical evolution of the principles that have governed youth justice in Canada is necessary to appreciate the significance of principles selected by the federal government in the *YCJA*.

1) The *Juvenile Delinquents Act*

In Canada, before the twentieth century, as in most of the western world, there was little legal recognition of the special needs of children and adolescents in the criminal justice system. By the turn of the twentieth century, however, the needs of children and adolescents were receiving increasing social and legal recognition. The *Juvenile Delinquents Act* of 1908 articulated a child welfare orientation. This simple, coherent philosophy was reflected in that Act's status offences — such as "sexual immorality or any similar form of vice" — and its overlap with the child welfare system. Under the *Juvenile Delinquents Act*, juveniles could be committed to training school for very minor offences with the objective of providing help and "saving" the child from a life of crime. The indeterminate length of committals to training school under the *Juvenile Delinquents Act* reflected the view that a juvenile should continue to receive the benefits of that placement until rehabilitation was effected. Juvenile court proceedings were informal, as state intervention was seen to be for the benefit of — and not for the purpose of punishing — children. There was very limited recognition of legal rights in the *Juvenile Delinquents Act*.

By the 1960s the juvenile justice systems that had been established at the beginning of the twentieth century were under attack in a number of countries. On one side, critics were arguing that a welfare-oriented philosophy was ineffective to protect society. They noted that many delinquent youth continued to offend despite the rehabilitative efforts of juvenile court judges and correctional programs. While the promotion of the welfare of youth and of rehabilitation are important objectives of a youth justice system, so too are accountability of offenders and the protection of society. Critics argued that the discretionary welfare orientation was often discriminatory and could be highly intrusive. At the same time it was becoming apparent that many youths were being subjected to abusive treatment in juvenile corrections facilities. These concerns spoke to a need for rights-based protection of youthful individuals against overreach of the state, however benevolent its intent.

2) The *Young Offenders Act*

After a decade and a half of debate over what principles and provisions were to govern youth justice in Canada, the YOA was enacted by Parliament in 1982 and came into force in 1984. This Act was a response to the criticisms of the *Juvenile Offenders Act*, as well as to the enactment of the *Canadian Charter of Rights and Freedoms*.[4] By the early 1980s Canada had become a rights-based society, clearly reflected by and reinforced through the introduction of the *Charter*, which guarantees rights to all Canadians but has special provisions to protect the

---

4   *Canadian Charter of Rights and Freedoms*, enacted as Part I of the *Constitution Act, 1982*, being Schedule B to the *Canada Act, 1982* (U.K.), 1982, c. 11 (subsequently referred to as the *Charter*).

vulnerable in society, such as women, Aboriginal peoples, and religious minorities. As the *Charter* was introduced at the same time the *YOA* was being enacted, it is understandable that the protection of legal rights of adolescents is one of the central themes of that Act.

The *YOA* is unquestionably criminal — and not child welfare — legislation. Its enactment marked a movement away from the welfare orientation of the *Juvenile Offenders Act* to a model of juvenile justice that placed a greater emphasis on holding adolescents accountable for their actions; it explicitly recognized the importance of the protection of the public in dealing with young offenders. While it was enacted as criminal law, the Act provided for a youth justice system for adolescents aged twelve through seventeen separate and distinct from the adult criminal justice system in several critical respects.

Although young people must be held accountable for criminal acts under the *YOA*, they generally were not to be held accountable in the same manner or to the same extent as adults. The Act extended legal protections to youth which were more extensive than those afforded adults in recognition of the vulnerability of adolescents. Perhaps most importantly, the *YOA* recognized that youths, because of their immaturity, have special needs and circumstances which call for special treatment. Justification for state intervention in the life of a youth under the Act was the violation of criminal law, rather than the promotion of a youth's best interests. This was in contrast to the explicitly, and theoretically solely, welfare-oriented approach of the *Juvenile Delinquents Act*. The *YOA* introduced a more formal youth justice system, in which a violation of the law had to be established by due process of law. If a criminal offence had occurred, the way in which a youth was dealt with under the Act was affected by the limited maturity and special needs of the adolescent. Recognizing the limited maturity and vulnerability of adolescents, the Act provided special legal protections for them and, despite its criminal-law structure, the *YOA* had provisions to divert less serious offenders from the youth court process.

The *YOA* did not have the same philosophical coherence of the *Juvenile Delinquents Act*, as the clearly articulated but singular welfare objective of the old law had proven to be overly simplistic. The philosophical tensions in the principles of the *YOA* reflect the very complex nature of youthful criminality and the inadequacy of taking a single-minded approach when dealing with young persons who violate the criminal law. The 1982 enactment of the *YOA* included, in section 3, an explicit Declaration of Principle, which was amended in 1995 to emphasize the Liberal government's view of the importance of crime prevention and rehabilitation.[5] Ultimately, the amended Declaration of Principle of the *Young Offenders Act* read:

3.(1) It is hereby recognized and declared that

(*a*)   crime prevention is essential to the long-term protection of society and requires addressing the underlying causes of crime by young persons and developing multi-disciplinary approaches to identifying and effectively responding to children and young persons at risk of committing offending behaviour in the future;

(*a.1*) while young persons should not in all instances be held accountable in the same manner or suffer the same consequences for their behaviour as adults, young persons who commit offences should nonetheless bear responsibility for their contraventions;

(*b*)   society must, although it has the responsibility to take reasonable measures to prevent criminal conduct by young persons, be afforded the necessary protection from illegal behaviour;

(*c*)   young persons who commit offences require supervision, discipline and control, but, because of their state of dependency and level of development and maturity, they also have special needs and require guidance and assistance;

(*c.1*) the protection of society, which is a primary objective of the criminal law applicable to youth, is best served by rehabilitation, wherever possible, of young persons who commit offences, and rehabilitation is best achieved by addressing the needs and circumstances of a young person that are relevant to the young person's offending behaviour;

(*d*)   where it is not inconsistent with the protection of society, taking no measures or taking measures other than judicial proceedings under this Act should be considered for dealing with young persons who have committed offences;

(*e*)   young persons have rights and freedoms in their own right, including those stated in the *Canadian Charter of Rights and Freedoms* or in the *Canadian Bill of Rights*, and in particular a right to be heard in the course of, and to participate in, the processes that lead to decisions that affect them, and young persons should have special guarantees of their rights and freedoms;

(*f*)   in the application of this Act, the rights and freedoms of young persons include a right to the least possible interference with freedom that is consistent with the protection of society, having

---

5   *An Act to amend the Young Offenders Act and the Criminal Code*, S.C.1995, c. 19, s. 1 added ss. 3(1)(a) and 3(1)(c.1).

regard to the needs of young persons and the interests of their families;

(g)   young persons have the right, in every instance where they have rights or freedoms that may be affected by this Act, to be informed as to what those rights and freedoms are; and

(h)   parents have responsibility for the care and supervision of their children, and, for that reason, young persons should be removed from parental supervision either partly or entirely only when measures that provide for continuing parental supervision are inappropriate.

Application of section 3 of the *YOA* was often contentious. The lengthy list of principles was criticized for being confusing and even incoherent. Most of the principles articulated in section 3(1) are broad, and there are some seeming inconsistencies or at least tensions among them. It was suggested by some that, in the absence of any statutory priorization, section 3 did little to direct decision-makers. Rather, it was argued that the vagueness and inconsistency in the principles left decision-makers a wide discretion to select and apply the principles as they saw fit.[6]

In a 1987 decision about whether to transfer a youth to adult court, Justice Laycraft of the Alberta Court of Appeal complained about the lack of clear direction in the Declaration of Principle of the *YOA*: "Section 3 contains some statements which directly conflict with other declarations of principle in the same section. The balance between these conflicting principles is, in the individual case, not easy."[7] Others argued that it was possible to reconcile and balance the principles of section 3 to derive a coherent message. The Supreme Court of Canada was more supportive of section 3, recognizing the tensions within the Declaration, but not regarding the principles to be contradictory. In the Supreme Court decision of *R. v. T.(V.)*, L'Heureux-Dubé J. wrote:

> while I am not unmindful of the apparent inconsistencies of the stated goals of the Act as contained in s. 3(1), in my opinion the better view is that advocated by Bala and Kirvan in . . . *The Young Offenders Act: A Revolution in Canadian Juvenile Justice* (1991). . . .
>
> While it may not be inaccurate to suggest that the Declaration of Principle reflects a certain social ambivalence about young

---

6   See, for example, P. Platt, *Young Offenders Law in Canada* (Butterworths, Toronto, 1989) at 2.18: "The difficulty is that they are not coherent and in some cases positively inconsistent." In the second edition (1995), Platt dropped this more trenchant critique but still observed that s. 3 "will remain a fertile ground for searching out Parliament's legislative intention."

7   *R. v. M.(S.H.)* (1987), 35 C.C.C. (3d) 515 (Alta. C.A.) at 524–25.

offenders, it is also important to appreciate that it represents an honest attempt to achieve an appropriate balance for dealing with a very complex social problem. The *Young Offenders Act* does not have a single, simple unifying philosophy, for there is no single, simple principle which can deal with all situations in which young persons violate the criminal law. While the Declaration as a whole defines new parameters for juvenile justice in Canada, each principle is not necessarily relevant to every situation. The weight to be attached to a particular principle will be determined in large measure by the nature of the decision being made and the specific provisions of the *Young Offenders Act* which govern the situation, as well as the views of the decision maker. There are situations in which there is a need to balance competing principles, but this is a challenge in cases in the adult as well as the juvenile system.[8]

In *R. v. M.(J.J.)* Justice Cory of the Supreme Court of Canada agreed with the need for a balancing of principles: "A quick reading of section 3 indicates that there is a marked ambivalence in its approach to the sentencing of young offenders. Yet that ambivalence should not be surprising when it is remembered that the Act reflects a courageous attempt to balance concepts and interests that are frequently conflicting."[9]

Whether the principles in the *YOA* in theory could be balanced to provide a clear guide for decision makers, in practice implementation and interpretation varied significantly. Implementation of the *YOA* by provincial governments differed from one province to another, and interpretations of the Act varied from one judge to another. Given the lack of statutory priorization of principles, different governments and professionals inevitably interpreted these principles differently, and placed greater weight on different principles. Substantial variation in the interpretation and application of the *YOA* throughout Canada resulted in very substantial variations among jurisdictions in rates of charging and diversion, rates of custody use, and rates of transfer of the most serious cases into adult court.[10] For example, under the *YOA*, Quebec consistently had a rate of charging youths that was less than half the rate in Ontario and,

---

8   *R. v. T.(V.)* (1992), 71 C.C.C. (3d) 32 at 44–45. This passage was again quoted with approval in *Re F.N.* , [2000] 1 S.C.R. 880.

9   *R. v. M.(J.J.)* [1993], 20 C.R. (4th) 295 (S.C.C.) at 299.

10 See, for example, A.N. Doob and L. Beaulieu, "Variation in the Exercise of Judicial Discretion with Young Offenders" (1992) 34 Can. J. Crim. 35, commenting on the effect of the lack of priorization of principles in s. 3 on the wide variations in the sentencing practices of youth court judges under that Act.

among those youths who were sentenced in youth court, Quebec judges consistently made less use of custody and more use of probation.[11] In the conservative jurisdiction of Alberta, relatively large numbers of youth were tried as adults, while in Quebec the administration of youth justice was based on a more rehabilitative model. This variation was related not to differences in offending behaviour among jurisdictions but to differences in response to youth crime.[12]

While the *YOA* was in force, it was a highly criticized, high-profile piece of legislation. During the late 1980s and the 1990s, as Anglo-Canadian politics became more conservative, public debates focused on such issues as reducing public spending and increasing public safety. Sensationalist media reports of youth violence and political responses outside of Quebec contributed to escalating public concerns about youth crime and public demands for a get-tough approach to young offenders. The *YOA* was amended first in 1986 and again in 1992 and 1995. While each set of amendments contained a range of provisions, the major political focus in each round was the provisions that dealt with transfer to adult court and sentences for murder. The need to be seen to be responding to the most serious and highly publicized youth crimes dominated the youth justice reform agenda in the late 1980s and 1990s. With each set of amendments, child advocates argued that the *YOA* became "a more punitive statute."[13]

Despite the facts that the *YOA* had been amended to toughen the Act, and that the youth crime rate was slowly falling during the 1990s,[14] by the later years of that decade there was a crisis of public confidence in how Canada dealt with youth crime. According to a 1997 national poll, 92 percent of Canadians thought youth crime was a "serious problem," and most people surveyed thought "harsher punishment" was the best way to solve that problem.[15] These public concerns were reflected in, and arguably increased by, the comments of many politicians opposed to the Liberal government in Ottawa. In 1998, the Ontario premier told an interviewer: "The *Young Offenders Act* is so per-

---

11   Statistics Canada, *Youth Court Statistics 1999–2000* (2001) 21:3 Juristat.

12   A. Doob and J. Sprott, "Is the 'Quality' of Youth Violence Becoming More Serious?" (1998) 40 *Canadian Journal of Criminology* 185.

13   Canadian Council of Provincial Children's Advocates, "Bill C-68: A Critical Analysis of the Proposed Youth Criminal Justice Act," April 12, 1999.

14   Statistics Canada, above note 11.

15   K. Orstad,"What Are We: The Myth of Youth Crime." *Saturday Night*, March 1997. See also M. Wente, "The Kids Aren't All Right," *Globe and Mail*, February 1, 2000.

missive that it actually seems to condone criminal behaviour."[16] At a time when Canadian politicians were expressing concerns that the youth justice system was "too soft," international comparisons showed that Canada had the highest rate of use of a formal court response to youth crime and one of the highest rates of custody use for adolescents in the world.[17] Such high custody rates raise serious questions about the application of the diversionary and rehabilitative ideals set out in the *YOA* principles. This discrepancy between youth crime statistics and political rhetoric prompted academic critics such as Bernard Schissel to allege bad faith on the part of those politicians advocating a get-tough approach to youth justice reform: "the logic and rhetoric of politics and news . . . [are] so flawed and poorly struck that malicious intentions cannot be dismissed."[18]

Whatever the motives of those attacking the *YOA*, a get-tough response struck a popular chord in much of Canada. One columnist noted that: "No politician likes to be depicted on a billboard with serial killer Clifford Olsen, and nobody wants to be seen as soft on youth crime."[19] Laws and policies that promised to get tough on young offenders received overwhelming popular approval.[20] The Ontario Crime Control Commission acknowledged in 1998 that "in spite of declines in official crime statistics, there is a strong public perception that crime is on the increase."[21] The Commission's approach responded to public perception rather than the statistics, recommending a crackdown on school violence as well as the enactment of legislation to impose civil liability on parents of young offenders. For some politicians, youth justice law had become a symbol of what was wrong with Canadian society and a metaphorical starting point for ideological change. For some conservatives, unruly youth are the dire consequence of changing social values, effected by a shift in family forms and

---

16 Premier Mike Harris quoted in "Tories Say New Act 'Wishy-Washy'," *Globe and Mail*, September 19, 1998.

17 As of 1997, the rate of incarceration of Canadian youth was two times higher than that of the United States and ten to fifteen times higher than the rate per 10,000 youth in the population in several European countries. See Canada House of Commons, *Renewing Youth Justice* (April 1997) Thirteenth Report of the Standing Committee on Justice and Legal Affairs at 17.

18 B. Schissel, *Blaming Children: Youth Crime, Moral Panic and the Politics of Hate* (Halifax, NS: Fernwood Publishing, 1997) at 99.

19 E. Greenspon, "Youth Crime Bill A Canny Balance," *Globe and Mail*, March 12, 1999.

20 J. Gray, "Teenage Breakdown?" *Globe and Mail*, June 3, 2000. The new code of conduct makes suspension and expulsion easier for teachers.

21 Ontario Crime Control Commission, "Tough on Crime," Report on Youth Crime (Toronto: 1998) at 12.

feminism. For these critics, the best response to youth crime would be a return to "traditional family values."[22] Undeterred by national crime rates hitting a twenty-year low, conservative politicians in the 2000 federal election campaigned on a justice platform stressing victims' rights and the intention to get tough on young offenders.[23] Others at the opposite end of the political spectrum argued that proposed reforms to Canada's young offenders law were unduly harsh. Youth justice was one of the few issues with national implications on which the separatist Bloc Québécois chose to engage in the 2000 election campaign, citing the more welfare-oriented treatment of young offenders in Quebec as emblematic of the distinctness of that province.[24]

Canada's Liberal government went through a long process of consultation, drafting, redrafting, introducing and reintroducing new youth justice legislation, ultimately enacting the YCJA in 2002. The new Act remained controversial, with the Quebec government challenging it in court, arguing among other things that its punitive approach violated the United Nations *Convention on the Rights of the Child*, while conservative federal and provincial politicians criticized the new law as too soft on youth crime.[25]

3) The *Youth Criminal Justice Act*

Enacted amidst controversy, the *Youth Criminal Justice Act* attempted to compromise between clashing political perspectives while at the same time dealing with some significant problems in the youth justice system. Although the decisions of the Supreme Court of Canada suggested that

---

22 An interesting trend in the United States challenges the argument that the decline in "family values" and the rise of feminism caused an increase in crime. The introduction of legalized abortion, emblematic of the decline of traditional social values and a rise in "right-based" autonomy, correlated with a decrease in crime rates. It has been argued that the falling American crime rates in the 1990s were a result of the legalization of abortion roughly twenty years earlier, and the decline in the numbers of "unwanted" children: J. Donohue and S. Levitt, "Legalized Abortion and Crime" (September 1999) Stanford Law School, Public Law and Legal Theory, Working Paper No. 1.

23 See, for example, "Day Unveils Law and Order Message," *Globe and Mail*, July 19, 2000.

24 H. Winsor, "Odd Couple Scuffle Over Crime Bill," *Globe and Mail*, February 10, 2001, noting that the Bloc "seized upon (youth justice) as a way to illustrate Quebec's differentness."

25 See, for example, "Feds Delay Implementation of Youth Crime Bill," *Law Times*, February 25, 2002: 4.

the balancing of principles provided by the *Young Offenders Act* gave significant direction to the courts, a key rationale offered by Justice Canada for enacting new youth justice legislation was that "the overarching principles [in the *YOA*] are unclear and conflicting."[26] It was the intent of the new Act's framers to provide clearer guidance.

Like the *YOA*, the new law contains an express Declaration of Principle. The new Act is, however, a much longer and more complex piece of legislation than the *YOA*. In addition to the Declaration of Principle, the *YCJA* has a Preamble that is intended to reveal the general intent of Parliament in enacting a new youth justice law and guide the implementation of the Act. The new Act also has more detailed declarations of principle that are intended to guide decisions to divert youth from the formal court system through the use of "extrajudicial sanctions" (section 4), as well as principles to guide decisions about sentencing (section 38) and youths in custody (section 83).

The drafters of the *YCJA* attempted to respond to the criticisms that the principles of the *YOA* were vague, inconsistent, and not prioritized. The Department of Justice asserts that the statements of principle in the *YCJA* offer more coherence than those in the *YOA*, claiming that the provisions of the newer Act "provide clear direction, establish structure for the application of principles and thereby resolve inconsistencies."[27]

One of the first versions of the *YCJA*, introduced in Parliament in 1999, actually had a statement that one principle was "primary." Under section 3(1)(a) of Bill C-3, the "principal goal of the youth criminal justice system is to protect the public" by means of preventing crime, imposing meaningful consequences for offences, and rehabilitating offenders. This principle was articulated as having greater legal weight than the others listed.[28] The version of the Act that was enacted by Parliament in 2002 did not, however, explicitly have a "primary" or "principal" objective. Consequently, the order in which the principles are listed in section 3 of the *YCJA* is of no legal significance. By the time it was enacted by Parliament in 2002, the Declaration of Principle had been redrafted to a point where it presented a list of principles without any explicit prioritization. Parts of section 3 of the *YCJA* restate parts of the Declaration of Principle in section 3 of the *YOA*, sometimes in slightly different language. The potentially competing objectives of the values

---

26 Canada, Department of Justice Press Release "Why New Youth Justice Legislation?" (February 2001).

27 *Ibid.*

28 Bill C-3, Second Session, Thirty-Sixth Parliament, First Reading, October 14, 1999: not enacted.

of holding young offenders accountable and effecting their rehabilitation must still be balanced. To this balance are added such objectives as reinforcing respect for social values; respecting the role of parents, victims, and communities; and responding to the gender, culture, and Aboriginal status of young offenders.

Governments responsible for the implementation the *YCJA* will have to continue to balance various principles and priorities in deciding how to allocate resources and formulate policies. In some important respects, the new Act gives provincial governments more discretion than they had under the *YOA* about how to shape responses to youth crime. Those charged with making decisions about individual youth, such as police officers, prosecutors and judges, will also have to balance various principles in the context of the resources available. Responding to youth crime and individual young offenders remains a complex problem that defies a simplistic legislatively directed solution, and requires a balancing of principles. There are inevitable tensions in deciding how to deal with the offending behaviour of adolescents. Decision-makers will continue to have significant discretion, and there is likely to be substantial variation across Canada in how the *YCJA* is implemented. Under the *YCJA*, as under the *YOA*, it is predominantly the provincial governments, justice system professionals, and youth justice court judges, not the federal Parliament, who will shape youth justice in Canada.

Nonetheless, in comparison to the *YOA*, the various provisions of the *YCJA* that articulate principles and philosophy provide a *clearer message* for those charged with the operation of the youth justice system and the making of decisions about individual young offenders. The principles of the *YCJA*, as set out in the Preamble and section 3, taken together with the more specific declarations of principle in section 4 on extrajudicial measures, section 38 on sentencing and section 83 on youth in custody, provide some important guidance to decision-makers in the system, and have the potential to increase consistency in the youth justice system across Canada.

The *YCJA* provides for a greater emphasis on diversion from the youth court system for a broader range of less serious offenders than occurred under the *YOA*. The *YCJA* is also intended to encourage use of a range of community-based dispositions and to restrict the use of custody for those youths sentenced by the court. For the relatively small number of youths who commit serious violent offences, however, there is a greater emphasis on protection of the public and accountability, with an increased likelihood of adult sanctions being imposed. The youth justice system is intended to rehabilitate young offenders and thereby prevent offending; at the same time, it is to ensure that there are meaningful consequences for offending. The new Act maintains the principle of the *YOA* that, in comparison to adults, there should be a lesser accountability than for adults and more emphasis on rehabilitation for young offenders. It is, however, significant that the *YCJA* clarifies the relationship between the objectives of accountability and rehabilitation. Sentencing is to be proportional to the offence, and the achievement of rehabilitative objectives cannot justify a more intrusive or severe response than would be merited by the circumstances of the offence. Section 38(2) of the Act, for example, makes clear that young offenders should never receive a more severe sanction than adults would for the same offence in similar circumstances.

The *YCJA* continues the recognition in the *YOA* of the importance of involving parents, victims and community members in the youth justice process, and has some provisions that may encourage their greater participation in the process of holding a young person accountable. The *YCJA* continues to recognize the principle articulated in the *YOA* that young offenders are entitled to due process of law, and to special legal protections due to their limited maturity. Some of the specific provisions of the new Act, however, provide less protection for the legal rights of youth than the provisions of the *YOA*.

There is a significant degree of overlap between the various guiding statements of the *YCJA* and even within specific sections. In particular in section 3 there is a significant degree of repetition of themes and principles. Those charged with the application and interpretation of the *YCJA* face a challenge in determining what the principles and priorities of the Act are. A careful reading of the Act shows that it does offer a more coherent set of principles and a more consistent set of priorities than the *YOA*. While the different guiding provisions of the *YCJA* are generally consistent with one another, the repetition and restatement of ideas makes it challenging to discuss and to understand the principles in the new Act. The discussion in this chapter focuses principally on the Preamble and section 3, relating it to some of the other provisions in the Act. The principles articulated in section 4, which govern extrajudicial measures, are discussed more fully in Chapter 5, and the principles in section 38 and 83 are discussed more fully in Chapter 8, which deals with sentencing. This chapter considers the themes and principles of the Preamble and section 3 but, to provide more structure and avoid undue repetition, the discussion does not always follow the sequence and structure of these statutory provisions.

4) The Preamble

Since the *YOA* was enacted in 1982, it has become more common for Parliament to include preambles in new criminal law legislation.[29] Preambles provide a brief explanation for the social context and policy concerns that motivated Parliament to enact a new law, and offer some general guidance for the implementation and interpretation of the Act. Some commentators have suggested that preambles are generally "too vague" or "too political" to be useful, and that the "free-ranging and overtly political character of preambles often serves political needs."[30] It is perhaps a reflection of the politically charged nature of the *YCJA* that this statute has a preamble. The rules of statutory construction make clear that a preamble has a different and lesser legal effect than the provisions in the legislation itself. Section 13 of the *Interpretation Act*[31] provides: "the preamble of an enactment shall be read as part of the enactment intended to assist in explaining its purpose and object."

Legal scholar Professor Ruth Sullivan explains that preambles "reveal legislative purpose."[32] Traditionally, preambles were not referred to by judges who were interpreting a statute unless the meaning of a legislative provision was unclear. Even when a preamble was used to discern the "true meaning" of a vague or ambiguous statutory provision, it was given little weight by the courts.[33] More recently, however, courts have been taking a less literal and more contextual and purposive approach to statutory interpretation, and preambles have been given greater weight by courts.[34]

It is now accepted that a preamble can be used to assist in determining a statute's purpose and object, even if the provisions of the law are clear. Further, a preamble can be given whatever weight a court considers appropriate in the circumstances.[35] Legislative purpose can be set out directly, or can be inferred from the concerns set out in a preamble; preambles are part of the legislative context in which a statute should be read. Legislative preambles have been invoked by judges to

---

29   K. Roach, "The Uses and Audiences of Preambles in Legislation" (2001) 47 McGill L.J. 129, in which the increased prevalence of preambles in new criminal law legislation is documented and discussed.

30   R. Sullivan, *Statutory Interpretation* (Toronto: Irwin Law, 1997) at 117.

31   *Interpretation Act*, S.C.1985, c. I, s. 21.

32   R. Sullivan, above note 30 at 117.

33   *A.G. v. Prince Ernest Augustus of Hanover*, [1957] A.C. 436 (H. L.).

34   See, for example, the concurring opinion of L'Heureux-Dubé J. in *N.B. (Minister of Health) v. G.(J.)*, [1999] 3 S.C.R. 46.

35   For example, in *Rawluk v. Rawluk*, [1990] 1 S.C.R. 70, a preamble was found to be significant in helping to interpret a statute.

help to establish a statute's general purpose and effect, and thereby assist with the interpretation of specific provisions. Nonetheless, if there is a conflict between a preamble and a substantive provision, the substantive provision prevails.

The Preamble of the *Youth Criminal Justice Act* reads:

> WHEREAS members of society share a responsibility to address the developmental challenges and the needs of young persons and to guide them into adulthood;
>
> WHEREAS communities, families, parents and others concerned with the development of young persons should, through multi-disciplinary approaches, take reasonable steps to prevent youth crime by addressing its underlying causes, to respond to the needs of young persons, and to provide guidance and support to those at risk of committing crimes;
>
> WHEREAS information about youth justice, youth crime and the effectiveness of measures taken to address youth crime should be publicly available;
>
> WHEREAS Canada is a party to the United Nations *Convention on the Rights of the Child* and recognizes that young persons have rights and freedoms, including those stated in the *Canadian Charter of Rights and Freedoms* and the *Canadian Bill of Rights*, and have special guarantees of their rights and freedoms;
>
> AND WHEREAS Canadian society should have a youth criminal justice system that commands respect, takes into account the interests of victims, fosters responsibility and ensures accountability through meaningful consequences and effective rehabilitation and reintegration, and that reserves its most serious intervention for the most serious crimes and reduces the over-reliance on incarceration for non-violent young persons.

This Preamble is in some respects more a policy statement than a declaration that will give direction to those who are making decisions about individual cases. Much of the Preamble supports the adoption of policies and programs that focus on prevention and addressing the underlying causes of criminal behaviour. It is hoped that administrators and politicians responsible for the establishment of programs and formulation of policies that deal with children and adolescents will be influenced by this focus, but it is not a legal requirement that they do so. The weight given to any preamble as an interpretative aid when dealing with individual cases is affected by its clarity and specificity: if a preamble itself is ambiguous, it may not be considered very helpful to a court. By virtue of its generality and complexity, most of the Preamble of the *YCJA* is likely to have only limited legal significance to individual cases in the youth justice system. Further, the Act has four explicit statements of principle (sections 3, 4, 38 and 83) which lessen the need for reliance on the Preamble to provide interpretative guidance.

There are, however, at least two aspects of the Preamble that may be legally significant: first, its reference to the *Convention on the Rights of the Child*, and second its articulation of the principle that the most serious intervention should be reserved for the most serious crimes.

One important way in which the Preamble of the *YCJA* is not simply a repetition of the Declaration of Principle in section 3 is that only the Preamble expressly mentions the *United Nations Convention on the Rights of the Child*. The *Convention* is the most comprehensive of a series of international agreements which set minimum standards for the treatment of children and youth, as well as standards for the civil, political, economic, social, and cultural rights of children. UNICEF describes the *Convention* as setting out "non-negotiable minimum standards and obligations" concerning the treatment of children by states parties.[36] The *Convention* is more fully considered later in this chapter, where it is argued that its legal significance for individual youth justice cases in Canada is likely to be very limited. This is both because of the wording of the Preamble — which merely refers to the fact that Canada is a party to the *Convention* — and because of the vagueness of the *Convention* itself.

Under the *YOA*, Canada had high rates of formal court processes for responding to youth crime and sent a relatively great number of youth into custody, most often for offences that did not involve violence.[37] The Preamble of the *YCJA* articulates the principle that the youth justice system should "reserve . . . its most serious intervention for the most serious crimes." This principle is relevant to a number of stages of the youth justice process, starting with the decision whether to lay charges

---

36 UNICEF, online <www.unicef.ca> (accessed 8 August 2002).

37 For example, in 2000–2001, of the 20,809 youth cases that resulted in a custody disposition, 23 percent were for theft and property-related offences, 11 percent for break and enter, 36 percent for failure to attend court or comply with a community disposition, and 7 percent for minor assaults; calculated from Statistics Canada, *Youth Court Statistics 2000–2001* (Ottawa, 2002) Juristat 22:3. For an international comparison, see N. Bala, J.P. Hornick, and H. Snyder, *Juvenile Justice Systems: An International Comparison of Problems and Solutions* (Toronto: Thompson Educational Publishers, 2002).

or divert a case to extrajudicial measures. It is also relevant to sentencing decisions and the decision whether to impose an adult sentence. In addition to articulating the principle that "the most serious intervention" should be reserved for the "most serious crimes," the Preamble also establishes the related objective of reducing Canada's "over-reliance on incarceration for non-violent offenders." There are more detailed statements in the various declarations of principles and detailed provisions that are intended to reduce the levels of intervention and use of custody under the YCJA from those achieved under the YOA. Still, counsel and judges may in some cases make reference to these general statements in the Preamble to guide decision making.

5) The Declaration of Principle

Section 3 of the YCJA is entitled the "Declaration of Principle." Section 3(1) has four broad and overlapping paragraphs that set out the principles intended to characterize and govern Canada's youth criminal justice system. Section 3(1)(a) provides that the purpose of the youth justice system is to promote the long-term protection of the public by addressing the underlying causes of offending behaviour, rehabilitating young offenders and ensuring that there are meaningful consequences for offending. Section 3(1)(b) describes the characteristics that distinguish the youth criminal justice system from the adult system: the youth justice places greater emphasis on rehabilitation, has limited accountability to reflect the limited maturity of youth, has special procedural protections to ensure that adolescents are treated fairly, and should respond in a timely fashion to reflect the rapid development and perception of time of adolescents. Section 3(1)(c) sets out the principles that are to guide the imposition of sanctions on youths who have violated the law. An overriding principle is that sanctions are to be based on accountability and to be proportionate to the offence, and not imposed solely to achieve social or therapeutic objectives. Sanctions imposed by means of extrajudicial measures or after a conviction in youth justice court should reinforce respect for societal values; have a restorative nature by encouraging the offender to repair harm done to victims and the community; be meaningful to the young person; and respect the needs and circumstances of the individual youth, including differences based on gender, ethnic, cultural, linguistic, and developmental needs, as well as Aboriginal status. Section 3(1)(d) sets out three special considerations that should characterize proceedings involving young persons: respect for the legal rights of youth; respect for the dignity and privacy of victims; and involvement of parents in youth justice court proceedings and supporting them in addressing the offending behaviour of their children.

The Declaration of Principle of the *YCJA* reads:

3.(1) The following principles apply in this Act:

(*a*) the youth criminal justice system is intended to
  (*i*)   prevent crime by addressing the circumstances underlying a young person's offending behaviour,
  (*ii*) rehabilitate young persons who commit offences and reintegrate them into society, and
  (*iii*) ensure that a young person is subject to meaningful consequences for his or her offence in order to promote the long-term protection of the public;
(*b*) the criminal justice system for young persons must be separate from that of adults and emphasize the following:
  (*i*)   rehabilitation and reintegration,
  (*ii*) fair and proportionate accountability that is consistent with the greater dependency of young persons and their reduced level of maturity,
  (*iii*) enhanced procedural protection to ensure that young persons are treated fairly and that their rights, including their right to privacy, are protected,
  (*iv*) timely intervention that reinforces the link between the offending behaviour and its consequences, and
  (*v*)   the promptness and speed with which persons responsible for enforcing this Act must act, given young persons' perception of time;
(*c*) within the limits of fair and proportionate accountability, the measures taken against young persons who commit offences should
  (*i*)   reinforce respect for societal values,
  (*ii*) encourage the repair of harm done to victims and the community,
  (*iii*) be meaningful for the individual young person given his or her needs and level of development and, where appropriate, involve the parents, the extended family, the community and social or other agencies in the young person's rehabilitation and reintegration, and
  (*iv*) respect gender, ethnic, cultural and linguistic differences and respond to the needs of aboriginal young persons and of young persons with special requirements; and
(*d*) special considerations apply in respect of proceedings against young persons and, in particular,

(i)   young persons have rights and freedoms in their own right, such as a right to be heard in the course of and to participate in the processes, other than the decision to prosecute, that lead to decisions that affect them, and young persons have special guarantees of their rights and freedoms,

(ii) victims should be treated with courtesy, compassion and respect for their dignity and privacy and should suffer the minimum degree of inconvenience as a result of their involvement with the youth criminal justice system,

(iii) victims should be provided with information about the proceedings and given an opportunity to participate and be heard, and

(iv) parents should be informed of measures or proceedings involving their children and encouraged to support them in addressing their offending behaviour.

Declarations of Principle are like preambles in that they reveal the purpose of legislation and draw attention to values and policies that are expected to inform the interpretation of the provisions of the Act.[38] The two differ, however, in that a declaration of principle is included in the body of the statute, and has direct statutory effect. Section 3(2) provides that the *Young Criminal Justice Act* should "be liberally construed to the end that young persons will be dealt with in accordance with the principles" set out in section 3(1). This reinforces the interpretive weight to be given to the Declaration of Principle.

Case law decided under the *YOA* indicates that the Declaration of Principle in the *YCJA* will be of substantial significance to the courts in interpreting the new Act. For example, in upholding the sentencing decision made by a trial judge under the *YOA*, the Supreme Court of Canada stated that the Declaration of Principle in section 3 of that Act "should not be considered as merely a preamble. Rather, it should be given the force normally attributed to substantive provisions."[39] The Court recognized a "certain ambivalence created by these disparate goals (or competing objectives),"[40] but emphasized the importance of the principles. The Court indicated that the principles should be used by decision makers for such purposes as determining whether to refer a youth to alternative measures,[41] deciding whether to admit a youth's

---

38   R. Sullivan, above note 30, at 118.
39   R. v. M.(J.J.), above note 9. See also R. v. T.(V.), [1992] 1 S.C.R. 749.
40   Binnie J. in *Re F.N.*, above note 8, at para. 10.
41   R. v. T.(V.), above note 8.

confession to the police,[42] and making disposition and transfer decisions.[43] Given the similarity between the role of the declarations of principle in the *YOA* and *YCJA*, it is likely that the courts will continue this practice under the new Act.

Some of the principles articulated in section 3 of the *YCJA* are directly applicable to proceedings in the youth justice system, and specific provisions of the Act reinforce their importance and facilitate their application. These statements of principle will have direct legal effect. The principles that govern sentencing are of this sort; the failure of a youth justice court judge to apply the appropriate sentencing principles may result in a successful appeal. Other principles articulated in section 3 must be viewed as more aspirational than legally binding. It is hoped that these statements will affect attitudes, practices, and policies but, if they do not, there may be no legal recourse. For example, the failure to have "timely intervention" or to respect the "dignity of victims" will likely have no legal significance, except in extreme cases. The fact that some of the statements in various declarations of principle may be directed to changing practices and attitudes without being legally binding in a court of law does not mean that they are without significance. Many of the most important changes that the new Act is intended to effect will only be achieved if there are changes in attitudes, practices, and policies.

6) Declarations for Extrajudicial Measures, Sentencing, and Custody

In addition to the Preamble and Declaration of Principle, the *YCJA* contains more specific declarations of principle for particular purposes. Section 4 introduces Part 1 of the *YCJA*, which governs the use of extrajudicial measures. Section 4 sets out a further declaration of principles to encourage diversion of less serious offenders from the formal court process and to encourage the use of these measures for young persons who violate the criminal law. Section 38, which introduces Part 4 of the Act and governs sentencing, establishes the purpose of sentencing: the imposition of just sanctions that have meaningful consequences and promote rehabilitation, thereby contributing to the long-term protection of society. Section 38 also articulates a set of principles that are intended to govern sentencing for those youth found guilty in youth justice court. It emphasizes the importance of proportionality, acknowledgement of harm to victims, and the imposition of the least restrictive

---

42   *R. v. T.(J.T.)*, [1990] 2 S.C.R. 755.
43   *R. v. M.(S.H.)*, [1989] 2 S.C.R. 446.

sentence that is capable of holding a young person accountable while promoting the youth's rehabilitation. Section 83, which introduces Part 5 of the Act and governs custody and supervision, establishes the purpose of custody as the carrying out of court-imposed sentences in a "safe, fair and humane" fashion that assists young persons to be rehabilitated and reintegrated into the community. Section 83 also articulates a set of principles that are to guide decisions about the placement of young offenders within the youth corrections system and their release into the community on supervision.

The declarations of principle that are set out in sections 4, 38, and 83 to govern extrajudicial measures, sentencing, and the use of custody expand on the themes and more general statements in the Preamble and section 3 of the *YCJA*. These more specific statements of principle will be considered in more detail later in this book,.

C. PURPOSE OF YOUTH JUSTICE: LONG-TERM PUBLIC PROTECTION

Section 3(1)(a) of the *Youth Criminal Justice Act* declares that the purpose of the youth criminal justice system is to promote the long-term protection of Canadian society. This emphasis on the protection of the public has been criticized by some advocates for youth as sending a law-and-order message and taking a punitive approach to young offenders.[44] It should, however, be appreciated that the focus of section 3(1)(a) is on the "long-term" protection of society. This provision recognizes that this objective will be achieved by:

- prevention of crime by addressing the circumstances underlying a youth's offending behaviour;
- rehabilitation and reintegration into society of youths who have committed offences; and
- ensuring that youths who commit offences are subjected to meaningful consequences.

The approach of section 3(1)(a) of the *YCJA* can be contrasted to section 718 of the *Criminal Code*, which establishes the "fundamental purpose[s]" for the sentencing of adult offenders. As for youth, the sentencing of adult offenders is to contribute to the maintenance of a "just, peaceful and safe society."[45]

---

44   "War on Crime to Target Young," *Globe and Mail*, June 1, 1998.
45   *Criminal Code*, R.S.C. 1985, c. C-46, s. 718.

Similar to sections 3 and 38 of the *YCJA*, section 718 of the *Code* states that a court sentencing adult offenders shall have "one or more of the following objectives: to denounce unlawful conduct . . . assist in rehabilitating offenders, to provide reparations for harm done to victims or the community; and to promote a sense of responsibility in offenders." The *Code* provision recognizes that in some cases an adult sentence may have the objective of "assisting" in the rehabilitation of an offender, but the wording also clearly indicates that in other cases rehabilitation of an adult offender might not be a factor. By way of contrast, sections 3 and 38 of the *YCJA* always require the youth justice court to consider the objectives of rehabilitation and reintegration of a young offender when imposing a sentence. Further, section 718 of the *Criminal Code* allows a court to promote the objective of having a peaceful and safe society by specifically having as the objective of the sentence for an adult "to deter the offender and other persons from committing offences [and to] separate offenders from society where necessary." That is, general deterrence and the incapacitation of offenders are legitimate objectives for the sentencing of adults.

The *YCJA* requires a youth justice court to hold young offenders accountable for their crimes, and to impose sanctions proportionate to their offences. Sentencing of this type by youth justice courts will serve a deterrent function and will result in some young offenders being placed in custody and removed from society, especially those who have committed serious violent offences or who have committed repeat offences and have failed to comply with the terms of community-based sentences. It is, however, significant that neither section 3 nor section 38 of the *YCJA* mention either deterrence or separation of young offenders from the community as specific sentencing objectives.

The *YCJA* has a quite different set of guiding principles for dealing with young offenders from those applied to adults. Greater emphasis is placed on preventing crime by addressing the causes that underlie a young person's offending behaviour and reintegrating him or her into the community. Under the *YOA*, many youth court judges took account of deterrence when dealing with young offenders, although case law indicates that, considering all of the provisions of section 3 of the *YOA*, deterrence was not to be as much of a factor for the sentencing of young persons as with adults.[46] Available social science research clearly supports the approach to youth justice that is reflected in the *YCJA*, which does not explicitly consider deterrence as a factor in sentencing

---

46   See for example, *R. v. M.(J.J.)*, above note 9; and *R. v. E.(R.K.)*, [1996] M.J. 14 (C.A.).

youth. Baron and Kennedy, Canadian criminologists, argue that certainty of criminal sanction affects youth offending rates more than the harshness of that sanction: "harsher penalties will not deter those most at risk for criminal behaviour."[47] Similarly Professor Anthony Doob, a leading Canadian criminologist, and some of his colleagues conclude:

> the likelihood of apprehension — or more importantly the perceived personal likelihood of apprehension, can be important for some offences in determining whether or not a young person will commit offences. However, a review of the literature on size of sanction suggests that this [i.e., length of sentence or even transfer to adult court] is likely to be irrelevant to whether or not a young person commits an offence . . . changing levels of punishment will not change youth crime.[48]

Most adolescents who offend commit relatively minor offences, and if apprehended, are likely to be sufficiently chastened by that experience that they are unlikely to reoffend. This is the case whether they are dealt with informally by extrajudicial measures, sent to youth justice court, or placed in custody. On the other hand, the relatively small group of young offenders who are most likely to reoffend are least likely to be deterred by the threat of harsh punishment.

In a study of Edmonton street youths, among whom a typical respondent committed a break and enter six times in the year prior to the study, criminologists found that living on the margins of society can alter perceptions of punishment. Deterrence does not threaten people on the margins of society in the same way as it does people in the mainstream. They concluded that conventional models of deterrence must be rethought when dealing with adolescents at risk, such as those with a history of offending.[49] Similarly a report on Toronto teens with experience with the youth court system reported that serving time in custody is a status symbol among some peer groups; if these youths spend time in custody "they come out a hero with their peer group."[50] Although under the new Act youths will continue to be sentenced to

---

47   S. Baron and L. Kennedy, "Deterrence and Homeless Male Street Youths" (1998) 40 Can. J. Crim. 27 at 52.

48   A.N. Doob, V. Marinos and K.N. Varma, *Youth Crime and the Youth Justice System in Canada* (Toronto: University of Toronto, Centre of Criminology, 1995) at 69.

49   See S. Baron and L. Kennedy, above note 47, for the findings of a study done on Edmonton male street youths in 1995.

50   E. Anderssen, "Crime Bills Aims to Reduce Rate of Incarceration," *Globe and Mail*, March 12, 1999.

custody, the *YCJA* is clearly intended to reduce the use of custody for adolescent offenders from its high level of use under the *YOA*.

1) Crime Prevention

The Preamble and section 3(1)(a)(i) of the *YCJA* both refer to the prevention of youth crime as an important means of achieving a safer society. These two provisions, however, use the term "crime prevention" in somewhat different ways. Growing public concerns made crime prevention an important political issue in the 1990s, and in 1995 the Liberal government amended the Declaration of Principle of the *YOA* in order to acknowledge its importance. The federal government established the twenty-five-member National Crime Prevention Council in 1994, composed of volunteers serving essentially advocacy and advisory functions. The Council recognized that the concept of "crime prevention" has several distinct meanings:

- measures designed to reduce an individual's inclination to commit crimes through intervention *after* an offence has been committed (i.e., rehabilitation);
- measures designed to reduce an individual's inclination to commit crimes through early preventative intervention in the lives of children and adolescents at high risk of offending *before* they commit any offences (also referred to as crime prevention through social development);
- measures taken to reduce the opportunity to commit crimes, such as increased policing, neighbourhood crime-watch programs, enhanced security, and lighting, as well as programs that assist the vulnerable and reduce the likelihood of individual victimization (also referred to as "situational" or opportunity-reduction crime prevention); and
- measures aimed at the apprehension and punishment of individual offenders, the goal being to prevent future crime either by deterring people from committing offences or, if incarceration results, by "incapacitation" of likely offenders.[51]

The National Crime Prevention Council noted that conventional crime prevention efforts in Canada focused on the third and fourth types of measures, although their effectiveness is limited. Situational crime-control efforts can reduce total levels of offending. Not infrequently,

---

51   National Crime Prevention Council, *Money Well Spent: Investing in Preventing Crime* (Ottawa: 1996) at 27.

however, these efforts tend to protect certain targets while those committing crime shift to other, less protected, locales. Longer custodial sentences have had little or no impact on rates of youth offending, and the Council endorsed placing a priority on "crime prevention through social development" as the most effective long-term method of reducing levels of crime in Canada.

In the 1990s, the federal government tried to appeal to those with differing views about crime prevention. Numerous significant legislative and administrative reforms were intended to take a law-and-order approach to "combat crime." This included the inclusion in the 1995 reforms to YOA provisions that facilitated the transfer of youths charged with serious offences to adult court and provided longer sentences for youths who commit murder.[52] In 1995, the Liberal government also added provisions to the YOA which reflected at least a symbolic commitment to an approach to crime prevention based on the Council's concept of "social development."[53] Section 3(1)(a) was added to the YOA to recognize that "crime prevention is essential to the long term protection of society and requires . . . identifying and effectively responding to children and young persons at risk of committing offending behaviour in the future." While this message in section 3(1)(a) may have had some symbolic value, and reflects sound social policy, it had very little practical significance. Although the federal government provided some short-term funding for some pilot projects directed at early intervention, the federal government and those working within the youth justice system have little direct responsibility over the type of crime-prevention measures referred to in section 3(1)(a) of the YOA. Those measures of crime prevention, aimed at children and adolescents who are *at risk* of becoming future offenders, are intended to prevent them from offending in the first place. It is the provincial governments and those who work in the health, education, and social-service fields who have the primary responsibility for taking proactive steps to reduce the likelihood of offending by children and adolescents at risk. The Preamble to the YCJA repeats the crime prevention theme of section 3(1)(a) of the YOA that

---

52   The ambivalence about the best approach to preventing youth crime — to get tough with offenders, especially violent offenders, or increased efforts at crime prevention through social development — was apparent in the report of Canada, House of Commons, *Thirteenth Report of the Standing Committee on Justice and Legal Affairs: Renewing Youth Justice* (Ottawa: Ministry of Supply and Services, 1997).

53   See, for example, House of Commons, *Twelfth Report of the Standing Committee on Justice and the Solicitor General: Crime Prevention in Canada: Toward a National Strategy* (Ottawa: Ministry of Supply and Services, 1993).

"reasonable steps [should be taken] to prevent youth crime by address-ing its underlying causes [and] to respond to the needs of . . . those at risk of committing crimes." Although these statements are of political rather than legal significance, they continue to provide rhetorical sup-port for crime prevention through social development.

In contrast to the essentially symbolic statements about crime pre-vention that are found in section 3(1)(a) of the *YOA* and in the Preamble of the *YCJA*, section 3(1)(a)(i) of the *YCJA* can have practi-cal significance in providing guidance for individual cases. That section uses the concept of crime prevention in a narrower sense than the Preamble of the *YCJA* or section 3(1)(a) of the *YOA*, as it recognizes that the youth criminal justice system focuses on *responding* to youth crime and, hence, this system can only play a relatively small role in preventing crime. The *YCJA* makes clear that the youth justice system, as opposed to other social institutions, is to focus on responding to those adolescents who have actually committed offences, and not deal with those at risk of committing future offences. Section 3(1)(a)(i) may be invoked in making a sentencing decision about a specific youth. It makes clear that the interventions of the youth justice system, whether through extrajudicial sanctions or a youth justice court sentence, should address the "circumstances underlying a young person's offend-ing behaviour" to the greatest extent possible.

The principle in section 3(1)(a)(i) in many respects reinforces the principle of section 3(1)(a)(ii), that the youth justice system should address the problems of youth that are causally related to their offend-ing behaviour and seek to rehabilitate young offenders. For example, the criminal behaviour of many young offenders is related to learning disabilities, and youth justice system intervention that identifies this disability and then affords the youth help in dealing with it will help prevent future offending behaviour. In appropriate cases, section 3(1)(a)(i) may be used as a basis for advocating a section 34 assess-ment, so that a court may learn about the underlying circumstances of offending behaviour, as well as to advocate for a sentence that address-es those circumstances. But section 3(1)(a)(i) also makes clear that the interventions of the youth justice system should focus on *offending* behaviour. If a youth has other social problems, whether a lack of ade-quate housing or engaging in self-destructive non-criminal behaviour, then the youth should be referred to other services. The need to focus the youth justice system on responding to offending behaviour is rein-forced by sections 29(1) and 39(5), which make clear that neither pre-trial detention nor custody should be used as a substitute for "appropriate child protection, mental health or other social measures."

Section 35 of the *YCJA* allows a youth justice court judge at any stage of a youth proceeding to refer a young person to a child welfare agency, so that the agency can conduct an assessment of whether the youth is in need of agency services.

Considerable social science research now supports the view that the youth justice system can only have a limited role in preventing crime and can have only limited impact on reducing reoffending. Most available research supports the view that crime prevention is most cost-effective and best achieved by early intervention in the community with children and adolescents at risk rather than harsher punishment in the youth justice system.[54] As Anne McLellan, then Minister of Justice, noted when introducing the first version of *YCJA* in 1998: "an effective approach for dealing with youth crime must reach beyond the justice system and include crime prevention and a host of other programs and services that help to support children and youth."[55]

Despite the statements of principle in the Act that recognize the limits of the youth criminal justice response in preventing youth crime, some provincial and local governments in Canada advocate using the criminal law in the wider preventative fashion — using the fourth definitional approach identified by the National Crime Prevention Council to focus on deterrence and incapacitation. As discussed in Chapter 1, this more punitive approach to crime prevention was most apparent in the position of Ontario's Conservative government which argued, when the *YCJA* was being enacted by Parliament, that the Act is too soft and will therefore encourage youth crime. While the weight of social science research clearly demonstrates that more use of custody, longer sentences in youth custody, and treating greater numbers of young offenders as adults do not have a significant effect on levels of youth crime, the political appeal to this approach to crime prevention is considerable.[56]

---

54   See, for example, L.J. Schweinhart, *et al.*, *Significant Benefits: The High/Scope Perry Preschool Study Through Age 27* (Ypsilanti, MI: High/Scope Press, 1993); and R. Peters, *et al.*, *Developing Capacity and Competence in the Better Beginnings, Better Futures Communities: Short-Term Findings Report* (Kingston, ON: Better Beginnings Research Unit, Queen's University, 2000).

55   Minister of Justice and Attorney General for Canada, "Notes for Remarks by the Honourable Anne McLellan," *Justice Information*, May 12, 1998 at 1.

56   See, for example, Ontario Ministry of the Attorney General, *No More Free Ride for Young Offenders Act* (Toronto, 2001). (Available online at time of writing at <www.attorneygeneral.jus.gov.on.ca>.)

2) Curfew as a Crime-Prevention Measure

Another approach to using the justice system to reduce levels of youthful offending is to impose a curfew on youth. A few Canadian municipalities[57] have followed a practice quite widespread in American cities and towns of enacting a municipal bylaw to require youth under the age of sixteen or eighteen to be in their residences by a certain time of the night, usually between 21:00 and 22:00 on week-nights and a little later on weekends, and lasting until sunrise or 6:00. Youth who violate the curfew may be arrested by the police and taken home or to a place of youth detention, although these bylaws invariably allow a youth to be out after the curfew if accompanied by a parent or guardian. The rationale for these bylaws is that youth who are out and unsupervised at night are prone to engage in offending behaviour, such as vandalism or violent offences.[58] The bylaws are also intended to protect juveniles from potential victimization, as well as to support parental efforts at supervision of their adolescent children.

The reality is that most offending at night is carried out by adults, and that most youth offending occurs during the daylight hours, generally peaking in the hours after school is released. Curfew measures have little or no effect on community safety. American cities that have curfews have had at best mixed results in using curfews to reduce levels of offending by or victimization of juveniles.[59] The effective enforcement of curfew laws by police requires significant police resources which could be more efficiently used in other types of crime prevention activities, and some American police forces make only minimal efforts at the enforcement of juvenile curfews. There are also concerns that the enforcement of curfew laws by police can be discriminatory, targeting low-income youth who are more likely to be on the street due to a lack of indoor recreational and social activities. Curfew enforcement is often intrusive, with police stopping young people at random to demand proof of age.

---

57   See, for example, "Town Puts 11 pm Curfew on Teenagers," *National Post*, July 7, 2001, regarding a 23:00 – 6:00 curfew on youth under sixteen years of age in Wilkie, Saskatchewan. See also the *Curfew Act*, R.S.B.C., 1979, c. 87, which specifically allows municipalities to enact this type of bylaw.

58   See, for example, Dick Illingworth, "Return of a Teenage Curfew is Needed," *Municipal World*, September 1996, 106:9 at 4–5.

59   See, for example, "Curfew Law Fails to Curb Violent Crime, Study Finds," Washington Crime News Services, February 20, 1998, 32:8; and "Curfews keep U.S. kids off city streets," *Toronto Star*, August 17, 1997.

A number of constitutional challenges have been made in the United States to the validity of juvenile curfew bylaws. Some American courts have upheld curfew bylaws, ruling that they are justified to protect adolescents, but other courts have ruled such bylaws unconstitutional. Bylaws that do not have exemptions allowing for employment and religious observance may be most vulnerable to constitutional challenge. Some American judges have held that such bylaws are constitutionally unacceptable regardless of how narrowly they are drafted, as they are unjustified discrimination on the basis of age.[60] There is no United States Supreme Court decision on the issue. In Canada, there are no reported cases on the constitutional validity of juvenile curfew bylaws, but a municipal bylaw that restricted access for youth under the age of sixteen to video arcades was held to be unconstitutional as unjustifiable discrimination on the basis of age and hence in violation of section 15 of the *Charter*.[61]

While responsible parents do attempt to monitor where their adolescent children are at night and have family curfews for them, there are real questions whether municipalities can validly enact bylaws to achieve this object. If such a bylaw is aimed at preventing crime among juveniles, it seems highly discriminatory. If such a law is intended to promote the welfare of adolescents, it seems to run contrary to the relatively narrow approach of the *YCJA* to the use of the criminal law power of the police and legal processes.

3) Accountability and Proportionality

A central premise of the *YCJA* is that adolescents are capable of independent thought and judgment and hence should be morally and legally accountable for their acts — but that they are psychologically, socially, and intellectually less mature than adults, which should affect the way in which they are held accountable. The law rests on the premise that young persons who violate the criminal law should be held accountable for their acts but, because of their relative immaturity and amenability to change, there should be a lesser accountability than for adults committing the same offences and there should be a greater

---

60   Patrick Chudy, "Doctrinal Reconstruction: reconciling conflicting standards in adjudicating juvenile curfew challenges" (2000) 85 Cornell L.Rev. 518–85.

61   *R. v. Music Explosion Ltd.* (1990), 59 C.C.C. (3d) 571 (Man. C.A.).

emphasis on rehabilitation in the way in which the justice system holds them accountable.[62]

Section 3(1)(a)(iii) makes clear that the youth justice system is intended to ensure that a youth who has committed an offence is subject to "meaningful consequences." Section 3(1)(b)(ii) provides an important qualification to the principle of accountability: the consequences imposed should be a "fair and proportionate" response to the offence and record of the youth, and should be "consistent with the greater degree of dependency of young persons and their reduced level of maturity." Further, while all young offenders should be held accountable in some fashion, in some cases the objective of promoting the protection of the public by promoting the rehabilitation and reintegration into society of a young offender may also mitigate the sanction imposed. Accountability of offenders may involve some element of "retribution," that is, the "imposition of a just and appropriate punishment." Retribution is not, however, equivalent to vengeance, as Chief Justice Lamer stated in a case dealing with the sentencing of adults: "Vengeance [is] motivated by emotion and anger, as a reprisal for harm inflicted. . . . Retribution . . . by contrast, represents an objective, reasoned and measured determination of an appropriate punishment *which reflects the moral culpability of the offender*, having regard to the intentional risk-taking of the offender, the consequential harm caused by the offender, and the normative character of the offender's conduct" [emphasis added].[63]

Since accountability and retribution are based on the moral culpability of the offender, adolescents should, in general, receive a lesser sanction than an adult would for any given offence. Because of their limited intellectual, moral, and psychological development, it is inappropriate to hold adolescents accountable in the same manner and to the same extent as adults. The immaturity and lack of judgment of youth are reasons for denying rights and privileges, such as those involving voting or driving, as well as for limiting accountability under the YCJA.

---

62 Two articles highlight contemporary debates in the United States concerning the capacity of adolescents and the effect that their capacity should have on juvenile justice policy. Common ground between them is that youths differ from adults in their propensity to take risks, and lack of experience, leading them to make unwise choices which adults would likely not make. Contrast S. Morse, "Immaturity and Irresponsibility" (1998) 88 J. Crim. L. and Criminology 15; and E. Scott and T. Grisso, "The Evolution of Adolescence" (1998) 88 J. Crim. L. and Criminology 137.

63 *R. v. M.(C.A.)*, [1996] 1 S.C.R. 500, at para. 80.

The *YOA* also recognized that young persons should have limited accountability in comparison to adults. In *R. v. M.(J.J.)*, a sentencing appeal under the *YOA*, Justice Cory of the Supreme Court of Canada wrote: "the Declaration [of Principle] in s. 3(1)(a) and (c) notes that young offenders cannot be held accountable in the same way as adult criminals because of their dependency on others and their obvious lack of maturity."[64] Section 3(1)(b)(iii) of the *YCJA* articulates the same basic premise: the greater dependency and limited level of maturity of young persons should affect how they are treated by the youth justice system. This will normally result in young persons receiving less onerous sanctions than adults in similar circumstances. It may also mean that a twelve-year-old youth should have a lesser degree of accountability and a lesser sanction than a seventeen-year-old who commits the same offence.

Contemporary understanding of the intellectual, psychological, and social development of adolescents have influenced the principles selected by Parliament to govern the youth justice system under the *YCJA*. Adolescents are now understood to be immature in comparison to adults but to have the capacity for considerable autonomy in their decision making.[65] Many researchers now believe the cognitive skills of youths are often as developed as those of an adult, although their moral development and judgment are generally not as fully developed.[66] Additionally, adolescents may lack the capacity for empathy and are more prone to take risks than adults.[67]

That adolescents should be held accountable for their actions but in a more limited way than adults is reflected by the inclusion of notions of proportionality in the *YCJA*, as well as in other areas of law. In a recent tort case, Abella J.A., writing for the Ontario Court of Appeal, held that teenagers should not be held to an adult standard of care in a civil tort law case. Her reasons help illustrate contemporary understanding of the immaturity of adolescents. She held that two sixteen-year-old boys who were driving their drunk friend home and let him out of their car at his request should not be held liable in negligence for this decision. She reasoned that they "had never been drunk and had no knowledge of how that would affect someone's ability to make decisions."[68]

---

64 *R. v. M.(J.J.)*, above note 9.
65 S. Morse, above note 62.
66 E. Scott and T. Grisso, above note 62.
67 T. Geraghty and S. Drizin,"The Debate Over the Future of the Juvenile Courts" (1998) 88 J. Crim. L. & Criminology 15.
68 *Nespolon v. Alford et al.* (1998), 40 O.R. (3d) 355 (Ont. C.A.).

Fair and proportionate accountability is the central sentencing principle of the *YCJA* found in section 3(1)(b)(ii), which is reinforced by the statement in the Preamble providing that the youth justice system should "reserve the most serious intervention for the most serious crimes." The principle of fair and proportionate accountability is also reflected in section 38(2) of the Act, which provides that a youth justice court sentence should:

- be proportionate to the seriousness of the offence and the degree of responsibility of the youth for the offence;
- be similar to the sentences imposed in the region on young persons found guilty of the same offence committed in similar circumstances; and
- not result in a punishment greater than that which would be appropriate for an adult who committed the same offence in similar circumstances.

Section 38, and other provisions of section 39 which restrict the use of custodial sentences, are clearly intended to structure judicial discretion in sentencing, and thereby achieve two of the objectives of the *YCJA* set out in the Preamble: namely, reserving "the most serious interventions for the most serious crimes" and reducing "over-reliance on incarceration for non-violent young persons."

Section 3(1)(a)(iii) requires "meaningful" consequences for young persons who violate the law, but the *YCJA* recognizes that there is a broad range of measures that may be meaningful ways of holding a young person accountable. What is "meaningful" will depend on such factors as the nature of the offence and the circumstances of the youth. In some measure, what is meaningful for an adolescent may differ from what is meaningful for an adult. Section 4 of the Act makes clear that for many youths who have committed an offence, some form of diversion from the formal youth court system through imposition of extrajudicial measures is the most appropriate response. This will result in some youth who have committed relatively minor offences being dealt with by means of an informal warning through a range of more formal extrajudicial sanctions. These sanctions may result in an apology to a victim, performance of services, or provision of counselling, but do not resort to formal court processes that would create a record of conviction. For more serious cases, accountability is achieved through the youth justice court, which may impose a range of sentences to ensure that a sanction is a fair and proportionate response to the offence.

Consistent with the principle that adolescents should be subjected to a lesser degree of accountability than adults, the maximum sentences that a youth justice court can impose are significantly less than the maximum sentences that can be imposed on an adult. The maximum sentence for most offences in youth justice court is two years in custody and, for most offences for which an adult could receive a sentence of life imprisonment, the maximum youth justice court sentence is three years.[69] For murder, the maximum youth justice court sentence is ten years, in contrast to life imprisonment for adults.[70] Even for those youth who have committed the most serious offences in the most serious circumstances and are to be subjected to an adult sentence, the age and immaturity of the offender are factors that may mitigate the length of the sentence, and for those youth who are sentenced as adults for murder and receive a sentence of life imprisonment, there is still earlier parole eligibility than for adults.[71]

Consistent with the notion that criminal liability is normally only imposed if a person has the requisite mental capacity to intend to commit a criminal act, an exception is made to a person being held accountable for illegal acts if, pursuant to section 16 of the *Criminal Code*, the person is found exempt from criminal responsibility by reason of a mental disorder that rendered that person "incapable of appreciating the nature and quality" of his or her acts or of "knowing that it was wrong." As discussed more fully in Chapter 7, if a youth is found to be not criminally responsible on account of a mental disorder, the youth may be committed for treatment to a mental health facility until it is considered safe to release the person. In these limited circumstances, the protection of the public and the interests of the mentally incompetent youth may justify confinement and separation from society that is not commensurate with the offence.

4) Respect for Social Values and Deterrence

Section 3(1)(c)(i) of the *YCJA* provides that "within the limits of fair and proportional accountability, the measures taken against young persons who commit offences should reinforce respect for societal values." There was no analogous provision in the *YOA*. The intent of this provision and the source of "societal values" that are to be respected is not totally clear, although there will be cases in which this provision may be relevant to sentencing. Section 3(1)(c)(i) might, for example, be

---

69   *YCJA*, above note 3, s. 42(2)(n).
70   *YCJA*, above note 3, s. 42(2)(q).
71   *Criminal Code*, above note 45, s. 745.1, discussed in Chapter 9.

cited by a Crown prosecutor to seek a more severe sentence if a crime committed by a young offender was motivated by racial or religious hatred, whether it be a property offence such as vandalism or a personal-injury offence such as an assault. One of Canada's societal values is the promotion of a tolerant and diverse society, and evidence of racial, religious, or other bias is an aggravating factor in the sentencing of adults under section 718.2(a)(i) of the *Criminal Code*. Although section 718.2 of the Code is not explicitly incorporated into the *YCJA*, to the extent that its provisions are not inconsistent with principles in the Act, it may be looked to as a source of societal values.[72] Similarly, it might also be an aggravating circumstance if an offence involves a breach of trust, such as sexual exploitation of a young child by an adolescent who is being paid to look after that child. While section 718.2 is not directly applicable to sentencing under the *YCJA*, these are circumstances in which societal values are implicated in the offence and that might suggest a higher degree of accountability.

Sections 38(2)(d)(iii) and 38(3)(b) of the *YCJA* make clear that when a youth justice court is imposing a sentence on a young offender, the court may have regard to the harm done to the "victim and the community" as aggravating circumstances in imposing a sentence. Offences that involve a breach of trust typically cause greater harm to victims. Criminal acts that are motivated by racial hatred or other types of bias cause greater psychological and social harm than the similar acts that may have different, more individualized motivations, as they represent an assault on human decency as well as physical integrity, and increase fears of victimization in the community among other members of the same group. Similarly offences that occur in schools or that are gang related may cause greater social and psychological harm to the broader community than similar offences that do not involve these circumstances, and may therefore merit a more severe sanction. "Respect for societal values" may be referred to in these circumstances and might affect the sanction imposed. In imposing a sanction on a young person, consideration may be given to the effect of the offence on a broader community as well as the victim, and the extent to which the offence implicates societal values beyond those associated with criminal activities. While this takes account of societal interests in imposing a sentence, it is not the same as considering the deterrent effect of a particular sentence.

---

72   *YCJA*, above note 3, s. 50 specifies that s. 718.2(e) of the *Criminal Code*, above note 45, on the sentencing of Aboriginal offenders, applies to young offenders, although no other paragraphs of s. 718.2 are directly applicable to the sentencing of youths under the *YCJA*.

Under the *YOA*, general deterrence was a legitimate factor to be taken into account in rendering a disposition, albeit of lesser significance than for adults. As stated by Cory J. in the Supreme Court of Canada in *R. v. M.(J.J.)*:

> There is reason to believe that *YOA* dispositions can have an effective deterrent effect. The crimes committed by the young tend to be a group activity. The group lends support and assistance to the prime offenders. The criminological literature is clear that about 80 percent of juvenile delinquency is a group activity, whether as part of an organized gang or with an informal group of accomplices. . . . If the activity of the group is criminal then the disposition imposed on an individual member of the group should be such that it will deter other members of the group. For example the sentence imposed on one member of a "swarming group" should serve to deter others in the gang. Having said that, I would underline that general deterrence should not, through undue emphasis, have the same importance in fashioning the disposition for a youthful offender as it would in the case of an adult. One youthful offender should not be obliged to accept the responsibility for all the young offenders of his or her generation.[73]

This general statement was used by youth court judges making dispositions under the *YOA* as the basis for making a more severe disposition in cases in which deterrence was considered significant, for example involving gangs[74] or occurring at school.[75]

Section 718(b) of the *Criminal Code* provides that, when sentencing an adult, one factor that a court may specifically have as an objective is "to deter the offender and others from committing offences." This provision is *not* directly applicable to sentencing in youth justice court under the *YCJA*. Despite the statements in the case law under the *YOA* about the consideration of deterrence, it is submitted that it would be an error of law for a youth justice court acting under the *YCJA* to identify deterrence of others as a factor in sentencing. While a youth justice court should not explicitly consider deterrence as a sentencing factor, it may take account of the harm done to victims and the community from offences, and of the need to reinforce respect for social values. Thus, an offence such as the burning of a cross on the lawn of a black-skinned family might result in a more severe sentence than a similar offence not having this type of symbolism. An offence that is motivated by racial or

---

73   *R. v. M.(J.J.)*, above note 9, at para. 30.
74   See, for example, *R. v. R.K.E.* (1996), 107 Man. R. (2d) 200 (Man. C.A.).
75   See, for example, *R. v. LeRoy B.* (1993), 18 W.C.B. (2d) 565 (Ont. C.A.).

religious hatred may cause particular degradation for the victim and apprehension in a broader community, and offends fundamental Canadian values.

An offence involving violence by a gang member may also result in a more severe sentence than the circumstances would otherwise warrant because of the fear and intimidation that such an offence may cause in the broader community. An assault of a teacher by a student may similarly result in a more severe sanction since the offence undermines the sense of safety in the school and thereby affects all students and teachers in the school, and undermines confidence and respect for the education system. Further, it would not be inappropriate for a youth justice court to explicitly recognize that there is a deterrent effect from young offenders knowing that they will be held accountable for their acts, and that aggravating factors which may result in a more severe sanction include the harm done to the broader community from an offence and the need to reinforce respect for social values. However, the deterrence of other offenders should not be a factor resulting in a more severe sanction for a young offender. In particular, the mere fact that a property offence, like theft of automobiles, is widespread in a particular community should not justify the imposition of a more severe sanction under the YCJA for a young person who is apprehended for that offence. While under the YOA, youth courts did take account of the prevalence of such offences and the need for deterrence when deciding what disposition to make, it is submitted that this should not be a factor in sentencing under the YCJA.[76]

D. RESTORATIVE JUSTICE AND MEANINGFUL RESPONSES

The requirement of section 3(1)(c)(iii) that consequences of offending behaviour for youth are to be "meaningful" speaks both to the manner in which the consequences are imposed and to their nature. Whether the offence is resolved by an informal warning from a police officer, extrajudicial sanctions, or a youth justice court sentence, the person imposing the sanction should attempt to engage the youth in the sentencing process. An attempt should be made to explain *what* sanction is being imposed and why this particular sanction is an appropriate response.

---

76   See R. v. J.M.C. (1994), 90 C.C.C. (3d) 385 (Man. C.A.).

Whether accountability is achieved through extrajudicial measures or in youth justice court, section 3(1)(c)(ii) suggests that whenever appropriate and feasible, the consequences for the youth should involve some form of compensation to the victim or the community. This provision states that sanctions imposed on a young person who has violated the law should "encourage the repair of harm." Some form of reparation of harm, whether by means of an apology, performance of services, or compensation to a victim, tends to make the consequences of offending more meaningful to the youth. Section 3(1)(c)(ii) reflects a "restorative justice philosophy"; that is, whenever possible, a sanction imposed on an offender should attempt to restore harmonious relationships between the offender and those who have been harmed by the offence, namely the victim and the community. This may require apologies as well as the possibility of some form of compensation being provided to the victim or the community.[77]

1) Rehabilitation and Reintegration

Canada's juvenile justice system has long been separate and distinct from the adult criminal justice regime. This is based at least in part on the belief that adolescents have different needs and are more amenable to rehabilitation than adults. In the late 1970s critics of the juvenile corrections system argued that efforts at rehabilitation of offenders were a failure, as offenders who went through programs oriented to rehabilitation and treatment in custody seemed as likely to reoffend as those who were simply incarcerated. This was sometimes referred to as the "nothing works" critique of juvenile corrections.[78] Since 1980 there has been a great deal of research and experimentation in youth corrections. There have been efforts to develop programs that are more effective in reducing recidivism, as well as more sophisticated research into the effectiveness of different types of programs for different types of offenders.

---

77 As discussed further in Chapter 5, the efficacy of the restorative justice approach to reducing recidivism remains controversial, and there are concerns over the potential for negative effects on victims who may feel coerced into participating: see, for example, K. Haines, "Some Principled Objections to a Restorative Justice Approach to Working with Juvenile Offenders" in L. Walgrave, ed., *Restorative Justice for Juveniles: Potentialities, Risks, and Problems for Research* (Leuven, BG: Leuven University Press, 1998) 93.

78 J. Shamsie, "Anti-social Adolescents: Our Treatments Do Not Work — Where Do We Go From Here?" (1981) 26 Can. J. Psychiatry 357. See also R. Martinson, "What works: Questions and answers about prison reform" (1976) 35 The Public Interest 22–54.

The present literature reveals that treatment programs that address the criminogenic needs of young offenders may reduce reoffending rates by 20 to 40 percent in comparison to conventional custodial programs for young offenders, which only provide access to education but do little to directly address the causes of criminal behaviour.[79] The programs that seem more effective at reducing recidivism address social and cognitive factors, such as problem-solving skills, attitudes, and beliefs about offending. Human-service programs, supported through court-based sanctions, contribute more to reductions in antisocial behaviour than sanctions alone, while deterrent-based programs that lack clearly identified human-service components are not effective in reducing recidivism. Determining what program is most likely to be effective for a particular young offender requires an understanding of that individual's needs and circumstances. For many young offenders, the most effective programs in terms of reducing the risk of further criminal activities are community based, as the youth must learn to deal with pressures and temptations within the community, if that youth is not to reoffend. If youths with a low risk of serious offending are placed in custody, there may be an increased risk of them reoffending. This is because, in custody, they are likely to associate with adolescents with more serious problems and more antisocial values.

The *Juvenile Delinquents Act*, with its child-welfare orientation, focused on the rehabilitation of delinquents, at least in theory. While the YOA placed a greater emphasis on accountability than the *Juvenile Delinquents Act*, the YOA also had a strongly rehabilitative focus, as the Supreme Court of Canada recognized in *Reference re. Young Offenders Act* s. 2 (P.E.I.). Chief Justice Lamer wrote: "It is clear . . . that the *Young Offenders Act* does not generally recognize any proportionality between the gravity of the offence and the range of sanctions. It rather recognizes the special situation and the special needs of the young offender and gives to the judge special options that are not available for adults. It is still primarily oriented towards rehabilitation rather than punishment or neutralization."[80]

In *R. v. M. (J.J.)*, the Supreme Court upheld a disposition under the YOA of two years in open custody for an Aboriginal youth convicted of

---

79 See G. Bernfeld, D. Farrington, and A. Leschied, eds., *Offender Rehabilitation in Practice: Implementing and Evaluating Effective Programs* (Baffins Lane, Chicester, West Sussex, UK: John Wiley Press, 2001). See also A.W. Lescheid, "Informing Young Offender Policy in Current Research: What the Future Holds" (2000) 12:2 [Corrections Canada] Forum.

80 *Reference re Young Offenders Act* s. 2 (P.E.I.), [1991] 1 S.C.R. 252, 62 C.C.C. (3d) 385 at 398.

three counts of break, enter, and theft, and one count of breach of probation. The Court acknowledged that this disposition was not warranted strictly on accountability principles but was concerned that the youth had a "depressing" family history, with parents prone to alcohol abuse, spousal violence, and physical abuse of their children. Justice Cory wrote about the relationship between "child welfare concerns and the proportionality principle" in sentencing youths under the *YOA*:

> The situation in the home of a young offender should neither be ignored nor made the predominant factor in sentencing. Nonetheless, it is a factor that can properly be taken into account in fashioning the disposition. . . . The aim must be both to protect society and at the same time to provide the young offender with the necessary guidance and assistance that he or she may not be getting at home. Those goals are not necessarily mutually exclusive. In the long run, society is best protected by the reformation and rehabilitation of a young offender. In turn, the young offenders are best served when they are provided with the necessary guidance and assistance to enable them to learn the skills required to become fully integrated, useful members of society.[81]

Although the *YCJA* is clearly criminal legislation, it is also distinct from the law applicable to adult offenders in its recognition that adolescents have special needs, and that those who commit offences may be impressionable and amenable to rehabilitation. Belief that adolescents are more likely to be rehabilitated than adults remains a fundamental principle of Canada's youth justice system under the *YCJA*. However, the *YCJA* rejects the approach of the *Juvenile Delinquents Act* and decisions under the *YOA* like *M.(J.J.)* which, in order to achieve child welfare objectives, allowed sanctions imposed by the juvenile justice system to be more intrusive than would be justified on accountability-based principles. Under the *YCJA*, concerns about rehabilitation and welfare may be considered to mitigate the rigours of a proportionality-based approach or to shape the nature of a non-custodial sentence, but they cannot be used to justify a longer sentence in custody than the nature and circumstances of the offence would justify.

Judges sentencing a young offender under the *YCJA* may require information from a section 40 pre-sentence report or a report under section 34 prepared by a psychologist, psychiatrist, or other mental-health professional. These reports may enable the court to understand a youth adequately and impose a sentence that is most likely to address the criminogenic needs of the youth and, thereby, reduce the risk of reof-

---

81   *R. v. M.(J.J.)*, above note 9 at paras. 25–26.

fending. However, both the statements of principle and specific provisions of the *YCJA* make clear that a youth court should not use concerns about child welfare or rehabilitation to impose a longer sentence than would otherwise be warranted on accountability-based principles by the nature and circumstances of the offence and record of the offender.

It is significant that the references to addressing the circumstances underlying the causes of youth crime and to rehabilitation and reintegration are in sections 3(1)(a) and (1)(b), which deal with the purpose and nature of the youth justice *system*. Parliament clearly expects the provincial and territorial governments, and non-governmental agencies that administer youth justice the programs and facilities, to place an emphasis on rehabilitative interventions. It is, however, section 3(1)(c) of the *YCJA* which provides direction to *judges* on the imposition of "appropriate sanctions on individual young offenders"; this provision clearly has an accountability-based model for sentencing. While section 3(1)(c)(iii) recognizes that youth justice court sentences are to be "meaningful [for the] needs and level of development" of the youth and, "where appropriate [should] involve . . . community and social or other agencies in the young person's rehabilitation and reintegration," this is very much qualified by the opening words of section 3(1)(c) which provide that any sentence should be "within the limits of fair and proportionate accountability." Therefore, a youth justice court could, for example, invoke section 3(1)(c)(iii) to impose a community-based sentence to achieve rehabilitative objectives instead of the custodial sentence that might be required by the circumstances on the basis of accountability principles. However, section 3(1)(c)(iii) should not be invoked to justify a custodial sentence in order to meet the needs of a young person merely because this is considered necessary to meet the needs of a youth.

Section 38 of the *YCJA* also makes clear that the sentencing of young offenders is to be based on the principle of accountability. While section 38(1) also recognizes that sentences should promote rehabilitation of young offenders, this is qualified by section 38(2), which makes clear that the sentence imposed on a young offender should not be more severe than that imposed on other youths in similar circumstances. Further, section 39(5) makes clear that custody should not be used as a substitute for child protection, mental health, or other social measures.[82] Various substantive provisions of this Act give youth jus-

---

82   The similarly worded s. 24(1.1)(a) of the *Young Offenders Act*, was added in 1995, above note 5, s. 15, in apparent response to the 1993 Supreme of Canada decision in *R. v. M.(J.J.)*, above note 9. The Court partially justified the longer

tice court judges a broader range of sentencing options than were available under the *YOA*, in order to allow the courts to promote rehabilitation and reintegration of young offenders into society. Some of these are new community-based sentencing options, such as provisions allowing "intensive" community-based support and supervision, or use of attendance centres. The *YCJA* also has provision for residentially based "intensive rehabilitative custody."[83]

Perhaps the most significant and novel features of the *YCJA* for the promotion of rehabilitation and reintegration of young offenders into society are the provisions that govern custodial sentences and provide for a period of supervision in the community after the custodial portion of the sentence is served. Section 83 of the Act specifies that the "purpose of the youth custody and supervision system is to contribute to the protection of society by . . . assisting young persons to be rehabilitated and reintegrated into the community as law-abiding citizens." Section 90 requires that while a youth is in custody youth corrections staff will develop a "reintegration plan" that "sets out the most effective programs" to maximize the youth's "chances for reintegration into his community." Section 91 provides for short-term "reintegration leaves" from custody to prepare a youth for return to the community under supervision.

In most situations, the last third of a custodial sentence for a young offender is to be presumptively served in the community, under the supervision and with the support of youth workers. Section 97(2) allows for the provincial director to impose conditions on the youth being released into the community to facilitate reintegration and protect the public. These conditions might govern where the youth will reside, whether the youth must attend school or work, or undertake counselling. These provisions recognize that the period after release from custody is often critical to a youth's successful rehabilitation and reintegration into society. There may be situations in which a youth justice court judge may decide that the young person is "likely to commit a serious violent offence" as a result of the failure of the youth to

---

custodial sentence on the basis that it was in "open custody": "Yet those facilities are not simply to be jails for young people. Rather they are facilities dedicated to the long term welfare and reformation of the young offender." Significantly the *YCJA*, above note 3, s. 88, only gives youth justice court judges the power to make a sentence of custody, so that they will not view "open custody" as a "soft option" and make custody orders for rehabilitative purposes (though allowing provinces to choose to give youth justice court judges rather than correctional officials the authority to make decisions about open or secure custody.)

83   *YCJA*, above note 3, s. 42(2)(r).

successfully engage in rehabilitative efforts while in custody, so as to justify requiring the youth to serve the full sentence in custody.[84]

For many adolescents involved in the youth justice system, their criminal behaviour constitutes an isolated and often not very serious act. For these youth, the provisions in the *YCJA* that encourage use of extrajudicial measures may be most relevant. For some youth, however, criminal behaviour is part of a pattern of more serious difficulties. It is essential to try to understand the special needs of these youths if their interests and the long-term interests of society are to be met. In particular, for purposes of making a sentencing decision, a youth court judge may order a pre-sentence report or an assessment under section 34 for a medical or psychological report in order to learn more about the needs and circumstances of a youth before the court. Many troubled youths who offend have ongoing needs that cannot all be met by the criminal justice system. There are cases where the needs of a young person who has committed an offence can best be met in the child protection, education or mental health systems, either concurrently with a youth justice response or instead of it.

Making various decisions about young persons, especially concerning sentencing, requires a careful balancing of the principles of accountability, protection of society, and responding to their needs. In some cases decisions are relatively easy, and it is possible to impose a sentence which holds a youth accountable while addressing treatment needs. For example, for some offences related to drug use, the best response for the youth, family, and society may be to have a probation term imposed, including a condition that the youth attend substance-abuse counselling. In some situations, a residential or custodial sentence may be made which also involves the provision of rehabilitative or treatment services. Other decisions are more difficult. Some youth commit very serious or repeat offences, and a judge may decide that accountability concerns may require a sentence that does not meet the needs of the youth. Perhaps the clearest choice between accountability and meeting the needs of a youth is when a decision is being made about whether to impose an adult sentence.

While prevention of crime, rehabilitation, and reintegration are important guiding principles for the youth justice system, their application must necessarily be realistic. Beyond the issue of whether access to appropriate rehabilitative resources, programs, and facilities (more fully discussed below) is available, it is necessary to recognize that not

---

84   *YCJA*, above note 3, S. 98.

all young offenders can be rehabilitated. Some youths lack the motivation, at least at some points in their lives, to engage in rehabilitative efforts. Treatment professionals can try to engage a youth, but a resistant offender cannot be rehabilitated. Further, no program or facility can rehabilitate all young offenders. Some youths will reoffend despite their participation in any available rehabilitative regime.[85] Even after youths have completed their sentence — let alone at the time the court is deciding what sentence to impose — it may not be possible to identify which youths are not amenable to rehabilitation.

2) The Role of the Youth Court Judge in Restorative Justice

Those who work in the youth justice system in Canada are frequently faced with the stark reality that the appropriate rehabilitative resources are not available to help a young offender who has significant problems related to his or her offending behaviour. While there are some excellent programs and facilities with good records for rehabilitating young offenders, in many places justice system professionals are often confronted by cases where there is a lack of real options. There may be no appropriate treatment available in the youth's community, and the only available custody facilities may offer little more than security, accommodation, and access to educational programming, or may not have treatment resources that can help the youth deal with his or her specific problems.[86]

In a 1996 Alberta case a judge decided to invoke section 3(1)(c.1) of the *YOA* as the basis for an order requiring the provincial government to pay for treatment services that were not otherwise available and that she believed were needed to prevent reoffending by a young offender. The youth was convicted of property offences related to painting graffiti on buildings (called tagging). He spent two months in detention pending adjudication and then pleaded guilty. Given the offence, a custodial sentence was clearly not warranted, especially since the youth had already been in detention for a significant period

---

85   A.W. Leschied, P.G. Jaffe, D. Andrews, P. Gendreau, leading Canadian proponents of rehabilitation for young offenders, have noted that: "it is now clear that the average effect of 'treatment' is the reduction of recidivism, *to at least a mild degree* [emphasis added], "Treatment Issues and Young Offenders" in R.R. Corrado, *et al.*, eds., *Juvenile Justice in Canada: A Theoretical and Analytical Assessment* (Toronto: Butterworths, 1992) at 360.

86   See, for example, Ontario Social Development Council, "Myths, Facts, and the Potential of the Treatment Option," in *Youth Justice in Crisis* (Toronto: 1994).

of time, but defence counsel requested an order of probation with the requirement that the youth attend for treatment at a drug addiction program, with a court direction that the provincial Ministry of Justice should pay the costs not otherwise covered. The Crown prosecutor argued that there was no authority in the YOA for a judge to order a government to pay for services needed by a youth on probation. The Crown and judge accepted that drug addiction was the root cause of the youth's problems. While acknowledging that there was no specific statutory power to allow a youth court to direct that a government provide or pay for services, Judge Cook-Stanhope noted the 1995 additions to the Declaration of Principle in section 3 of the YOA, specifically referring to the importance of crime prevention and rehabilitation. She concluded that these amendments created:

> a positive duty on this youth court to assess and then to address, appropriately, the needs and circumstances of every individual young person . . . with a view to ameliorating those risks which are likely to cause the individual to continue to exhibit offending behaviours. . . . If the principles enunciated in s. 3 are to be more than just hollow-sounding rhetoric, youth courts must be equipped with the authority to ensure that their orders will take effect. Failing that, this statute will not operate effectively as a special code for young persons. . . . If the youth courts are not possessed of such powers to attend to the rehabilitative requirements of young persons, public clamour for more and harsher punitive measures instead of more effective rehabilitative ones will continue to build and eventually completely overtake other informed debate concerning appropriate . . . measures to deal with our young people who come into conflict with the law.[87]

One can appreciate the judge's frustration in the face of provincial unwillingness to provide appropriate rehabilitative services and can sympathize with her desire to ensure that the words of section 3 of the YOA did not have a hollow ring, especially in regard to the provision of preventive and rehabilitative services.

The Crown did not appeal Judge Cook-Stanhope's decision, but when another Alberta judge relied on her decision to make a similar order requiring the provincial government to pay for community-based drug treatment services for a young offender, the Crown did appeal. In 2000 the Alberta Court of Appeal ruled that very specific statutory language would be needed before legislation could be construed so as to give the judiciary the power to order governments to pay for specific

---

87   R. v. A.(L.), [1996] A.J. 957 (Alta. Prov. Ct.). The decision was not appealed.

programs. In the absence of a clear statutory power or a *Charter* violation, it is inconsistent with the generally accepted judicial role in
Canada for a judge to assume such authority.[88] The Appeal Court commented on the role of the sentencing judge in youth court:

> In order to arrive at an appropriate sentence judges consider only the
> facts of the case before them. Governments are not confined to evi-
> dence in individual cases, but may rely on information gathered from
> a variety of sources, including the courts, when making policy choic-
> es. For example, while a judge may weigh the objectives of rehabili-
> tation and protection of society in crafting an appropriate disposition
> for an offender, the government must weigh the costs and benefits of
> funding particular programs against comparable programs in light of
> available resources. A judge, within the confines of a particular case,
> is in no position to undertake the same evaluative process.
>
> Governments control public spending by allocating a finite num-
> ber of budgeted dollars among competing programs. If judges were
> empowered to order the government to make specific additional
> expenditures, they too would have their hand in taxpayers' pockets,
> for ultimately governments would have to raise taxes to pay the extra
> costs. The government has wide latitude in discharging its duties
> under the *YOA*. The judiciary "need not and should not tell the gov-
> ernment . . . what specific delivery systems should [be] employed."[89]

The Saskatchewan Court of Appeal dealt with the same issue in *R.
v. L.E.K.*, where the trial judge — Judge Turpel-Lafond, one of Canada's
few Aboriginal judges — had ordered that provincial officials develop
a treatment and education plan to meet the special needs of an
Aboriginal female offender suffering from fetal alcohol syndrome. The
Saskatchewan Court of Appeal held that the trial judge had exceeded
her authority under the *YOA*, ruling that

> the general principles of the Act in s. 3 do not create or confer juris-
> diction on the youth court that has not specifically been conferred
> elsewhere. The Act carefully defines the powers and duties of the
> youth court judge, the provincial director, the offender and the

---

88   See, for example, *Regional Municipality of Peel* v. *MacKenzie* (1982), 68 C.C.C.
     (3d) 289 (S.C.C.) (no jurisdiction under the *Juvenile Delinquents Act*, above note
     1, for court to order municipality to pay for services); *R.* v. *B.(K.)* (Alta. Q.B.,
     5 November 1992, per Deyell) (no jurisdiction to order government to pay for
     s. 22 *Young Offenders Act*, above note 2, treatment order: that provision has since
     been repealed.
89   *R.* v. *R.J.H.*, [2000] A.J. No. 396 (C.A.), at paras. 35–6.

Attorney General. It is the responsibility of the province to provide the programs and facilities necessary to enable the terms of the statute to be carried out but, s. 3(1) does not impose a mandatory duty on the director to create a specific kind of program. The youth court's jurisdiction is limited not only by the terms of the statute which created it but also by fundamental constitutional principles relating to the separation of powers between the judiciary, whose role it is to impose sanctions, and the executive, whose role it is to administer the sanctions. Moveover, while s. 3(2) of the Act requires a liberal interpretation be given to the legislation, it is subject to the overriding principle that the normal principles of statutory interpretation apply.[90]

Even if the *YOA* or the *YCJA* explicitly provided for youth court judges to order provincial governments to pay for specific programs — and they do not — such an exercise of statutory jurisdiction might be deemed unconstitutional. In *R.J.H.*, the Alberta Court of Appeal suggested that, even if the federal government were to enact legislation specifically granting youth court judges the power to order provincial governments to pay for treatment programs for young people, the legislation would infringe on the power of provincial governments under section 92(14) of the *Constitution Act, 1867*,[91] which grants the provinces exclusive jurisdiction over the administration of justice.

While section 3 and the Preamble of the *YCJA* recognize the value of a crime prevention strategy that addresses the underlying causes of youth crime, there is nothing in the principles or provisons of the Act to require spending on preventative, social, or educational programs that could actually prevent youth offending from occuring in the first place. Further there is nothing in the *YCJA* to allow a youth justice court to order any particular type of program or service to be provided to a young offender as part of a sentence imposed by the court. The judge can, within limits, impose a sentence that requires a youth to attend an available counselling or treatment program, or that requires the youth to be confined to a place of custody where it is expected that such services will be provided, but the judge cannot require that the government actually provide any services to the youth. Although the judge may recommend that particular rehabilitative services should be provided, it is the responsibility of provincial correctional authorities to decide what services should actually be provided to a youth under a sentence imposed by the court.

---

90   *R. v. L.E.K.*, [2000] S.J. No. 844 (Sask C.A.), para 20.
91   *R. v. R.J.H.*, above note 89. *Constitution Act, 1867* (U.K.), 30 & 31 Vict. c.3, s. 92(14).

It is understandable that youth court judges want to ensure that appropriate rehabilitative services are provided to the offenders with whom they deal. The appeal court decisions, however, make clear that the YOA did not allow for youth court judges to assume this role. Nor do principles and provisions of the YCJA contemplate a judicial role in deciding what services are to be provided to young offenders. However, as is more fully discussed in Chapter 8, a youth court judge may make recommendations for the provision of specific services, and frequently these recommendations will be followed. Further, a sentence may be imposed in the expectation that particular services will be provided, and if they are not provided, this may be the ground for the review of the original sentence and early release, but this will not result in the provision of services needed by the youth.

The statements in the Declaration of Principle of the YCJA about the importance of crime prevention and rehabilitation require a youth justice court judge to consider the rehabilitative value of different sentences that might be imposed in accordance with principles of "fair and proportionate accountability." Rehabilitative concerns might, for example, result in a youth court judge deciding that a term of probation should be imposed rather than a custodial sentence that would be warranted on purely accountability-based principles in light of the rehabilitative potential of an *available* community-based treatment program that could help reduce the likelihood of a young offender committing further offences. However, the proportionality principle of sentencing and provisions like section 39(5) of the YCJA make clear that a youth justice court cannot impose a longer custody sentence than would be justified by the nature and circumstances of the offence if the objective is to provide rehabilitative or social services to the youth.

Judges are critical decision makers in the youth criminal justice system. Their attitudes, demeanour, and decisions profoundly affect the treatment of individual youth. However, judges cannot effect rehabilitation or prevent crime. Rehabilitation and crime prevention are missions of the entire youth justice and corrections systems. Judges can make orders that may allow various professionals and agencies to work toward the objectives of rehabilitation and reintegration, but judges must also appreciate that their role is limited.

3) Timely Intervention

The youth justice system is often fraught with delay and it is not uncommon for cases involving adolescents to be adjourned many times before resolution. In 2000–2001, under the YOA, some 17 percent of youth court cases were completed on a first court appearance, and a total of 50 percent were resolved within two months or less of a youth's first appearance; 17 percent of youth court cases took six months or longer to complete.[92] Delay is a problem throughout the justice system, but it is a special concern in cases involving children and adolescents. Adolescents have a different perception of time and less well-developed memories than adults. As a result, the response to offending behaviour will have a greater impact on a young person if it occurs within a relatively short time of the offence. Further, if a youth has serious problems, it is better that they are addressed as quickly as possible. There were no provisions in the YOA that addressed these concerns, although most judges and professionals who work with adolescents are aware of them.

The Declaration of Principle of the YCJA has statements that explicitly acknowledge the importance of resolving cases in the youth justice system as expeditiously as possible. Section 3(1)(b)(iv) of the YCJA states that " timely intervention . . . reinforces the link between the offending behaviour and its consequences," while section 3(1)(b)(v) emphasizes that "persons responsible for enforcing" the Act should respond with "promptness and speed . . . given young persons' perception of time." Some youth justice court cases are complex and take time to resolve. The most serious cases are often the most time consuming. Under the YOA for the most serious cases there was the possibility of a pre-adjudication transfer to adult court. This could be a very time-consuming pre-trial procedure. One of the reasons that YCJA deals with the issue of the possibility of the imposition of an adult sentence on a post-adjudication basis is that this should allow for a more expeditious resolution of these cases. Nevertheless, in those very serious cases, where there is the possibility of an adult sentence (and in any case with a murder charge), the YCJA allows for a preliminary inquiry, a jury trial, and a more complex sentencing process, all procedural steps that will lengthen the time taken to complete proceedings.

Many youth justice court cases, however, are not inherently complex and the delays that occur are often a result of institutional constraints rather than being necessary to resolve the case. There can be adjournments to allow a youth to apply for legal aid, to permit the Crown to disclose its evidence and to allow for the preparation of reports. Court dates are set to meet institutional pressures and the busy schedules of the professionals involved in the justice system, whether they are Crown or defence lawyers, police, judges, or probation officers, rather than to meet the needs of youth. While it is beneficial for

---

92   Statistics Canada, *Youth Court Statistics 2000–2001* (2002), Juristat 22:3.

youth to have an expeditious resolution of their cases, many of them do not seek this and may actually prefer to have the proceedings delayed. In some cases the youth may hope that the prosecution's case will weaken over time, as memories fade or witnesses become unavailable. In some cases a youth may want to postpone the prospect of punishment or irrationally hope that, if proceedings are delayed, "the whole thing may disappear."

The desire of a youth to seek delay, or at least not to seek an expeditious resolution, is not a reason for the prosecution or court to permit the proceedings to be unnecessarily delayed. Sections 3(1)(b)(iv) and (v) are intended to remind court administrators, judges, lawyers, and others of the need to give priority to the expeditious resolution of youth justice court cases. These provisions might, for example, be cited by counsel or a judge if there is a disagreement about scheduling. They might also be relevant if a youth is arguing that the case should be stayed because there has been a violation of the guarantee in section 11(b) of the *Charter* of the right to be tried within a reasonable time; what may be a "reasonable period" for an adult may not be reasonable for a twelve-year-old youth. One of the reasons for making use of extrajudicial measures is that these relatively informal methods of dealing with adolescent offenders are typically more expeditious than the formal youth justice court process.

4) Extrajudicial Measures

Section 3(1)(d) of the Declaration of Principle in the *YOA* made explicit reference to "taking no measures or taking measures other than judicial proceedings." There is no direct equivalent of this statement of principle in section 3 of the *YCJA*. It is, however, clear that in enacting the *YCJA*, Parliament intended to increase the use of non-judicial methods of dealing with young persons who violate the criminal law. The use of what are referred to in the *YCJA* as "extrajudicial measures" can help achieve a number of the objectives of section 3 of the *YCJA*, ensuring that a young person who has violated the criminal law experiences "meaningful consequences" (s. 3(1)(a)(iii)) in a more "timely" way than is typically possible in the court system (ss. 3(1)(b)(iv) and (v)). Extrajudicial measures typically allow for the engagement of victims and for apologies or restitution to them (ss. 3(1)(c)(i) and 3(1)(d)(iii)), and may engage parents and community agencies (s. 3(1)(c)(iii)). Section 3(1)(c) requires that the response to youth offending is to be based on "fair and proportionate accountability" for determining the "measures." The use of the more inclusive term "measures" indicates that, in some cases, extrajudicial measures will be appropriate, while in others a youth justice court sentence may be the appropriate method of imposing accountability.

Further, section 4 of the *YCJA* is a Declaration of Principles that deal explicitly with what the Act refers to as "extrajudicial measures," encouraging the diversion of less serious adolescent offenders from the formal youth court system. These measures range from the decision of a police officer to informally warn a young person who is believed to have to committed a minor offence not to reoffend, through more formal programs of police and prosecutorial cautioning of youth and screening of charges, to community-based programs of extrajudicial sanctions that might involve an apology or restitution to a victim. A response based on some form of extrajudicial measures is often the most appropriate method of dealing with less serious offences. Section 4 creates a presumption that non-violent first offenders should be dealt with by means of extrajudicial measures, while making clear that they can be used in other cases as well.

Although the *YCJA* is clearly intended to increase the use of a range of extrajudicial measures, section 3(1)(d)(i) also makes clear that a youth has no right to any sort of a hearing before a decision is made about whether his or her case is dealt with in the courts or diverted to some form of extrajudicial measures. Section 3(1)(d)(i) reaffirms the judgment of the Supreme Court of Canada in R. v. T.(V.),[93] a case decided under the *YOA*, which held that the decision about whether to divert a youth from the formal youth court system is to be made by the police officer, prosecutor, or community agency dealing with the youth and is not subject to review or appeal to the courts.

If a judge believes that a youth should have been dealt with by means of extrajudicial sanction rather than in court, the judge has no legal authority to divert the case from the court system. Some youth justice court judges may be inclined to suggest to a prosecutor that it would appear that a case might be better dealt with by means of extrajudicial measures; while some prosecutors may accept this suggestion, there is no judicial power to require this to be done. If a judge feels that a case should have been dealt with by means of extrajudicial measures, however, this may affect the sentence that the court imposes, and may for example result in the court imposing a mere reprimand or absolute discharge. In appropriate cases a judge can also make a referral under section 35 of the *YCJA* to a child protection agency to require the agency to

---

93   R. v. T.(V.) (1992), 71 C.C.C. (3d) 32 (S.C.C.).

assess whether the youth requires the agency's services, but that agency and not the court will determine whether the services are required.

The *YCJA* encourages provincial governments, police, prosecutors, and community groups to consider a range of extrajudicial measures to divert youths from the justice system, and various federal funding initiatives are supporting these efforts. However, the Act also makes clear that young persons do not have a legally enforceable right to be dealt with in this way.

5) Rights of Young Persons

One of the central themes of both the *YOA* and the *YCJA* is that young persons are entitled to all of the due-process rights afforded to adults. Further, because of their vulnerability and immaturity, they are to have special legal protections not afforded to adults. The Preamble of the *YCJA* declares that "Canada . . . recognizes that young persons have rights and freedoms" under Canada's *Charter of Rights* and *Bill of Rights*, as well as acknowledging that Canada is a party to the *United Nations Convention on the Rights of the Child.* Section 3(1)(b)(iii) makes clear that young persons are entitled to "enhanced procedural protection" in light of their immaturity and of the difficulties which they experience in enforcing their rights. Section 3(1)(d)(i) emphasizes that young persons can exercise their "own rights" and reiterates that young persons should have "special guarantees of their rights and freedoms."

Youths have all of the protections afforded adults under the *Canadian Charter of Rights and Freedoms* at the time of arrest and in the criminal process. Further, the *YCJA* affords youths greater rights than are provided to adults. In particular, young persons are entitled to have access to legal representation paid by the state if they are unable to obtain counsel. The *YCJA* also retains a number of provisions that are intended to protect the privacy of young persons and limit use of their records. There are special obligations on the police when questioning a young person,[94] and youth justice court judges have special duties, when a young person who is not represented by counsel wishes to plead guilty, to ensure that the youth appreciates the significance of this step.[95]

The underlying rationale for giving greater legal protections to young persons than to adults — like the rationale for the limited accountability of adolescents — is their intellectual, social, and psychological immaturity. Adolescents are less likely to appreciate the sig-

---

94   *YCJA*, above note 3, s. 146.
95   *YCJA*, above note 3, s. 32(3).

nificance of the legal process and the legal consequences of the decisions that they are expected to make. They generally do not fully
understand and appreciate their rights and are likely to be unable to
exercise them fully without assistance. Adolescents are also likely to
have greater difficulty in formulating realistic plans and advocating for
their views in the youth justice system. Adolescents may also be more
vulnerable to pressure from the police and other agents of the state. As
Carol Letman, co-chair of the Criminal Lawyer's Association's Youth
Justice Committee has pointed out, young people's comprehension of
their rights is often limited: "most don't understand them even after
they are explained by the police."[96]

The granting of special rights to young persons has been questioned by those who believe that allowing youths to be acquitted on
"technicalities" is inconsistent with the principles of protection of society and accountability for criminal behaviour. This is a familiar debate
in the criminal justice field, one certainly not restricted to juvenile justice. However, in the context of youth justice court proceedings, the
debate may have an added poignancy as it can be argued that the exercise of legal rights may serve to defeat the needs of a young person.[97]

This type of concern is expressed by victims, police, and Crown
prosecutors, and sometimes also by parents, who expect their children
to be held accountable for their wrongs and hope that they may receive
needed help from the youth justice system. Parents may feel under-
mined in their efforts to raise their children to be honest and law-abiding, if there are acquittals on such bases as the failure of the police to
caution a youth adequately before a statement is made. Prominent
defence lawyer Edward Greenspan acknowledged this "dilemma of due
process":

> Due process is a costly, time consuming process and the procedural
> safeguards which make up "due process" are not always self-evident.
> . . . In ordinary circumstances, the child is urged to tell the truth and
> confess; under due process, the young person may be acquitted even
> though he has acknowledged responsibility to his lawyer. The dilem-
> ma of due process results in "some young people receiving the wrong

---

96   "The Youth Criminal Justice Act," *Law Times*, March 28, 1999.

97   See, for example, A.W. Lescheid, *et al.*, "Treatment Issues and Young Offenders"
in Corrado *et al.*, eds., *Juvenile Justice in Canada* (Toronto: Butterworths, 1992):
"rhetoric that has minimized the contribution of rehabilitation to lowered recidivism [has] established a system in which young people in conflict with the law
are represented by lawyers who 'protect' kids from rehabilitation while ensuring
their clients receive just punishment" (at 359).

message as to the appropriateness of their behaviour and the values underlying our system of justice."

Due process has undoubted benefits for the child, who is now "entitled to protection from arbitrary or well meaning but mistaken government." The young person can no longer be removed from his/her home unless there has been "a scrupulous determination of the facts."[98]

Different defence lawyers have varying views about how aggressively to defend the strict legal rights of adolescents, and different judges also have differing views about how to respect those rights strictly.[99] Further, despite that fact, in principle, Canada's youth justice system is premised on respect for the legal rights of young persons (more fully discussed in Chapters 4 and 6), many young persons who are involved in the youth justice system do not appreciate the significance of their rights and waive them.

Despite the strong rights rhetoric in the *YCJA* and the fact that the Act affords greater protections to young persons than to adults, there are some important respects in which the *YCJA* provides less protection for legal rights than had the *YOA*. A very significant procedural entitlement that has been weakened under the *YCJA* is the right to have an order for counsel paid by the government if the youth is "unable" to retain counsel. This statutory right for young persons is substantially broader than the constitutional "right to retain counsel." Adults who are unable to afford counsel must typically rely on legal aid, which has increasingly strict criteria for granting access to legal services. While indigent adults charged with more serious offences are eligible for legal aid, many adults of limited means are charged with less serious offences and may be forced to go through the criminal justice system without legal representation.[100]

---

98 Quoted in Ontario Social Development Council, *Y.O.A. Dispositions: Challenges and Choices* (Toronto: 1988) at 14.

99 Contrast the views of Cory J. and L'Heureux-Dubé J. in R. v. J.(J.T.), [1990] 2 S.C.R. 755. See Chapter 6.

100 See R. v. *Prospero* (1994), 92 C.C.C.(3d) 352, 33 C.R. (4th) 85 (S.C.C.), ruling that there is generally no obligation on the state to provide counsel for adult accused persons. In some very serious cases involving adult accused persons, the trial judge may invoke s. 7 of the *Charter*, above note 4, to order that proceedings are to be stayed (suspended) unless the state ensures that counsel is provided for an adult accused without the resources to privately retain counsel. This discretionary authority is only exercised in complex, serious cases and is clearly narrower than the statutory authority under *YCJA*, above note 3, s. 25, to order that counsel is to be appointed for any young person who is unable to obtain a lawyer and wants one, no matter how minor the charge.

As under the *YOA*, young persons who are unable to obtain counsel are entitled to have an order made under the *YCJA* that counsel be provided and paid by the government. The assessment of the ability to afford to pay a lawyer continues to be based primarily on the youth's means. It is recognized that parents with resources may decide not to retain a lawyer for their child and, further, if the parents are paying for a lawyer that may have an influence on how the case is handled. However, under section 25(10) of the *YCJA* (which had no equivalent in the *YOA*), provincial governments are authorized to establish programs that will allow the government, after the completion of youth justice court proceedings, to recover from the young person's parents the costs of providing legal services. This change may result in parents, knowing that they will ultimately have to pay for any lawyer provided, pressuring their children to waive the right to counsel, or to plead guilty and avoid the expense of a trial.

While the *YCJA* continues many of the protections of privacy that were in the *YOA*, under the new Act, publication of identifying information about a young offender is permitted if the youth has committed a very serious offence, even if the court does not impose an adult sentence.[101]

Another important special protection for youths was found in section 56 of the *YOA*, which required a judge to exclude from a trial any statement made by a young person to the police if the police failed to provide the youth with a special caution before the statement was made. Most notably, the police were obliged to advise the youth of the right to remain silent and of the right to consult with a parent or lawyer, and to have them present when a statement is made to the police. Section 146 of the *YCJA* retains the requirements of the *YOA* for a special police caution for young persons who are being questioned, but under section 146(6) the youth justice court may admit a statement if there has been a "technical irregularity" in complying with the caution requirements. Although giving the court some discretion to admit a statement despite a "technical irregularity" in the police caution, it is significant that in exercising its discretion under section 146(6), the youth justice court should only admit the statement if "satisfied that its admission would not bring into disrepute the principle that young per-

---

101 See *YCJA*, above note 3, ss. 110 and 75(3), which allow a youth justice court to prohibit the publication of identifying information about a youth who has committed a very serious offence if the "court considers it appropriate in the circumstances, taking into account the importance of rehabilitating the young person and the public interest."

sons are entitled to enhanced procedural protections to ensure that they are treated fairly and their rights are protected." While the *YCJA* may weaken some of the special procedural protections afforded to youths under *YOA*, Parliament continues to provide significant legal protections to young persons that are not afforded to adults. The new Act has attempted to balance the costs of diminution of rights against resource issues and concerns with the administration of justice.

6) Respect for Diversity and Special Needs

Section 3(1)(c)(iv) of the Declaration of Principle of the *YCJA* provides that "within the limits of fair and proportionate accountability, the measures taken against young persons who commit offences should . . . respect gender, ethnic, cultural, and linguistic differences and respond to the needs of aboriginal young persons and of young persons with special requirements." (Chapter 1 provides a more detailed discussion of some of issues pertaining to young offenders who are female or of Aboriginal or other ethnicity that constitutes a social minority.) This provision is addressed both to those responsible for the establishment and administration of programs and facilities for young offenders, and to those making decisions about individual young offenders.

Decisions about the youth justice system in general as well as about individual young offenders should be made in a way that recognizes that the needs of a young person are affected by the youth's gender, ethnicity, cultural heritage, and Aboriginal status. Further, many young offenders have special requirements that might, for example, reflect learning disabilities, a history of having been abused, or drug addiction. Those making decisions about the sanctioning of individual young offenders, whether in regard to a referral to a program of extra-judicial sanctions or imposing a sentence, should know about the background of the individual youth and available resources. If, for example, the program that best meets the rehabilitative needs of a particular young offender is only available in the community and not in custody, this might affect the sentence which a court imposes.

As much as possible, young persons should receive services from those who are familiar with and sensitive to their linguistic and cultural background. In Canada this conventionally meant providing services in English or French, as appropriate, but Canada has become an increasingly diverse society. There are now a number of programs for young offenders, especially ones that are community based, that are directed toward youths from particular cultural or ethnic backgrounds. If a young person is placed in a custodial facility that does not meet his or her needs, this might be a ground for seeking a sentence review under section 94 of the *YCJA*, especially if there was an expectation from the court when the youth was sentenced that the youth would be placed in a facility that would meet cultural or special needs.

Issues of sensitivity to cultural differences and needs are perhaps most significant for Aboriginal young offenders. Many Aboriginal young offenders come from socially and economically deprived backgrounds, or may have experienced abuse or neglect in their homes. In addition to being a marginalized minority, subjected to systemic discrimination, and the "poorest of the poor,"[102] Canada's Aboriginal peoples have a unique constitutional status. Section 718.2(e) of the *Criminal Code*, which is incorporated into the *YCJA*,[103] requires that courts sentencing aboriginal offenders are to give "particular attention to the circumstances of aboriginal offenders" in considering alternatives to imprisonment. While the Supreme Court of Canada made clear in *R. v. Gladue* that this does not necessarily mean that the sentence imposed on an Aboriginal offender should automatically be reduced, this provision does require a sentencing judge to pay especially close attention to the circumstances of the offender and to consider culturally sensitive community-based sentencing options.[104]

Female young offenders also face special challenges in receiving access to programming and services that meets their special needs. In comparison to male young offenders, female adolescent offenders are more likely to have suffered from sexual abuse and are more likely to experience depression or engage in self-destructive behaviour. Because there are relatively few female young offenders in custody, programming tends to be geared to meeting the needs of boys. A case decided under the *YOA*, *R. v. C.(J.A.)*,[105] illustrates some of the difficulties in providing custodial facilities which respond appropriately to female young offenders. A female young offender in Manitoba received a disposition of six months' open custody, but because no adequate open custody facilities were available for girls, she was placed in a secure custody facility for

102 National Council of Welfare, *Justice and the Poor* (Ottawa: 2000).

103 *YCJA*, above note 3, ss. 38(2)(d) and 50.

104 *R. v. Gladue*, [1999] 1 S.C.R. 688. The issue of whether to give special sentencing treatment to aboriginal offenders remains controversial. See s. S. Anand, "The Sentencing of Aboriginal Offenders, Continued Confusion and Persisting Problems: A Comment on the Decision in *R. v. Gladue*" (2000) 42 Can. J. Crim. 412; P. Stenning and J. Roberts, "Empty Promises, Parliament, The Supreme Court, and the Sentencing of Aboriginal Offenders" (2001) 64 Sask. L.Rev. 137, and generally "Colloquy on Empty Promises," (2002) 65:1 Sask. L.Rev.

105 *R. v. C.(J.A.)*, [1999] M.J. No. 400 (Man. C.A.).

female young offenders. Justice Twaddle, writing for the Manitoba Court of Appeal, issued a declaration that her detention in the secure custody facility was unlawful, and that she was to be released unless she was immediately transferred to an appropriate open custody facility.

The *YCJA* requires that decisions about the level of custody are to "allow for the best possible match of programs to the young person's needs and behaviour." The *YCJA* gives a province the option of having decisions about the level of placement initially made by a youth justice court as part of the sentencing process, or having the initial decision about the level of custody made by a provincial director with a process of review board hearings for placement decisions made by a provincial director. In provinces where the initial decisions about the level of placement are to be made by provincial directors, there will be less scrutiny and control under the *YCJA* than was available to protect the interests of the girl in *C.(J.A.)*. Provincial directors and review boards may feel more pressure than youth justice court judges to make decisions based on resource and administrative concerns rather than based on the needs of individual young offenders.

7) Victims' Involvement and Rights

Historically victims did not play a significant role in Canada's criminal justice system, except as witnesses. By the 1990s there was a growing recognition that the justice system often failed to give sufficient respect to the concerns of victims. A central feature of the public discourse in Canada about crime in the 1990s was the rise of those advocating victims' rights.[106] Some aspects of this movement grew out of the concerns of feminists about the inadequacies of the justice system in responding to sexual assault and spousal abuse, but there were broader concerns about the treatment of victims by the justice system. In many localities programs were established to provide support to victims and witnesses involved in the justice system, while prosecutors and police began to communicate more effectively with victims and to provide them with more support. One of the 1995 amendments to the *YOA* was to make clear that victim impact statements are admissible at the time of sentencing of a young offender, and in the late 1990s some provinces enacted legislation that purported to give greater rights to victims in the criminal justice system.[107]

---

106 See, for example, Kent Roach, *Due Process and Victims' Rights: The New Law and Politics of Criminal Justice* (Toronto: University of Toronto Press, 1999).

107 *Victims' Bill of Rights*, S.O. 1995, c. 6.

While the Declaration of Principle of the *YOA* made no explicit mention of victims, the Declaration of Principle in the *YCJA* contains explicit statements about the important role of victims in the youth justice system, and there are other specific provisions that offer victims some limited new legal rights. Section 3(1)(c)(ii), for instance, states that the sanctions imposed on young persons who commit offences, whether in a program of extrajudicial sanctions or as a sentence in youth justice court, should "encourage the repair of harm done to the victims and the community." Section 3(1)(d) provides that those responsible for the administration of the youth justice system should give "special consideration" to the needs of victims in the youth justice process, declaring that:

> (ii) victims should be treated with courtesy, compassion and respect for their dignity and privacy and should suffer the minimum degree of inconvenience as a result of their involvement with the youth criminal justice system; [and]
>
> (iii) victims should be provided with information about the proceedings and given an opportunity to participate and be heard.

Many prosecutors and police acting under the *YOA* treated victims with "courtesy, compassion and respect," although there was no explicit statutory statement that this was expected. The *YCJA* reinforces the desirability of this type of professional demeanour. It is, however, practically impossible to legally enforce expectations that victims will be treated with courtesy, compassion, and respect. Litigation concerning provincial legislation containing vague statements similar to sections 3(d)(ii) and (iii), about victims' rights, such as Ontario's *Victims' Bill of Rights*, indicates that these types of general statements in the *YCJA* do not have strictly legal significance.[108] These statements do not, for example, place a legal obligation on a prosecutor to discuss a case with a victim. Although as a matter of good practice a prosecutor should usually discuss a possible plea bargain with a complainant, especially if the case involves violence, there is no legal obligation to do so. However, victims who are not treated with courtesy, compassion, and respect, or who are not provided with adequate information about proceedings, may well have legitimate ground for complaint through various administrative or political channels.

---

108 Examples of cases where plaintiffs encountered difficulties in asserting claims under the Ontario *Victims' Bill of Rights* include *Crawford v. Edwards*, [2001] O.J. No. 2750 (Ont. Sup. Ct.) and *Belesky v. Rose*, [1998] O.J. No. 597 (Ont. Ct. of Justice).

The *YCJA* does have a few substantive features that give victims some clearer rights in the youth justice process than were recognized under the *YOA*. For example, the *YCJA* makes clear that victims are entitled to information about cases involving young persons that are resolved by extrajudicial sanctions,[109] as well as information concerning youths dealt with in court. As under the *YOA*, there are provisions in the *YCJA* enabling a youth justice court judge who is sentencing a young offender to have information about the impact of a crime on the victim.[110]

In some cases, a desire to have the offender "repair the harm" done to the victim may result in adopting a restorative justice approach to the case. Restorative justice is an approach to dealing with offending that differs from the conventional punitive and adversarial models of the criminal justice system."[111] While the concept of "restorative justice" has a range of related meanings, the focus is on restoring the relationship between the offender and the victim, as well as restoring the relationships of the offender with his or her family and the broader community. Often a restorative justice approach focuses on repairing harm done to a victim or community by providing some form of compensation to the victim or community. Aboriginal communities in particular are making considerable use of a range of community-based restorative justice approaches. While they are modelled to some extent on Aboriginal customs, the utility of such panels is not limited to cases involving Aboriginal offenders.[112] As Baron and Kennedy note,[113] a sense of belonging to and being sanctioned by a particular community can have powerful deterrent effects, detracting from the peer influence which often makes adolescents susceptible to offending behaviour.

Often, some form of conference (or meeting) involving the victim, the offender and family members of the offender, and others in the community may be the most effective way to allow a discussion of the offence, and the needs of both the offender and the victim. The conference may result in the offender apologizing to a victim and providing some form of compensation. The conference may be an aspect of extra-judicial measures, or may result from a referral from a youth justice court judge in order to have a sentencing recommendation made to the

---

109 *YCJA*, above note 3, s. 12.
110 *YCJA*, above note 3, s. 40(2)(b); s. 50 of the *YCJA* provides that s. 722 of the *Criminal Code*, above note 45, governing victim impact statements applies to youth court sentencing.
111 J. Braithwaite, "Restorative Justice and Social Justice" (2000) 63 Sask L.Rev. 185.
112 S. Nolen, "Where Jail is Sometimes the Only Way out of Town," *Globe and Mail*, March 21, 2000.
113 S. Baron, and L. Kennedy, above note 47.

court or may even be supervised by the judge. An integral element of restorative justice approaches is the involvement of the victim. Victims must voluntarily agree to be involved in any conferencing or restorative justice efforts and must be supported through the process. Core elements of restorative justice are healing relationships, community deliberation, victim involvement, and in the case of youths, parental involvement.

The restorative justice movement seeks to address criminality in a manner that focuses on crime as a "problem," rather than on the individual offender. According to proponents of restorative justice, the right punishment for the criminal offence may not be the entire solution to the problems created by or reflected in the criminal offence. The YCJA clearly encourages greater use of restorative justice approaches, although they will not be appropriate for all cases. The statements in sections 3(1)(c)(ii) and (d)(ii) and (iii) focus on the treatment of victims in the youth justice process, including an encouragement for the adoption of restorative justice approaches. These statements do not, however, deal explicitly with the psychological trauma and fears of victims, especially victims of violent crime. It is important to appreciate that adolescents and children are more likely to be victimized by youth crime than are adults.[114] In particular, adolescents who are victims of violence or intimidation in their schools or communities may fear continued exploitation and may be concerned that the youth justice system will not protect them. At least in some measure, the sentencing provisions of the YCJA — which provide for custodial sentences for violent offenders and that require the youth justice courts to consider the "harm done to victims" in imposing a sentence — address some of these concerns of victims.[115]

Beyond issues related to conferences, compensation, and sentencing, victims may have special concerns in regard to the apprehension and detention of alleged offenders, especially in situations that arise in schools where the alleged victims and offender might be forced to remain in contact pending any resolution of the case. As discussed more fully in Chapter 4, victim concerns should be communicated with the court through the prosecutor or police so that the judge can decide whether it is appropriate for these concerns to be reflected in conditions placed on the release of an alleged offender pending resolution of a case. However, at the pre-adjudication stage, the justice system faces a difficult challenge in balancing the need to protect victims

---

114 National Council of Welfare, above note 103.
115 YCJA, above note 3, s. 38(3).

and communities with the rights of an accused person who is presumed innocent. It is also important to appreciate that, until the accused is convicted, as a matter of law, there is only an "alleged victim" — or a "complainant," to use the term in the *Criminal Code*. Judges in particular need to maintain an impartial attitude to all witnesses, and have a duty not to presume that there is a victim until there has been a finding of guilt. Conversely, there will be cases in which an accused young person will be acquitted because of the difficulty of the Crown in satisfying the criminal burden of proof, even though the accused was in fact guilty. In these cases the victim may be entitled to compassion, respect, and support, despite the acquittal.

8) Parents' Involvement

One effect of an adolescent's contact with the youth justice system can be the undermining of the relationship between the parents and their child. Often considerable tension arises as a result of the involvement of the police and courts in the family. It can be very disruptive to a family to have state agencies assuming the role of disciplinarian. Despite such familial tension, for many young offenders the most effective way to prevent future offending is to engage their parents in the youth justice process and to seek their support for any rehabilitative efforts. The *YCJA* recognizes that parents have an important responsibility for their children and that adolescents can often be best helped in a familial context. Section 3(1)(c)(iii) recognizes that measures taken against young persons who commit offences should be "meaningful" for the youth and should "*where appropriate*, involve parents, [and] the extended family" [emphasis added]. Section 3(1)(d)(iv) declares that "parents should be informed of measures or proceedings involving their children and encouraged to support them in addressing their offending behaviour." These statements of principle recognize that the problems of young persons which underlie their criminal behaviour are often most likely to be effectively resolved if parents are involved in any treatment or dispositional plan. Most young offenders will remain with or return to their families after their involvement with the justice system is completed.

It is, however, important not to romanticize the role of parents and families in the lives of their children, especially for those youths who are serious or repeat offenders. Often involvement in the youth justice system reflects problems with the parent-child relationship or a lack of appropriate parenting. Some young offenders have been victims of physical, emotional, or sexual abuse at the hands of their parents or other relatives. Some adolescents have ceased to have meaningful relationships with their parents before they are involved in the youth justice system. Further, the fact that a youth is charged with a criminal offence frequently strains the relationship with parents, and those dealing with young offenders should be realistic about the role that parents are likely to play in their children's lives.

In some cases the parents are the victims of a young person's offence, for example, a theft or an assault; indeed a significant portion of youth homicides involve cases in which adolescents have killed their parents.[116] Sometimes the police are called by parents who feel that they cannot "control" their child and who are looking to the youth justice system to "help" their child; the parents may even want a custodial sentence, feeling that they can no longer have their child live at home.

Like the *YOA*, the *YCJA* has a number of provisions that require the involvement of parents in the youth justice process. The new Act provides that parents are to be notified of the arrest of their child and of youth justice court proceedings,[117] as well as of extrajudicial sanctions.[118] If the presence of parents in youth justice court is considered "necessary or in the best interests of a youth," the parents may be ordered to attend court.[119] Youth justice court decisions about such issues as pre-trial detention and sentencing are to be made taking into consideration the desirability of parental supervision. Further, parents are normally interviewed in the course of the preparation of a pre-sentence report. Parents also have the right to make submissions to the court prior to a decision being made about a sentence, although often they feel intimidated and reluctant to speak in a relatively formal setting like a youth justice court hearing.

It is important to appreciate that, while parents are encouraged to be involved, they are not parties to a youth justice court proceeding. It is only the youth who can retain and instruct counsel; parents are sometimes confused about this issue and want to be involved in directing a case. Indeed, some defence lawyers may be influenced by parental views about their child's "best interests" rather than taking directions from their young clients, although this is contrary to the ordinary professional conduct rules about following a client's instructions. There is a particular concern about parental influences on counsel if parents are paying the legal bills.

---

116 W. Meloff and R.A. Silverman, "Canadian Kids Who Kill" (1992) 43 Can. J. Crim. 15.
117 *YCJA*, above note 3, s. 26.
118 *YCJA*, above note 3, s. 1; there was no equivalent provision in the *Young Offenders Act*, above note 2.
119 *YCJA*, above note 3, s. 27.

The *YCJA* requires police to advise young persons who are being questioned in connection with a suspected offence of the right to see their parents before making a statement, as well as the right to consult a lawyer.[120] Justice Kearns of the Alberta Court of Appeal recognized that: "Sometimes at least, the young person needs to speak to someone other than a lawyer. Affection, empathy, love and comfort do not fall within the scope of traditional legal services."[121] There is, however, real ambiguity about the role that parents should play when meeting with a child who has been arrested by police and faces questioning. While a lawyer is clearly going to focus on the youth's legal rights, and is very likely to advise the youth to remain silent at the investigative stage, parents may encourage their children to do the "right thing" and make a confession, which may entail very serious consequences for a youth. For example, an Ontario mother who met with her son before police questioning in connection with a sexual assault charge advised him to tell the police everything he knew, believing that he had done nothing wrong and that the police would release her son as soon as a statement was made. The youth gave a statement but was not released; the statement was later used to help secure a conviction against him in court.[122] In hindsight, the mother's advice may have contributed to her son's serious legal difficulties.

Like the *YOA*, the *YCJA* recognizes that Canada has diverse family forms and that, for many young offenders, the adults carrying out a parenting role are not their biological or adoptive parents. The term "parent" is broadly defined in section 2 of the Act to include "any person under a legal duty to provide for the young person, or who has, in law or in fact, the custody or control" of the youth. Section 3(1)(c)(iii) recognizes the important role of the "extended family" in the lives of many adolescents, which may include grandparents, or aunts and uncles, or older siblings. The care and guidance provided by extended family members may be especially important for Aboriginal children. Most of the provisions of the Act that require notification or involvement of a parent provide for some other adult whom the youth knows to be involved if the parent is unavailable.

The old *Juvenile Delinquents Act* provided that parents could be fined if they did any act "contributing" to their children becoming delinquent, or "knowingly . . . neglect[ed]" to do something that would

---

120 *YCJA*, above note 3, s. 146 (2)(c).
121 *R. v. S.(J.L.)* , [1995] A.J. No. 213 (Alta. C.A.).
122 *R. v. M.(Steven)* (1996), 28 O.R. (3d) 776 (Ont. C.A.).

have tended to prevent their child from committing a delinquent act.[123] The *YOA* eliminated parental liability, requiring that young persons alone should be responsible for their illegal acts, while recognizing that parents may have an important role in their children's rehabilitation.[124] The rationale for eliminating parental liability in the *YOA* was that efforts to "punish the parent" can heighten family tensions and thereby have negative effects on rehabilitation. Further, holding parents liable may produce manipulative behaviour by some adolescents.

The inappropriateness of imposing liability on parents for crimes committed by their children was recognized by the 1965 federal government report on the *Juvenile Delinquents Act*, commenting on the provision of that Act which allowed the juvenile court to fine parents of delinquents: "the effect is to aggravate still further an already disturbed family relationship. The parent tends to respond to punishment by increasing . . . hostility to, and rejection of, the child. The child in turn reacts to the parent's anger by getting into further trouble. Moreover, such a law places a tremendous weapon in the hands of an angry child."[125] While youthful offending can often be related to some form of parental abuse, neglect, or inadequacy, this is clearly not always the case. Some parents try very hard to prevent their children from offending, but biological or genetic factors, learning disabilities or the influence of peers or the community may overwhelm parental efforts.

Often, parents of offenders are not deliberately neglectful but rather lack parenting skills; parents may themselves be challenged by their own problems such as poverty, substance abuse, or mental illness. Even if parental inadequacy is demonstrable, assigning parental financial responsibility for youth offending is not likely to result in better parenting. Indeed, parental responsibility laws may exacerbate family tensions or lead to situations where further criminal acts are committed by manipulative adolescents, in addition to increasing deprivations experienced by the other non-offending children in these often impoverished families.[126] As Doob and Jenkins point out, survey research

---

123 *Juvenile Delinquents Act*, above note 1, s. 37. See, for example, *Re. S.(A.C.)* (1969), 7 C.R.N.S. 42, 7 D.L.R. (3d) 62 (Que. S.C.).

124 Of course under the *YCJA*, above note 3 — as under the *Young Offenders Act*, above note 2, and the *Juvenile Delinquents Act*, above note 1 — a parent who directs or helps a child in the commission of an offence can be charged as a party to the offence under s. 21 of the *Criminal Code*, above note 45.

125 Department of Justice Committee on Juvenile Delinquency, *Juvenile Delinquency in Canada* (Ottawa: Government of Canada, 1965) 203.

126 See, for example, R. Tripp, "Putting Onus on Parents Called Foolish," *Kingston Whig-Standard*, August 16, 2000.

shows that only a minority of parents know about the misbehaviour of their children, and "adolescents work hard at keeping their parents ignorant of certain aspects of their lives."[127]

By the mid 1990s, however, there were some moves in Canada to reimpose parental liability, at least to provide compensation to victims of their children's offences. Some Canadian stores began to send letters to parents of youthful shoplifters seeking significant monetary payments as purported "compensation." In a 1996 Manitoba case a youth was caught stealing about $60 worth of merchandise at a Zellers store and sent to alternative measures by the police. Although the goods were recovered, the store demanded $225 from his mother to "compensate [for the] incremental" costs associated with shoplifting, such as employing loss prevention officers and surveillance equipment.[128] The mother, feeling psychological guilt and wanting to avoid any possible legal repercussions, paid the money but then changed her mind about this payment and sued Zellers in civil proceedings to recover the money she had paid. In ordering the store to repay the mother the $225, the court ruled that, at common law,[129] a parent has no liability for the acts of a child unless it is proven that the parent was directing the act, or was in some way negligent, for example by permitting access to a firearm that was used in a shooting.[130]

In the 1990s, there were growing demands to amend the YOA to hold parents liable to victims,[131] echoing an American movement to

---

127 A. Doob and J. Jenkins, "Comment: Loaded Dice in the Parenting Game," *Globe and Mail*, August 16, 2000.

128 Every year, Zellers catches 50,000 people shoplifting, and had collected $1 million from such letters in three years of operation of the policy, making such letters quite profitable for the chain: "Stores Cannot Fine Shoplifters, Court Says," *Globe and Mail*, July 17, 1996.

129 Under Quebec's *Code Civile*, art. 1459, parents are in theory liable for the delicts (wrongful acts) of their children unless the parents can show an absence of fault in their supervision, though in practice there does not seem to be any effort in Quebec to use that provision to pursue the parents of youths committing criminal offences. In some provinces there is legislation imposing liability of parents for damages caused by their children to school property; for example, the British Columbia *School Act*, s. B.C. 1989, c. 61, s. 10, interpreted narrowly so as to exclude parental liability in *Central Okanagan School District No. 23 v. Brazeau* (1996), 7 E.L.J. 308 (B.C. Prov. Ct.).

130 *B.(D.C.) v. Zellers Inc.*, [1996] M.J. 362 (Q.B.).

131 "Let Parents Pay for Crimes by Children, Manning Urges," *Globe and Mail*, June 8, 1993. Reform (now Alliance) justice critic Chuck Cadman, himself the father of a boy murdered by a youth who was supposed to be supervised by his parents on pre-trial release at the time of the killing, proposed a parental responsibility amendment to the YOA to increase parental responsibility. Justice Minister Anne

hold parents financially accountable for their children's criminal conduct. California was first to enact parental responsibility legislation, in 1985, and was followed with all of the other states enacting some type of parental responsibility law. Parental responsibility legislation has been challenged in the United States but the courts in that country have upheld the constitutional validity of this type of law.[132] Some of these American state laws impose civil liability to victims on parents of offenders, although many of them focus on requiring parents of youthful offenders to participate in some form of parenting course or treatment related to their child. Led by Manitoba in 1996, a few of Canada's more conservative provincial governments have enacted legislation that imposes limited civil liability to victims by parents of young offenders.[133] Under the Manitoba law, parents are liable to a victim for up to $5000 for deliberate property damage caused by their child, unless they can show that they "exercised reasonable supervision over the child [and made] reasonable efforts in good faith to prevent or discourage the child from engaging in the kind of activity that resulted in the property loss." British Columbia, Ontario, and Nova Scotia have enacted similar legislation, intended to compensate victims and to encourage parents to take their parental responsibilities more seriously.[134] There is, however, considerable doubt that this type of legislation will do much to either compensate victims or deter youth crime. It seems difficult to reconcile the emphasis in the YCJA on the accountability of young

---

McLellan has stated that this concern is addressed in s. 139(1) of the YCJA, which increases the penalty for wilful failure to comply with an undertaking to supervise a youth; see C. Hoy, "It's a Crime: Blaming the Parents," Law Times, March 21, 1999. One can question whether the federal criminal law jurisdiction under the Constitution Act, 1867, above note 91, s. 91(27) would allow Parliament to impose civil liability on parents whose children have violated the law but who themselves have broken no criminal laws. The Juvenile Delinquents Act, above note 1, only provided for the fining of parents for the offence of "contributing to delinquency" if they "knowingly . . . neglected" to do something which contributed to their child's delinquent acts, with the fines were payable to the government.

132   In the Interest of B.D,. 720 So. 2d 476, Miss. Lexis 574 (1998), constitutional challenge to the Mississippi parental responsibility statute was rejected. Mississippi Supreme Court upheld the legislation as the parent/child relationship gave a rational connection between the actions of the child and parental liability. Further, the statute was seen as reasonably encouraging parents to exercise a guiding role over their children.

133   Parental Responsibility Act, S.M. 1996, c. 61.

134   Ontario: Parental Responsibility Act, 2000, S.O. 2000, c.4; British Columbia: Parental Responsibility Act, S.B.C. 2001, c. 45; Nova Scotia: "N.S. to Enact Parental Responsibility Law," Lawyers Weekly, June 30, 2000.

offenders with notions of parental responsibility. If parents are responsible for the behaviour of a young person, this may send a message to youths that they are not responsible for their own conduct, or at least have less responsibility than they otherwise might have. Further, imposing parental responsibility may weaken already strained family ties. Not infrequently, the relationship between a young offender and his or her family may be strained or even severed by the time the offence is committed.[135]

The common law provides for civil liability for parents for damage caused by their children if it can be proven that the parents either incited their children to commit crimes or were negligent, in the sense that their conduct fell below the standard of conduct normally expected of parents. Parental liability may be established at common law if the child had a propensity to do the harm, which the parent knew and the parent failed to take reasonable steps to supervise the child, or if the parent left the child unsupervised with access to a dangerous instrument, such as a gun, and injury resulted.[136] The fundamental change brought about by the provincial parental liability legislation is a shift of the onus to parents to prove that they were not negligent. In practice, the legislation seems to have been used rarely, at least in part because parents are able to rebut the presumption of negligence[137] or have such limited means that suing them civilly will accomplish little.

The *YCJA* does not impose financial liability on parents for the crimes of their children and the Declaration of Principles does not

---

135 For example, the mother of a boy charged with manslaughter said of her twelve-year-old son: "I do not acknowledge him as my flesh and blood. I wash my hands of him." The father of an adolescent charged with three murders said: "If they kill him, I don't want to know where they bury him." Both parents quoted are socially marginalized, one a single mother, the other a poor immigrant father. M. Valpy, "I Wash My Hands of Him," *Globe and Mail*, February 16, 1996.

136 *Trevison v. Springham*, [1995] B.C.J. No. 2563 (S.C.B.C.) The adopted son of the defendants set fire to the house of the plaintiffs when he was seventeen. Although the boy had a history of getting into trouble and had set another fire previously, failure to supervise adequately was not established, and no parental liability was imposed. However, in *School Division of Assiniboine South N. 3 v. Hoffer* (1972), 21 D.L.R. (3d) 608 (Man. C.A.), a parent was found liable for injuries suffered in a snowmobile accident because of negligence in instructing his fourteen-year-old son in the use of snowmobiles.

137 See *Shannon v. T.W.*, [2002] O.J. 2339 (Ont. Sm. Cl. Ct.), the first reported decision under Ontario's *Parental Responsibility Act*, where the court found that the parents of a boy, aged 10, had discharged the burden of proving that adequate supervision was provided; a 14-year-old was hired to babysit the younger boy, and the two boys broke into a house while the parents were at work.

mention parental responsibility, but in comparison to the *YOA* one of the themes of the *YCJA* is an increased emphasis on parental responsibility. The most significant change in the Act from the previous law in terms of increased parental liability is section 25(10), which permits provincial governments to seek reimbursement from parents for the costs of providing legal services to youths. This new provision is very likely to result in increased pressure from parents on young persons to waive their right to representation, and increased tensions between parents and adolescents dealt with in the youth justice system. The *YCJA* also increases the maximum penalty to two years' imprisonment for "wilfully" failing to comply with an undertaking made to supervise a youth on pre-trial release — although this is a largely symbolic change since the same provision in the *YOA*, with a maximum penalty of six months' imprisonment, was rarely if ever used.[138]

E. INTERNATIONAL STANDARDS AND YOUTH JUSTICE SYSTEMS

When considering the principles articulated in the *YCJA*, it is important to be aware of international standards for dealing with youth. It is also helpful to understand how different countries respond to youth crime, to situate Canadian approaches to youth crime in an international context and to appreciate the range of possible responses to youth crime.[139] As discussed earlier in this chapter, the *United Nations Convention on the Rights of the Child* is an international treaty that recognizes the need for special protections, services and rights for children, defined as those under the age of eighteen years.

1) The *United Nations Convention on the Rights of the Child*

In 1991 Canada ratified the *United Nations Convention on the Rights of the Child*,[140] joining over one hundred other countries in pledging to

---

138 *YCJA*, above note 3, s. 139.

139 For a further discussion of the *Convention* and juvenile justice issues in a number of countries around the world, see L. Palme, "No Age of Innocence: Justice for Children," in *The Progress of Nations 1997* (online at the time of writing at <www.unicef.ca>.)

140 U.N. Doc A/44/736 (1989), adopted by United Nations General Assembly, November 20, 1989. Another document that Canada has adopted is also relevant

adhere to certain internationally accepted principles and minimum standards for government treatment of children in a whole range of matters including health, education, welfare, and juvenile justice. The Preamble of the *YCJA* acknowledges that Canada is a party to the *Convention*. One of the most significant provisions of the *Convention* is Article 4, which provides: "State parties shall undertake all appropriate legislative, administrative and other measures for the implementation of rights recognized in the present *Convention* . . . to the maximum extent of their available resources."[141]

The *Convention*, which was the product of a decade of debate and compromise at the United Nations, applies to "children" up to the age of eighteen, setting out the general principle that in "all actions concerning children . . . the best interests of the child shall be *a* primary consideration."[142] The tiny but crucial qualifying term to the use of "best interests" — that this factor shall be "*a*" primary consideration — indicates that considerations other than the best interests of the child may also be factors in decision making about children.

Of particular relevance to youth justice systems is Article 40 of the *Convention* on the Administration of Juvenile Justice:

> 40(1) State parties recognize the right of every child alleged as, accused of, or recognized as having infringed the penal law to be treated in a manner that is consistent with the promotion of the child's sense of dignity and worth, which reinforces the child's respect for the human rights of and fundamental freedoms of others and which takes into account the child's age and the desirability of promoting the child's reintegration and the child's assuming a constructive role in society.

Article 40(2) to (4) set out a number of specific rights that should be afforded children, including the rights

- to have the matter determined without delay by a competent, impartial authority or judicial body, in the presence of legal or other assistance [40(2)(iii)];
- not to be compelled to give testimony or to confess guilt [40(2)(iv)];

for determining international standards, the *United Nations Standard Minimum Rules for the Administration of Juvenile Justice* [the Beijing Rules], adopted by General Assembly Resolution 40/33 November 29, 1985.

141 *United Nations Convention on the Rights of the Child*, full text from "Defence for Children International." (Available online at time of writing at <http://child-abuse.com>).

142 *Ibid.*, Art. 3(1).

- to have his or her privacy fully respected at all stages of the proceedings [40(2)(vii)].

Governments are expected to have special laws and institutions for dealing with children separate from adults, including establishing:

- a minimum age below which children shall be presumed not to have the capacity to infringe the penal law [40(3)(a)];
- whenever appropriate and desirable, measures for dealing with children without resorting to judicial proceedings, providing that human rights and legal safeguards are fully respected [40(3)(b)]; and
- a variety of dispositions to ensure that children are dealt with in a manner appropriate to their well being and proportionate to their circumstances and the offence[40(4)].

Although the *Convention* has been ratified by Canada, it does not have the same legal status as a Canadian statute, let alone such constitutional instruments as the *Charter*. The mention in the Preamble to the *YCJA* that Canada is a party to the *Convention* does not in itself give the *Convention* the full force of law in Canada.[143] Only if Parliament itself enacted legislation to explicitly adopt the *Convention* as having the force of law could it be used to negate or override a Canadian statute. While the *Convention* can be used in the case of ambiguity as an aid to the interpretation of the *YCJA* or the *Charter*, it does not have the full force of law in Canada.[144] The reference to the *Convention* in the Preamble to the *YCJA* is an "interpretative aid" for situations where legislation is ambiguous or silent rather than an independent source of legal rights.[145] This limited approach is reinforced by the specific word-

---

143 Under the common law doctrine of transformation, international treaties are not enforceable at domestic law unless and until they are expressly incorporated into the body of a domestic statute. See, for example, *Thomson v. Thomson*, [1994] 3 S.C.R. 551. This is reflective of the constitutional division of powers in Canada and the principle of Parliamentary sovereignty, which require that states have power over their own legal systems and that only Parliament can enact laws that have binding effect in Canada (or the provincial legislatures acting within their fields of jurisdiction).

144 On the limited effect of the *Convention* in Canada, see. A. Bayefsky, *International Human Rights Law: Use in Canadian Charter of Rights and Freedoms Litigation* (Toronto: Butterworths, 1992), esp. 94–103. For a *Young Offenders Act* case where the *Convention* was cited by the court but not ultimately used, see *R. v. H. (Adam)* (1993), 12 O.R. (3d) 634 (C.A.).

145 In *Baker v. Canada (Minister of Citizenship and Immigration)*, [1999] 2 S.C.R. 817, L'Heureux-Dubé, J. wrote for a majority of the Supreme Court and used the *Convention* to require immigration authorities to consider the "best interests" of any Canadian children as one factor in determining whether to allow a parent to

ing of the Preamble: "Canada is a party to the convention and recognizes that young people have rights and freedoms." These words recognize the fact that Canada has ratified the *Convention*, and indicate that young people have rights that have a variety of legal sources, including the *Charter* and the *YCJA* itself. It is, however, apparent that the *Convention* is an interpretative aid rather than an independent source of legal rights and remedies.[146]

Canadian courts do occasionally cite the *Convention* and look at other internationally articulated standards to guide their interpretations of Canadian legislation. In 2000 in *Re. F.N.*,[147] a case concerning the disclosure of youth court records, Binnie J., writing for the Supreme Court of Canada, cited the provisions of *The United Nations Standard Minimum Rules for the Administration of Juvenile Justice* — known as the *Beijing Rules* — to help interpret the protection of privacy provisions of the *YOA* in a way that protected the privacy of young offenders.[148] The *Beijing Rules* are also an international treaty, which was adopted before the *Convention*, that sets more detailed standards for some youth justice issues. The Court in *Re. F.N.* clearly indicated that this international treaty could be used to help interpret Canadian legislation but did not suggest that it might be used to override or invalidate clear legislative pronouncements.

When ratifying the *UN Convention on the Rights of the Child*, Canada specifically made a "reservation" with respect to Article 37(c).

---

remain in Canada. The dissent of Cory and Iacobucci JJ. expressed concerns that the majority judgment in the case eroded the international law doctrine of transformation, and in effect gave the international treaty the full force of Canadian law even though it was not enacted by Parliament. However, a close reading of the reasons L'Heureux-Dubé J. in *Baker* does not support the view that international treaties which Canada has ratified are now directly enforceable under domestic Canadian law. While that case raises questions about the precise legal effect of international treaties that have not been incorporated into domestic law, it clearly allowed the *Convention* to be used as an "interpretative aid" to Canada's *Immigration Act*, R.S.C. 1985, c. I-2, despite the fact that the statute made no mention of the *Convention*. See S. Aiken and S. Scott, "Baker v. Canada and the Rights of Children" (2000), 15 J. L & Soc. Pol. 211–54.

146 Article 44 of the *Convention*, above note 139, sets out a scheme for monitoring each country's compliance with its provisions. Under that scheme, reports of levels of compliance are made public every five years. Canada, like other countries, receives bad publicity and the prospect of political criticism if its level of compliance is low.

147 *Re F.N.*, above note 8.

148 At para 16. These are the *"Beijing Rules"* of General Assembly Resolution A/RES/40/33. November 29, 1985.

This article requires that children who are deprived of their liberty "shall be separated from adults unless it is considered in the child's best interest not to do so . . . save in exceptional circumstances." The fact that Canada filed a reservation, accepting the general principle of Article 37, but "reserving" the right to detain youths with adults where separate detention is not "appropriate or feasible,"[149] seems to indicate that, apart from this express reservation, the federal government intends to adhere to the *Convention* in general.

Advocates for youth should primarily view the *Convention* as a political tool that can be used to influence how Canada's youth justice policy evolves. Indeed, during the Parliamentary hearings on the 1995 *YOA* amendments, there was criticism of the transfer provisions based on the violation of Article 37(c) of the *Convention*, even though Canada had reserved that provision.[150] Not surprisingly, a document like the *Convention*, which is intended to have broad application in many very different countries, is frequently vague and provides only very general guidance. One might, for example, question whether some provisions of the *YCJA*,[151] allowing publication, under specified circumstances, of a young offender's identity, violate the privacy protection stipulation in Article 40(2)(vii), but it is difficult to be certain whether there is a violation, as that article of the *Convention* is not specific about what the "respect of privacy" entails.

On the whole, the principles and provisions of the *YCJA*, like those of the *YOA*, seem broadly consistent with the *Convention*, although arguably some parts of the Act may fail to meet international standards.[152] All of these international documents require a balancing of interests, including a recognition of the importance of accountability, while in general placing rehabilitation in "*a*" primary position. However, if some of the more drastic law-and-order proposals for changes to Canada's youth justice laws had been accepted — for example, to lower the minimum age of adult court jurisdiction to sixteen or to publicize the names of all young offenders — there would clearly have been violations of the *Convention*.

---

149 See *Young Offenders Act*, above note 2, ss. 7(2), 16.1, 16.2 for provisions allowing detention with adults.

150 See, for example, Testimony of R.W. Hatton, Senate Committee on Justice and Legal Affairs, April 3, 1995.

151 *YCJA*, above note 3, s. 110.

152 For a discussion of the extent to which the *YCJA* complies with the *Convention*, see R.B. Howe and K. Covell, "Youth Justice Reform and the Rights of the Child: A Step Forward or Backward?"(2002) 20 Can J. Comm. Mental Health 91.

2) International Comparisons

All developed countries and most less developed nations have a distinctive rehabilitation-focused legal regime for dealing with children and juveniles who have violated the criminal law and have juvenile correctional facilities that are separate from those for adult offenders. There is, however, very significant variation in approaches to juvenile justice in different countries. One may gain a better understanding of the choices that have been made in Canada about how to approach youth crime by considering the processes used in some other countries. While Canada's rate of incarceration of adult offenders is much higher than for many countries in the world, it is relatively low in comparison to countries like the United States and Russia.[153] However, under the *YOA*, Canada had one of the highest rates in the world of the use of a formal youth court response for adolescents, making much less use of diversion into informal programs for handling adolescent offenders than other countries, and Canada's youth courts made significantly greater use of custodial sentences for adolescent offenders than the courts in other countries.[154]

Under the *YOA*, in Canada only about one-quarter of young offenders were diverted from the formal youth court process, while over half of all young offenders coming into contact with the police were diverted in the United States (53 percent), England (57 percent), and New Zealand (61 percent).[155] Further, the rate of use of custodial sentences for Canadian youth was roughly twice that of the United States, and ten to fifteen times higher than the rate in several European countries.[156]

---

153 R. Walmsley, "World Prison Population List," 2d ed. (London: U.K. Home Office Research, 1999) Development and Statistics Directorate Research Findings no. 116. The average daily population world prison population was 8.6 million people in 1998–99.

154 According to the U.S. Department of Justice, Canada imprisons young people more often than the United States or any other industrialized country. See L. Chialkowska, "Canada Tougher on Youth Crime than U.S.," *National Post*, May 18, 2000. See also "Youth Justice Statistics," Department of Justice News Communiqué, March 29, 1999 (Ottawa).

155 "Youth Justice Statistics," *ibid.*

156 *Renewing Youth Justice*, Thirteenth Report of the Standing Committee on Justice and Legal Affairs (Ottawa: Canada, 1997) at 17.

a) The United States

The first juvenile courts were established in the United States at the very end of the nineteenth century.[157] The original American juvenile courts had an informal, discretionary child-welfare approach, serving as a model for the first juvenile courts in Canada and many other countries. Ironically, given the leadership America provided a century ago, at the start of the twenty-first century the United States has probably gone further than any country in enacting punitive juvenile justice statutes, with a particular focus on treating juvenile offenders as adults. There is even debate in the United States over whether to continue having juvenile courts.[158] With rising rates of juvenile crime in the late 1980s, youth crime became a major political issue in the United States with various efforts to get tough on juvenile offenders.[159]

While originally the statutory statements of principle for dealing with juvenile offenders focused on the welfare of juveniles, in the past two decades most states have adopted statements of principle that have emphasized the protection of the public and accountability of juvenile offenders.[160] Most states have moved away from indeterminate welfare-oriented sentences to determinate juvenile sentencing. Washington State has adopted a specific juvenile sentencing grid, which takes account of the nature of the offence and prior record to guide juvenile court judges in their sentencing decisions.[161] In the 1980s and 1990s,

157 See H. Snyder, "Juvenile Crime and Justice in the United States of America" in N. Bala, J.P. Hornick, and H. Snyder, eds., Juvenile Justice Systems (Toronto: Thompson Educational Publishing, 2002); and J.P. Hornick, N. Bala, and J. Hudson, *The Response to Juvenile Crime in the United States: A Canadian Perspective* (Calgary: Canadian Research Institute for Law and the Family, 1995).

158 T. Geraghty and S. Drizin, "The Debate Over the Future of the Juvenile Courts" (1997) 88 J. Criminal Law and Crim. 1.

159 There is evidence that juvenile crime rates in the United States may have peaked in the early 1990s. Although the causes for the decline, or at least levelling off, of juvenile crime rates in the USA are not certain, many experts believe that improved policing may be playing a role, while doubting that "tougher" laws have had any impact: "After 10 Years, Juvenile Crime Begins to Drop," *New York Times*, August 9, 1996. See also H. Snyder, "Juvenile Crime and Justice in the United States of America" in N. Bala, J.P. Hornick, and H. Snyder, eds., *Juvenile Justice Systems: An International Comparison of Problems and Solutions* (Toronto: Thompson Educational Publishing, 2002).

160 C. Hemmens, E. Fritsch, and T. Caeti, "Juvenile Justice Code Purpose Clauses: The Power of Words" (1998) 8 Criminal Justice Policy Review 221.

161 R. Lieb, "Washington State's Solo Path: Juvenile Sentencing Guidelines" (1999) 11 Federal Sentencing Reporter 273.

most states enacted laws to make it easier to have youths transferred to adult court, and in some states children as young as seven can now be tried as adults for certain crimes.[162] American states and cities are increasing their range of legal responses to youth crime, including the introduction of juvenile curfews, parental responsibility laws, and automatic school suspensions for students found in possession of weapons. All states have provision for juvenile transfer (or waiver) into adult court.

Since 1992, almost all American states have made punitive amendments to their laws governing their response to serious and violent juvenile offenders.[163] In an increasingly large number of states, transfer is automatic for certain serious offences or is a matter for prosecutorial discretion, while a minority of states have a judicial pre-adjudication transfer model, similar to that in Canada under the YOA. Because of the differences in age jurisdiction between Canada and the United States, it is not possible to get an accurate comparative picture of numbers of adolescents treated as adults. However, it is clear that the rate at which adolescents in the United States under the age of eighteen are placed in prison with adults is many times the Canadian rate. In a number of states, there is the possibility of capital punishment for juveniles sixteen or older at the time of commission of a murder.[164] This is contrary to Article 37(a) of the *United Nations Convention on the Rights of the Child*, but the United States is not a signatory to the *Convention*.

If get-tough strategies were effective tools for reducing youth crime, then the United States ought to have one of the lowest youth crime rates in the world: to the contrary, the United States has one of the *highest* rates. While the rates of property offences committed by youths are roughly comparable in Canada and the United States, the American rates of youth violence, and in particular youth homicide, are much higher. The United States has one of the highest levels of youth homicide in the world, some of which is attributable to a range

---

162 H. Snyder, "Juvenile Crime and Justice in the United States of America" in N. Bala, J.P. Hornick, and H. Snyder, eds., *Juvenile Justice Systems: An International Comparison of Problems and Solutions* (Toronto: Thompson Educational Publishing, 2002).

163 S. Morse, "Immaturity and Irresponsibility," (1998) 88:1 J. Criminal Law and Crim. 15.

164 In 1993 twelve states expressly allowed capital punishment for those under 18. Challenges to constitutionality of capital punishment for juveniles based on the argument that it is "cruel and unusual punishment" have failed; *Stanford* v. *Kentucky*, 109 S. Ct. 1969 (1990); *Arizona* v. *Jackson*, 216 Ariz. Adv. R. 9 (1996).

of social and cultural factors. Differences in access to firearms clearly play an important role. Although most American states have enacted laws to prevent adolescents from possessing firearms, teenagers in the United States still have relatively easy access to guns. Angry and immature adolescents with access to firearms are especially dangerous.

Criminal law in the United States is largely a matter of state responsibility, with substantial variation throughout the country. Most states rely on the common law to set the minimum age of juvenile court responsibility at seven, while legislation specifies that adult jurisdiction starts at sixteen to nineteen years of age. The U.S. Supreme Court has held that juveniles have a right to due process and to state-provided lawyers if they cannot afford to retain counsel,[165] but in practice many judges and parents discourage juveniles from having a lawyer unless the charges are very serious.

While the emphasis is on more punitive and interventionist responses to violent youth crime in the United States, there is also substantially more use of informal diversion programs for offenders committing property and less serious offences, and a lower rate of juvenile court committals to custody than in Canada.[166] There are also innovative programs in a number of localities that attempt to respond to youth crime by dealing with the underlying problems that youth face, generally involving family members and community-based dispositions.

b) England

England has three categories of youthful offenders who can be dealt with under criminal law.[167] Children are those ten to thirteen years of age, who are presumed to be incapable of committing an offence but who may be dealt with by the courts if the presumption is rebutted. Children ten and over charged with homicide are dealt with in adult court. Young persons, those who are fourteen to seventeen, are dealt with by youth court except for the most serious offences. Young adults are eighteen to twenty years inclusive and they are dealt with in adult court but with special provisions for sentencing and special correctional facilities.

---

165 *Re Gault*, 87 S. Ct. 1428 (1967).

166 See J.P. Hornick, N. Bala, and J. Hudson, *The Response to Juvenile Crime in the United States: A Canadian Perspective* (Calgary: Canadian Research Institute for Law and the Family, 1995).

167 This section also draws on J.P. Hornick and S. Rodal, *The Use of Alternatives to Traditional Youth Court: An International Comparison* (Calgary, Canadian Research Institute for Law and the Family, 1995); P. Platt, *Young Offenders Law In Canada*, 2d ed. (Toronto: Butterworths, 1995) at 577.

English policies toward youthful offenders have been in a state of considerable flux.[168] By the 1980s quite extensive use was being made of informal police cautioning for dealing with youthful offenders outside of the courts, but there was still concern about the excessive use of custodial dispositions for young persons under welfare-oriented legislation. This led to the enactment of the *Criminal Justice Act, 1991*, containing provisions intended to limit the use of custody. However, with increasing concerns about juvenile crime, some of the key provisions of the 1991 Act were amended in 1993 and 1994 to permit more use of custodial dispositions, especially for fourteen- to seventeen-year-olds. In the late 1990s, the Labour government introduced a number of administrative and legislative reforms to try to deal more effectively with youth crime, including a greater emphasis on police cautioning and restorative justice, introduction of a range of new community-based sentencing options, and more effective monitoring of program delivery.

c) New Zealand

Dramatic political and economic changes in New Zealand have led to major emphasis on having a more market-oriented economy, a smaller government, and a lower debt. At the same time, the country has moved to adopt innovative approaches to juvenile justice, by enacting the *Children, Young Persons and Their Families Act, 1989*, for those aged ten through sixteen years.[169] The Act encourages resolution of youth crime problems outside of the formal court system, having as its first guiding principle: "unless the public interest requires otherwise, criminal proceedings should not be instituted against a child or young person if there is an alternative means of dealing with the matter."[170]

The New Zealand statute specifically encourages the process of police street cautioning of youths for minor offences, as well as more elaborate warnings provided to youths and their parents at police stations by members of the specialist Youth Aid Section. The legislation

---

168 For a more thorough discussion of changes to juvenile justice law in that country, see J. Graham, "Juvenile Crime and Justice in England and Wales" in N. Bala, J.P. Hornick, and H. Snyder, eds., *Juvenile Justice Systems: An International Comparison of Problems and Solutions*, (Toronto: Thompson Educational Publishing, 2002).

169 This section draws on H. Lilles, "Canada's *Young Offenders Act*: Some International Perspectives for Reform" (1995) 5 J. Law & Social Work 41; and G. Maxwell and A. Morris, "Juvenile Justice in New Zealand" in N. Bala, J.P. Hornick, and H. Snyder, eds., *Juvenile Justice Systems: An International Comparison of Problems and Solutions* (Toronto: Thompson Educational Publishing, 2002).

170 Section 208, *Children, Young Persons and Their Families Act, 1989*, New Zealand.

also provides for family group conferences, based loosely on the Indigenous Maori methods of responding to offending behaviour. At these conferences a youth and family members, the victim, and a support person, a police representative, and possibly a social worker or probation officer can meet with a Youth Justice Coordinator to discuss the offence and arrange an appropriate (non-custodial) resolution that takes account of the concerns of the victim and the needs of the youth and family, as well as the interest of society. The youth is encouraged to be actively involved in this process and to take responsibility for his or her acts. Research indicates a substantial degree of victim satisfaction with these conference outcomes, although some victims continue to feel excluded from or disappointed with the process.[171]

The introduction of these reforms in New Zealand has resulted in a very substantial reduction in the use of custody, and the closing of a number of custodial facilities. There is also an indication that offending rates among young adults are falling, leading one New Zealand judge to "suggest that the new youth court [legislation] is producing adults who are less likely to be prosecuted in the adult courts."[172] Only about 10 percent of the youth cases in which police are involved in New Zealand come to the youth court, a fraction of the rate of court use in Canada. The cases referred to court involve serious violent or recurrent offending, or deeply disturbed families where court is the only appropriate response, and a custodial disposition or residential treatment are considered likely to be necessary, but the rate of custody use in New Zealand is also substantially lower than in Canada. For the most serious cases, transfer to adult court is possible; it is automatic for murder and manslaughter charges.

d) Sweden

Like several other European countries, Sweden has a relatively high minimum age of criminal responsibility (fifteen years of age) and a rehabilitative system for those aged fifteen to twenty, which includes young adults.[173] Youths younger than fifteen are dealt with exclusively by the child-welfare authorities and may not be sentenced under the *Penal Code*. Youths up to eighteen years of age may be referred by the prosecutor to the child-welfare authorities, provided that they confess

---

171   J.P. Hornick and S. Rodal, *The Use of Alternatives to Traditional Youth Court: An International Comparison* (Calgary: Canadian Research Institute for Law and the Family, 1995) 37.

172   F.W.M. Macelrea, "Restorative Justice: The New Zealand Youth Court — A Model for Developments in Other Courts?" (1994) 4 J. Judicial Admin. 36 at 53.

173   This section draws on P. Platt, *Young Offenders Law in Canada*, 2d ed. (Toronto: Butterworths, 1995) at 590–91.

guilt; if they deny guilt, a criminal trial is held, but only in rare and serious cases is imprisonment allowed for a child under eighteen. Only about 15 percent of youth cases are sent to court by prosecutors. A prison sentence is allowed for young people between eighteen and twenty-one years of age, only if the crime is especially serious, and life imprisonment is not permitted for a crime committed by anyone younger than twenty-one.

Youth cases are dealt with by the same judges as for adult prosecutions, although youths sent to custody are placed in separate correctional facilities. Judges may order a youth to be placed in the care of welfare authorities instead of imposing a custodial sentence. The minimum penalties that apply to some adult offences do not apply to youths. In law, youths face the same maximum penalties for most offences as adults, with a maximum sentence of sixteen years' imprisonment, but in practice judges are far more lenient with youth offenders and custodial sentences are relatively rare.

F. THE ROLE OF YOUTH JUSTICE IN RESPONDING TO YOUTH CRIME

In every society there are real limits to the potential of criminal laws and the youth justice system to protect society and reduce youth crime. Public policies related to health, education, child welfare, law enforcement, and gun control, as well as a range of cultural and social factors are much more important for determining a country's youth crime rate than its youth justice system. It is clear from the American experience that merely enacting juvenile justice laws that require longer sentences or greater numbers of adolescents treated as adults does not reduce youth crime.

In Canada, the appropriate role of the youth justice system and the principles that are to guide that system have been subjects of long-running debates. The *Juvenile Delinquents Act* of 1908 established a highly discretionary regime with little regard for the rights of children and, at least in theory, a focus on the welfare of the juvenile offender. The *YOA*, which came into force in 1984, had a clearer criminal law orientation and greater emphasis on due process. However, the *YOA* continued to give judges a significant degree of discretion, and, perhaps not surprisingly, resulted in a regime with substantial variation throughout the country in how the Act was applied, especially in terms of the use of court and custody.

The *YCJA* has a number of statements in the Preamble and in sections 3, 4, 38, and 83 which are intended to establish a new set of principles to direct the youth justice system. Although these provisions might have been drafted in a more elegant and concise fashion, when read together they do offer a more coherent set of principles than those in the *YOA*. While the Preamble clearly recognizes the value of a range of social, educational, and health programs to address the underlying causes of youth crime and prevent youth crime, the Act is premised on a narrower, more focused role for the youth justice system. The youth criminal justice system is intended to respond to adolescent offending that has already occurred. A central principle of the *YCJA* is that there is to be fair and proportionate accountability, which, for many adolescents, may mean an informal response by means of a police warning or some form of extrajudicial measures. The Preamble of the *YCJA* makes clear that an objective of the Act is to reduce over-reliance on custody, especially for non-violent offenders. The *YCJA* continues to recognize the importance of attempting to rehabilitate young offenders, and thereby prevent future offending, but the attainment of this objective cannot be used to justify a longer custodial sentence. While the new Act may offer a more coherent set of principles than the *YOA*, those responsible for the implementation and interpretation of the Act will continue to face challenges in making decisions on both a systemic and individual case basis. The application of the Act to individual young persons will continue to require professional judgment and a balancing of principles and concerns, made in the context of the resources available.

The more coherent message of the *YCJA* should increase consistency in how principles are applied in different parts of Canada and should result in less use of custody. However, the Act continues to allow for substantial variation among provinces and territories in terms of policies and resources available to deal with young offenders and for some issues there may be even greater variation than under the *YOA*. The *YCJA* may also erode protection of legal rights for youth and, in particular, it may have the practical effect of discouraging youths from seeking access to legal representation.

The principles in the *YCJA* are important but their significance will depend on the actions of justice system officials. In individual cases, these principles will be applied by police officers, prosecutors, judges, and youth court workers, exercising their individual professional judgment. As under the *YOA*, judges dealing with individual young offenders will be constrained by what resources and programs are available. As under the *YOA*, the policy and resource decisions of provincial governments will continue to have a profound effect on Canada's youth justice system and on how principles are applied in individual cases. Ultimately, it will be the cumulative effect of these decisions by provincial and territorial governments and by individual professionals that determines whether the hopes of Justice Canada for the new Act are achieved, namely the aspiration that "the *YCJA* will correct fundamental weaknesses of the *YOA* and result in a fairer and more effective youth justice system."[174]

FURTHER READINGS

ANAND, S.S., "The Good, the Bad and the Unaltered: An Analysis of Bill C-68, The Youth Criminal Justice Act" (2000) 4 Can. Crim. L.Rev. 249

BALA, N., J.P. HORNICK, & H. SNYDER, *Juvenile Justice Systems: An International Comparison of Problems and Solutions* (Toronto, ON: Thompson Educational Publishers, 2002)

BALA, N., J.P. HORNICK, M.L. MCCALL, & M.E. CLARKE, *State Responses to Youth Crime: A Consideration of Principles* (Ottawa, ON: Department of Justice, 1994)

CANADA, FEDERAL–PROVINCIAL/TERRITORIAL TASK FORCE ON YOUTH JUSTICE, *A Review of the Young Offenders Act and the Youth Justice System in Canada* (Ottawa, ON: Ministry of Supply and Services, 1996) cc. 1–2

CANADA, HOUSE OF COMMONS STANDING COMMITTEE ON JUSTICE AND LEGAL AFFAIRS, *Reviewing Youth Justice* (Ottawa, ON: Ministry of Supply and Services, 1997)

HORNICK, J.P., N. BALA, & J. HUDSON, *The Response to Juvenile Crime in the United States: A Canadian Perspective* (Calgary, AB: Canadian Research Institute for Law and the Family, 1995)

HORNICK, J.P., & S. RODAL, *The Use of Alternatives to Traditional Youth Court: An International Comparison* (Calgary, AB: Canadian Research Institute for Law and the Family, 1995)

---

174 Department of Justice Press Release, "Why New Youth Justice Legislation?" (February 2001).

LILLES H., "Canada's Young Offenders Act: Some International Perspectives for Reform" (1995) 5 J. L. & Social Work 41

WINTERDYK, J.A., *Juvenile Justice Systems: International Perspectives*, 2d ed. (Toronto, ON: Canadian Scholars Press, 2002)

CHAPTER 3

JURISDICTION OF THE YOUTH JUSTICE COURT

A. YOUTH JUSTICE COURTS AND SERVICES

The *Youth Criminal Justice Act* specifies, in section 13(1), that each province and territory has the responsibility to designate a court as its youth justice court.[1] The *Young Offenders Act* had a similar provision,[2] except that the term "youth court" was used under the old law. The word "justice" was added to the definition of "youth court" in the *YCJA* to give a sense that the court represents a relatively formal response to youth offending and that, in this forum, the community can expect fairness, accountability, and respect for victims. The *YCJA* consistently refers to "youth justice courts" and this is the term that should be used in formal documents. It seems inevitable, however, that justice system professionals and the public will tend to use the simpler, shorter term "youth court," to refer to the court with special procedures and powers that deals with "young persons" as distinguished from "adult

---

1   *Youth Criminal Justice Act*, S.C. 2002, c. 1 (royal assent February 19, 2002, to come into force April 1, 2003), often referred to in this book as the *YCJA*.
2   *Young Offenders Act*, R.S.C 1985, c. Y-1, enacted as S.C. 1980–81–82–83, c. 110. The Act was also amended in 1985 through *An Act to amend the Young Offenders Act, the Criminal Code, the Penitentiary Act, and the Prisons and Reformatories Act*, R.S.C. 1985 (2d Supp.), c. 24, in force September 1, 1986 and November 1, 1986, and in 1995 through *An Act to amend the Young Offenders Act and the Criminal Code*, S.C. 1995, c. 19.

court."[3] One may also hear the terms "young offenders' court" and "YO court" used, but these terms should be avoided, as they imply that all youths who appear are guilty.[4]

One might expect that the "youth justice court" should be a "special" court, with judges who have experience or educational qualifications to equip them for dealing with troubled youth, and having judges with a distinctive philosophy, or at least with a physical locale that is separate from the adult courts. In some places in Canada and elsewhere in the world, the courts that deal with adolescent offenders have some or all of these special characteristics, but under the *YCJA* the provinces and territories have a great deal of discretion about the designation, staffing, and resources of youth justice courts, with substantial variation in how these courts operate throughout the country.

Quebec established a specialized youth court under the *YOA* with provincially appointed judges with jurisdiction over youth court proceedings, child protection, and adoption cases,[5] and which generally sat in special courthouses separate from where adults appear. In comparison to judges in other provinces, youth court judges in Quebec took an approach to young offenders that emphasized the *limited* accountability and rehabilitation of adolescents, and that resulted in lower rates of custody use than elsewhere in Canada. The approach of judges in Quebec is broadly consistent with the institutional structures adopted in that province, as the youth justice system is closely linked to the child-welfare system. Quebec has a broad range of social policies that are among the most supportive of children and youth in Canada.

---

3   The *YOA, ibid.*, used the term "ordinary court" to refer to the court in which adults were prosecuted, and to which the most serious cases involving young persons might be transferred, though it was colloquially called "adult court." The *YCJA*, above note 1, has no explicit term for "adult" or "ordinary" court, since there is no provision for transfer of charges to any other court. The *YCJA* does, however, have references to the "superior court" deemed to be sitting as a "youth justice court" for purposes of dealing with the most serious charges for which a sentence of more than three years may be imposed (s. 13(3)).

4   There are of course also a range of other slang expressions used for "youth justice court" including "Kiddies Court," which is sometimes used by police or prosecutors as a derogatory allusion to the limited penalties, and "Juvie Court," probably owing to the influence of the American media where the term "Juvenile Court" is commonly used. The term "Juvenile Court" used under Canada's *Juvenile Delinquents Act*, enacted as S.C. 1908, c. 40; subject to minor amendments over the years, finally as *Juvenile Delinquents Act*, R.S.C. 1970, c. J–3., until 1984.

5   Known technically as the Youth Division of the Court of Québec, and commonly as the Youth Court (Tribunal de la Jeunesse), *Courts of Justice Act*, R.S.Q. c. T–16, s. 83.

In most provinces and territories, jurisdiction for *YCJA* cases is to be given to the judges of the provincial or territorial court who generally deal with adult criminal cases, although adult and youth cases will generally be scheduled for hearings at different times. These judges are appointees of the provincial or territorial government, and all have had legal training. In some provinces, like Ontario, legislation requires a minimum of ten years' experience as a lawyer before being eligible for appointment to the provincial court. The common practice of scheduling youth and adult cases for different times or days facilitates transport from youth detention facilities and appearances by professionals who deal with youth, as well as reducing the possibilities for youth to be influenced by adult offenders in such places as court waiting rooms. The fact that judges with a responsibility for adult criminal cases deal with cases under the *YCJA* means that these judges are familiar with the substantive criminal law and evidentiary issues that arise in youth cases, although there is a concern that some of these judges may not take a very different approach with youths than they do with adults.

In some jurisdictions, such as Manitoba, under the *YOA* the primary responsibility for youth cases was given to judges who also have jurisdiction over a range of family and domestic matters, such as child protection and spousal support. The rationale for this approach is that these judges may be more understanding of the family problems faced by many young offenders, and may be more familiar with the types of community resources that are available to assist them. In some places in Canada jurisdiction for *YOA* cases was given to the federally appointed judges who deal with a broad jurisdiction over all family law issues, including divorce and child protection. This more family-oriented approach seems likely to continue under the *YCJA* in the jurisdictions that took this approach under the previous Act, although even in these jurisdictions the judges who sit on youth cases, especially outside of major urban centres, may have a more diverse caseload that includes adult criminal cases. In a number of jurisdictions, such as British Columbia and the Yukon, the provincial or territorial court has responsibility for both criminal and family cases. While as a matter of practice some judges, especially in urban centres, may tend to deal more frequently with some types of cases, there is no judicial specialization.

Ontario and Nova Scotia adopted a two-tier youth court model when the *YOA* came into force in 1984. As was the practice under the *Juvenile Delinquents Act*, twelve- to fifteen-year-olds continued to be dealt with in Family Court, while sixteen- and seventeen-year-olds appeared in the adult Criminal Division of the Provincial Court, albeit with adult criminal court judges nominally sitting as youth court judges. Critics argued that by maintaining the court jurisdiction in effect under the *Juvenile Delinquents Act*, these jurisdictions simply acted in an expedient fashion and failed to implement the spirit of the *YOA*.[6] It was also argued that the older youths were subjected to harsher treatment by the judges with adult criminal law jurisdiction and that these youths may have less access to certain kinds of rehabilitative services than the younger age group.[7] The Ontario Court of Appeal, however, ruled that the two-tier implementation model was permitted under the *YOA* and did not violate the *Canadian Charter of Rights and Freedoms*,[8] since the judges in both courts "have the same powers and duties, but for administrative purposes some sit in the Criminal Division, some sit in the Family Division, and some in both. All of these judges are qualified to sit as judges in the youth court."[9]

In 1990 the Ontario government began a process of court restructuring, merging the Family and Criminal divisions into the Ontario Court of Justice (Provincial Division), while slowly extending the Unified Family Courts.[10] The government at that time planned to slowly transfer responsibility for all young offenders cases to judges with a family-law focus as part of a plan for restructuring the Ontario judicial system and as a response to the problem of overcrowding in the criminal courts. However, when the Progressive Conservatives took power in 1995, they decided to give the adult criminal court judges the primary responsibility for youth cases, which was consistent with its get-tough approach to youth crime. The process for this transfer has proceeded slowly. In Nova Scotia, there has also been a process of gradual transfer of responsibility for youth justice cases to the provincially appointed judges with primarily criminal law jurisdiction.

---

6   D. Stuart, "Annotation to *R. v. C.(R.)*" (1987), 56 C.R. (3d) 185.

7   Ontario Social Development Council, *Young Offenders Act Dispositions: Challenges and Choices* (Toronto: 1988) at 99.

8   *Canadian Charter of Rights and Freedoms*, enacted as Part I of the *Constitution Act, 1982*, being Schedule B to the *Canada Act, 1982* (U.K.), 1982, c. 11 (subsequently referred to as the *Charter*).

9   *R. v. C.(R.)* (1987), 56 C.R. (3d) 185 at 187 (Ont. C.A.)

10   Under s. 96 of the *Constitution Act, 1867* (U.K.), 30 & 31 Vict. c. 3, courts with provincially appointed judges can only be given limited jurisdiction over family matters such as child support, child protection, and adoption. However, federally appointed judges, such as those in Ontario's Unified Family Court or the New Brunswick Court of Queen's Bench (Family Division), can have jurisdiction over a full range of family matters, including divorce and property division as well as support, child protection and adoption.

In addition to initially having a two-tier youth court jurisdiction, Ontario also maintained division of ministerial responsibility in the provision of services, such as alternative measures, probation, detention, and correctional services for youths. Twelve- to fifteen-year-olds (known as "Phase 1" youths) were dealt with by employees of the social services ministry, which also had responsibility for child protection and other children's services, while sixteen- and seventeen-year-olds ("Phase 2" youths) received services from the corrections ministry, which has responsibility for adult offenders, fewer resources, and a reputation for placing less emphasis on treatment and rehabilitation than the social services ministry. In 2001 the Ontario government announced that all probation, corrections, and community support services for young offenders would be provided by the corrections ministry. The government claimed that this was being done to improve the efficiency of the youth corrections system. However, the transfer of all responsibility for services to the corrections ministry is reflective of the get-tough rhetoric of the Conservative government, as services for young offenders will no longer be provided by the Ministry of Community, Family and Children's Services, the government department with a stronger welfare orientation.

All jurisdictions in Canada now have a single ministry to provide all community and custody-based services for young offenders. In most provinces, responsibility for the provision of services for young offenders is with the ministry responsible for adult correctional services. In Quebec, since the *YOA* came into force, there has been a different approach to youth justice from most other jurisdictions, with young offenders and child welfare services being closely linked and the province having one of the lowest rates of use of youth court and custody in Canada. In the late 1990s the British Columbia government consolidated the responsibility for the delivery of many services for children and youth in a ministry with more of a child welfare orientation.[11] Until that time, youth justice services were administered together with services for adult offenders. In the late 1990s, the children and family development ministry became responsible for youth justice services, adolescent mental health and child welfare services. The ministry has an integrated service delivery model, with significant emphasis on

---

11   The impetus for this administrative change was a judicial inquiry into the death of a young child as a result of child neglect. The report was highly critical of the lack of coordination of services for vulnerable children, youth and families. See Tom Gove, *Report of the Gove Inquiry into Child Protection in British Columbia* (Vancouver, BC: Attorney General, 1995).

prevention and a community orientation. Under the *YOA*, British Columbia, like Quebec, had one of the lowest rates of custody use for young offenders in Canada.

1) Appointment of Youth Justice Court Judges

The *Youth Criminal Justice Act* allows the provincial or territorial government to "designate" one of its courts as its youth justice court, under section 13(1). In most places in Canada, the governments will designate the judges of the provincial or territorial court as the youth justice court judge. In some places, the provincial governments are also likely to give federally appointed judges of the unified family court jurisdiction over youth justice cases.

Under the *Young Offenders Act*, the practice of having provincially appointed judges dealing with youth justice cases was challenged on the ground that it violated the *Constitution Act, 1867*, section 96, which provides that only the federal government can appoint judges to sit in the "superior" courts (i.e., the Court of Queen's Bench and the Unified Family Court). It was argued that the youth courts were in effect exercising the jurisdiction of superior courts by dealing with serious criminal charges against young persons, and hence must have federally appointed judges. This argument was rejected by the Supreme Court of Canada in *Reference re. Young Offenders Act (P.E.I.)*,[12] in which the Court held that the *YOA* created "a complete and comprehensive scheme [for dealing with young offenders,] . . . designed to respond to what was a novel [i.e., post–Confederation] concern of society" and, hence did not interfere with the jurisdiction that was historically exercised by superior courts.[13] This decision is clearly applicable to the *YCJA*, so that provinces may designate provincially appointed judges to deal with cases. The Supreme Court of Canada also accepted that while the provinces could appoint youth court judges, this did not preclude provincial governments from designating federally appointed "superior" court judges as youth court judges, thus validating the scheme of provinces such as New Brunswick, where the federally appointed Family Division of the Court of Queen's Bench was the youth court.[14]

---

12   *Reference re Young Offenders Act (P.E.I.) s. 2*, [1991] 1 S.C.R. 252.

13   *Ibid.* at paras. 19 & 31.

14   A superior court judge in New Brunswick had earlier ruled that giving his court jurisdiction for youth court cases was inconsistent with the "accepted . . . role and status of Superior Courts" and hence contrary to s. 96 of the *Constitution Act, 1867*, above note 10, but the Supreme Court of Canada rejected this argument: see *R. v. D.(Y.)* (1985), 67 N.B.R. (2d) 269 (Q.B.).

In every jurisdiction except New Brunswick the primary responsibility for youth cases rests with judges appointed by the provincial or territorial government. The YCJA provides that, in cases where a youth might face an adult sentence after conviction, the youth has the right to have the case dealt with by a federally appointed superior judge. If the youth faces the possibility of an adult sentence, the youth should have the same procedural rights as an adult, which includes the right to a preliminary inquiry and a jury trial. Adult sentences can only be imposed for the most serious cases, generally involving serious or repeated violence. (See Chapter 9.) Jury trials and preliminary inquiries can only be held in cases dealt with by federally appointed superior court judges. Accordingly sections 13(2) and (3) of the YCJA provide that a youth facing the possibility of an adult sentence has the right to elect a trial before a superior court judge, with a jury if the youth requests it. In these cases, the superior court judge is deemed to be a "youth justice court judge" and the proceeding is still governed by the YCJA, for example, for such issues as pre-trial detention and prohibitions on identifying publicity.

The process for appointment of judges to the youth justice court varies among jurisdictions. Each government has its own process for selecting candidates for appointment to the bench. While historically judges were appointed at the discretion of the government, and appointment decisions could be affected by patronage or political influence, in recent years there has been an effort to reduce political pressures in the appointment process and screen out unsuitable candidates, although some appointments may still be politically influenced.[15] There is no requirement that judges appointed to deal with youth justice court cases have any particular background or training. Once appointed, judges are encouraged to attend various judicial-education programs, which are generally organized by judges' organizations or the National Judicial Institute, but there is no requirement to do so.

2) Justices of the Peace

The lowest level of judicial officer in Canada is the justice of the peace, often referred to as the "J.P.," who is appointed by the provincial or territorial government. Most justices of the peace are lay persons and receive some training and supervision from Provincial Court judges, although some recent appointees have been lawyers. Justices of the

---

15   See, for example, G.L. Gall, *The Canadian Legal System*, 4th ed. (Toronto: Carswell, 1995) at 263–79.

peace generally deal with procedural aspects of cases within the jurisdiction of the Provincial Court.

Under the *Criminal Code*, justices of the peace usually have responsibility for a range of procedural issues, such as pre-trial detention (bail) hearings and issuing summons to witnesses, as well as commencing proceedings by issuing summons or warrants for the accused, and can adjourn cases.[16] Although their responsibilities vary from one province to another, in adult cases justices of the peace also have the authority to accept pleas and to sentence for a range of less serious (or summary) offences under the *Criminal Code*, as well as to conduct trials under such provincial legislation as highway traffic laws. The *YCJA*, section 20, provides that justices of the peace have the same procedural jurisdiction in youth justice court proceedings as they do in adult proceedings. However, section 20(1) also specifies that a justice of the peace cannot accept a plea, preside over a trial, or sentence a young person.[17] This restriction reflects the belief that youth cases are more sensitive than those involving adults and hence should be presided over by more qualified judicial officers.

Only a youth justice court judge can satisfy the requirements of section 32(3) of the *YCJA* to ensure that a youth who is not represented by counsel understands the charges and is given an explanation of the option to plead guilty or not guilty. Also, section 36 requires that, before accepting a youth's guilty plea, the judge must be satisfied that "the facts support" this plea. The intent of these provisions — which have no statutory equivalents in adult proceedings — is that a youth justice court judge, who has legal training, can provide more protection for the rights of a young person.

The *YOA* originally provided that, because of their sensitive nature, all pre-trial detention hearings had to be conducted by youth court judges and could not be presided over by justices of the peace. However,

---

16   Under s. 21 of the *YCJA*, above note 1, a clerk of a youth justice court may, in the absence of a youth justice court judge, adjourn a case. This power may, for example, be exercised if the judge is sick or unavailable.

17   In recent years there has been a growing recognition of the importance of justices of the peace and their judicial role. They are not mere civil servants but judicial officers who have an important role in protecting the liberty of individuals. Governments have an obligation to ensure the judicial independence of justices of the peace by having appropriate policies governing salary and removal from office for cause; see, for example, *Ontario Federation of Justices of the Peace Association* v. *Ontario* (1999), 43 O.R. (3d) 541 (Div. Ct.); and *R.* v. *974649 Ontario Inc.*, 2001 SCC 81, 206 D.L.R. (4th) 444.

amendments to the *YOA* were enacted in 1985 to ease the burden on judges and facilitate administration of justice in locales where judges were not readily accessible.[18] Justices of the peace may now conduct pre-trial detention hearings for youths (as well as adults), but section 33 of the *YCJA* provides that a pre-trial detention and release decision made by a justice of the peace may be subject to reconsideration by a youth justice court judge, with the rehearing considered "as an original application." In practice it seems that justices of the peace still more commonly deal with pre-trial detention of adults than young persons, and that pre-trial detention decisions about youths are often made by judges.

In some remote northern areas with large Aboriginal populations, there are special programs to give some justices of the peace a relatively broad authority in youth justice court proceedings to accept pleas and conduct trials, in order both to provide better access to courts in remote locales and to allow Aboriginal justices to have more responsibility for their communities. For example, in the Yukon, the more serious youth cases must be dealt with by the legally trained judges of the Territorial Court, who reside in Whitehorse and travel to the smaller localities as needed, but justices of the peace who reside in these smaller communities have a relatively broad set of responsibilities for youth justice cases. In *R. v. G.(A.P.)* the Yukon Territory Court of Appeal upheld the validity of legislation that deems all justices of the peace of the Yukon Territorial Court to also be judges of the Yukon Youth Court, with jurisdiction to accept pleas, conduct trials, and impose sentences in less serious youth cases.[19] The Appeal Court concluded that section 6 of the *YOA* — the equivalent to section 20 of the *YCJA* — which prevents justices of the peace from conducting trials, applies only to justices of the peace who are not also specifically appointed as youth court judges. The Court of Appeal noted that there is technically no requirement in the *YOA* for youth court judges to have legal training. The same reasoning should apply to the *YCJA*, and a territory or province therefore can choose to give specific justices of the peace the powers of youth justice court judge: as under the *YOA*, this is most likely to happen in remote or Aboriginal communities.

---

18   *An Act to amend the Young Offenders Act, the Criminal Code, the Penitentiary Act and the Prisons and Reformatories Act*, above note 2, s. 4.

19   *R. v. G.(A.P.)* (1990), 57 C.C.C. (3d) 496 (Y.C.A.), leave to appeal refused (1991), 61 C.C.C. (3d) vi (note) (S.C.C.).

3) Offence Jurisdiction

Under the old *Juvenile Delinquents Act*, juvenile courts had a very broad offence jurisdiction. The violation by a juvenile of any federal, provincial, or municipal law, or the commission by a juvenile of any act of "sexual immorality or any similar form of vice," constituted the offence of "delinquency." If a juvenile committed any "act of delinquency," the juvenile court had the authority to impose any disposition available under the *Juvenile Delinquents Act*.[20] As explained in Chapter 1, the vaguely worded offence of "sexual immorality and any similar form of vice" was a "status offence," that is, an offence that only those with the "status" (age) of a juvenile could be found guilty of. Status offences were intended to give juvenile courts a protective mandate, although in practice the provisions were often applied in a discriminatory fashion, with courts much more likely to intervene in the lives of girls and children from low-income families. When the *YOA* came into force in 1984, that Act narrowed the offence jurisdiction of the youth court, focusing on violations of the criminal law. Consistent with the due process and accountability orientation of the *YOA*, the concept of status offences was abolished under federal law.[21] The *YCJA* maintains a

---

20   *Juvenile Delinquents Act*, above note 4, ss. 2(1) and 3.

21   One remaining status offence under provincial law, truancy, is the wilful failure to attend school for those under sixteen years of age. Under the *Juvenile Delinquents Act*, above note 4, it was quite common for children to be prosecuted for truancy and even to be sent to training school for failing to attend school. In a number of provinces, like Quebec, legislation now specifies that only parents are liable to prosecution if their child fails to attend school or otherwise receive an appropriate education (for example, by parental instruction at home). In other provinces, however, a youth may still be prosecuted under legislation like Ontario's *Education Act*, R.S.O. 1990, c. E.2, s. 30 for a wilful failure to attend school or otherwise receive an education, but in practice in recent years some judges have shown reluctance to impose even probationary sentences on youths who violate school attendance laws, preferring to view this as strictly an educational issue and unsuitable for resolution in the court system; *R. v. R.(B.)*, [1996] O.J. No. 980 (Gen. Div.) (QL). Other judges may, however, still place a youth who fails to attend school on probation; the failure to attend school then becomes a breach of probation for which the youth may receive a custodial sentence. A judge acting under the *YCJA*, above note 1, may make school attendance a condition of probation for a youth who commits a criminal offence if it is felt that the offence occurred because the youth "had too much time on his hands." Many youths who commit offences have school attendance problems, and may find it difficult to comply with this type of probationary term, resulting in further "offending" behaviour, this time a breach of probation charge.

focus on criminal offences. Subject to a few exceptions, section 14 gives the youth justice court exclusive jurisdiction over alleged violations by young persons of the federal criminal law, which includes violations of the *Criminal Code* and other federal statutes that create criminal offences, principally related to drug offences.

Under the *YOA*, young persons were charged with offences under the relevant legislation, such as the *Criminal Code*. It was not technically necessary for court documents (i.e., the information that commences the prosecution) to state that a young person was involved, although this was a common practice.[22] Under the *YCJA*, charges will continue to be laid for violations of the specific legislation. Technically it is not necessary in the information to expressly state that a young person is involved or that proceedings are under the *YCJA*. Violations of such provincial or territorial laws as the highway traffic code, and violations of such municipal bylaws, as, for example, the regulation of noise, are technically not dealt with under the *YCJA*.

Most provinces (and territories) have enacted legislation which governs the procedure and sentencing for those between the ages of twelve and seventeen who are charged with violations of municipal bylaws and provincial laws. Most jurisdictions afford young persons charged under provincial and municipal laws some of the protections that they are afforded under the *YCJA*, such as requiring parents to be notified of charges. These statutes also give the youth justice court jurisdiction to deal with these less serious offences, although there are some differences in the proceedings; for example, in most provinces, a youth charged under provincial or municipal laws will not have the same access to a lawyer paid by the government as is afforded under section 25 of the *YCJA*.

Section 14(1) of the *YCJA* makes clear that violations of federal regulatory laws — as opposed to the more serious criminal laws — may be dealt with pursuant to the federal *Contraventions Act*. This Act generally adopts the approach of the province in which an alleged violation of a regulatory federal laws has occurred for dealing with young persons in regard to such an offence.[23] This applies to less serious non-criminal offences, for example motor vehicle offences on such federal property as military bases, and might, for example, allow for an offence like this to be resolved by means of a ticket rather than a court appearance.

---

22   *R. v. C.(P.)* (November 27, 1984), (Ont. Prov. Ct.) [unreported] [summarized (1984), 13 W.C.B. 227].

23   *YCJA*, above note 1, s. 14.

4) Recognizances

Under section 14(2) of the *YCJA*, a youth justice court judge has jurisdiction to hold a hearing to determine whether a youth should be
required to enter into a recognizance (or peace bond) under sections
810, 810.01, or 810.2 of the *Criminal Code*. Section 810 is a preventive
justice provision that allows a court to require a youth to enter a recognizance when there are "reasonable fears" that he or she will commit an
offence that will cause injury to another person. To require a youth to
enter a recognizance, the court only needs evidence on the civil standard of proof that there are reasonable fears that the youth will commit
an offence; this is not a strictly criminal process.[24] The recognizance is
a promise to "keep the peace and be of good behaviour" and is in effect
for up to twelve months. A youth who fails to comply with the recognizance may forfeit a stated sum of money and may also be convicted
of the offence of "breach of recognizance" under s. 811 of the *Code*.

Although there can be a trial about whether a recognizance should
be imposed, commonly a person will consent to entering into a recognizance as a means of resolving the criminal process. The recognizance
is not infrequently used by a Crown prosecutor as a means of resolving
charges against an accused without requiring a full trial and conviction.
For example, as a result of plea bargaining about an assault charge, the
Crown prosecutor and defence counsel might agree that the accused
will enter into a recognizance and the assault charge will be discontinued; this might be an appropriate response to a situation where a victim has evidence of being threatened by a youth or has been the victim
of a less serious assault, but the victim does not need to go through a
full trial. The court may impose conditions on a recognizance, such as
that the youth refrain from direct or indirect communication with a
specific person or stay away from a specific place, which may afford
some protection to a victim. While a recognizance does not in itself
prevent a youth from offending, the fact that a youth is brought into
court to enter the recognizance may have a psychological effect, and
the recognizance is entered into the Canadian Police Information
Centre computer files, facilitating a police response if there is a violation of the recognizance. Sections 810.01 and 810.2 of the *Criminal
Code* allow for a recognizance to be required if there are reasonable
grounds to believe that a youth may be involved in a criminal organization or commit a serious personal injury offence. Conditions that

---

24   See, for example, *R. v. Budreo* (1996), 27 O.R. (2d) 347 (Gen. Div.).

may be imposed under these provisions can include the surrender of any firearms or weapons, or reporting to the police periodically.

There was no explicit provision in the *YOA* to allow a youth court to require a youth to enter a preventative recognizance, and some decisions held that the youth court could not do this.[25] The silence of section 14(2) of the *YCJA* with respect to section 810.1 of the *Criminal Code* makes clear that this provision does not apply to youth. Section 810.1 allows an order to be made restricting the freedom of an adult to be in contact with children under fourteen when there are reasonable grounds to believe that the person may commit a sexual offence; this provision is, for example, used to restrict the freedom of pedophiles released from prison.[26] It is not appropriate to use section 810.1 for youths since they are much more likely to be in contact with children in their living and school situations, but it is possible to place restraints on a youth who has been convicted of a sexual offence as long as the youth justice court sentence is in effect through the imposition of a probation term.

5) Jurisdictional Exceptions for Members of the Armed Forces

A limited number of exceptions to the exclusive jurisdiction of the youth justice court to deal with a criminal charge against a young person are allowed for under the *YCJA*. Section 14(1) specifies that the Act does not apply to discipline or court martial proceedings under the *National Defence Act* against a member of the armed forces who is under eighteen. A seventeen-year-old can join the armed forces with parental consent, although in recent years it has been less common for youths under the age of eighteen to be accepted into the Canadian armed forces. The rationale for this exception to youth justice court jurisdiction reflects the fact that those in the armed forces undergo a change of legal status and, if considered mature enough to join the forces, they should be subject to its discipline.

The armed forces would be very reluctant to have members who are not subject to its discipline code and procedures. However, youths who join the cadets (who are twelve to nineteen years of age) are not subject to the legal discipline of military courts. Similarly, youths who are not members of the forces but commit offences on military premises, such as children of military personnel, may be charged with

---

25   See, for example, *R. v. P.R.*, [1996] N.S.J. 581 (N.S. Yth. Ct.); and *R. v. S. (J.L.)* (2001), 163 C.C.C. (3d) 560 (B.C.C.A.).

26   *R. v. Budreo*, above note 24.

offences under the *National Defence Act* (for example, destruction of base property) but are dealt with under the *YCJA* in youth justice court.

6) Contempt of Court

Section 15 of the *YCJA* deals with the complex issue of jurisdiction over contempt of court charges. Sections 15(1) and (3) of the *YCJA* provide that the youth justice court has jurisdiction to cite any person involved in proceedings in that court for any contempt "in the face of the court," whether that person is an adult or a young person. This gives a youth justice court judge the authority to deal with such matters as disrupting the court's proceedings or refusing to testify. Under section 15(3) the youth justice court also has a concurrent jurisdiction to deal with youths who may have committed a contempt "in the face of" another court. In one legally significant contempt case that ended in the Supreme Court of Canada, a youth who was already in custody for other offences was called by the Crown as a witness to testify at a preliminary inquiry in the Provincial Court against two adults charged with attempted murder. In the witness box, the youth threw the Bible on the floor, crossed his arms, put his foot on the railing of the witness box, and told the clerk of the court that he would not testify. The following exchange took place between the youth (B.K.) and the judge:

B.K.:   Fuck it, man, I ain't testifying.
Judge: I'm sorry, I didn't hear you.
B.K.:   I ain't testifying, man. Fucking charge me. Whatever you fucking want, man. I ain't testifying.
Judge: I find you guilty of contempt in the face of this Court.
B.K.:   Up yours, you dick.
Judge: And I sentence you to a period of six months consecutive to any —
B.K.:   Fuck you, you goof.
Judge: — time now being served.
B.K.:   Goof.
Judge: Get him out of here.
B.K.:   Fucking goof.[27]

The Provincial Court judge immediately made a finding that the youth's conduct constituted contempt of court and sentenced the youth to an additional six months in custody. After the youth left the witness box and was taken back to custody, the Crown indicated that it had no

---

27   *R. v. K.(B.)*, [1995] 4 S.C.R. 186 at 190–91.

other witnesses to call, and the two men accused of attempted murder were immediately discharged. The youth appealed the trial judge's conviction and the six months' sentence for the contempt charge. The Supreme Court ruled that the trial judge was "amply justified" in citing (charging) the youth for this contempt "in the face" of the court. However, even in such an obvious case, the rules of natural justice require that a person should be given notice that he is being cited for contempt of court for his behaviour and given the opportunity to consult counsel and make submissions before a ruling is made on whether he or she is guilty of contempt and about what sentence is imposed.[28]

Under section 15(3) of the *YOA*, a charge for contempt "in the face of the court" (that is, misconduct in a courtroom) may be dealt with by the court in which it occurs, or the case might be referred by the presiding judge to a youth justice court to resolve the contempt charge. Section 15(2) of *YCJA* gives the youth justice court jurisdiction over a contempt charge for a young person against any court that occurred "otherwise than in the face of the court." Contempt outside the face of a court occurs when an order of the court that affects behaviour in the community is disobeyed. Section 47(2) of the *YOA* had a similar provision, although it purported to give the youth court "exclusive jurisdiction" to deal with contempt by a youth "outside the face of the court" for all courts.

In *Macmillan Bloedel Ltd.* v. *Simpson*,[29] an order was made by the British Columbia Supreme Court to prohibit the protest activities of environmentalists which interfered with logging in Clayoquot Sound. A seventeen-year-old youth was charged in the court, along with other adult protesters, for being in contempt of the court order, an example of contempt "outside the face of the court." As a young person, he applied to have his case dealt with in youth court pursuant to section 47(2) of the *YOA*, presumably hoping for more lenient and sensitive treatment in youth court. The superior court judge refused the application, found him guilty, and sentenced him to forty-five days' imprisonment and a $1000 fine. The youth appealed; the fine was removed but the custodial sentence was affirmed by the British Columbia Court of Appeal.

The youth appealed to the Supreme Court of Canada on the jurisdictional issue. The dissent of L'Heureux-Dubé J. would have applied section 47(2) of the *YOA* and allowed the youth court, with its expertise and experience, to have exclusive jurisdiction to deal with the defiant young person. The majority of the Court, however, ruled that

---

28   *Ibid.* at 197–98.
29   *Macmillan Bloedel Ltd.* v. *Simpson*, [1996] 2 S.C.R. 1048.

section 47(2) of the *YOA* violated section 96 of the *Constitution Act, 1867*, to the extent that it gave *exclusive* jurisdiction over contempt of a "superior" court order to an "inferior" court,[30] such as a youth court. However, the Supreme Court accepted the validity of concurrent jurisdiction so that the contempt of an order of a superior court judge could be dealt with by that court, if the judge of that court wishes to exercise jurisdiction, or the contempt citation may be referred to a youth court.

Sections 15(2) and (3)of the *YCJA* must be read as qualified by the Supreme Court decision in *Macmillan Bloedel Ltd.* v. *Simpson*. Although a youth justice court can be asked to deal with contempt charges against youth arising out of proceedings in other courts, in most situations it is a concurrent jurisdiction. The Crown or judge citing a youth for contempt of court "in the face of the court" can have the issue dealt with by the court in which the contempt occurred, or may decide that the contempt citation should be dealt with by the youth justice court. Contempt "out of the face of the court" most commonly involves superior courts, since these courts issue injunctions that affect members of the public. For contempt "out of the face of the court" by a youth involving orders of a superior court, there is also a concurrent jurisdiction between the court which made the order and the youth justice court. Regardless of which court deals with contempt by a young person, under section 15(4) of the *YCJA*, the sentencing provisions of the Act apply, so that the maximum penalties are those set out in the Act and a youth who receives a custodial sentence will serve it in a youth custody facility.

Under section 15 of the *YCJA*, a youth justice court may deal with contempt of court by any person who is in the courtroom, whether a youth or an adult, who is disrupting the proceedings. Most youth justice court judges are aware that they are dealing with cases that may be

---

30   The term "superior court" refers to a court with a federally appointed judge under s. 96 of *Constitution Act, 1867*, above note 7, who exercises the inherent general jurisdiction that judges of the superior courts had in 1867. "Inferior" courts have provincially appointed judges with a jurisdiction that is defined by statute. Although the terms "superior" and "inferior" have historical roots and are intended to be technical, they obviously have certain connotations, and inferior court judges, who deal with most cases involving children, youth, and the poor, are paid less money and given less respect by the legal profession than the superior court judges, who deal with cases involving large sums of money as well as the most serious adult criminal charges. However, the Supreme Court of Canada has affirmed that provincially appointed inferior court judges have the same constitutionally guaranteed judicial independence as federally appointed judges: *Reference re Remuneration of Judges of the Provincial Court of Prince Edward Island*, [1997] 3 S.C.R. 3.

highly emotional for the individuals affected, and that young persons may lack the self-control and maturity of adults. While youth justice court judges expect that appropriate decorum will be maintained, these judges may be a little more restrained in their exercise of the contempt power than judges sitting in adult proceedings, especially when dealing with unruly youths.

7) Jurisdiction Over Offences in the *Youth Criminal Justice Act*

Although most of the cases dealt with in youth justice court involve charges under the *Criminal Code* or federal drug legislation, the *YCJA* itself creates certain offences related to the administration of the Act. The *YOA* had similar offence provisions, with by far the most frequently used provision being section 26, which created an offence for a youth who wilfully failed to comply with a youth court disposition imposed under the Act (e.g., by breaching a probation order). Section 137 of the *YCJA* creates the offence of failure to comply with a community-based youth justice court sentence, such as by breaching a probation order. A youth who wilfully fails to comply with a community-based sentence may be charged under this section and prosecuted in youth justice court. However, if a person who was a youth at the time of an offence and receives a community-based sentence under the Act breaches the terms of that sentence after becoming an adult, then that person will be charged in adult court for the violation of the *YCJA* order, and subject to all of the procedural and sentencing rules of adult court.[31]

The *YCJA* also has provisions that regulate the conduct of police and other adults responsible for the administration of the Act. Section 138 creates an offence for unauthorized disclosure or publication of information about young persons in youth justice courts while section 139(3) makes it an offence to ask for restricted information about youth offender records for employment purposes.

There are also offences created by the Act that may be committed by parents or other adults who are responsible for the care of young persons. Section 139(1) makes it an offence for persons to fail wilfully to comply with their undertaking to supervise a youth released pending trial. Section 27(4) creates the offence of contempt of court for a parent to disobey a judge's order to attend youth justice court; the

---

31   See, under the *YOA*, *R. v. M.(R.E.)* (1988), 46 C.C.C. (3d) 315 (B.C.S.C.); and
     R. v. Ellsworth (1991), 68 C.C.C. (3d) 246 (Nfld. S.C.).

youth justice court has jurisdiction over this type of contempt. Section 136(1) creates a number of offences related to situations of wilful interference with a sentence imposed on a young offender, including inducing or assisting a youth to escape from a custody facility. Under section 136(2), a charge under this provision is within the exclusive jurisdiction of a provincial court judge.

Charges against police, parents, or other adults under these provisions of the *YCJA* are likely to be rare. However, when they occur, those who are charged with violating any of these provisions (unless they happen to be youths) will be prosecuted in adult court proceedings, although the Act specifies that they are to be dealt with by a provincial court judge. In practice, this is likely to mean that they may appear before a judge who regularly deals with youth cases, albeit not sitting as a youth justice court judge.

B. AGE JURISDICTION

Youth justice courts generally have jurisdiction over a criminal offence committed by a "young person," defined in section 2(1) of the *YCJA* as a person starting from his or her twelfth birthday and ending at his or her eighteenth birthday, a period roughly corresponding to the stage of human development known as adolescence. From the perspective of criminal law and section 2(1) of the Act, a "young person" is between the stage of being a "child" — a person under the age of twelve and without criminal liability — and being an "adult" — a person with full legal accountability. The date for determining whether a youth justice court has jurisdiction is the date of the alleged offence, so that a person who is seventeen years of age at the time of the alleged offence will be dealt with under the Act, even if that person is over seventeen years of age when charged or brought to youth justice court.

There were cases under the *YOA*, especially involving sexual offences, where the victims delayed reporting their allegations to the police because of guilt, fear, or embarrassment. Alleged perpetrators, in their twenties when the charges were laid, were dealt with under that Act since the allegations related to a time when they were "young persons."[32] Under section 14(5) of the *YCJA*, proceedings against those eighteen

---

32   See, for example, *R. v. Daniels*, [1995] S.J. No. 577 (Q.B.) (QL), where the complainant was nine years old at the time of the alleged sexual abuse and did not report it until she was nineteen, by which time the accused "young person" was twenty-six years of age. The youth court had jurisdiction.

years of age or older and alleged to have been committed while they were under the age of eighteen are to be dealt with under the *YCJA* in youth justice court. Hence these "young persons" are entitled to be sentenced under and are entitled to most of the protections of the Act, such as having the right to the court-ordered provision of legal counsel and the ban on publication of identifying information. This is intended to prevent any unfairness that could arise to youths if their cases are not resolved until after the eighteenth birthday has passed; it also gives individuals the benefit of more lenient treatment for the "mistakes of their youth."

Section 146(2) of the *YCJA*, however, provides that the special requirements for police cautioning as a condition of admissibility of statement only apply to a "young person who is under the age of eighteen" at the time of questioning. This portion of section 146(2) is a statutory clarification of an issue that was ambiguous in the *YOA*. It is, however, consistent with a Supreme Court of Canada decision which held that the protections of section 56 of the *YOA* did not apply to "young persons" eighteen years of age or older at the time of questioning by the police. Writing for a majority of the Court, Lamer C.J.C. observed that: "[p]ersons over the age of 18 have long been deemed to possess sufficient maturity and control over the situation they may find themselves in to no longer require the watchful eye of a parent."[33] If a person is a young person at the time of commission of an offence but over the age of eighteen at the time of conviction and it is a very serious offence, the age of the offender might be a factor that affects the decision of the court case to impose an adult sentence under section 72 of the *YCJA*.

If an adult sentence is imposed under section 72, adult rules regarding parole and allowing publication of identifying information apply. Further, section 89 of the *YCJA* provides that if a "young person" is twenty years of age or older at the time that a sentence is imposed by a youth justice court for an offence that occurred when that person was under the age of eighteen, then if a custodial sentence is imposed, that person shall be committed to a provincial correctional facility for adults to serve the sentence. If the sentence is for longer than two years, the court may also require the sentence to be served in a federal penitentiary. There is also provision in section 92 of the Act allowing youth correctional officials, after giving the "young person" an administrative hearing, to have the "young person" transferred to an adult correctional facility. If a "young person" is placed in an adult correctional facility under sections 89 or 92, the prohibitions on the use of records and the publication of identifying information that apply to

---

33 *R. v. Z.(D.A.)*, [1992] 2 S.C.R. 1025 at 1053.

young persons continue to apply, though the adult rules about parole and early release from prison will apply.[34] These provisions, which allow a custodial sentence imposed on a "young person" who has become an adult to be served in an adult correctional facility, are intended to ensure that such a person will not disrupt the environment or exploit the more lenient conditions of a youth facility.

1) Establishing the Age of a "Young Person"

Section 2(1) of the *YCJA* specifies that a young person is one "who is or, in the absence of evidence to the contrary, appears to be" between the ages of twelve and eighteen. Generally, at the time of charging or arrest the police will establish age by asking a person who appears to be a youth his age, and then confirming age by checking with a parent[35] or by examining a birth certificate or other record. It is not necessary for the Crown to prove the age of the accused young person as part of its case or to establish that the youth justice court has jurisdiction. Unless the accused or the judge raises the question, a youth justice court does not need to address the issue of age to have jurisdiction to deal with a case.[36]

If the jurisdictional age issue is raised, then section 148 of the *YCJA* provides that age can be established by the testimony of a parent, by a birth certificate, or by "any other information . . . that [the court] considers reliable," as well as allowing the court to draw inferences of age based on a "person's appearance" or from statements made by the person during direct examination or cross-examination.[37] Occasionally, young persons who are arrested by the police will lie about their age, perhaps to avoid having their parents notified or as part of a ruse to deceive the police about their true identity. In this situation, the police may fail to afford the youth the special protections of section 146 of the *YCJA*. Section 146(8) provides that a statement by a youth to the police

---

34   Ss. 89(3) and 92(3) of the *YCJA*, above note 1.
35   At common law, only a mother, or a father who was present at a child's birth, could establish age, since other evidence was "hearsay," including testimony from an individual about his or her own birthday. In a technical sense, a person does not have first-hand knowledge of his or her birth date but can only relate the evidence of another person: *R. v. Hicks* (1968), [1969] 4 C.C.C. 203 (B.C.S.C.).
36   See, for example, *R. v. H.(D.W.)* (1986) 62, Nfld. & P.E.I.R. 55 (Nfld. S.C.T.D.). Under the *Juvenile Delinquents Act* proof of age was an "essential element" of the Crown's case, and if the Crown failed to prove a juvenile's age, a juvenile was entitled to an acquittal: *R. v. Crossley* (1950), 10 C.R. 348 (B.C.S.C.).
37   S. 148 of the *YCJA*, above note 1, is similar to s. 57 of the *YOA*, above note 2.

will be admissible even if the police failed to comply with the special cautioning provisions of the Act, provided that the youth held out him- or herself as being eighteen years of age or older and there were reasonable grounds to believe that this was true.[38] In this situation, detention with adults would also be permissible until the police learn the age of the adolescent, who until that point would not be a "young person." Once the correct age is established, however, the case must be dealt with in youth justice court and the youth detained separately from adults.

In a number of cases under the *YOA*, jurisdictional issues arose because the accused was close to his or her eighteenth birthday and there was uncertainty as to exactly when the offence occurred. For example, in *R. v. A.(E.A.)*[39] the accused was convicted in youth court of the sexual assault of a young child whom he was babysitting. While the child could testify about the alleged assault, the precise time it occurred could not be established because the victim was too young to have an accurate sense of time. It was established that the offence occurred sometime between nine o'clock at night and one o'clock the following morning, while at midnight the accused began his eighteenth birthday. The Ontario Court of Appeal upheld the jurisdiction of the youth court to deal with the case: "Under such circumstances, it would be most favourable to [him] . . . to conclude that the time of the commission of the offence was when he was a young person since the disposition . . . available under the *YOA* [is] . . . more favourable to the appellant than if he were tried in an adult court."[40]

Section 16 of the *YCJA* largely codifies the approach of *R. v. A.(E.A.)*, providing that, if a person is "alleged to have committed an offence during a period which includes the date on which the person attains the age of eighteen," then the youth justice court has jurisdiction. If the accused in this situation is convicted and it is proven beyond a reasonable doubt that the offence was committed after the accused reached his eighteenth birthday, a sentence will be imposed as applicable to an adult, and adult release and parole provisions will apply. If, however, the accused is convicted but there is uncertainty about his age at the time of the offence, or it is clear that the offence occurred before the eighteenth birthday commenced, the person will be sentenced under the *YCJA*, with the sentence review and release provisions of the Act applicable.

---

38 S. 146(8) of the *YCJA*, above note 1, is identical to s. 56(5.1) of the *YOA*, above note 2, which came into effect in 1995.

39 *R. v. A.(E.A.)* (1987), 22 O.A.C. 83 (C.A.).

40 *Ibid.* at 84.

2) Maximum Age: The Policy Decision

Under the *Juvenile Delinquents Act* the provinces had significant flexibility in the establishing of minimum and maximum ages for juvenile court jurisdiction, with the minimums varying from seven to fourteen years of age, and the maximum from the sixteenth to the eighteenth birthday. The *YOA* established a uniform national age jurisdiction, a measure that was widely considered to be required by the "equality under the law" provision of section 15 of the *Charter of Rights*, which came into effect in April 1985.[41] Establishing uniformity required almost every province and territory to make some changes to its age jurisdiction. Given the practical and philosophical effects of the age jurisdiction for the youth justice system, it is not surprising that age-jurisdiction issues remain the subject of intense political controversy.

The most widely debated issue among politicians at the time of enactment of the *YOA* in 1982 concerned the maximum age for youth court jurisdiction. Under the *Juvenile Delinquents Act*, only Manitoba and Quebec had eighteen years of age as the start of adult jurisdiction; most of the provinces had sixteen years as the beginning of adult responsibility. Those provinces that were required to raise their age jurisdiction as a result of enactment of the *YOA* faced the costs and administrative difficulties associated with this change. There was also a widespread view that sixteen- and seventeen-year-olds should be held more fully accountable than younger adolescents and, hence, should be dealt with in the adult system. This view is still expressed by some critics of the *YOA* and the *YCJA* who continue to advocate lowering the maximum age for youth justice jurisdiction so that adult responsibility would start at sixteen.[42]

Any maximum (or minimum) age level that is chosen for youth justice court jurisdiction will have arbitrary aspects, with some whose chronological age is above the line seeming less mature than some below the line. Having a clear line, especially for the maximum level, is generally preferable to having individualized assessments of competence, responsibility or maturity since a clear age-based system is much

---

41   *Canadian Charter of Rights and Freedoms*, above note 8, s. 15.

42   In September 2000, members of the Canadian Alliance (formerly, Reform) Party of the House of Commons Committee studying the *YCJA* proposed amendments that would have changed the age jurisdiction for youth justice court to ten years of age to the sixteenth birthday. The Reform Party also favoured lowering the start of adult jurisdiction to sixteen; see, for example, Canada, House of Commons, Standing Committee on Justice and Legal Affairs, *The Reform Party Report on Amending the Young Offenders Act* (Ottawa: Ministry of Supply and Services, 1997).

easier to administer. The adult sentencing provisions offer some individual flexibility for treating older youths who are charged with the most serious offences in a fashion similar to adults.

The eighteenth birthday was chosen as the start of adult criminal court jurisdiction at least in part because for most civil law purposes adulthood starts at that age. For many individuals, the eighteenth birthday roughly marks the end of their physical and neurological maturation process, as well as the start of adulthood in a social sense with the end of high school. Society considers seventeen-year-olds too young to vote; why should they be considered old enough to be as fully accountable as adults?[43] The *United Nations Convention on the Rights of the Child* also sets eighteen years of age as the start of adulthood, and many countries with rehabilitation-oriented youth justice and correction systems are for youths up to that age or even older.

While there are good reasons for having chosen eighteen as the start of adult criminal responsibility, the issue has remained controversial and the 1995 YOA amendments created a presumption that sixteen- and seventeen-year-olds who are charged with the most serious offences should be transferred to adult court.[44] The contentious debate surrounding the enactment of the YCJA resulted in a lowering of the presumption for the imposition of adult sentences to those youths fourteen years of age and older convicted of very serious offences. The YCJA retains a presumption that any youth who is under the age of 18 will serve at least the initial part of any sentence in a youth custody facility, even if an adult-length sentence is imposed.[45]

3) Minimum Age of Twelve: History and Policy

The English common law set seven as the minimum age of criminal responsibility. Children between seven and thirteen could also rely on the defence of *doli incapax* (incapacity to do wrong).[46] These children

---

43   Some Canadian teenagers are challenging the age of eighteen as the minimum age for voting: see "Teens Fight for Right to Vote — Constitutional Challenge: Seek Suffrage for 16-year-olds," *National Post*, August 18, 2001. If this challenge is successful it might weaken the argument for having eighteen as the minimum age of criminal court responsibility, although it would not necessarily require a reduction in the age of youth justice court jurisdiction.

44   YOA, s. 16(1.01), enacted by the 1995 amendments to the Act, above note 2, s. 8(1).

45   YCJA, above note 1, s. 76(2)(a). These provisions are more fully discussed in Chapter 9.

46   For a discussion of the early history and evolution of this defence, see S.S. Anand, "Catalyst for Change: The History of Canadian Juvenile Justice Reform" (1999) 24 Queen's L.J. 515, 517–21.

were only to be convicted if the prosecution could prove beyond a reasonable doubt that the child had sufficient mental capacity to be held criminally accountable. The common law presumption of incapacity was incorporated into Canada's *Criminal Code* in 1892[47] and thus was applicable under the *Juvenile Delinquents Act*. Until the YOA came into force in 1984, it was theoretically necessary for the prosecution to prove that a child who was between seven and fourteen years of age was "competent to know the nature and consequences of his conduct, and to appreciate that it was wrong."[48]

In practice, the issue of incapacity was infrequently raised in juvenile court proceedings, and judges tended to assume that children had the capacity to appreciate the nature and consequences of their acts, especially as they approached the age of fourteen.[49] There were, however, cases in which this defence was successfully raised. For example, in 1977 in *R. v. C.(B.)*, a twelve-year-old boy charged with the murder of his stepmother was acquitted on the basis of the *doli incapax* defence.[50] However, relatively few children under twelve were being brought before the juvenile courts, and, as the process of reform of the *Juvenile Delinquents Act* began, it was widely felt that the minimum age of seven was too low.

The 1965 Department of Justice Committee report, *Juvenile Delinquency in Canada*, recommended a minimum age of ten, or at most twelve. In 1975, a report of the Solicitor General's Committee, "Young Persons in Conflict with the Law," recommended fourteen as a minimum age. Although Quebec supported this proposal, there was considerable concern expressed in other provinces about such a high minimum age. In 1977 the federal Department of the Solicitor General recommended twelve as a minimum age, and this was reflected in the YOA as enacted in 1982. While the selection of twelve was in part a

---

47   The *Criminal Code*, 1892, S.C. 1892, c. 29, ss. 9 and 10; later *Criminal Code*, above note 16, ss. 12 and 13.

48   *Criminal Code*, above note 16, s. 13.

49   See J.L. McLeod, "*Doli Incapax*: The Forgotten Presumption in Juvenile Court Trials" (1980) 3 Can. J. Fam. L. 251.

50   *R. v. C.(B.)* (1977), 39 C.C.C. (2d) 469 (Ont. Prov. Ct.). The boy had "abnormal psychiatric features" and the judge observed: "The evidence of the doctors indicates that the accused may not realize that his stepmother is dead; that he had no concept that what he allegedly did was morally wrong; that he did not appreciate what kill means. Such evidence leaves doubts regarding the competency of the accused and his ability to appreciate when an act is wrong" (at 475). The judge concluded his decision by recommending that the boy should receive "immediate and appropriate treatment" under provincial mental-health legislation.

political compromise, for most youths the ages of twelve through seventeen correspond roughly with the period of maturation known as "adolescence," the twelfth birthday marking the approximate beginning of puberty and its concomitant changes in physical, moral, psychological, and sexual development. For many children, twelve also marks the approximate age of leaving primary or elementary school and the beginning of an intermediate or senior elementary school program, reflecting the different social and intellectual needs of children and adolescents.[51]

At the time that the *YOA* was enacted, the minimum-age issue received much less attention than the change in maximum age, and only British Columbia advocated a lower minimum age than twelve. However, after the Act came into force there was growing criticism of the designation of twelve as the minimum age of criminal responsibility. The *YOA* was premised on the assumption that children under twelve years of age who commit criminal offences will be dealt with by their parents or, if state intervention is needed, it will be provided by the child-welfare or mental-health authorities. Further there was a concern that it was inappropriate to have younger children involved in a court process that was more criminally and due-process oriented than the informal welfare-oriented model of the *Juvenile Delinquents Act*.

One theme of media reports and political criticism of the *YOA* was that the legal system was not responding adequately to offending behaviour by children under twelve, and as a result this type of criminal conduct was increasing.[52] Public anxiety was heightened in 1993 by the brutal slaying of a toddler in England by two ten-year-old boys.[53] While the two boys were tried as adults in England, the Canadian law would not be adequate to deal with such a case. This was chillingly emphasized by a highly publicized 1996 Toronto sexual assault perpetrated by

---

51 Any community or residential program intended to respond to children under twelve involved in offending behaviour must recognize their distinctive needs and abilities. Pre-adolescent children are in crucial respects different from adolescents and require separate and distinctive treatment.

52 See, for example, "Law Courts Spawn Fagans, Officials Fear," *Globe and Mail*, November 9, 1985.

53 The brutal killing by the two ten-year-olds has remained very controversial. While they were tried as adults, they were entitled to earlier release. The trial of these two boys in an adult proceeding, with great formality and judges wearing wigs, was later found to be inconsistent with the *European Convention of Human Rights*. The English courts ruled that, because of their notoriety, the boys should be released before they were to be transferred from a youth custody facility and placed in an adult prison population, which caused a great public outcry in England. See "Toddler's Murderers to be Freed: British Officials to Give Teens New Identities in Face of Bitter Controversy", *National Post*, June 23, 2000.

an eleven-year-old boy against a thirteen-year-old girl. The boy evidently knew that he could not be charged, reportedly telling the police officer who arrested him: "You got me. So what are you going to do?"[54]

Some of the media reports may have exaggerated the problems posed by this case, since this particular child was removed from parental care pursuant to child-welfare legislation and placed in a group home where he could receive appropriate supervision and treatment for his behavioural problems; this did little, however, to reduce public anger at the inadequacy of the legal response.

Further, children under twelve commit a relatively small proportion of all offences. For example, in 1983, the last full year that the *Juvenile Delinquents Act* was in force, less than 2 percent of all juvenile charges were laid against children under twelve; seven- to eleven-year-olds had a charge rate of 1.3 per 1000, while twelve-year-olds had a charge rate of 12.9 per 1000 and seventeen-year-olds a rate of 103 per 1000.[55] A 1992 Statistics Canada study of police records indicated that children under twelve committed about 1 percent of all crimes, compared to 21 percent for young offenders (aged twelve to seventeen) and 78 percent for adults; if all children under twelve had been charged, this would have represented about 5 percent of youth crime. While some of the reports of offending behaviour involve children as young as four or five, the police reports indicate that almost two-thirds of the offences by children under twelve involved ten- and eleven-year-olds; males accounted for 89 percent of the children involved. Although most of the crimes committed by children under twelve were property related (especially mischief, theft, and break and enter), one offence of serious concern was arson: about 13 percent of all arson cases involved children under twelve. About 6 percent of the offences by children under twelve involved violence.[56]

A 1994 Canadian study raised some disturbing questions about sexual offending by children under the age of twelve.[57] Based on police

---

54   See, for example, H. Hess, "Police can't charge 11-year-old accused of rape," *Globe and Mail*, May 18, 1996: A12.

55   Statistics Canada, Canadian Centre for Justice Statistics, *Juvenile Court Statistics 1983* (Ottawa: Statistics Canada, 1984).

56   While not conclusive, this type of information should tend to dispel the perception created by some media stories that children under twelve are commonly being exploited by adults for such purposes as drug dealing. However, such cases have occurred in Canada.

57   J.P. Hornick, F.H. Bolitho, and D. LeClaire, *Young Offenders and the Sexual Abuse of Children* (Ottawa: Department of Justice, 1994) at 47, 67.

records, about 20 percent of all adolescent sex offences were committed by youths under eighteen: of these, about 10 percent (2 percent of all sexual offences) were committed by children under the age of twelve. Many of the acts committed by this youngest age group were intrusive acts such as oral sex and vaginal penetration, and typically involved younger victims. Those sexual offenders under twelve were more likely to act with co-perpetrators, while older sexual offenders were more likely to act alone. While this type of sexual offending behaviour by children under the age of twelve is disturbing and should be the subject of a societal response, it is not clear that with offenders who are so young a criminal prosecution would be in the interests of the victim, society, or the offender.

At least part of the rationale for choosing twelve as the minimum age of criminal responsibility was that it marked the approximate beginning of adolescence. Further, there were concerns that younger children might not fully appreciate the consequences of their acts, or at least would have difficulty in comprehending and meaningfully participating in the youth justice process. Even quite young children who engage in offending behaviour have some awareness that their acts are wrong, though this does not necessarily mean that they should be held accountable in the youth justice system. There is controversy among psychologists about how age affects the ability to understand crime or the court process, and little empirical work has been done to help policy makers determine an appropriate minimum age for youth court jurisdiction.

Dr. Michele Peterson-Badali, a Toronto psychologist, has observed: "One of the most interesting and important, and yet unstudied, areas of developmental psychology involves the cognitive capacities and development of children as they relate to public policy, which in its ultimate form is often embodied in law. . . . [N]o study has systematically examined the relevance of the ages set out in our juvenile legislation to the issues in development as they have been studied by psychologists."[58] She concluded that twelve years of age appears to be a "reasonable minimum" for the application of formal criminal sanctions, although she notes that many children in the twelve-to-fourteen age group lack a "more refined understanding" of such matters as the relativistic nature of liability or knowledge of the age boundaries of youth court jurisdiction. However, in a more recent focused experimental study of competency to make plea decisions, Peterson-Badali and Abramovitch concluded that "a majority of even the 10 year old

---

58   M. Peterson-Badali, "Children's Understanding of the Juvenile Justice System: A Cognitive-Developmental Perspective" (1988) 30 Can. J. Crim. 381 at 382–83.

subjects used legal rather than moral criteria in making their plea decisions [for hypothetical scenarios]. The actions of these children clearly indicate their ability to distinguish a legal domain, with its own set of rules and principles, from the domain of morality."[59] This type of research suggests that, to the extent that the establishment of a minimum age for youth justice court jurisdiction is based on assessments about the capacity of children to participate meaningfully in legal processes that affect them and to understand the criminal justice system, consideration could be given to lowering the minimum age of criminal responsibility from twelve years of age.

4) Offenders Under Twelve: Child Welfare Responses

The most common police response to offending behaviour by a child under twelve is to take the child home and discuss the situation with the parents.[60] The police may caution the child directly and, if the behaviour is more serious or repetitive, they may make a referral to an appropriate agency for voluntary assistance. If the police are aware of a program that deals specifically with offending behaviour by children under twelve, a referral may be made to such a program; there are a few of these programs in major urban centres in Canada.[61]

Only if the behaviour is very serious or if the police have other protection concerns, such as apparent parental abuse or neglect, is a referral likely to be made to child welfare authorities. When a child welfare agency receives reports of offending behaviour by a child under twelve

---

59 M. Peterson-Badali and R. Abramovitch, "Grade Related Changes in Young People's Reasoning about Plea Decisions" (1993) 17 Law & Human Behaviour 537 at 548. See also J.T. Dalby, "Criminal Liability in Children" (1985) 27 Can. J. Crim. 137.

60 For studies of the adequacy of police and child welfare responses to offending by children under the age of twelve, see Leena K. Augimeri, *et al.*, *Canadian Children Under 12 Committing Offences: Police Protocols* (Toronto: Earlscourt Child and Family Centre, 1999); Ken Goldenberg, *et al.*, *Canadian Children Under 12 Committing Offences: Legal and Treatment Approaches* (Toronto: Earlscourt Child and Family Centre, 1999). (Both publications funded by Justice Canada were available online at the time of writing at <http://canada.justice.gc.ca>.)

61 The Earlscourt Project in Toronto has the one of the largest and most sophisticated array of programs for children under twelve, including special programs for girls, sexual offenders, and fire setters. (See <www.earlscourt.on.ca>.) Another much smaller pilot program in British Columbia is described in: Sibylle Artz, *A Community-Based Approach for Dealing with Chronically Violent Under-Twelve-Year-Old Children* (Ottawa: Department of Justice, 1999).

years of age, which may come from police or other sources, the agency will investigate whether there are parental abuse or neglect concerns that would in themselves merit intervention, with the offending behaviour being considered primarily as a symptom of the child's response to an unsatisfactory home situation. If parental abuse or neglect concerns are present, the agency will intervene. If abuse or neglect is not evident but offending behaviour is a serious concern, the response of child-welfare agencies will vary. Some agencies appear quite willing to respond to the offending behaviour by children under twelve years of age, at least by meeting with parents and perhaps making a voluntary referral to another agency, but in many child welfare agencies these cases have a low priority for overburdened staff. Police officers are often aware of agency priorities and are concerned that cases of offending by children under the age of twelve may "fall through the cracks." Police may be reluctant to make a referral if they expect that the agency will not take action, as this may be futile or even give the child the impression that there will be no consequences for offending behaviour.

In every Canadian jurisdiction there is in theory the possibility of a child welfare or mental health response in the case of serious offending behaviour by a child under the age of twelve. However, there are real legal and practical limitations to these responses. In every province the primary legal basis for a response to offending by children under twelve is child welfare law. When parents[62] are considered unwilling or unable to care properly for their children, child welfare legislation authorizes involuntary intervention by a state-sponsored child welfare agency.[63] The agency can become involved in a broad range of circumstances, including physical, emotional, or sexual abuse, physical or emotional neglect, parental death, a parental desire to have a child placed for adoption, and other situations where parents are unwilling or unable to care for their children, such as when an adolescent is "out of control."

---

62   The concept of "parent" is broadly defined in child welfare legislation, and generally includes biological parents, legal guardians, and other persons such as grandparents, if they have had responsibility for the care of the child.

63   Child welfare agencies in Canada are under provincial government control and receive all, or almost all, their funding from government. In most provinces, the agency operates as part of a government department, and the staff are civil servants. In some provinces, like Ontario, there are semi-autonomous Children's Aid Societies, which have local boards but still operate under government control and regulation. Increasingly, Aboriginal child welfare agencies are being established in various parts of Canada to work with Aboriginal children and families, within the legal framework of provincial child welfare legislation.

Under the legislation, child welfare workers, and in most jurisdictions police officers, have the authority to apprehend a child believed to be in need of protection. A police officer or child welfare worker who is dealing with a child under twelve who is believed to have committed an offence may have grounds for immediately apprehending the child, although this is only to be done if there are serious and pressing child-welfare concerns. A child who is apprehended is removed from parental custody and usually placed in a foster home or a temporary care facility. If a child is apprehended, there must be an interim-care hearing in Family Court within a relatively short period to review the apprehension and either return the child to parental care, perhaps under agency supervision, or confirm the removal pending trial. While legislation varies from one jurisdiction to another, there is always an onus upon the agency to justify an apprehension as necessary to protect a child from harm, since apprehension represents a great intrusion into the life of the child and family.

Although not a perfect analogy, the power to apprehend under child welfare legislation can be viewed as similar to the authority of police to arrest and detain a person charged with a criminal offence, especially in the context of offending behaviour by children under twelve. In child welfare proceedings, however, the sole focus in justifying such an apprehension at an interim-care hearing must always be on protecting the child from harm, and not with protecting society or possible victims.

When a case comes before the court for a full child welfare hearing, the judge has essentially four options:

- dismiss the application;
- return the child to parental care, subject to some form of supervision by the agency;
- place the child in the temporary guardianship (or wardship) of the agency, with the child being placed by the agency in a foster home, group home, or treatment facility, or with a relative of the child under agency supervision (in some provinces, there are provisions to restrict the placement of children by agencies in secure treatment facilities and mental health facilities); and
- make the child a permanent ward of the agency.

This final option may result in a termination of visitation and other parental rights, with the possibility of adoption by another family. With children involved in offending, adoption is very unlikely to occur, if such a child is not returned to parental care, it is likely that the child will remain in long-term agency care. While each child welfare statute has its own criteria for decision making, in a broad sense the decision about what type of order to make rests on an assessment of the "best interests" of the child. In some Canadian provinces, there are provisions for children to have their own legal representation in child welfare proceedings.[64] Other jurisdictions, however, give only parents the formal right to be involved in such proceedings, an approach premised on the view that the adults involved (the parents and the agency) can fully represent the interests of the child. If a central issue in a child welfare case is an allegation that the child has been engaging in offending behaviour, there may be a greater need to have independent legal representation for the child, and it can be argued that section 7 of the *Charter of Rights* requires this, even if it is not provided for in provincial legislation.[65]

A child welfare proceeding can be highly adversarial and involve a lengthy, contested trial. It is, however, quite common for these cases to be resolved on the basis of the parents and agency — and where legally required, the child — agreeing to a particular disposition. While each Canadian jurisdiction has its own unique child welfare legislation, it is possible to classify the statutes according to how they deal with offending behaviour by children under twelve:

- offending behaviour by a child under twelve is itself a ground for intervention (in Newfoundland, New Brunswick, Yukon Territory, Nunavut, and Northwest Territories);
- offending behaviour *combined* with parental inability to act is ground for intervention (in Nova Scotia, Ontario, and Saskatchewan);
- offending behaviour is not mentioned in the definition of "child in need of protection," but special provisions are included for police reporting or apprehension in the event of offending behaviour (in Alberta, British Columbia, and Prince Edward Island); and
- offending behaviour is not specifically referred to, but child-welfare legislation may in more serious situations be invoked under more general criteria, such as on the basis of being a child "beyond the control of the person caring for him" (in Manitoba and Quebec).

---

64 Ontario and Quebec have the most extensive programs for representation for children. In most other jurisdictions, such representation occurs only on an exceptional basis. In Manitoba, *The Child and Family Services Act*, R.S.M. 1987, c. C80, s. 34(2), provides that only a child twelve years of age or older can instruct counsel. Similarly, under Nova Scotia's *Children and Family Services Act*, S.N.S. 1990, c. 5, s. 7(2), legal representation is provided only to a child twelve or older. See S.G. Himel, "Representing Children" in N. Bala, J. Hornick, and R. Vogl, eds., *Canadian Child Welfare Law* (Toronto: Thompson Educational Publishing, 1991) at 196–205.

65 *New Brunswick (Minister of Health)* v. *G.(J.)*, [1999] 3 S.C.R. 46.

If offending by a child is at issue in a child welfare proceeding, the standard for proving that the offence occurred is only the civil standard of proof. If the court accepts that the offending occurred and that the child is in need of protection due to the circumstances in the home, the focus of the child welfare proceeding becomes the "best interests" of the child.

5) A Mental Health Response for Offenders Under Twelve

In some cases, offending behaviour is a manifestation of a mental disorder and the child may pose a serious threat to his or her own safety or the safety of others. Sometimes mental health professionals provide services for such children (and families), either on a voluntary basis or as part of a child welfare order involving supervision in the community. In cases involving more severe or disruptive behaviour, consideration may be given to having the child placed in some type of mental health facility for treatment of a behavioural or emotional problem, although this is less common than involving a child welfare agency. Mental health facilities generally have some degree of security and can provide a degree of social protection as well as treatment. Although mental health legislation will allow for apprehension and confinement of the child for an indefinite period, it can provide only a limited response to cases of offending behaviour by the most seriously disturbed children since it focuses exclusively on treatment and mental health. The legal issues surrounding the use of mental health facilities for young children are complex, and there is little legal literature available in Canada on the subject.[66] In some provinces there are overlapping services and legislative regimes, with some facilities governed by mental health legislation and others by child welfare legislation. As with other types of children's services, in many localities there are resource and other restrictions on access to children's mental health services and facilities. Many children's mental facilities in Canada have significant waiting lists, although cases involving very disruptive or disturbed behaviour may receive priority for admission.

Facilities also have policies that restrict admission. In one of the few reported cases involving a legal response to offending behaviour by a child under twelve, the Nova Scotia Hospital refused admission to a ten-year-old boy with a severe conduct disorder who had been engag-

---

66   See, for example, G.B. Robertson, *Mental Disability and the Law in Canada*, 2d ed. (Toronto: Carswell, 1994) at 374–77; and B.M. Knoppers, ed., *Canadian Child Health Law* (Toronto: Thompson Educational Publishing, 1992) at 171–75.

ing in behaviour that was dangerous to himself and others. The boy's parents were not willing to consent to his admission, and the hospital's treatment program restricted admission to children whose parents were willing to consent and to be active participants in the treatment process. The child welfare authorities, who had legal guardianship of the boy under the provincial *Children's Services Act*, believed that the hospital nevertheless had the only suitable program in the province and applied for a court order requiring his admission. Judge Niedermayer of the Nova Scotia Family Court recognized that there was no express statutory basis for making such an order, but he ruled that the general statements in the provincial child welfare legislation about court action being guided by "the principle that the welfare of the child is the paramount consideration" gave him the authority to order the hospital to admit the boy.[67] While the decision is legally questionable, one can sympathize with the judge's decision to resolve a dispute between two government-funded agencies in a manner that appeared to promote both the child's best interests and the protection of society. This case illustrates the complexity of the interrelationship of different public agencies serving children.

As a result of the general common law rules about parental consent for the provision of medical services and the silence of the bulk of mental health legislation on this subject, in most Canadian provinces only a parent's or guardian's consent is legally required for a child under twelve to be admitted to a mental health facility; legislation or hospital policies also require that the medical staff must be satisfied that the child has an emotional or mental disorder that justifies such confinement.[68] Children who are admitted in this way must be released if a parent or guardian withdraws consent; however, in this situation attending medical staff may seek involuntary admission if they believe that the child poses a significant danger to him- or herself or to others. In some provinces, like Ontario, legislation requires court review of parental decisions placing children in mental health facilities.[69]

---

67 N.S. (*Minister of Community Services*) v. *P.(K.)* (1991), 101 N.S.R. (2d) 405 (Fam. Ct.). See also M. Boyle, "Children's Mental Health Issues: Prevention and Treatment" in L.C. Johnson and R. Barnhorst, eds., *Children, Families and Public Policy in the 90's* (Toronto: Thompson Educational Publishing, 1991) at 73–104; and S. Moyer, *Summary Report of Survey of Legislation, Procedures and Services in Six Jurisdictions* (Ottawa: Department of Justice, 1990) at 12.

68 In Saskatchewan, the *Mental Health Services Act*, S.S. 1984–85–86, c. M–13.1, s. 17, permits a voluntary admission only at a person's "own request." This suggests that parents cannot request their child's "voluntary admission" in Saskatchewan. See Robertson, above note 66, at 375.

69 See, for example, Ontario, *Child and Family Services Act*, R.S.O. 1990, c. C.11, s. 124.

All Canadian jurisdictions have civil-commitment legislation that allows a person who is considered dangerous to be placed "involuntarily" in a mental health facility, which for children means placement without the consent of a parent or guardian; except in Ontario, the same legislation governs involuntary commitment for both children and adults. While a detailed consideration of such legislation is beyond the scope of this book, the basic scheme involves an initial assessment of dangerousness and committal by a doctor, and the possibility of a review of that decision by a court or review board. The exact criteria for commitment vary from jurisdiction to jurisdiction, depending on the relevant legislation, although there are also broad similarities in that individuals are only subject to continuing committal if they are suffering from a "mental disorder" *and* pose a significant risk to themselves or others.

It should be appreciated that most offending behaviour by children under twelve is *not* the result of a "mental disorder," and a response involving confinement under mental-health legislation is very rarely appropriate, although the provision of mental health services in the community is sometimes an appropriate part of the response to such behaviour. Only a relatively small number of cases involving significant violence fit the criteria for confinement under existing mental health legislation, and then only if there are facilities with resources to deal with the specific needs of the child. In most provinces the admission to such a facility may be made by a parent or guardian or, if necessary, on an involuntary basis by court order. Any involuntary use of mental health facilities is subject to the child being released when treatment personnel, or a review body, are satisfied that the child no longer presents a sufficient, immediate risk to the community or to him- or herself. In practice, the criteria for involuntary committal are interpreted in a fairly narrow way, since this involves a great incursion in personal liberty and may result in invasive treatment, such as the use of psychotropic drugs.

There are complex challenges in diagnosing and treating children under the age of twelve for mental health problems; most standardized clinical tests to determine psychological status are not reliable with this age group and conventional therapeutic interventions, which are based on verbal communication, can be difficult to implement with young children. Given the limited mental health facilities suitable for children, and the intrusive nature of placement in such facilities, confinement there is only rarely a response to offending by children under twelve.

6) Offending Behaviour by Youths under Twelve: Is Law Reform Needed?

Offending behaviour by children under twelve is a significant social problem that is not addressed in a totally satisfactory way by existing Canadian programs and legislation. At present, the most common police response to such behaviour is to contact parents, discuss the situation with them, and perhaps make a referral to an agency or program for voluntary assistance. For most child offenders, this may be all the intervention that is needed. The offending behaviour of most children under the age of twelve is relatively minor, and even among those children engaging in aggressive behaviour, a significant portion will cease that behaviour in reponse to the efforts of parents and teachers without requiring legal or therapeutic intervention.[70] Some children under twelve, however, have serious behavioural problems that are unlikely to be resolved without appropriate intervention. In general, early intervention is desirable. Adolescents with serious youth justice court records typically had more serious behavioural and offending problems than other children when they were under the age of twelve.[71] Further, children under twelve with significant offending problems often have a range of other social problems.[72]

While some large communities have special programs to which police can make such voluntary referrals, in many localities there are no such programs, and only a general voluntary referral can be made, such as to a family doctor. More serious cases, either in terms of frequency of offending behaviour or the nature of the behaviour — or because of parental unwillingness to take appropriate measures to deal with their child's misbehaviour — may be referred to child welfare authorities. The most severe cases may be considered for placement in a mental-health facility. While all jurisdictions have child welfare and mental health legislation that has potential applicability to some situations

---

70   See, for example, J.B. Sprott, A.N. Doob, and J.M. Jenkins, "Problem Behaviour and Delinquency in Children and Youth" (2001) 21:4 Juristat, presenting data from the large-scale National Longitudinal Study on Children and Youth, indicating that 45 percent of children aged ten and eleven reported by teachers and parents as engaging in highly aggressive behaviour were not exhibiting such behaviour two years later.

70   See, for example, T.E. Moffitt and A. Caspi, "Childhood Predictors Differentiate Life-Course Persistent and Adolescent-Limited Antisocial Pathways among Males and Females" (2001) 13 Development and Psychopathology 355–75.

72   See, for example, J.B. Sprott and A.N. Doob, "Bad, Sad and Rejected: The Lives of Aggressive Children" (2000) 42 Can. J. Crim. 123–33.

involving offending behaviour by children under twelve, there are also problems with the present legal responses.

One major problem is that offending behaviour is often not a priority for child welfare agencies, unless there is other evidence of abuse or neglect. The institutional priorities of child welfare agencies and the professional orientation of their staffs tend to restrict the ability of these agencies to respond to offending behaviour. The result is that too often victims, police, and citizens may feel that little or nothing is being done in these cases, although the more serious the offending behaviour, the more likely child welfare authorities are to respond. In at least some of the cases where child welfare agencies are not becoming involved because of either legal or resource constraints, an opportunity for earlier and potentially more effective intervention is being lost and the child must pass his or her twelfth birthday before there is a societal response. While for some families and children a voluntary referral may result in the provision of appropriate services for a child, there are also parents who are unwilling or unable to follow up on a voluntary recommendation that assistance is needed. There are a few good programs in Canada for children under the age of twelve who have behavioural problems, but these largely operate on a voluntary basis and there is a concern that some of the children most in need of help are not receiving it.

Although most children under twelve who commit offences should be dealt with informally, or under child welfare or mental health legislation, there is a strong argument that present child-welfare and institutional arrangements are not totally adequate. For some cases it may be inappropriate to have an approach that focuses solely on the "best interests" of the child and appears to give no weight to accountability, the concerns of victims, or the protection of society. The present responses may be seen as failing to meet the needs of victims. Further, while there is substantial evidence that longer sentences do not deter youths from committing offences, the perception of some relatively sophisticated children under the age of twelve that "nothing happens" may encourage them to engage in offending behaviour.[73] Further, the criminal law has an important symbolic value for society in general and

---

73   See, for example, S. Moyer, *Summary Report of Survey of Legislation, Procedures and Services in Six Jurisdictions* (Ottawa: Department of Justice, 1990) at 24. The existence of a more effective and consistent child welfare response combined with greater professional and public awareness of its existence could also serve to alter the perception that there is not an adequate response to children under twelve offending.

victims of crime in particular. The public's sense of injustice at the lack of accountability of offenders under twelve may have negative implications for the entire justice system and certainly frustrates victims, the police, and in some cases the parents of child offenders as well.

It is for these reasons that the 1997 report of the House of Commons Justice Committee recommended lowering the age of criminal responsibility to ten, with restrictions to ensure that a criminal response is used in an appropriate, restrained fashion.[74] While many conservative politicians favoured lowering the minimum age of youth justice court jurisdiction to ten, at least for serious cases, the Liberal government rejected the Committee recommendation. In part, the decision to keep the minimum age of youth justice court jurisdiction in the *YCJA* at twelve was based on a desire to gain support for the new law in Quebec, where opposition to the lowering of the age jurisdiction was strong.

The decision to keep twelve as the minimum age of youth justice court jurisdiction also reflected a view that it is inappropriate to use formal criminal justice for pre-adolescent children. Nova Scotia Family Court Judge Niedermayer observed in a case involving a ten-year-old boy with a severe conduct disorder: "It is well-recognized in medical/social work literature and thought that it is inappropriate to mix pre-adolescents with adolescents; these are two separate types of individuals who require different programs. The personnel who are clinically involved with these groups require a different type of training."[75] While the federal government remains committed to retaining the age of twelve as the minimum age for youth justice court jurisdiction, research supported by Justice Canada continues to conclude that present social and legal approaches to offending by children under the age of twelve is not satisfactory.

A 1999 study surveyed respondents across Canada and found significant numbers of child offenders "falling through the cracks."[76] These researchers, from Toronto's Earlscourt Child and Family Centre, who work exclusively with offenders under twelve, concluded that the primary means of responding to child offending should be through

---

74 Canada, House of Commons, *Thirteenth Report of the Standing Committee on Justice and Legal Affairs: Renewing Youth Justice* (Ottawa: Ministry of Supply and Services, 1997) at 59–61.

75 *Nova Scotia (Minister of Community Services)* v. *P.(K.)*, above note 67, at 406–7.

76 Ken Goldenberg, *et al.*, *Canadian Children Under 12 Committing Offences: Legal and Treatment Approaches* (Toronto: Earlscourt Child and Family Centre, 1999). (Funded by Justice Canada, it was available online at the time of writing at <http://canada.justice.gc.ca>.)

support of parents and schools, including access to community-based treatment programs and projects that allow a role for victims. It was also recognized that police can have an important role in terms of responding to cases, and co-ordinating access to various services. Whatever legal regime is in place, police and other professionals need special training to communicate and work effectively with this younger population. The researchers also recognized the need for a more effective legal framework, as the present approaches based on voluntary assistance or child welfare intervention are too frequently inadequate. Instead of either a pure youth justice or child welfare response, these researchers advocated the enactment of special provincial legislation focused on children under twelve who commit offences, providing for police apprehension powers and for the possibility of involuntary intervention, including a judicially controlled power to place a child in treatment-oriented facilities, separate from older adolescents. They also recommended that special community committees or agencies should be established to deal with the problems of child offenders

It should be appreciated that whatever legal regime is in place for dealing with children under the age of twelve will have little effect in terms of reducing criminal behaviour of children in this age group unless steps are also taken to ensure that appropriate services are available, services premised on the recognition that children under twelve have different needs and capabilities than older youths and must be treated distinctly. For the vast majority of children in this age group, the most appropriate responses will be informal and involve parents and schools. It must also be recognized that, even if new legislation were enacted or the *YCJA* were amended to lower the age of youth justice court jurisdiction, there will continue to be an important role for child welfare agencies and the mental health system for dealing with offending behaviour by children.

There is growing evidence that by the age of six children who require intervention can be identified by suitably trained professionals. Certainly it is possible to identify by the age of ten children who are already engaging in serious or persistent offending behaviour and have a high risk of future offending.[77] Early identification and effective intervention with children at risk of future criminal behaviour are probably the most effective means of ensuring the long-term protection of society.

---

77   See, for example, D. Day and A. Hunt, *Predictive Validity of a Risk Model with Under-Twelve Offenders* (Toronto: Earlscourt Child and Family Service Centre, 1993). These researchers conclude that aggressiveness and variety of antisocial behaviour were the best predictors of future delinquent behaviour, and that these were highly correlated with the early-age onset of problem behaviour.

FURTHER READINGS

DALBY, J.T. "Criminal Liability in Children" (1985) 27 Can. J. Crim. 137

CANADA, FEDERAL–PROVINCIAL/TERRITORIAL TASK FORCE ON YOUTH JUSTICE, *A Review of the Young Offenders Act and the Youth Justice System in Canada* (Ottawa: Ministry of Supply and Services, 1996) c. 3

LESCHIED, A.D.W., & S.K. WILSON, "Criminal Liability of Children Under Twelve: A Problem for Child Welfare, Juvenile Justice, or Both?" (1988) 30 Can. J. Crim. 17

PLATT, P. *Young Offenders Law in Canada*, 2d ed. (Toronto: Butterworths, 1995) cc. 4, 5, 6, 9, and 18

WILSON, L.C., "Changes to Federal Jurisdiction Over Young Offenders: The Provincial Response" (1990) 8 Can. J. Fam. L. 303

CHAPTER 4

ARREST, POLICE QUESTIONING, AND PRE-TRIAL DETENTION

A. COMMENCING THE YOUTH JUSTICE PROCESS

Police may become involved in responding to the suspected criminal behaviour of a young person in several ways. They may directly observe the occurrence of what they believe to be an offence, for example, if they observe an assault happening on the street or if they stop the driver of a car who appears to be impaired. More often, police become involved after an alleged offence has occurred in response to a report from a member of the community, such as the victim, a witness, or some other person who knows about the offence. The police will respond to a report of an alleged crime initially by providing immediate assistance to anyone who has been injured and by beginning an investigation. The nature and sophistication of the investigation will depend on the seriousness of the offence.

In less serious cases, especially those involving first offenders, the police may decide to respond to a case outside the formal youth justice court process, perhaps by informally discussing the situation with the youth who is believed to have committed the offence. The officer may issue a warning against the commission of further offences or may refer the youth to be dealt with informally by a community-based program. The police discretion not to formally charge and arrest is an important aspect of the justice system, in particular when young people are concerned. The importance of the police discretion not to charge is underlined in sections 3 and 4 of the *Youth Criminal Justice Act*,[1] which emphasize that police are empowered to employ extrajudicial measures, for example, by cautioning youths or by referring them to a program of extrajudical sanctions. (Diversion from the formal youth justice court process through various forms of extrajudicial measures is discussed in more detail in Chapter 5.) Generally, adolescents tend to be less cautious criminals than adults, and the crimes they commit are usually less difficult for police to solve than those perpetrated by adults. Compared to adults, adolescent offenders are less likely to take steps to hide their identity, and they are more likely to inform friends of their involvement in a crime. Police investigations of crimes often focus on interviewing the victim and witnesses, although some cases involve sophisticated forensic investigative techniques, including fingerprinting, DNA analysis,[2] and such electronic surveillance techniques as wiretapping.

If police have reasonable grounds to believe that a young person has committed a criminal offence for which judicial sanction is an appropriate response, they are in a position to commence a criminal proceeding. This may be done by arresting the suspect or by issuing a document to that person requiring his appearance in court. A youth who is arrested or suspected of committing an offence will usually be interviewed by police. Since many offences committed by adolescents occur in groups, and it is relatively easy to establish that they were in some way involved in the offence, often the greatest challenge for the police is to determine the nature of the involvement and the degree of

---

1   *Youth Criminal Justice Act*, S.C. 2002, c. 1 (royal assent February 19, 2002, to come into force April 1, 2003), often referred to in this book as the *YCJA*.

2   DNA analysis refers to the comparison of human tissue, such as blood, semen, or hair samples, left at a crime scene, with the tissue of a suspected offender. The term DNA, short for deoxyribonucleic acid, refers to the substance that forms the basis of human cells and is distinctive for almost every person; identical twins share the same DNA. Under ss. 487.05 to 487.09 of the *Criminal Code*, R.S.C. 1985, c. C-46, the police can obtain a warrant from a provincial court judge to take tissue samples from a person suspected of committing certain listed, serious offences. The taking of a DNA sample requires the taking from a suspect of a small amount of blood, hair, or saliva (i.e, through a buccal swab from the mouth, a quick, painless, non-invasive procedure). Under s. 487.07(4)–(5), if police are executing a DNA warrant on a young person, they must afford the youth special protections for legal rights similar to those which apply when a statement is being taken from a youth. The young person must be afforded the right to consult with a parent and lawyer before the sample is taken, and to have that person present while the sample is taken. The youth may waive this right in a written, audio- or videotaped waiver.

responsibility of each participant in the crime; in this type of investigation, police interviews with the suspects may be critical to establishing exactly what occurred.

The arrest, questioning, and any detention of a suspected youth offender are governed by the *Canadian Charter of Rights and Freedoms*,[3] the *Criminal Code*, and the *Youth Criminal Justice Act*. At this initial stage of the court process, the *YCJA* provides that young persons have special rights that are intended to afford them special protection and to involve their parents in the justice process. This chapter focuses on the legal issues that arise at the beginning of the youth justice process as a case moves through a police investigation to arrest and possible pre-trial detention. The discussion in this chapter pays particular attention to the special rights of youths under the *YCJA*.[4] There are frequent references in this chapter to judgments decided under the *Young Offenders Act*;[5] although the *Youth Criminal Justice Act* makes some important changes to the law governing police questioning and pre-trial detention, significant portions of that Act are virtually identical to provisions in the *Young Offenders Act* and much of the case law under it remains relevant.

B. SEARCH AND ARREST POWERS AND THE *CHARTER*

In addition to those rights guaranteed to all those who are arrested under the *Criminal Code* and the *Charter*, the *YCJA* affords special rights and protections to young persons who are arrested. Some of these provisions are premised on the recognition that adolescents generally

---

3   *Canadian Charter of Rights and Freedoms*, enacted as Part I of the *Constitution Act, 1982*, being Schedule B to the *Canada Act, 1982* (U.K.), 1982, c. 11 (subsequently referred to as the *Charter*).

4   The general law applicable to the arrest, questioning, and detention of accused persons, both adults and youths, is complex and will only be summarized here. For a more detailed consideration, see, for example, R. Delisle and D. Stuart, *Learning Canadian Criminal Procedure*, 6th ed. (Toronto: Carswell, 2000) c. 2; D. Stuart, *Charter Justice in Canadian Criminal Law*, 3d ed. (Toronto: Carswell, 2001) and T. Quigley, *Procedure in Canadian Criminal Law* (Toronto: Carswell, 1997) cc. 4–11.

5   *Young Offenders Act*, R.S.C 1985, c. Y-1,enacted as S.C. 1980–81–82–83, c. 110. The Act was also amended in 1985 through *An Act to amend the Young Offenders Act, the Criminal Code, the Penitentiary Act, and the Prisons and Reformatories Act*, R.S.C. 1985 (2d Supp.), c. 24, in force September 1, 1986 and November 1, 1986, and in 1995 through *An Act to amend the Young Offenders Act and the Criminal Code*, S.C. 1995, c. 19.

lack the maturity and sophistication to appreciate their situation fully and, hence, require special legal rights. Other provisions are intended to involve parents in the process. Parents are involved under the *YCJA* both to protect the rights of children and to recognize the supportive role that parents may play.

Under section 495(1) of the *Criminal Code*, police officers can, without a warrant, arrest a person who they reasonably believe has committed an indictable or hybrid[6] offence. The police can search any person who has been arrested in order to preserve evidence that might otherwise be lost.[7] If an officer arrests a person for a summary or hybrid offence, like theft under $5000, pursuant to section 495(2) the officer should release the person with a notice to appear in court on a specified date unless the officer believes that detention is necessary to:

- establish the identity of the person;
- secure or preserve evidence;
- prevent the commission of another offence; or
- ensure the attendance of the person in court.

Unless police officers observe a person committing a summary offence, they must go before a justice of the peace to get a warrant to arrest a person believed to have committed a purely summary offence. Ordinarily, the police commence a proceeding for summary offences without making an arrest, and issue a summons or notice to appear in court.

---

6   In the *Criminal Code*, above note 2, offences are categorized as: indictable, summary, and hybrid. Indictable offences are the most serious offences, like robbery and homicide, for which longer sentences may be imposed. Adults charged with indictable offences generally have the right to a preliminary inquiry and a jury trial. A relatively small category of the least serious offences are summary offences, and adults charged with these offences must be tried by a "summary" process without a jury. Many offences, like sexual assault and theft, are hybrid, with the Crown having an "election" (or choice) to proceed summarily or by indictment; for adults, if the Crown elects to proceed summarily, the maximum penalty is a shorter jail term, but the accused loses the opportunity to have a jury trial.

7   *R. v. Stillman*, [1997] 1 S.C.R. 607, discussed later in this chapter, deals with the scope of police authority to search an accused after arrest. The accused was a seventeen-year-old youth charged with sexual assault and murder, who was transferred for trial to adult court. The Supreme Court ruled that hair samples, buccal swabs, and dental impressions taken from the youth after his arrest without his consent violated his rights under the *Charter*, and were inadmissible. The Court held that the relatively intrusive methods needed to take this evidence were not part of a lawful arrest. The arrest in *Stillman* occurred in 1991; since 1995 the *Code*, s. 487.05, can be used by the police to obtain a warrant to take hair samples and buccal swabs for purposes of DNA analysis and comparison to tissue (semen or blood) samples found on the body of a victim.

Section 494 of the *Criminal Code* provides that individual citizens who are not police officers can make an arrest of a person who is in the act of committing an indictable offence. Further, the owner of property, or any individual authorized by the owner, can arrest a person found committing any offence in relation to the property. This arrest power is typically exercised by private security guards or store personnel, who may use "reasonable force" to effect an arrest. However, individuals exercising this arrest power are obliged to contact the police as soon as they make a "citizen's arrest," so that the police can take charge of the person who has been apprehended.

The *Criminal Code* protects an individual from prosecution when making a citizen's arrest as long as the person has reasonable and probable grounds for doing so. Such persons must be cautious, however, in exercising their power to make a citizen's arrest and can be subject to civil liability if they act unreasonably. In a British Columbia civil case, the employees of a store were sued after making a citizen's arrest on a thirteen-year-old boy whom they believed was shoplifting. The claim for compensation for wrongful arrest was ultimately unsuccessful, as the employees were found to have reasonable grounds for their actions — and even perhaps an obligation to make the arrest on the part of their employer. The case highlights the need for caution for those exercising the power to make a citizen's arrest.[8]

1) *Charter* Protections

The rights that are guaranteed to all persons under the *Charter* are doubtless of special significance to young persons, since they are particularly vulnerable to police supervision or deprivations of their rights by adults with good intentions. Sections 8–10 of the *Charter* protect the rights of individuals who have been detained or arrested, providing:

> 8. Everyone has the right to be secure against unreasonable search or seizure.
> 9. Everyone has the right not to be arbitrarily detained or imprisoned.
> 10. Everyone has the right on arrest or detention
>   (*a*) to be informed promptly of the reasons therefor;
>   (*b*) to retain and instruct counsel without delay and to be informed of that right; and
>   (*c*) to have the validity of the detention determined . . . and to be released if the detention is not lawful.

---

8   *Parlee (Guardian ad litem of)* v. *Port of Call Holdings Ltd.*, [2000] B.C.J. No. 698.

The right of an arrested person under section 10(b) of the *Charter* to consult a lawyer on arrest and have a lawyer present during police questioning is, for youths, in addition to the statutory rights under the *YCJA*, such as the right of a young person to consult a parent before making a statement.[9]

If the police violate the *Charter* — for example, by carrying out an illegal search in which they discover incriminating evidence — this does not result in an automatic exclusion of the evidence in later court proceedings. There is generally an onus on the person alleging a *Charter* violation to establish on the civil standard of proof, the "balance of probabilities," that his or her rights have in fact been violated. Then the judge must apply section 24(2) of the *Charter* and determine whether "having regard to all the circumstances, the admission of it in the proceedings would bring the administration of justice into disrepute," which requires an assessment of the seriousness of the *Charter* breach as well as consideration of whether the police were acting in good faith (that is, not knowingly violating the rights of the accused) and whether the evidence was likely to have been obtained even without the rights violation.[10]

In *R. v. V.(I.C.)*, a police officer observed a fifteen-year-old girl chatting quietly on a street corner in a place known by the officer to have an "almost magnetic appeal for children who have run from home, some of whom have become the so-called 'street kids,' and acts as a focal point for many persons involved in prostitution and drug trafficking."[11] The officer believed that she was either "loitering" (an offence removed from the *Code* before the case arose) or was "possibly a runaway," and he purported to arrest her under provincial child welfare legislation.[12] A strug-

---

9   *R. v. I.(L.R.)*, [1993] 4 S.C.R. 504.

10 See *R. v. Stillman*, above note 7, a case involving a transferred young offender, for a case interpreting s.24(2) of the *Charter*, above note 3.

11 *R. v. V.(I. C.)* (25 September 1985) (Ont. Prov. Ct.) [unreported] [summarized 15 W.C.B. 31], per Main Prov. J. The location was the Yonge and Dundas corner of the Eaton Centre in Toronto.

12 Under Ontario's child welfare legislation, *Child and Family Services Act*, R.S.O. 1990, c. C.11, s. 41(4), a peace officer may apprehend a child under sixteen without a warrant, if there are reasonable grounds to believe that the child has left the lawful care of a Children's Aid Society and there is a "substantial risk" to a child's health or safety. Under s. 40(8), a child welfare worker may apprehend a child without a warrant, if there is a "substantial risk to the child's health or safety"; a peace officer may assist in such an apprehension. Under s. 43 of the Act, parents may obtain a warrant from a justice of the peace to have a child under sixteen apprehended by police if the child has left parental care and it is believed that a child's health or safety is at risk. Of course, with the consent of a youth, an officer who considers the youth to be in an "undesirable" location may take the child from that place to his or her home or some other safe place.

gle ensued and the girl was charged with assaulting the police officer. In acquitting the girl of this charge, the judge observed:

> [T]he evidence presented . . . is more than sufficient to find that Christina V.'s rights were infringed under ss. . . . 8 and 9 of the *Charter* . . . she was deprived of her liberty, the security of her person was invaded, her property was unjustly seized and searched and she was arbitrarily detained and imprisoned. These gross violations of her fundamental rights were totally out of proportion with the situation and prescribed nowhere by law. . . . The phenomenon of the runaway child is, in the first instance, a social problem. Left unaddressed, it too often escalates into a legal issue involving either or both child welfare authorities and law enforcement officers. The magnitude of the problem as it relates to downtown Toronto . . . requires an urgent response. Undoubtedly, as a result of pressure from concerned parents, politicians and business people in the area, the . . . Police Department has felt obliged to provide that response. Unfortunately, the standard law enforcement approach to the problem is woefully inadequate as well as improper.
>
> As exhibited in this case, good faith and a sense of duty on the part of the police fall far short of addressing the situation. The runaway child who has been reported missing but has not committed any criminal offence may be a child at risk. That is the issue which must be addressed first and it can only be accomplished in a competent and caring fashion by trained child-care workers.[13]

In *R. v. W.(J.P.)* a police officer obtained some information which suggested that a particular youth might be in possession of stolen property, but the officer did not have sufficient evidence to obtain a search warrant, let alone charge the youth.[14] The officer went to the youth's home but he was not there. The officer obtained the permission of the father to search the youth's room, where he discovered some stolen items. While the search was in progress, the youth returned home and was arrested; his permission for the search of his room was not sought. Judge Howard of the British Columbia Provincial Court ruled that the father could not waive his son's "reasonable expectation of privacy" and his rights under section 8 of the *Charter*. The evidence was excluded and the youth acquitted. The judge observed that: "Young persons, like adults, are fully entitled to the rights secured by the *Charter*. . . .

---

13   *R. v. V.(I. C.)* , above note 11.

14   *R. v. W.(J.P.)*, [1993] B.C.J. No. 2891 (Youth Ct.) (QL). See also *R. v. L.R.M.* (1988), 5 W.C.B. (2d) 432 (N.S.Fam Ct.).

What more private place could teenagers have than their bedroom. . . . The risk that a parent might [lawfully] enter a teenager's bedroom does not destroy the right that a young person has against unlawful and unreasonable intrusion by the agents of the state."[15] The decision in *R. v. W.(J.P.)* illustrates that judges are prepared to protect the rights of accused young persons and encourage police compliance with the law, even if this means that youths who are in fact guilty are acquitted.

While this principle is accepted by all judges, the issue of police searches of a youth's room with only the permission of a parent is contentious and the Alberta Court of Appeal took a different approach to this type of search from that by Judge Howard. In *R. v. D.M.F.*,[16] the Alberta Court of Appeal dismissed the appeal of a sixteen-year-old youth for the violent sexual assault of two women in which crucial evidence had been obtained as a result of a search of the youth's room without his permission. The case arose out of the sexual assault of two women, each of whom had been raped at a different time by an unknown assailant, whose face was partially covered. Each victim had been taken to a doctor by the police and a semen swab taken from her vagina, enabling the police to obtain DNA identifying the assailant. As a result of their investigations and prior knowledge of him, the police suspected that D.M.F. might be the assailant, but they lacked sufficient evidence to arrest him. He agreed to be questioned by the police but did not confess to the crime.

A few days after they questioned him, the police went to his home in the hope of obtaining some items of his clothing that would allow them to do a DNA identification. The youth was not at home but the police officers spoke to his mother, who had previously contacted them to complain about his behaviour, including her suspicions that he had defrauded her by charging long-distance telephone calls to her number without her permission. The officers asked to search his room, briefly explaining to the mother the implications of a DNA identification of her son as the assailant in the sexual assaults. The mother took the officers to her son's room. The door was closed but not locked. The officers took two pairs of boxer shorts that were lying on the floor and later DNA analysis identified semen on the shorts which matched the semen of the assailant.

A major issue at the trial of the youth, D.M.F., was the legality of the seizure of his boxer shorts. Although other forensic evidence was later gathered to link him to the sexual assaults, at the time the shorts were

---

15   *R. v. W.(J.P.)*, *ibid.* at paras. 23–25.
16   *R. v. D.M.F.*, [1999] A.J. No. 1086 (C.A.)

taken the police did not have a warrant to search his room. The lawyer for the youth argued that the shorts had been taken in violation of section 8 of the *Charter*, which protects against "unreasonable [and unlawful] search and seizure." The trial judge and Court of Appeal held that the shorts had been obtained lawfully because the mother consented to the search. Justice Hetherington in the Court of Appeal wrote:

> Mr. D.M.F. was not present when the detectives searched his bedroom. Certainly he had possession of this room, but he did not have control of it. He could not regulate access to it. The trial judge made the following findings . . . :
>
>> Mrs. M.L.F. imposed house rules that she expected the accused to follow. These rules included a curfew, no girlfriends staying overnight, and no smoking in his bedroom. There was a lock on the accused's bedroom door, but it was easily unlocked with either a coin or a piece of metal.
>>
>> Mrs. M.L.F. entered the room a couple of times a week to pick up dirty clothing for the laundry, return clean clothing and to tidy the room. Although the accused objected on occasion, she told him that she would continue to enter the room until he assumed the responsibility for the laundry and for keeping the room clean.
>
> In addition, Mrs. M.L.F. testified that several other occupants of the house went into Mr. D.M.F.'s room without his permission. One of them sometimes borrowed his clothes.
>
> There was nothing in the evidence to suggest that Mr. D.M.F. had a subjective expectation of privacy, and such an expectation would have been unreasonable in the circumstances.
>
> In conclusion, Mr. D.M.F. did not have a reasonable expectation of privacy in relation to his bedroom or its contents. It follows that neither the search of his bedroom by Detective Holland and Detective Vogan, nor their removal of the boxer shorts from the room, violated Mr. D.M.F.'s right under s. 8 of the *Charter*.[17]

It is a common practice for the police to obtain a warrant before searching a youth's room, even with the parent's consent, as this avoids entering into the uncertain area of search without consent. Since 1998 it has also been possible for the police to obtain a warrant to directly take DNA samples from a suspect, usually by plucking a few hairs from him or obtaining a saliva swab from his mouth.[18] However, in *D.M.F.*,

17 *Ibid.* at paras. 81–84.
18 See ss. 487.05 to 487.09 of the *Criminal Code*, above note 2.

when the police seized the youth's shorts, the police may not have had the reasonable grounds needed to obtain a search warrant.

In some cases, the youthful victims of an improper police arrest may obtain monetary compensation for false arrest and imprisonment, as occurred in *Walkley v. Canada (A.G.)*[19] A storekeeper in a small British Columbia town noticed that a teddy bear was missing immediately after three girls left the store, but she had not seen them take anything. A person outside the store reported to the storekeeper that through the window he had seen one of the girls take the teddy bear. The police were immediately notified and two officers soon located the girls, two of whom were twelve, and the other was eleven years old. The officer questioned the girls, who denied taking the teddy bear. They had been Christmas shopping and produced receipts for all the goods in their possession; at an officer's request they opened their jackets and emptied their pockets but no teddy bear was discovered. The officers nevertheless concluded that the girls had committed the theft and told one of them that she was a "liar and a thief." She was arrested, handcuffed, and taken to the police station; the other girls were also accused of lying and taken to the station. Upset and crying, the girls were questioned by the police and were eventually placed in a holding cell.

Shortly after the arrest, a parent of one of the girls was located but was told by the police that it would be "a good lesson for the girls" to leave them longer at the police station. The parents did not come to take the girls home for more than two hours after they were arrested. No teddy bear was ever recovered and the girls were not charged. The girls, acting through their parents as litigation guardians, sued the police officers and government, and each girl was awarded $10,000 for what the court characterized as "an extremely traumatic experience . . . which was entirely unnecessary."[20] The judge accepted that the initial questioning of the girls was reasonable and lawful but that, thereafter, the conduct of the police was unacceptable since the circumstances and nature of the alleged offence did not justify the arrest and imprisonment of the girls:

> [L]iberty is a hallmark of our society . . . [and] children in our society ought to be the constant object of our nurturing and support. In cases such as this where people and property are not at risk, where there is no violence, where the demeanour of the children is normal, where there is no attempt to be evasive and where time and distance

---

19   *Walkley v. Canada (A.G.)*, [1997] B.C.J. No. 599 (S.C.) (QL).
20   *Ibid.* at para. 78.

allow a quick check on identification, there can be no justification for the arrest and imprisonment of 11 and 12 year old children.[21]

This case illustrates that police cannot take the law into their own hands and seek to punish youths to "teach them a lesson."

Just as police cannot take the law into their own hands, neither can they take events into their own hands by manipulating circumstances to induce a youth to commit a crime and then arrest the youth. Undercover police surveillance operations may become so intrusive as to constitute entrapment and charges based on the youth's conduct in such circumstances will be stayed as an abuse of the legal process. The entrapment defence was successful in R. v. J.S., a case in which the a youth was arrested for trafficking in marijuana as a result of a $10 sale to undercover police officers outside the site of a Marilyn Manson music concert. The youth was going to the concert with some friends, bringing with him $30 worth of marijuana which he had purchased, intending to smoke it at the concert with the friends. While standing outside a fast-food restaurant near the concert site, the youth was approached by two undercover officers dressed in the attire of Manson concert-goers (i.e., white face makeup and black wigs). One of the officers approached the youth, after making a comment that he was unable to find any drugs in Hamilton, and asked if anyone knew where he could "score some weed." The youth asked how much the officer was looking for. The officer replied that he just wanted enough "for a few joints . . . a dime." While the youth discussed with his friends whether he should sell any of the marijuana, the undercover officer continued to press for the sale.

At his trial, the youth testified that he was hungry and wanted to buy some food but he did not have any money; he also stated that he had had some concerns about his safety if he refused to make the sale as the purported buyers were much bigger and older than him. The youth told the officer to meet him in the washroom of a fast-food restaurant, where he sold them $10 worth of marijuana and was then arrested. The Ontario Court of Appeal held that this was a case of "entrapment" as the conduct of the police went "beyond providing an opportunity to commit the crime [and actually] induce[d] the commission of an offence."[22] The Court of Appeal concluded that the youth would not have sold the marijuana had he not been pressured by the undercover officers into making the sale, and stayed the proceedings as an abuse of process.

---

21 *Ibid.* at para. 67.
22 *R. v. J.S.* , [2001] O.J. No. 104 (C.A.) at para 5.

2) Searches and Investigations by School Officials

A significant amount of offending behaviour occurs in schools, including thefts, assaults, intimidation, and drug dealing. Concerns that this type of offending behaviour by some students can intimidate or injure other students and staff and may undermine the educational environment are understandable. A public perception exists that there have been dramatic increases in drug dealing and violence in Canadian schools.[23] Politicians and school boards have responded to these concerns with safe-school and zero-tolerance policies, which require notification of police as well as suspension or expulsion from school for students who have violated school policies about drugs, violence, or possession of weapons.

It is important that students are not subjected to bullying, intimidation, or injury from other students, and that there are appropriate responses to the use of drugs or alcohol in school. However, there are concerns that school authorities and police may be responding to certain types of less serious offending in an overly intrusive manner. It is a common perception of teachers that violence and drug use by students are more serious concerns than in the past. However, many situations of minor offending in schools, which in the past would have been dealt with by school officials, are now resulting in the police being called and youths being subject to inappropriate charges in the youth justice system.[24] As well, there are concerns that sometimes the responses of school officials may result in the violation of the rights of students.

A tragic Ontario incident highlights the dangers that may arise if school officials decide to involve police in the questioning of students about suspected violations of school rules without notifying the parents of the students involved. A high-school student with an excellent record was the editor of the student yearbook which, as a prank, contained material describing fictitious sexually improper conduct by some of the staff members — material which was clearly inappropriate for a student yearbook (or any other medium). Instead of disciplining the student and informing his parents, the school authorities called the police, who interviewed the youth and threatened him with possible legal sanctions as a result of the publication prank, without his parents

---

23   See "Schools are More Violent: Poll," *Globe and Mail*, September 8, 1998. In *R. v. M.R.M.*, [1998] 3 S.C.R. 393, Cory J. remarked, without citing any evidence: "Schools today are faced with extremely difficult problems which were unimaginable a generation ago" (at para 3).

24   See, for example, W.N. Welsh, "Effects of Student and School Factors on Five Measures of School Disorder" (2001) 18 Justice Quarterly 911–47.

being notified of the investigation.[25] A few days later, without the parents knowing what had transpired and with no charges being laid, the boy committed suicide. The coroner's inquest recommended that schools should notify parents if their children are involved in a police investigation as a result of events related to the school. The report also recommended a uniform approach across the province to access to students by police at school. While this case is tragic and extreme, it does illustrate the need for sensitivity in responding to allegations of misconduct by adolescents in the schools and for involving parents at an early stage in any investigative process so that they can provide appropriate support to their children.

In 1998 the Supreme Court of Canada decided *R. v. M.R.M.*,[26] ruling on the constitutionality of searches conducted by school officials. The vice-principal of a high school was told by several student informants that another student was selling drugs at the school, and was told by one of the informants that it was likely the student would be carrying drugs that evening at a school dance. When the student arrived at the school the vice-principal telephoned the police, in accordance with school policy about drug searches. The vice-principal then approached the student and a friend and asked them to come to his office. In his office, the vice-principal asked each of the students if they were in possession of drugs, which they denied, and the vice-principal said that he wanted to search the students. A plain-clothes police officer conferred briefly with the vice-principal, and then entered with the vice-principal the room where the students were waiting. The vice-principal then asked the students to empty their pockets and roll up their pant legs. Noticing a bulge in the sock of the student suspected of selling drugs, the vice-principal then removed a cellophane bag from the student's sock, which he gave to the officer. The officer identified the contents as marijuana and arrested the youth, informing him of his right to counsel.

At issue in the Supreme Court was the legality of the search by the vice-principal. If the search had been conducted by the police officer directly, it would have violated sections 8 and 10 of the *Charter*, since the students were detained without being advised of their constitutional rights and it was a warrantless search of an individual prior to arrest. Justice Cory, writing for a majority of the Supreme Court, held that in this case the school official's "primary motive" was the enforcement of school discipline and he was "not acting as an agent for the police"

---

25   Green, S. "Schools Must Keep Parents Informed, Inquest Says," *Globe and Mail*, July 11, 1998.

26   *R. v. M.R.M.*, [1998] 3 S.C.R. 393.

and, hence, should not be held to the same legal standards as the police. The Court concluded that students in school have a "reduced expectation of privacy," observing that teachers and principals must be able to act quickly to enforce discipline and protect the school environment. While in some cases school officials might be viewed as "agents of the state" and held to the same standards as police officers, they should generally not be held to the same standards as police officers when questioning a youth or conducting a search.

Accordingly, as long as a school official has reasonable grounds to believe that a violation of school regulations or discipline has occurred, a reasonable search and interview of a student may be conducted. An important factor in deciding whether the search of a student is reasonable includes a consideration of the credibility and specificity of the information which resulted in the search. In M.R.M., several students whom the vice-principal believed to be credible specifically identified the suspect as dealing in drugs at the school, and one identified a specific time when it was likely that he would have drugs in his possession. The Court also held that searches to be carried out must be "reasonable," taking account of the age and gender of the student, as well as the purpose and intrusiveness of the search. The Court specifically mentioned that a search for a weapon might have to be carried out more quickly and intrusively, and observed that a search for drugs of a female student by a male teacher may well be "inappropriate and unreasonable."

The majority of the Supreme Court concluded that, in this case, the search of the student was reasonable and hence legal. Justice Cory emphasized that the lower constitutional expectations for the conduct of school officials only applies if they are acting to "maintain order, discipline and safety within the school."[27] It was significant in M.R.M. that the vice-principal had contacted the police officer and invited him to be present, and the officer was a "mere observer" during the search. If, however, a school official is contacted by the police for assistance in a police investigation, it would seem that, for the purposes of the Charter and the YCJA, the school official would become an "agent of the police" and a student would be entitled to all of the constitutional and statutory protections that apply before the police can detain and search a person.

In a dissenting opinion in R. v. M.R.M., Major J. agreed that in principle students have a lowered expectation of privacy when in school and that school officials who are enforcing school discipline are not bound by the same restraints as the police. In this case, however, he argued that, since the police officer spoke to the vice-principal before

27   Ibid. at para. 55.

the search was conducted and the officer was present during the search, the vice-principal became an "agent of the police" and the youth should have been afforded the same rights as if the search were conducted directly by the police. The majority judgment in M.R.M. has been criticized by commentators for reducing the rights of students.[28] Professor Wayne MacKay argues that, by lowering the expectations for the conduct of school officials, there has been a "fusion of roles, the parental, the educational and the police enforcer," resulting in a situation in which the rights of students in schools are "diluted to level of those enjoyed by prison inmates and other institutionalized citizens."[29]

Shortly after M.R.M. was decided, an incident at a school near Windsor, Ontario, drew national attention to the issue of school officials searching teens. In that incident, a male teacher and a male vice-principal were trying to recover some money that a student had reported stolen. They asked the twenty male grade-nine students in the victim's gym class if any of them had taken it, and they all denied it. The teacher and vice-principal then strip-searched all of the boys but still failed to find the stolen money. Some of the boys were very upset and told their parents, who contacted lawyers and the media. The strip-search drew national attention to the issue of student rights and resulted in the suspension of the teacher and the vice-principal. While no criminal charges were laid against the school officials, a civil action was launched by the boys, which resulted in a settlement being paid by the school board.[30] This incident led to a public outcry, which prompted many school boards to develop policies prohibiting strip-searches by school officials and clarifying policies about the search of students by teachers.[31]

A strip-search of an adolescent is a highly intrusive act, and it would be extremely difficult to ever legally justify a school official doing this to a student. If there is a sufficiently high level of concern about suspected serious criminal activity, school officials should contact the police, who can decide whether there are sufficient grounds to justify an arrest and a strip-search. Police have also been criticized for

---

28 See D. Stuart, "Reducing *Charter* Rights of School Children" (1999), 20 C.R. (5th) 230.

29 A.W. MacKay, "Don't Mind Me, I'm From the R.C.M.P" (1997), 7 C.R. (5th) 24 at 33 (annotation to NSCA in R. v. *M.R.M.*). See also A.W. MacKay, "Students as Second Class Citizens Under the *Charter*" (1987), 54 C.R. (3d) 390.

30 See M. Philp, "Strip-Search Teachers Suspended for Reviews," *Globe and Mail*, December 10, 1998; also "No Charges Laid Against Teachers Who Strip-Searched Boys," *Globe and Mail*, December 19, 1998; V. Galt, "Settlement Ends Students' Strip-Search Lawsuit," *Globe and Mail*, October 27, 1999.

31 R. Brennan, "Education Minister Orders New Guidelines After Ontario Strip Search," *National Post*, December 9, 1998.

inappropriate strip-searches of adolescents, such as one involving a thirteen-year-old girl after an alleged incident of shoplifting.[32] While police officers do have the right to strip-search individuals who have been arrested, the Supreme Court of Canada has made clear that a strip-search is a "serious infringement of privacy and personal dignity."[33] Even with suspected adult drug dealers, such searches by the police are only constitutionally valid if they are conducted as an incident to a lawful arrest: for the purpose of discovering weapons in the detainee's possession, in order to ensure the safety of the police, the detainee, and other persons; or for the purpose of discovering evidence related to the reason for the arrest and to prevent its disposal by the detainee. In addition to reasonable and probable grounds justifying the arrest, the police must establish reasonable and probable grounds justifying the strip-search. Generally, strip-searches should be conducted only at the police station, except where there are exigent circumstances requiring that the detainee be searched prior to being transported there, and should be conducted by an officer of the same gender as the detainee.

Since *R. v. M.R.M.*, judges have generally been prepared to uphold the legality of the search of a locker by a teacher or vice-principal. The courts have observed that the search of a student's locker in a school is less intrusive than the search of a student's person. Further, since school officials generally have a master key for locks and a policy that makes clear to students that lockers may be searched, "the degree of control that the school administration maintains over [the lockers lowers] . . . the expectation of privacy" that students should have in regard to their lockers.[34] Even the search of a student's locker has to be done on reasonable grounds; if school authorities decided to search every locker in the school in the hope that some illegal objects might be found, there would be a significant question as to whether any evidence obtained would be regarded as legally seized.

B. POLICE QUESTIONING

Often the most important part of a police investigation of a crime is the questioning of a suspect with the view to obtaining a confession of guilt, or information that would implicate others or perhaps serve to

---

32   See K. Makin, "Humiliating Police Strip Search Still Haunts 13 year old Girl," *Globe and Mail*, January 15, 1999.

33   *R. v. Golden*, [2001] S.C.J. 81, 159 C.C.C. (3d) 449.

34   See, for example, *R. v. S.M.Z.* (1998), 21 C.R. (5th) 170 (Man. C.A.).

exonerate a suspect. While a confession is often evidence of guilt, it may also be used as the basis for discovering other physical evidence of guilt. If there are multiple perpetrators, as is common with offences committed by adolescents, a statement by one party to an offence may serve to induce others involved to give a statement as well, in order to give their version of the events in question. Further, if a suspect confesses — even if there might be some doubt about the admissibility of the confession because of violation of legal rights — it may serve as a psychological inducement to plead guilty later.

A number of constitutional and common law rules govern the admissibility of statements made by adult suspects to the police. Because adolescents have less knowledge and sophistication than adults, and are less likely to appreciate the consequences of making a statement to the police, there are added legal requirements in the YCJA and the case law that the police are expected to follow when questioning young persons. These special requirements are intended both to protect the legal rights of adolescents and to reduce the possibility that they will be induced to make a false confession to a crime that they did not in fact commit. Despite the existence of these protections, adolescents are more likely than adults to make a confession to the police.

Because of the complexity of the rules about the admissibility of the statements of youths and the importance of this type of evidence of guilt, one of the most frequently litigated issues in the trials of young persons is the admissibility of their statements. Despite the relatively large number of trials dealing with the issue and the large body of reported case law, it should be appreciated that the police often satisfy all of the legal requirements for the taking of a statement from a youth, and the confession is the basis of a guilty plea or a conviction. The cases that are most likely to result in trials where the admissibility of a statement is a central issue are those in which there is some argument that the police failed to comply with all of the legal requirements for the taking of a statement. The legal requirements for the admissibility of a young person's statements in the YCJA are quite similar to those found in the YOA, although, as a result of the lobbying efforts of police and the provincial attorneys general, there have been a number of changes that will make it a little easier for the Crown to persuade a youth justice court that a confession made by a youth to the police should be admitted.

Police officers have extensive training in the questioning of suspects. Police training includes instruction on the basic legal rules for the admissibility of statements as well as on a variety of psychological tactics that can be used to induce a suspect to start to talk to police and eventually make a statement.[35] Most suspects do not initially want to talk to the police but, not infrequently, they may be induced to make a statement that will be admissible in court. The police may, for example, start off the questioning simply by telling a suspect that the police want to hear his or her side of the story. After the suspect gives a version of the events, or denies any knowledge of them, the police may confront the suspect with evidence they have obtained that is inconsistent with the story the suspect has told. The police may then, for example, suggest that the suspect will feel better if he confesses.

1) False Confessions

The police sometimes use a variety of forms of deception when attempting to obtain a statement from a suspect. The police may, for example, tell a suspect that they have evidence implicating him or her which they do not have, such as falsely saying they have a statement from an alleged co-perpetrator that implicates the suspect. More typically the police will not actually lie, but they may inflate the reliability of the incriminating evidence that they have implicating the suspect. In *R. v. Rothman*, Lamer J. remarked: "[T]he investigation of crime and the detection of criminals is not a game to be governed by the Marquess of Queensbury rules. The authorities, in dealing with shrewd and often sophisticated criminals, must sometimes of necessity resort to tricks or other forms of deceit and should not through the rule be hampered in their work. What should be repressed vigorously is conduct on their part that shocks the community."[36]

Police are subject to organizational and social pressures to solve crimes. The desire for an expeditious resolution to an investigation may threaten the presumption of innocence and result in pressures to secure a confession from a person who is not in fact guilty.[37] While false confessions may be relatively rare, they do occur.[38] Police-induced

---

35   See, for example, John E. Hess, *Interviewing and Interrogation for Law Enforcement* (Cincinnati, OH: Anderson Pub. Co., 1997).

36   *R. v. Rothman*, [1981] 1 S.C.R. 640 at 679.

37   See also J. Williams, "Interrogating Justice: A Critical Analysis of the Police Interrogation and its Role in the Criminal Justice Process" (2000) 42 Can. J. Crim. 209.

38   For example, an American case illustrates the increased possibility of adolescents making false confessions. In that case, the adolescent brother of a murder victim and some of his friends were suspects in the killing of a young girl. The teenage suspects were questioned for two days alone without parents or a lawyer present, and ultimately made false confessions. Police had told the boys a series of lies during the course of the interrogations, which helped induce the false

false confessions can result in significant miscarriages of justice, and are more likely to occur as a result of the questioning of suspects who are mentally handicapped, or otherwise vulnerable, such as adolescents.[39] The problem of false confessions being induced from vulnerable witnesses was recognized as a real concern by the Supreme Court of Canada in *R. v. Oickle*, where the Court quoted with approval several American scholars who have done research on the issue of false confessions, including Welsh White, who observed: "False confessions are particularly likely when the police interrogate particular types of suspects, including suspects who are especially vulnerable as a result of their background, special characteristics, or situation, suspects who have compliant personalities, and, in rare instances, suspects whose personalities make them prone to accept and believe police suggestions made during the course of the interrogation."[40]

While the Supreme Court does not give a clear idea of what type of police conduct is unacceptable, the decision in *Oickle* indicates that, with an adult suspect, there is significant scope for psychological inducements to the making of a statement without rendering a statement inadmissible. The police may, for example, assure a suspect that he will "feel better" and receive psychiatric help to deal with the problems that led to his criminal behaviour if he confesses. The Court indicated, however, that police trickery could be a ground for ruling a statement inadmissible. Justice Iacobucci noted that the issue of police trickery was related to but distinct from concerns about the "voluntariness" of a statement made to the police, concluding: "There may be situations in which police trickery, although neither violating the right to silence nor undermining voluntariness *per se*, is so appalling as to shock the community."[41]

The implication of the statements of Lamer J. in *Rothman* and Iacobucci J. in *Oickle* is that, when police are questioning naive and unsophisticated youths who may be easily misled, there should be less judicial tolerance for any forms of police trickery or deception than when they are questioning more mature or sophisticated adults. The

---

confessions. A paranoid schizophrenic transient was later found to have committed the murder. See S. Crowe, "The Confession," *CBS News*, June 20, 2000, online at <cbsnews.cbs.com>.

39   R. Ofshe and R. Leo, "The Social Psychology of Interrogation" (1997) 16 Studies in Law, Politics & Society 189; and R. Leo and R. Offshe, "The Consequences of False Confessions" (1998) 88 J. Crim. L. & Criminology 429.

40   W.S. White, "False Confessions and the Constitution: Safeguards against Untrustworthy Confessions" (1997) 32 Harv. C.R.–C.L. L.Rev. 105 at 120, quoted with approval in *R. v. Oickle*, [2000] 2 S.C.R. 3 at para. 42.

41   *R. v. Oickle*, above note 40 at para. 67.

relative immaturity and lack of sophistication of most adolescents suggest that the courts should exercise greater scrutiny when considering police inducements or trickery that may have induced a confession. In particular, if the police confront a witness with the existence of "evidence" that does not in fact exist, some suspects, especially relatively naive and vulnerable adolescents, may confess to crimes that they did not in fact commit.[42]

The statutory and common law rules that afford youths special protections when being questioned by the police, such as section 146 of the *YCJA*, are in part a response to concerns about the possibility of the police inducing an adolescent into making a false confession. There is also a recognition that adolescents generally lack the knowledge, sophistication, and experience to appreciate the implications of making a statement to the police, and accordingly are entitled to special cautions and legal protections. It must, however, be emphasized that individual youths, after being properly advised of their legal rights, may decide to waive their legal rights and make a statement. As long as they have been properly advised of their rights and have not been subjected to improper inducements or threats, a confession made by a young person to the police will be admitted in court. Indeed, even after being advised of their rights, adolescents seem more likely to confess their crimes to the police than adults in similar circumstances.

2) Special Protection When Police Question Youths: Section 146

In addition to the general protections afforded to all persons at the time of arrest under the *Charter*, special provisions in section 146 of the *YCJA* are intended to ensure that there is no improper questioning of young persons by police or other persons "in authority." Despite these protections, most youths who are questioned by the police will ultimately make a statement that implicates them in the offence. The taking of a statement from a youth is often an important part of a police investigation and, later, of the Crown's case in court against the youth. In practice most cases are ultimately resolved by a guilty plea, but if there is a trial, one of the issues most likely to be litigated is the admis-

---

42 *Ibid.* Iacobucci J wrote: "Another theme is the *danger of* using non-existent evidence. Presenting a suspect with entirely fabricated evidence has the potential either to persuade the susceptible suspect that he did indeed commit the crime, or at least to convince the suspect that any protestations of innocence are futile" (at para. 43).

sibility of the youth's statement to the police. So the taking of statements is an important issue for police officers who work on young offenders' cases, as well as for judges and lawyers in youth justice court.

The statutory provision that governs the admissibility of statements made by young persons, and accordingly regulates police practice, is section 146 of the YCJA. The rules governing police questioning of young persons set out in section 146 of the new Act are similar to those in section 56 of the YOA. Section 146 of the YCJA provides:

> **146** (1) Subject to this section, the law relating to the admissibility of statements made by persons accused of committing offences applies in respect of young persons.
>
> (2) No oral or written statement made by a young person who is less than eighteen years old, to a peace officer or to any other person who is, in law, a person in authority, on the arrest or detention of the young person or in circumstances where the peace officer or other person has reasonable grounds for believing that the young person has committed an offence is admissible against the young person unless
>
> (*a*) the statement was voluntary;
>
> (*b*) the person to whom the statement was made has, before the statement was made, clearly explained to the young person, in language appropriate to his or her age and understanding, that
>
> > (*i*)   the young person is under no obligation to make a statement,
> >
> > (*ii*) any statement made by the young person may be used as evidence in proceedings against him or her,
> >
> > (*iii*) the young person has the right to consult counsel and a parent or other person in accordance with paragraph (c), and
> >
> > (*iv*) any statement made by the young person is required to be made in the presence of counsel and any other person consulted in accordance with paragraph (c), if any, unless the young person desires otherwise;
>
> (*c*) the young person has, before the statement was made, been given a reasonable opportunity to consult
>
> > (*i*)   with counsel, and
> >
> > (*ii*) with a parent or, in the absence of a parent, an adult relative or, in the absence of a parent and an adult relative, any other appropriate adult chosen by the young person, as long as that person is not a co-accused, or under investigation, in respect of the same offence; and

(*d*) if the young person consults a person in accordance with paragraph (c), the young person has been given a reasonable opportunity to make the statement in the presence of that person.

(4) A young person may waive the rights under paragraph (2)(c) or (d) but any such waiver

(*a*) must be recorded on video tape or audio tape; or
(*b*) must be in writing and contain a statement signed by the young person that he or she has been informed of the right being waived.

(5) When a waiver of rights under paragraph (2)(c) or (d) is not made in accordance with section (4) owing to a technical irregularity, the youth justice court may determine that the waiver is valid if it is satisfied that the young person was informed of his or her rights, and voluntarily waived them.

(6) When there has been a technical irregularity in complying with paragraphs (2)(b) to (d), the youth justice court may admit into evidence a statement referred to in section (2), if satisfied that the admission of the statement would not bring into disrepute the principle that young persons are entitled to enhanced procedural protection to ensure that they are treated fairly and their rights are protected.

(7) A youth justice court judge may rule inadmissible in any proceedings under this Act a statement made by the young person in respect of whom the proceedings are taken if the young person satisfies the judge that the statement was made under duress imposed by any person who is not, in law, a person in authority.

(8) A youth justice court judge may in any proceedings under this Act rule admissible any statement or waiver by a young person if, at the time of the making of the statement or waiver,

(*a*) the young person held himself or herself to be eighteen years old or older;
(*b*) the person to whom the statement or waiver was made conducted reasonable inquiries as to the age of the young person and had reasonable grounds for believing that the young person was eighteen years old or older; and
(*c*) in all other circumstances the statement or waiver would otherwise be admissible.

Section 146(2)(a) provides that a youth's statement must be "voluntary," and so the common law jurisprudence on the general concept of "voluntariness" applies to the statements of youths. If the issue of the voluntariness of a statement arises, the onus is on the Crown to prove "beyond a reasonable doubt" that the statement is truly voluntary.[43]

While there is a large body of jurisprudence defining the elusive concept of "voluntariness," the classical articulation of the principle is from the 1914 Privy Council decision in *Ibrahim v. the King*. In that case it was held that an incriminating statement made by a suspect to a "person in authority" is only admissible if it is proven beyond a reasonable doubt to have been made without "fear of prejudice or hope of advantage exercised or held out by a person in authority."[44] In its decision in 2000 in *R. v. Oickle*, the Supreme Court of Canada observed that this old rule is too narrow, and a broader set of circumstances may be considered as rendering a statement "involuntary." A statement may also be considered involuntary if it is not the product of an "operative mind" or if it is the product of oppressive circumstances. Justice Iacobucci summarized the law:

> While the foregoing might suggest that the confessions rule involves a panoply of different considerations and tests, in reality the basic idea is quite simple. First of all, because of the criminal justice system's overriding concern not to convict the innocent, a confession will not be admissible if it is made under circumstances that raise a reasonable doubt as to voluntariness. Both the traditional, narrow *Ibrahim* rule and the oppression doctrine recognize this danger. If the police interrogators subject the suspect to utterly intolerable conditions, or if they offer inducements strong enough to produce an unreliable confession, the trial judge should exclude it. Between these two extremes, oppressive conditions and inducements can operate together to exclude confessions. Trial judges must be alert to the entire circumstances surrounding a confession in making this decision.

---

43   In general the onus is on the accused to establish a violation of the *Charter*, above note 3, on the balance of probabilities: *R. v. Collins*, [1987] 1 S.C.R. 265. An exception to this rule arises in the context of the admissibility of a statement, where the onus is on the Crown to prove all issues related to the admissibility of the statement beyond a reasonable doubt. This includes a Crown onus to establish that there was a proper waiver of the *Charter* right to consult with counsel: see *R. v. Leclair*, [1989] 1 S.C.R. 3 and D. Stuart, *Charter Justice*, above note 4, at 41–42. Placing the onus on the Crown to establish a waiver of the *Charter* right to consult with counsel is especially appropriate for young persons, since for a youth the duty on the police to advise of the right to consult with counsel arises both under the *Charter* and the statute.

44   *Ibrahim v. R.*, [1914] A.C. 599 at 609 (P.C.).

The doctrines of oppression and inducements are primarily concerned with reliability. However . . . the confessions rule also extends to protect a broader conception of voluntariness "that focuses on the protection of the accused's rights and fairness in the criminal process.". . . Voluntariness is the touchstone of the confessions rule. Whether the concern is threats or promises, the lack of an operating mind, or police trickery that unfairly denies the accused's right to silence, this Court's jurisprudence has consistently protected the accused from having involuntary confessions introduced into evidence. If a confession is involuntary for any of these reasons, it is inadmissible. . . .

I would also like to emphasize that the analysis under the confessions rule must be a contextual one. . . . Instead, a court should strive to understand the circumstances surrounding the confession and ask if it gives rise to a reasonable doubt as to the confession's voluntariness, taking into account all the aspects of the rule discussed above.[45]

A statement made in response to police threats of violence is involuntary and hence inadmissible. The police telling a youth "You might as well tell us the whole truth instead of getting yourself into more trouble," may also be regarded as a threat rendering a statement involuntary and inadmissible.[46] A youth's statement made after police tell him that they will help him secure a lesser sentence if he co-operates with them and makes a statement will be viewed a "promise of advantage" that will render a statement involuntary.[47]

A court must consider all of the circumstances of a case when deciding whether a statement is voluntary and may consider whether the statement was made in "oppressive conditions," such as when the suspect was deprived of food, water, or sleep, or was subjected to prolonged, excessively aggressive questioning.

A statement is voluntary only if it is the product of an "operating mind." Statements have been ruled inadmissible because of the suspect's impairment by drugs or alcohol;[48] this can apply to those adolescents who are in an impaired physical or emotional state when being questioned by the police.[49] There is a clear onus on the Crown to establish that a statement that was made to the police or another person in

---

45 *R. v. Oickle*, above note 40, at paras. 68–71.
46 *R. v. C.(D.E.)* (11 August 1986), (Ont. Prov. Ct. (Fam. Div.)) [unreported] [summarized [1986] W.D.F.L. 2047], Morrison Prov. J.
47 *R. v. C.(D.J.)* (1993), 124 N.S.R. (2d) 371 (C.A.).
48 *R. v. Clarkson*, [1986] 1 S.C.R. 383.
49 See, for example, *R. v. R.(No.1)* (1972), 9 C.C.C. 274 (Ont. Prov. Ct. (Fam. Div.)).

authority was truly voluntary. Often there are very significant differences in the testimony of the police and an accused person about what was said during an interrogation session that resulted in a statement being made to the police. Increasingly the courts expect police to video- or audiotape all of the interrogation of a suspect.

In *R. v. Moore-MacFarlane*, the Ontario Court of Appeal ruled inadmissible an alleged confession made by a young adult male to police officers. The accused claimed that he was coerced into making a false confession after he was assaulted and interrogated while naked. The police denied that any assault had occurred and said that the accused was in his underwear and socks. Justice Charron observed:

> the Crown bears the onus of establishing a sufficient record of the interaction between the suspect and the police That onus may be readily satisfied by the use of audio, or better still, video recording. Indeed, it is my view that where the suspect is in custody, recording facilities are readily available, and the police deliberately set out to interrogate the suspect without giving any thought to the making of a reliable record, the context inevitably makes the resulting non-recorded interrogation suspect. In such cases, it will be a matter for the trial judge on the *voir dire* to determine whether or not a sufficient substitute for an audio or video tape record has been provided to satisfy the heavy onus on the Crown to prove voluntariness beyond a reasonable doubt.[50]

Where the suspect being questioned is an adolescent, there may be heightened difficulties with resolving any discrepancies in the testimony of the youth and the police about what transpired during the interrogation. Making a video or audio recording is even more important.

Section 146(2)(b) requires the police to inform youths fully of their rights prior to a statement being made. The warning in section 146(2) is substantially broader than that given an adult under the *Charter*. An adult only has to be informed of the reason for arrest and of the right to retain counsel. An adult in law has no obligation to answer police questions but, in Canada, the police have no obligation to advise an adult of the right to silence. As well, police may question an adult who has retained counsel in the absence of that legal adviser, unless the accused asks for counsel to be present.[51] Under section

---

50   *R. v. Moore-MacFarlane* (2001), 56 O.R. (3d) 737 (C.A.) at para. 65. The Supreme Court of Canada in *R. v. Oickle*, above note 40, at para. 46, also encouraged the videotaping of a police interrogation, without making it an absolute requirement.

51   *R. v. Hebert*, [1990] 2 S.C.R. 151.

146(2)(b) a youth must be advised of the right to silence and warned of the potential use of any statement against him or her, as well as of the right under section 146(2)(c) to consult with counsel and a parent, and under (2)(d) to have those persons present while a statement is being made. While these rights may be waived by the youth, under section 146(4) any such waiver must be video- or audiotaped, or must be in writing and signed by the youth.[52] By way of contrast, an adult may give an oral waiver of the *Charter*-based right to counsel, and, provided there was an earlier warning of the right, may be deemed to have waived the right to counsel by answering police questions.

If an adequate caution is given, the fact that a youth signs a document waiving the right to consult with a parent or a lawyer before making a statement and to have such a person present during questioning is likely to be taken as a clear act of waiving rights. More difficult issues can arise if the purported waiver is oral and captured on video- or audiotape. In *R. v. C.L.M.* a fourteen-year-old girl was arrested at 23:00 for a second-degree murder charge and given the *Charter* caution for adults. She was placed in a detention cell where she fell asleep and was woken by the police at 04:00 and taken to a room with videotaping equipment. While being filmed, she was advised of her rights and it was apparent that she understood them. The police arranged for her to consult with a legal aid lawyer and she spoke to the lawyer for a couple of minutes. She then said that she wanted to speak to her mother or another relative. The police tried to contact her relatives but were unable to do so. They asked her if she wanted to wait for them. She did not answer that question but began to talk about what happened the night before, when the killing occurred. The police then began to ask detailed questions, which she answered. After several minutes she again asked to call her mother but was unable to reach her. The court held that the statement was not admissible as there was not a clear waiver of rights: "[G]iving an answer to the question asked of her by the police officer did not constitute a clear and unequivocal waiver of her legal rights. I am convinced, on the basis of her demeanour and conduct dur-

---

52   This is consistent with *YOA* case law, where courts consistently held that there must be some demonstration that a youth understood the waiver he or she was making. See, for example, *R. v. A.L.*, [1998] S.J. No. 861, where a mere reading of a form to a youth was held insufficient for a young person being questioned by the police. Further, something more than a checked box was required as proof that an accused had understood and waived his or her rights as under s. 56 of the Act. See also *R. v. A.M.J.* (1999), 137 C.C.C. (3d) 213 (B.C.C.A.), where the fact that a waiver form was improperly completed by a youth was taken as evidence that the adolescent did not understand the waiver.

ing the interview as evidenced by the videotape, that had she been asked directly if she was waiving her right to consult with an adult or have an adult present, she would have answered in the negative."[53]

Since it is only necessary for an accused to raise a reasonable doubt as to whether the Crown has established the voluntariness and other elements for the admissibility of a statement,[54] if the police are relying on a waiver of rights on video- or audiotape, they should take steps to ensure that it contains a clear and unequivocal waiver. As *C.L.M.* illustrates, the fact that a youth answers questions after having been informed of his or her rights and without insisting on the exercise of those rights, the youth will not be taken to have waived the exercise of those rights under section 146(4).

Section 146 of the *YCJA* is premised on the recognition that young persons may lack the sophistication and maturity to appreciate their legal rights fully or the consequences of making a statement, and so require special protections when being questioned by police. A significant body of social-science research indicates that adolescents do not have the same understanding of legal concepts as adults and are less likely to appreciate the consequences of making a statement confessing guilt or waiving the right to consult a lawyer.[55] Adolescents may, for example, only think that it is useful to contact a lawyer if they are truly "innocent" (i.e., unjustifiably charged). As a result, even after being cautioned the majority of youths who are questioned by police waive their rights to consult a lawyer and make an inculpatory statement confessing guilt.

Some advocates for youths argue that section 146 does not go far enough to protect youths, and that the law should require consultation

---

53   *R. v. C.L.M.* , [2000] S.J. No. 176 (Q.B.) at para 13, per Baynton J.

54   The Supreme Court has held that when the issue of the admissibility of a statement arises, the Crown bears the evidentiary and legal burden of proving beyond a reasonable doubt that an accused has waived *Charter* rights in connection with the taking of the statement: *R. v. Prosper*, [1994] 3 S.C.R. 236. The Crown also had the evidentiary and legal burden of proving beyond a reasonable doubt that the police complied with the cautioning requirements of s. 56(2) of the *YOA*: see, for example, *R. v. B.S.M.* (1995), 100 Man. R. (2d) 151 (C.A.) and *R. v. D.(R.)* (1997), 35 W.C.B. (2d) 191 (Ont. Prov. Ct.). It is thus clear that the evidentiary and legal burden is on the Crown to prove beyond a reasonable doubt that there has been compliance with s. 146(2) of the *YCJA*.

55   See, for example, R. Abramovitch, M. Peterson-Badali, and M. Rohan, "Young People's Understanding and Assertion of their Rights to Silence and Legal Counsel"(1995) 37 Can. J. Crim. 1; R. Abramovitch, K. L. Higgins-Biss, and S. R. Biss, "Young Persons' Comprehension of Waivers in Criminal Proceedings" (1993) 35 Can. J. Crim. 309.

with a lawyer before a statement can be made. In advancing this position, a Toronto legal-aid clinic that specializes in representing adolescents graphically described some of its concerns:

> We are frequently faced with youth who advise us that they are frightened and intimidated at the police station. Youth are often told of their right to counsel but then that right is not translated into action, that is, they are not given a telephone, or they are left to wait for some considerable time. Often, there are youth who sign the waivers and don't know why they are doing so or can't recall whether or not they have signed anything. Many youth have a vague recollection of being told their rights but do not truly understand what their rights entail. Youth are often left in the interrogation room for long periods of time and are separated from other youth that they are charged with. We are also aware of youth left in the interrogation room without any clothes on. Many of our clients . . . were advised of their right to counsel and . . . did sign a waiver . . . however, when asked [by us] to articulate what the waiver meant they are unable to do so. . . .
>
> In our experience, fear, apprehension and the belief that the police will "give them a break," encourage young persons to make statements that they may not otherwise have made. At the time of arrest and detention, young persons are in an extremely vulnerable position. Often they are afraid of the police and the reaction of their parents. Thus it is not surprising that few youth want to talk to their parents or have their parents present when making a statement. Yet youth are not encouraged to speak to counsel. . . . [O]n numerous occasions we have heard from youth: "Well I thought of calling a lawyer but I didn't know one.". . . Despite the fact that police are obliged to tell young persons about duty counsel, the concept of contacting a lawyer (usually a stranger) is itself intimidating for a youth.[56]

Under the *YOA*, a statement made by a youth to the police was inadmissible if the police had not fully complied with section 56 of that Act. The importance of strict compliance with section 56 was emphasized in the 1990 decision of the Supreme Court of Canada in *R. v. J.(J.T.)*, where the confession of a seventeen-year-old youth to the police about the brutal sexual assault and murder of a three-year-old

---

56   Justice for Children and Youth, *Submission of the Canadian Foundation for Children, Youth and the Law on the Importance of Statement Protections Under the Young Offenders Act Section 56* (Toronto, 1995).

child was excluded, with the Court ruling that under the circumstances the remaining admissible evidence would permit him only to be tried for manslaughter and not murder.[57] In *R. v. J.(J.T.)*, the police invited the youth to come to the police station for questioning, without charging him. At that time the police suspected that the youth had killed the child but lacked the evidence to lay charges. After several hours of questioning, the youth made a statement in which he implicated himself. The police then charged him and advised him of his rights under the *Charter*, as well as of his right under the *YOA* to consult an adult relative and a lawyer. The youth met in private with an adult relative and then with a lawyer.

After the lawyer left, the police again asked the youth whether he wanted to make a statement, to which he responded: "No. [The lawyer] told me not to." The police told the youth about some of the evidence which they had obtained that appeared to implicate him and then asked further questions, which the youth answered. However, prior to resumption of questioning, the police failed to advise the youth again of his right to consult and have present an adult and a lawyer during questioning. After the youth made a statement confessing guilt, he refused to sign a written waiver of his right of consultation as required by section 56(4) of the *YOA*. The Supreme Court of Canada ruled all three of the statements inadmissible, with Cory J. stating:

> By its enactment of s. 56, Parliament has recognized the problems and difficulties that beset young people when confronted with authority. It may seem unnecessary and frustrating to the police and society that a worldly wise, smug 17-year-old with apparent anti-social tendencies should receive the benefit of this section. Yet it must be remembered that the section is to protect all young people of 17 years or less. A young person is usually far more easily impressed and influenced by authoritarian figures. No matter what the bravado and braggadocio that young people may display, it is unlikely that they will appreciate their legal rights in a general sense or the consequences of oral statements made to persons in authority; certainly they would not appreciate the nature of their rights to the same extent as would most adults. Teenagers may also be more susceptible to subtle threats arising from their surroundings and the presence of persons in authority. A young person may be more inclined to make a statement, even

---

57   The youth was ultimately tried as an adult, convicted of manslaughter, and sentenced to life imprisonment: *R. v. J.(J.T.)* (1991), 73 Man. R. (2d) 103 (C.A.).

although it is false, in order to please an authoritarian figure. It was no doubt in recognition of the additional pressures and problems faced by young people that led Parliament to enact this code of procedure.[58]

Justice Cory went on to explain the importance of applying the general statutory rule to all youths.

Section 56 itself exists to protect all young people, particularly the shy and the frightened, the nervous and the naive. Yet justice demands that the law be applied uniformly in all cases. The requirements of s. 56 must be complied with whether the authorities are dealing with the nervous and naive or the street-smart and worldly-wise. The statutory pre-conditions for the admission of a statement made by a young person cannot be bent or relaxed because the authorities are convinced, on the basis of what they believe to be cogent evidence, of the guilt of the suspect. As soon as the requirements are relaxed because of a belief in the almost certain guilt of a young person, they will next be relaxed in the case of those whom the authorities believe are probably guilty, and thereafter in the case of a suspect who might possibly be guilty but whose past conduct, in the opinion of those in authority, is such that he or she should be found guilty of something for the general protection of society. Principles of fairness require that the section be applied uniformly to all without regard to the characteristics of the particular young person.[59]

The 1995 amendments to the *YOA* made clear that the caution requirements of section 56(2) applied whenever the police have "reasonable grounds for believing that the young person has committed an offence," even if the youth has not yet been formally charged. This will continue to be the law under the *YCJA*, although, if the police are questioning a youth only as a potential witness or victim, section 146 of that Act has no application.[60]

---

58   *R. v. J. (J.T.)*, [1990] 2 S.C.R. 755, at 766.
59   *Ibid.* at 768.
60   In *R. v. J. (J.)* a fourteen-year-old girl reported to a social worker and a police officer that she had been sexually abused. She was warned about the seriousness of her allegation but not advised of her rights under s. 56 of the *YOA*, which was not surprising since she was viewed as a victim at that time. It was later discovered that the girl had deliberately made a false accusation and she was charged with mischief. At her trial on the mischief charge, the statement was held admissible by the Ontario Court of Appeal, with Cory J.A. concluding that s. 56(2) "must refer to young persons *accused* of committing offences" ((1988), 65 C.R. (3d) 371 at 383 (Ont. C.A.)) [emphasis added]. See also N. Bala, "Annotation," (1988) 65 C.R. (3d) 372–76.

The test of "reasonable grounds" for believing that the young person has committed an offence — and hence must receive a caution before making a statement — is the same as that used in the *Criminal Code* as being the basis for the laying of charges. Hence, section 146 does not apply when police are asking a "potential suspect" questions based on a mere hunch or police intuition. This was illustrated by the decision under the *YOA* of the Ontario Court of Appeal in *R. v. W.(J.)*. Two police officers were patrolling in an industrial neighbourhood at 02:00 when they observed two youths leaving the parking lot of a business, with one carrying a knapsack. The officers approached the youths and asked what they were up to. One youth responded: "We're going over to a friend's place." The police asked to look in the knapsack that the other youth was carrying and he said "sure." As the knapsack was being searched, the first youth said: "There's a . . . crowbar in there which belongs to my friend. . . . It's my buddy's, and I was just borrowing it to take a dent out of my mom's car."[61]

Only after this statement was made did the officers have *reasonable grounds* to suspect that the youths had been trying to break into the business premises, a suspicion subsequently confirmed when the police found fresh footprints in the snow leading from one window to another. The youths were then arrested and advised of their rights. At issue was the admissibility of the first youth's statement to the police on a charge of being in possession of a burglary tool contrary to section 351 of the *Criminal Code*. Without that statement, the Crown could not link him to the tools, since the other youth had physical possession. The Ontario Court of Appeal ruled the statements inadmissible since section 56 was not satisfied, stating that section 56 in its original form applied to any statement made by a youth to a police officer investigating an offence.[62] Justice McKinlay contrasted the law applicable to *R. v. W.(J.)* with the law that came into effect later under 1995 amendments to the *YOA*:[63] "Section 56(2), which came into force in December of 1995, makes it clear that the protection of the section now applies only to young persons arrested or detained, or where the peace officer involved has reasonable grounds for believing that the young person

---

61   *R. v. W.(J.)* (1996), 30 O.R. (3d) 342 at 349 (C.A.).

62   Justice McKinlay did, however, recognize an exception for a situation like *R. v. J.(J.)*, *ibid.*, where the statement forms the *actus reus* [guilty act] of the crime. This exception to the need for a police caution before a young person makes a statement continues to apply under the *YCJA* to cases where that person makes an intentionally false statement to lead the police to believe that he or she has been the victim of a crime when this is not in fact the case.

63   Amendment to *YOA*, above note 5, s. 35.

has committed an offence. . . . [I]n this case . . . [the] statements were made by the appellant at a time when he was neither detained by the police nor [reasonably] suspected of any crime."[64]

In a strict legal sense, when the youths were first stopped and questioned by the police, the youths were not being legally detained or reasonably suspected of an offence; in theory, the youths could have kept walking and refused to answer any questions, although they undoubtedly felt obliged to answer the questions posed by the police. The police may not have had reasonable grounds to believe that the youths had committed an offence and so could not legally arrest the youth before the first statement was made, although they undoubtedly had a hunch that the youths were involved in wrongdoing. The judgment of McKinlay J.A. in *R. v. W.(J.)* suggests that as a result of the 1995 *YOA* amendments the courts should take a narrower view of the circumstances in which youths need to receive a special caution. This approach affords the police a little more latitude to ask questions of a youth without giving a caution than they were allowed by the Supreme Court in *R. v. J.(J.T.)* in 1990; a mere police hunch or "suspicions *without reasonable foundation*" would not require cautioning before questioning.

Other cases, however, suggest that a youth who is answering police questions under a feeling of psychological compulsion, but without having been legally arrested, should be entitled to the cautions required by the *Charter* and the youth justice legislation, especially if this is done in a situation in which the police suspect the youth being questioned of being guilty of the offence charged.[65] *R. v. Stillman* is an example of the court taking a fairly broad approach to the situations in which a young person who is being questioned by the police is entitled to a special caution. The accused, who was seventeen years old at the time of the alleged offence, had been charged with first-degree murder and transferred to adult court for trial. At issue was the admissibility of two statements, one oral and one in writing, made by Stillman to one of the investigating officers, Constable Blinn. The officer claimed that when he took these statements, Stillman was only a witness, but the officer later admitted that he had previously been alerted to Stillman's possible guilt by the suspicions of the victim's mother. When Constable Blinn spoke to Stillman, the officer asked a series of short questions about rape and death of Pamela Bischoff. Justice Larlee concluded that the statements were voluntary but were not admissible due to the failure to have a special youth caution:

---

64   *R. v. W.(J.)*, above note 61, at 349.
65   See, for example, *R. v. Hawkins* (1992), 102 Nfld. & P.E.I.R. 91 (Nfld. C.A.).

Did Cst. Blinn consider Mr. Stillman to be a witness when he interviewed him? I am not convinced that Mr. Stillman was considered a witness. Instead I find as a fact that he was a suspect on April 14, 1991 [when the first oral statement was made]. Mrs. Bischoff had expressed an opinion to Cst. Blinn and in the course of a short interview he asked Mr. Stillman, "Did you kill Pamela Bischoff?" That is not a question one poses to a witness but to a suspect.

Nobody else was interviewed between April 14 and April 16, 1991 so Cst. Blinn decided to obtain a written statement. During the interview he asked Mr. Stillman a series of short questions that touch on the question of assault. Mr. Stillman at that point was clearly not a witness but a suspect.

Since I conclude that Mr. Stillman was a suspect the taking of the statements clearly falls within the category of "in circumstances where the peace officer has reasonable grounds for believing that the young person has committed an offence", the wording of the 1995 amendment to s. 56(2) of the Act. . . . The two statements are not admissible because the criteria in s. 56(2) have not been met.[66]

This decision illustrates that, even in a very serious case — and perhaps especially in this type of case — the courts will strive to protect the rights of a young person who is being questioned by a police officer who suspects that the youth may be guilty of an offence, even if the youth was not actually charged at that time. The argument for applying section 146 of the YCJA in such situations seems strong, since youths lack knowledge of their legal rights and generally feel compelled to answer a police officer's questions. Such an interpretation would encourage police officers to respect the rights of adolescents and would be consistent with the principles in section 3, and the commitment to the protection of legal rights in the Preamble of the YCJA.

Another important question which can arise in connection with the admissibility of statements under section 146 of the YCJA is whether a statement that is made after an appropriate special youth caution will be considered tainted by an earlier statement which was not properly obtained. This issue arose under the YOA. The analysis of the issue of possible tainting is identical under the YCJA to under the YOA, and the case law under the YOA on this issue will continue to be applicable. The 1993 decision of the Supreme Court of Canada in R. v. I.(L.R.) dealt with tainting and the admissibility of statements made by a sixteen-year-old youth charged with second degree murder. The Supreme Court

---

66   R. v. Stillman (1997), 196 N.B.R. (2d) 211, at 218–19.

ruled that, if a youth makes a statement that is inadmissible because of an inadequate police caution, a subsequent statement made after a proper caution may be tainted and ruled inadmissible unless precautions are taken by the police. Justice Sopinka wrote:

> [T]he admissibility of a confession . . . which has been preceded by an involuntary [inadmissible] confession . . . [involves] a factual determination based on factors designed to ascertain the degree of connection between the two statements. These . . . include . . . the time span between the two statements, advertence to the previous statement during questioning, the discovery of additional incriminating evidence subsequent to the first statement, the presence of the same police officers at both interrogations and other similarities between the two circumstances. . . . An explanation of one's rights either by a police officer or counsel may not avail in the face of a strong urge to explain away incriminating matters in a prior statement.[67]

In *R. v. I.(L.R.)*, the second statement was taken only after a proper caution. It was taken, however, the morning after the youth made an inadmissible statement and without any effort to advise the youth that the earlier statement might be inadmissible or to advise that the youth should feel no compulsion to explain the earlier statement.[68]

Similarly, in *R. v. D.O.* the Ontario Court of Appeal ruled inadmissible a statement from a youth given at the police station after a proper caution a few hours after the youth had made a statement to the same officers at the court house which was clearly inadmissible, owing to improper inducements. The Court of Appeal held that the "questioning at the police station was no more than a continuation and completion of an interrogation that began . . . earlier in the afternoon."[69] The Court believed that the inducements made earlier in the day "could not have helped but [led the youth] to conclude that it was in his best interests to provide the written statement requested." On the other hand, the Ontario Court of Appeal has also held that, depending on the circumstances, if an initial statement is inadmissible and then a later statement is taken with an appropriate caution, the second statement may be admissible. It is not an absolute requirement that, prior to the second statement, the police must give a specific warning to the youth that the earlier statement might not be admissible. There are no "hard and fast rules for the admissibility of a statement assuming, of

---

67   *R. v. I.(L.R.)*, above note 9, at 526–27.
68   *R. v. H.(C.G.)*, [1996] M.J. No. 628 (Prov. Ct.) (QL).
69   *R. v. D.O.* (1990), 41 O.A.C. 145 at para. 12.

course, that the statutory criteria [for the second statement]have been met."[70] The critical issue is that the court must be satisfied that any improper inducements or threats that were made prior to the making of the first statement were "no longer operative," and that the youth did not feel pressure as a result of the making of that first statement to confirm or clarify the statement.

It should be noted that section 146 of the *YCJA* only imposes requirements for the admissibility of a written or oral statement from a youth and does not preclude the admission of physical evidence that might be recovered as the result of a youth making a statement to the police without an appropriate caution and waiver of rights. (This was also the case with section 56 of the *YOA*.) However, if the physical evidence was also obtained in violation of *Charter* rights, such as after the failure to properly advise of the right to retain counsel, under section 24(2) of the *Charter* the physical evidence may be excluded if its admission would "bring the administration of justice into disrepute." In general, if an accused is alleging a *Charter* violation, the onus is on the accused to establish on the balance of probabilities the factual basis for the violation and to persuade the court that the admission of the evidence would bring the administration of justice into disrepute.[71]

3) An Explanation "Appropriate to Age and Understanding:" Section 145(2)(b)

Section 146(2)(b) of the *YCJA* continues the requirement of section 56 of the *YOA* that when the police advise a youth of his or her rights under the Act, the explanation that is offered must be "in language appropriate to his or her age and understanding." With an adult, a statement will generally be admissible if the police advise an arrested person of his or her rights using the language of the *Charter* — the police have printed cards with the caution on them to assist in doing this — provided that the person has an adequate understanding of the language the officer is speaking. The *YCJA*, however, presents police

---

70   R. v. J.L. (2000), 129 O.A.C. 95 at 96 (C.A.). The Court emphasized that in this case the youth "had an overwhelming desire to acknowledge" his guilt when making the second statement, and hence tainting was not a concern.

71   R. v. *Collins*, [1987] 1 S.C.R. 265. One exception to the rule that the onus is on the accused to establish a *Charter* violation is that as an aspect of proving the admissibility and voluntariness of a statement, the Crown must prove beyond a reasonable doubt that there was a waiver of the *Charter* right to consult with counsel; see R. v. *Leclair*, [1989] 1 S.C.R. 3; and D. Stuart, *Charter Justice*, above note 4, at 41–2.

officers who are questioning a youth with a significantly greater challenge. A simple reading of rights will not suffice; rather, an explanation must be given to the youth that is appropriate, having regard to the youth's language skills and developmental stage. Providing an appropriate caution for a youth takes much longer than for an adult, and police should have specific training about the requirements of the YCJA.

According to psychological research, by about the age of ten, most children can understand basic legal concepts. However, even by the age of twelve, most children lack specific information about the legal system and do not understand the role of a defence lawyer, or even that of the police. Adolescents are more likely than adults to misunderstand the plea of not guilty as a claim of innocence. This lack of understanding raises questions about the ability of younger adolescents to participate in a traditional lawyer-client relationship, as well as underlining the need for special protections of adolescents' procedural rights These questions are particularly significant as children who are socially deprived or at risk of offending are less likely to understand the justice system.[72]

In 1986, in R. v. M.(M.A.), a sixteen-year-old youth with a learning disability had been charged with gross indecency. The police officer who arrested the youth purported to inform him of his rights by reading from a form which recited the words used in section 56(2) of the YOA. The young person then signed a statement in which he waived his right to consult with and have present a lawyer or parent, in accordance with section 56(4). In upholding the ruling of the trial judge that the statements were inadmissible, Hinkson J.A. of the British Columbia Court of Appeal wrote:

> [I]t appears . . . that the learned trial judge was confronted with the requirements of s. 56 and concluded that having the contents of the two forms read to him, the young person did not know what to do in the circumstances and did not know why a lawyer would be necessary. . . . In my opinion, the course followed by the police officer in the present case did not meet the requirements of s. 56 of the Young Offenders Act. The forms themselves appear to be clear, but Parliament indicated the requirement that before the statement was made there must be a clear explanation to the young person. I am not persuaded that reading the contents of those two forms met the requirements imposed by Parliament before the statement could be taken from the young person. . . .

---

72   M. Peterson-Badali et al., "Young Children's Legal Knowledge and Reasoning Ability" (1997) 39 Can. J. Crim. 145.

Parliament has paid special attention to the needs of young people for protective advice and has called on the police to provide it. There should be a genuine endeavour by the person in authority to describe the function of the lawyer and the benefits to the young person of having a lawyer, or parents, or relatives, or an adult friend present. That endeavour should be designed to lead to an appreciation on the part of the young person of the consequences of the choices that he makes.

Even had this young person been a person without any learning disability, the mere reading over of these two statements and then asking the young person to sign them, without any explanation to him whatsoever, would not, in my opinion, have been compliance with . . . s. 56 of the *Young Offenders Act*.[73]

Given that the wording used in section 146(2)(b) of the *YCJA* is essentially identical with that in section 56(2)(b) of the *YOA*, this type of reasoning will be highly persuasive under the new Act.

Strictly speaking, section 146(2)(b) of the *YCJA* does not require that the youth actually understand the advice provided — that is, the test for the adequacy of a caution is not subjective — but only that the explanation must be in language appropriate to the youth's age and understanding, meaning that the test is objective, but nonetheless takes into account the age and capacities of the particular youth being questioned. However, in practice, police should try to ensure that the particular youth being questioned actually understands the caution being given. Generally, this requires a caution that avoids or explains such technical terms as "counsel" and "retain." A useful practice is for the police to test a youth's understanding by asking the youth to state in his or her own words the meaning of the caution that was provided.

In the 1990s police forces increasingly started to make audio- or videotapes of cautions made in accordance with the *Charter* and section 56 of the *YOA* to demonstrate that appropriate care was taken. Use of an audio- or videotape is also encouraged by section 146(4)(a) of the *YCJA*, which allows a video or audio recording as one way of showing a waiver has been made, and by case law which has held that the failure of the police to video- or audiotape a caution and statement when the equipment to do this is available may render the statement inadmissible.[74] Another option is to have the youth write out, preferably in his or her own words, the cautions that have been given.

---

73   *R. v. M.(M.A.)* (1986), 32 C.C.C. (3d) 567 at 571 and 573 (B.C.C.A.).

74   See *R. v. Moore-MacFarlane* (2001), 56 O.R. (3d) 737 (C.A.), at para. 65, discussed above.

When advising a youth of the right to consult with a lawyer prior to making a statement and to have a lawyer present when a statement is made, the police should specifically mention that, if a youth is unable to afford a lawyer, one can be obtained without charge through legal aid or by order of a court. The police should also indicate the means by which a legal aid lawyer can be contacted for advice prior to police questioning (i.e., by providing a telephone number), if a youth expresses the desire to consult with a lawyer. There is an obligation on the police to facilitate this contact and allow for a private consultation.[75] While most provinces have programs in place for consultation twenty-four hours a day, often by means of a toll-free consultation with a lawyer (generally known as "duty counsel"), for adults there is no legal obligation on the government to provide this type of service. However, if a youth wishes to consult a lawyer and one is not immediately available, the police should not question the youth.

A 1993 decision of the Supreme Court of Canada, *R. v. I.(L.R.)*, dealt with the admissibility of statements made by a sixteen-year-old youth charged with second-degree murder.[76] The Supreme Court emphasized that a youth must be advised of the right to consult and have present both a lawyer *and* a parent (or another adult, if a parent is not available). The parent and lawyer have different roles, and the youth should understand that both may be consulted and present during a police interview.[77] The youth is not expected to choose between consulting a lawyer or a parent. Another issue raised in *R. v. I.(L.R.)* was whether police must ensure that the youth has an awareness of "the extent of his or her jeopardy" when making a statement. In particular, if the offence is serious and the youth is fourteen or older, are the police required to advise the youth of the *possibility* that the youth may be subject to adult sanctions? The Supreme Court acknowledged that there was no express requirement in section 56(2) of the *YOA* that a youth must be warned of the possibility of transfer. The Court pointed out, however, that cases before the *YOA* on the voluntariness of state-

---

75   See *R. v. Brydges*, [1990] 1 S.C.R. 190; and *Re C.(V.K.)*, [1991] A.J. No. 382 (Prov. Ct. (Youth Div.)); *Re A*, [1990] Y.J. 97 (Yk. Terr. Ct.) (QL); *R. v. Bartle*, [1994] 3 S.C.R. 173.

76   *R. v. I.(L.R.)*, above note 9. In 1995 s. 56(2)(b) was amended to reflect this Supreme Court decision; the original wording of s. 56(2) was less clear than the present wording about whether a youth could consult either a parent *or* a lawyer, or both a parent *and* a lawyer. See *YOA* 1995, above note 5.

77   Similarly, even if a parent is actually consulted, a youth must still waive in writing or on videotape the right to consult counsel and have counsel present: *R. v. D.(M.)*, [1996] O.J. No. 1162 (Prov. Div.) (QL).

ments of adolescents suggested that it was a good practice for police to include such information in their cautions.[78]

The Supreme Court ruled that: "a warning that a young person may be raised to adult court should not be interpreted as an absolute requirement. . . . [but it] is one factor to be considered in determining voluntariness, the importance of which will vary depending on the other facts of the case, including the age, level of understanding and sophistication of the young person, and whether or not the young person has consulted with counsel."[79] Justice Sopinka clearly indicated that it would "be preferable" for a warning of the possibility of transfer to be given, even if before the statement was made the youth had consulted with counsel who would be expected to provide such advice. The Supreme Court did not rule that the failure to give this warning about the possibility of an adult sanction was necessarily fatal to the admissibility of a statement but rather indicated that it was one factor relevant to the voluntariness of the statement.

The 1996 Ontario Court of Appeal decision in R. v. M.(S.) upheld the admissibility of a statement made by a seventeen-year-old youth in connection with a sexual assault, despite the failure to warn of the possibility of transfer to adult court.[80] The Court of Appeal noted that R. v. I.(L.R.) did not set out a "mandatory requirement" for such a caution. The Court of Appeal stated that in murder cases such as R. v. I.(L.R.), a warning of the possibility of an adult sanction may be most appropriate since the difference between adult and youth sanctions is greatest in that context.[81]

Although not expressly mentioned by the Supreme Court in R. v. I.(L.R.), the warning concerning the possibility of adult sanction will be most appropriate if the charge is very serious, making the likelihood of an adult sanction greater. In R. v. I.(L.R.), the youth was not in fact transferred, although the Crown had made an unsuccessful transfer application before his trial in youth justice court. Under the YOA if the youth had been transferred, the failure of the police to have warned of this possibility was likely to be viewed negatively by the adult court when deciding whether to admit the statement. Conversely, if, as in R. v. M.(S.), no attempt was made to seek an adult sanction, the absence of this warning was less significant.

---

78   See, for example, R. v. Yensen, [1961] O.R. 703 (H.C.J.).

79   R. v. I.(L.R.), above note 9, at 524, Sopinka J.

80   R. v. M.(S.) (1996), 28 O.R. (3d) 776 (C.A.).

81   For murder, the maximum sentence in youth justice court is ten years, whereas in adult court the automatic sentence is life imprisonment, although transferred youth are eligible for parole in five to ten years. Transfer is discussed in Chapter 9.

While the *YCJA* changes the process for imposition of an adult sanction from a pre-adjudication transfer hearing to a post-adjudication sentencing decision, the *YCJA* requires that the youth have notice before trial that an adult sentence might be sought. (Discussion of adult sentencing is in Chapter 9.) The principle of *R. v. I.(L.R.)* should be equally applicable to cases under the *YCJA* as it was under the *YOA*. In cases involving very serious charges against youths aged fourteen or older, the failure of the police to warn of the possibility of an adult sanction may be considered a factor in assessing the admissibility of the statement, and police would be well advised to provide such a warning in these cases. However, even for serious cases, the failure to provide such a caution does not automatically result in the exclusion of the statement.

Another aspect of ensuring that a statement is voluntary and that the youth understands the "extent of his or her jeopardy" is that the youth must know the charges that are being investigated. It is a requirement of section 10(a) of the *Charter* that the police inform individuals of the reasons for their arrest at the time of arrest (that is, individuals must be informed of the charges they face). Concerns arise when a youth is arrested for one offence and, during the course of making a statement to the police, begins to confess to other, unrelated crimes. The courts have articulated a general principle in interpreting the right to counsel, guaranteed by section 10 of the *Charter*, namely, that the police must restate the accused's right to counsel when there is a fundamental and discrete change in the purpose of the investigation, one involving a different and unrelated offence or a significantly more serious offence than that contemplated at the time of the warning.[82]

There is a similar duty on the police to re-caution an accused youth of rights under the *YCJA* if questioning is "redirected to a new topic" so that the youth can appreciate the consequences of making the statement. In *R. v. Z.(C.)*, the police arrested three youths in connection with the robbery of a convenience store and, after an appropriate caution and waiver, questioned each of the youths separately. After one of the youths made a confession to the robbery, the officer then began to ask that youth about the robbery of another store the day before, believing that the three youths had also been responsible for that offence, but without re-cautioning the youth. The judge ruled that the statement was not admissible in regard to a charge for the robbery of the second store because of the failure of the police officer to charge the youth with that offence and again satisfy the requirements for the special youth

---

82   *R. v. Evans*, [1991] 1 S.C.R. 869 at 893.

caution: "Although these offences are of the same delict, they are sufficiently distinguishable in time and place and participation of all
involved so as to give rise to different possibilities for a defence to any
or all of the perpetrators."[83]

A 1997 British Columbia case raised the issue of whether section 56
applied to statements overheard by an undercover police officer while a
youth is in custody. For adults, the Supreme Court of Canada has held
that, as long as an undercover officer makes no attempt to elicit a statement, there is no need for the Crown to prove voluntariness or comply
with the *Charter*, as there is no basis for the accused to believe that the
officer is acting as an agent for the state.[84] However, in *Re G.(D.B.)*, it was
held that different rules apply to youths.[85] In that case, two youths were
arrested in connection with a serious fire that they were believed to have
started. They refused to make a statement and at 04:00 were placed in
separate cells in the police station, with the intent to take them to a
youth facility in the morning. An undercover police officer was placed
in an adjacent cell, where he pretended to be a prisoner, sleepy and disinterested. During the next few hours, the youths conversed and made
several incriminating statements that the officer overheard.

Judge Ehrcke ruled the statements inadmissible since the officer
had not satisfied section 56 of the *YOA*: "The youths were not aware
they were making statements to a peace officer. . . . Freedom of choice
for a youth who is detained requires that the youth is cognizant of the
fact that he is speaking to or in the presence of a police officer, at least
where an intentional police tactic is invoked. . . . It may be that in other
circumstances, where an officer unintentionally overhears something,
a youth can be taken to have accepted the risk."[86] In reaching this decision, the judge cited *I.(L.R.)*. While a statement made by an adult in
similar circumstances would be admissible, "the special situation of
youths" demanded protection of "their vulnerability," at least while
they are in detention.[87] As noted previously, given the virtually identical wording of the provisions in the *YCJA* and the *YOA*, the case law
decided under the *YOA* clearly remains relevant.

---

83   *R. v. Z.(C.)*, [1995] O.J. No. 4010 (Prov. Div.) (QL) 1 at para. 17.
84   *R. v. Hebert*, [1990] 2 S.C.R. 151.
85   *Re G.(D.B.)*, [1997] B.C.J. No. 1203 (Prov. Ct.) (QL).
86   *Ibid.* at paras. 78 and 79.
87   See *R. v. E.(O.N.)* (2000), 47 W.C.B. (2d) 401 (B.C.S.C.), where statements made
      by a youth in the community to an undercover investigative officer who was
      posing as a drug dealer were held to be admissible.

4) Admission of Statement Despite "Technical Irregularity:" Sections 146(5) and (6)

Unlike a *Charter* violation, which gives a judge a discretion to admit evidence if satisfied that doing so would not bring "the administration of justice into disrepute,"[88] a failure to comply fully with cautioning and waiver provisions of section 56 of the *YOA* resulted in a mandatory exclusion of a statement. The courts held that even a relatively minor failure to comply with the requirements of section 56 would result in the exclusion of any statement.[89] Section 56 was highly controversial with police, Crown prosecutors and provincial attorneys general complaining about its complexity, and with members of the public expressing outrage at such decisions as *R. v. J. (J. T.)*, which caused the exclusion of confessions to horrendous crimes as a result of seemingly minor failures to comply strictly with the cautioning provisions for young persons. In response to these concerns, the *YCJA* changes the rule about the mandatory exclusion of statements taken without full compliance with the special cautioning rules for young persons, creating a relatively narrow judicial discretion to admit statements if there has been a "technical irregularity" in the way in which the youth has been cautioned or waived his or her rights.

Section 146(5) of the new Act allows a judge to admit a statement despite a "technical irregularity" in the manner in which the youth has waived his or her rights of consultation under section 146(4), provided that the judge is "satisfied that the youth was informed of his or her rights, and voluntarily waived them." Section 146(6) provides that, where there has been a "technical irregularity" in the cautioning of a youth under section 146(2)(b) to 2(d), the court may admit the statement if satisfied that "the admission of the statement would not bring into disrepute the principle that young persons are entitled to enhanced procedural protection to ensure that they are treated fairly and their rights are protected." The new discretion in section 146 of the *YCJA* to admit statements despite the failure of the police to comply fully with cautioning and waiver requirements further complicates the process for deciding whether a statement is admissible, although the discretion to admit the statement is relatively narrow.

---

88   The *Charter*, above note 3, s. 24(2).
89   There is an abundance of cases illustrating the unwillingness of the courts to admit the statement of a young person if there was any failure to comply with s. 56(2) of the *YOA*: see, for example, *R. v J. (J. T.)*, [1990] 2 S.C.R. 755, discussed above.

It is significant that section 146, as enacted, is substantially narrower than earlier versions of the statute which Parliament considered. Bill C-3, an earlier version of the *YCJA* which died on the Parliamentary order paper when the fall 2000 federal election was called, would have allowed for balancing between competing interests when judges exercised their discretion. In Bill C-3, a judge would have had the power to admit a statement despite a defect in the cautioning of the youth or in the waiver of rights if satisfied that doing so would not "bring the administration of justice into disrepute."[90] This would have given judges a broad discretion to admit statements on the basis of a balancing similar to that under section 24(2) of the *Charter*. The broad judicial discretion to admit statements allowed by Bill C-3 was met with strong opposition from the defence bar and advocates for youth who were concerned that this would encourage the police to disregard the need to give special respect to the rights of young persons.[91] As a result of these concerns, the provision enacted in the *YCJA* confers a significantly narrower judicial discretion than what was provided for in Bill C-3.

The term "technical irregularity" is not defined in either the *YCJA* or the *Criminal Code*. *Black's Law Dictionary*[92] defines "technical" as "immaterial, without affecting substantial rights, without substance," while the definition of "irregularity" includes a "violation or nonobservance of established rules and practices." A "technical irregularity" is therefore a relatively minor procedural deficiency in the way in which a youth was advised of his or her rights, and the exercise of the waiver of those rights. Section 146(5) makes clear that the youth must actually be informed of his or her rights, and must voluntarily waive them. The granting of the power to a court to cure a "technical irregularity" is granted in some other statutes, such as the *Federal Court Act*.[93] In interpreting that curative provision, Muldoon J. suggested that it "ought to cool out any notions of putting before the court any undotted 'i's or uncrossed 't's."[94] The courts have also invoked the concept of "technical irregularity" to uphold the validity of criminal proceedings

---

90 Bill C-3, Second Session, Thirty-Sixth Parliament, First Reading, October 14, 1999, s. 145 (not enacted).

91 See Cohen, G. "The *YCJA*," Law Times, March 22, 1999.

92 Black's Law Dictionary, 5th ed. (Minnesota: West Publishing Co., 1979). There is no listing for the term "technical irregularity" in The Dictionary of Canadian Law (Toronto: Carswell, 1995).

93 *Federal Court Act*, R.S.C. 1985, c. F-7, s. 18(5)(b).

94 *Kelly v. Canada (Commissioner of Corrections)*, [1993] F.C.J. 149 (F.C.T.D.). See also, for example, *General Truck Drivers Union, Local 939 v. Hoar Transport*, [1969] S.C.R. 634, where the Supreme Court of Canada considers the concept of "technical irregularity" in the context of labour law legislation.

in which the Crown omitted certain words in information that did not materially prejudice the accused or hinder his ability to mount a defence.[95] The omission of the word "arrest" from an arrest warrant that was otherwise valid and complete has been held to be a mere "technical irregularity" that did not affect its validity.[96]

Section 146(5) and (6) permit a judge to admit a statement of a youth despite a "technical irregularity" in the administering of a caution or in the waiving of rights. As with most other issues with respect to the admission of statements, the onus in an application to invoke this provision is on the Crown, and any factual matter must be proven beyond a reasonable doubt.

It is submitted that there must, at a minimum, have been a good faith effort by the police to ensure that there was compliance with the Act, and that the youth must in fact have been informed of his or her rights and actually chose to waive them. A situation in which section 146(5) might be invoked would be one in which a youth was properly cautioned and intended to waive all rights but accidentally checked one of the wrong boxes on the form, erroneously indicating that the right was not being waived. On the other hand, if there was only an oral waiver of rights with no attempt to obtain a written waiver, or to video- or audiotape a waiver of rights, this would not seem to be an appropriate case for invoking section 146(5). Section 146(4) imposes a clear obligation on the police to take special steps to attempt to impress on a youth the significance of the waiver of rights and to preserve a record of this: totally ignoring this provision by only seeking an oral waiver is not a situation in which section 146(5) should be invoked.

Clearly section 146(5) and (6) of the YCJA will not be applicable if the police are aware that the person whom they are questioning is a young person, or should reasonably be aware of this, and comply only with the Charter cautioning requirements for adults but not with any of the special requirements of the YCJA for dealing with youth. As the Supreme Court of Canada observed in R. v. (J.T.), the fact that a young person may be close to the age of eighteen and has "street smarts" owing to prior involvement with the youth justice system does not justify disregarding the special protections afforded all those under eighteen when they are questioned.[97]

---

95   Lavallee, Rackel & Heintz v. Canada (A.G.), [1997] A.J. 109 (Alta Q.B.).
96   Pigeau v. Crowell (1990), 96 N.S.R. (2d) 412 (C.A.)
97   R. v. J.(J.T.), [1990] 2 S.C.R. 755 at 766–68. In that case, in her dissenting opinion L'Heureux-Dubé J. advocated adoption of a "totality of the circumstances" approach to assessing whether there had been a satisfactory cautioning of the

5) Who is a "Person in Authority"?

Section 146(2) of the *YCJA* requires a "peace officer or other person who is, in law, a person in authority" to advise youths of their rights for a statement (or apparent confession) to be admissible. The requirement for providing cautions under section 146 and the *Charter* applies only to "persons in authority," since only these individuals are considered to be agents of the state in a position to coerce or induce a youth into making a statement. Otherwise, a statement from any party to litigation (i.e., accused young person) to someone who is not a person in authority is an "admission" as opposed to a "confession,"[98] and it will generally be received in evidence against that party without any concern about whether it was voluntary or whether the party who made it was cautioned. An exception to this general rule is found in section 146(7), where judges are given a discretion to rule inadmissible a statement made to a person not in authority, if it was done under "duress."

A difficult question is the extent to which individuals such as school-teachers, probation officers, social workers, and even parents may be regarded as "persons in authority." In practice, individuals other than police officers lack the training and knowledge to provide an appropriate caution or otherwise respect the rights of a youth. If they are considered to be "persons in authority" or "agents of the state," a statement made to them by a youth will inevitably be excluded for a failure to comply with the requirements of the *Charter* and section 146 of the *YCJA*. In a psychological sense, a youth is likely to view adults such as social workers, teachers, and parents to be just as much persons in authority as police officers, and may feel pressured by them into answering questions. However, section 146 of the *YCJA* refers to an individual who, *in law*, is a "person in authority." Section 146(9) provides: "For the purpose of this section, a person consulted under paragraph (2)(c) is, in the absence of evidence to the contrary, deemed *not* to be a person in authority."

---

youth, including consideration of whether the youth had "indicia of adulthood." Sections 146(5)–(6) of the *YCJA* do not adopt this type of wide discretionary approach to the admission of statements in situations where there has been a failure to comply with s. 146(2).

98   Some legal authorities distinguish between a "confession" and an "admission." A "confession" is generally defined as an inculpatory statement made by an accused person to a police officer or other person in authority; at common law it is admissible in evidence only if it is voluntary. An "admission" is any statement accepting responsibility by a party to litigation (such as an accused) that is not covered by the "confession rule." Admissions do not need to be proven to be voluntary to be received in evidence. Neither type of statement needs to be a full admission of guilt to be admissible against the accused.

The jurisprudence under the *YOA* and the common law of voluntariness takes a narrow approach to the concept of who is, in law, a "person in authority," focusing on the question of a person who is in a position to affect the legal prosecution of a case rather than on who may actually exercise control over a young person. In *R. v. Hodgson*, Justice Cory wrote for the Supreme Court of Canada:

> the question as to who should be considered as a person in authority depend[s] . . . on the extent to which the accused believed the person could influence or control the proceedings against him or her. . . . The subjective approach to the person in authority requirement has been adopted in this Court. . . . However, to this statement I would add that the accused's belief that he is speaking to a person in authority must also be reasonable, in the context of the circumstances surrounding the making of the statement. . . . A parent, doctor, teacher or employer all may be found to be a person in authority if the circumstances warrant, but their status, or the mere fact that they may wield some personal authority over the accused, is not sufficient to establish them as persons in authority for the purposes of the confessions rule.[99]

In *R. v. B.(A.)*, a youth was charged with having committed sexual offences against his two young half-sisters. An important piece of evidence against the youth was a statement he had made to his mother admitting that he had abused the girls, after she promised to "get some help" for him if he told her the truth about what happened. Two similar statements that the youth made to two physicians who later treated him were also significant evidence of his guilt. The Ontario Court of Appeal ruled that neither the mother nor the physicians were "persons in authority," and there was no need for the Crown to establish the voluntariness of the statements or prove that section 56(2) of the *YOA* was satisfied. Justice Cory, then on the Ontario Court of Appeal, wrote:

> As a general rule, a person in authority is someone engaged in the arrest, detention, examination or prosecution of the accused. It need not be a police officer. The test for who is a person in authority, for non-obvious persons in authority, is whether there is realistic expectation that they are associated with the investigation. The onus is not always on the defence to request a *voir dire* concerning the admissibility of the evidence; in such rare cases the trial judge is to make an inquiry into whether a *voir dire* should be held even in the absence of a defence request to hold one. When the word "examination" is used

---

99   *R. v. Hodgson*, [1998] 2 S.C.R. 449 at paras. 32–35.

. . . it refers to interrogation by police officers, detention or security guards and members of the Crown attorney's office. . . . Certainly, in the ordinary sense of the term, A.B.'s mother was a person in authority. To a boy of 13, his mother must be an authoritative figure. . . . most particularly in a position of authority in light of her maternal desire to protect her young daughters.[100]

The Court concluded that the mother was not a person in authority, emphasizing that, when she had asked her son about his acts, she had had no intention of calling the police or instituting court proceedings, but rather had wanted to find out what had happened so that she could get him psychiatric help. While recognizing that there might be circumstances in which a parent could become a "person in authority," Cory J.A. observed: "Only the most serious continued and flagrant misconduct could ever be expected to lead parents to call the authorities about their own child. Until that time, parents would not, in law, be persons in authority."[101]

In *R. v. H.*, a thirteen-year-old student was charged with the theft of money in a school and the prosecutor wanted the court to hear about statements made by the youth admitting guilt to his teacher and the school principal. Prior to the statements being made, the teacher had promised that, if the money was returned, nothing further would happen. Not surprisingly, neither the teacher nor the principal had complied with the *Charter* or section 56 of the *YOA*, since they had no training in the taking of legally admissible statements. Judge Russell of the Alberta Youth Court ruled that the youth's statements to the teacher and principal were inadmissible because of the violation of the *YOA* and section 10 of the *Charter*. The decision in *R. v. H.* does not require school personnel to advise adolescent students of all their legal rights, such as the right to counsel, in all situations where disciplinary action is being taken, but it does indicate that, if these rights are not afforded a youth prior to questioning, statements which are made may later be ruled inadmissible in youth court proceedings.[102]

As discussed above, the Supreme Court of Canada held in *R. v. M.R.M.*[103] that a vice principal did not need to satisfy all of the require-

---

100 *R. v. B.(A.)* (1986), 50 C.R. (3d) 247 at 256–57 (Ont. C.A.).

101 *Ibid.* at 259.

102 *R. v. H.* (1985), 43 Alta. L. R. (2d) 250 (Prov. Ct. (Youth Div.)), Russell Prov. J. To a similar effect, see *R. v. R.(F.)* (10 November 1988), (Man. Prov. Ct. (Fam. Div.)) [unreported] [summarized [1988] W.D.F.L. 2561]; and *R. v. J.(A.R.)* (1992), 16 W.C.B. (2d) 282 (Ont. Prov Ct.).

103 *R. v. M.R.M.*,[1998] 3 S.C.R. 393.

ments of the *Charter* when searching a student for marijuana, and was not held to the same standard as a police officer in regard to the search. That decision was set in the context of an investigation into a violation of school rules about the possession of drugs, and did not deal with a situation in which the legal consequences are so significant that it is inevitable that the principal becomes an "agent of the police in detecting crime," for example, as might be the case in an investigation into a serious crime, such as a sexual assault or a homicide. In such a situation, the failure to respect legal rights and properly caution a youth might result in the evidence obtained being ruled inadmissible. Further, *M.R.M.* dealt with the admissibility of physical evidence obtained from a search, which was clearly and independently probative of the fact that the crime in question had been committed and would probably have been discovered in the course of a legal search that a police officer could have carried out.

On the other hand, *R. v. H.* involved only an incriminating statement that might not have been made if the youth's rights had been respected, and the *YOA* has special provisions precluding the admission of such statements if rights have been violated. In situations where there has been a violation of rights, the courts generally have a more restrictive attitude toward the admission of confessions (so-called "conscriptive evidence") than they do toward the admission of physical evidence that could have been legally obtained even without the cooperation of the accused.[104] This suggests that on the particular facts of *R. v. H.*, a case in which the teacher was not only investigating a breach of discipline but also made a representation about how the matter would be handled by the school authorities, the teacher might well be found to be a "person in authority" under the *YCJA*, notwithstanding the Supreme Court decision in *M.R.M.*

A probation officer has generally been viewed as a person in authority, that is, one who can effect or control a prosecution against the youth. As a result, in the course of supervising a youth who is on probation, a purported confession of guilt made by a youth to a probation officer may not be admissible for the purposes of establishing guilt for the offence of breach of probation, unless the probation officer specifically cautions the youth, an unlikely event.[105] When a youth makes a statement to a staff person in a group home, however, there is

---

104 *R. v. Stillman*, above note 7.
105 *R. v. H.(C.)*, [1995] O.J. No. 932 (Prov. Div.) (QL), Lenz Prov. J. Statements made by a youth to a probation officer for the purpose of preparing a pre-sentence report or progress report will be admissible for that purpose, but will not be admissible to establish proof of any other offence: *YCJA*, above note 1, s. 40(10).

a tendency not to view the staff as "persons in authority," presumably because they have no direct role in the administration of justice or prosecution of offences.[106] Because of the use in the *YCJA* of virtually identical wording to that in the *YOA* concerning who constitutes a "person in authority," the judicial precedents under the *YOA* are likely to be highly persuasive under the new Act.

6) Who is a "Young Person"?

In *R. v. Z.(D.A.)*, the Supreme Court of Canada held that the police do not need to comply with section 56 of the *YOA* for a statement to be admitted in evidence if a youth was seventeen at the time of the alleged offence but had passed his eighteenth birthday at the time of police questioning. While for purposes of jurisdiction and disposition he was a "young person" to be dealt with under the *YOA* in youth court, he did not have to be given the special protections of section 56. Writing for a majority of the Supreme Court, Lamer C.J.C. commented: "Persons over the age of 18 have long been deemed to possess sufficient maturity and control over the situation they may find themselves in to no longer require the watchful eye of a parent"[107] This position is now reflected in the explicit opening words of section 146(2) of the *YCJA*, which makes clear that this provision only applies to a statement made by a young person who is under the age of eighteen when the statement is made.

Sometimes youths who are arrested by the police lie about their age,[108] perhaps to avoid having their parents notified, or to be kept in detention with older friends, or as part of a ruse to deceive the police about their true identity. If this happens, the police may fail to comply with section 146 of the *YCJA* in regard to questioning. The *YOA* was amended in 1995 to deal with this type of situation, and section 146(8) of the *YCJA* adopts this provision of the *YOA*, giving a youth justice court judge the discretion to admit a statement made by a young person to the police — even if they have failed to comply with section 146 — provided that the youth held him- or herself as being eighteen or older. This provision only applies if the police conducted "reasonable inquiries" about the age of the person that they were questioning, and had "reasonable grounds" to believe that the person was over the age of eighteen, based both on what that person said and on his or her

---

106 *R. v. B.(L.J.)* (January 16, 1986), (Man. Prov. Ct. (Fam. Div.)) [unreported] [summarized [1986] W.D.F.L. 550].

107 *R. v. Z.(D.A.)*, [1992] 2 S.C.R. 1025 at 1053.

108 See, for example, *R. v. H.(K.J.)* (27 October 1984), (Ont. Prov. Div.) [unreported] [summarized [1995] W.D.F.L. 83].

appearance, and on any other information available to the police. In this situation, the statement must of course be considered voluntary under the rules applicable to adults, and there must have been compliance with the *Charter*. While a statement made without a youth caution may be admissible under section 146(8) if the young person deceived the police about his or her age while being questioned, the case must be dealt with in youth justice court once the correct age has been established.

7) Spontaneous Statements: Section 146(3)

Section 146(3) of the *YCJA* provides that the requirements of section 146(2)(b) do not apply in respect of "oral statements . . . made spontaneously" by a youth if the police have not had a "reasonable opportunity" to comply with the cautioning requirements of section 146(2) before the statement was made. This provision recognizes that there are situations in which a youth spontaneously makes a statement and since, in such cases, the police cannot reasonably have been expected to comply with section 146(2), the use of the statement is not an infringement of the rights of the youth. Further, the circumstances in which these statements are made provide some assurance that they are not the product of coercion. To ensure that the police did not exploit section 56(3) of the *YOA*, which is identical to section 146(3) of the *YCJA*, the courts interpreted the exception for spontaneous statements narrowly. The Crown was required to prove beyond a reasonable doubt that a statement was spontaneous, with the courts indicating that "any doubt as to whether the statement is spontaneous should be resolved in favour of the young person."[109] The same legal and evidentiary onus should apply under section 146(3) of the *YCJA*.

In a 1987 Quebec case, the police arrested a youth for a sexual assault and gave him a caution satisfying the *Charter*, although not section 56(2) of the *YOA*.[110] The alleged victim's father was making threatening gestures toward the youth and the police quickly put the youth in a patrol car and drove him to the police station, a few minutes away. In the patrol car on the way to the police station, the youth made two statements. The court refused to invoke section 56(3) of the *YOA* and excluded the statements made in the patrol car. While there was not enough time for the police to allow the youth to consult with parents or counsel before the statements were made, the police had sufficient

---

109   *R. v. W.(J.)* (1996), 30 O.R. (3d) 342 at 349 (C.A.), at 346; see also *R. v. N.(P.)* (1999), 42 W.C.B. (2d) 81 (B.C. Prov. Ct.).
110   *R. v. L.(M.)*, [1987] R.J.Q 709 (Youth Ct.).

opportunity to give him at least the rudiments of the more elaborate caution to be given to youths under section 56(2), in particular to advise him of the right to silence and of the right to consult with a parent and counsel before making a statement.

Section 56(3) of the *YOA* was invoked by courts to admit statements that youths made just as they were being arrested, for example, as a gratuitous response to being informed of the reason for the arrest as required by the *Charter*.[111] It was also used to admit statements made to an officer who was speaking to a youth without suspecting that this individual had committed an offence, when the youth blurted out a confession. An interesting example of the application of section 56(3) is provided by *R. v. H.(K. J.)*,[112] where a youth had been apprehended at a store for shoplifting and had given the police officer who came to the store a false name and birth date, one which indicated that he was an adult. The officer was suspicious of the youth's identity and took him to the police station, telling the youth that if his identity were not established, the police would bring him before a justice of the peace to seek to have him detained. At that point, the police had no intention of taking a statement. The youth told the officer: "I will tell you who I am if you give me a cigarette." The officer nodded acquiescence and said : "Who are you?" The youth replied: "Kevin H. I tried to kill Gavin N. two days before my birthday, September 17." The officer then asked further questions, without cautioning the youth. On charges related to the attempted homicide, Hardman Prov. J. ruled that the first statement admitting the killing was spontaneous and admissible under section 56(3), although the later responses to the questions were not admissible since the officer had an opportunity to warn the youth that serious charges might be laid and to caution about his rights.

The courts have held that when a police officer is questioning a youth who is suspected of committing an offence but has not been arrested, section 56(3) did not apply since the statement should be viewed not as spontaneous but rather as a response to a police question.[113] An example of a statement found not to be spontaneous is *R. v. A.N.*, where the mother of a youth who had learned that the police suspected her son of having committed a break and enter brought her son to the police station in the middle of the night. The police were not expecting them to arrive and, in the foyer of the police station, she

---

111 *R. v. M.(C.J.) (No. 2)* (1986), 43 Man. R. (2d) 138 (Q.B.)
112 *R. v. H.(K.J.)* above note 108.
113 *R. v. W.(J.)*, above note 109.

directed her son to "tell" the police officer on duty "something." The youth then made a verbal admission to committing the break and enter. The officer then arrested the youth. The police later questioned the youth; while he was cautioned about the statements made after the arrest, there was no waiver of his right to consult with counsel and those later statements were not admissible. Judge LeGrandeur also ruled that the first statement made in the foyer of the police station was not admissible either. Since that statement was in the presence and for the benefit of the police officer, section 56 applied. There had been no attempt to provide a caution before the statement was made, and it was not a spontaneous statement but rather was "given in response to external stimulus, that is the direction of his mother."[114]

There may, however, be situations in which a youth is in custody and a statement will be ruled spontaneous. In *R. v. Wilson*, a youth was arrested on murder charges arising out of the beating death of a man. The youth was fully advised of his rights and had the opportunity to meet with his parents and a lawyer. The youth told the investigating officer that he did not want to make a statement. After thirty-eight hours in detention in a cell, an officer on guard duty became concerned about the youth's emotional state and advised the investigating officer, who came to his cell. The investigating officer found the youth crying and shaking uncontrollably. While still in his cell the youth said: "I couldn't quit. I kept getting madder. They tried to stop me. They wouldn't let me. I just couldn't." Concerned by the youth's uncontrollable shaking, the investigating officer took the youth to an interview room where the youth sat at a desk facing the open door. There the youth said: "I can't believe I did it. I kept seeing blood. I got madder."[115] The British Columbia Court of Appeal upheld the decision of the trial judge to admit the statements as a "spontaneous outburst." The Court noted that the statements were not made in response to questions and the officer gave the youth no inducements to speak.

C. THE ROLE OF COUNSEL AT THE POLICE STATION

Section 146(2) of the *YCJA* and section 10 of the *Charter* provide a right for youths to consult a lawyer on arrest and before making a statement. This is reinforced by section 25 of the *YCJA*, which provides:

---

114 *R. v. A.N.*,[1998] A.J. No. 855, at para. 17.
115 *R. v. Wilson* (2001), 156 C.C.C. (3d) 74 at 81 (B.C.C.A.).

> 25. (1) A young person has the right to retain and instruct counsel without delay, and to exercise that right personally, at any stage of proceedings. . . .
>
> (2) Every young person who is arrested or detained shall, on being arrested or detained, be advised without delay by the arresting officer or the officer in charge, as the case may be, of the right to retain and instruct counsel, and be given an opportunity to obtain counsel.

Section 25 requires that on arrest the police should advise the youth of his or her right to be represented by counsel and take steps to facilitate contact between the youth and counsel. Many adolescents, relying on images from television and the movies, naively believe that lawyers only have a role in helping the innocent and most waive their right to consult with a lawyer after arrest and before making a statement to the police. However, some youths, especially those who are more familiar with the youth justice system or who are more sophisticated, do exercise their right to consult a lawyer. If a youth expresses a desire to consult with a lawyer, whether by telephone or in person, the youth has a right to a private consultation with the lawyer. To satisfy section 25 of the *YCJA* and the *Charter*, police should offer a youth access to a telephone and a list of lawyers paid by legal aid who will, without charge to those in detention, provide summary advice to those detained by the police. In most places in Canada legal aid plans have toll-free numbers that allow those who have been arrested to have access to legal advice at this critical stage in the legal process, with a roster of lawyers in private practice or from a clinic available for this purpose.

When contacted in this situation, it is generally premature for the lawyer to discuss the offence with the youth in the emotionally stressful state immediately after arrest, even if there is a time and place to do so. A lawyer should, especially at this stage, take care to communicate in clear and comprehensible language with the youth. Social research has shown that defence lawyers, and even youths themselves, are likely to overestimate an adolescent client's understanding of the legal system.[116] Some of the things that the lawyer should do at this initial consultation include:

- advising the youth that whatever is told to the lawyer is confidential and cannot be shared with others without the client's permission, but that the youth's conversations with others, including parents or cellmates, may later be used against him or her;

---

116 M. Peterson-Badali, and C. Koegl, "Young People's Knowledge of the *Young Offenders Act* and the Youth Justice System" (1998) 39 Can. J. Crim. 127.

- advising the youth that there is no obligation to give police any information other than name, age, and parents' identity. At this initial stage lawyers will invariably strongly urge a client not to make a statement, show the police evidence, or otherwise co-operate with the police investigation. There will be ample time to offer an explanation or plead guilty at a later point, when there has been an opportunity for reflection and the lawyer has had disclosure of the Crown's case;
- cautioning the youth that the police may use different techniques to try to induce a youth to make a later statement — for example, they may try to confront the youth with purported evidence of his or her guilt that may be inaccurate or that may not be admissible at a trial, such as a statement from an alleged accomplice;[117]
- advising the youth of the right to have a lawyer present if a statement should later be made to the police;
- warning of the possibility, if the circumstances appear to warrant, of an adult sentence;
- discussing the possibility of pre-trial detention and beginning to prepare for a bail hearing; it would be helpful for the lawyer to ascertain what the position of the police and Crown will be about pre-trial detention;
- obtaining information about the youth and parents, such as addresses and telephone numbers, and discussing with the youth what level of parental involvement is desired in regard to such issues as pre-trial detention and communication with counsel;
- ascertaining what has happened since the arrest (i.e., has a statement been made to the police already?);
- ascertaining the youth's present physical and emotional state (i.e., is medical attention needed?); and
- advising the youth, if a statement has been made, against offering any further explanations to the police at this time.[118]

Assuming that the youth accepts the lawyer's advice about not talking to the police at this time, the lawyer should obtain the youth's instructions to inform the police that a statement will not be made. If the youth insists on making a statement to the police at this time, the

---

117 The issue of the admissibility of a confession of an accomplice is complex and depends at least in part on whether the youths are charged jointly, and have one proceeding, or are charged separately. Counsel will not be able to advise the youth fully about this issue at such an early stage. See, for example, *R. v. B.(K.G.)*, [1993] 1 S.C.R. 740; and *R. v. S.(R.J.)*, [1995] 1 S.C.R. 451.

118 For a more detailed discussion, see S. Scott, M. Wong, and B. Weagant, *Defending Young Offender Cases*, 2d ed. (Toronto: Carswell, 1997) cc. 1 and 2.

lawyer should offer to be present, with a view to ensuring that there is no coercion and that questions are clear and fair.

If the youth has chosen to retain this particular lawyer to provide advice and representation, it will also be important to inform the youth about how to contact the lawyer if the need arises in the future, emphasizing that the police are obliged to facilitate contact if the youth is in detention. If the lawyer providing this initial advice was contacted through the legal aid toll-free telephone number, the lawyer should explain how the youth can go about getting legal representation. One potential difficulty for lawyers at police stations, and throughout their representation of adolescents, may arise when the interests and wishes of that adolescent conflict with those of his or her parents. Section 25(10) of the *YCJA*, which empowers the provinces to seek recovery of the costs of proving counsel from parents after the completion of the proceedings, may make this situation particularly difficult. It is likely that in some cases lawyers will experience considerable pressure from parents who feel that legal services for which they may ultimately have to pay should serve their interests. However, it is clear that counsel is to represent the interests of the youth, not those of the parents, and that it is the youth alone who is to instruct counsel.

D. PARENTS AT THE POLICE STATION

Section 146(2)(c)of the *YCJA* requires the police to advise a youth of the right to consult a parent before being questioned. The youth is entitled to decide whether to consult a parent or, if a parent is not available, another adult relative or an adult known to the youth. Some youths will want to see their parents to obtain emotional support and advice, although many who are arrested feel either too embarrassed or frightened, or too estranged to have their family immediately involved. The police are also obliged under section 26(1) of the Act to inform a parent "as soon as possible" whenever a young person has been arrested and detained in custody pending an appearance in court. This will apply in situations where a youth is being detained, regardless of the wishes of the youth and whether or not the youth is being questioned. This provision makes clear that the police have a duty to let parents know if their children are in detention.

It has been held that if a youth whom the police want to question expresses a desire to see a parent, the police have an obligation to permit a meeting as soon as the parent is available. In *R. v. P.(S.)*, a fourteen-year-old youth went to the police station with his parents and was arrested in their presence on a charge of sexual assault. He was taken to an interview room alone while his parents waited in the public area of the station. The police advised him of his rights and read him a waiver form. The youth said he wanted his father present during the interview. The officers then left the youth alone for forty minutes, without telling the parents anything. The officers returned and again explained his rights, at which point the youth said that he would make a statement without his father being present, and signed a waiver. The youth's statement was largely exculpatory, although he admitted that he had hugged the complainant. While the trial judge admitted the statement and convicted the youth, the Ontario Court of Appeal ruled that the statement was not admissible and set aside the conviction: "It is obvious . . . that the police failed to observe both the letter and spirit of this section. Once the [youth] . . . had stated unequivocally that he wanted his father present during the interview, he was entitled to have that right implemented immediately, where, as here, the father was already at the police station."[119]

Courts have also ruled statements inadmissible when youths have in some way been "misled" about the availability of a parent or when they have not been informed about the arrival of a parent at the police station during questioning, even if the right of consultation has been previously waived.[120] This is consistent with the recognition in principle of the important role of parents in the YCJA and the fact that a waiver of the rights in section 146(2) must be a knowing waiver. That is, a youth who believes that a parent is not readily available may want to get things over with and decide to waive the right of consultation, whereas if the youth had known that a parent was available for immediate consultation, he or she might have wanted to exercise that right.

While the YCJA and the Charter are premised on the expectation that a lawyer whom the youth might choose to consult will provide legal advice and protect the youth's legal rights, the role of parents at the point of police investigation is less clear. Some parents will feel that their role is similar to a lawyer's and take steps to protect their child's rights, advising the youth to remain silent until legal assistance is obtained. Other parents, however, may be more inclined to try to establish the truth and advise their child to speak up. While some parents

---

119 R. v. P.(S.) (1991), 44 O.A.C. 316 at 317 (C.A.).
120 R. v. S.(J.L.) (1995), 162 A.R. 388 (C.A.); R. v. M.(M.), [1995] M.J. No. 654 (Prov. Ct.) (QL).

may be supportive of their children, others may feel anger or embarrassment, or even think the "the kid had it coming."

An American study based on the actual observation of parents meeting with their children after arrest revealed that most parents do not offer any advice about legal rights such as the right to silence or the right to obtain legal representation.[121] Similarly, British research indicates that the presence of parents during a police interview with a youth has little effect on police tactics; the parents usually remained silent during the police questioning and, if they did intervene, they were as likely to be helpful to the police as to their child.[122]

While it is clear that the right of a youth to consult with a lawyer is the right to speak to that lawyer in private, the ambiguity about the role of the parent at this stage is reflected in the conflict in the case law over the nature of the consultation that is to occur between the parents and their children. In *R. v. M.-B.(M.)*, Garfinkle Prov. J. emphasized the supportive and advisory nature of the parental role, excluding a youth's statement because the Crown failed to show that there had been full compliance with the provisions of section 56 of the *YOA*, including those requiring that a youth should have a "reasonable opportunity" to consult meaningfully with a parent.[123] Satisfactory consultation requires that the youth and parent should be able to have a confidential conversation. The parent should also be given sufficient information by the police about the charges to enable a proper consideration of the issues to be undertaken. The judge in this case ruled the youth's statement inadmissible since, before the father consulted the youth, the police had not informed the father of the charges or the nature of their investigation and of the use they intended to make of the youth's statement. The judge felt that without this information, the father could not have a meaningful consultation with his child. The judge also suggested that the statement was inadmissible because the officer remained close to where the consultation between the father and son occurred and could have overheard it, a fact that raised concerns about lack of confidentiality.

The approach of *R. v. M.-B.(M.)* may be contrasted with that of Hardman Prov. J. in *R. v. B.(C.)*, where a statement was admitted despite

---

121 T. Grisso, *Juvenile Waiver of Rights: Legal and Psychological Competence* (New York: Plenum Press, 1981).

122 National Association for the Care and Resettlement of Offenders, "The Police and Criminal Evidence Act of 1984 and Young Offenders: The Role of an Appropriate Adult" in *National Association for the Care and Resettlement of Offenders Briefing* (London: 1996) at 6.

123 *R. v. M.-B.(M.)* (1995), 29 W.C.B. (2d) 416 (Man. Prov. Ct.); see also *R. v. D.K.D.*, [1998] A.J. No. 1508 (Prov. Ct.)

the failure of the police to give the parent an opportunity for a private consultation:

> There are clearly many reasons to view the role of counsel as different from that of parent. Lawyers are a specifically trained group of professionals who are governed by a stringent set of rules regarding their conduct. . . . As such their consultation with a client is protected by a special privilege. While parents have a special role under the Act, it is clearly a different role that would in a very practical way speak against making consultations always private with parents. There are situations where a young person may not want to be alone with a parent, particularly one who is angry. . . . What is reasonable will no doubt depend on the circumstances including the wishes of the young person and the parent. There may be security issues in some situations which would speak against private consultation with a parent.[124]

Section 146 of the *YCJA* does not resolve the issue of whether the police are obliged to allow for a private meeting between a youth and a parent. It is submitted, however, that, in the absence of security or safety concerns, there should be the opportunity for a private meeting; if there are security concerns, the police should be able to observe but not overhear the conversation. This approach seems most consistent with the protection of the rights of young persons and with encouraging parents to have a supportive role for their children. There may, of course, be situations in which it is not appropriate to allow for a consultation with one parent, such as if that person is a co-accused, but there may still be the possibility of consultation with the other parent or some other appropriate adult. Related to the issue of the privacy of any consultation between the parent and child is the question of the legal characterization of a statement from the youth confessing guilt to a parent. Parents will normally not be considered "persons in authority," and statements made to them by their children will usually be admissible against the child, despite the absence of any form of caution.[125] This common law position is reinforced by section 146(9), which provides that a person consulted by a youth pursuant to section 146(2)(c) "shall, in the absence of evidence to the contrary, be deemed not to be a person in authority."

In *R. v. B.(A.)*, where the Ontario Court of Appeal ruled that parents are not ordinarily in law "persons in authority," Cory J.A. discussed the

---

124 *R. v. B.(C.)*, [1995] O.J. No. 2303 (Prov. Div.) (QL).
125 *R. v. B.(A.)*, leave to appeal refused (1986), 50 C.R. (3d) xxv (note) (S.C.C.); see text with note 100. See also *YCJA*, above note 1, s. 146(9).

role of parents in their children's lives and the significance of a discussion in which a child might admit responsibility for a wrong act:

> From the point of view of the family, conversations such as this one are of great importance. . . . Whether it be directed to tracing a lost hockey stick, discovering who was . . . bullying a younger child, or investigating a broken window . . . the parental goals of discovering the truth and counselling, guiding and assisting the child will remain the same. . . . [F]amily discussions leading to the identification of problems and the provision of assistance without judicial intervention are encouraged by the Act.[126]

One could argue that, because parents are so important in the lives of their children, the law should give special protection to conversations between a parent and child, and should regard them as privileged and not admissible in court against the interest of the child — in the same way that communications between spouses or between a lawyer and client are privileged. Some American courts have accepted this argument to recognize a parent-child privilege,[127] but this has not been the Canadian approach.

While the effect of these decisions is ordinarily to render a statement made by a youth to a parent admissible, section 146(7) allows a youth court judge to rule inadmissible any statement given by the young person if the youth satisfies the judge that "the statement was given under duress imposed by any person who is not, in law, a person in authority." This provision, which is essentially identical to section 56(5) of the *YOA*, places an onus on the youth to satisfy the court, on the balance of probabilities, that there were physical threats or psychological pressures that resulted in the youth being unable to exercise proper judgment or acting without free will.[128] This provision may be relevant to some situations in which parental pressure has coerced a youth into making a confession to the police. In *R. v. L.(S.)*, the judge

---

126   *R. v. B.(A.)*, *ibid.*, at 258–59.
127   See, for example, *Re. A. & M.*, 403 N.Y.S. 2d 375 (S.C. App. Div. 1978).
128   There was little reported case law under this provision of the *YOA*, above note 5. In *R. v. E.(O.N.)* (2000), 47 W.C.B. (2d) 401 (B.C.S.C.), a case involving a threatening atmosphere by an undercover police officer, the court held that this provision only applied if the youth made the statement "devoid of free will and independent mind." S.S. Anand and J. Robb, "The Admissibility of Young People's Statements Under the Proposed *YCJA* (2002), 39 Alta L.Rev. 771, at 783, argue that in interpreting s. 46(7), youth justice courts should refer to the civil law concept of duress, which is used in contracts cases, with its "emphasis on exercise [of lack of] proper judgment is particularly pertinent to young persons."

felt that a father who became actively involved with the police in the questioning of his son about a suspected homicide in effect became a "member of the investigation team." The court ruled the youth's confession inadmissible, saying:

> There is no doubt that most well-thinking parents in a situation involving the death of a youngster would be anxious to co-operate in finding the truth, but when that involves co-operating with the police and obtaining some incriminating evidence against their own child, and without being made aware of all the information that the police had against the child, it is, I feel, not a rightful situation and can constitute an abuse of the very special relationship of authority and influence that a parent has on his child.[129]

The definition of "parent" in section 2(1) of the *YCJA* is broad enough to include any person or legal body "under a legal duty to provide" for a youth, or in fact or law having "custody or control" of a child. Accordingly, when a youth has been a ward of a child-welfare agency — for example, because of abuse or neglect at home — the agency becomes a parent for the purposes of section 146. When the child is a ward and an agency worker is playing the role of parent, concerns about duress and confidentiality may be heightened. If there is an allegation of an offence against another ward of the agency — in a group home, for example — there may also be concerns about a potential conflict of interest for the agency worker. In *R. v. C.(D.E.)*, the judge ruled that a statement which a sixteen-year-old ward of a child-welfare agency made to the police confessing to a sexual assault on a younger child was inadmissible because it was involuntary and section 56(2)(b) of the *YOA* was not satisfied. Judge Morrison remarked that a significant factor in determining that the statement was inadmissible was the role played by the agency worker who, although accompanying the youth to the police station where the statement was made, co-operated fully with the police and took no steps to advise or assist the youth:

> I am not suggesting that whenever a ward is under criminal investigation . . . there is an . . . obligation [on the agency] to automatically and immediately retain counsel. I am suggesting, particularly when a charge is a serious one, that the statutory guardian ought to offer the ward the same advice and direction one would expect to be forthcoming from a reasonable parent. A reasonable parent when informed or aware of the child's apparent complicity in an offence would . . . make a conscious and serious attempt to speak to their child in a private and

---

129 *R. v. L.(S.)* (Ont. Prov. Ct. (Fam. Div.)), summarized (1984), Y.O.S. 84–020.

meaningful way in a manner consistent with child and community interest and then determine the course of action to be adopted, including the appointment of counsel.[130]

While it may not be easy to define the role of agency workers when a ward is charged with a criminal offence, at the very least they have an obligation to take steps to ensure that a youth has adequate information to make an informed decision about whether to make a statement. Given the complexity of the position of the workers, obtaining the services of a lawyer for the youth will often be the best way to help fulfil the obligations to the ward.

1) Notification of Parents: Section 26

If a young person is arrested by the police and detained pending an appearance in youth justice court for a judicial interim release hearing, a parent must be notified "as soon as possible," orally or in writing, so that the parent knows where the child is and can provide assistance. This notification requirement is found in section 26(1) of the *YCJA*: "if a young person is arrested and detained in custody pending his or her appearance in court, the officer in charge at the time the young person is detained shall, as soon as possible, give or cause to be given to a parent of the young person, orally or in writing, notice of the arrest stating the place of detention and the reason for the arrest." If a youth is arrested and perhaps questioned, but then released on a promise to appear, section 26(2) requires that "a parent" must be notified in writing of the date of the youth justice court hearing, although there is no requirement for immediate notification of a parent of the fact that his of her child has been arrested. Section 26(2) also requires that, if a youth is not detained by the police and court proceedings are commenced by the issuance of a summons or appearance notice, which requires the youth to attend court on a specified date, a parent must be notified in writing of the date of the youth justice court hearing.[131] The purpose of notice under section 26(2) is to allow parents to facilitate the attendance of their child in court, as well as to attend themselves.

---

130 *R. v. C.(D.E.)* (11 August 1986), (Ont. Prov. Ct. (Fam. Div.)) [unreported] [summarized [1986] W.D.F.L. 2047], per Morrison Prov. J.

131 *YCJA*, above note 1, s. 26(6) provides: "Any notice under this section shall, in addition to any other requirements under this section, include (a) the name of the young person in respect of whom it is given; (b) the charge against the young person and . . . the time and place of appearance; and (c) a statement that the young person has the right to be represented by counsel."

Section 26(1) applies if a youth is detained by the police for the purpose of being brought to court for a judicial interim release hearing, and requires notification of the detention "as soon as possible." If the police are only detaining a youth for a relatively brief period of time for the purposes of investigating the offence or questioning the youth, they are only legally obliged to contact a parent if the youth requests a consultation with a parent in connection with the making of a statement. In practice, however, most police officers will attempt to contact parents whenever they arrest a youth so that the parents can take their child home. This may also give the police officer an opportunity to discuss the situation with the parents, perhaps including the possibility of extrajudicial sanctions, and to serve the parents with any notice required under section 26(2). If the parents cannot be located, however, the police may release the youth and later arrange for the parents to be served with the written notice required under section 26(2).

The notice provisions in the YCJA only require notice to be given to "a parent," indicating that notice to one parent is sufficient, on the assumption that one parent will usually inform the other. As noted above, the definition of "parent" in section 2(1) of the YCJA is broad, and includes "any person who is under a legal duty to provide for the young person or any person who has, in law or in fact, the custody or control of the young person." If the parents have separated this definition would certainly allow the police to notify a non-custodial parent, although it would be most common practice to serve the custodial parent. This definition includes a step-parent, guardian, or other adult who resides with the youth and exercises parental responsibilities for the youth. Normally at the time of arrest, the police will ask the youth about the identity of parents and about how to locate them. Section 26(4) provides that if a parent cannot be located or is not available, the police may give notice of detention and of the court hearing to an adult relative or other appropriate adult who is "known to the young person and likely to assist the youth." If there is doubt about to whom notice should be given, an application can be made to a youth justice court under section 26(5) for directions from the court about who should receive the parental notice.

Under the Juvenile Delinquents Act, in effect until 1984, the failure of the Crown to prove that a parent was served with notice of a delinquency proceeding would take away jurisdiction of the juvenile court to deal with the case, even if the parent actually attended court.[132] If the Crown prosecutor was careless and forgot to prove compliance with

---

132 R. v. Côté (1976), 31 C.C.C. (2d) 414 (Sask. Q.B.).

the *Juvenile Delinquents Act* notice provision, charges could be dismissed. Section 26(9)–(11) of the *YCJA* adopts the approach of the *YOA*, limiting the situations in which the failure to give notice will render proceedings invalid.[133]

If the youth is not detained in custody and no notice is given to a parent of the youth justice court proceeding under section 26(2) of the *YCJA*, the proceedings are not invalid if the parent attends court with the youth, despite the failure to receive formal written notice. Further, if, before a finding of guilt is made, the Crown realizes that a parent has not been served, section 26(10) gives the youth justice court a broad power to take steps to remedy the failure to give notice by dispensing with notice or ordering service on some other appropriate person than a parent. However, a finding of guilt and any sentence can be invalidated if the youth has not been in detention and the police failed to give any parent notice of the court proceedings; the failure to give any parent notice will not invalidate the proceedings if a parent attends court or a judge dealt with the notice issue under section 26(10).

Under section 26(9), if a youth is detained in custody after arrest and not released pending trial, the failure to give a parent notice of the detention under section 26(1) does not invalidate the proceedings, although the judge should inquire about whether a parent has received notice and may adjourn proceedings. If no parent or other appropriate adult has received notice, the court may adjourn the proceedings and order that notice shall be given in a manner and to a person that the court specifies, or the court may dispense with notice. While the Crown and police have an obligation to ensure that a parent is notified of the detention of the youth and about the proceedings, in these more serious cases where a youth has been detained, Parliament did not consider it appropriate to invalidate the proceedings because of a delay or failure to given notice.[134] If their child is in detention, parents who have not been notified but are concerned about their children are very likely to contact the police and learn of the proceedings.

Section 27 allows a youth justice court to order that a parent attend any proceedings if such attendance is considered "necessary or in the best interests of the young person." While parents are not parties to youth justice court proceedings, they have a statutory right to address the court prior to sentencing. Parents will often attend proceedings voluntarily but, sometimes, especially with older youths or youths with a history of offending, relations between the parent and child may be

---

133 For similar provisions of the *YOA*, above note 5, see s. 9(7) to (9).
134 *R. v. M.(L.J.)* (1995), 128 Sask. R. 134 (C.A.)

strained. Ordering the attendance of parents who are unwilling or unable to attend youth justice court with their child will rarely be useful. One of the few reported cases where a judge made such an order under the *YOA* involved a ward of the child-welfare authorities, who appeared to be abandoning the youth to the justice system.[135]

E. FINGERPRINTS AND PHOTOGRAPHS

Section 113 of the *YCJA* allows the police to fingerprint and photograph a young person charged with an indictable offence, which for this purpose includes any hybrid offence.[136] It is common police practice to have fingerprints and photographs taken, even if this is not necessary for the investigation of the offence charged, to assist in possible future investigations.[137] In serious cases, the fingerprinting and photographing may be done as soon as charges are laid, while in less serious cases the youth will be released after initial apprehension and given a notice requiring attendance at the police station a few days after the charges are laid so that this may be done.[138] Unlike the situation with an adult, section 113(2) of the *YCJA* specifies that a young person cannot "consent" to a police request for fingerprints for "investigative" purposes in circumstances where he or she has not been charged with

---

135 *R. v. H.(R.)* (November 26, 1984), (Alta. Prov. Ct.) [unreported] [summarized (1984), 13 W.C.B. 170]. However, the Canada, House of Commons, *Thirteenth Report of the Standing Committee on Justice and Legal Affairs: Renewing Youth Justice* (Ottawa: Ministry of Supply and Services, 1997) recommended, without explanation, that parents should be required to attend youth court except in "exceptional circumstances" (at 68).

136 *Lunney v. H.(M.)* (1984), 56 A.R. 250 (Q.B.), aff'd. (1985), 21 C.C.C. (3d) 384 (Alta. C.A.).

137 As discussed earlier in this chapter, in investigations involving sexual offences and other serious offences, under s. 487.05 of the *Criminal Code*, above note 2, the police can also obtain a warrant to take a DNA sample from a suspect, including a youth.

138 Failure to attend for required fingerprinting is a punishable offence under s. 145 of the *Criminal Code*, above note 2. In *R. v. K.(P.A.)* (4 June 1997), (Ont. Prov. Ct.) [unreported] [summarized *Lawyers Weekly*, August 15, 1997, no. 1713–008], Scott J. held that a youth could be convicted under this provision only if a parent was also notified of the requirements to attend; although the *YOA*, above note 5, did not explicitly refer to such notice, the judge interpreted s. 9(6) of that Act to require this so that parents "can provide guidance and assistance to ensure those obligations are understood and complied with." This is not explicitly dealt with in the *YCJA*, above note 1, and the same reasoning may well apply.

an indictable offence. This affords special protections to youths who may be vulnerable to manipulation by the police and who might not appreciate the significance of "consenting" to have their fingerprints taken.[139] If the youth is found not guilty of the offence, then section 119(2)(b) specifies that three months after the acquittal, no further use can be made of any fingerprints or photographs of a young person. If the youth is found guilty, the period of use is determined by section 119, and depends on the seriousness of the offence and its disposition.

If the young person is found guilty, the police force that took the fingerprints and photographs is required to send a record of them to the central repository kept by the Royal Canadian Mounted Police, as part of the computerized Canadian Police Information Centre (CPIC), where they may be accessed by any force in Canada for investigative purposes in any future situations.[140] If the youth is found guilty, the period of use by CPIC is determined by section 119, and depends on the seriousness of the offence and its disposition. If the youth is found not guilty, under section 128(2) the CPIC registry must ensure that, within three months of the acquittal, any fingerprints or photographs of the young person that may have been received from a local force during an investigation are destroyed.

F. FIRST APPEARANCE AND PRE-TRIAL DETENTION

If a youth has been arrested, the arresting police officer or the officer in charge at the police station may decide to release the youth, either with or without questioning about the alleged offence, or may decide that it is appropriate to seek to have the youth detained pending trial. Under the *YOA*, there were concerns that pre-trial detention was being overused, and the *YCJA* seeks to address this problem. The provisions of the *Criminal Code* that govern the arrest of both adults and youths, sections 494–502, require the police to release a person who has been arrested unless it is in the "public interest" to detain that person, having regard to:

- the need to establish the identity of the person;
- the need to secure or preserve evidence;

---

139 *R. v. D.(F.D.)* (11 May 1984), (Ont. Prov. Ct.) [unreported] [summarized (1984), 12 W.C.B. 152].

140 *YCJA*, above note 1, s. 115(2). See Chapter 7 for a fuller discussion of access to records and disclosure.

- the need to prevent further offending by the person; and
- the concern that the person will fail to attend court.[141]

The police may release a youth with a document requiring the youth to appear in youth justice court on a specified date. For the least serious cases, a youth may be given an appearance notice which simply requires the youth to appear in court on the specified date. If the police release the youth on a recognizance or a promise to appear, there may be conditions imposed, such as abstaining from communicating with potential witnesses or the complainant.

Youths who are arrested for relatively minor charges are normally released pending a hearing, but those charged with more serious offences, or who have records of prior findings of guilt, or who might not appear in court, may be detained pending trial. The detention process is controlled by the youth justice court, pursuant to Part XVI of the *Criminal Code* and the *YCJA*. Section 30(3) of the *YCJA* requires that, following arrest, a youth should be detained "separate and apart" from adults, although section 30(7) allows the police to "temporarily restrain" a young person with an adult after arrest, provided that the youth is under the "supervision and control" of an officer and the youth is transferred "as soon as is reasonably practicable" to a temporary detention facility or brought before a court.

While in general the *YCJA* seeks to protect youths from possible exploitation or abuse by adults and requires separate detention, section 30(7) gives police some flexibility at the time of arrest and when taking a youth to the police station. It is not, for example, necessary to transport youths separately from adults when taking them from the scene of arrest to the police station, provided that an officer is supervising the youth and can prevent any exploitation by adults. In general, however, once detained, the conveyance of youth to court and detention facilities must be separate from adults.

Ordinarily, youths are to be detained in separate facilities from adults, but section 30(3) of the *YCJA* allows a youth justice court judge or a justice of the peace to order a young person to be detained with adults if this is necessary for "his own safety or the safety of others," or if there is no youth detention facility available within a "reasonable distance." This provision is occasionally invoked, for example, if an older

---

141 See, for example, *Criminal Code*, above note 2, ss. 495(2)(d)–(e) and 498(1)(i)–(j). The focus of the discussion here is on issues related to the pre-trial detention of young persons; for a much fuller discussion of issues related to pre-trial detention, see Gary Trotter, *The Law of Bail in Canada*, 2d ed. (Scarborough, ON: Carswell, 1998).

youth appears to be a security risk and is threatening other youths or staff in a youth detention facility.[142] While pre-trial detention is usually separate from adults, youths who are waiting for trial are often kept in the same facilities as young offenders who have been convicted and are serving sentences in custody. In some provinces adolescents who have been taken into the care of a child-welfare agency may be placed with young persons awaiting trial under the YCJA. Although young offenders sometimes have problems similar to those adolescents in agency care, there are concerns about the appropriateness of this arrangement for youths in the care of child-welfare agencies.[143]

If the police decide that a youth should be detained, the youth should be brought to court within twenty-four hours or, if a judge or justice of the peace is not available within that time, "as soon as possible" thereafter.[144] A "judicial interim release hearing" should ordinarily be held within twenty-four hours of arrest but, in practice, some youths may be detained for a few days before being brought before the court, especially if the arrest is on the weekend or there are difficulties in locating parents.[145] These judicial interim release hearings are called "bail" or "show cause" hearings, because the onus is generally on the Crown to show why the accused should be detained.

Although at least in theory the Crown prosecutor will make the decision about whether to seek an order for detention or what conditions to request if the youth is to be released, in practice the views of the police — usually communicated to the Crown prosecutor in a written brief — are likely to be very influential. If the youth is on probation or supervision at the time of the arrest, the probation officer responsible for supervising the youth may also be consulted. In the case of a youth not represented by counsel, the police are obliged under section 25 of the YCJA to inform him or her about the right to counsel and the process to be followed to obtain access to legal services.

---

142 See, for example, *R. v. P.*, [1979] 2 W.W.R. 262, 8 R.F.L. (2d) 277 (Man. Q.B.), which was decided under a similar provision of the *Juvenile Delinquents Act*, R.S.C. 1970, c. J-3.

143 See, for example, *Re B.(J.A.)*, (12 October 1984), (Ont. Prov. Ct. (Fam. Div.)) [unreported] [summarized [1984] W.D.F.L. 1522].

144 *Criminal Code*, above note 2, s. 503(1).

145 See, for example, J. Gandy, *Judicial Interim Release (Bail) Hearings* (Toronto: Policy Research Centre for Children, Youth and Families, 1992). This study of three Ontario cities found that some youths had to wait in detention for up to a week before appearing in court. Youths with a lawyer can take steps to prevent such abuses from occurring. In theory a lawyer could bring an application for a writ of *habeas corpus* to a superior court, but in practice a call from a lawyer to the police or Crown prosecutor will invariably suffice.

For youths who appear in court for a bail hearing without having obtained the services of a lawyer, there may be a duty counsel (i.e., a lawyer paid by the government) to provide some assistance with that hearing and to help the youth begin the process of obtaining a lawyer to deal with the charges. The charge is also read at the first appearance, unless counsel for the youth waives this.[146] While a pre-trial judicial interim release for young persons is often dealt with by youth justice court judges, section 20 of the *YCJA* also allows a justice of the peace to deal with this issue — except for murder cases[147] — since a youth court judge may not be readily available. Under section 20, if a justice of the peace makes an initial order concerning pre-trial detention, a new detention hearing may be held before a youth justice court judge who will deal with the issue as an "original application," not as a review or appeal. There is also the further right to have a review by a higher court of the decision of a youth justice court judge about judicial interim release.[148]

Pursuant to the *Criminal Code* section 525, if a youth is ordered to be detained there must be a periodic rehearing of the detention decision, every thirty days for a summary offence and every ninety days if the offence is hybrid or indictable. If a youth is not released and is held in detention, a case will generally receive some priority in scheduling of a trial date, although it is not uncommon for a youth to spend weeks, or even months, in detention without having been found guilty of any offence. At least in theory, the decision to order that a youth should be detained pending trial is to be made on the same legal basis as that applicable to adults. In general, the onus is on the Crown to show why an accused should be detained pending trial. However, where the person is charged with murder or a serious drug offence, or is charged with a serious offence while on release for other serious charges, it will be a "reverse onus" situation, with the accused required to show why he or she should be released.[149] There is also a "reverse onus" if the youth is charged with failure to appear in court pursuant to an earlier release.

---

146 *YCJA*, above note 1, ss. 32(1) and (2).
147 *Criminal Code*, above note 2, ss. 515(1) and 469 list a few offences for which a justice of the peace cannot deal with judicial interim release. Murder is the only offence on the list that a youth is likely to be charged with, as the others are such offences as mutiny, treason, and piracy.
148 *Criminal Code*, above note 2, ss. 520 and 521; *YCJA*, above note 1, ss. 33(5)–(7). The review is generally by a superior court judge; if the youth justice court judge is a superior court judge, the review is by a judge of the court of appeal.
149 *Criminal Code*, above note 2, ss. 515(6) and 522.

The grounds for detention are set out in section 515(10) of the *Criminal Code,* which provides that detention is justified only:

(a) where the detention is necessary to ensure . . . attendance in court . . .

(b) where the detention is necessary . . . for the protection or safety of the public, having regard to all the circumstances including any substantial likelihood that the accused will, if released from custody, commit a criminal offence or interfere with the administration of justice [for example by threatening a witness] . . . and

(c) . . . where the detention is necessary in order to maintain confidence in the administration of justice, having regard to all the circumstances, including the apparent strength of the prosecution's case, the gravity of the nature of the offence, the circumstances surrounding its commission and the potential for a lengthy term of imprisonment.

Under the *YOA,* the courts accepted that, if a youth had no previous record, in light of the provisions of the *Criminal Code* and the *YOA* and "in particular the principles set out in s. 3 . . . it is only in exceptional cases that pre-disposition custody of a young offender would be justified."[150] Detention was more likely to be considered when the youth has a significant record of prior offending, thereby raising a concern that there may be a "substantial likelihood" of further offending, or if there is a history of failing to comply with court orders, or of non-attendance at court. There is significant evidence that, under the *YOA,* there was over-reliance on pre-trial detention for young persons, just as custody was overused as a sentence.[151] For example, in 1997–98, pre-trial

---

150 *R.* v. *G.(C.)* (1993), 79 C.C.C. (3d) 446 (Ont. C.A.), Labrosse J.A. Even when a youth faces a murder charge and hence has the onus of justifying release, if there is no prior record and parents can provide adequate supervision, the "court must lean against institutional confinement . . . in favour of parental custody" and release the youth: *R.* v. *L.(D.C.)* (15 February 1991), (B.C.C.A.) [unreported] [summarized (1991), 16 W.C.B. (2d) 137]. See also *R.* v. *L.(D. B.)* (1994), 155 A.R. 64 (C.A.), where the court appeared to accept this approach but was not satisfied by the youth's evidence of the adequacy of parental supervision.

151 *YCJA,* above note 1, s. 30(8), also allows provincial governments to require the approval of an official or board before a youth is detained pending trial, although few jurisdictions are likely to invoke this provision by creating another step in the process; rather provinces are likely to deal with any government concerns about pre-trial detention by establishing non-legally enforceable guidelines for police or Crown prosecutors.

remand represented 60 percent of total admissions of youths into custodial facilities in Canada.[152] Despite the focus in section 515(10) of the *Code* on the issues of ensuring court attendance and preventing reoffending, under the *YOA* some youth court judges and other justice system personnel took a range of social factors into account in deciding whether to detain a youth. Also, some judges may have misused detention, by in effect imposing it as a form of punishment.

The Preamble to the *YCJA* emphasizes the need to reduce Canada's "over-reliance on incarceration for non-violent young persons." In some measure the overuse of custodial facilities has been a result of youths being held in pre-trial detention for social or punitive purposes. Given the slow pace of proceedings in the youth justice system, pre-trial detention may be considered by some to be a response that is developmentally appropriate and in the best interests of some youth. Canadian child psychiatrist Eric Hood argues that a "taste of custody" through pre-trial detention may sometimes teach "a more immediate lesson" than the slow-moving justice system."[153] While a swift response to crime is desirable, a judge should not impose a sanction before the youth is found guilty and sentenced, even if the judge is certain that the youth is guilty.

In one Saskatchewan case under the *YOA* a sixteen-year-old Aboriginal youth with a prior record of two property offences pleaded guilty to three more non-violent offences. The youth court judge ordered the youth remanded (i.e., detained) in custody pending sentencing, saying: "This has got to stop, and if no one is around who cares about this young person — his parents didn't come with him — then I think what else am I to think about the guidance that's necessary to prevent young people from developing this way to do these things." This pre-adjudication detention decision was reversed by an appeal judge, who remarked that the youth court judge did not remand the youth in detention "for either of the purposes referred to in section 515(10); namely, to ensure his attendance in court, or for the purpose of protecting the public.... [The judge,] in remanding [the youth] ... in custody ... without sentencing him ... did so because he was not certain what sentence he wished to impose, and he apparently wished

---

152 Statistics Canada, "The Use of Custodial Remand," *The Daily*, November 25, 1999: available online at time of writing at <www.statcan.ca>.

153 See J. Saunders, "Hamilton Mother Hopes Tough Love Straightens out Son," *Globe and Mail*, April 18, 1998.

to provide . . . a 'wake up' call. Neither of these 'purposes' would qualify a person for detention under section 515(10)."[154]

It is likely that there will be cases in which youth justice court judges will believe that a youth with a prior record is probably guilty of the new charges and will be tempted to give this individual an immediate "short, sharp shock" by ordering detention following arrest. It may be difficult to establish that a judicial decision to detain a youth was motivated by an intent to punish. While in theory sanctioning must not be a factor at this stage, judges are entitled to take account of a prior record at a bail hearing for the purpose of determining whether there is a "substantial likelihood" of reoffending pending resolution of the case. Indeed, this is an important, relevant factor at the bail hearing. The late Ontario youth court judge A.P. Nasmith expressed concern that youths are more likely to be subject to pre-adjudication detention than adults facing the same charges and that detention may be misused, thereby contributing to the "excessive criminalization of children." The judge cited the disturbing finding of American researchers that a large portion of juveniles who were detained before trial were released after trial, indicating that detention was not justified. The judge quoted the researchers' conclusion: "Detention is used more to punish youngsters than to protect them, or society. The ease with which juveniles can be detained provides an enormous temptation to judges . . . to lock youngsters up for a few days, or longer, to 'teach them a lesson.'"[155] Judge Nasmith expressed similar concerns about the situation in Canada.

Section 29(2) of the *YCJA* is a partial response to the potential misuse of pre-trial detention. Section 29(2) provides that "in considering whether the detention of a young person is necessary for the protection or safety of the public under paragraph 515(10)(b) of the *Criminal Code*, a youth justice court judge . . . shall presume that detention is not necessary under that paragraph if the young person could not, on being found guilty, be committed to custody on the grounds set out" in

---

154 *R. v. Y.(D.H.)* (1995), 132 Sask. R. 107 at 111 (Q.B.). In 1997, s. 515(10) of the *Criminal Code* was amended by the *Criminal Law Improvement Act, 1996*, S.C. 1997, c. 18, s. 59(2) to allow a court to consider the gravity of the offence and the effect of release on "maintain[ing] [public] confidence in the administration of justice." While this amendment may result in more youths (and adults) facing serious charges to be detained, it should not be used to allow "punishment before disposition," especially for non-violent offences. See *R. v. Hall*, [2002] S.C.J. No. 65 (QL), upholding the constitutional validity of this provision.

155 A.P. Nasmith, *Judicial Interim Release for Youths: The Law and Other Exigencies* (Canadian Association of Provincial Court Judges, New Judges Program, 1993), quoting C.E. Silberman, *Criminal Violence, Criminal Justice* (New York: Random House, 1978) at 321–22.

section 39(1)(a)–(c) of the *YCJA*. As discussed in Chapter 8, section 39(1) restricts the situations in which a custodial sentence can be imposed on a youth who is found guilty of an offence which does not involve violence. Section 29(2) therefore creates a presumption that, if a custodial sentence could not be imposed if the youth is later convicted, the youth should not be detained unless there is evidence of a substantial likelihood that the youth will not attend court, justifying pre-trial detention under section 515(10)(a) of the *Criminal Code*.[156]

It is also apparent that a host of socio-legal factors related to a youth's family situation and personal background can affect detention decisions.[157] It is, to some extent, legitimate for youth justice court judges to take account of these factors, since they may affect the youth's likelihood of reoffending or not appearing in court, but caution should be exercised so that a judge is not detaining a youth as a means of providing social supports or in an effort to try to assist parents or child welfare workers in dealing with a troublesome youth or a "runner." It should also be appreciated that the kind of social and family problems that can affect detention decisions are also correlated to ethnicity, Aboriginal status, and low income: there are concerns that pre-trial detention under the *YOA* may have operated in a discriminatory fashion in Canada. Some judges may, for example, have been influenced into ordering pre-trial detention because the youth is living on the street, or because the parent or guardian is reluctant to provide accommodation.

It is not difficult to understand the reasons for some judges to be tempted to use pre-trial detention as a social measure for adolescents who may be homeless or engaging in such self-destructive behaviour as juvenile prostitution. Section 29(1) of the *YCJA*, however, makes clear that a youth justice court judge or a justice of the peace shall not detain a young person in custody prior to being sentenced as a "substitute for appropriate child protection, mental health, or other social measures."

---

156 If a youth is charged with a failure to appear pursuant to an earlier release, ss. 515(6)(c) and 10(a) of the *Code* continue to make this a situation where the onus is on the youth to justify release from detention.

157 See, for example, P.J. Carrington, S. Moyer, and F. Kopelman, "Factors Affecting Pre-Dispositional Detention and Release in Canadian Juvenile Courts" (1988) 16 J. Crim Justice 463; and S.A. Fortugno and M. Rogstad, *A Socio-Legal Analysis of Youth Justice in Saskatoon* (Saskatoon: John Howard Society of Saskatchewan, 1994). There were substantial variations under the *YOA* in the rates of pre-trial detention use, with Manitoba and Alberta having three times as many youths (per 10,000 youth population) in detention as Quebec and Newfoundland; S. Moyer, "A Profile of the Juvenile Justice System in Canada," *Federal–Provincial/Territorial Task Force on Youth Justice* (Ottawa: Ministry of Supply and Services, 1996) at 65.

Further, section 35 of the *YCJA* allows a youth justice court judge to refer troubled youths to a child welfare agency for an assessment to determine whether the young person is in need of child welfare services, although it is for the agency and not the court to decide if it will provide services. Section 35 is intended to increase the integration between the social welfare and justice systems, and to help connect youths to the community services of which they are in need. There are, however, likely to continue to be concerns about how these systems interact. Under the *YOA*, wards of child welfare agencies accounted for a substantial portion of all youths who were placed in detention. While in theory child welfare or mental health laws should be invoked to deal with such social problems, the reality has been that overburdened child welfare agencies and mental health facilities often seem reluctant to deal with the troubled adolescents who are charged with offences.

Not infrequently, the charges are actually laid as a result of agency or group-home staff seeking police assistance in situations where a parent might not call the police, and then informing the court at a judicial interim release hearing that the adolescent is "non-compliant" and not suitable for agency care. Although a concern about a youth's welfare should not be a justification to remand the youth in custody, under the *YOA* this may have been be a factor contributing to the over-reliance on pre-adjudication detention and custody, as child welfare agencies transferred difficult cases into the youth justice system.

At a bail hearing the court can admit evidence considered "credible or trustworthy," which permits the Crown to rely on evidence that may not be admissible at trial.[158] A summary of the circumstances of the alleged offence and the strength of the Crown's case, including any statement from the youth and the youth's previous record, if any, will normally be presented to the court, either by a police officer testifying or, with the consent of the accused, by having the prosecutor read this evidence from a report or file.[159] There may also be evidence about any prior releases and about any history of failing to attend court, and possibly some background information about the youth and family situation, if this is known from the police investigation or prior court involvement.

The youth has an opportunity to present evidence and, if appropriate, a plan for supervision in the community pending trial. If supervision by a parent or other person is contemplated, that person will normally testi-

---

158 *Criminal Code*, above note 2, s. 518(1)(e).

159 In theory the Crown may introduce evidence only through witnesses, but it is common at a bail hearing for the accused to consent to the prosecutor "reading in evidence" from the file without calling witnesses: *R. v. Hajdu* (1984), 14 C.C.C. (3d) 563 (Ont. H.C.J.).

fy. If the youth testifies, the prosecutor cannot ask questions about the alleged offence, unless the youth raises this issue.[160] A bail hearing will result in the court ordering either the detention or the release of the youth. There is also a broad authority under section 515 to impose "reasonable conditions" on an individual who is being released, either to ensure attendance in court or to reduce the likelihood of reoffending. These conditions might include a requirement that the youth reside under the supervision of parents or some other person, maintain a curfew, and refrain from contacting co-accuseds or victims of the alleged offence. A judge may also require that an accused provide some form of financial security or that some other person act as a surety or guarantor that the accused will attend court, with the possibility of a financial penalty if the accused fails to attend. Imposing financial stipulations on the release of youths from custody pending trial is generally inappropriate.

Section 31 of the *YCJA* allows a court to release a young person whose detention would otherwise be justified under section 515(10) of the Code into the care and control of a "responsible person," such as a parent or other adult. Section 31(1) provides that a youth may be placed in the care of a "responsible person" instead of being detained in custody if the youth justice court judge or justice of the peace is satisfied that the youth would, but for this section, be detained in custody, and the court is satisfied that the person is "willing and able to take care of and exercise control over the young person." An order shall only be made under this provision if the youth is "willing to be placed in the care" of the "responsible adult," and that person undertakes in writing to take care of and to be responsible for the attendance of the young person in court and to comply with any other conditions imposed by the court, such as ensuring that the youth maintain a curfew and refrain from consuming alcohol pending trial. A similar provision in the *YOA*, section 7.1, was not used frequently, since, if the court felt that detention was appropriate, it was reluctant to permit an adult in the community to supervise a youth pending trial, particularly if the individuals coming forward offering supervision had previously failed in their efforts to supervise the youth. Courts were also reluctant to accept supervision by parents who had criminal records, which may disadvantage youths from families with a criminal history.[161]

An adult who "wilfully fails" to comply with an undertaking made under section 31 commits an offence under section 139 of the *YCJA* and, if convicted, is liable to imprisonment for up to two years. This is

---

160 *Criminal Code*, above note 2, s. 518(1)(b).
161 *R. v. S.(K.)*, [1996] O.J. No. 2346 (Prov. Div.) (QL).

a substantial increase in the penalty to which a responsible person may be liable if he or she wilfully fails to meet conditions of placement from the six months' imprisonment allowed for under section 7.2 of the *YOA*. This increase in the maximum penalty reflects a movement toward increased parental responsibility for their children, although prosecutions under this provision rarely if ever occurred.

In some localities innovative bail-supervision programs have been established to allow supervision in the community by professionals of youths released pending trial. These programs have had some success in preventing youths from being unnecessarily placed in detention. Youths under the supervision of these programs often reside at home with their families — although they may be placed in a group home or may be living on their own — and are required to meet regularly with a supervisor who monitors their behaviour and arranges community supports. This type of program may help to reduce disproportionate pre-trial detention of youths whose parents have prior criminal records, who are Aboriginal, or who belong to a visible minority, by providing them with an appropriate community supervisor.

While the supervisors in these programs have a professional responsibility for youths in their caseload, they will not be "responsible persons" for the purposes of having an order made under section 31(1). At least some of the youths released under bail-supervision programs may be at a relatively high risk of offending and it would be inappropriate to hold these professionals accountable through the criminal justice system for the misconduct of these youths. However, if there are significant failures in the level of supervision provided in a particular community, this will undoubtedly affect the willingness of courts to release youths into the care of that bail-supervision program.

Pre-trial detention has the potential of being highly disruptive and stressful to a young person, since it may result in the sudden removal from familiar surroundings and placement in an often intimidating, institutional environment. While some localities have quite good youth-detention facilities with social supports and programs to meet the needs of youths at this stressful time,[162] there is great variation in available facilities. Many youth-detention facilities have inadequate programs and resources and may just be jails for adolescents. There are concerns that youths placed in detention may be subjected to harassment or abuse from other young offenders and to the negative influences of such envi-

---

162 See, for example, A.W. Leschied, G.W. Austin, and E. Riley, "Description and Assessment of a Crisis Consultation Program in a Youth Detention Centre" (1989) 31 Can. J. Crim. 145.

ronments. The inadequacies of some youth-detention facilities were graphically demonstrated in a 1991 Ontario decision, *R. v. M.(T.)*, where Judge King found that the conditions in which youths were detained pending court appearance in downtown Toronto constituted "cruel and unusual" treatment, in violation of section 12 of the *Charter*. The holding cells where youths under sixteen were detained were hot, smelly, overcrowded, and dirty. There was nothing for them to do for hours at a time. The staff had no training in dealing with youths, and all youths were handcuffed when outside the cells. While the conditions at this particular facility improved after this case was decided, the decision is illustrative of the problems that arise with pre-trial detention.[163]

Pre-trial detention is highly intrusive since it occurs without any finding of guilt; in certain respects, it is inconsistent with the presumption of innocence. Pre-trial detention will significantly interfere with familial and peer relationships and will likely totally disrupt schooling or employment. Even if there are good staff and resources in the facility where the youth is detained, it is difficult to establish a meaningful educational or rehabilitative program for a youth whose detention begins abruptly and is of an indeterminate and often relatively short duration. Further, a youth who is in detention and uncertain about the future may feel considerable pressure to plead guilty to get things over with, even if the youth is not in fact guilty.[164] It is, therefore, important for counsel to make a serious effort to obtain the release of a young client at this stage. Bail hearings are often a challenging proceeding for a lawyer since there may be little time to meet the client and, if needed, to prepare a suitable plan for supervision in the community.[165]

---

163 *R. v. M.(T.)* (1991), 4 O.R. (3d) 203 (Prov. Div.). Another Ontario youth court judge, Bean Prov. J., emphatically stated: "[I]n most detention facilities . . . [t]he programs are terrible. The physical facilities usually stink. There's nothing for them to do. They just sit there and rot" (quoted in "Ont. Judge Stresses Importance of Bail in Young Offender System," *Lawyers Weekly*, June 30, 1989: 22.

164 See G. Kellough and S. Wortley, "Remand for Plea: Bail Decisions and Plea Bargaining as Commensurate Decisions" (2002) 42 Brit. J. Crim. 186. This article reports on a study of adults in detention in Toronto, and concludes that those who are in detention are considerably more likely to plead guilty than those facing the same charges and with similar records who were released.

165 Under s. 516 of the *Criminal Code*, above note 2, it is possible to have a three-day adjournment (or longer with the consent of the accused) in a pre-trial release hearing, and counsel for a youth will sometimes want to seek an adjournment to have time to prepare a plan. Plans might involve parents, relatives, or other adults, or a child welfare agency, a youth shelter, or some other social agency. Sometimes non-profit agencies outside the child welfare system are willing to provide assistance; if the youth is a ward of a child welfare agency, the agency may be willing, or obliged, to provide financial support during the release period.

Section 38(3)(d) of the *YCJA* makes clear that if a youth is found guilty, the youth justice court judge who imposes a sentence shall "take into account . . . the time spent in detention by the young person."[166] As discussed more fully in Chapter 8, there is a strong argument that the youth should receive extra credit for the time in pre-trial detention since the conditions and programming are often worse than those in custody, and a portion of the custodial sentence that is imposed is presumptively spent in the community under supervision. This, however, is no reason for counsel and the courts not to take very seriously the decision to detain a youth prior to adjudication.

If a youth is released into the community as a result of a judicial interim release hearing, it is important that any conditions imposed are realistic and necessary to ensure attendance in court or to prevent offending. Sometimes parents or social workers will want a judge at a pre-trial release hearing to impose detailed behavioural conditions on a youth, for example, in regard to curfews, school attendance, or behaviour. Even if the youth is originally charged with a relatively minor offence, the conditions of release may place strict limits on his or her behaviour for potentially lengthy periods of time until final resolution of a case. Given the circumstances and temperament of some youths, complying with strict behavioural conditions may be unrealistic. While a failure to comply with the conditions may not pose any threat to the safety of society, if there is a breach of a condition of release and a charge laid for this, the judge may be more likely to view this breach as a serious offence, since it shows disrespect for the justice system, and impose a custodial sentence. Thus, a relatively minor initial charge has the potential to result in a spiraling series of administration-of-justice charges and serious involvement with the youth justice system. This concern suggests the need for only imposing conditions that relate to attendance in court or prevention of offending behaviour. For some troubled youths the new provisions of the *YCJA* allowing for referral from the justice system to child welfare may provide a way out of this spiral.

---

166 Taking account of pre-trial detention was already a common practice when sentencing youths under the *YOA*, above note 5; see *R. v. K.(M.)* (1996), 28 O.R. (3d) 593 (C.A.).

G. RELEASE OF CHARGED YOUTHS AND SCHOOL CONCERNS

Victims of an alleged offence (i.e., complainants) may have concerns about the release of an accused young person pending trial, especially if there will be ongoing contact with the possibility of intimidation or further offending. This type of concern is especially likely to arise if the accused and the complainant attend the same school, where frequent contact is likely and where they may have many common associates. Other concerns arise in schools with the judicial interim release of accused youths. It may be one of the conditions of bail that the accused youth attend school, because of a concern that if the youth is not in school there is a heightened risk of offending. Or it may be a condition of release that the accused youth not attend the same school as the complainant, in which case school authorities may be obliged to find another school for a youth to attend. Concerns of school officials will be heightened if the alleged offence involved violence or occurred on school property.

There has been a growing concern about violence in schools, and research indicates that many students are afraid of violence, extortion, and bullying.[167] While there is a growing awareness of the effects that violence and bullying can have on the physical safety and psychological well-being of students, as with other questions related to youth offending, there is debate about how unsafe Canadian schools really are, and about how to respond to such issues as violence and drug dealing in the schools. Some politicians and school officials claim that there is a rising tide of violence, weapons and disorder in the schools, and that students and teachers[168] are increasingly afraid of being victimized in or around their schools. These observers point both to the school shootings in Tabor, Alberta, and Littleton, Colorado, as well as to suicides by students who have been affected by school bullying.[169] The policies that

---

167 L. Sarick, "School Violence Worse Than Expected Ontario Survey Says," *Globe and Mail*, September 28, 1993: A20; C. Ryan, F. Matthews, and J. Banner, *Student Perceptions of Violence* (Toronto: Central Toronto Youth Services, 1993); "Shakedowns in the Schoolyard," *Globe and Mail*, October 4, 1997: A1.

168 See, for example, L. Perreaux, "Teachers flee school after threats, lies," *National Post*, March 15, 2002.

169 See, for example, *R. v. D.W.*, [2002] B.C.J. No. 627 (Prov. Ct.) (criminal harassment conviction for youth in case where victim committed suicide); K. Cox, "Suicide Boy Told to Pay or be Beaten," *Globe and Mail*, April 12, 2002; and "Everyday War Zone," *Globe and Mail*, March 10, 2002.

tend to flow from these concerns include establishing school conduct codes and requiring students to wear uniforms, as well as an increased police presence in the schools, more use of suspensions and expulsions, and a greater use of the youth justice system. Other commentators argue that the actual problem of school violence is no worse than a decade ago; it is the perception or awareness of such problems as bullying and violence that have increased over the past decade rather than their actual incidence.[170] While recognizing that school violence is an important issue, these commentators express a concern that some politicians and school boards may be overreacting to school violence issues. They recognize a role for police and the youth justice system in responding to serious cases of violence in the schools, but express concerns that too many students are being subject to suspension or expulsion, often with negative effects on public safety.[171] While recognizing the potentially serious effects of school violence and the need to create an environment in which victims feel safe to disclose bullying or intimidation, they tend to favour policies that change school environments and work toward extrajudicial resolutions for most student offending. They point out that most assaults in schools are relatively minor, and many cases of student conflict have elements of fault on both sides, as for example, demeaning taunts that result in physical retaliation.[172]

The weight of social science evidence is that, despite the rhetoric in the media and among some politicians, it is far from clear that there is *more* violence in schools than was the case a decade ago. Schools are still relatively safe places for adolescents, with much more youth offending occurring outside schools than inside. It is, however, important for schools to take steps to reduce bullying and violence in schools to make students and teachers feel safer.

In *Peel Board of Education v. B.*, Reid J. of the Ontario High Court held that several male students facing serious charges involving alleged sexual assaults on a female student at another school could not be suspended or expelled pending judicial resolution of their *YOA* charges. The 1987 decision rested on the judge's interpretation of section 38 of

---

170 See, for example, V. Schiraldi and J. Ziedenberg, *Schools and Suspensions: Self-reported Crime and Growing Use of Suspensions,* Justice Institute Policy Brief (September 2001) online at the time of writing at <www.cjcj.org>.)

171 E.P. Mulvey and E. Cauffman, "The Inherent Limits of Predicting School Violence" (2001) 56 *American Psychologist* 797; and W.N. Welsh, "Effects of Student and School Factors on Five Measures of School Disorder" (2001) 18 Justice Q. 911.

172 See, for example, W.R. Dolmage, "One Less Brick in the Wall: The Myths of Youth Violence and Unsafe Schools" (1996) 7 E.L.J. 185.

that Act, which prohibited "publication" of identifying information about a young person appearing in youth court, since the judge ruled that the effect of expulsion of the students would inevitably be to identify the students within their school. The judge observed: "Rumour and gossip to the effect that the students have been expelled and must therefore be guilty of the offences with which they have been charged are . . . the almost inevitable consequences of an expulsion." The judge also said that the expulsion of the students prior to resolution of the charges "comes distressingly close to expulsion without trial. . . . That is wholly contrary to the fundamental principle of our system of justice."[173] Justice Reid further suggested that, even if the youths were convicted of these offences, it might not, in itself, be grounds for expulsion. It should be noted that the *Peel* case involved allegations that students at one school sexually assaulted a student at another school; this type of situation should generally call for different treatment in terms of school-board response than one involving an alleged victim in the same school as the accused.

Justice Reid's approach to section 38 was overruled in 1994 by the Ontario Divisional Court in *G.(F.)* v. *Scarborough (City) Board of Education*, where Montgomery J. concluded that the *YOA* was never intended to "deprive principals and school boards of the ability to enforce order and discipline in their schools."[174] The court accepted that school officials have the authority under such legislation as the Ontario *Education Act* to suspend or expel a student who has engaged in "conduct . . . so refractory that the pupil's presence is injurious to other pupils." The school officials do not need to wait until the completion of any youth justice court proceedings but may exercise their civil jurisdiction as soon as the charges come to their attention, as long as the requirements of education law are followed.[175]

Responding to growing pressure from politicians, teachers and parents, most Canadian school boards have adopted "safe school" or "zero tolerance" policies for incidents of violence and weapons in schools. While it is important for schools to have policies and programs to respond to harassment, bullying, violence and other criminal acts committed by students in and around schools, a policy that requires automatic suspension or expulsion for even minor incidents of violence

---

173 (1987), 59 O.R. (2d) 654 (H.C.J.) at 661.
174 (1994), 68 O.A.C. 308 at 312 (Div. Ct.)
175 See, for example, A.F. Brown and M.A. Zuker, *Education Law* (Toronto: Carswell, 1994) at 151–58; and J. Wilson, *Wilson on Children and the Law* (Toronto: Butterworths, 1994) at paras. 8.35 to 8.47.

may not be appropriate.[176] While the summary removal of a youth from the school pending trial may seem inconsistent with the presumption of innocence, the expulsion of youths who may pose a serious threat to the safety of others may be justified. Expulsion can create problems for youths who often have significant social and educational needs, although increasingly school boards have some programs for alternate education for students who have been suspended or expelled.[177]

The addition in 1995 of section 38(1.13) to the *YOA* allowed the police and probation services to share information with school officials about young persons involved in the youth justice system. This provision is essentially continued in section 125(6) of the *YCJA*, allowing a police officer or youth worker to disclose information about a young person involved with the youth justice system with "any professional or other person engaged in the supervision or care" of the young person, including a "representative of any school board if the disclosure is considered necessary" to:

(a) ensure compliance of the youth with any order of a youth justice court, such as a condition of bail release or a term of probation.
. . .

(b) ensure the safety of staff, students or other persons; or

(c) to facilitate the rehabilitation of the young person.

Section 125(7) requires school officials to keep information received from the police or youth justice system separate from other information about their students, to restrict access to the information to necessary staff, and to destroy any records of this information when it is no longer required. These restrictions are intended to reduce the risk of labelling youth as offenders or delinquents, although this type of legal regulation may not prevent the inappropriate oral dissemination of information regarding accused youths within their schools.

---

176 See, for example, Ontario *Safe Schools Act*, S.O. 2000, c. 12. Even with these types of policies in place, some teachers and school administrators may ignore or minimize legitimate concerns of victims of bullying and harassment, especially if the victims are viewed as different and, hence, tacitly regarded by school personnel as the appropriate objects for social isolation by their peers, for example if the victims are disabled, homosexual, or members of other social, racial, or cultural minorities. See V. Malarek, "Ontario teens suing school board over bullying," *Globe and Mail*, June 3, 2002.

177 See, for example, J. Lewington, "Expelled students to get new chance," *Globe and Mail*, September 13, 1994: A6; and T. Blackwell, "Last Chance School," *National Post*, February 17, 2002.

In *Re F.N.* the Supreme Court of Canada considered section 38(1.13) of the *YOA*, which is virtually identical to section 125(6) of the *YCJA*, ruling that school boards should not be provided with copies of youth court dockets, as there would be many less serious youth cases before the courts about which school officials should not be informed, although recognizing their need to know about other cases.[178] Justice Binnie acknowledged that:

> School boards do have a legitimate interest in knowing of members of its student body that could present a danger to themselves or others. The schools may well desire the information for their own purposes . . . timely information from the Youth Court has in the past assisted schools . . . to address legitimate safety concerns, including assignment of a student assistant to monitor a student charged with arson to ensure no incidents of arson occurred; preparation of risk assessments in cases where students have been charged with serious violent offences; placement of a student in another school after an attack on a classmate to reduce the risk of further assault or confrontation; and restriction of a student's movement within a school so as to reduce the safety risk to other students. . . .
>
> Once the information is lawfully in the hands of the school, of course, the school may take steps to address its safety concerns (as, of course, it is entitled to do on the basis of any information that raises safety issues). This remedial action may include, where appropriate, an expulsion hearing . . . or other restrictions even prior to trial where necessary. . . As stated by Smith Prov. Ct. J. in *R.G. (Re)*, [1999] B.C.J. No. 1106 . . . "As important as privacy is for youth records under the *Young Offenders Act*, there is an overriding importance, in certain circumstances, of allowing disclosure in order to protect other children."[179]

In some cases school authorities will want the youth justice court to impose restrictions on youths who are released pending adjudication. When an offence under investigation appears to relate to a youth's school, it is desirable for police officers to consult with school authorities prior to a bail hearing, and this information should be communicated to the Crown prosecutor in the police brief. Where, for example, the alleged offence involved complainants who are students in the same school, an order precluding attendance at that school might be sought as an appropriate condition of release; if possible such an order

---

178 *Re. F.N.* , [2000] 1 S.C.R. 880.
179 *Ibid.* at paras. 35 and 53.

could be co-ordinated with a plan by educational officials to transfer the youth to another school or provide alternate schooling. In cases where the allegations are less serious and there is no other school within a reasonable distance, however, it may be necessary for the accused and the complainant to continue to attend the same school, with the provision that the accused not contact the complainant, and some rearrangement of schedules for classes and activities.

Some judges will make obtaining employment or school attendance a condition of pre-adjudication release or probation, in the belief that the absence of structured activity may have contributed to the offending behaviour; for a youth who cannot find work, this becomes an order to attend school, which may make the school officials uneasy. If such a condition is imposed — or, better, before it is imposed — the police or prosecutor should be in contact with school officials to make appropriate educational and safety plans and to ensure that compliance is monitored.

Educators and police are increasingly aware of the role that schools can play in dealing with youthful offending. Many adolescents with serious offending problems also have learning disabilities or difficulties with school, and dealing effectively with educational problems can also help resolve offending behaviour. Schools are also establishing programs to deal with aggression and bullying in schools in a positive manner, at the same time that police are becoming involved in working more closely with teachers and in having more of a presence in schools.[180]

H. FITNESS TO STAND TRIAL AND ASSESSMENTS

In some cases questions may arise about the mental fitness or competence of a youth to understand and meaningfully participate in court proceedings, whether because of the youth's limited intellectual capacity or mental illness. The *YCJA* takes essentially the same approach to fitness to stand trial and the disposition of "not criminally responsible due to mental disorder" as the *YOA*. Section 141 of the *YCJA* largely adopts the provisions of Part XX.I of the *Criminal Code*, with some modifications to take account of the age and special needs of a young person, and to allow parents to participate in the decision-making

---

180 See, for example, V. Galt, "Stemming the tide of school violence," *Globe and Mail*, February 2, 1996: A1.

processes that will affect their child. The issue of fitness to stand trial may arise at any stage of the process. It is sometimes apparent when a youth is arrested or first appears in court that the youth is out of touch with reality or significantly mentally disabled.[181] In other cases, the issue of lack of capacity may not become apparent until the youth meets with defence counsel.

If the issue of fitness is raised, the court will hold a hearing to determine fitness to stand trial. Under section 2 of the *Criminal Code* a person is considered "unfit to stand trial" if the person is

> unable on account of mental disorder to conduct a defence . . . or to instruct counsel . . . and, in particular, unable . . . to
> (*a*) understand the nature or object of the proceedings,
> (*b*) understand the possible consequences of the proceedings, or
> (*c*) communicate with counsel.

The *Criminal Code* section 672.11 allows for a pre-adjudication mental-status psychiatric assessments of a young person if the court will be considering the issues of fitness to stand trial or not criminally responsible due to mental disorder. A person may be detained for up to sixty days for the purpose of conducting this type of an assessment, although statements made by a youth in the course of such an assessment are admissible only as the basis of the opinion of the psychiatrist about the youth's mental status. Any confession concerning the offence is not admissible to establish the guilt of the accused.

The threshold for finding an accused fit to stand trial is low. For example, in *R. v. S.D.*,[182] the Nova Scotia Youth court had to rule on an

---

181 In some cases involving adolescents, issues of immaturity and mental disability, emotional disturbance, and mental disorder may all be operative, as occurred in a 1977 Ontario case where a twelve-year-old boy killed his stepmother: *R. v. C.(B.)* (1977), 39 C.C.C. (2d) 469 (Ont. Prov. Ct.). Psychiatric evidence established that the youth was suffering from a personality disorder and did not appreciate that his act was wrong or even that the woman was no longer alive, and he was accordingly ruled "insane." Under the *Juvenile Delinquents Act*, above note 142, which was in force at the time, this resulted in the discharge of the juvenile, although he could be detained under provincial mental-health legislation. Today this might be found to be a situation in which there was either unfitness to stand trial or a finding of not criminally responsible on account of mental disorder.

182 *R. v. S.D.*, [1998] N.S.J. No. 325 (N.S. Youth Court). See also Webster and Rogers, *et al.*, "Assessment and Treatment of Mentally Disordered Young Offenders" in A.W. Leschied, Peter Jaffe, and Wayne Willis, eds., *The Young Offenders Act: A Revolution in Juvenile Justice* (Toronto: University of Toronto Press, 1991) 197–229.

application concerning the fitness to stand trial of a thirteen-year-old young person. The boy had likely suffered organic brain damage before birth resulting from his mother's use of drugs and alcohol during pregnancy, and he was assessed to be in the "intellectually deficient range." Judge Daley observed that there is an onus on the party (or counsel for that party) claiming unfitness to satisfy the court of lack of capacity, and concluded that the youth was fit to stand trial:

> He does not have a sophisticated thought pattern nor an information base of an average person of his age. With sensitivity, thoughtful interpretation and patience, he has the ability to understand the charges against him, to converse with counsel and to participate with understanding, in the process involving these charges. In many ways, he is, in my view, in a situation similar to that of an accused from another country or culture. Interpreters are used to convey information and to aid with understanding. S.D. can manage his participation in a proper manner, provided counsel and the court exercise the patience and interpretive skills required to ensure he completes the exercise with understanding and proper participation.[183]

In finding the accused young person fit to stand trial, the judge explained that there is a low threshold for being found fit to stand trial; the test for being fit to stand trial is a basic understanding of the nature and object of proceedings, and the ability to communicate instructions to counsel meaningfully.

If a youth is found unfit to stand trial, under section 672.58 of the *Criminal Code* a youth justice court may order that the youth is to be detained for involuntary treatment for up to sixty days. If at the end of this period, the youth is still considered by the court to be unfit to stand trial, the youth justice court must decide whether the youth should be absolutely discharged, discharged into the community subject to supervisory conditions, or detained in a secure mental health facility or hospital indefinitely. If the youth is detained, the detention is to be reviewed by a board at least once every twelve months to determine whether the youth has gained fitness to stand trial, in which case the matter should be referred to court for a trial, or whether the youth ought to be released into the community despite being unfit to stand trial.[184] For a youth, the consequences of being found unfit to stand trial

---

183 *R. v. S.D.*, *ibid.*, at para. 14.

184 *YCJA*, above note 1, s. 141(10); for adults who are subject to indefinite hospital detention, there must be a review at least once every two years; s. 672.33(1) of the *Criminal Code*, above note 2.

can be much more serious than a finding of guilt in youth justice court since, unlike the limited custodial sentence for those found guilty in youth justice court, there may be indefinite committal. However, a youth found unfit may also be released on conditions that are similar to a youth justice court sentence in terms of control and support in the community.

In addition to the youth and counsel for the youth being notified of any court hearing or review board hearing that deals with fitness to stand trial, the parents of the youth are to receive notice and have the right to participate. In making the decision about whether to detain the youth or release the youth, the court or review board shall impose the "least restrictive" disposition taking into consideration:[185]

- the need to protect society from dangerous persons;
- the age, special needs and mental condition of the youth;
- the supports available to the youth in the community; and
- the desirability of reintegrating the youth into society.

In *R. v. D.(C.L.)*, an Aboriginal youth facing a sexual assault charge was found unfit to stand trial. Although he had "limited cognitive ability" and some idea of the nature of the proceedings, a psychiatric assessment confirmed that his understanding was not sufficient to enable him to give proper instructions to counsel. The initial judicial finding was later confirmed by a review board hearing, which decided that the youth could be released subject to a restrictive community-based disposition placing him under virtual "house arrest" with "responsible members of [his] reserve looking after him and protecting the community against him."[186]

It is often difficult to find community members willing to supervise those found unfit to stand trial. A court may postpone the hearing into the issue of fitness until the conclusion of the prosecution's case, since, if there is insufficient evidence to convict the accused, it would be unfair to detain the accused under criminal legislation. In some cases, even if charges are dropped or the person is acquitted, the person may still be detained in a mental-health facility under provincial mental-health legislation, if there is clear evidence that they suffer from a mental illness and pose a serious risk to their own safety or the safety of others.

---

185 *Criminal Code*, above note 2, s. 672.54.
186 *R. v. D.(C.L.)*, [1995] B.C.J. No. 2863 (Prov. Ct.) (QL). Review Boards conduct hearings to determine when to release those found unfit to stand trial or not criminally responsible by reason of mental disorder. They generally have a chair who is a lawyer, a psychiatrist, and one other member. Release may be subject to conditions. Review Boards deal with both youths and adults.

The issue of fitness to stand trial concerns the capacity of the youth to participate in the court process at the time of the proceedings. Assuming that the youth is fit to stand trial, a distinct but related issue is whether a court should find the youth not criminally responsible on account of mental disorder under section 16 of the *Criminal Code*, which requires the court to be satisfied that at time of the offence the youth was "suffering from a mental disorder that rendered that person incapable of appreciating the nature and quality of the act . . . of knowing that it was wrong."

A determination that an individual is either unfit to stand trial or not criminally responsible for an act by reason of mental disorder does not mean that person has no rights. In the initial sixty-day period in which a person who is detained as a result of unfitness to stand trial he or she may be subject to involuntary treatment to attempt to restore his or her capacity. After that, however, a person who is detained in a hospital owing to mental disorder is not to be subjected to involuntary treatment unless there is also a finding under provincial mental-health laws that the person lacks the capacity to make a decision about treatment.[187] If a person is found unfit to stand trial or not criminally responsible on account of mental disorder, requirements for treatment in the community may be imposed with the person facing the possibility of return to a secure mental-health facility if those conditions are breached. Some of the issues related to mental disorders and the finding of not criminally responsible are further explored in Chapter 7.

FURTHER READINGS

ANAND, S.S., & J. ROBB, "The Admissibility of Young People's Statements under the Proposed *Youth Criminal Justice Act*"(2002) 39 Alta. L. Rev. 771–88

BALA, N., & H. LILLES, eds., *Young Offenders Service* (Toronto: Butterworths, 1984) section 56

CANADA, FEDERAL–PROVINCIAL/TERRITORIAL TASK FORCE ON YOUTH JUSTICE, *A Review of the Young Offenders Act and the Youth Justice System in Canada* (Ottawa: Ministry of Supply and Services, 1996) cc. 5, 10, and 11

---

187   See *Criminal Code*, above note 2, s. 672.55; and *Starson* v. *Swayze*, [2001] O.J. No. 2283 (Ont. C.A.).

DELISLE, R.J., & D. STUART, *Learning Canadian Criminal Procedure*, 6th ed. (Toronto: Carswell, 2000) c. 2

PLATT, P., *Young Offenders Law in Canada*, 2d ed. (Toronto: Butterworths, 1995) cc. 4, 5, 6, 9, and 18

QUIGLEY, T., *Procedure in Canadian Criminal Law* (Toronto: Carswell, 1997) cc. 4–11

ROHER, ERIC M., *An Educator's Guide to Violence in Schools* (Aurora, ON: Canada Law Book, 1997)

SCOTT, S., M. WONG, & B. WEAGANT, *Defending Young Offender Cases*, 2d ed. (Toronto: Carswell, 1997) cc. 1, 2, 3, and 4

STUART, D., *Charter Justice in Canadian Criminal Law*, 3d ed. (Toronto: Carswell, 2001)

TROTTER, GARY, *The Law of Bail in Canada*, 2d ed. (Toronto: Carswell, 1998)

CHAPTER 5

DIVERSION AND EXTRAJUDICIAL MEASURES

A. THE CONCEPT OF DIVERSION

While the primary legal response to youthful offending is through the court system, there are many youths who are diverted from the formal justice system and dealt with in a less intrusive, more informal, and more expeditious fashion. The value of alternatives to the conventional judicial response was, for example, recognized in the 1993 Martin Committee report:

> [T]he criminal law is a blunt instrument of social policy that ought to be used with restraint. The criminal law aims to achieve rehabilitation, specific deterrence, general deterrence, and the protection of society. However, there is no reason to think that the criminal law is the only method of achieving these socially desirable goals. Accordingly, it is clearly in the public interest to consider the . . . alternatives to any given prosecution, and their efficacy, remembering that these alternatives may be able to deal more sensitively and comprehensively with the particular problem at hand, while at the same time meeting the goals of the criminal justice system.[1]

---

1   Ontario, Ministry of the Attorney General, *Report of the Attorney General's Advisory Committee on Charge Screening, Disclosure and Resolution Discussion* [Martin Committee Report] (Toronto: Queen's Printer, 1993) at 96.

Alternatives to the formal criminal response are especially worthy of consideration if it is an adolescent who breaks the law, as this may reflect youthful immaturity. For many adolescent offenders, apprehension by the police and some form of non-judicial response may be sufficient to hold the youth accountable and deter any further offending. Under the *Juvenile Delinquents Act*,[2] alternatives to formal charging were widely employed. Most frequently, diversion was informal: although the Act had no express provisions dealing with diversion, it was a common practice for police who apprehended juveniles for minor offences to release them after talking to the youths and warning them that if they were caught committing further offences, they would be charged and taken to court. By the 1970s, more formal diversion programs were being established by various social agencies in Canada and other countries. Police or prosecutors were sending youths to these community-based programs rather than to juvenile court.

One of the rationales offered for the first formal juvenile diversion programs in the early 1970s was a sociological doctrine known as labelling theory. The theory is that youths who are labelled as "delinquents" may come to think of themselves as offenders, as well as being referred to by parents, teachers, and others as "deviant." It is thought that such labelling might contribute to future offending or "secondary deviance."[3] Proponents of this theory argue that some youths may be unnecessarily harmed by being labelled as "young offenders" through the formal court process, and that they may be less likely to reoffend if they are diverted to a relatively informal process. Labelling theory has never been clearly demonstrated to reflect reality, and empirical research is at best equivocal about whether merely identifying and describing a youth as an "offender" actually increases the likelihood of reoffending. It has not been conclusively proven that use of formal diversion programs as opposed to youth court charging *reduces* recidivism.[4] It is,

---

2   *Juvenile Delinquents Act*, enacted as S.C. 1908, c. 40; subject to minor amendments over the years, finally as *Juvenile Delinquents Act*, R.S.C. 1970, c. J–3.

3   See, for example, S. Moyer, *Diversion from the Juvenile Justice System and Its Impact on Children: A Review of the Literature* (Ottawa: Department of Justice, 1980) at 67–74.

4   There is no clear empirical support for the proposition that the process of 'labelling" which results from a court-based response to youth crime has a higher recidivism rate than a less formal response by a community-based program of "alternative measures" (to use the term under the *Young Offenders Act*, below note 9) or "extrajudicial sanctions" (the term used under the *Youth Criminal Justice Act*, below note 6). There is, however, significant empirical support for the proposition that, even taking into account prior offending and the seriousness of

however, clear that, in most situations where it is employed, the use of diversion does *not increase* the likelihood of a youth reoffending and that most youths who are sent to these programs do not reoffend.

The fact that diversion may not, in itself, necessarily *reduce* reoffending does not mean that diversion programs are without value. Diversion programs have the potential to resolve a case in a way that is more expeditious and less expensive for society than a court-based response. Further, in comparison to the formality and adversarial nature of youth justice court — a forum that tends to preclude open discussion by the individuals concerned with a crime — a properly designed diversion program can offer youths, parents, and victims an opportunity to engage actively in achieving a resolution for the situation caused by the offending which may prove more satisfactory to all involved. There may also be an important role for members of the community in diversion programs. Such community involvement may, for example, be especially important for Aboriginal communities, although it may be very appropriate in other communities as well.

The term "restorative justice" is increasingly being used to characterize responses to offending that involve the victim, the offender, family members, and community members in a process of discussion about the offence and its effects on the victim and the community, and the joint development of a plan to provide compensation to the victim and to help prevent recurrence of offending behaviour. Restorative justice is distinguished from the retributive principles of the conventional criminal justice model by its focus on restoring relationships between the offender and victim, and between the offender and the community. While courts can make use of restorative justice principles in dealing with offenders, a range of diversion programs are especially well suited to applying restorative justice principles.[5]

---

the offence, a court-based response which places the youth in custody disrupts relationships with parents and results in the youth being seen as a relatively serious offender, which does increase the likelihood of recidivism: see E.A. Stewart, *et al.*, "Beyond the Interactional Relationship Between Delinquency and Parenting Practices: The Contribution of Legal Sanctions" (2002) 39 J. Res. in Crime & Delinquency 36.

5   Gordon Bazemore and Lode Walgrave, eds., *Restorative Juvenile Justice : Repairing the Harm of Youth Crime* (Monsey, NY: Criminal Justice Press/Willow Tree, 1999); Bruce Archibald, "A Comprehensive Approach to Restorative Justice" in Don Stuart, *et al.*, eds, *Towards A Clear and Just Criminal Law: A Criminal Reports Forum* (Toronto: Carswell, 1999); J. Braithwaite, "Restorative Justice and Social Justice" (2000) 63 Sask L.Rev. 185; and R. Prashaw, "Restorative Justice: Lessons in Empathy and Connecting People" (2001) 20 Can. J. Comm. Mental Health 23.

Responses to youth crime based on labelling theory and restorative justice principles have not been conclusively proven to reduce recidivism, but there is the prospect that some types of diversion programs can reduce reoffending among some youths. Many different models of diversion are being tried in Canada and some may actually have the potential to reduce recidivism. Some diversion programs provide responses that are quite similar to those used by the courts, albeit without being imposed after a judicial process, and these are likely to have similar recidivism rates to court-based responses. There are, however, now some programs that offer responses to offending that are not available through the conventional youth court system. Innovative programs allow for the interaction of victims, families of offenders, and community members with the youth in a way that is not possible in court. Some programs may have access to counselling resources and an ability to engage youth in a way that is not possible in the court system. These innovative programs need to be assessed to determine whether they actually reduce recidivism.

Diversion is an important potential response to youthful offending, and the *Youth Criminal Justice Act*[6] has a number of provisions that are intended to encourage a range of diversionary responses, or extrajudicial measures, as they are known under the Act. As well as enacting provisions of the Act that encourage diversion, the federal government is providing additional funding to support community-based responses to youth crime.

Diversion, which has been underused in Canada, should be encouraged. Even so, there remain legitimate concerns about its potential misuse that need to be addressed, such as the possibility that diversion may jeopardize the rights of young persons or victims, or may fail to take sufficient account of the interests of society. There is also the potential for diversion to be applied in a discriminatory fashion, with youths from certain disadvantaged or socially marginalized backgrounds less likely to be dealt with outside of the court system. Similarly, the efficacy of some restorative justice programs for reducing recidivism among youthful offenders has been questioned. Some researchers believe restorative justice processes have been shown to greatly reduce recidivism.[7] Others, however, maintain that the empirical research does not support such optimistic conclusions and have expressed concerns that family or

---

6   *Youth Criminal Justice Act*, S.C. 2002, c. 1 (royal assent February 19, 2002, to come into force April 1, 2003), often referred to in this book as the *YCJA*.

7   See, for example, J. Braithwaite, "Restorative Justice and Social Justice" (2000) 63 Sask. L.Rev. 185.

group conferencing, for example, can have a negative impact on victims of youth crime.[8] These concerns should be kept in mind when designing, implementing, and evaluating such programs.

B. ALTERNATIVE MEASURES UNDER THE YOUNG OFFENDERS ACT

The drafters of the *Young Offenders Act*[9] wanted to encourage the practice diversion as it developed under the *Juvenile Delinquents Act*, although they also wanted to regulate certain aspects of it. The Declaration of Principle in section 3(1)(d) of the *YOA* expressly recognized that "where it is not inconsistent with the protection of society, taking no measures or taking measures other than judicial proceedings [under the *Young Offenders Act*] should be considered for dealing with young persons who have committed offences." Section 4 of the *YOA* created a legislative framework for alternative measures to deal with young persons who were believed to have committed criminal offences.

Alternative measures were a form of diversion from the court process, which allowed a youth to be dealt with in a relatively expeditious, informal fashion and enabled a youth to avoid a formal youth court record. Alternative measures were generally used for youths who committed less serious offences and who did not have a history of offending. There was, however, substantial variation in how section 4 was applied, with some provinces taking a more expansive approach and permitting youths facing more serious charges and with a prior record of offending to be considered for alternative measures.

The drafters of the *YOA* intended to increase the use of various informal alternatives to the formal youth justice system. It is now clear, however, that, after the Act came into force, fewer young offenders were dealt with by means of screening or diversion than was the case under the more informal *Juvenile Delinquents Act*. The use of court-

---

8   See, for example, K. Haines, "Some Principled Objections to a Restorative Justice Approach to Working with Juvenile Offenders" in L. Walgrave, ed., *Restorative Justice for Juveniles: Potentialities, Risks, and Problems for Research* (Leuven, BG: Leuven University Press, 1998) at 93.

9   *Young Offenders Act*, R.S.C 1985, c. Y-1,enacted as S.C. 1980–81–82–83, c. 110. The Act was also amended in 1985 through *An Act to amend the Young Offenders Act, the Criminal Code, the Penitentiary Act, and the Prisons and Reformatories Act,* R.S.C. 1985 (2d Supp.), c. 24, in force September 1, 1986 and November 1, 1986, and in 1995 through *An Act to amend the Young Offenders Act and the Criminal Code,* S.C. 1995, c. 19.

based responses to youth crime actually increased under the *YOA*; the reasons for this are complex. This general trend to make greater use of courts rather than informal responses to youth crime was not uniform across Canada.

It is significant that in some provinces, most notably Quebec, the introduction of the *YOA* was not accompanied by an increase in use of a court-based response to youth crime. In Quebec, the government established programs and policies that encouraged police and Crown prosecutors to divert less serious offenders from the youth court system to either informal community-based alternatives or the child-welfare system. Under the *YOA*, Quebec had the lowest rate of use of youth court in Canada.[10] In other provinces, however, the introduction of the *YOA* in 1984 was accompanied by a phenomenon known as "net widening." Alternative measures programs were established, but the police did not actually divert youth from the court system. Rather, youth who committed minor offences which under the *Juvenile Delinquents Act* would have resulted in an informal caution by the police were sent to the new programs, while charge rates in court remained the same or actually increased.

The *Young Offenders Act* came into force about the same time as the *Charter*,[11] and together these two legal instruments created a more formal and rights-oriented response for police and courts to follow in dealing with youth offending. The *YOA* did not preclude the use of informal responses. Indeed, some of the statements in the Declaration of Principle actually tried to encourage diversionary responses. Nonetheless, many police and prosecutors were influenced by the more formal approach to youth justice reflected in the Act to move away from informal responses to youth crime toward one that focused on courts.

Perhaps more significantly, the increased use of court following the enactment of the *YOA* may in part have been a police response to the growing public pressure "to do something" about youth crime. Arresting youths who in the past might have been dealt with informal-

---

10   Canadian Centre for Justice Statistics reported a youth court charge rate of 2.0 percent of the youth population in Quebec, compared to 4.5 percent in Ontario, and 8.7 percent in Manitoba ("Alternative Measures in Canada 1998–99" (2000) 20:6 Juristat). The Centre reported an annual charge rate per 10,000 youths of 196 in Quebec, compared to a national rate of 417, with Ontario having a rate of 428 and Manitoba having a rate of 700 ("Youth Court Statistics 1999–2000" (2001) 21:3 Juristat).

11   *Canadian Charter of Rights and Freedoms*, enacted as Part I of the *Constitution Act, 1982*, being Schedule B to the *Canada Act, 1982* (U.K.), 1982, c. 11 (subsequently referred to as the *Charter*).

ly was one police response to community demands to get tough with young offenders. In some provinces the use of court-based responses was also encouraged by provincial policies that restricted the use of alternative measures or, for a time, precluded it altogether.

Under the *Juvenile Delinquents Act*, the issue of juvenile diversion received little or no attention from most provincial governments. Local programs, police forces, and Crown prosecutors could exercise their discretion to divert quite a broad range of cases. When provincial governments began to develop formal policies about referring youths to alternative measures programs under the YOA, these policies were often more restrictive than the practices of police, prosecutors, and operators of diversion programs under the *Juvenile Delinquents Act* and encouraged a more formal response to youth offending.

A narrow approach to the alternative measures provisions of the YOA was most apparent in Ontario. When the YOA came into force in 1984, Ontario's opposition to alternative measures reflected a general political resistance by the provincial government to the federally enacted statute. With an attitude that critics referred to as a provincial failure to comply with "the spirit of the new law,"[12] the Ontario government also argued that the research into the effectiveness of diversion in terms of reducing recidivism was "ambiguous and conflicting," and expressed concerns about the potential for the abuse of the rights of youths in these programs as well as about widening the net.[13] Ontario provided no new funding for the establishment of diversion programs, and refused to implement section 4 of the YOA. Section 4(1)(a) provided that "[a]lternative measures may be used . . . *only if* . . . the measures are part of a program authorized" (emphasis added) by the provincial government, and the Ontario government decided not to formally authorize any programs.[14]

---

12   See K. Makin, "Ontario Move on Young Offenders Backed," *Globe and Mail*, Toronto ed., June 29, 1990: A7. Another example of Ontario's resistance to the YOA was the two-tier age implementation, with older adolescents dealt with in the criminal courts and by the adult corrections ministry. See discussion in Chapter 3.

13   Ian Scott, then the Attorney General of Ontario, quoted in Ontario Social Development Council, *Young Offenders Act Dispositions: Challenges and Choices* (Toronto: 1988) at 16.

14   In practice, some of the diversion programs in Ontario established before the YOA came into force in 1984 continued to operate with the co-operation of local police and prosecutors, and even with some funding from the community and social services ministry. The opposition to alternative measures in the Ontario government in the 1984–90 period was largely centred in the Ministry of the Attorney General.

Since all the other provinces and territories established programs to give adolescents access to alternative measures, it is not surprising that the decision of Ontario not to implement section 4 of the YOA was challenged as a violation of the principle of "equality under the law" guaranteed by section 15 of the *Charter*. In 1988, in R. v. S.(S.),[15] the Ontario Court of Appeal held that the absence of such programs in Ontario constituted a "denial of equal benefit and protection of the law" on the basis of province of residence, and hence was in violation of section 15 of the *Charter*. The government of Ontario responded to the Court of Appeal decision by establishing alternative measures programs across the province, albeit on an "interim basis," but it also appealed to the Supreme Court of Canada.

In June of 1990 the Supreme Court reversed the Ontario Court of Appeal decision in R. v. S.(S.). The Supreme Court observed that section 4(1) of the YOA provided that "[a]lternative measures *may* be used" [emphasis added], indicating that there was a discretion granted the provincial government as to whether to establish any of these programs. The Court held that it was constitutionally valid for Parliament to delegate authority to the provinces under section 4(1)(a) to decide whether to establish alternative measures. Under Canada's federal system, it is not a violation of the *Charter* to have youths in one province denied access to alternative measures. Although some types of interprovincial differences in treatment under the criminal law would be unconstitutional, the Supreme Court adopted an approach that required an assessment of all the circumstances of a particular delegation of responsibility to provincial governments to determine whether there is a *Charter* violation. Chief Justice Dickson observed that:

> diversity in the criminal law, in terms of provincial application, has been recognized . . . as a means of furthering the values of federalism . . . the question of how young people found to have committed criminal offences should be dealt with is one upon which it is legitimate for Parliament to allow for province-based distinctions. . . . benefits . . . derive from the adaptability of a program of alternative measures to the needs of different regions and communities.[16]

In a decision rendered at the same time as R.v. S.(S.), the Supreme Court also accepted that if provinces choose to establish alternative measures programs, they may develop their own criteria for eligibility. If a province chose to have narrower offence criteria for its alternative

---

15 (1988), 63 C.R. (3d) 64 (Ont. C.A.).
16 R. v. S.(S.), [1990] 2 S.C.R. 254 at 290–91.

measures programs than other provinces, that did not render its program unconstitutional.[17]

Despite the Supreme Court of Canada decisions, which would have allowed Ontario to have no alternative measures programs, the Ontario government continued and actually expanded its "interim" alternative measures programs. Shortly after *S.(S.)*, the Supreme Court gave its decision in *R. v. Askov*,[18] ruling that delays in the Ontario courts were denying accused persons — principally adults but also youths — the constitutionally guaranteed right to a trial within a reasonable time. The *Askov* decision placed great pressure on the Ontario government to deal with the problem of overcrowding in the court system and provided a strong impetus for moving less serious cases out of the courts by making greater use of alternative measures programs. Accordingly, the Ontario government decided to join all other governments in Canada and permanently establish alternative measures programs to relieve pressure on the courts.

Even after deciding to adopt alternative measures, Ontario maintained the most restrictive alternative measures policies in Canada. Ontario was the only province to have alternative measures policies that operated exclusively on a post-charge basis. Before a referral could be made, it was generally necessary for the youth to appear in youth court, where an initial decision about referral to alternative measures was made by the Crown prosecutor. If a youth was referred to alternative measures, the court case would be adjourned. This type of post-charge process is cumbersome and relatively intrusive for the youth and parents. Further, the offence criteria established by the Attorney General of Ontario to help determine eligibility for alternative measures were narrow:

> For a youth charged with a property offence where the value is under $5000 and without a prior record of offending, there is a presumption that the youth is eligible unless there are "exceptional circumstances" (for example, vandalism that is motivated by racial hatred). If there is a record of offending in the previous year, the youth should ordinarily be sent to court, although there is still a discretion to send the youth to alternative measures.
>
> For a youth charged with: a property offence where the value is over $5000, a minor assault, giving a false name when arrested, or a credit card offence, the prosecutor has a discretion to refer a youth to alternative measures (consideration should be given to the views of the victim, the seriousness of the allegations, any prior record of the

---

17   *R. v. S.(G.)*, [1990] 2 S.C.R. 294.

18   *R. v. Askov*, [1990] 2 S.C.R. 1199.

youth, and any other information relevant to the youth's background or circumstances. More serious offences, such as any sex offence, assaults causing injury, alcohol related driving offences, and failure to comply with terms of a probation order or to attend court, are ineligible for alternative measures.[19]

The official Ontario criteria thus excluded some quite common non-violent offences, in particular break and enter. In most other provinces a youth charged with this offence could be considered for alternative measures. As a result of its narrow policy, Ontario had one of the lowest rates of use of alternative measures in Canada.[20]

In contrast with Ontario, Quebec had the broadest criteria for the use of alternative measures, with the prosecutor having a discretion to send any charges to alternative measures and a requirement that all less serious cases be referred, usually on a pre-charge basis.[21] In Quebec, youths could be sent to alternative measures even with a prior record of offending. As noted, because of this extensive use of alternative measures, Quebec had the lowest rate of youth court charging in Canada.

The drafters of the YOA had hoped to encourage use of diversion programs and informal responses to youth crime, especially for less serious cases. By the middle of the 1990s, alternative measures programs were operating in all Canadian jurisdictions. However, Canada's response to youth crime was much more formal and intrusive than that of other countries. Comparative data released in 1998 indicated that in Canada only about 25 percent of youth cases with which police came into contact were diverted by the police or referred to alternative measures. In the United States the rate was 53 percent, while in Great Britain it was 57 percent.[22]

The YCJA[23] is intended to bring Canada into closer conformity with other countries and encourage greater use of a range of diversionary measures by police, prosecutors, and communities. However, the YCJA does not change the basic effect of the Supreme Court decision in R. v. S. (S.) It remains the responsibility of provincial governments to determine the extent to which they establish diversionary programs and policies.

---

19 Ontario, Ministry of the Attorney General, *Alternative Measures Program: Policy & Procedures Manual* (Toronto: Queen's Printer, 1995).

20 Canadian Centre for Justice Statistics, 2000, above note 10.

21 See P. Platt, *Young Offenders Law in Canada*, 2d ed. (Toronto: Butterworths, 1995) at 162; and N. Bala and H. Lilles, eds., *Young Offenders Service*, looseleaf ed. (Toronto: Butterworths, 1984) vol. 1.

22 Justice Canada, *A Strategy for Youth Justice Renewal* (Ottawa, 1998) at 20.

23 Above note 6.

C. EXTRAJUDICIAL MEASURES UNDER THE *YOUTH CRIMINAL JUSTICE ACT*

The *YCJA* abandons the *YOA* terminology of "alternative measures" and adopts the two new terms: "extrajudicial measures" and "extrajudicial sanctions." The broader concept of "extrajudicial measures" is defined in section 2 of the *YCJA* as "measures other than judicial proceedings . . . used to deal with a young person alleged to have committed an offence." Extrajudicial measures are all types of diversion and include the exercise of police discretion not to charge, as well as more formal diversion programs. Sections 4 and 5 of the Act set out general principles and objectives for the use of extrajudicial measures and are clearly intended to encourage their use by police, prosecutors, youth workers, and community groups. Section 2 of the Act also refers to "extrajudicial sanctions," which is the new term for "alternative measures." Extrajudicial sanctions are one type of extrajudicial measure, the more formal type of pre-adjudication diversion schemes whose operation is governed by sections 10, 11, and 12 of the Act.

Section 4 of the *YCJA* sets out principles that are to govern the establishment of policies and programs about extrajudicial measures, as well as to be taken into account in making decisions about individual youth. Section 4 provides:

> 4(*a*) extrajudicial measures are often the most appropriate and effective way to address youth crime;
>
> (*b*) extrajudicial measures allow for effective and timely interventions focused on correcting offending behaviour;
>
> (*c*) extrajudicial measures are presumed to be adequate to hold a young person accountable for his or her offending behaviour if the young person has committed a non-violent offence and has not previously been found guilty of an offence; and
>
> (*d*) extrajudicial measures should be used if they are adequate to hold a young person accountable for his or her offending behaviour and, if the use of extrajudicial measures is consistent with the principles set out in this section, nothing in this Act precludes their use in respect of a young person who
>
> > (*i*) has previously been dealt with by the use of extrajudicial measures, or
> >
> > (*ii*) has previously been found guilty of an offence.

Section 4(c) of the *YCJA* creates a presumption that police and prosecutors should not respond through the laying of charges in youth justice court to youths who have no prior record of offending and are believed to have committed non-violent offences. Section 4(d) makes clear that extrajudicial measures may also be appropriate for some youths with prior records of offending, depending on the nature of the offence, the previous record and the circumstances of the youth.

Encouraging the use of extrajudicial measures for those with prior police involvement is significant. In practice, under the *YOA* there was a strong presumption that alternative measures were only to be used once, with only 2 percent of the youth involved in alternative measures having a history of prior participation in such a program, and less than 1 percent having a prior youth court record.[24] Section 4(d) of the *YCJA* recognizes that adolescents often make more than one relatively minor mistake. Taking into consideration the attitude of the victim and the youth, the seriousness and circumstances of the offence, and the likelihood of reoccurrence, it may be appropriate to give a youth more than one opportunity to avoid court. It is not clear that a youth justice court will have a more effective or even a more punitive sanction than some form of extrajudicial measure. Indeed, an appearance in court is often a less engaging experience than participation in an extrajudicial sanctions program, although the long-term consequences of going to court may be more serious, especially if the youth acquires a significant record of offending.

Section 5 sets out criteria that should be considered by those establishing programs and policies about the use of extrajudicial measures. This section indicates that notions of restorative justice are an important aspect of extrajudicial measures. While responses to youth offending outside the court system are intended to be informal, they should encourage youths to take responsibility for their acts, engage with their families and communities, and repair harm done to victims. Section 5 provides:

5. Extrajudicial measures should be designed to

(a) provide an effective and timely response to offending behaviour outside the bounds of judicial measures;

(b) encourage young persons to acknowledge and repair the harm caused to the victim and the community;

(c) encourage families of young persons — including extended families — and the community to become involved in the design and implementation of those measures;

---

24   Canadian Centre for Justice Statistics, 2000, above note 10.

(d) provide an opportunity for victims to participate in decisions related to the measures selected and to receive reparation; and

(e) respect the rights and freedoms of young persons and be proportionate to the seriousness of the offence.

While sections 4 and 5 encourage the use of extrajudicial measures, they do not give youth a legal right to be dealt with outside the court system. It is clear that the *YCJA* is not intended to change the effect of judicial precedents rendered under the *YOA* which held that federal legislation which encourages use of informal methods of responding to youth crime do not give any individual youth the legal right to be dealt with outside the court system. It is the police and prosecutors who decide who is charged and taken to court, perhaps acting with the advice of probation officers or community agencies and taking account of the views of victims. It remains a matter of provincial government policy, as implemented by police officers and Crown prosecutors exercising their professional discretion, whether a youth receives the benefit of extrajudicial measures.

After the *YOA* came into force in 1984, there were some youth court judges who believed that the judiciary had a right — and perhaps even an obligation — to refer cases to alternative measures which they did not consider suitable for prosecution in the courts.[25] However, in a number of Supreme Court decisions it has been held that the prosecutor and police have the *discretion* to refer cases to alternative measures, and that this discretion is not reviewable by the courts.[26] In its 1992 decision in *R. v. T.(V.)*[27] the Supreme Court of Canada considered a case in which a fourteen-year-old girl who was living in a group home, apparently pursuant to child welfare legislation, had been charged with mischief, assault, and uttering threats as a result of a dinner-time altercation. This was a situation that a parent might well have resolved without calling the police. It appears that charges were laid only because a police officer had happened to come to the group home that evening on an unrelated matter.

The British Columbia Court of Appeal considered the effect of section 3(1)(d) of the *YOA*, which provided that "where it is not inconsistent with the protection of society, taking no measures or taking measures other than judicial proceedings . . . should be considered for dealing with young persons who have committed offences." The Court felt that under section 3(1)(d) of the *YOA* the prosecuting authorities

---

25   See, for example, *R. v. B.(J.)* (1985), 20 C.C.C. (3d) 67 (B.C. Prov. Ct.).

26   See, for example, *K.P. v. Desrochers*, [2000] O.J. 5061 (Sup. Ct.).

27   *R. v. T.(V.)*, [1992] 1 S.C.R. 749.

were required to "consider" whether to use measures other than court and, if they have failed to do so, a youth court judge had "ultimate responsibility" for a case and could dismiss the charges. The Court of Appeal suggested that a youth court judge could dismiss a charge for a relatively minor offence if it involved a person in a "parent-like role" (such as a group-home staff member) making use of the court system for "minor disciplinary infractions" for which a parent would not ordinarily resort to the courts. However, the Supreme Court of Canada reversed the decision of the Court of Appeal.

The Supreme Court ruled that, except in cases of a clear "abuse of process," a judge has no discretion as to whether charges should be laid or dealt with by a court. The Supreme Court held that Crown prosecutors and the police are the appropriate officials to exercise authority under section 3(1)(d) of the YOA and refer a case to alternative measures or decide that a prosecution is appropriate. While an adult advocate for a youth, whether a lawyer, a parent or a social worker, can sometimes play a useful role in informally communicating with the prosecutor or police about why a youth should be diverted, the exercise of discretion by the police and prosecutor is not reviewable by a court. There was no obligation to give a youth any sort of notice that consideration was being given to whether to refer a case to alternative measures. Nor was there an obligation to conduct any sort of a hearing to decide whether a youth will be diverted from court.[28] The Supreme Court indicated that, if a judge felt that a youth had been charged for a relatively minor offence that should have been dealt with outside the courts, the appropriate response would be at the sentencing stage, where an absolute discharge might be appropriate.[29]

The statements of principle in the YCJA that are intended to encourage the use of extrajudicial measures are more detailed than those found in the YOA. They do not, however, reverse the effect of the Supreme Court of Canada decision in R. v. T.(V.), which denies the existence of a legally enforceable right to be dealt with outside the court system.[30] There is only a narrow judicial power to dismiss charges that should have been dealt with by way of extrajudicial measures if there has been an "abuse of process." Such an abuse might, for example,

---

28 W.(T.) v. Smith (1986), 45 Sask. R. 191 (Q.B.); R. v. B.(G.) (December 1994), (Y.S.C.) [unreported] [summarized (1994), 26 W.C.B. (2d) 48].

29 R. v. T.(G.) (1987), 57 C.R. (3d) 388 (Alta. Youth Ct.).

30 R. v. T.(V.), [1992] 1 S.C.R. 749. YCJA, above note 6, ss. 6(2) and 10(6), discussed below, make clear that the failure of the police or Crown prosecutor to consider screening or extrajudicial sanctions does not give rise to a right of a judicial power to stay charges.

arise if there were a police or prosecutorial decision about the use of extrajudicial sanctions that discriminated on the basis of gender or ethnicity.[31] Another example of the narrow judicial authority of a judge to review the Crown's decision to prosecute arises if there is bad faith; for example, if charges are laid only because the victim of a crime did not receive expected financial compensation from an offender, charges should be stayed as an "abuse of process."[32]

In addition to the formal, narrow judicial power to stay proceedings as an abuse of process, some judges, in appropriate cases, are likely in practice to suggest that the Crown prosecutor refer the youth to some form of extrajudicial measures. A judge might, for example, make this type of suggestion at a pre-trial conference, which is a meeting held in many jurisdictions between prosecutor, defence counsel, and a judge, that typically resolves procedural issues and explores whether the entire case can be resolved without trial. This judicial power of "suggestion" for use of extrajudicial measures is not legally binding, but may be quite influential with some prosecutors. It would seem most appropriate for a judge to make this type of suggestion in situations where the prosecutor or police appear to lack familiarity with youth justice court processes and programs, or where there appears to be a persistent failure by local police or prosecutors to use the provisions of the Act that require consideration of extrajudicial measures. If there has been a failure by the prosecutor or police to deal with an appropriate case by means of extrajudicial measures, the judge might take account of this at the time of sentencing. This might, for example, result in a reprimand or an absolute discharge for a case that the judge thought should have been resolved by extrajudicial measures.

---

31   While a youth justice court judge cannot refer a case to an extrajudicial sanctions program, there is a narrow residual discretion in any case for a judge to stay proceedings where compelling the accused to stand trial would contravene "the community's basic sense of decency and fair play and thereby . . . call into question the integrity of the [justice] system." *R. v. O'Connor*, [1995] 4 S.C.R. 441 at 457. The abuse of process power is to be exercised only in the "clearest of cases" and might, for example, be invoked if there was a lengthy delay in laying charges after a police investigation, or a person were tried several times resulting in hung juries and further prosecution seemed "oppressive." There is also a doctrine known as *de minimis non curat lex* (about trifling things do not go the law), which has occasionally been invoked by Canadian judges to dismiss charges, as, for example, in drug cases where a small quantity of drugs are discovered. But it would appear that, since *R. v. T.(V.)*, *ibid.*, this doctrine cannot be used in youth justice court to deal with cases that might have been diverted. See D. Stuart, *Canadian Criminal Law*, 4th ed. (Toronto: Carswell, 2001) at 594–99.

32   *R. v. Thore*, [2001] B.C.J. 720 (S.C.).

1) Police and Crown Discretion: Sections 6–9

In Canada, the police have the initial responsibility for investigating suspected offences and deciding whether to commence formal legal proceedings against a person believed to have committed a criminal offence. In most provinces, the police have the authority to commence the proceedings by appearing before a justice of the peace to swear an information (also referred to as "laying charges"). In some provinces, such as British Columbia, a crown prosecutor screens cases before police proceed to swear an information.

In all provinces, the police have a critical role in deciding whether to begin a process that could lead to a formal response to a suspected crime. For adolescents who are apprehended for relatively minor offences, a police officer may decide not to invoke the formal processes of court or even of an extrajudicial sanctions program. The officer may decide that a youth should be dealt with informally, sometimes by warning the youth about not committing further offences. This practice, commonly known as "police screening," was widely employed when the *Juvenile Delinquents Act* was in force, at a time when there were few formal programs for diversion from the juvenile court.[33] Police screening was especially common with delinquents under twelve, but it was used with juveniles of all ages. Under the *Juvenile Delinquents Act*, some police forces kept records of "police cautions" so that they could determine when a youth had "run out of chances." The practice of police screening reflects the belief that some cases do not warrant the time and effort of formal charging. They also reflect an understanding that the cautioning of a youth by a police officer is an effective, low-cost way of holding the youth accountable and, in some cases, to arrange for compensation to a victim. Further, the warning that there will be more serious consequences if there are further criminal acts can have a significant deterrent impact with some youths.

The *YOA* recognized the value of this police practice, with section 3(1)(d) acknowledging that "where it is not inconsistent with the protection of society, taking no measures . . . should be considered for dealing with young persons." Indeed, when that Act was enacted, there was a concern that the introduction of formal alternative measures programs should not result in net widening: that is, alternative measures programs were intended to be a true alternative to youth court and not

---

33   See, for example, J.M. Gandy, "The Exercise of Discretion by the Police as a Decision-Making Process in the Disposition of Juvenile Offenders" (1970) 8 Osgoode Hall L.Rev. 329; and Moyer, above note 2.

a means of dealing formally outside court with youths who would have been informally screened by police under the *Juvenile Delinquents Act*. In some localities, however, the introduction of the *YOA* and the establishment of alternative measures programs resulted in police charging youths who, under the *Juvenile Delinquents Act*, would have been dealt with informally by the police.[34] Pressures from schools and others in the community for a greater police response to youth crime also played a part. The police decision to charge under the *YOA* rather than simply caution was influenced by the expectation that the youth who was charged with a less serious offence was still likely to be diverted to alternative measures and not dealt with by the youth court.

Most countries make substantially more use of police screening of youthful offenders than Canada.[35] New Zealand, for example, has policies to encourage officers to caution youths in their home and to allow the administration of a caution in the presence of the parents at a police station by a senior officer. Specially trained youth officers are able to arrange for restitution and an apology to a victim or community service work. About three-quarters of the youth offenders with whom the police come into contact in New Zealand are handled by the police, who keep a record of their cautioning. It is not unusual for a youth to be diverted more than once. About one-eighth of cases are resolved at a family group conference, and only about one-eighth of cases are dealt with in the youth courts. The cases that go to court in New Zealand are only the most serious ones or those where the youth is denying guilt and wants a trial.[36]

It has been recognized that more extensive use of police screening would also be appropriate in Canada, although subject to some important qualifications. To encourage more use of police cautioning, as well as to provide some consistency and regulation of the practice, some provisions of the *YCJA* make explicit reference to police cautioning. The exercise of discretion by the police not to charge is an important

---

34   See, for example, J. Kenewell, N. Bala, and P. Colfer, "Young Offenders" in R. Barnhorst and L.C. Johnson, eds., *The State of the Child in Ontario* (Toronto: Oxford University Press, 1991) 160 at 165; and J. Hackler and D. Cousins, *Police Screening Patterns in Five Western Canadian Cities* (Edmonton: Centre for Criminological Research, University of Alberta, 1989).

35   J.P. Hornick and S. Rodal, *The Use of Alternatives to Traditional Youth Court: An International Comparison* (Calgary: Canadian Research Institute for Law and the Family, 1995).

36   G. Maxwell and A. Morris, "Juvenile Crime and Justice in New Zealand" in N. Bala, J.P. Hornick, and H. Snyder eds., *Juvenile Justice Systems: An International Comparison of Problems and Solutions* (Toronto: Thompson Educational Publishing, 2002).

type of extrajudicial measure and, as such, is encouraged by the general statements in sections 4 and 5. These statements stress the importance of responding outside the court system to adolescent offenders, especially if they have no prior record of offending and the offence does not involve violence. Often a non-court police response is the most effective, most humane, and least expensive way of dealing with an adolescent who has made a mistake. In appropriate cases, an informal, relatively rapid response of a police officer — especially an officer with sensitivity and experience in dealing with youths — can have as much or more impact in terms of deterrence and accountability than a much delayed, often perfunctory appearance in youth justice court.

Unlike the *YOA*, which only alluded to police screening in vague terms, sections 6 and 7 of the *YCJA* are specifically directed to the police. Section 6 explicitly states that, before taking steps to begin a formal court process against a youth, a police officer "*shall . . . consider* whether it would be sufficient to warn the young person, administer a caution . . . or refer the young person to a community-based program" [emphasis added]. In making a decision not to proceed to court, the officer who deals with a young person believed to have committed a crime is expected to take into account section 4, with its presumption that non-violent first offenders should not be charged. More generally, the officer should consider the seriousness of the offence, the prior record and attitude of the youth, and the views of the victim, as well as any policies of the specific police force.

While police officers have an obligation to consider whether to deal with a youth outside the court system, section 6(2) of the *YCJA* makes clear that this is an entirely discretionary matter, specifying that the "failure of a police officer" to consider any form of extrajudicial measures "does not invalidate" any subsequent court proceedings and is technically not reviewable by a judge. However, if it appears that an officer has failed to consider some form of diversionary measures, the prosecutor may decide to divert the case.

When considering how to respond to a youth suspected of an offence, an officer may have a number of different options, depending on local resources and policies. The least intrusive response is for the officer who first comes in contact with the youth to personally warn the youth not to commit any further offences. The *YCJA* refers to both the police "warning" in section 6 and the police "caution" in section 7. There is ultimately no legal difference between a warning and caution, but the caution is seen as a more formal or intrusive response. Even so, it is still administered by the police without any need for charges to be laid and without any sanctions being imposed. The police warning is to be administered informally by the officer handling the case, although it may include the officer meeting with the parents of a youth. The officer may contact the parents, telling them that their child is believed to have committed an offence. The officer may discuss with the parents whether the offending behaviour is related to other problems that might be assisted by a social agency or doctor, or whether the child's school or church might be able to provide help, leaving it for the parents to decide what help to seek. The officer might arrange for a simple apology to a victim or a return of stolen property. If there is to be much involvement between the offender and victim, a referral to an extrajudicial sanctions program is likely appropriate. Police forces generally now have policies that require a report of a police warning to be filed, so that if there is a repetition of offending behaviour, there may be a more intrusive response.

In Australia and some other countries, programs have been established that allow a senior officer at the police station to meet with the youth and parents to discuss offending behaviour and administer a more formal caution against repetition of offending. Section 7 of the *YCJA* encourages provincial governments to have programs and policies for police cautioning, perhaps modelled on the programs in Australia with the caution being administered by a specially trained officer who is sensitive to youth and aware of community resources. A caution may involve the sending of a "caution letter" by the police or prosecutor to the youth and parents warning of the consequences of further offending. The cautioning process may also involve a voluntary referral for further help from a social agency or community resource.

In Canada, if the youth's behaviour or situation seems more serious, or there is a victim who expects or would benefit from some type of restitution or meeting with the offender, the youth may be referred by the police to a formal extrajudicial sanctions program. In most provinces the police can refer a youth directly to such programs without charging the youth. In some provinces a referral to a pre-charge program can only be made by a Crown prosecutor after charges have been laid, although the views of the police officer who has been handling the case are usually considered by the prosecutor in deciding whether to make a referral.

Section 8 of the *YCJA* allows the provincial governments to implement programs to have prosecutors administer cautions to youths instead of starting or continuing judicial proceedings. Prosecutors have always had the authority to discontinue a case, but this type of program would encourage them to exercise this discretion in appropriate cases, after warning the youth against committing further offences. The prosecutor might also meet with the parents or make a referral to a community agency.

Section 23 of the *YCJA* allows provincial governments to establish programs to have prosecutors screen youth cases before charges are laid. In appropriate cases, the prosecutor may decide that charges should not be laid; the youth might be referred to a program of extrajudicial sanctions or the prosecutor might decide to personally caution the youth or to send a caution letter. In some jurisdictions, prosecutorial screening of youth charges was a common practice before the *YCJA* was in force; section 23 is intended to encourage this practice. Nonetheless, it is for provincial governments to decide whether to have this type of program. Giving the prosecutor a formal screening role can ensure that the police have complied with any provincial policies about diversion. Further, in cases that may seem a little more contentious, the prosecutor may be more willing than a police officer to take responsibility for deciding not to have a case dealt with by the courts.

Prior to the enactment of the *YCJA*, it was theoretically possible for a victim who disagreed with the decision of the police or prosecutor to screen or divert a case to commence a "private prosecution" against a youth to bring a case to court. This involved the victim appearing before a justice of the peace to swear an information to commence the proceeding and then appearing in court to prosecute the case. This did not happen frequently under the *YOA*, but when it did it could be quite intrusive since the victim appeared to have control over the youth's future; this could result in a case which would otherwise have been dealt with informally being dealt with by the courts. It was already a common practice under the *YOA* for the Crown Prosecutor to review private prosecutions, and either take over the prosecution or exercise the Crown discretion to stay the prosecution, which minimized the potential for the abuse of this kind of process. Section 24 of the *YCJA* codifies the practice of Crown involvement in youth justice prosecutions, requiring the consent of the provincial attorney general to any private prosecution of a young person. This should ensure that a private prosecution does not occur in circumstances in which a youth should be diverted from the court system, although the views of the complainant or private prosecutor should be considered by the police and prosecutor when deciding how a case should be dealt with.

Decisions by the police or a prosecutor to caution a youth or to refer a youth to a program of extrajudicial sanctions do not require any finding or formal admission of guilt by the youth. However, section 10(2)(e) requires that as a condition of participation in extrajudicial sanctions the youth must "accept responsibility" for the offence. Since there is no formal finding or legal admission of guilt, section 9 of the *YCJA* provides that the fact that the police or prosecutor has cautioned a youth or has referred a youth to extrajudicial sanctions cannot be used against the youth as proof of guilt in connection with that offence. In any event, once a case is referred to extrajudicial sanctions, it is rare for the case to be referred to court. However, if there is a subsequent finding of guilt for another offence in youth justice court, at the sentencing stage the court may be informed of the prior participation in extrajudicial sanctions (or alternative measures), as this may be indicative of the failure of this type of response to have an effect on offending behaviour. The fact of prior participation in extrajudicial sanctions may be taken into account as an aggravating circumstance if there is a subsequent offence. Accordingly, the police and prosecutor should keep a record of the fact that a youth has been diverted or screened. Prior use of extrajudicial measures is likely to be relevant in considering how any subsequent offending behaviour should be dealt with. If the youth is later found guilty in court in connection with another offence, then at the sentencing stage the court may receive evidence about the use of extrajudicial sanctions in the two preceding years.[37]

Before deciding whether to caution a youth, make a referral to a program of extrajudicial sanctions or send a case to court, a police officer will usually discuss the offending behaviour with the youth. The fact that the youth acknowledges the offending behaviour and expresses remorse could be a significant factor in deciding that a formal court response is not required. An admission of guilt by the youth in such a situation is very likely inadmissible in court. If there is any suggestion by the police that they will not proceed with formal charges if the youth confesses, any statement is likely to be considered induced by "hope of advantage" and, hence, involuntary and inadmissible. Section 10(4) of the *YCJA* provides that any statement made by a young person "as a condition of being dealt with by extrajudicial measures is inadmissible" against the youth in any civil or criminal proceedings; this provision would probably be applicable in this situation. Further, the

---

37   *YCJA*, above note 6, s. 119(4), provides that records of cases that involve use of extrajudicial measures other than extrajudicial sanctions (i.e, a caution or informal diversion) can only be shared with: (a) a police officer or Crown considering whether to again use extrajudicial measures for a later offence; (b) participants in a conference considering whether to use extrajudicial measures; (c) a police officer, Crown or conference participant dealing with the offence in question; or (d) a police officer investigating a later offence. The record of involvement with extrajudicial sanctions can only be used for two years: s. 119(2)(a).

statement is inadmissible if the police have not fully advised the youth of his or her legal rights in accordance with the *Charter* and section 146 of the *YCJA*. (For a fuller discussion of the admissibility of statements-made by youths, see Chapter 4.)

The decision not to divert or screen a charge involves a significant exercise of police or prosecutorial discretion referred to as "low visibility." There is a potential that this discretion may be exercised in a discriminatory fashion. Some research reveals a concern by youth belonging to visible minorities that police are less likely to exercise their discretion not to charge when dealing with minority youth than when dealing with youth not belonging to visible minorities.[38] Beyond the issue of systemic discrimination, there may be a tendency for officers to "give a break" to youths from "good families," thereby effectively prejudicing youths from disadvantaged backgrounds. The exercise of police and prosecutorial discretion to screen or divert to extrajudicial sanctions should be guided by appropriate policies and training to assure fair and effective application. Further, there should be adequate record keeping to ensure that youths are not being repeatedly screened by different officers on different occasions.

2) Committees and Conferences

To encourage the use of extrajudicial measures and community involvement in responding to youth crime, the *YCJA* has provisions authorizing conferences and youth justice committees. While both were used under the *YOA*, it is expected that their use will increase with the enactment of the *YCJA*.

a) Youth Justice Committees: Section 18

Although the manner and extent of their use depends on provincial policies and local initiatives, the federal government is encouraging this type of response to youth crime by providing educational materials, as well as funding support for operation and evaluation of model programs. The *YOA* section 69 allowed provincial governments to establish local volunteer youth justice committees "to assist . . . in any aspect of the administration" of that Act, or in any programs or services for young offenders. A significant number of these committees were established in different parts of Canada, in particular in Manitoba and

---

38   J. Warner, *et al.*, "Marijuana, Juveniles, and the Police: What High-School Students Believe about Detection and Enforcement" (1998) 40 Can. J. Crim. 401 at 414.

in some Aboriginal communities. In each locality the committee had membership drawn from those in the community who have an interest in assisting young persons in trouble with the law. These committees had a range of functions, such as monitoring and supporting the administration of the youth justice system, but their most common function was to administer "alternative measures programs," the term used in the *YOA* for what the *YCJA* refers to as "extrajudicial sanctions." To emphasize the continuity in approach to youth justice committees, section 165(4) of the *YCJA* stipulates that any youth justice committee established under the *YOA* is deemed to continue under the new Act.

Section 18 of the *YCJA* is similar to the youth justice committee provision in section 69 of the *YOA*, but has added a long list detailing possible functions for youth justice committees. The previous Act required that the members of these committees were to serve "without remuneration." While the members of these committees will continue to be drawn from the community, the requirement that all members serve without remuneration has been deleted. This clarifies that in addition to volunteers, professionals who work for community agencies or schools, or police officers may be members. It also allows for possible payment of a person serving in the role of co-ordinator. It is expected that youth justice committees will continue to serve an important role in individual cases, especially in situations where extrajudicial measures are being used. A committee may, for example, under section 19 of the *YCJA*, accept a referral from the police or a prosecutor to arrange a meeting involving an offender and a victim, and then make a recommendation for an appropriate extrajudicial measure. A committee may also be involved in providing support for victims and assisting in their reconciliation with offenders.

A youth justice committee may have a role in arranging for support or supervision of young offenders in the community, whether referred by a court or as a result of extrajudicial measures. Section 18(2) of the *YCJA* makes clear that youth justice committees may be asked to play a role in monitoring the implementation of the Act, advising federal and provincial governments about how to improve the youth justice system, and providing information to the public about the youth justice system. A youth justice committee may also be asked to play a role in co-ordinating the efforts of local child welfare agencies, social agencies, and schools in working with young offenders. Some youth justice committees are also involved in responding to offending by children under twelve, in conjunction with parents, police and child welfare agencies. The way in which a youth justice committee operates depends on the role that it is expected to play. If it is dealing with individual youth, it is important that a committee has appropriate policies and a training program to ensure that volunteers understand their mandate. While the whole group may deal with policy issues, frequently only a subgroup of committee members deals with individual cases.

b) Youth Justice Conferences: Sections 19 and 41

Related to section 18 of the YCJA, which governs youth justice committees, are sections 19 and 41, which deal with conferences. While youth justice committees may act as a conference, the two institutions are distinct. The concept of the conference in the YCJA was in part inspired by the "family group conference," as developed in New Zealand, which is based on the traditional responses to offending by that country's indigenous Maori population. The conference concept is also based on the traditional practices of many Canadian Aboriginal communities for dealing with offending. Indeed, in many communities, as well as in many schools and families, there are long traditions of responding to certain types of less serious offending behaviour by having a meeting with the offender, the victim, and others to discuss the behaviour and develop a consensus about a just response. The YCJA recognizes a flexible concept of the conference as having a role in responding to youth crime.

A "conference" is defined in section 2 of the Act as "a group of persons who are convened to give advice" concerning a specific young person having difficulty with the law. This definition is broad, so that a "conference" may function and be used in a range of different ways. Conferences involve meetings between offenders, victims, and community members, and typically have an emphasis on restorative justice and on providing compensation to victims for injury caused by offenders. While offenders should be held accountable for what they have done through the conference process, this does not necessarily mean that a punishment needs to be imposed. Sometimes a youth will be held accountable by attending a conference, apologizing, undertaking not to reoffend, and perhaps providing some form of compensation to the victim.

The YOA did not have specific provision for having conferences, although in practice in some places they were used under that Act, especially in dealing with youth from Aboriginal communities and in regard to alternative measures under that Act. Under the YOA, some alternative measures programs operated on a model premised on having offenders, their families, victims (where appropriate), and community members meet together to discuss the offence and develop a mutually acceptable plan. This type of response is one example of the *YCJA* concept of the conference. Under the *YOA* some judges also made use of "sentencing circles" for dealing with Aboriginal offenders, especially those living on reserves and in northern communities. The judge would invite the offender, members of the offender's family, the victim and supporters, and community members to come to court and express their views about an appropriate sentence. Often some form of reconciliation between the victim and offender was an objective of this process, although this was not always attainable. The concept of the conference under the *YCJA* includes the sentencing circle, although the conference is clearly a broader concept.

Section 19 of the *YCJA* provides that a police officer, a provincial director or a youth justice court judge may convene a conference to provide advice about any decision to be made under the Act. Although not explicitly stated in the Act, it is expected that conferences will typically include the youth and parents, members of the community, and, where appropriate, the victim. The community members might be volunteers, respected Elders in an Aboriginal community, or such professionals as social workers or teachers who have worked with the youth. There will normally be a discussion about the offence and the youth, with a sharing of perspectives and information. In less serious cases, a conference may advise the police or a prosecutor about whether the youth is suitable for extrajudicial sanctions. If the case involves extrajudicial sanctions, there may be no formal record of the deliberations of a conference, and only a brief record of its conclusion.

Police forces in Canada are increasingly involved in establishing their own programs of extrajudicial sanctions, with conferences playing an important role in many localities. A growing number of police officers have training in conducting conferences involving offenders, family members, victims, and community members. Youth justice committees and community agencies are also making increasing use of the conference as an aspect of extrajudicial sanctions programs. A conference may be used in more serious cases to provide advice to a judge about whether to release a youth from detention pending trial, as well as advising at the time of sentencing or sentence review. Section 19 of the *YCJA* expressly allows a youth justice court judge to refer a case to a community conference to provide advice for any judicial decision that will be made, such as a decision about pre-trial release or about sentencing.

Under the *YOA*, some judges combined aspects of community-based conferencing with court-based sentencing and would, for example, refer a youth to a community conference *after* a finding of guilt and before a youth was sentenced.[39] This practice is encouraged by section 19 of the *YCJA*, which allows for a judicial referral to a community agency to arrange a post-adjudication meeting between the victim and the offender and the supporters of each. As a result of the conference, a restorative justice proposal may be made by the offender to the victim. The conference facilitator may then send a report to the court about the conference, including the proposal made and the attitude of the victim. The sentencing judge may then consider using the restorative proposal and any recommendation from the conference as the basis of the sentence.

Section 41 reinforces section 19, making clear that there can be conferences *after* a finding of guilt and before a sentence is imposed. A judge may invoke section 41 to convene and sit at a conference, for example in "circle sentencing," or may direct that a conference is to be convened in the community to provide advice about sentencing to the court. The conference may have a restorative and conciliatory effect on the participants, and can serve an important role in providing the offender with an understanding of the consequences of his or her acts, and in holding the offender accountable to the victim and society. The practice of "circle sentencing," a form of judicially convened conferencing, is becoming a more common way of dealing with both youth and adult offenders, especially in Aboriginal communities.[40] If a judge convenes a conference, it will be held as part of the court proceeding under section 41 of the *YCJA*. In this situation, the participants in the conference are technically not witnesses who are subject to cross-examination by counsel, although there may be a dialogue involving the judge, lawyers, and members of the conference.

If a conference is presided over by a judge, a record of the proceedings should be kept and may be used by the judge for the purposes of making decisions about the youth. The judicial conference is intended to bring the community and the court closer together, and requires trust and co-operation between members of the community and the judiciary. Although section 41 makes clear that the recommendation of a conference is not binding on the court, in practice judges are likely to follow the recommendations of a conference, since these recommendations reflect a consensus of the victim and members of the community.

Family group conferences may also be used as a response to offending behaviour by children under the age of twelve, although participation

---

39   Lynn Cook-Stanhope, "Red Necks Meet Bleeding Hearts" (2000) 24:2 Prov. Judges J. 34.
40   See Heino Lilles, "Youth Justice Initiatives in the Yukon" (2000) 24:2 Prov. Judges J. 18.

for the parents and child must be voluntary. There may be cases in which a family group conference for a child under twelve may be an alternative to the commencement of child welfare proceedings.

Youth justice committees and conferences are similar but distinct. Youth justice committees are established in specific communities and have a continuing existence and fixed membership. Committees may deal with individual cases or systemic issues, while conferences deal only with individual cases and have a membership determined to deal with specific cases. The mandate of a youth justice committee may include the convening of conferences about youths from a particular community, perhaps with some or all of the committee members participating in the conferences. The YCJA enables youth justice committees and conferences to play an important role in supplementing the role of the youth courts. However, their actual role ultimately depends on the willingness of provincial governments to implement the provisions of the Act and provide financial support for this type of response to youth offending, and on the interest of community members and justice system professionals to support these non-judicial methods of responding to youth offending.

There are some concerns about how community-based conferences will function. For example, will the interests of victims be adequately protected? Will victims feel intimidated by the presence of the accused or silenced by the presence of supporters for the accused? In some cases, a committee might want to impose a sanction that is harsher than the sentence that a youth justice court might impose. Because of these concerns, section 19(3) allows the provincial government to establish rules for the operation of community-based conferences, for example, to ensure that its members have some training and that fair procedures are followed and appropriate sanctions are imposed. If introduced by a provincial government, these rules will, for example, govern cases that are referred by the police or Crown prosecutor for extrajudicial sanctions. Section 19(3) also specifies that any provincial rules that are promulgated do not apply to community conferences dealing with a youth on referral from a judge or to judicially convened conferences. Sections 19(1) and 41 make clear that a youth justice court judge may refer a matter to a conference to provide the court with a recommendation, or the judge may directly convene and preside over a conference. Since these types of conferences operate under judicial control, direct provincial regulation would not be appropriate. However, even judicially convened conferences may be difficult to operate effectively without a level of support from various government-funded agencies, such as probation services and the police.

Section 119(1)(j) allows for the sharing of information about the young person with those involved in the conferencing process. Staff, volunteers, and community members need to be instructed about their obligation to keep this type of information confidential.

D. EXTRAJUDICIAL SANCTIONS

The process for referring a youth to an extrajudicial sanctions program varies significantly from one jurisdiction to another, and sometimes between programs within the same province.[41] In some provinces a youth may be referred to an extrajudicial sanctions program without charges being laid (referred to as pre-charge programs), but in others charges must be laid before a case can be sent to extrajudicial sanctions (i.e., post-charge programs). Some provinces use both pre- and post-charge programs.

In most pre-charge programs, the police refer youths directly to the program, perhaps after some form of consultation with the Crown prosecutor's office, without even commencing a youth justice court proceeding. It is also possible to have a pre-charge program for which referrals are made by the Crown prosecutor as a result of referral after Crown screening of charges. In post-charge programs, a court proceeding is commenced, and the youth is issued a summons or appearance notice for court. If the youth is charged, the youth may be fingerprinted and photographed; under section 119(2)(a) of the *YCJA*, if the case is dealt with by extrajudicial sanctions, two years from the date that the youth consents to participate in the program no further use can be made of those records, and the centralized Canadian Police Information Centre records will be destroyed at that time.

With post-charge programs, the youth will generally have a first appearance in court before the Crown prosecutor decides whether the youth should be referred to the program. If the case is referred to an extrajudicial sanctions program, the court case is adjourned pending a decision about which sanction should be imposed and the charges will be dismissed by the court if the youth satisfactorily completes the program. Generally, the Crown prosecutor will arrange for the formal dismissal of the charges without the youth reappearing. Post-charge programs are more cumbersome. However, when extrajudicial sanctions are not completed, it is easier to bring a case to court if proceedings have already been commenced.

---

41   Canadian Centre for Justice Statistics, 2000, above note 10.

The initial decision about whether to divert a youth from the court system to an extrajudicial sanctions program is made by the police or prosecutor. Thus, the support of local police and prosecutors is essential for the success of this type of program. Police officers and prosecutors are most likely to be supportive if they have an understanding of how the program operates and have a good relationship with the program administrators. In some communities, police officers may directly operate the extrajudicial sanctions programs, but even in these communities the officers who operate the program need to enlist the support of other officers and satisfy them that this is an appropriate way to hold youth accountable. Section 10(2)(b) of the *YCJA* specifies that the person "who is considering whether to use [an] extrajudicial sanction [program] . . . [should be] satisfied that it would be appropriate, having regard to the needs of the young person and the interests of society." The making of this decision requires consideration of the threat posed to society by the youth's behaviour, the youth's circumstances, and the effect of the offence on the victim. In practice, the decision to refer will be governed by the provincial or local policy that regulates the exercise of discretion by the prosecutor or police when deciding whether a youth is eligible for extrajudicial sanctions. These policies typically specify that only certain offences are eligible for diversion. However, under the *YOA* there was substantial variation among provinces in eligibility policies and criteria, and this is likely to continue under the *YCJA*.

A common model is to have the Crown prosecutor, generally acting with the advice of the police, make the decision about whether to divert a youth to an extrajudicial sanctions program instead of dealing with the case in the courts. In some provinces, the Crown prosecutor may have a report prepared by a probation officer to assist in deciding whether a youth is suitable for extrajudicial sanctions or, as in Quebec, the local child welfare agency may be involved in consulting with the prosecutor. In many places, a pre-charge extrajudicial sanctions program may accept referrals directly from the police without the involvement of the Crown prosecutor's office — for example, the pre-charge program operated by Royal Canadian Mounted Police at Sparwood, British Columbia involving resolution conferences.

There is a duty imposed under section 10(2)(f) of the *YCJA* on the Crown prosecutor, or an agent of the Crown (such as a designated police officer), to form the "opinion" that there is "sufficient evidence to proceed with the prosecution of the offence." Section 10(2)(g) also specifies that extrajudicial sanctions cannot be used where the "prosecution of the offence is . . . in any way barred at law," for example, by the passage of the six-month limitation period for a strictly summary offence. These provisions are intended to prevent "net widening" and ensure that extrajudicial sanctions are not used as a way of responding informally to a case that is "too weak" to take to court. Cases with insufficient evidence for a prosecution should not be dealt with by the justice system at all, although it will sometimes be appropriate for a police officer in such a situation to speak informally with the youth and warn against engaging in criminal behaviour.

The referral to extrajudicial sanctions by the police or prosecutor will involve the transmission to the program operator of documents that explain the nature of the alleged offence, and will provide some information about the youth to the program operator. A meeting will be arranged between the program operator and the youth. In some localities, responsibility for meeting with the youth and arranging for the supervision of extrajudicial sanctions is given to a community agency with paid staff or volunteers or to a youth justice committee, while in other places government social workers or juvenile probation staff are responsible.[42] Increasingly, police forces in Canada are also being involved in various extrajudicial sanctions programs, which may be operated by officers with special training and interest in young offenders. Some police forces, for example, arrange family group conferences as a part of extrajudicial sanctions, and may as a result of a conference require restitution for victims.

Aboriginal communities in particular are establishing extrajudicial sanctions programs and youth justice committees that involve meetings with offenders and their family members, victims, and community members such as respected Elders. This is consistent with Aboriginal principles of traditional justice, which resemble restorative justice and emphasize the importance of restoring relationships within the community; it is also consistent with section 5 of the *YCJA*.

Under the *YOA*, in some provinces the offence criteria for referral of Aboriginal youth to alternative measures were broader than for non-Aboriginal youth, in recognition that there are social, political, and constitutional reasons for dealing with Aboriginal youths outside of the conventional justice system, a system that has clearly failed to deal adequately with Aboriginal offending.[43] A wider offence jurisdiction for extrajudicial sanctions for Aboriginal youth under the *YCJA* may also be appropriate. Extrajudicial sanctions programs that give Aboriginal

---

42   *Ibid.*
43   The courts have accepted that it does not violate s. 15 of the *Canadian Charter of Rights and Freedoms*, above note 11, to offer alternative measures to Aboriginals in circumstances where others do not have the same opportunity: *R. v. Willcocks* (1995), 22 O.R. (3d) 552 (Gen. Div.).

communities greater responsibility for their troubled adolescents have the potential to permit more effective healing-based non-adversarial responses to youthful offending.[44]

If a youth is referred to extrajudicial sanctions, the person or agency responsible for the program meets with the youth to ascertain what response is appropriate and available, and to ensure that the response is acceptable to the youth. In some localities, the meeting is very informal, with just a youth worker and the young person present. Section 11 of the *YCJA* requires that parents must be notified, orally or in writing, of any sanction that is imposed, but it is a common practice to involve parents in the process before a decision is made about how to proceed. Normally the meeting will result in the development of a plan, response, or sanction that will be reflected in a written agreement; programs generally have forms that help structure these agreements. Increasingly, programs are being established in Canada that involve victims, parents, and possibly members of the community meeting with the youth and a facilitator to attempt to achieve some form of reconciliation and develop a suitable plan. Section 5 of the *YCJA* makes clear that extrajudicial sanctions programs should encourage the involvement of families of young persons and victims in determining an appropriate response to the offence and that, if possible, this should be a restorative response that repairs the harm caused to the victim and community.

Section 12 gives a victim the right to request and obtain information about how a youth who has been sent to an extrajudicial sanctions program has been dealt with. This is, however, a minimum requirement and, consistent with sections 3 and 5 of the *YCJA*, many extrajudicial sanctions programs are trying to involve victims more actively in the process. It is important for victims to have a sense that justice has been done and, in appropriate cases, to meet with offenders or receive some form of compensation for the harm that they have suffered.[45] It is a common practice to notify the victim before sanctions are imposed and, often, to invite the victim to a meeting with the youth, at which the offence is discussed and an appropriate response developed. While these meetings can provide an important opportunity for victims to feel

---

44   See, for example, R. Ross, *Returning to the Teachings: Exploring Aboriginal Justice* (Toronto: Penguin, 1996);and R. Green, *Justice in Aboriginal Communities: Sentencing Alternatives* (Saskatoon: Purich, 1998).

45   See, for example, K.J. Pate and D.E. Peachey, "Face-to-Face: Victim-Offender Mediation under the *Young Offenders Act*" in J. Hudson, J. Hornick, and B. Burrows, eds., *Justice and the Young Offender in Canada* (Toronto: Wall and Thompson, 1988) 105.

vindicated and for offenders to gain an appreciation of the effects of their conduct, the meetings must be conducted with sensitivity to ensure that neither the victim nor youth feels intimidated by the experience. If appropriate, extrajudicial sanctions may include some form of restitution, apology, or personal service by the youth to the victim.

Victim-offender reconciliation may be an object for some extrajudicial sanction meetings — such as when the victim and offender attend the same school — and most programs place some emphasis on restorative justice objectives. Although a meeting may be an important restorative act for some victims, other victims want nothing to do with the offender. When a large corporation is victimized, as often occurs in shoplifting cases, it may be a less appropriate participant as a "victim" engaged in the extrajudicial sanctions. Even in these cases, it is important for a youth to understand that harm has been done, and a security officer or manager may represent the victim and explain the effects of the crime on society as a whole.

In some cases, it may be desirable to give the youth an opportunity to reflect on and acknowledge the offence by asking him or her to write an essay or prepare a poster on the subject, although account should be taken of the youth's abilities in imposing any requirements for written work. Or it may be appropriate for the youth to do some community-service work or make a donation to a charity, to make clear to the youth that offending behaviour harms the whole community. In some cases, especially if there has already been a suitable parental response to the offending behaviour or some form of reparation has been made to the victim, it may be that no further response is required after a meeting with the program operator. In some provinces, a common response is a letter sent to the parents and youth that warns the youth not to commit further offences and leaves it to the parents to determine an appropriate response. In Manitoba, it is called a "parental action letter" while, in Alberta and British Columbia, it is referred to as a "caution letter." The decision to impose no further sanctions will depend on the nature of the offence and may be influenced by the attitudes of the victim and the youth, as well as by the youth's reactions at the meeting.

Usually extrajudicial sanctions are arranged with just one meeting between the youth and others involved in the process. Sometimes more than one meeting is held, for example if the participants feel that there is a need to gather more information, involve others, or consider their position. A plan may be arranged that will involve a reconvening of the group to monitor the youth's progress. In some localities, extrajudicial sanctions programs may make use of a range of responses that are not merely sanctions but that try to address the causes of a youth's offending behaviour. In some communities programs are directed at certain types of offending behaviour, such as shoplifting. One option may be to require a youth to attend a values development course directed at adolescents with offending problems. This type of course is commonly used in Quebec. In some places, there may be a requirement for a community supervisor or mentor, or a referral may be made for some form of counselling. Such counselling might be provided by a therapist, doctor, or community agency; in an Aboriginal community, a youth may be required to enter into a relationship with a respected Elder as mentor.

A response recommending therapy or counselling is premised on the belief that some offending behaviour is a symptom of an emotional, social, behavioural, or substance-abuse problem. Responding to the underlying problem is most likely to prevent further offending, as well as being generally beneficial to the youth. Some extrajudicial sanctions programs, however, are not permitted to make a referral to counselling a requirement of participation; these programs take a non-interventionist approach, believing that a referral to counselling is too intrusive a response to the relatively minor charges that they deal with and should only be imposed by a court.[46] Even if the policies that govern an extrajudicial sanctions program preclude imposition of conditions of counselling, the staff or volunteers who meet with a youth may, in appropriate cases, make a referral to a youth or parents for further counselling, treatment, or support, explaining that this is a suggestion for help they may wish to obtain, and is not a condition of participation.

While most youths who are sent to extrajudicial sanctions programs in Canada have not committed serious offences and are not likely to reoffend, there is a minority who may pose a future threat to society. If such youth do not have their needs addressed at this early stage of involvement with the youth justice system, they will likely commit subsequent, more serious offences. Extrajudicial sanctions programs that respond to the problems of youths at risk are consistent with section 3(1)(a)(ii) of the YCJA, which recognizes the importance of "addressing the circumstances underlying a young person's offending behaviour." This suggests that counselling or treatment conditions may be appropriate options for some of the most troubled youths referred to extrajudicial sanctions programs.

---

46   This is, for example, the official policy in Ontario. Counselling is not considered "an appropriate measure," although program workers provide "information about counselling and a referral might be appropriate as part of the negotiation process" (Ontario, Ministry of the Attorney General, *Alternative Measures Program: Policy & Procedures Manual* (Toronto: Queen's Printer, 1995) at 15).

1) Role and Rights of Youths

An extrajudicial sanctions program can offer a youth the opportunity for an expeditious, informal response to an alleged violation of the law. If the case is resolved by extrajudicial sanctions, the youth and parents will generally feel less intimidated than if the case goes to court, and they are likely to participate more fully in any discussions about the offence and their circumstances than in the more formal, adversarial court setting. So it is not surprising that research reveals that parents and youth may be more likely to perceive themselves as having been treated fairly in a diversion program than in court.[47] For the youth and parents, diversion avoids the stigma of having a "youth justice court record." The parents may also encourage their child to choose extrajudicial sanctions, since there is no need to incur the expense of having a lawyer and there may be less need to take time away from work or other activities to attend court. As a result, there may be considerable pressure on a youth to participate in extrajudicial sanctions. There is the potential for a fairly intrusive response to a quite minor offence with extrajudicial sanctions, or even for participation by a youth who is not guilty of any offence. While the *YCJA* has provisions that are intended to minimize the risk of an abuse of the rights of a youth, there are fewer protections if a youth goes to an extrajudicial sanctions program than if the youth goes to court.

Extrajudicial sanctions programs are not designed to be "informal courts." Under section 10(2)(e) of the *YCJA* extrajudicial sanctions may be used "*only* if . . . the young person accepts responsibility for the act . . . that forms the basis of the offence that he or she is alleged to have committed" [emphasis added]. Typically this provision is satisfied at the meeting between the youth and program operator to develop a plan of extrajudicial sanctions. The youth will be asked to discuss the circumstances of the alleged offence, explaining the nature of his or her participation in the offence alleged. Often a youth will make a full admission of guilt, but section 10(2)(e) technically does not require that the youth accept full legal guilt for the specific offence alleged. Sometimes a youth may question some aspect of the specific charge or police report, but accepts that he or she was in some way responsible for an illegal act.

---

47   See, for example, M.E. Morton and W.G. West, "An Experiment in Diversion by a Citizen Committee" in R.R. Corrado, M. LeBlanc, and J. Trépanier, eds., *Current Issues in Juvenile Justice* (Toronto: Butterworths, 1983) 203 at 211.

While section 10(2)(e) does not require a full legal admission of guilt, it at least requires a recognition of involvement and an acceptance of moral responsibility for the offence alleged. A youth who "denies his participation or involvement" or who expresses the wish to be dealt with in youth justice court cannot be dealt with by an extrajudicial sanctions program (section 10(3)). If this occurs, the program operator should refer the case to the Crown or police so that the matter can be dealt with in youth justice court. A trial to determine whether or not a youth is guilty can be conducted only in youth justice court.

Section 10(2)(d) requires that a youth must be advised of the right to legal representation and given a reasonable opportunity to consult with counsel before consenting to participate in extrajudicial sanctions. Most programs ensure that at an early stage of the extrajudicial sanctions process the youth accepts responsibility for the offence alleged, agrees to participate, and is aware of the right to consult a lawyer. However, unlike the situation for youths who are dealt with in youth justice court — for whom section 25 of the *YCJA* provides for access to legal representation if they are unable to afford to pay for a lawyer — for youths referred to extrajudicial sanctions, there is no statutory provision dealing with access of legal services. Some youths do consult a lawyer before agreeing to participation. If the program is post-charge, the youth may have an opportunity to have a brief meeting with duty counsel at youth justice court before the case is referred to extrajudicial sanctions. A few programs arrange for duty counsel to assist at their meetings but, in times of increasing fiscal restraint, it is difficult to obtain a commitment from legal aid authorities to fund this. There are concerns that some youths may in effect waive their legal rights, perhaps because of a "desire to get things over with" or because of parental pressure, without fully appreciating their position. This may happen even if a youth has not committed the act alleged or would have a valid defence to the allegations.

Whether or not there is successful completion of the extrajudicial sanctions plan, section 10(4) of the *YCJA* specifies that no statement or confession made by the youth "accepting responsibility" for the offence as a condition for being dealt with by extrajudicial measures may be used in any later civil or criminal court proceedings. Section 10(4) is intended to reassure youths and their advisers, as well as to encourage youths to accept responsibility and participate in extrajudicial sanctions. The provision may also reflect a concern that there may be cases in which there is the potential for a youth to feel coerced into "accepting responsibility" in order to gain access to extrajudicial sanctions, despite the fact that the youth is not actually guilty. Even without section 10(4), in many cases there would be an argument that a statement made by a youth as a condition of participation in alternative measures was induced by a "hope of advantage" (i.e., the dismissal or staying of charges) and, hence, would be involuntary and inadmissible in any subsequent prosecution.(See Chapter 4 on voluntariness.)

Under section 10(2)(c) a youth must agree to the specific extrajudicial sanction that is developed for him or her. If the youth objects that the plan is too onerous and the appropriateness of the sanction is not resolved by discussion, then the case must be referred to court. In some cases, the plan developed in extrajudicial sanctions may be more onerous or intrusive than the sentence which a youth justice court judge would impose, but the youth without legal assistance may not be aware of the discrepancy and may erroneously believe that any alternative measures plan is less than the sanction a court would impose. One Crown prosecutor, John Pearson, commented on the problems that can arise from the lack of access to legal assistance in connection with alternative measures under the YOA. These comments remain relevant to the YCJA:

> If parents and young persons have difficulty appreciating the need for counsel when they are going through the court system, how likely is it that they will recognize the need when a "non-judicial" resolution is being proposed? Once alternative measures are invoked, the young person is dealt with by a system that has none of the mechanisms required in order for legal representation to be effective. A well-meaning diversion committee, from which there is no appeal, determines society's response to the young person's criminal conduct. The philosophy behind the juvenile-court movement is played out on another stage.[48]

Pearson expressed concern that in some respects the "diversion movement" is similar to the informal paternalistic court of the *Juvenile Delinquents Act*, where government actions that were intended to promote the best interests of adolescents could result in a much more intrusive response than the offence warranted.

It would be desirable to ensure that all youths who are referred to extrajudicial sanctions have actually had access to legal advice before waiving their right to go to court, especially since the youth's participation may be held against him or her if there were a later prosecution for another offence. However, given the less serious nature of the

---

48   J.C. Pearson, "Legal Representation under the *YOA*" in A.W. Leschied, P.G. Jaffe, and W. Willis, eds., *The Young Offenders Act: A Revolution in Canadian Juvenile Justice* (Toronto: University of Toronto Press, 1991) 114 at 118.

offences and the fact that only community-based sanctions can be imposed, the drafters of the *YCJA* (and the *YOA*) did not give youths referred to extrajudicial sanctions the statutory right to counsel. With scarce resources, legal aid plans generally do not provide access to legal services for youths referred to these programs. Even parents with financial means may feel reluctant to pay a lawyer for a case that they believe is being dealt with informally. Those who administer extrajudicial sanctions programs should be aware of the potential for violations of rights, and in particular of the potential that a youth may feel coerced by parents or others into accepting responsibility for an offence that he or she did not actually commit, as well as for the possibility that an unduly onerous plan may be imposed on a youth.

2) Consequences of Participation in Extrajudicial Sanctions

If a young person agrees to participate and successfully completes the extrajudicial sanction plan agreed to, the case cannot proceed to court. Section 10(5)(a) of the *YCJA* specifies that if the case is brought to youth justice court, the judge must dismiss the charges. If an extrajudicial sanction plan is developed and agreed to, but the youth does not fully complete it, there may be another meeting between the youth and the program administrator to discuss any problems that the youth may be having. The program administrator may decide to refer a youth who has not fully complied with the sanction plan to the police or prosecutor, who may bring the case to court. Non-completion is most likely to result in referral to court if the offence was more serious and the non-completion was wilful and substantial. Under section 10(5)(b) the judge has a discretion where there is only partial completion of extrajudicial sanctions. If the prosecution is considered to be unfair, the judge may dismiss the charge or take account of the partially completed plan when sentencing the youth. The judge should consider how much of the plan was completed, the reasons the plan was not fully carried out, and whether the extrajudicial sanctions have had an effect on the youth.

Section 119(2)(a) of the *YCJA* provides for a two-year "period of access" for records relating to extrajudicial sanctions, running from the date that a youth consents to the specific sanction. During the two-year period of access, section 119(1) lists individuals who can obtain access to the records of an extrajudicial sanctions program, including the youth, the victim, and youth corrections or probation staff. If within the two-year period a youth is charged with and convicted of an offence, then section 40(2)(d)(iv) of the *YCJA* specifies that a pre-sentence report prepared to assist the judge in sentencing the youth shall include "the history of alternative measures under [the *Young Offenders Act*] . . . or extrajudicial sanctions used to deal with the young person and the response of the young person to those measures or sanctions."

In theory, it might be argued that prior participation in an extrajudicial sanctions (or alternative measures) plan, should not be weighted as heavily against a youth as a prior formal youth justice court finding, since there has been no judicial finding of guilt. However, at a subsequent sentencing hearing, the prior involvement is a "part of the history of the person being sentenced" and may demonstrate that a more intrusive or punitive response may be appropriate for that individual.[49] Prior participation in extrajudicial sanctions is generally a negative factor at any subsequent sentencing, even if the participation arose out of a pre-charge program. Prior participation makes it unlikely that a court will merely reprimand the youth or impose an absolute discharge. The possibility of later use of a record of judicial sanctions emphasizes the need to ensure that those youths who waive their right to go to youth justice court are truly accepting responsibility for their acts and are aware of the consequences of participation.

Some extrajudicial sanctions programs, especially those that are community based, have a policy of actually destroying a youth's record of participation two years after the youth consented to participation in the program. However, while no use is to be made of the record after two years, program operators are not technically obliged to destroy the records. After two years, no use may be made of any records kept in regard to an offence sent to extrajudicial sanctions. Also, after two years the Canadian Police Information Centre is obliged to destroy any of its records relating to the offence and the youth, as well as the fingerprints and photographs of the youth, assuming that there are no further offences that result in the taking of fingerprints or photographs (section 128(4)). If a police force has records, including photographs or fingerprints, relating to a youth who has been sent to extrajudicial sanctions who is not convicted of any further offences in the two-year period, the force should not make use of these records, although it is not obliged to physically destroy or delete its records. After two years, many police forces will, on request, retrieve and destroy records relating to a youth who was sent to extrajudicial sanctions and has had a conviction-free period.

---

49 *R. v. Drew* (1978), 7 C.R. (3d) S-21 (B.C.C.A.).

3) Judicial Referral to a Child Welfare Agency

Under the *Juvenile Delinquents Act*, the juvenile justice and child welfare systems were closely linked. Juvenile court judges had the authority to commit delinquents to the care of a child welfare agency as a sentencing alternative to a custodial sentence. It was common under that Act for delinquent youth and "children in need of protection" to be placed in the same juvenile care facilities. The *YOA* was intended to effect a sharper separation between the child welfare and youth justice systems, based on the premise that children who are abused or neglected should not be treated in the same way as young offenders. There are good arguments for separating youthful offenders from adolescents who are in the child welfare system as a result of parental abuse or neglect, since those youths who are victims of parental failings should not feel as although they are being punished for not having a suitable home. Further, the needs of youth who have been victims of abuse or neglect can be quite different from those who are offenders.

One of the legal changes brought about by the enactment of the *YOA* was the increase in the minimum age of criminal responsibility from seven years of age, as it had been under the *Juvenile Delinquents Act*, to twelve years of age. This tended to increase the separation between the juvenile justice and child welfare systems, as the overlap between the two systems was greatest for children under twelve. Child welfare agencies often have difficulty effectively providing services for adolescents with a history of having been abused or neglected, as these youth generally mistrust adults and tend to run away from child welfare facilities. After the *YOA* came into force, some child welfare agencies may have tended to transfer some troubled adolescents into the youth justice system, for example, by having youth who resided in agency group homes charged for relatively minor offences that involved misconduct in these facilities. Rather than dealing with these relatively minor offences as behavioural problems in the child welfare system, there was a tendency for child welfare agencies to have these more difficult cases charged and handled by the youth justice system.

The separation between the two systems was also increased by administrative changes made in several provinces at the time the *YOA* came into force. Influenced by that Act's criminal justice orientation, some provincial governments transferred administrative responsibility for young offenders from their social services ministry to their corrections ministry. There was also an increasing tendency to have young persons appearing in front of judges who regularly dealt with adult offenders, as opposed to judges dealing with child welfare and family law issues. In some provinces, however, most notably Quebec, there continued to be close links between the child welfare and youth justice systems under the *YOA*.

In Quebec, a separate set of judges sat in Youth Court, dealing exclusively with children and adolescents, both in the youth justice and child-protection contexts. Troubled adolescent offenders were frequently diverted from the youth justice system to child welfare programs and facilities, and Quebec had the lowest rate of youth court use in Canada.[50] British Columbia was one of those provinces which, after the *YOA* came into force, transferred responsibility for youth probation and corrections from the ministry responsible for child welfare services to the adult corrections ministry. Interestingly, in the latter half of the 1990s, administrative changes were made in that province to again more closely link all services for children and adolescents. The B.C. government decided that youth corrections, youth probation, child-protection services, and mental health services for adolescents were all to be provided by the children and families ministry. This change improved the co-ordination of services and contributed to British Columbia achieving one of the lowest rates under the *YOA* of use of youth court and custody by the year 2000.[51]

While the promotion of the welfare of a young offender is an important factor in the youth court process, appeal courts acting under the *YOA* ruled that it was wrong to impose a youth court sentence merely to meet a youth's needs. In a 1985 decision reducing a long custody sentence that a youth court judge had imposed under the *YOA* on a youth who had committed a relatively minor offence, Thorson J.A. of the Ontario Court of Appeal stated:

> The fact that this young offender may require some long-term form of social or institutional care or guidance if there is to be any real prospect of his rehabilitation does not mean that the vehicle of the *Young Offenders Act* can be employed for that purpose. Here, as under the *Criminal Code*, it is a cardinal principle of our law that . . . the punishment should fit the crime but should not be stretched so that it exceeds it, even where that might be thought desirable by some in the interest of providing some extra protection for the public.[52]

---

50   Canadian Centre for Justice Statistics, 2000, above note 10.
51   See Tom Gove, "Youth Court in British Columbia" (2000) 24:2 Prov. Judges J. 28.
52   *R. v. I.(R.)* (1985), 44 C.R. (3d) 168 at 178 (Ont. C.A.). See also *R. v. B.(M.)* (1987), 36 C.C.C. (3d) 573 (Ont. C.A.).

This approach, which restricts the use of the youth justice system as a basis for intervention in a youth's life, is reinforced by the enactment in 1995 of section 24(1.1)(a) of the YOA, which specified that a youth should not be placed in custody as "a substitute for appropriate child protection, health and other social measures."[53]

The Declaration of Principles and sentencing guidelines in section 38 of the YCJA further reinforce the principle that a youth justice court sentence should not be more severe or intrusive than is necessary to hold an offender accountable in order to satisfy child welfare objectives. The YCJA maintains a clear theoretical distinction between the child welfare and youth justice systems, with section 39(5) restating the provision of the YOA stipulating that a youth justice court "shall not use custody as a substitute for appropriate child protection, mental health or social measures."

Section 29 of the YCJA similarly provides that a youth is not to be detained pending trial because the youth needs child welfare or other social services. It must, however, be acknowledged that, despite these legislative and judicial pronouncements, some youth justice court judges may be tempted to take account of social circumstances when dealing with the detention or sentencing of troubled adolescents. For instance, a judge may be tempted to place a youth who is living on the street in custody when this is not warranted by the circumstances of the offence. There may also be a tendency for child welfare and mental health agencies to try to transfer clients who face charges into the youth justice system so that: "this kid is no longer our problem."[54]

Those who work in the youth justice system, whether as police, prosecutors, probation officers, or defence counsel, need to be familiar with the resources available outside the youth justice system, in particular in the child welfare, mental health, and education systems. Youth

---

53   This provision only came into force in 1995; prior to that date (and perhaps even later), it was clear that an inadequate home situation and child welfare concerns may have influenced some youth court judges in making dispositions under the YOA, above note 9: see R. v. J.J.M., [1993] 2 S.C.R. 421 and discussion in Chapter 9.

54   See, for example, J. Gandy, Judicial Interim Release (Bail) Hearings (Toronto: Policy Research Centre on Children, Youth, and Families, 1992). Consider also the tragic case of James Lonee, a sixteen-year-old offender killed by another youth in an Ontario custody facility. Lonee was "devastated" when the child welfare agency terminated his long-term wardship once he was in custody under the YOA; the agency had expressed concern about "double-resourcing." This ended Lonee's involvement with the agency social worker, which had been the longest, most committed relationship he had experienced in his sad, short life (K. Toughill, "A life in pain," Toronto Star, September 22, 1996).

justice system professionals should try to communicate effectively with professionals in those other systems to ensure that there is an appropriate response to each youth, while respecting the mandate of the *YCJA*. Sometimes a youth who has committed an offence should be dealt with outside the youth justice system *instead* of being prosecuted. In other cases, different resources from outside the youth justice system may be used *as part of* a youth justice response; for example, a requirement that a youth attend alcohol counselling provided by a community agency might be a term of probation.

To help ensure that adolescents needing child welfare services are not inappropriately dealt with in the youth justice system, section 35 of the *YCJA* provides that in "addition to any other order that it is authorized to make, a youth justice court may, at any stage of proceedings . . . refer the young person to a child welfare agency for assessment to determine whether the young person is in need of child welfare services." Lawyers for youths can play a role in obtaining appropriate assistance, and they should be familiar with the resources in the youth justice system and elsewhere that are available to assist their clients and be prepared to explore various options. Defence counsel may also have an important informal advocacy role, communicating and working with different agencies and with parents to develop a suitable plan for a young offender, provided always that the lawyer is acting on the client's instructions and respecting any confidential information that may have been received. Some youths, even after careful explanation, would rather be dealt with by the youth justice system than some other agency, and a lawyer advocating for that young client must respect this decision in presenting a plan to the court.

Under the *YCJA* a youth justice court should not impose a sentence that is inappropriately onerous, given the circumstances of the offence and the record of the offender. An appropriate judicial response may consider both rehabilitation and accountability and in doing so may well serve to promote the welfare of a youth. While there are arguments for the complete separation of the child welfare and youth justice systems, there are also significant reasons for having some degree of overlap between the two systems. Many abused and neglected youth have emotional and behavioural problems that lead to criminal activities.

In some cases it may be a matter of chance or institutional arrangement whether a particular adolescent with a history of abuse or neglect becomes involved in the child welfare or youth justice system. Section 35 of the *YCJA* may be used to have child welfare services provided *in addition* to a youth justice response. This provision may, for example, be used at the sentencing stage. Section 35 can also be invoked at the time of a pre-trial detention hearing, for example to ascertain whether a child who is living on the street or engaging in juvenile prostitution should receive child welfare services before the case is resolved by the youth justice court. While the provision of child welfare services after a section 35 referral might affect a decision by the Crown about whether to proceed with charges or seek pre-trial detention and may affect the sentence imposed by a youth justice court after conviction, the referral is not in itself a sentence or means of concluding proceedings under the *YCJA*.

While a referral under section 35 of the *YCJA* must come from the court, the judge's referral may be made at the suggestion of defence counsel, a probation officer, the prosecutor, a parent, or anyone else. The judge may also make the decision to refer under section 35 without anyone making a suggestion, although it would normally be appropriate for a judge to advise all the parties that this was being considered and ask for their submissions before a referral is made. The referral need not take any particular form, although it would normally be in writing. The judge should normally direct that relevant portions of the youth's records should be provided to the child-welfare agency, making an order under section 119(1)(s) of the *YCJA* to allow disclosure to the agency.

The *YOA* did not have an equivalent provision to section 35 of the *YCJA*, and this provision was enacted to remind those who work in the youth justice system that a youth justice court response is not likely to meet all of the needs of a young person who has violated the criminal law. While a section 35 referral will not necessarily conclude proceedings in youth justice court, it may facilitate some form of diversion of some adolescents from the youth justice system to the child welfare system or at least affect how their cases are dealt with in youth justice court. A youth justice court judge cannot use section 35 to order that child welfare services are to be provided or that a youth is taken into the care of a child welfare agency. Indeed, in contrast to section 34 of the *YCJA*, which allows the judge to order an assessment by a psychologist or psychiatrist, a literal reading of section 35 might not even require the agency to actually conduct an assessment under section 35, although the agency will have a duty under provincial child welfare legislation to investigate any report that a child may be "in need of protection" or "endangered," including a report made by a judge.

It is clear that the youth justice court cannot order the detention of the youth for an assessment to be carried out under section 35. In practice, however, one would expect that a child welfare agency receiving a referral from a youth justice court judge would take the matter seriously. One would also expect that ordinarily the youth would agree to engage in the assessment process, as the youth justice court retains jurisdiction over the case. If, on the basis of the agency assessment, whether based on meetings with the youth or a file review, the youth is considered by the agency to need its services, there is an obligation on the agency under provincial child welfare laws to provide those services, and a power under child welfare legislation to apprehend and detain the youth, subject to judicial review under child welfare laws. Although not explicitly stated in the *YCJA*, it seems to be implicit in section 35 that the child welfare agency is expected to report to the youth justice court on whether child welfare services will be provided.

Section 35 of the *YCJA* reflects the practice of some judges under the *YOA* who were already making informal referrals to child welfare agencies. Section 35 reminds all judges of the need for a flexible, socially appropriate response to youth offending. However, its ultimate value will depend on the extent to which child welfare agencies have the resources and commitment to provide help to troubled adolescents. Further, in most provinces there are age restrictions on the youth who can receive such services; for example, in Ontario there are statutory restrictions on child welfare agency involvement for youths sixteen or older. While some of those in the child welfare system have expressed concerns that this provision might be used inappropriately, the child welfare agencies retain control over whether to provide services. Although some young offenders have problems that can be best dealt with in the child welfare system, most of them are best dealt with in the youth justice system, with its focus on accountability and protection of the public.

E. THE FUTURE OF DIVERSION

Under the *Young Offenders Act*, there was substantial variation in the use of police screening, and alternative measures differed in different provinces, but on the whole Canada made far more use of the formal youth court processes to respond to adolescent offending than other countries and less use of various diversionary practices. Canada's extensive reliance on a court-based response to youth offending was both expensive and associated with a high rate of use of youth custody. Experience in other countries clearly indicates that Canada can extend the use of various diversionary programs, including making more extensive use of police screening and cautioning, as well as other community-based programs, without increasing the risk of reoffending. Indeed, some of the international experience suggests that diversionary programs based on such models as the New Zealand family group conference may result in reductions in youth crime,[55] especially in Aboriginal communities where the conventional court-based approaches employed in Canada have proven notably unsuccessful in preventing reoffending.

Various types of diversionary schemes represent a socially useful and cost-effective response to many situations of youth offending. The *YCJA* and related federal funding initiatives are intended to significantly increase the use of various diversionary measures, including police or prosecutorial screening and community-based extrajudicial programs. An expeditious, informal response may be preferable to a delayed, formal adversarial court experience for many adolescents, parents, and victims. Indeed, diversion programs are also starting to be established for adult offenders in Canada.[56] There is still, however, surprisingly little research, in particular in Canada, on whether use of various types of diversionary schemes can actually reduce the risk of reoffending: clearly, this question merits study.

One would expect that the effectiveness of extrajudicial measures in terms of reducing recidivism might depend on the nature of the program and the types of cases dealt with, as well as on whether the program has good links to counselling and community supports that can assist youths at serious risk of reoffending in dealing with their problems. Some of those involved in operating diversionary programs claim that programs that have higher levels of victim involvement are more likely to be effective, both in engaging offenders and in reducing recidivism. Conversely, it seems that non-involvement of victims may reduce the impact of the diversionary process on the young offender and hence reduce the effectiveness of this type of program.[57] While various types of youth diversion programs can make some use of volunteers and provide a less expensive alternative to adolescent offending than sending a youth to court, they still require appropriate funding. These programs are most likely to be effective if they have trained competent staff with enough time to meet with victims and offenders before a conference is held, and to monitor and follow up with a youth after a diversionary decision is made. Clearly research and monitoring of different types of diversionary programs would be desirable.

There will always be a role for a formal court-based response for those adolescents who commit more serious offences or who are not

---

55   J.P. Hornick and S. Rodal, *The Use of Alternatives to Traditional Youth Court: An International Comparison* (Calgary: Canadian Research Institute for Law and the Family, 1995) at 50.

56   *Criminal Code*, s.717, enacted as S.C. 1995, c.22.

57   Donald Schmid, "Survey of New Zealand Youth Justice Coordinators" (2001).

responsive to informal intervention. There is also an important role for the court system in protecting legal rights. Extrajudicial sanctions and other forms of diversion must be structured and monitored to ensure that the rights of youths are not abused. There is substantial scope for the extension of various diversionary schemes in Canada.

FURTHER READINGS

BAZEMORE, G., & L. WALGRAVE, eds., *Restorative Juvenile Justice: Repairing the Harm of Youth Crime* (Monsey, NY : Criminal Justice Press/Willow Tree, 1999)

BRAITHWAITE, J. "Restorative Justice and Social Justice" (2000) 63 Sask L. Rev. 185

CANADA, FEDERAL–PROVINCIAL/TERRITORIAL TASK FORCE ON YOUTH JUSTICE, *A Review of the Young Offenders Act and the Youth Justice System in Canada* (Ottawa: Ministry of Supply and Services, 1996) c. 4

CANADIAN CENTRE FOR JUSTICE STATISTICS, "Alternative Measures in Canada 1998–99" (2000) 20:6 Juristat

GREEN, ROSS G. *Justice in Aboriginal Communities: Sentencing Alternatives* (Saskatoon, SK: Purich Publishing, 1998)

HORNICK, J.P., & S. RODAL, *The Use of Alternatives to Traditional Youth Court: An International Comparison* (Calgary, AB: Canadian Research Institute for Law and the Family, 1995)

HUDSON, J., J.P.. HORNICK, & B.A. BURROWS, eds., *Justice and the Young Offender in Canada* (Toronto, ON: Wall and Thompson, 1988) cc. 7 and 8

PLATT, P., *Young Offenders Law in Canada*, 2d ed. (Toronto, ON: Butterworths, 1995) c. 7

SCOTT, S., M. WONG, & B. WEAGANT, *Defending Young Offender Cases*, 2d ed. (Toronto, ON: Carswell, 1997) c. 4

TOMBS, J., & S. MOODY, "Alternatives to Prosecution: The Public Interest Redefined" [1993] Crim. L.Rev. 356

CHAPTER 6

LAWYERS IN THE YOUTH JUSTICE PROCESS

A. THE IMPORTANCE OF LAWYERS IN A DUE-PROCESS JUSTICE MODEL

The *Canadian Charter of Rights and Freedoms*[1] and the *Youth Criminal Justice Act* are premised on a due process model of justice. Section 3(1)(d)(i) of the Act's Declaration of Principle affirms that youths are to have all of the legal rights afforded adults, as well as recognizing that because of their immaturity, they require "special guarantees of their rights and freedoms."[2] In the due process model of justice, legally trained professionals inevitably play a key role. Like the *Young Offenders Act*,[3] the *Youth Criminal Justice Act* has provisions which are intended to ensure that youths can have access to legal assistance at every stage of the youth justice process. Lawyers are responsible for deciding how the case for the prosecution and defence will be presented to the judge, another legally trained professional. The lawyers also resolve a large number of cases without significant judicial involvement. Crown prosecutors often have

---

1 The *Canadian Charter of Rights and Freedoms*, Part I of the *Constitution Act, 1982*, being Schedule B to the *Canada Act*, 1982 (U.K.), 1982, c. 11 (referred to subsequently as the Charter).

2 The *Youth Criminal Justice Act*, S.C. 2002, c. 1 (royal assent February 19, 2002, to come into force April 1, 2003), often referred to in this book as the *YCJA*. S. 3, Declaration of Principle.

3 The *Young Offenders Act*, R.S.C 1985, c. Y-1,enacted as S.C. 1980–81–82–83, c. 110.

responsibility for deciding whether a young person will even go to youth justice court or will be diverted to extrajudicial measures, as discussed in Chapter 5. As discussed in Chapter 7, in practice, many of the cases dealt with in youth justice court are resolved by means of a plea bargain negotiated by the lawyers and only formally ratified by a judge.

While legally trained professionals now play a crucial role in society's response to adolescents who are alleged to have violated the law, this is a relatively recent development. The role of lawyers in the youth justice system continues to evoke controversy, as well as questions whether the system has become excessively legalized. At the same time, there are concerns that, while the YCJA in theory appears to ensure that youths whose cases are dealt with in court will have access to legal assistance, in practice many youths are either inadequately represented or not represented at all. Most of the provisions of the YCJA that deal with protection of legal rights and access to legal services for young people are similar to those in the YOA. There is, however, a concern that some provisions of the YCJA may make it less likely that youths will have access to legal representation than was the case under the YOA. This chapter describes how young persons are provided access to legal services and considers some of the contentious issues related to the role and effectiveness of both defence counsel and Crown prosecutors.

B. LAWYERS UNDER THE *JUVENILE DELINQUENTS ACT*

While Canada's present youth justice legislation has provisions intended to ensure that young persons have access to legal representation, in 1908 the drafters of the *Juvenile Delinquents Act* contemplated an explicit prohibition on the appearance of lawyers in juvenile court. In the end, the drafters settled for an Act that made no mention of the issue of legal representation but created a statutory regime that explicitly allowed for informality and precluded the reversal of a judicial decision on the grounds of any "irregularity" as long as the disposition of the case was in the "best interests of the child."[4] The emphasis under the *Juvenile Delinquents Act* was on having judges and the juvenile court system making expeditious decisions to allow interventions that would promote the best interests of delinquent youth. Throughout

---

4   The *Juvenile Delinquents Act*, 1908, S.C. 1908, c. 40, later *Juvenile Delinquents Act*, R.S.C. 1970, c. J-3, s. 17.

much of the twentieth century, few juvenile court judges had legal training and lawyers rarely appeared in that court.

In one 1958 Manitoba case, a lawyer appeared in juvenile court with a fourteen-year-old youth charged with indecent assault and requested an adjournment before entering a plea, so that the lawyer could have time to investigate the circumstances of the alleged offence. The juvenile court judge noted that the lawyer had not asked him for permission to represent the youth. The judge suggested that the lawyer's presence was "gumming the works up and [would] . . . make it considerably more difficult" for the juvenile. Further, the judge threatened that, if there was going to be a not-guilty plea and a trial, the juvenile might be transferred to adult court, which under the *Juvenile Delinquents Act* the juvenile court judge could do on his own motion without the request of the Crown. The lawyer withdrew from the proceeding, and the juvenile was convicted. Although the conviction was eventually overturned by the Supreme Court of Canada on procedural grounds,[5] the comments of the juvenile court judge reflected an attitude held by many at that time, namely, that lawyers were expected to play a very limited role in juvenile courts.

By the 1970s many of the judges in juvenile court were legally trained and, as a result of provincial legal aid schemes being established, more lawyers began appearing in juvenile court. In the United States there was a growing recognition of the need to afford juveniles due process of law. The 1966 Supreme Court decision in *Kent v. United States* inaugurated the process of bringing constitutional considerations into American juvenile courts, with Fortas J. observing:

> While there can be no doubt of the original laudable purpose of juvenile courts, studies and critiques in recent years raise serious questions as to whether actual performance measures well enough against theoretical purpose to make tolerable the immunity of the process from the reach of constitutional guarantees applicable to adults. . . . [T]here may be grounds for concern that the child receives the worst of both worlds: that he gets neither the protections accorded to adults nor the solicitous care and regenerative treatment postulated for children.[6]

---

5   *R. v. S.(G.)*, [1959] S.C.R. 638, rev'g (1958), 28 C.R. 100 (Man. C.A.). Although Locke J. in the Supreme Court and Adamson J.A. in the Manitoba Court of Appeal remarked on the "astonishing" attitude of the juvenile court judge toward defence counsel, the majority of appellate judges declined to comment on or were actually supportive of the approach of the trial judge to the presence of defence counsel.

6   *Kent v. United States*, 383 U.S. 541 at 555–56 (1966).

In 1967 the U.S. Supreme Court ruled in *Re. Gault* that, like an adult facing a term of imprisonment, a juvenile facing a custodial disposition is entitled to the assistance of counsel and, if the parents are unable to afford counsel, the state must provide access to representation. Justice Fortas wrote:

> Ultimately . . . we confront the reality . . . of the Juvenile Court process. . . . The boy is committed to an institution where he may be restrained of liberty for years. It is of no constitutional consequence — and of limited practical meaning — that the institution to which he is committed is called an Industrial School. . . . [H]owever euphemistic the title, [it] is an institution of confinement in which the child is incarcerated.
>
> . . .
>
> The juvenile needs the assistance of counsel to cope with problems of law, to make skilled inquiry into the facts, to insist upon the regularity of the proceedings, and to ascertain whether he has a defense and to prepare and submit it. The child "requires the guiding hand of counsel at every step in the proceedings against him."[7]

The American Constitution, as interpreted by the U.S. Supreme Court, theoretically gives juveniles the right to legal representation; in practice juveniles in that country not infrequently feel pressured by judges or parents to waive their right to counsel, so that the resolution of their cases are expeditious and relatively inexpensive.[8]

In Canada, juvenile court judges and probation officers became increasingly accustomed to the presence of defence lawyers in the 1970s, but juvenile justice professionals continued to express the view that many, if not most, juveniles did not require legal representation.[9] Further, it was clear that most professionals involved in the juvenile courts, including many defence lawyers, saw the role of the lawyer as quite different from that in adult court. Writing in 1972, one Ontario juvenile judge questioned the role of a privately retained lawyer for an accused child, if the lawyer considered his "primary objective . . . [as] to free his client from the jurisdiction of the court." The judge felt that a "much better job" was done by "legal aid or duty counsel lawyers [who] are committed to the proposition that they are paid by the State to protect the legal rights of children while at the same time taking

---

7   *Re Gault*, 387 U.S. 1 at 27 and 36 (1967).
8   B.C. Feld, *Justice for Children: The Rights to Counsel and the Juvenile Courts* (Boston: Northeastern University Press, 1993).
9   R.S. Stubbs, "The Role of the Lawyer in Juvenile Court" (1974) 6 Man. L.J. 65 at 76.

advantage of all of the potential powers of the Court to promote the best interests of the child."[10]

A study of thirty lawyers who appeared in juvenile court in Toronto in 1970 revealed that, while some of them saw themselves in the usual advocate's role, most of them did not think that they had the same adversarial role as in adult court. One of them, for example, emphasized that a defence lawyer "shouldn't twist evidence or the juvenile would get the wrong idea of the system."[11] Many lawyers felt that part of their role was to work with other professionals in the juvenile court in order to promote the best interests of the youth before the court. While some lawyers for youths charged under the YOA continued to have this paternalistic attitude, it was clearly much more prevalent among lawyers acting under the *Juvenile Delinquents Act*.

C. THE RIGHT TO COUNSEL FOR YOUTHS

The YCJA has a number of provisions that are intended to ensure that youths are aware of their legal rights and have the opportunity to exercise their rights to have access to legal representation. As discussed in Chapter 4, under section 146 of the YCJA, if the police want to question a youth suspected of having committed an offence, they must advise the youth of the right to counsel and, if the youth chooses to waive the right to counsel, the police must obtain a signed or audio- or videotaped waiver from the youth. Even if the police do not want to question a youth, section 25(2) of the YCJA as well as section 10(b) of the *Charter* require that, on arrest or detention by the police, a youth shall be informed of the right to representation by counsel and given an opportunity to contact a lawyer.

A youth who is taken to a police station for a breathalyzer test to determine the level of alcohol consumption must be given a reasonable opportunity to consult counsel before taking the test. However, despite the fact that section 25(1) of the YCJA gives a youth the right to retain counsel "without delay," police officers who have stopped a youth who is driving for a preliminary screening with a roadside device can do so with-

---

10   W.T. Little, "The Need for Reform in the Juvenile Courts" (1972) 10 Osgoode Hall L.J. 224 at 227.

11   I. Dootjes, P. Erickson, and R.G. Fox, "Defence Counsel in Juvenile Court: A Variety of Roles" (1972) 14 Can J. Crim. 132 at 137. See also P.G. Erickson, "The Defence Lawyer's Role in Juvenile Court: An Empirical Investigation into Judges' and Social Workers' Points of View" (1974) 24 U.T.L.J. 126.

out first giving the youth an opportunity to consult a lawyer.[12] The breathalyzer result is normally admissible as evidence of intoxication in court; however, a roadside screening is used to determine only if an individual should be taken to the station for the more accurate test, a fact that justifies not requiring access to counsel before the roadside test is taken.

Although the police generally provide the legally required cautions about the right to legal counsel, most youths who are arrested do not appear to appreciate the value of obtaining legal advice, or feel too intimidated by the situation in which they find themselves, and will come to court on their first appearance without having consulted a lawyer.

Section 25(3) of the YCJA requires that, if a youth appears in youth justice court without a lawyer, the presiding judge shall inform the youth of the right to be represented by counsel and give the youth a reasonable opportunity to obtain a lawyer.[13] If the youth is "unable to obtain counsel," the judge shall refer the youth to the local legal aid office to determine whether legal aid will be provided. While there is some variation among provinces in criteria for legal-aid eligibility, the two most significant factors for determining eligibility are the seriousness of the case and the resources available to the person applying for legal aid. In general, if there is the likelihood that a youth will receive a custodial sentence, or if the youth is already in pre-trial detention or custody, the case is serious enough to merit legal aid. Even if a case is serious, legal aid will only be provided to those with very limited resources. Typically only those adults living on social assistance or earning slightly above social assistance levels of income are eligible for legal

---

12 *R. v. Frohman* (1987), 60 O.R. (2d) 125 (C.A.). This decision interpreted s. 11(1) of the *YOA*, above note 3. The relevant portion is identical to s. 25(1) of the *YCJA*, above note 2.

13 *YCJA*, above note 2, s. 25, provides that, if a youth is unable to obtain counsel at "any stage of the proceedings," the court shall direct that counsel is to be provided. S. 25(3) specifies that this order for representation may be made for a pretrial detention hearing, a trial, a sentencing hearing including a hearing to determine whether an adult sentence should be imposed, and for a hearing to review a youth justice court sentence or a decision about the level of custody. These provisions do not give any right to counsel in regard to an appeal. A youth who wishes to appeal a youth justice court decision can apply for legal aid, which may be granted depending on the seriousness of the issue and whether there is a reasonable prospect for success. If an appeal is made to the provincial Court of Appeal, there is authority in s. 684 of the *Criminal Code*, R.S.C. 1985, c. C-46 for a judge of that court to assign counsel for the accused, to be paid by the government; while the appeal court has a discretion, it is more likely to make an order for representation in cases involving youths than for appeals by adults: see *R. v. M.(A.)* (1996), 30 O.R. (3d) 313 (C.A.).

aid. For youths, legal-aid officials will generally determine financial eligibility taking account of parental income, so that, if a youth's parents have even modest employment income, legal aid may be denied.

Section 25(4)(b) requires that, if a youth "wishes to obtain legal counsel" but is unable to do so and has been denied legal aid, the youth justice court judge is required to "direct that the young person be represented by counsel." If an order is made for representation under section 25(4)(b), then the lawyer is to be paid for by the provincial government. In most jurisdictions, a youth who obtains an order under section 25(4)(b) is likely to be referred again to the local legal-aid office with a copy of the order. The legal-aid office will arrange for legal representation to be provided pursuant to that court order rather than under direct legal-aid eligibility, with funding for this coming from the provincial government but not from the legal-aid budget. This can be a confusing and frustrating process for a youth; it also causes delay, since the youth may have to appear in court on at least a couple of occasions before getting legal representation.

Section 25(4) of the *YCJA* gives youths a significantly broader right than the adult right to "retain counsel." Adults who are unable to pay privately for a lawyer will generally only have a government-paid lawyer if they meet financial eligibility criteria *and* have a case considered sufficiently complex or serious to meet legal-aid criteria. With government funding constraints for legal aid, the financial and case-seriousness criteria for adults are becoming increasingly narrow.[14] Youths can obtain a government-paid lawyer for even the most minor criminal charges that are being dealt with in youth justice court, because without legal representation an adolescent is likely to lack the ability to prepare properly for, understand, and participate in the proceedings. Even with a sympathetic and helpful judge, an adolescent is likely to find the courtroom a confusing and intimidating environment.

Section 25(4)(b) is intended to ensure that a youth who is facing a less serious charge that is not eligible for legal aid for an adult can have access to legal representation. It is, however, clear that this provision does not give a youth the unfettered right to choose which counsel will represent him. For example, in a case decided under the identical provision of the *YOA*, a youth who was charged with a number of motor

---

14   There is no obligation under the *Charter*, above note 1, or the *Criminal Code*, above note 13, for governments to provide legal representation to those who are arrested or accused in court: *R. v. Prosper*, [1994] 3 S.C.R. 236. However, there is a residual judicial discretion under the *Charter*, ss. 7 and 11(d), to order that proceedings should be stayed if an indigent accused adult does not receive legal representation.

vehicle offences was granted legal aid and referred to a clinic staff lawyer, although the youth preferred to be represented by a lawyer in private practice who had represented him in previous cases. The youth appeared with his preferred lawyer and requested an order under the equivalent of section 25(4)(b) of the *YCJA*. The Legal Services Society indicated that, for financial reasons, it would only allow youths to be represented by outside counsel if the charge was very serious or there were "extraordinary circumstances, such as a total breakdown in the relationship between the counsel and the client." The youth court judge held that this was not a proper case in which to make an order under this provision, as the youth was not unable to obtain counsel. The judge did, however, observe:

> The only obligation imposed by the section is that Legal Services appoint counsel, and in the absence of a substantive reason for the discharge of that counsel, and I think the onus lies upon the accused here, the court will not consider directing the Attorney General to appoint counsel. I make it clear here that the Young Person is entitled to discharge his lawyer without giving a reason, provided that he is not using such action to interfere with the trial process; however, he is not entitled to have counsel appointed by the Attorney General at public expense without advancing a reason for such an application.[15]

This recognizes a residual judicial discretion to direct that a youth is to be represented by a lawyer other than one appointed through the legal aid office but indicates that judges will only invoke this authority if there is a good reason for the youth to object to the particular lawyer appointed.

In another case under the *YOA*, a youth who had been charged with a number of property offences, as well as failure to comply with the conditions of an undertaking to abide by the conditions of his release pending trial and failure to appear in court, was granted legal aid because his family was on social assistance. A legal-aid staff lawyer was appointed but he withdrew from the case because the youth failed to answer telephone calls or attend meetings, as well as failing to appear in court with the lawyer. The youth then appeared in court with another lawyer, who asked for an order directing that counsel be appointed under the equivalent of section 25(4) of the *YCJA*, but the youth court judge refused to make an order. In upholding the decision of the youth court judge,

---

15   *R. v. B.W.*, [1997] B.C.J. No. 3056 (B.C. Yth Ct.), per Rae. Prov. J. at para 8. If there is no lawyer willing to take a case at the rate of pay offered by Legal Aid, the Attorney General my have to pay a higher rate to ensure that an order under s. 25(4) can be satisfied; see *R. v. M.R.*, [2002] O.J. 3189 (Ct. J.)

Wilkinson J. observed that a judge is obliged to make an order for representation if a youth is denied legal aid and unable to obtain counsel. However, in interpreting the provision, the courts must be sensitive to the limited public resources and must consider the conduct of the youth and the effect of making an order on the court process:

> if . . . the young person is correct and the inquiry as to inability to obtain counsel is limited solely to financial inability some manifestly absurd results could follow. A young person without financial assistance could, ad infinitum, disqualify himself from legal representation by his own misconduct or discharge his counsel for whatever reason and repeatedly insist on the appointment of substitute counsel.[16]

These decisions indicate that the courts will make *reasonable* efforts to ensure that a young person has legal representation but, at some point, the courts may require a youth to appear unrepresented if the youth is unwilling to take advantage of the legal services offered by the legal aid program. There is, however, also some suggestion in these cases that if the charges are more serious, with the possibility of a lengthy custody term or even an adult sentence, there should be more flexibility in how section 25(4) is interpreted.

D. CONTRIBUTIONS FROM PARENTS AND YOUTH: SECTIONS 25(4) AND (10)

Legal aid plans which provide legal representation generally seek partial or total reimbursement from clients with assets or income. For an adult client with a low-paying job, total or partial repayment may be made over a period of time or, if the client has an asset such as a house, a lien may be placed on the house so that when it is sold, legal aid will be repaid. With many adult clients, such as those on social assistance or those who are incarcerated, no effort may be made to seek reimbursement. For those older youths who may have employment, government authorities do seek at least partial reimbursement for legal services provided. Most youths, however, especially those involved in the criminal justice system, do not themselves have any income or assets, and legal aid plans will not seek reimbursement from them.

One of the most controversial issues in regard to the application of section 25 and the similar provision of the *YOA* is how to deal with

---

16 *R. v. C.L.D.*, [2001] S.J. No. 459 (Q.B.), at para 13.

cases in which legal aid was denied not because a youth has the means to retain counsel but because a youth's parents have the means to retain counsel or to contribute to the cost but are unwilling to do so. A parent of limited means but who owns a home may, for example, refuse the request of legal aid to have a lien placed on the family home to secure repayment of the cost of hiring a lawyer for a child facing charges in the youth justice system.

After the *YOA* came into force in 1984, there were some judges who interpreted section 11(4) of that Act, which is virtually identical to section 25(4) of the *YCJA*, as giving the youth court the authority to conduct an inquiry as to whether youths or their parents had the resources to contribute to the cost of retaining a lawyer. However, in 1993 in *R. v. C.(S.T.)* Russell J. of the Alberta Court of Queen's Bench ruled that there is no statutory basis for having such a hearing:

> [T]he court has no discretion to decline to direct the appointment of counsel where the young person has been unable to obtain legal aid [provided that the court is satisfied that the youth does not have his own resources to hire counsel and hence is "unable" to obtain counsel.] The Youth Court need only be satisfied that the young person wishes to obtain counsel but has been unable to do so because legal aid is not available for any reason. An affidavit to that effect, or in the alternative [a] simple inquiry into those facts alone should suffice. The court has no discretion to determine whether a young person should be provided with a lawyer out of public funds.[17]

Since relatively few youths have the financial means to retain a lawyer, the effect of *R. v. C.(S.T.)* was that youths dealt with under the *YOA* had the right to have a lawyer paid by the government, regardless of their parents' financial status.

In the 1990s, with increasing pressures to reduce government spending, provincial governments were expressing concerns about orders made under section 11(4)(b) of the *YOA* in situations in which parents could afford to pay for a lawyer for their child. One response of some provincial governments was to raise in the courts again the issue of parental resources for retaining counsel in hearings under section 11(4) of the *YOA*. In 1999, in *R. v. J.H.*, the Ontario Court of Appeal considered a challenge by the Ontario government as to how youth court judges dealt with cases in which legal aid had been refused and an order was sought under section 11(4)(b) of the *YOA*. In this case, the trial judge had followed the common practice of making the order

---

17   *R. v. C.(S.T.)* (1993), 140 A.R. 259 at 267 (Q.B.).

under section 11(4)(b) without inquiring about whether a youth's parents could afford to retain counsel for their child.

The Court of Appeal held that a youth court judge was obliged to hold "some sort of inquiry, however cursory, to determine why the young person was refused legal aid [to] . . . ensure that there is actually an inability to obtain counsel."[18] As part of this inquiry, the youth court judge should "include a consideration of the young person's ability to access the resources normally available to a youth, including having reasonable recourse to the financial resources of their parents." In coming to the conclusion that this type of inquiry is justified, the Court of Appeal emphasized that the courts have a role in ensuring that the "limited resources [of the state are] husbanded for those who are most in need of representation and to ensure that the [legal aid] plan is not taken advantage of by accused persons who have directly or indirectly the resources to retain counsel."[19]

The Court of Appeal, however, also recognized that in situations where parents had the financial resources to pay for a lawyer for their child but were unwilling to do so, a youth court judge had no authority to order the parents to provide counsel or to require them to contribute to the cost of providing counsel. If after inquiry it was apparent that the parents had the funds to pay a lawyer but the youth was not given access to those or other funds, then the youth court was obliged to find that the youth was effectively "unable to obtain counsel." Thus, the Ontario Court of Appeal indicated that before an order was made under section 11(4)(b) of the YOA, the youth court judge was expected to ascertain if the parents were willing to pay for a lawyer for their child, but could not order them to pay for a lawyer if they were unwilling to do so. Section 25(4)(b) of the YCJA is essentially identical to section 11(4)(b) of the YOA, so this will continue to be the expectation under the new Act.

There is understandably some uncertainty about exactly how these inquiries are to be conducted, since the statute gives no indication of how the application is to be made, what type of evidence is required or who bears the onus of proof.[20] It would seem that the practice of most youth court judges has been to conduct fairly brief inquiries under section 11(4)(b) of the YOA. The Crown prosecutor, understandably,

18   R. v. J.H., [1999] O.J. 3894, 28 C.R. (5th) 129 (sub nom. R. v. M.(B.)) (C.A.); see also annotation N. Bala, "Trying to Make Parents Pay for Their Children's Lawyers" (1999), 28 C.R. (5th) 140.

19   Ibid., at para 17.

20   See R. v. B.L.A., [2002] O.J. 531(Ont. Ct. J.), per Kukurin J., discussing the problematic nature of s. 11(4)(b) of the YOA, above note 3.

would take no role at this stage of the process, and the youth would usually have the assistance of duty counsel to make an oral application for a direction for the appointment of counsel. If the youth provided a letter from the legal aid office denying eligibility and offered a brief explanation about parental inability or unwillingness to pay as well as about his or her own lack of resources, this generally was a sufficient basis for an order. It seems likely that under the *YCJA* judges will continue to play an inquisitorial role when dealing with section 25(4)(b) applications, asking questions and assisting the youth as necessary.

Some parents are prepared to retain and pay for counsel for their child without going through any kind of a legal process. They feel a sense of moral obligation to their child and may want to ensure that their child has immediate access to the best possible legal services. It takes several weeks for a lawyer to be obtained through legal aid or under a court order. Further, some more experienced lawyers are unwilling to represent clients if they will be paid by legal aid or as a result of a direction from the court, as the rate of pay is relatively low; these lawyers will only accept clients who are able to pay their normal rates, which may be substantially higher than the rates paid by the government. While some parents are willing to pay for lawyers for their children, legal services can be expensive and many parents are reluctant to spend money on a child whom they may feel has been acting badly. Many parents are embarrassed or angry when their child is charged with a criminal offence and are unwilling to divert money from other family spending to pay for a lawyer for their child. In some cases, the parents may feel indirectly victimized by their child's conduct. In others, the parents or other family members may be the victims of the acts that have resulted in the charges before the court.

For a period of time under the *YOA*, the Alberta legal aid authorities decided that in situations in which youths were granted legal aid or orders were made for legal representation under section 11(4) of the Act, reimbursement would be sought from parents if they had financial resources. There was, however, no legislative provision in the Act to expressly allow for provincial governments to seek reimbursement from parents; questions were raised about the legality of this scheme, which was discontinued.[21] Some provincial governments, notably the Conservative governments in Alberta and Ontario, wanted parents to contribute to the cost of counsel for their children and lobbied the fed-

---

21 Canada, FederalProvincial/Territorial Task Force on Youth Justice, *A Review of the Young Offenders Act and the Youth Justice System in Canada* (Ottawa: Ministry of Supply and Services, 1996) at 530.

eral government to include provisions in the *YCJA* to allow for this. Section 25(10) of the *YCJA* permits provincial governments to establish "a program to authorize the recovery of the costs of a young person's counsel from the young person or parents" if counsel is paid by the government, whether under the legal aid scheme or pursuant to a direction under section 25(4)(b).

Section 25(10) stipulates that the costs may be recovered only "after the proceedings have been completed," including any appeal. Parents may be required to reimburse the government regardless of whether or not the youth is convicted. At least on its face, section 25(10) is intended to ensure that any counsel appointed for the youth is paid by the government and independent of direct parental influence. The restriction on seeking reimbursement before completion of any proceedings is intended to minimize parental pressure to end the proceedings in a way that will jeopardize legal rights for the sake of minimizing legal expenses. There is, however, real concern that in provinces that introduce this type of cost-recovery program, parents will pressure their children to waive the right to seek counsel or will encourage their children to resolve the proceedings by means of a guilty plea rather than with a potentially expensive trial.

In this era of limited fiscal resources, it is understandable that governments are looking to parents to provide financial support for youths involved in the justice system. It should, however, be appreciated that many youths come from impoverished backgrounds and no money will be available. Further, given the tensions around the court process and the problems that arise when parents pay for lawyers for their children, it would have been preferable for the state not to look for reimbursement for this type of expense. It would have been a better policy choice for governments to look for parental financial contributions for youths placed in custody, provided parents have the means to pay.

Any provincial schemes to seek reimbursement will not expect contributions from those who are on welfare or who have very low incomes. It is disturbing that the parental pressure to waive the right to counsel or have a trial is most likely to be effective in middle income families where there is a good relationship between the parents and youth. Upper-income parents may be less inclined to pressure their children to waive legal rights, as they can more easily afford the costs of legal services. In families where there is a poor relationship between the youth and parents, the youth may not be concerned about the financial burden on their families of them having legal representation. At time of writing, it is not known which provinces will introduce cost recovery schemes under section 25(10) of the *YCJA*, or exactly how they will operate. There is genuine concern that any jurisdiction which institutes such a program may see increasing numbers of youths waiving their right to representation, significantly compromising the ability of youths to meaningfully participate in the youth justice court process.

The relationship of parents to the lawyer representing their child has long raised some difficult questions. After the *YOA* came into force in 1984, some judges ruled that since young persons are minors, they lack the legal capacity to retain counsel without the involvement of a parent or guardian.[22] However, the *YOA* was amended in 1986 so that section 11(1) explicitly stated that young persons can "exercise . . . personally" the right to retain counsel or may personally waive that right. The same words are in section 25(1) of the *YCJA*, making clear that youths charged under the Act have the legal capacity to retain counsel, although they may choose to waive that right.

Before the enactment of the *YOA* it was not uncommon for a parent with financial resources to hire a lawyer to represent a child charged under the *Juvenile Delinquents Act*. Even under the *YOA* some parents paid for a lawyer for their child, either because of a sense of moral obligation or because they were not satisfied with the lawyer provided under the government-representation plan. At least in theory, the client in a youth court proceeding is the youth who is charged with the offence, regardless of who pays the lawyer, and only the youth should instruct the lawyer. It is, for example, preferable for a lawyer representing a youth not to meet with the parents of a youth without the young person being present, as this may confuse the youth or the parents about the lawyer's role, or may cause the youth to be concerned that the lawyer is communicating confidential matters to the parents without the youth's permission. In practice, however, if parents are paying for a lawyer there may be some confusion as to who is instructing the lawyer. Section 25(8) of the *YCJA*, which is virtually identical to section 11(8) of the *YOA*, provides that a youth justice court judge shall ensure that a youth is "represented by counsel independent" of the parents, if it appears that the interests of the youth and parents conflict or the best interest of the youth require representation by his or her own counsel.

Even in the usual case where lawyers for youths are paid by the government, some lawyers appear uncertain of their role and relationship with parents. This is most obviously illustrated by the failure of some lawyers, especially when acting as duty counsel at youth justice court, to interview the youth alone. A youth may choose to have parents present

---

22   See, for example, *R. v. W.(W.W.)* (1985), 34 Man. R. (2d) 134 (C.A.).

during an interview with a lawyer; however, there should always be some time for a private interview, at least to get the permission of the youth for the parents to be present for the rest of the interview. Parents can provide important support, information, and advice to their child, but their presence can also be intimidating or embarrassing to a child and may cause a youth to be less candid with counsel. Indeed, a lawyer should communicate with the parents only with the consent of the youth, and the lawyer must refrain from sharing any confidential information provided by the youth with the parents. It is sometimes difficult for parents to accept that an unknown professional will be playing an important role in their child's life, especially if the youth is relatively young or the lawyer appears to be offering advice that differs from the parents' views about the case.

E. DELIVERY OF LEGAL SERVICES

Under section 25(5) of the *YCJA*, if a youth justice judge directs that representation is to be provided to a youth, it is the responsibility of the provincial attorney general to establish a scheme to provide representation. Several different models for delivery of legal services to youths have evolved. A common element in legal aid schemes in Canada is the provision of duty counsel, a lawyer who is available at the court to provide summary assistance to any person lacking a lawyer; they are not available at all courts, or may only be available at certain times, for example, when first appearances are scheduled. Some duty counsel are staff lawyers hired by legal-aid plans, but many are lawyers in private practice hired at an hourly rate. Duty counsel are usually available to assist unrepresented individuals at bail hearings; with obtaining an adjournment to give time to apply for legal aid or to retain a lawyer privately; in entering a plea; and at the time of sentencing. Duty counsel can generally meet individuals only for a relatively brief interview before court. They often have difficulty in properly assisting with matters like bail hearings or sentencing, and they generally lack the time or resources to assist meaningfully with a trial.[23]

A duty-counsel scheme is preferable to having individuals appear in court without any opportunity for legal advice or representation, not only in terms of protecting legal rights and advising individuals but for

---

23   See *R. v. Ford* (2001), 52 O.R. (3d) 142 (Sup. Ct. J.), on the inability of duty counsel to provide effective assistance at trial. Sometimes, however, in relatively simple cases, duty counsel my provide assistance to unrepresented persons at trial.

court efficiency. However, many adolescents have difficulty in communicating effectively with unfamiliar adults, especially in the context of a rushed interview in an intimidating setting. Canadian research indicates that adolescents often do not understand the role of duty counsel and may not appreciate the advice being provided in this setting.[24] These concerns are heightened if the duty counsel lacks familiarity with youth justice court or is inexperienced in dealing with adolescents. Duty counsel can help a youth apply for legal aid or may make a request to a judge for a direction under section 25(4)(b) for representation by counsel. If a direction is made under section 25(4)(b) for the provision of counsel, duty counsel will not suffice, since a lawyer must have adequate time to meet with a youth and prepare for court.

One of the most common methods for provision of legal services to youths is by lawyers in private practice, paid by the government. In some provinces, a youth can choose any lawyer who is willing to accept the relatively low fees paid pursuant to the legal aid plan scheme or the section 25(4)(b) representation plan. Because the fees are limited, some more experienced lawyers are unwilling to do much (or any) work under the government schemes, although some junior members of the bar may have practices based largely or exclusively on this type of work.

In some provinces, such as Manitoba, in an effort to reduce costs, under the YOA, the government tried block-fee schemes, under which law firms bid on providing representation for a specified number (e.g., fifty) of young offenders cases, and youths were directed exclusively to firms that have the arrangement. This block-fee scheme has only been used for the less serious cases that do not qualify for legal aid and were the subject of a court order for representation. While this type of scheme reduces costs, it has been heavily criticized for its potential to reduce the quality of representation.[25] Despite this concern, in Canada's current fiscal environment, other jurisdictions may adopt this type of scheme for less serious cases. In some provinces, most notably Alberta, Saskatchewan, Nova Scotia, and Quebec, legal aid clinics that deal exclusively with youths have been established in larger cities. These

---

24   K. Catton and P. Erickson, *The Juvenile's Perception of the Role of Defence Counsel in Juvenile Court* (Toronto: University of Toronto, Centre of Criminology Working Paper, 1975), in N. Bala, H. Lilles, and G. Thomson, eds., *Canadian Children's Law* (Toronto: Butterworths, 1982) at 711.

25   See L. Keller, "Legal Aid Manitoba to Seek Bids from Lawyers for Blocks of YOA s. 11 Cases," *Lawyers Weekly*, April 23, 1993: 2; and T. Onyshko, "LSUC committees will study proposals to reduce fees paid by Legal Aid Plan" *Lawyers Weekly*, February 18, 1994: 1.

clinics have staff lawyers, and in some cases have access to clinic social workers to assist in dealing with cases. While youths charged with the most serious offences can choose to have government-paid counsel from private practice, the clinics deal with the majority of youth justice cases in the cities where they have been established.

A major motivation for having youth legal aid clinics is that they can be less expensive than other models of service delivery. Such clinics allow lawyers to specialize and establish a sufficiently large case load in the area that they can operate more efficiently than lawyers in private practice.[26] It is also possible to recruit a relatively small group of lawyers with personalities and backgrounds that suit them to this type of work, and to ensure that they have knowledge of the law, facilities, and programs that affect youth. There are, however, concerns that the existence of clinics reduces the opportunity for youths to choose a lawyer, and that staff lawyers might come to see themselves more as civil servants than as advocates for often disadvantaged youths. There may also be some stigma attached to the clients of legal aid clinics, since they may be more readily identified as disadvantaged youths.

Given the importance of legal representation in the justice system and the financial implications for lawyers in private practice of any extension of legal aid clinics, it is scarcely surprising that the subject of clinics — their costs, independence, and effectiveness — remain controversial.[27] There is Canadian research which indicates that clinic lawyers can provide less costly service and equally or more effective service — as measured by findings of guilt and length of sentence — for adult clients.[28] While none of the research relates directly to adolescent clients, there may be special reasons for clinics for adolescents, since these clients often lack the ability to make a meaningful selection

---

26 J. Mahony, "Province's Public Defender Pilot Project Could Lead to Dismantling of Legal Aid, Alta. Lawyers Fear," *Lawyers Weekly*, February 25, 1994: 2; and "Alberta May Keep Youth Court Public Defenders," *Law Times*, February 10, 1997. A study in Ontario recommended more extensive use of specialized youth clinics in that province, along with some continuing representation by lawyers in private practice: Ontario Legal Aid Review, *Report of the Ontario Legal Review: A Blueprint for Publicly Funded Legal Services* [the McCamus Report] (Toronto: Government of Ontario, 1997) 158. See Ron Levi, "The Provision of Legal Aid Services Under the *YOA*," Vol. 3 of *Report of the Ontario Legal Aid Review*.

27 See, for example, C. Schmitz, "Welfare Council Slams Legal Aid System," *Lawyers Weekly*, January 27, 1995: 1; and M. Zapf, "B.C. Bar Raps Discussion Paper on Public Defended Feasibility" *Lawyers Weekly*, February 28, 1992: 14.

28 National Council on Welfare, *Legal Aid and the Poor* (Ottawa: 1995) at 50.

of a lawyer and have special needs that support staff and lawyers in a clinic may be able to address better than lawyers in private practice. It is, however, clear that if the clinics are not adequately funded, staff lawyers may become overburdened and unable to provide adequate representation.

At least in theory, section 25 of the *YCJA* assures that every youth who wants representation has the right to have a lawyer. However, in reality, many youths have their cases resolved without legal representation. The process for obtaining counsel may be slow and frustrating, often requiring several court appearances and a rejection by legal aid prior to a court making an order that representation should be provided. Even if parents are not required to contribute to the cost of a lawyer, the parents may well feel humiliated by the whole experience and may encourage a youth to resolve his or her case without having a lawyer.

A disturbing 1994 study of the Saskatoon Youth Court revealed that more than one-third of all youths entered a plea and were sentenced without having a lawyer present. Although many of those youths were charged with less serious property offences, some were charged with violent offences or were being dealt with in situations where pre-trial detention or a custodial sentence was imposed. There is an indication in this study that Aboriginal youth, who were more likely to appear without a parent or guardian, were also more likely not to have a lawyer. Further, Aboriginal male youths who appeared without counsel were more likely to be detained at a bail hearing than those who had representation at the bail hearing. The researchers concluded:

> Youths who plead guilty without counsel may do so out of ignorance, apathy or the belief that a lawyer will make no difference in the outcome — especially if they have a prior conviction. . . . a lack of familiarity with procedure and available dispositions may compound the decision not to elect counsel. . . . youth often plead guilty to avoid prolonging proceedings by seeking an adjournment to obtain legal counsel. . . . Given that a youth is most likely to plead guilty, to be held for [pre-trial detention at a] show cause [hearing] and to be sentenced to custody when appearing without a lawyer, it is imperative that efforts be made to have youth represented by counsel on first appearance and throughout court proceedings.[29]

---

29   S.A. Fortugno and M. Rogstad, *A Socio-Legal Analysis of Youth Justice in Saskatoon: The Behaviour of the System Toward Aboriginal and Non-Aboriginal Youth* (Saskatoon: John Howard Society of Saskatchewan, 1994) at 61.

Section 25(7) of the *YCJA* allows a judge to permit a youth who is not represented by a lawyer to be assisted by an adult whom the judge deems suitable, such as a parent or relative. While such assistance may be preferable to having a youth appear in court without any help, judges are reluctant to use this provision. As noted by one Ontario judge, interpreting the virtually identical provision of the *YOA*:

> The court may be sensitive to the fact that a young person may prefer to be assisted by a known and trusted adult rather than professional counsel, but also be alert to the dangers of an overbearing adult imposing upon the young person in a possibly well-intentioned but misguided manner. . . .
>
> Even on a relatively minor charge where the young person wishes to plead guilty, I would find it difficult to be satisfied that a parent, for instance, has the required expertise and objectivity to properly advise the young person. . . . Parents may be guided by many motives, including the seeking of help for a troubled young person and encourage a totally inappropriate guilty plea, or on the other hand be so unaware of the legal issues as to believe that a defence exists [that] is not valid. I would expect that very few lay advisors will be accepted by the courts as appreciating the complexity or seriousness of the matters . . . and courts may refuse to permit the adult to assist the youth and might well, at that time, remind the youth of the right to retain counsel . . . although . . . there is no authority, aside from the issue of insanity at the time of trial, to force counsel upon a young person who does not wish to be represented.[30]

These judicial concerns about allowing non-lawyers to assist youths also reflect on the problem of youths being totally unrepresented in court. If governments make efforts to have parents or youths pay for counsel, this may well result in more youths appearing without lawyers. It may also produce more cases where youths request the assistance of parents in court, which, given the complexity and potential consequences of youth justice court proceedings, would be unfortunate.

---

30   *R. v. A.(H.E.)* (13 June 1984), (Ont. Prov. Ct.) [unreported] [summarized [1984] W.D.F.L. 1024], Pedlar Prov. J. This case dealt with s. 11(7) of the *YOA*, above note 3.

F. CONTROVERSY OVER THE ROLE OF DEFENCE COUNSEL

While there is probably a greater consensus now than in the past among lawyers about the role that they should adopt in representing adolescent clients charged with criminal offences, there continues to be significant variation and controversy about the role of defence lawyers in the youth justice system. The governing body for the legal profession in Ontario, the Law Society of Upper Canada, issued a report in 1981 advising lawyers about the role which they should adopt in representing juveniles charged under the *Juvenile Delinquents Act*, advising that:

> Even where a child may lack the capacity to properly instruct counsel, there is no place . . . for counsel representing a child [charged under the *Juvenile Delinquents Act*] to argue what is in his opinion in the best interests of the child. Counsel should not be deciding whether training school would be "good" for the child . . . it is advice with respect to the legal rights of the child which is being provided to the child, not to the parents, not to the court, and not to society, but to the child.[31]

A 1986 Manitoba study indicated that many lawyers who represented youths charged pursuant to the *YOA* adopted this representational approach, often known as the advocate role, which involves taking instructions from an adolescent client and treating that client in essentially the same way that a lawyer would treat an adult client.[32] The coming into force of the *YOA* in 1984, with its clearly criminal orientation replacing the welfare approach of the *Juvenile Delinquents Act*, caused more lawyers to adopt the advocate role.

Lawyers adopting the advocate role will, at their initial meeting with a youth, emphasize the right to remain silent and will typically advise against co-operation with the police during their investigation. At trial, they will be prepared to raise any legal defence or challenge — provided that the client does not instruct counsel to plead guilty — for example, seeking to exclude inadmissible evidence, even if the youth is in fact guilty. A lawyer adopting the advocate role will, in an appropriate

---

31   Law Society of Upper Canada, *Report of the Subcommittee on Legal Representation of Children* (Toronto: Law Society of Upper Canada, 1981).

32   H.A. Milne, R. Linden, and R. Kueneman, "Advocate or Guardian: The Role of Defence Counsel in Youth Justice" in R.R. Corrado, *et al.*, eds., *Juvenile Justice in Canada: A Theoretical and Analytical Assessment* (Toronto: Butterworths, 1992) 313.

case, also be prepared to advise the youth that the Crown's case appears very strong and suggest that a guilty plea may be appropriate, especially if the prosecutor is prepared to enter into a plea bargain, perhaps dropping some charges or offering a joint submission about the sentence in exchange for a guilty plea. The advocate will always, however, respect the right of the client to decide how to plead to the charges. At the sentencing stage, the advocate will again follow the client's instructions, which will often involve seeking the least severe sentence.

While many defence lawyers see their role as solely that of an advocate for the youth, others still adopt more of a "guardian" role, preferring to take into account the views of probation officers, social workers, and parents as well as those of the youth, in formulating a position that is based on the lawyer's assessment of the best interests of the young person. As one Manitoba lawyer with experience in representing youths commented: "My attitude to the practice of law is not adversarial. I am aware of the legal issues and the fact that I am a lawyer, but I am concerned with rehabilitation. I do take the role of a stern parent."[33] An American lawyer who favours this approach commented:

> In juvenile court cases "beating the rap" is . . . not only detrimental to the public safety but is likely to prove harmful to the juvenile offender himself. To assume that it is best for juveniles who have committed serious violations of the law to be exonerated on technical legal grounds is tantamount to endorsing the notion that juveniles should be free to steal, commit burglary, or engage in other serious offences with complete immunity.[34]

Lawyers adopting a guardian role will attempt to achieve an acquittal if the youth denies guilt, but they may not be as aggressive in pursuing more technical defences (for example, by raising evidentiary issues relating to a statement to the police admitting guilt). The guardian role may be especially significant at the sentencing stage, with the lawyer seeking a sentence that promotes rehabilitation, even if it is not the least restrictive alternative and the youth does not want it; the lawyer taking this approach may aim to persuade the client that the disposition is in the youth's best interests.

Many lawyers are neither purely advocates or guardians, adopting an approach that may have elements of both and may vary with the nature of the case, the age and attitude of the young person, and the

---

33   *Ibid.* at 333.
34   D. Bogen, "Beating the Rap in Juvenile Court" (1980) 31:3 Juv. & Fam. Ct. J. 19 at 21.

stage of the proceedings. These lawyers may be more inclined to take more of an advocate's stance prior to a finding of guilt, strictly protecting the youth's legal rights, but more of a guardian's approach at the sentencing stage, attempting to persuade a young client to accept a "rehabilitative" sentence. It is apparent that members of the defence bar have differing views about their role in the youth justice system, and sometimes individual lawyers will vary their approach from one case to another, depending on the circumstances of the case and the position of the youth. In some measure, the uncertainty of some defence lawyers toward their role in youth justice court may reflect the ambivalence in the *YCJA* and society as a whole about the question of how to balance concerns with due process against the special needs and vulnerability of youth.

The *YOA* clearly placed much more emphasis on due process than the *Juvenile Delinquents Act*, supporting the adoption by lawyers of an advocate's role. The *YCJA*, with its emphasis on sentencing that is proportionate to the offence and provisions that prohibit use of detention and custody in the youth justice system as a substitute for appropriate child welfare or mental health services, would seem to reinforce the view that defence counsel should adopt an advocate's role in youth justice court. However, some provisions of the new Act may still suggest that a guardian's role is sometimes appropriate. In particular, section 34(9) of the *YCJA* provides that a judge may order that a medical or psychological assessment, prepared for such purposes as a detention or sentencing, shall not be disclosed to the youth whom it concerns if "in the opinion of the court . . . disclosure of the report might be prejudicial to the young person." While the youth may be denied access to the report, in whole or part, counsel for the youth will have access to the complete report, but if an order is made under section 34(9) the lawyer is not permitted to discuss it with the client. This provision is intended to promote the youth's well-being and might, for example, be used to keep sensitive information from the youth about the family's history if there is a concern that disclosure might affect the treatment of the youth or relationships within the family.

In order to be consistent with the *Charter* provisions assuring a fair trial, there is provision in section 34(11) of the *YCJA* to allow a judge to permit disclosure of a report to the youth despite the fact that this might be prejudicial to the youth's well-being if this is considered "essential" for the "interests of justice." Despite this narrowly worded exception, section 34(9) clearly modifies the traditional relationship of lawyer and client, where there is expected to be a full sharing of all information that the lawyer has about the case. Section 34(9) may in some cases compromise the youth's ability to instruct counsel fully and effectively in the proceedings. Counsel may have considerable difficulty in knowing how to respond to the report without having information and instructions from the client. Such reports may be influential in the proceedings, and, as one Crown prosecutor pointed out in connection with a similar provision in the *YOA*, it "places counsel for the young person in the impossible position of having access to information that cannot be divulged to the client."[35]

Lawyers inevitably make many decisions about the handling of a case without seeking specific instructions from their clients — for example, about tactics relating to evidentiary and advocacy issues. There are, however, two major decisions that all clients are expected to make: whether to plead guilty and whether to testify. Although the lawyer is expected to provide informed advice about these decisions, the client is expected to make these two critically important decisions about the case.[36] For adult clients there is generally not much difficulty in obtaining instructions about these two issues, but lawyers for adolescents sometimes have difficulty obtaining instructions from their young clients. In some situations, a youth may not want to decide about an issue on which the lawyer is seeking instructions, or the youth may be ambivalent or inconsistent. A lawyer may also be concerned about the intellectual or emotional capacity of an adolescent to appreciate fully the consequences of a decision.[37]

The American Bar Association has developed a detailed set of professional standards for lawyers who are representing persons who are under the age of eighteen in delinquency and protection proceedings.[38] The Bar Association recognizes that a youth's capacity to give instructions to a lawyer is, in significant measure, affected by the youth's rela-

---

35   J.C. Pearson, "Legal Representation under the *YOA*" in A.W. Leschied, P.G. Jaffe, and W. Willis, eds., *The Young Offenders Act: A Revolution in Canadian Juvenile Justice* (Toronto: University of Toronto Press, 1991) 114 at 123.

36   See *Boudreau v. Benaiah* (1998), 37 O.R. (3d) 686 (Gen. Div.).

37   There is a small but growing body of empirical research on the capacity of adolescents to understand the legal process and provide instructions to counsel: see M. Peterson-Badali and C. Koegl, "Young People's Knowledge of the *YOA* and the Youth Justice System" (1998) 40 Can J. Crim. 12752; M. Peterson-Badali & R. Abramovitch, "Children's Knowledge of the Legal System: Are They Competent to Instruct Counsel?" (1992) 34 Can J. Crim. 13960.

38   American Bar Association, Council for Family Law Section, "Proposed Standards of Practice for Lawyers Who Represent Children in Abuse and Neglect Cases" (1995) 29 Fam. L.Q. 375; and IJA-ABA Joint Commission on Juvenile Justice Standards, *Juvenile Justice Standards Relating to Counsel for Private Parties* (New York: The Commission, 1990).

tionship with the lawyer and the information received from the lawyer. The lawyer should provide a clear explanation of the youth's position and the choices that the youth has, as well as giving an indication of the possible consequences of different choices. All communication should take account of the individual youth's age, level of education, cultural context, and degree of language skill. An apparent lack of capacity should be viewed as "contextual, incremental and may be intermittent." That is, the youth's capacity to provide instructions may increase over time, and, even if a youth fails to give clear instructions at one time, the lawyer should attempt to seek instructions later. The association also suggests that in some cases a lawyer may need the assistance of a social worker or other professional to communicate effectively with a youth. Ultimately, if a youth is unable to give instructions, the lawyer should advocate for the "least restrictive intervention."[39]

None of the governing bodies of the legal profession in Canada has provided the kind of detailed direction for lawyers that has been provided by the American Bar Association. However, a Quebec Bar Committee issued a lengthy consultation paper dealing with a range of issues related to the legal representation of children and adolescents. This Committee suggests that a lawyer must adopt an "adviser and attorney" (i.e., advocacy) role and follow the directions of a youth with the capacity to give instructions. Further, consistent with the *YCJA*, there should be a presumption that a youth who is twelve years or older has the capacity to instruct a lawyer. The Quebec Committee did not deal explicitly with the question of the role that a lawyer for a youth facing criminal charges should adopt if a youth lacks the capacity to give instructions, although it indicated that a lawyer should always ensure that the "rights and procedural guarantees of the child are respected."[40] The Committee noted that the general code of ethics for lawyers applies to those representing children and youth, but it urged the adoption of special provisions for lawyers involved in these cases. The need for special ethical guidelines is greatest when younger children are involved and proceedings are civil, and focus on the best interests of the child.

For lawyers representing youths charged under criminal legislation such as the *YCJA*, the rules for professional conduct governing those who represent adults charged with criminal offences offer significant direction. The Ontario and Quebec Bar Committees make clear that lawyers owe the same duties of advocacy and confidentiality to youths

---

39   *Ibid* at 82.

40   Quebec Bar Committee, "The Legal Representation of Children" (1996) 13 Can J. Fam. L. 49 at 105.

as they do to adult clients. The lawyer's role is to present the youth's views and to protect the youth's rights in court; no other professional involved in the process has this role. Despite the importance of this general guidance, it would be helpful to provide lawyers with some specific direction on such issues as a youth's capacity to instruct a lawyer, and the relationship between parents and the lawyer for a youth.

G. CONCERNS ABOUT THE EFFECTIVENESS OF COUNSEL IN YOUTH JUSTICE COURT

While most youths who appear in youth justice court will be represented by lawyers, there are concerns that some of these lawyers may not be communicating well with their young clients and may not be providing them with as effective representation as these youths should receive. These concerns about effectiveness, as well as about the costs of due process, both in financial and human terms, have led some observers to argue that there should be fewer lawyers involved in the youth justice process. Others, however, favour the continued involvement of lawyers for youths, while arguing that there should be better training and supervision for this type of sensitive work. While there is not enough research to get a clear picture of how effectively lawyers in Canada have represented adolescents in the youth justice system, there are indications that some lawyers may not be as effective as they should be. One study of duty counsel from the 1970s revealed that many lawyers did not provide youths with an adequate explanation of their professional role and, as a result, the youths did not really understand the function of defence counsel.[41] Effective communication with adolescents generally requires more skill and patience than communication with an adult. Some lawyers may, for example, not be taking the time to interview their young clients properly before court.

In one reported 1996 Ontario case, the mother of a youth charged with sexual assault under the *YOA* had approached a lawyer to represent her son, who was in pre-trial detention.[42] The lawyer agreed to

---

41 Catton and Erickson, above note 24.

42 *R. v. B.(L.C.)* (1996), 27 O.R. (3d) 686 (C.A.). For a review of jurisprudence on the criteria that must be satisfied before a an accused will be able to get relief because of the inadequacy of representation provided by defence counsel, see *R. v. Appleton* (2001), 55 O.R. (3d) 321 (C.A.); and *R. v. B.(G.D.)*, [2000] 1 S.C.R. 520. The incompetence must be more than a mere error of judgement, and must have resulted in a "miscarriage of justice."

represent the youth but failed to attend at several bail hearings and adjournments, and the youth remained in detention pending trial. The lawyer spoke to the youth only by telephone, explaining: "I don't do jails." The lawyer apparently felt that the fee received from legal aid for representation of the youth did not make a personal visit economically justifiable. The lawyer first met the youth in person on the day of the trial. The youth was convicted of sexual assault and appealed. While the Ontario Court of Appeal was critical of defence counsel's "somewhat casual approach," the Court ruled that this did not affect the outcome in the particular case. This may well have been a correct legal decision, but one can also appreciate why the youth was not satisfied with the representation provided.

Various researchers have carried out studies to determine the effect that the presence of counsel has on the outcomes of cases in juvenile courts. This type of research is difficult to do in a methodologically sound fashion, since youths who have more serious or complicated cases are more likely to have lawyers. Merely comparing the outcomes of cases where youths had a lawyer with those where they were unrepresented does not offer a proper basis for assessing the effect of representation on outcomes. Some researchers have done studies that attempt to provide a control for the nature and seriousness of cases, but such controls are not easy to devise and apply. Another complicating factor is that the effect of representation may depend on the attitude of the judges, with judges who are more due process oriented giving greater effect to the type of representation and argument that a lawyer is likely to bring to the court.[43]

A major research project conducted in several Canadian cities in 1981–82, when the *Juvenile Delinquents Act* was still in effect, revealed that youths with legal representation were more likely to enter not-guilty pleas and had fewer convictions than unrepresented juveniles.[44] Once a juvenile was convicted, the presence of a lawyer seemed to have limited impact on the sentence. In some localities the presence of counsel was associated with more severe sentences, while in other

---

43   See, for example, S.H. Clarke and G.G. Koch, "Juvenile Court: Therapy or Crime Control, and Do Lawyers Make a Difference?" (1980) 14 Law & Soc. Rev. 263.

44   P.J. Carrington and S. Moyer, "The Effect of Defence Counsel on Plea and Outcome in Juvenile Court" (1990) 32 Can J. Crim 621; P.J. Carrington and S. Moyer, "Legal Representation in Canadian Juvenile Courts: Its Nature, Extent and Determinants" (1992) 34 Can J. Crim. 51; and P.J. Carrington and S. Moyer, "The Impact of Legal Representation on Juvenile Court Dispositions" (1990) Canadian Sociology and Anthropology Annual Meeting.

locales representation was associated with less severe sentences or appeared to have no impact. It is difficult to draw conclusions about the effect of counsel from these studies, since youths are more likely to seek legal representation if their case is serious or they intend to plead not guilty. As noted above, a 1994 Saskatchewan study found that Aboriginal male youth who appeared without representation were more likely to be detained at a bail hearing and to be sentenced to custody than those represented by a lawyer.[45]

A 1988 study of youth court judges in Ontario suggested that lawyers were generally effective in dealing with legal issues at the trial stage of proceedings but often failed to be involved actively in the youth court sentencing process. The researcher concluded:

> Both Crown and defence counsel are failing to provide effective assistance to the court with respect to appropriate dispositions. The comments of the judges amount to an indictment of the performance of counsel, particularly defence counsel. Judges report that most defence counsel failed to call character witnesses on behalf of the offender, failed to offer any statement by the offender to explain the offence, failed to produce independent evidence about the offender's special needs, and failed to provide detailed disposition recommendations suited to the offender.[46]

Beyond concerns about the effectiveness of legal representation in terms of securing more acquittals and less severe sentences, some observers question the effect of lawyers on the adolescents who appear in youth justice court. The lawyer will speak for the youth, sometimes giving the youth a sense of being a spectator in court. It is not uncommon to see adolescents in court who appear bored and disinterested in the proceedings. It may be argued that the increased involvement of lawyers has resulted in youths sometimes feeling less responsible for their acts, first because they may be advised by their lawyer that they have a chance of getting off even though they are guilty, and secondly because they may feel disengaged from the court process, even when being sentenced.[47]

---

45   Fortugno and Rogstad, above note 29 at 61.

46   D.K. Hanscom, *The Dynamics of Disposition in Youth Court*, 1988, LL.M. Thesis, University of Toronto. See commentary "Lawyers Knock Report Suggesting Counsel to Blame for Increase in Young Offenders Act Custody Rate" *Law Times*, April 9–15, 1990.

47   See, for example, P. Gabor, I. Greene, and P. McCormick, "The *YOA*: The Alberta Youth Court Experience in the First Year" (1986) 5 Can. J. Fam. L. 301; J. Hackler, "The Impact of the Young Offenders Act" (1987) 29 Can. J. Crim. 205.

These types of concerns have led some to argue that there are too many lawyers involved in the youth justice process: it is argued that their presence is often ineffective and unnecessary, contributes to delay, and diverts resources from badly needed treatment for youths. In one widely reported speech in 1985, James Felstiner, a youth court judge in Ontario who had worked as a social worker before going to law school and being appointed as a judge, aroused controversy when he suggested that there was an excessive use of lawyers in youth court. The judge was concerned that the lawyers' "criminal court games" were causing delays and resulting in youths pleading not guilty even if they were admitting guilt: "[A] very great majority of children are guilty of their offence, or something close to it. I think a great majority don't need a lawyer."[48] Judge Felstiner's comments, for which he was criticized by the Ontario Judicial Council, do not appear to reflect the views of most judges.[49]

Most judges accept that the formal model of criminal justice contemplated by both the *Young Offenders* and the *Youth Criminal Justice Acts*, with an emphasis on accountability and due process, requires the active involvement of lawyers. The court proceedings are unlikely to be comprehensible to a youth without representation. A youth without representation is unlikely to understand the proceedings or their consequences, and will have great difficulty participating meaningfully in the court process. While many youths who are charged are in fact guilty, the police sometimes charge the innocent, whether because of investigative errors, bias, or excessive zeal. The consequence of having a criminal justice system that respects individual liberty is that some who are in fact guilty are acquitted; a system that ensured that all of the truly guilty are convicted would inevitably also convict some who are in fact innocent. Defence counsel have an important role in ensuring

---

and "An Impressionistic View of Canadian Juvenile Justice: 1965 to 1999" (2001) 20 Can J. Comm. Mental Health 17, who comments on the changes from the informal juvenile court under the *Juvenile Delinquents Act* to the more legalistic youth court of the YOA: "The vast increase in the number of judges, prosecutors, defence lawyers and closed-custody institutions is the result of one profession, law, expanding into an area previously dominated by another, social work . . . but it is too late to go back. Lawyers have replaced social workers as the main players in juvenile justice. We must work with them" (at 18–21).

48   K. Makin, "Use of Criminal Lawyers in Youth Courts Assailed," *Globe and Mail*, Toronto ed., November 5, 1985: A1 at A2.

49   M. Strauss, "Judge Receives 'Slap on Wrist' for Comments," *Globe and Mail*, Toronto ed., February 15, 1986: A16. Judge Felstiner claimed that his remarks were taken "out of context" but acknowledged that some of them were "badly expressed."

that the justice system functions properly and that the rights of citizens, even young ones, are not violated.

Defence counsel can also have a very significant role at the sentencing stage, not only in calling evidence on behalf of the youth but also in challenging the views of various professionals who are proposing to help the youths. Sometimes the good intentions of these professionals outstrip their expertise, and intrusive sentencing plans are proposed that may be unrealistic or unlikely to help the youth. There is, for example, a tendency for some professionals to minimize the harmful effects of a custodial placement in terms of peer abuse and transmission of negative values from other young offenders, while over-emphasizing the rehabilitative potential of the programming available in custody.

Defence counsel needs to be aware of the availability and benefits of community-based dispositions and should be prepared to challenge professionals who are recommending custody. One of the most creative and satisfying roles that defence counsel can play is to help the youth to formulate plans that can be put before the youth justice court in regard to pre-trial release or at the time of sentencing or sentencing review. To be acceptable to the court a plan should have a realistic chance of meeting the youth's needs, and this will usually require consultation with the parents and family, as well as with professionals and agencies. Even a lawyer who adopts a strong advocacy stance at the sentencing hearing — following a young client's instructions, which typically is to seek the least intrusive sentence possible — is most likely to be effective if the judge is persuaded that a proposed sentence meets the needs of the youth that are related to the offending behaviour.

A Nova Scotia youth court judge remarked at a disposition review hearing under the *YOA*: "Counsel for an accused [youth] must take an active role in assisting the client, not a passive one. That is one of the purposes of ensuring counsel be available. . . . It is not simply the traditional criminal law role, and lawyers who work in Youth Court must be aware of this difference."[50] The reason for having different expectations of counsel in youth justice court at the sentencing stage rests, in part at least, on the difficulty that a youth will have in formulating a realistic plan without an experienced, knowledgable adviser and facilitator. Defence counsel, however, too rarely play this demanding role, lacking the interest, time or knowledge, and tending to rely on plans

---

50   *R. v. R.(K.)* (1987), 80 N.S.R. (2d) 61 at 64 (Youth Ct.), per Niedermayer J.Y.C.

put forward by agents of the state, such as probation officers or correctional staff. There are a few pilot programs in Canada which are intended to provide defence counsel with assistance in developing plans for proposed sentences that meet the needs of individual youth, typically involving community-based sentences.[51]

Defence counsel should have an important role in the youth justice system, but measures may be needed to improve the quality of representation that youths actually receive. Some lawyers who represent youth are excellent — sensitive, dedicated, and knowledgeable — but others may not be so satisfactory. One of the difficulties with the present system is that, except where there are clinics, there are no screening or supervision, or educational or training requirements for lawyers who do this type of work. Adolescents are, in general, vulnerable and unsophisticated consumers of legal services: they may not be able to make an appropriate selection of a lawyer for their case; may not be in a good position to assess the quality of services they are receiving; or know how to complain if they are not receiving adequate representation. These types of concerns led the Quebec Bar Committee to recommend a process for "accreditation" of lawyers who represent children and adolescents, as well as the creation of an ombudsman's office to supervise the provision of legal services to minors.[52] To be accredited, a lawyer would have to meet educational and training requirements.

The 1997 Ontario Legal Aid Review made a similar recommendation: that those lawyers who represent young persons involved in the youth justice system should be part of a "specialized defence panel . . . trained and evaluated in relation to this idea of expertise."[53] Lawyers who do this type of work should be aware of relevant services and facilities in their communities, as well as of applicable laws. They should also be familiar with the problems and developmental stages of adolescence and have an understanding of the role of the different professionals who work with young offenders. Finally, they should be able to communicate and work effectively with parents, bearing in mind the duty of confidentiality to their client and the need to act only on the youth's instructions.

---

51 One prominent example of such a program is Operation Springboard in Toronto.
52 Quebec Bar Committee, above note 40 at 126.
53 Ontario Legal Aid Review, above note 26, Volume 1, at 158.

H. THE ROLE OF THE PROSECUTOR IN YOUTH JUSTICE COURT

Under the *Juvenile Delinquents Act*, it was common for probation or police officers to appear for the Crown, with a lawyer appearing for the prosecution only in the most serious cases. The lack of legal representation generally did not seriously hinder the prosecution since the proceedings tended to be relatively informal and juveniles were often unrepresented. Further, judges under the *Juvenile Delinquents Act* often tended to take on some of the prosecutorial functions,[54] and, for example, had the authority under section 9 of that Act to commence and decide an application for transfer to adult court without a request coming from the Crown.

With the enactment of the *Young Offenders Act*, defence counsel began to appear regularly in youth court, and Crown prosecutors' offices felt that the Crown should also be represented by legally trained personnel, both to respond to the more legalistic demands of the Act and to be able to reply to arguments of defence lawyers. There are now experienced, knowledgeable Crown prosecutors in some youth justice courts, but too often these courts are given a low priority or are viewed in the Crown's office, somewhat derisively, as a training ground. Representation is often provided by articling students, junior lawyers, or part-time prosecutors. In some locales, less serious cases may still be prosecuted by police officers.

While there may be some controversy over the role of defence counsel in youth justice court, there is agreement, at least in theory, about the role of the Crown prosecutor, whether in adult or youth court, as explained in *Boucher* v. *R.* by Rand J:

> It cannot be over-emphasized that the purpose of a criminal prosecution is not to obtain a conviction, it is to lay before a jury [or judge] what the Crown considers to be credible evidence relevant to what is alleged to be a crime. . . . The role of the prosecutor excludes any notion of winning or losing; his function is a matter of public duty . . . in public life there can be none charged with greater personal responsibility.[55]

---

54   P.G. Erickson, "The Defence Lawyer's Role in Juvenile Court: An Empirical Investigation into Judges' and Social Workers' Points of View" (1974) 24 U.T.L.J. 126 at 138.

55   *Boucher* v. *R.*, [1955] S.C.R. 16 at 23–24.

Prosecutors play a dual role as both administrators of justice and as advocates. While as advocates they have a responsibility to present the prosecution's case in "forcible and direct language," they must avoid making inflammatory or unfair comments about the accused or witnesses.[56] As officers of the court with a responsibility for the administration of justice, Crown prosecutors have a responsibility to see that the innocent are not prosecuted or convicted, and they have a duty to discontinue a prosecution if there is not a reasonable likelihood that a conviction will be obtained.

An important example of the difference between the prosecutor and the defence counsel is in regard to pre-trial disclosure. The courts, relying on the *Charter*'s guarantees for a fair trial and the role of the prosecution in a criminal case, have held that there is an obligation on the Crown to disclose to the accused information obtained by the Crown in the course of investigating the offence, whether or not the Crown intends to put the evidence before the court.[57] Defence counsel has no corresponding duty and may decide not to reveal any information before trial.[58] While Crown prosecutors work with the police and such other agents of the state as probation officers, it is said that the prosecutor's only client is the public. That is, unlike a defence counsel, who takes instructions from the accused, or a lawyer in a civil case who receives direction from the client, the Crown prosecutor generally decides what to do based on his or her own sense of justice, not on the basis of instructions from a client.

In Canada, the function of the police as investigators is quite separate from the office of the Crown prosecutor. An Ontario judge observed of Crown prosecutors that they "act as an independent reviewing body of the [police] . . . to ensure that prosecutions are not only thorough but fair."[59] In a complex case, the Crown prosecutor may be asked to give advice to the police about what evidence to obtain or

---

56   G. Mackenzie, *Lawyers and Ethics: Professional Responsibility and Discipline* (Toronto: Carswell, 1993) at 64. See also *R. v. F.S.* (2000), 47 O.R.(3d) 349 (Ont. C.A.).

57   *R. v. Stinchcombe*, [1991] 3 S.C.R. 326. The Crown may decline to disclose certain limited types of "privileged" information, such as the identity of an informer.

58   While in general in Canada there is no duty on the accused to provide any form of pre-trial disclosure, in limited circumstances, such as when the accused seeks to rely on alibi evidence to establish a defence, the failure to provide notice of this to allow the Crown to investigate before trial may affect the credibility of this type of evidence.

59   *R. v. Moscuzza* (2001), 54 O.R. (3d) 459 (Sup. Ct.) per Gans J.

whether to lay charges in a particular case. Local Crown prosecutors are not, however, independent in the way that judges are; they are accountable to the attorney general or minister of justice[60] and are subject to government policies, although they should not be subject to political interference. The Crown prosecutor is not the lawyer for the complainant (or victim). Yet, while the Crown prosecutor should not be taking directions from victims about how to handle a case, there have been concerns that too often victims have been left uninformed and unsupported in the criminal process. Recently there have been increased efforts to provide support and information for victims, in particular in cases involving violence or abuse and especially for children (e.g., to prepare them adequately for testifying in court and to reduce the trauma of the court experience).

Provisions in the Declaration of Principle of the *YCJA*, with no direct equivalent in the *YOA*, were enacted to remind prosecutors, police, and others in the youth justice system of the importance of respecting victims. Sections 3(1)(d)(ii) and (iii) of the Act declare that "victims should be treated with courtesy, compassion and respect [and] should be provided with information about the proceedings and given an opportunity to participate and to be heard." There is clearly a need to appreciate that too often, the needs of victims have been disregarded in the justice system. It is, however, primarily the responsibility of the police and various workers in victim services to provide support to victims. The Crown prosecutor should not be seen as accountable to the victim for how a case is handled. While a Crown prosecutor may, for example, consult with the victim before deciding whether to refer a case to extrajudicial measures, accept a plea bargain, or make submissions to the court about an appropriate sentence, there is no legal obligation to do so.

It would be inappropriate for a Crown prosecutor to base decisions about the handling of a case solely on the views of the victim. Some victims may be more compassionate toward young offenders, while other victims may, perhaps understandably, expect a more punitive attitude than the principles of the *YCJA* allow. While section 3(1)(d)(iii) of *YCJA* creates the expectation that the Crown prosecutor will meet with the victim to explain why a particular position was taken with respect to sentencing, accepting a plea, or referring a case to extrajudicial measures, the prosecutor must take account of many factors in

---

60   The primary responsibility for the prosecution of cases against young persons under the *YCJA*, above note 2, rests with the provincial governments. Some offences, in particular those involving violations of drug laws, are the responsibility of federally appointed prosecutors.

deciding how to deal with a case and cannot be bound by the views of the victim.

At the sentencing stage in youth justice court, the Crown prosecutor should be working with numerous different professionals, including police, mental-health professionals, social workers, and the provincial director of probation and corrections staff, as well as communicating with the victim, to ensure that all necessary evidence is before the court, and the prosecutor should be advocating for a sentence that accords with the principles of the YCJA.[61] While much of the co-ordinating and planning for sentencing hearing, at least on the "government" side, will usually be done by the provincial director, in principle the Crown prosecutor has an important role in ensuring that appropriate information is before the court. The prosecutor should also offer submissions about an appropriate sentence and, according to the principles of the YCJA, this requires consideration of both the interests of society and the needs of youth. In practice, however, many Crown prosecutors have heavy case loads and may not have the time to prepare sufficiently for youth justice court. These problems are compounded if the prosecutor is not familiar with the relevant laws, facilities, and programs. There is relatively little research about the effectiveness of prosecutors in the youth justice system; however, the research available indicates that, as with the concerns about the lack of involvement of defence lawyers in the sentencing process, judges have expressed concern that some Crown prosecutors are ill-prepared and contribute little to the sentencing process. This type of concern has led to calls for better training for Crown prosecutors who appear in youth justice court.[62]

---

61 See, for example, R. S. Stubbs, "The Role of the Lawyer in Juvenile Court" (1974) 6 Man. L.J. 65 at 82; and IJA-ABA Joint Commission on Juvenile Justice Standards, above note 38.

62 Hanscom, above note 46; Ontario Social Development Council, *Young Offenders Act Dispositions: Challenges and Choices* (Toronto: 1988) at 129.

FURTHER READINGS

CORRADO, R., *et al.*, eds., *Juvenile Justice in Canada: A Theoretical and Analytical Assessment* (Toronto: Butterworths, 1992) c. 7

IJA-ABA JOINT COMMISSION ON JUVENILE JUSTICE STANDARDS, *Juvenile Justice Standards Relating to Counsel for Private Parties* (New York: The Commission, 1990)

PEARSON, J., "Legal Representation Under the Young Offenders Act: in A.W. Leschied, P.G. Jaffe, & W. Willis, eds., *The Young Offenders Act: A Revolution in Canadian Juvenile Justice* (Toronto: University of Toronto Press, 1991) c. 5

MARTIN, G.A., & J.W. IRVING, *Essays on Aspects of Criminal Practice* (Toronto: Carswell, 1997) cc. 6 and 7

ONTARIO LEGAL AID REVIEW, *Report of the Ontario Legal Aid Review: A Blueprint for Publicly Funded Legal Services* (Toronto: Government of Ontario, 1997), vol. 1, c. 9 and vol. 3, c. 11

PLATT, P., *Young Offenders Law in Canada*, 2d ed. (Toronto: Butterworths, 1995) c. 15

PROULX, M. & D. LAYTON, *Ethics and the Canadian Criminal Lawyer* (Toronto: Irwin Law, 2001)

CHAPTER 7

THE YOUTH JUSTICE COURT PROCESS

A. YOUTH JUSTICE COURT PROCEEDINGS ARE SUMMARY

Section 142 of the *Youth Criminal Justice Act* provides that proceedings in youth justice court are generally governed by the provisions of the *Criminal Code* that are applicable to "summary conviction offence[s] [in adult court,] except to the extent that these provisions are inconsistent with this Act."[1] Thus the fundamental rules and processes that apply in adult court also govern youth justice court and it is, for example not sufficient for the Crown to prove that a youth is probably guilty; rather, the ordinary criminal standard of proof "beyond a reasonable doubt" must be satisfied.[2] However, since proceedings are summary, this means that youth justice court proceedings are in general less complex and more expeditious than those which are applicable to "indictable offences" in adult court. In particular, in youth justice court there is usually no preliminary inquiry, and almost all trials are conducted by a judge alone (i.e., without a jury).

---

1 See also ss.140–41 of the *Youth Criminal Justice Act*, S.C. 2002, c. 1 (to come into force April 1, 2003), often referred to in this book as the *YCJA*; s. 142 refers to Part XXVII of the *Criminal Code*, R.S.C. 1985, c. C-46, ss. 785–840, which govern summary proceedings.
2 *R. v. M.B.*, [1997] B.C.J. No. 2184 (B.C.C.A.).

In adopting a summary procedure for youth justice court, the *Youth Criminal Justice Act* continues the approach of the *Young Offenders Act*[3] and the *Juvenile Delinquents Act*,[4] allowing for a more expeditious resolution of cases. From the perspective of an adolescent, the youth justice court will seem like a very formal and unfamiliar environment. The resolution of most cases without a jury, however, makes the court setting less intimidating than it might otherwise be. It has been held that the denial of the right to a jury trial to young persons in the youth justice court process does not violate the provisions of the *Charter* which guarantee equality (s. 15) and the right to a jury trial to persons facing imprisonment of five years or more (s. 11(f)).[5]

In *R. v. L.(R.)*, the Ontario Court of Appeal upheld the provisions of the *Young Offenders Act* which denied a youth the right to a jury trial. While an adult facing the same indictable charges (a number of offences including three for break and enter) would have been entitled to the procedure for trial by indictment with a preliminary inquiry and a jury, the adult would also face a much greater possible maximum penalty. In rejecting the *Charter* challenge, the Court of Appeal emphasized that the maximum penalty in youth court is three years, much less than an adult would face for the same offence. Justice Morden wrote:

> the *Young Offenders Act* is intended to provide a comprehensive system for dealing with young persons who are alleged to be in conflict with the law which is separate and distinct from the adult criminal justice system. While the new system is more like the adult system than was that under the *Juvenile Delinquents Act*, it nonetheless is a different system. As far as the aftermath of a finding of guilt is concerned, the general thrust of the *Young Offenders Act* is to provide for less severe consequences than those relating to an adult offender. . . . the establishment of the legal regime . . . for dealing with young persons, which is separate and distinct from the adult criminal justice system, is of sufficient importance to warrant the overriding of the equality right alleged to be infringed in this proceeding.[6]

---

3   *Young Offenders Act*, R.S.C 1985, c. Y-1,enacted as S.C. 1980–81–82–83, c. 110, s. 52.

4   *Juvenile Delinquents Act*, enacted as S.C. 1908, c. 40; subject to minor amendments over the years, finally as *Juvenile Delinquents Act*, R.S.C. 1970, c. J–3.

5   *Canadian Charter of Rights and Freedoms*, being Schedule B of the *Constitution Act, 1982*, enacted as *Canada Act, 1982*, (U.K.), c. 11 (subsequently referred to as the *Charter*).

6   *R. v. L.(R.)* (1986), 52 C.R. (3d) 209 at 219 and 225 (Ont. C.A.); to the same effect, see *R. v. B.(S.)* (1989), 76 Sask. R. 308 (C.A.).

This line of reasoning will doubtless apply to the *YCJA*. The general adoption of the summary procedure provisions of the *Criminal Code* and denial of the right to a jury trial for young persons should be accepted as constitutionally valid.

There is a range of very serious cases in which a young person may face a sentence of more than three years. Section 11(f) of the *Charter* guarantees any person facing a maximum possible sentence of five years or longer the right to "the benefit of trial by jury."[7] Accordingly, the *YCJA* allows youth facing sentences of five years or longer to have the right to choose to have a preliminary inquiry and a trial by jury. Thus, a youth facing a murder charge, for which the maximum youth justice court sentence is ten years, has the right to a jury trial and a preliminary inquiry. Further, for very serious charges other than murder where there is also the prospect of an adult sentence, the youth also has the right to a jury trial and a preliminary inquiry.

Because of section 96 of the *Constitution Act, 1867*,[8] a jury trial must be conducted by a federally appointed superior court judge (e.g., a Queen's Bench or Superior Court judge). Generally, youth justice court proceedings are presided over by judges of the provincial or territorial court. Section 13(2) of the *YCJA* provides that if a youth is charged with murder or there is the possibility that an adult sentence may be imposed, the youth has the right to be tried by a federally appointed superior court judge, who has the jurisdiction to conduct a jury trial. Section 14(7) specifies that a superior court judge dealing with a youth proceeding shall be, "deemed to be a youth justice court judge for the purpose of [that] proceeding, [but] retains the jurisdiction and powers" of a superior court judge, for example in regard to issues of contempt of court and control of the jury process. The superior court judge in this situation is deemed to be sitting as a youth justice court judge and subject to the provisions of the *YCJA* governing such matters as the right to counsel and protection of privacy.

While technically the *YCJA* has expanded the range of cases in which there may be a jury trial in the youth justice system, in reality young persons will have access to a jury trial in the same types of cases under both statutes. Under the *Young Offenders Act*, only if a youth was facing a murder charge in youth court, where the maximum sentence was ten years, was there the right to a jury trial.[9] However, under the

---

7   The *Charter*, above note 5, s. 11(f).

8   *Constitution Act, 1867* (formerly, the *British North America Act, 1867*) (U.K.) 30 & 31 Vict., c. 3.

9   *An Act to amend the Young Offenders Act and the Criminal Code*, S.C. 1995, c. 19, s. 19(4). This provision increased the maximum youth court sentence for murder from five years less a day in custody to ten years.

Young Offenders Act, youth facing very serious charges could be subjected to a process that would result in their cases being transferred into adult court, where they would face the possibility of an adult sentence but also have the right to a jury trial and preliminary inquiry.

The real significance of this change is that under the *YCJA* young persons facing the prospect of adult-length sentences will have their jury trials in youth justice court, conducted under a regime that gives them special protections, such as the prohibitions on the publication of identifying information and detention separate from adults. As discussed more fully in Chapter 9, on adult sentencing, if after conviction a youth offender is subjected to an adult sentence under the *YCJA*, at that point the youth will lose the protections of the Act and may, for example, be subjected to identifying publicity.

1) Crown Election for Hybrid Offences

Legislation that creates offences, such as the *Criminal Code*, generally specifies whether an offence is indictable or summary, with a more severe maximum penalty if the offence is indictable. Some offences are hybrid, generally with a maximum sentence of six to eighteen months' imprisonment if the case is proceeded with summarily, and a longer maximum penalty if the case is proceeded with by indictment. In cases involving adults charged with hybrid offences, the Crown prosecutor is required to elect (i.e., to inform the court about the decision) whether to proceed summarily or by indictment before the accused enters a plea. The Crown election is noted on the court file and will govern the manner of trial for an adult. If the Crown elects to proceed by indictment, there is a more severe maximum penalty, but the accused generally has the right to a preliminary inquiry and jury trial.

Although the *YCJA* provides that proceedings in youth justice court are to be summary, offences in youth justice court retain their character as summary, hybrid, or indictable for such purposes as: the possibility of an adult sentence; the maximum length of a custodial sentence;[10] the length of time that records concerning the offence may

---

10   The maximum penalty for an adult charged under a summary procedure is generally six months in prison, though with some hybrid offences like sexual assault the maximum sentence under a summary proceeding is eighteen months. The *YCJA*, above note 1, s. 38(2)(a) specifies that the maximum custodial sentence that may be imposed on a youth shall be no longer than that which could be imposed on an adult for the same offence.

be kept; and the limitation period for commencing a prosecution.[11] Accordingly, the Crown prosecutor dealing with a hybrid charge in youth justice court should indicate to the judge and the accused, prior to the youth entering a plea, how the Crown elects to treat the charge.

The issue of Crown election for hybrid offences has more practical significance in adult proceedings where it can affect the manner of a trial and the right to a preliminary inquiry, and has less significance for young persons. In some cases under the *YOA*, the Crown prosecutor neglected to elect in regard to a hybrid charge; the youth court generally treated these cases as summary for such purposes as the maximum sentence and records.[12] One rationale for this approach is that the youth might not have pleaded guilty if the Crown had elected to treat the offence as indictable. A further rationale is that, if the Crown makes a mistake and fails to make an election, the young person should have the benefit of the more protective regime.[13] This type of analysis should also apply under the *YCJA* so that, if the Crown prosecutor fails to make an election before a youth pleads to elect for a hybrid offence, it should be treated as summary.[14]

2) Adjournments and Delay

A youth justice court proceeding is generally commenced with an "information" being sworn before a justice of the peace and the youth being served with a summons, appearance notice, or other document requiring him or her to attend court on a specific date. As discussed in Chapter

---

11   The limitation period for a summary offence is generally six months (*Criminal Code*, above note 1, s. 786(2)), whereas if an offence is proceeded with by indictment there is generally no limitation period; see, for example, *R. v. C.(F.)*, [1995] O.J. No. 3832 (Prov. Div.) (QL).

12   See *YCJA*, above note 1, s. 37 (for appeal purposes hybrid offence treated as summary unless election), and s. 121 (for records purposes hybrid offence treated as summary unless election). See also *R. v. M.(F.H.)* (1984), 30 Man. R. (2d) 190 (Q.B.) (for maximum-sentence purposes, hybrid offence treated as summary unless election). But see the *Interpretation Act*, R.S.C. 1985, c. I–21, s. 34(2).

13   However, under the *YOA*, it was held that, if it was clear from the expiry of the six-month summary limitation period before the information was laid that the charge must have been treated as indictable, the Crown will be deemed to have elected to have the youth court proceeding indictable: *R. v. B.(I.)* (1994), 20 O.R. (3d) 341 (C.A.).

14   If the Crown has no reasonable opportunity to elect prior to plea, a Crown election after plea may be accepted: *R. v. J.(H.W.)* (1992), 71 C.C.C. (3d) 516 (B.C.C.A.).

4, in cases involving more serious charges or a youth with a history of failing to attend court, the youth may be detained in custody pending trial, subject to the right to seek bail (i.e., judicial interim release).

Some cases are resolved with a single court appearance by the youth. This is usually the case only if the charge is less serious and referred to a post-charge extrajudicial sanctions program, or if the youth is prepared to plead guilty at his or her first appearance in court. A guilty plea on a first appearance is likely only in less serious cases, since the youth is unlikely to have had an opportunity to consult fully with a lawyer before a first appearance, although there may be a brief meeting with duty counsel. If the case is more serious or the youth wants to obtain legal advice, the judge will adjourn the proceedings to allow the youth time to consult a lawyer. Often, several brief court appearances and adjournments are needed while a youth applies for legal aid and then finds a lawyer or, if necessary, returns to court to obtain a direction for representation under section 25 of the YCJA. There may be further adjournments while defence counsel obtains disclosure from the Crown, investigates the circumstances of the case or does legal research, and meets with the client to provide advice about how to plead.

If a not-guilty plea is entered, there must be a court appearance to set a trial date. The judge setting the trial date will try to ensure that there is sufficient court time available to complete the trial. With government funding constraints, courts are frequently very busy and trial dates are sometimes set months away, or a trial has to be conducted on several different dates spread over a period of weeks or even months. The adjournments and delays that are common in the Canadian justice system give rise to concerns when dealing with adults — and even more so when they affect young persons. Adolescents' lives develop and change rapidly, and their memories may fade more quickly than adult memories. A slow judicial response in youth justice court is highly problematic. Delay may affect the efficacy of rehabilitative treatment available through the youth justice system and weaken the deterrent impact from involvement in the youth justice system.

The YCJA explicitly recognizes the concerns about delay in the youth justice system and the need for timely intervention. The Declaration of Principle, section 3(1)(b), has statements that address these concerns in general terms, providing:

> 3. (1) (b) the criminal justice system for young persons must be separate from that of adults and emphasize the following . . . :
>
> (iv) timely intervention that reinforces the link between the offending behaviour and its consequences, and

(v) the promptness and speed with which persons responsible for enforcing this Act must act, given young persons' perception of time.

There was no equivalent to section 3(1)(b)(iv) and (v) of the *YCJA* in the *YOA*. Beyond these general statements in the *YCJA*, however, there are no provisions in the Act that deal with the problems of delay before sentencing.[15] Indeed, there is a concern that the complexity of the *YCJA* in comparison to the *YOA* may exacerbate problems of delay, although the encouragement to use extrajudicial measures has the potential to reduce case-loads in the youth justice system, and thereby allow for faster resolution of the cases that are in the courts.

In *R. v. M.(G.C.)*, the Ontario Court of Appeal indicated that the right of an accused person to a trial "within a reasonable time," guaranteed by section 11(b) of the *Charter*, has special significance for young persons when judges are considering so-called "Askov applications"[16] to determine whether proceedings should be stayed because of an unreasonable delay in having a case brought to trial. While the Ontario Court of Appeal in *R. v. M.(G.C.)* declined to impose a fixed judicial "limitation period" within which youth court proceedings need to be completed, Justice Osborne remarked:

> There is a particular need to conclude youth court proceedings without unreasonable delay, consistent with the goals of the *Young Offenders Act*. . . . it seems to me that, as a general proposition, youth court proceedings should proceed to a conclusion more quickly than those in the adult criminal justice system. Delay, which may be reasonable in the adult criminal justice system, may not be reasonable in the youth court. There are sound reasons for this. They include the

---

15   There are some provisions of the *YCJA* that deal explicitly with the problem of delay in obtaining sentence review for a youth in custody. For example, s. 98(2) provides that if there is an application to the youth justice court to continue to detain a youth in custody past the date scheduled for release on supervision in the community and the application is not completed before that date, the youth shall be released unless there are "compelling reasons" for keeping the youth in custody.

16   The term "Askov application" refers to the Supreme Court decision in *R. v. Askov*, [1990] 2 S.C.R. 1199, where the Court invoked s. 11(b) of the *Charter*, above note 5, to issue a stay of proceedings where there had been an "unreasonable delay" in having a trial. In determining whether a delay was unreasonable, the court should consider: the duration of the delay; the explanation for the delay; waiver of delay by the accused; and any prejudice to the accused arising from the delay. *R. v. Morin*, [1992] 1 S.C.R. 771, increased the emphasis placed on the prejudice to the accused, although it is clearly not the only factor.

well established fact that the ability of a young person to appreciate the connection between behaviour and its consequences is less developed than an adult's. For young persons, the effect of time may be distorted. If treatment is required and is to be made part of the *Young Offenders Act* disposition process, it is best begun with as little delay as is possible.

From a conceptual standpoint, the basis of the need to try young persons with reasonable dispatch is best analyzed and understood if it is viewed as a part of the consideration of prejudice, one of the four factors referred to in *Askov*. These four factors have to be balanced in each case to determine if an accused, young or old, has been brought to trial within a reasonable time.[17]

Justice Osborne went on to suggest, as an "administrative guideline, [that] in general, youth court cases should be brought to trial within five to six months, after the neutral period required to retain and instruct counsel, obtain disclosure, etc." However, it is interesting to observe that, in *R. v. M.(G.C.)*, the Court of Appeal refused to stay proceedings in which there was a delay of over ten months from the setting of the trial date until the commencement of the trial.

In its brief 1992 decision in *R. v. D.(S.)*, the Supreme Court of Canada noted that "account [must] be taken of the fact that charges against young offenders [should] be proceeded with promptly, [but the youthfulness of the accused] is merely one of the factors to be balanced with others."[18] In that case the Supreme Court refused to grant a stay, despite the fact that it took two and a half years for the youths to be brought to trial; the delay was largely a result of a transfer hearing and two subsequent appeals of the original transfer decision. The Supreme Court accepted that this type of delay was inherent in cases where the Crown seeks transfer and there are appeals. However, a delay of that length would not be acceptable in an ordinary youth court case.[19]

---

17   *R. v. M.(G.C.)* (1991), 3 O.R. (3d) 223 at 230–31 (C.A.). Statistics Canada, *Youth Court Statistics 2000–01* (2002) Juristat 22:3 reports 17 percent of youth court cases were completed on a first appearance, 50 percent were processed within two months and 83 percent of cases were processed within six months. The median time elapsed for all cases was 60 days, with Manitoba having the longest at 91 days, followed by Alberta (84 days), Saskatchewan (82 days), and Ontario (73 days).

18   *R. v. D.(S.)*, [1992] 2 S.C.R. 161 at 162, rev'g (1991), 4 O.R. (3d) 225 (C.A.).

19   The *YCJA*, above note 1, abolishes the pre-trial transfer process, though allowing for a post-adjudication process for imposition of an adult sentence; one of the reasons for changing the process is to allow for a more expeditious process of resolution of cases.

While efforts have been made to reduce delays in courts by judges and governments since the early 1990s, there continue to be cases where delays are long. It is apparent that a delay which may be constitutionally acceptable is far longer than one that is optimum in terms of adolescent development and needs. The issue of Askov applications in youth justice court is likely to remain contentious.[20] The enactment of section 3(1)(b)(iv) and (v) of the *YCJA* supports the principle that there is a stronger presumption of prejudice arising from delay "when young people are involved."[21]

B. PREPARING FOR PLEA

A lawyer consulted by a youth who is charged with an offence will generally be reluctant to give much advice about how to plead until the lawyer has had an opportunity to obtain disclosure from the Crown prosecutor, in order to ascertain the evidence that the police have gathered. The courts have held that, as an aspect of the *Charter* guarantee to make a "full answer and defence," all accused persons, including youths, have a right to disclosure of information obtained by the police in the course of their investigation.[22]

1) Disclosure of Information

The right to disclosure is quite broad. It applies to all information that the Crown intends to introduce in court as well as material in the possession of the Crown that will not be used as part of its case, whether the information is helpful to the accused or the prosecution. Generally, disclosure of the Crown's information will be given to a youth's lawyer

---

20   In *R. v. S.(M.T.)* (1991), (N.S. Youth Ct.) [unreported] [summarized *Lawyers Weekly*, June 7, 1991: 24] Niedermayer Prov. J. held that s. 11(b) of the *Charter*, above note 5, should be invoked when the police waited almost a year to execute an arrest warrant issued in connection with a young person's failure to appear on theft charges. In staying the charges, the judge observed that this was a case where the police failed to make "reasonable, concerted efforts" to locate the youth and compel his attendance.

21   *R. v. B.(J.)*, [1995] O.J. No. 3113 (Prov. Div.) (QL), Sheppard Prov. J. The judge invoked s. 11(b) of the *Charter*, above note 5, to stay youth court proceedings that took nineteen months from the alleged offence to come to trial; the first trial that was scheduled resulted in a mistrial due to the failure of the Crown to provide adequate disclosure.

22   *R. v. Stinchcombe*, [1991] 3 S.C.R. 326.

under the supervision of a Crown prosecutor. There are a few narrow exceptions to the rule about disclosure. For example, some information in the Crown's possession may be regarded as privileged and is not subject to disclosure (i.e., the name of a police informer — a person who provides the police with information that assists in an investigation but who will not be called as a witness in court).

If the defence counsel and prosecutor disagree about whether there has been satisfactory disclosure or whether some information is privileged, an application may be made to the youth justice court to have the judge hold a hearing to resolve their disagreement.

If the police discover new information as a result of an investigation continuing, the defence lawyer must be informed of this after the initial disclosure session. A failure by the Crown adequately to disclose may result in a case being adjourned to allow disclosure to occur, or, if the failure is more serious and cannot be fairly remedied by an adjournment, a mistrial may be declared or the prosecution may be stayed by the judge.[23] A defence lawyer who has had disclosure will be in a better position to advise a client about the strength of the Crown's case and about whether the client should consider pleading guilty. While a lawyer will usually offer advice about how to plead, the ultimate decision about how to plead should be made by the client, even if the client is an adolescent.

Defence counsel may also want disclosure of third-party records (i.e., records that might have information related to the offence that are *not* made by agencies responsible for the investigation or prosecution of the offence). Defence counsel may, for example, believe that there may be information in school records or child-protection files about an alleged victim or witness whose records might be used to try to impeach that person's credibility. In certain cases, especially those involving sexual offences, in order to prepare for trial defence counsel will want access to the records of third parties, such as those of the therapist for a victim of an alleged offence. These types of information are often very personal and sensitive. As a result, those affected may feel threatened if such information is disclosed, especially to the lawyer for the accused in a criminal case. Nevertheless, there may be cases in which this type of information could be significant for a criminal trial. Sections 278.1 to 278.9 of the *Criminal Code* govern the pre-trial dis-

---

23   In *R. v. B.(S.)* (1990), 75 O.R. (2d) 646 (Fam. Ct.), a mistrial was declared when it was discovered that the Crown had inadvertently failed to give complete disclosure; the case provides a description of disclosure practices and policies in a youth case.

closure to accused persons, including youths, of third-party records relating to complainants and witnesses.

In the context of proceedings against a young person, the application for disclosure is made to the youth justice court that has jurisdiction over the case. Before the court makes a decision about disclosure, the person to whom the records relate as well as the professional or agency that made the records should have notice that a court will consider this issue, and will have the right to contest the application for disclosure.[24] The accused must satisfy a judge that the information in the record is likely to be "relevant" to an issue in the proceedings or to the competence of a witness to testify, and that disclosure would be "necessary in the interests of justice."[25] The judge may personally review the records before deciding whether they should be disclosed. In deciding whether the record should be disclosed, the court will weigh the privacy interests of the person to whom they relate against the right of the accused to a fair trial. The court will usually impose conditions on the disclosure of any such records to the lawyer for the accused to ensure they are used only for the court proceedings and not further disseminated.

2) Pleas and Plea Bargaining

Most criminal charges, whether against adults or young persons, do not result in trials, but rather are resolved by guilty pleas or the charges being dropped by the Crown before the case comes to trial. Frequently accused young persons recognize that they have committed an offence and wish to plead guilty in order to have a quick resolution of the court proceedings. A youth who is determined to plead guilty will often decide not to consult a lawyer before the day scheduled for a first appearance in court. In most places, there is a duty on counsel available outside the courtroom to meet with unrepresented youths and provide some form of summary legal advice. Section 32(3)of the *YCJA* imposes an obligation on the youth justice court judge, before accepting a plea from an unrepresented youth, to explain that the young person may plead guilty or not guilty, and that the youth has the right to obtain legal representation. The court must also satisfy itself that an unrepresented youth understands the charge.

If the charge is very serious and the unrepresented youth faces the possibility of an adult sentence, the judge has special obligations under

---

24 *A.(L.L.) v. B.(A.)*, [1995] 4 S.C.R. 536.
25 See *R. v. Mills*, [1999] 3 S.C.R. 668.

section 32 to ensure that the youth understands the consequences of the proceedings. In this type of case, a judge is especially likely to urge a youth to seek legal representation; even if a guilty plea is appropriate, a lawyer representing a youth may have an important role in the sentencing process, particularly if the consequences are very serious. If the judge is not satisfied that an unrepresented youth understands the charge or the consequences of an adult sentence, the judge is obliged to enter a plea of not guilty and direct that the young person shall be represented by counsel.[26]

If a youth enters a guilty plea, the Crown prosecutor will read a summary of the evidence against the youth. The defence counsel or the youth, if unrepresented, will be asked if he or she agrees with the facts as alleged by the Crown. If there is a substantial disagreement about a significant fact that is material to the offence, there may have to be a trial; typically, though, minor disagreements are resolved by the Crown amending its statement of the facts. Section 36 of the YCJA requires a judge in youth justice court to be satisfied that the facts read by the Crown at the time of a guilty plea support the charge. If the facts do not reveal that all material elements of the offence have been committed, the judge must enter a plea of not guilty and order that the case proceed to trial.

For youths with representation, the judge is likely to place significant reliance on the assessment of counsel that the facts support the charge; the reading of facts is likely to be significant primarily for sentencing purposes. However, with unrepresented youths the judge is obliged to be fully satisfied that the facts admitted by the youth constitute all the material elements of the offence and do not reveal a defence that is likely to succeed. If an unrepresented youth pleads guilty, implicit in section 36 is the expectation that the judge should also be satisfied that the youth is genuinely admitting guilt and not merely giving in to parental or other pressure to plead guilty. Sections 32 and 36 of the YCJA recognize that youths are unlikely to understand the charges that they face or appreciate the significance of a guilty plea as fully as an adult.[27] Judges in adult court do not have the statutory obli-

---

26   YCJA, above note 1, s. 32(4) and (5). See also Criminal Code, above note 5, s. 616(1.1) on obligations of a judge accepting a plea of guilty.

27   The courts have recognized that age is relevant to a person's capacity to make an appropriate plea. In R. v. T.W.B., [1998] B.C.J. 1044 (B.C.C.A.), a fourteen-year-old youth entered a guilty plea and sought to change it one month later. On appeal, a new trial was ordered and a plea was struck. The B.C. Court of Appeal discussed when and why pleas can be changed, noting that it is "not insignificant

gation to make these types of inquiry when an unrepresented accused person appears in court and enters a guilty plea.

It is not uncommon for a guilty plea to be the product of a plea bargain, or resolution discussions. A "plea bargain" is typically the result of informal discussions between the Crown prosecutor and the lawyer representing the accused about how to resolve a case. These discussions may occur at a session at which the Crown is disclosing information, or informally at the courthouse. Sometimes a plea bargain will be made partway through a trial. Increasingly in the Canadian youth justice system, more formal judicial pre-trial conferences are held, where lawyers meet with a judge to narrow the issues in dispute and discuss a possible resolution without a trial. A judge may help focus the discussion and, if counsel reach an agreement, may impose a sentence in accordance with their resolution; if the case is not settled the judge from the pre-trial conference ordinarily cannot preside at the trial. As a result of the discussions at a judicial pre-trial, if there is a trial, counsel for the accused may admit certain facts that the Crown is alleging in order to shorten the trial. Before entering into a plea bargain, the Crown prosecutor may consult the investigating officer and perhaps the complainant (i.e., the victim). However, the prosecutor is entitled to make a decision about a plea bargain without consulting anyone and is not obliged to have the concurrence of the complainant.

The discussions between the Crown prosecutor and the lawyer for the youth may produce an agreement to plead guilty to certain charges in exchange for the dropping of other charges or an agreement that there will be a joint submission or a request by the Crown to the court for a particular sentence. If there is a plea bargain resulting in a joint submission concerning sentencing, the judge is not bound to impose the sentence agreed to by counsel, although the court usually accepts it.[28] In some cases the two lawyers will meet privately with the judge for an off-the-record conversation to ascertain whether the judge is likely to accept the joint submission as regarding sentence.

Sometimes the Crown offers the accused some advantage, such as dropping some charges or offering a joint submission as to sentence, in

---

that this case involves a young offender who was 14 at the time he entered the guilty plea" (at para. 10). The Court held a number of circumstances may give rise to "valid grounds" for changing a guilty plea. Whether such a plea can be changed is a case-specific determination based on the "circumstances of the case and the interests of justice" (at para. 15). Although the young person had consulted with counsel before entering a plea, it was apparently not a long meeting.

28   For a discussion of what considerations are significant in determining whether to accept a plea bargain, see *R. v. Dewald* (2001), 54 O.R. (3d) 1 (C.A.).

exchange for the accused testifying against a co-accused or producing some evidence (i.e., the gun used in a killing). At least in theory, only the Crown prosecutor, and not the police can enter into a plea bargain with the accused, since the prosecutor is responsible for the case in court. The Supreme Court of Canada has made clear that the prosecutor and police have a duty to ensure that the accused has a full opportunity to have legal advice before accepting a plea bargain; they should not attempt to have the accused accept an offer for a plea bargain when defence counsel is not available: "[T]o the extent that the plea bargain is an integral element of the Canadian criminal process, the Crown and its officers engaged in the plea bargaining process must act honourably and forthrightly."[29] If there is a clear agreement and the accused has carried out his or her side of the bargain, the courts will not allow the Crown to renege on the deal and request a sentence other than that which was agreed to,[30] though the judge is not obliged to accept the joint submission.

Although plea bargaining remains controversial in Canada,[31] it is a common practice. A guilty plea can spare victims from having to testify. From the perspective of the Crown prosecutor, plea bargaining reflects the need to try to resolve a significant number of cases without trials, as there is not enough court time for every accused person to have a trial. Plea bargaining also offers the assurance of a finding of guilt for at least some charges, while a trial has the possibility of resulting in a total acquittal. There are also advantages to accused persons from having more certainty about the likely outcome and often a less severe sentence than might occur if there is a trial.

Appellate courts have accepted that a joint submission after negotiations between counsel is "important to the administration of the criminal justice system." While sentencing judges "should seriously consider a joint submission, they are not required to accept it . . . if accepting it would be contrary to the public interest or would otherwise bring the administration of justice into disrepute."[32] In particular, in youth justice court, the judge should be satisfied that any sentence

---

29   R. v. Burlingham, [1995] 2 S.C.R. 206 at 230–31, Iacobucci J.

30   R. v. Agozzino, [1970] 1 O.R. 480 (C.A.); see also R. v. D.(E.) (1990), 73 O.R. (2d) 758 (C.A.).

31   See, for example, "Plea Bargain Slammed," Southam Newspapers, November 30, 1996, concerning criticism of a plea bargain for a seventeen-year-old youth initially charged with second-degree murder in the shooting death of his girlfriend. The Crown accepted a guilty plea to a manslaughter charge with a Crown recommendation for two years in youth custody.

32   R. v. Dewald (2001), 54 O.R. (3d) 1, per Laskin J.A., at para. 29.

based on joint submissions accords with the Act. It cannot be so lenient that it disregards principles of proportionality. Further, even if there are joint submissions, in particular for a custodial sentence, the sentence cannot be more intrusive than justified by the facts or permitted under the *YCJA*, even if counsel for the youth and the parents consider that a sentence that is proposed would be in the best interests of the youth.

Defence counsel as well as the judge have responsibilities when engaging in plea bargaining, as illustrated by *R. v. K.(S.)*.[33] In this 1995 *YOA* case from Ontario, a youth was facing ten charges of sexual assault. The Crown prosecutor had offered to drop six of them and to support a recommendation for a non-custodial sentence, if the youth would plead guilty to the four least serious charges. The defence lawyer met with the youth and his parents; while stressing that the decision about how to plead rested with the youth, the lawyer outlined the "dangers of seeking to defend the more serious counts and the likelihood of a significant custodial sentence" if the youth were convicted of those offences. The youth told the lawyer that the allegations were not "the truth," and the lawyer responded by indicating that "criminal courts do not necessarily deal in truth, but they deal in evidence and explain[ing] . . . what the difference was."[34] The youth then instructed his counsel to enter a plea of guilty to the four charges, and the Crown dropped the other six. When the case was adjourned for sentencing, the youth told the probation officer preparing the pre-sentence report that he was innocent.

The youth court judge imposed a sentence of sixty days in open custody followed by twenty-two months' probation with a number of conditions, including treatment in the community. In rejecting the joint submission for a non-custodial sentence, the judge emphasized that the youth was not just displaying a lack of remorse but was "adamantly declaring innocence." The youth actually served his custodial sentence but decided to appeal after his probation officer told him that, unless he admitted that he committed the acts alleged, he could not receive the treatment that was a condition of probation and he would be charged with breach of probation for failure to undergo treatment.[35] The Ontario Court of Appeal set aside the guilty pleas and

---

33 *R. v. K.(S.)* (1995), 24 O.R. (3d) 199 (C.A.). See also M. Proulx and D. Layton, *Ethics and Canadian Criminal Law* (Toronto: Irwin Law, 2001), c. 8.

34 *Ibid.* at 201.

35 Unlike the U.S. system, where a common aspect of plea bargaining is for an accused to plead guilty while maintaining innocence, in Canada, a plea of guilty should not be accepted if the accused denies guilt.

ordered a new trial. The Court of Appeal noted that the *Rules of Professional Conduct of the Law Society of Upper Canada* require a defence lawyer representing an accused person who is offered a plea bargain to be satisfied that a client is prepared to admit the necessary factual and mental elements of an offence before entering a plea of guilty, concluding:

> The court should not be in the position of convicting and sentencing individuals, who fall short of admitting the facts to support the conviction unless guilt is proved beyond a reasonable doubt. Nor should sentencing proceed on the false assumption of contrition. . . . [P]lea bargaining is an accepted and integral part of our criminal justice system but must be conducted with sensitivity to its vulnerabilities.[36]

Plea bargaining is now an integral part of Canada's adult and youth justice systems but some reforms would be desirable. The 1993 Martin Committee recommended the continuation of the practice of plea bargaining but with provisions to ensure a more open and accountable process by involving victims in the process and by ordinarily requiring the Crown prosecutor to indicate in court that plea bargaining has occurred.[37] The Committee also suggested that judges should refuse to accept joint submissions about sentences only in narrow circumstances, to avoid bringing the administration of justice into disrepute.[38]

Section 606(1.1) of the *Criminal Code* (in force September 23, 2002), requires that judges should always ensure that a person pleading guilty is doing so voluntarily and knowingly, and with an understanding that an agreement between defence counsel and the Crown prosecutor does not necessarily bind the court. The judge is also obliged to be satisfied that the accused understands that a guilty plea is an admission of the essential elements of the offence. This type of judicial inquiry is particularly appropriate in youth justice court, since adolescents may have less comprehension of their situation than adults.

---

36   *R. v. K.(S.)*, above note 33 at 204.

37   Ontario, Ministry of the Attorney General, *Report of the Attorney General's Advisory Committee on Charge Screening, Disclosure and Resolution Discussions* [the Martin Committee] (Toronto: Queen's Printer, 1993) at 291–348.

38   In law, a judge is not bound by joint submissions arising out of a plea bargain, although, as joint submissions are entitled to great weight, good reasons must be given for rejecting them: *R. v. Rubenstein* (1987), 41 C.C.C. (3d) 91 (Ont. C.A.). In practice, some judges will allow an accused to withdraw a guilty plea and have a trial before another judge if they are not prepared to uphold the agreement, although this is a matter of discretion.

C. THE TRIAL

Young persons who have a trial have the constitutionally guaranteed right to the presumption of innocence.[39] The onus or burden is on the Crown to prove the guilt of the accused beyond a reasonable doubt.

1) The Youth Justice Court Trial

During a youth justice court trial, the Crown must call witnesses to establish its case and each witness may be subject to cross-examination. The youth is entitled to call witnesses and to testify, subject to the Crown prosecutor's right of cross-examination, but there is no obligation on the accused to adduce any evidence or to testify. After all the witnesses have testified, there will be submissions or arguments by the lawyers to summarize their positions and address any legal issues. The judge will then render the verdict. If the case is relatively simple, the trial and verdict may be over in a few hours, with the judge rendering an oral decision as soon as the evidence and submissions are completed. If the case is complex, the trial may last for several days and the judge may reserve judgment, adjourning the case to decide whether to convict the youth and to allow time to prepare detailed written reasons for the judgment.

If, after hearing all the evidence and submissions, the judge is satisfied beyond a reasonable doubt that all elements of the offence charged have been proven, the judge makes a finding of guilt and the case proceeds to sentencing under the YCJA.[40] Otherwise, the court must find the youth not guilty (i.e, acquits the youth). While an acquittal ends the youth justice court prosecution, a youth justice court judge still has the jurisdiction at this point to make a referral under section 35 of the YCJA to a child welfare agency for assessment whether the young person is in need of the agency's services.

---

39   The *Charter*, above note 1, s. 11(d).

40   Technically, youth justice court does not make convictions, only findings of guilt. These two concepts are similar, but the technical difference between a "finding of guilt" for a youth and a "conviction" for an adult is significant in terms of some of the employment and civic disqualifications that accompany a conviction for certain offences. Even so, there are circumstances in which a youth justice court finding of guilt is similarly admissible in later proceedings to a conviction. For example, in *R. v. Joel Alexander C.*, [1998] O.J. No. 5580 (Gen. Div.), it was held that an adult may be cross-examined on his youth court record even though findings of guilt are not convictions. Such cross-examination was found to be authorized by the language of the *YOA*, above note 3 (1982), s. 27.

2) The Role of the Judge

The youth justice court process, like all criminal trial processes in Canada, is based on an adversarial model of justice. It is the responsibility of the parties — the Crown and the youth, usually acting through counsel — to decide what witnesses to call and what questions to ask those witnesses. The judge is expected to control the trial process as an impartial arbiter, resolving disputes that the lawyers may present about the admissibility of evidence, for example, whether the police failed to comply adequately with section 146(1) of the YCJA and thereby rendered a youth's statement inadmissible. At the end of the case, the judge must decide whether the Crown has proven, beyond a reasonable doubt, that the youth is guilty of the offence charged.

After the lawyers have finished questioning each witness, a judge may sometimes ask a few questions by way of clarification, but judges must be cautious about this. If a judge is seen to descend into the proceedings by asking questions too often, too aggressively, or too supportively, an appeal court may overturn the verdict. Judges may find sexual assault cases particularly challenging, since the judiciary has been criticized for insensitivity to victims, especially young ones. But if a judge responds by being too supportive of a victim, or too aggressive in questioning an accused, a new trial may be ordered. In a 1996 Newfoundland case involving a teacher accused of sexually assaulting a pupil, the Court of Appeal wrote: "It is clear that while a trial judge has the right to intervene, the judge must not do so [in such a fashion] as to give the impression that he or she is aligned with one side or the other. . . . Indeed it is the duty of the trial judge to intervene to ensure the element of fairness and, in particular, to ensure that the accused person gets a fair trial."[41] Concern about the appearance of impartiality is greatest at the trial stage, in determining whether the accused is guilty of the offence charged. There is a broader scope for judicial questioning of witnesses at the sentencing stage, particularly in youth justice court where the judge is concerned not only with the interests of society but also with the needs of the youth. Judges can also take a more active role in the proceedings should an issue of mental disorder arise, especially if

---

41   R. v. Riche, [1996] N.J. No. 293 (C.A.) (QL). See also R. v. A. (J.F.) (1993), 82 C.C.C. (3d) 295 (Ont. C.A.), where a trial judge was criticized for telling an eight-year-old girl, after she testified: "Thank you. I think you were a terrific witness, one of the best I have ever seen." The appeal court was concerned that this statement might lead an observer to conclude that the judge believed the child, which would be unfair since the accused had not yet presented any evidence.

the lawyers have chosen not to raise the matter. In this situation, a judge may even decide to call a witness, usually a psychiatrist who has examined the accused, if neither lawyer will call one;[42] usually a suggestion by a judge that this type of evidence is of concern to the court will prompt the Crown to call any necessary witnesses.

Under the *YOA*, although it was not uncommon for youths to be unrepresented at disposition hearings, fortunately it was relatively rare for a youth to have a trial without a lawyer. When an accused is unrepresented, judges have a broader scope to intervene in proceedings. For example, a judge may raise issues about the inadmissibility of Crown evidence and take an active role in the questioning of witnesses. This modification of the judicial role is necessary to serve the interests of justice, especially if the unrepresented accused is an adolescent, but it places the judge in a difficult position. There is a concern, as discussed in Chapter 6, that the provision of the *YCJA* that allows for provincial governments to seek reimbursement for legal services from parents will result in more youths being unrepresented at trial. More unrepresented youths are likely to present greater challenges to youth justice court judges.

It is inherent in the judge's role that reasons for the decision be provided, so that the accused and others will understand why the court rendered a particular judgement and so that the lawyers for the parties can advise about whether the judge has made an error of law that would justify an appeal.[43] In urban communities where there are many youth justice court judges, it is possible that several different judges will deal with a youth in a single case (e.g., one at a bail hearing, others through several adjournments, and yet another at trial). If one judge starts to hear evidence in a trial, that judge must adjudicate on the issue of guilt; if that judge should die or be unable to render a decision, section 131 of the *YCJA* allows for another youth justice court judge to deal with the case; however, that judge must "recommence the trial as if no evidence had been taken." The judge who finds a youth guilty should normally also render the sentence, since that judge will know the most about the circumstances of that case. Section 131 does allow another judge to make a sentence decision after adjudication, should the trial judge be incapacitated.

---

42   Justice Hartt, "Panel Discussion: Problems in Ethics and Advocacy," [1969] Special Lectures of the Law Society of Upper Canada 279 at 314.

43   *R. v. Sheppard*, 2002 SCC 26.

D. ASSAULTS

In general, the same laws that govern the admissibility of evidence in adult court apply in youth justice court, and the substantive offences found in the *Criminal Code* and other legislation as well as the statutory and common law defences are also applicable to youths. A youth may have a defence to some offences, however, to which an adult may not. One obvious statutory example is that an adult who has sexual relations with a person under fourteen commits the offence of sexual assault even if the younger person consents (i.e., the Canadian equivalent of "statutory rape").[44] However, a youth who is no more than two years older than the younger party can raise the defence of consent to a sexual assault charge.

For an assault charge, one defence that is available to both adults and youths but that may more frequently be relevant to youths is the defence of "consent." Assault is defined as the intentional application of force to another person without their consent.[45] Those who engage in a sport, like hockey, impliedly consent to the bodily contact that is inherent in the game, a fact that gives players a degree of legal immunity for conduct that would otherwise be criminal. Yet even in the context of a hockey game, there is no implied consent to an overtly violent attack made with the intent to injure.[46]

1) The Consent Defence for Youths in "Schoolyard Scuffles"

It is not uncommon for people, especially adolescents, to engage in consensual fights. In 1991 the Supreme Court, in *R. v. Jobidon*,[47] accepted that consent could be a defence to an assault charge arising out of consensual fights; however, the Court also articulated a policy-based limitation to the consent defence that, if a fight involves adults, there can be no consent (implicit or explicit) to an assault causing bodily harm or death. Justice Gonthier indicated that the Supreme Court ruling was

> restricted to cases involving adults[;] the phenomena of the "ordinary" schoolyard scuffle, where boys or girls immaturely seek to resolve with their hands, will not [necessarily] come within the scope

---

44   *Criminal Code*, above note 1, s. 150.1.
45   *Ibid.*, s. 265(1).
46   *R. v. Le Clerc* (1991), 4 O.R. (3d) 788 (C.A.).
47   *R. v. Jobidon*, [1991] 2 S.C.R. 714.

of this limitation [that consent is no defence if there is an intent to kill or cause serious bodily harm]. . . . I would leave open the question as to whether boys or girls under the age of 18 who . . . ultimately cause more than trivial bodily harm, would be afforded the protection of a defence of consent.[48]

As the Supreme Court noted, there have been cases in which youths have been able to rely on the consent defence even if very serious harm has occurred. One was *R. v. Barron*,[49] where the accused was a student who had pushed a classmate, resulting in the classmate falling down a flight of stairs in a school, hitting his head, and dying. The court accepted that the victim had implicitly consented to the roughhousing that led to his death, and that there had been no intent by the accused to injure — let alone cause death. The accused was acquitted of a manslaughter charge.

In its 1994 decision in *R. v. W.(G.)*, the Ontario Court of Appeal articulated limitations to the consent defence for adolescents. The case arose out of a fight between two sixteen-year-old high school students. For reasons that were never explained in court, both of them were "spoiling for a fight." In front of a number of other students, they exchanged words, which led to pushes, followed by blows. The fight was brief. The accused, who was the larger of the two, landed three blows in the other's face and the fight ended when the smaller youth's nose began to bleed profusely. He required medical assistance and missed several days of school as a result of his injuries. The trial judge found that the accused had intended to cause serious harm and convicted him of assault causing bodily harm. The Ontario Court of Appeal upheld the conviction, rejecting the argument that the accused could rely on his victim's consent to fight. Justice Doherty wrote:

> It may be that, where a young person engages in a consensual fight, not intending to cause harm, the other person's consent to the fight could negate liability even if serious bodily harm occurs. . . . Where . . . an accused intends to cause serious harm to his or her opponent, the adolescence of the accused provides no policy reason for recognizing consent as a "defence" to a charge of assault causing bodily harm.
>
> [T]he fight occurred between two students at a school, during school hours, and in the presence of a number of students. Those facts . . . make my conclusions all the more compelling. Violence involving young persons within the school system is an ever-growing

---

48   *Ibid.* at 768.
49   *R. v. Barron* (1985), 48 C.R. (3d) 334 (Ont. C.A.).

concern. . . . Schools must foster mutual tolerance and respect for the physical integrity of others. Students must realize that acts of violence intended to cause serious harm, which in fact do bodily harm, will not be countenanced.[50]

These cases indicate that there may be consensual fights between adolescents, which do not result in serious injury and criminal convictions but which clearly violate school policies to maintain discipline. As a matter of social reality, if not law, there will be more situations in which adolescents as opposed to adults can rely on the defence of consent. However, if there is an intent to injure and injury does occur, adolescents will be not be able to invoke the consent defence and will be criminally liable.

2) Alternate Approaches to School Bullying

In the past few years, a significant increase about bullying and violence in schools has raised concerns and resulted in substantial changes in attitudes and policies. Many school boards have adopted zero tolerance policies, requiring suspension or expulsion of students engaging in acts of violence. Despite the rhetoric in the media and among some politicians, it is far from clear that there is *more* violence in schools than was the case a decade ago. Rather, schools are relatively safe places for adolescents.[51] It is, however, still important for schools to take steps to reduce bullying and violence in schools to make students and teachers feel safer. If students who are being victimized know that there will be a swift and effective response to their complaints about victimization, they will be more likely to report to school authorities, and violence in schools is likely to be reduced. Not every act of violence in a school, however, should result in the commencement of proceedings in youth justice court. In some cases a fight between students is truly a consensual, if immature, response to a conflict between aggressive adolescents.

While school authorities should respond to such incidents, charging youths involved is not always appropriate and, in some cases, will not result in a conviction. Even in cases in which it is clear that one

---

50   R. v. W.(G.) (1994), 18 O.R. (3d) 321 (C.A.) at 324–25. See also R. v. M.(J.), [2001] O.J. No. 3752 (C.A.).

51   See A. Doob and J. Sprott, "Is the 'Quality' of Youth Violence Becoming More Serious?" in R.M. Mann, ed., *Juvenile Crime and Delinquency: A Turn-of-the-Century Reader* (Toronto: Canadian Scholars Press, 2000); and E.P. Mulvey and E. Cauffman, "The Inherent Limits of Predicting School Violence" (2001) 56 American Psychologist 797.

student is the physical aggressor, a response through some type of mediation or extrajudicial or restorative justice may be appropriate. Students involved in a fight are likely to have a continuing relationship, and working on an approach to restore or improve that relationship may be more valuable to the victim than prosecution in court.

In some cases an assault between adolescents may be a response to verbal taunting or provocation. While this might not be a defence to an assault charge in youth justice court, it may be more appropriate for school authorities to understand the assault in its context and attempt to deal with the underlying issues than resort to the court system. The problematic nature of a criminal response may, for example, be obvious if a student who is the subject of racist comments from classmates responds by hitting one of his or her tormentors. If charges are laid and a case goes to trial, it may take months for a resolution to be reached and this process may heighten adversarial feelings. The criminal justice model is premised on an offender-victim understanding of what may be a more complex relationship: a swift, fair, school-based response may be appropriate. In more serious cases of school violence or situations in which there is a concern that violence may escalate, however, charges in youth justice court may be the most appropriate response. If charges are laid, the court may have to impose pre-trial conditions on the accused, to try to balance concerns about the protection of the alleged victim against not unduly restricting the freedom of a youth who has not yet been found guilty of an offence and is presumed innocent. School authorities are not obliged to await the completion of the youth justice court process before imposing suspension, expulsion, or school transfer, although — as discussed in Chapter 4 — they too have an obligation to treat students fairly.

E. FITNESS TO STAND TRIAL AND MENTAL DISORDER

In relatively rare cases, a youth suffers from a mental disorder that affects the youth justice court process. Because of the potentially serious legal consequences and the relative narrowness of the legal concept, issues related to mental disorders are not frequently raised prior to adjudication; typically, the emotional and psychological problems of a youth are raised at the sentencing stage. (Issues related to emotional, psychological, and mental disorders which arise at the sentencing stage, are discussed in Chapters 8 and 9.) Essentially, two issues related to mental disorders can arise prior to the completion of the adjudication of guilt or innocence. One issue — fitness to stand trial — is whether the accused has sufficient mental capacity to participate meaningfully in the court process. The other issue is whether, at the time of the commission of the offence, the accused suffered from a mental disorder of such a nature that he or she should be relieved of criminal responsibility. Although both of these issues may arise in a single case, it is also possible that only one is a concern. The legal issues that arise, as well as the mental health issues, can be complex. As one judge dealing with conflicting evidence of mental disorder noted: "psychiatry is an inexact science."[52] Assessments of mental capacity and prognosis for treatment and future dangerousness are inherently uncertain for adults, and even more so for adolescents. Mental health research and concepts developed for adults may be difficult to apply to younger, developing age groups and there is less available research related to adolescents.[53] Also, issues of cognitive development and learning disability may overlap with emotional and mental problems.

The *YCJA* takes essentially the same approach to fitness to stand trial and the disposition of "not criminally responsible due to mental disorder" as the *YOA*, with section 141 of the *YCJA* largely adopting the provisions of Part XX.I of the *Criminal Code*, with some modifications to take account of the "age and special needs" of the young person. Section 141(6) provides that parents of youths who are involved in the justice system must receive notice of hearings that raise mental disorder issues, so that the parents can attend and support their children and, if appropriate, participate in the proceedings. As discussed in Chapter 4, the concept of being unfit to stand trial refers to a situation in which an accused person lacks the capacity to participate meaningfully in the court process. If the issue of fitness arises, a youth justice court judge will usually order a psychiatric assessment under section 672.11 of the *Code*, with a presumption that the accused will remain in the community during the assessment process; the youth may, however, be detained for a total of up to sixty days to allow an assessment to be carried out. A person may be unfit at one point in time but, if his or her condition improves, may later be regarded as fit to stand trial. A court may order up to sixty days in detention in a mental health facility to allow treatment of a person found unfit to stand trial, in the hope that this may result in the person becoming fit for trial. A person found

---

52   *R. v. C.(S.A.T.)*, [1996] S.J. No. 492 (Q.B.) (QL).
53   See, for example, D. Seagrave & T. Grisso, "Adolescent Development and the Measurement of Juvenile Psychopathy" (2002) 26 Law & Human Behaviour 219.

unfit to stand trial may be discharged into the community with or without conditions, or detained indefinitely in a mental health facility, subject to periodic review of mental status.

If the accused is found fit to stand trial based on competence at the time of the proceedings, a related but distinct issue may arise, namely, whether the accused suffered from a mental disorder at the time of the offence. Since the Canadian legal system is premised on notions of moral accountability, it is considered unfair to punish people who, on account of mental disorder, were unable to appreciate the consequences of what they were doing.[54] There may be a justification for detaining them in a mental health facility if they continue to suffer from a mental disorder and pose a danger to the public. Section 16 of the *Criminal Code* provides that a person may be found "guilty but not criminally responsible by reason of mental disorder [if their condition rendered them] incapable of appreciating the nature and quality of the act [charged] or of knowing that it was wrong." If the issue of mental disorder arises, a youth justice court will invariably order an assessment of the "mental condition" of the youth under section 672.11 of the *Code*; the court may require the detention of the youth for a total of up to sixty days to allow an assessment to be carried out. Statements made by an accused for the purpose of an assessment to determine fitness to stand trial or to determine whether the accused suffered from a mental disorder at the time of the commission of the offence are directly admissible only in regard to these issues and cannot be used as part of the Crown's evidence to convict the accused, or to challenge the credibility of the accused if the accused should choose to testify.[55] In addition to a court-directed assessment, in a case in which mental disorder is an issue, counsel for the accused will invariably also retain a psychiatrist to do an assessment.

A court which finds a person guilty but not criminally responsible by reason of mental disorder will have a hearing to decide on an appropriate legal disposition, which may result in a discharge into the community, often with conditions, or an indefinite committal to a mental health

---

54 In addition to cases where the accused may have suffered from a mental disorder such as to relieve from criminal liability, the accused may raise defences based on "automatism" or "intoxication," which both reflect some form of lack of mental capacity at the time of commission of the offence. If successful, these defences will result in an acquittal. The scope of the intoxication defence was tightly restricted by the enactment of s. 33.1 of the Code in 1995 by *An Act to amend the Criminal Code (self-induced intoxication)*, S.C. 1995, c. 32, s. 1. See K. Roach, *Criminal Law*, 2d ed. (Toronto: Irwin Law, 2000), cc. 6 and 7.

55 See *R. v. G.(B.)*, [1999] 2 S.C.R. 475.

facility. A person who is detained in a hospital as a result of being found not criminally responsible on account of mental disorder is not to be subject to involuntary treatment, unless there is also a finding under provincial mental health laws that the person lacks the capacity to make a decision about treatment.[56] For a youth, the consequences of being found unfit to stand trial or not criminally responsible by reason of mental disorder can be much more serious than a finding of guilt in youth justice court. Unlike the limited custodial sentence for those found guilty in youth justice court, there may be indefinite committal. However, a youth found unfit or not criminally responsible on account of mental disorder may also be released on conditions that are similar to a youth justice court sentence in terms of control and support in the community.

The parents of the youth are to be notified of these hearings and have a right to participate. In making the decision about whether to detain the youth or release the youth, the court or review board shall impose the "least restrictive" disposition taking into consideration:

- the need to protect society from dangerous persons;
- the age, special needs and mental condition of the youth;
- the supports available to the youth in the community; and
- the desirability of reintegrating the youth into society.[57]

Review boards conduct periodic reviews of those who are detained to determine whether they pose a risk to society or may be safely released. For young persons, parents must also be notified of the review board hearings, which must be held at least once a year.[58]

Amendments to the *Criminal Code* enacted in 1992 were intended to cap the period of indefinite detention of a person found unfit to stand trial or not responsible for an offence by reason of mental disorder. The cap will be the maximum sentence that a person could face if convicted. For a young person, the cap will be the maximum sentence under the *YCJA*. Section 141(8) allows the Crown to apply to the youth justice court to allow an adult-length cap, if the youth is charged with a presumptive offence or the Crown has given notice that it intends to seek an adult-length sentence. Despite the enactment of cap provisions for both youth and adults, at the time of writing, none of these provisions had been declared in force. There is some question as to whether the federal government will ever proclaim the cap provisions in force,

---

56   See *Criminal Code*, above note 1, s. 672.55; and *Starson* v. *Swayze*, [2001] O.J. No. 2283 (Ont. C.A.).

57   *Criminal Code*, above note 1, s. 672.54.

58   *YCJA*, above note 1, s. 141(10).

although, if this occurs, the cap provisions will be retroactive and apply to those still in detention as a result of previous findings of unfitness or mental disorder. As a result, to the present time, youths found to have a mental disorder affecting their fitness to stand trial or criminal responsibility may face indefinite committal, a potentially more severe consequence than a sentence imposed under the *YCJA*. Counsel for a youth will often resist seeking a finding of mental disorder, unless a youth faces a murder charge with the prospect of life imprisonment.[59]

Cases where issues of fitness to stand trial or mental disorder arise pose special tactical and ethical problems for lawyers. Such problems may be especially acute when the client is an adolescent. A lawyer may, for example, have concerns about taking instructions from a client who appears to lack the capacity to understand the nature of the proceedings or their consequences. Sometimes a client who appears mentally disordered will instruct his or her counsel to resist raising issues related to their condition. This might draw on fears of stigmatization, or might relate to the consequences of a finding of mental disorder being more severe than a conviction. The resistance to being labelled mentally disordered can also be a symptom of being mentally ill.

The ethical rules governing lawyers do not explicitly deal with these complex situations. It would appear that if a lawyer doubts the capacity of an adolescent client to provide instructions, the lawyer should consult parents, mental health professionals, and others who know the client to help form an opinion about the client's capacity. Ultimately, if the lawyer believes that a client lacks capacity, it is not unethical for the lawyer to raise the questions of fitness to stand trial or mental disorder, despite the client instructing the lawyer not to do so.[60]

---

59   *R. v. C.(S.A.T.)*, above note 52: transferred fourteen-year-old youth facing murder charge found guilty but not criminally responsible by reason of mental disorder.

60   See A.S. Manson, "Observations from an Ethical Perspective on Fitness, Insanity and Confidentiality" (1982) 27 McGill L.J. 196; and M. Proulx and D. Layton, *Ethics and Canadian Criminal Law* (Toronto: Irwin Law, 2001) 151–58. This can be very problematic, however, as illustrated in the celebrated Morin case. Morin was charged with murdering a nine-year-old girl and denied guilt, although the police had some circumstantial evidence of guilt. His lawyer at trial, despite Morin's objection, introduced psychiatric evidence that Morin was a schizophrenic capable of committing the murder and suppressing the memory. Although Morin was acquitted at the first trial, this psychiatric evidence convinced police and prosecutors of Morin's guilt and, after a Crown appeal, he was retried and convicted, serving several years in jail before DNA evidence established his innocence. Morin was profoundly critical of his lawyer at the first trial, maintaining — rightly as it turned out — that he was both innocent and sane. See K. Makin, "Hostility Erupts at Morin Probe," *Globe and Mail*, February 14, 1997: A1.

Even if the defence does not raise the issue, the Crown prosecutor or judge may raise the issue of fitness to stand trial; if necessary, a judge may even call witnesses to resolve an issue of fitness to stand trial. The Crown prosecutor may also raise the issue of an accused not being criminally responsible owing to mental disorder, even if the accused fails to do so. However, if the accused is fit to stand trial, the Crown can only do this after the accused has been found guilty.[61]

F. APPEALS: SECTION 37

Under the *Juvenile Delinquents Act*, the appeal of a decision of a juvenile court was discouraged, requiring special leave (i.e., permission) to establish that the appeal was "essential in the public interest or for the due administration of justice."[62] This restrictive approach was premised on the view that it was important to have a speedy, final resolution of cases involving adolescent offenders. Section 27 of the YOA changed the approach of the *Juvenile Delinquents Act*, recognizing that unless there is a conviction in accordance with the correct legal principles, there is no "offender." The YOA granted youths the same rights of appeal as those applicable to adults. Section 37 of the YCJA continues the general approach of the YOA on this issue, affording rights of appeal that are similar to those afforded to adults.

Under section 37 of the YCJA, if an offence is summary — or a hybrid offence for which the Crown made no election — there is a right of appeal from a final adjudication or sentence[63] of a youth justice court to a judge of the superior trial court, and then to the provincial Court of Appeal.[64] If the offence is indictable, or hybrid where the Crown has elected to treat it as indictable, the appeal is directly to the Court of Appeal. There is the possibility of appeal to the Supreme Court of Canada from the decision of a provincial Court of Appeal in regard to a youth justice court proceeding but only with leave of the Supreme Court.[65] The decision about whether to grant leave, or permission, to

---

61   *R. v. Swain*, [1991] 1 S.C.R. 933.

62   *Juvenile Delinquents Act*, above note 4, s. 37.

63   The *YCJA*, above note 1, s. 37(11) provides that there is no appeal from a sentence review under ss. 59 and 94 to 96.

64   If a province chooses to have the superior court designated as a youth justice court, then even for summary offences the appeal is directly to the Court of Appeal.

65   *Criminal Code*, above note 1, s. 691, *YCJA*, above note 1, s. 37(10).

appeal is made by a panel of three members of the Supreme Court, based on documents filed by the lawyers for the parties. Because of the desire for an expeditious and final resolution of cases involving adolescents and the relatively short sentences that they face compared to adults, the Supreme Court may be reluctant to grant leave to appeal in cases under the *YCJA*.[66] Experience under the *YOA* makes clear that the Supreme Court will grant leave to appeal in youth justice cases that raise important legal issues that may affect a significant number of youths.

Appeals do not involve a full rehearing of the evidence in a case but only a review of the transcript to find if there has been an error of law. However, in regard to sentence appeals, especially those related to young offenders who are in custody, appellate courts are generally willing to receive information concerning the progress of the youth in custody and they may take account of this to reduce a sentence.[67]

G. PRIVACY AND PUBLICITY

In keeping with the principles of section 3 of the *YCJA* that emphasize the limited accountability and rehabilitation of young offenders, the Act has a number of provisions intended to protect the privacy of young persons involved in the youth justice system. These provisions are intended to reduce the stigmatization of adolescent offenders and thus reduce the risk of reoffending. Justice Binnie in the Supreme Court of Canada in *Re F.N.* observed that: "stigmatization or premature 'labelling' of a young offender still in his or her formative years is well understood as a problem in the juvenile justice system. A young person once stigmatized as a lawbreaker may, unless given help and redirection, render the stigma a self-fulfilling prophecy. In the long run, society is best protected by preventing recurrence."[68] The sections of the *YCJA* that protect the privacy of youths are similar to provisions in the *YOA*, by restricting access to records and the disclosure of information relating to youths involved in the justice system, and generally prohibiting the publication in the media of identifying information about adolescents involved in the youthful offences. Those who violate the protection of privacy provisions may be subject to prosecution.

---

66   See comments of Supreme Court discouraging the granting of leave in such cases: *R. v. C.(T.L.)*, [1994] 2 S.C.R. 1012.

67   See, for example, *R. v. D.(S.)* (7 December 1992), (Ont. C.A.) [unreported] [summarized (1992), 18 W.C.B. (2d) 167].

68   *Re F.N.*, [2000] 1 S.C.R. 880 at para. 14.

Politicians who violate these provisions by identifying a young offender in the legislature or Parliament might not be subject to prosecution
on the defence of "Parliamentary privilege," but they may suffer political consequences for disregarding the interests of youth.[69]

Section 12 of the old *Juvenile Delinquents Act*, while less detailed
than the provisions of the *YOA*, also required that juvenile court hearings were to be held "without publicity" and without the public in
attendance.[70] Because of the history of protection of privacy for adolescent offenders, there is little Canadian experience with publication of
identifying information about youths. However, available research
from the United States, where some states allow for the publication of
the identity of adolescents in the juvenile courts, indicates that rehabilitation of young offenders can be significantly hindered if their identities are publicized.[71] Identifying publicity can increase a youth's
self-perception as an offender, disrupt the ability of a youth's family to
provide support, and negatively affect interaction with peers, teachers,
and the surrounding community.

Soon after it was enacted, the constitutionality of the privacy provisions of the *YOA* was challenged as a violation of freedom of the press
by a major Canadian newspaper chain. In *Southam Inc.* v. *R.*,[72] the
Ontario Court of Appeal upheld the validity of sections 38 and 39, noting that these provisions do not constitute a complete ban on media
reporting but restrict it in a limited fashion by preventing the media
from reporting information that would serve to identify a youth being
dealt with under the *YOA*. Expert testimony was presented about the
desirability of a ban on the publication of identifying information in
terms of the rehabilitation of youths, and the Court of Appeal accepted
that this was an objective of "superordinate importance" which justified
a restraint on freedom of the media. The importance of the media as
"representatives of the community" has, however, been recognized. The
media can give the public significant information about the youth justice courts and, accordingly, if a reporter learns of a youth justice court

---

69   "Ontario Throne Speech Investigation Clears Runciman," *Globe and Mail*, July
     25, 1998.

70   See *C.B.* v. *R.*, [1981] 2 S.C.R. 480.

71   D.C. Howard, J.T. Grisso, and R. Neems, "Publicity and Juvenile Court
     Proceedings" (1977) 11 Clearinghouse Review 203; and K.M. Laubenstein,
     "Media Access to Juvenile Justice: Should Freedom of the Press Be Limited to
     Promote Rehabilitation of Young Offenders?" (1995) 68 Temple L.Rev. 1897.

72   *Southam Inc.* v. *R.*(1984), 48 O.R. (2d) 678 (H.C.J.), aff'd (1986), 53 O.R. (2d)
     663 (C.A.).

proceeding but has not attended, the reporter should ordinarily be viewed as a person with a "valid interest" in the proceedings and given access to the transcript pursuant to section 119 of the *YCJA* in order to permit reporting of the proceedings, without identifying the youth.

The privacy provisions of Canadian youth justice laws remain controversial with some justice system professionals as well as with the public and the media. Some professionals feel unduly constrained in carrying out their jobs by these provisions, in particular by the provisions that may prevent the sharing of information with other professionals. Members of the public tend to criticize the prohibitions on publication of identifying information, expressing a concern that they may promote a lack of accountability among young offenders, as well as about their inability to protect themselves from offenders if they do not know their identity. The media tend to view these provisions as an unwelcome restraint on freedom of the press.[73]

Amendments to the *YOA* were intended to make it easier for professionals to share information and allow disclosure, in limited circumstances, of information about potentially dangerous young offenders. The *YCJA* makes some further changes that expand the scope for the disclosure of certain types of information by professionals as well as allowing for the publication of identifying information about serious violent offenders in a broader range of situations. Even so, there remain very significant differences between the treatment afforded adults and that afforded young persons in regard to the protection of privacy.

Two important related concepts in the area of protection of privacy are "disclosure" and "publication." Both are defined in section 2 of the *YCJA*, where "publication" means "the communication of information by making it known or accessible to the general public through any means, including print, radio or television broadcasting [or such] electronic means" as the Internet. "Disclosure" is defined to mean the "communication of information other than by way of publication" and may for example occur if one professional shares information about a youth involved with another professional by sending a letter or document, or by means of an oral conversation. While section 110 in general *prohibits* the publication of *identifying* information in the media about youths involved in the youth justice system, sections 113–129 restrict the disclosure of any information about youths in the justice system.

---

73   See, for example, Editorial, "Young offenders and the power of the press," *Globe and Mail*, February 10, 2000: A14.

1) Prohibition on Publication: Section 110

Section 110(1) prohibits the publication of *identifying* information about youths involved in the justice system, although the media can and do publish information about youths involved in the justice system without naming them or otherwise identifying them. Section 110(2)–(6) creates some important exceptions that allow the media to name and otherwise identify youths who are being dealt with under the Act. The publication of identifying information is permitted:

- if a young person is convicted and receives an adult sentence (s. 110(2)(a));
- if a young person is convicted of a one of the very serious "presumptive offences" and not subject to an adult sentence, publication of identification information may be permitted, but this is subject to judicial control (s. 110(2)(b));
- if the publication is made "in the course of the administration of justice, if it is not the purpose of the publication to make the information known in the community" (s. 110(2)(c));
- if the young person has reached the age of eighteen and is not in youth custody, and publishes or permits to be published identifying information (s. 110(3));
- if an order is made by a youth justice court allowing publication because a youth is at large and is believed to be a "danger to others" and that the publication of the name, photo or other identifying information would "assist in apprehending the young person" (s. 110(4)); and
- if a young person obtains an order from a youth justice court permitting the publication of identifying information on the basis that this would "not be contrary to the young person's best interests or the public interest" (s. 110(6)).

Some of these statutory exceptions to the prohibition of identifying information in the *YCJA* are very similar to those in the *YOA*.

Section 110(2)(c) of the *YCJA* allows for the publication of information "in the course of the administration of justice, if it is not the purpose of the publication to make the information known in the community." This is virtually identical to section 38(1.1) of the *YOA*. This provision makes clear that police officers, court clerks, and others involved in the administration of justice may make limited disclosures of the identity of a youth involved in the justice system to members of the public. It allows a court clerk to announce in a public waiting room the name of a young person who is being called into the youth justice court. Section 110(2)(c) may also, for example, allow for the disclosure of a youth court record or other document, such as a pre-sentence report, to an assessor who is preparing a report for use by a family court in a custody dispute between the parents of the youth. The disclosure of information about the youth's offending and the pre-sentence report to the assessor might ultimately help the family court judge to make a more informed decision about the young person or a sibling.[74] If such a disclosure is necessary for the understanding of the needs of a child, it is permitted, even though this might result in the creation of other documents (i.e., a custody assessor's report) that might make reference to the involvement of a youth in the justice system and that might find their way into public files. Even in this situation, however, the publication of any identifying information to a broader community — for example, through a law report — is prohibited by the YCJA. A law report about such a family court decision could therefore only use the initials of the parties.

In addition to section 110(2)(c) of the YCJA, section 125 has additional, more explicit provisions protecting police officers who may disclose information about youth involved in the justice system in the course of conducting an investigation, and Crown prosecutors who may disclose such information in the course of a prosecution.

Section 110(4) of the YCJA allows police officers to apply to the youth justice court for a order permitting the media to publish information about the identity of youths who are at large and who are believed to "pose a danger," if the publication of such information is "necessary to assist in apprehending the young person." If an order is made under section 110(4), it ceases to have effect after five days.[75] Section 110(4) of the YCJA is modelled on section 38(1.2) of the YOA. In R. v. N.(K.),[76] Kimelman A.C.J.M. held that to obtain an order under section 38(1.2) the police must satisfy the court that all "reasonable and continuing efforts" to locate the youth have been exhausted without publication, and there is a perceived necessity to publicize the youth's identity.

One example of the effective and appropriate use of an order under this provision involved an Ontario youth who had escaped from youth

---

74   L.(R.) v. D.(E.) (2000), 52 O.R. (3d) 537 (Ont Ct. J.). See also D.(M.) v. R. (1998), 40 R.F.L. (4th), (Ont. Prov. Ct.) where a young offender's records were released to that youth's father and an assessor for possible use in a custody dispute between the custodial parents of an eleven-year-old child, after the young offender committed several acts of violence against that child and mother while residing with them.

75   YCJA, above note 1, s. 110(5).

76   R. v. N.(K.) (1989), 51 C.C.C. (3d) 404 (Man. Prov. Ct.).

custody in 1995. The police made efforts to locate the youth over the next two years. In 1997 the Ontario Provincial Police obtained an order under section 38(1.2) of the YOA to get permission to release identifying information to the media. The youth turned himself in the day after the court order and identifying information was made public.[77]

Section 110(2)(a) of the YCJA allows for the publication of identifying information about a young person who has been convicted and received an adult sentence. This provision is similar to section 38(1)(a) of the YOA, which allowed for the publication of identifying information about a youth transferred to adult court. However, under the YOA, such publication could occur as soon as the pre-adjudication transfer order was made, which could result in identifying publicity about trials involving adolescents, even if the youths were acquitted or only convicted of a less serious charge than the original charge. Under the YCJA, publication under section 110(2)(a) is only to occur after conviction and after a decision is made that the case is so serious as to merit an adult sentence.

Section 110(2)(b) of the Act is the significant change to the publication regime of the YOA, allowing for the publication of identifying information about young offenders who have committed very serious offences but who are not subject to adult sanction. The enactment of this provision is a response to the demands for greater accountability of young offenders and to the demands for more public access to information about those youth who have committed the most serious offences. Such publication is only permitted, however, after there is a conviction. Section 110(2)(b) is generally applicable only when a youth fourteen years of age or older at the time of the offence is convicted of a "presumptive offence," which is defined in section 2(1) of the YCJA as a conviction for murder, attempted murder, manslaughter, aggravated sexual assault, or a third "serious violent offence." When there is prosecution for a presumptive offence, at any stage of the proceedings the Crown prosecutor may give notice that it will not be seeking an adult sentence, in which case section 65 also requires that the youth justice court must impose a ban on the publication of identifying information. Even if there is a conviction for one of the very serious presumptive offences, the publication of identifying information can be prevented by a decision of the Crown prosecutor or a youth jus-

---

77 See "Police Seek Help Tracking Teenager on the Lam," *Kingston Whig-Standard*, March 5, 1997; and "Wanted Teenager Turns Himself in," *Kingston Whig-Standard*, March 6, 1997.

tice court judge. Section 110(2)(b) may also apply if a youth is fourteen years or older and convicted of any indictable offence for which an adult could receive a sentence of longer than two years and the Crown prosecutor has given notice before trial that an adult sentence will be sought.

If there is a conviction in either of these two situations, the youth justice court must decide whether an adult sentence should be imposed. If an adult sentence is to be imposed, then section 110(2)(a) allows for the publication of identifying information. If the court decides not to impose an adult sentence, then either the Crown prosecutor or the young person may apply for an order under section 75(3) prohibiting the publication of identifying information. The judge is obliged under section 75(1) to ask if such an order is to be requested, but if there is no application for a publication ban, then the media is free to publish identifying information about the young offender, even if an adult sentence is not imposed.

If a order is sought prohibiting the publication of identifying information, the youth justice court judge must hold an inquiry under section 75(3) to decide whether it is "appropriate in the circumstances, taking into account the importance of rehabilitating the young person and the public interest." Section 75(3) does not provide much guidance about how the youth justice court judge should balance concerns about rehabilitation and the "public interest." The concept of the "public interest" is ambiguous. Among some members of the public there is a considerable degree of concern and interest in learning the identities of young offenders who commit serious offences, even if they do not receive adult sentences. It is, however, submitted that the public interest is broader than the interest or curiosity of members of the public.

The interpretation of the concept of the "public interest" and section 75(3) should be guided by the Declaration of Principle, section 3 of the YCJA, which recognizes the principles of limited accountability and protection of privacy for youths. Section 3 also recognizes the importance of ensuring that there are meaningful consequences for young offenders, but it stresses the importance of rehabilitation and reintegration of young offenders into society as the best way to promote the long-term protection of society. The available research strongly suggests that rehabilitation is more likely to be achieved if young offenders are not identified in the media. It is submitted that, in cases in which a judge has decided under section 72 that accountability concerns do *not* require the imposition of an adult sentence, the principles articulated in section 3 of the YCJA will ordinarily suggest that the youth justice court should not allow the publication of identifying information.

One situation where it might be appropriate to allow for the publication of identifying information under section 75(3), despite the fact that a youth sentence has been imposed, is when the youth has already been publicly identified as a result of an order under section 110(4) as a youth at large and posing a danger to the public. In this situation, the public would likely have a concern about the outcome of the case involving a specific, known young person and there would be limited harm to the youth from further identification. As discussed below, if there is a concern that the presence of a particular young offender in the community poses a risk of serious harm, section 127 of the *YCJA* permits an order to be obtained from the youth justice court to allow disclosure of information to specified persons, such as the neighbours of a young offender who is being released into the community. The provisions of the *YCJA* that deal with presumptive offences and adult sentences, more fully discussed in Chapter 9, are complex.

2) Protecting the Privacy of Young Victims: Section 111

It is not only youthful offenders but also child and youth victims whose privacy is protected by the *YCJA*. With some exceptions, section 111(1) of the *YCJA* prohibits the publication of information that would identify "any child or young person" as the victim of an offence or an alleged offence committed by a young person, or who is a witness in connection with such an offence. This provision recognizes the vulnerability of children and youths who may have been victimized and attempts to protect them from the glare of publicity and possible embarrassment or stigmatization in the community.

Section 38 of the *YOA* also prohibited the publication of information that would identify children or youths involved as victims or witnesses in the youth justice system. That provision, however, allowed for no exceptions. In *R. v. Thompson Canada Ltd.*[78] a newspaper was prosecuted for violating section 38 of the *YOA* by publishing pictures and identifying information about two older adolescents who were victimized in a school shooting. The stories concerned the acknowledgement within their community of their suffering and bravery, and described the recovery of one of the youths who had been very seriously injured in the shooting. The stories were published with the permission of the youths and their parents. Justice Agrios of the Alberta Court

---

78   *R. v. Thompson Canada Ltd.*, [2001] A.J. No. 1544 (Alta. Q.B.).

of Queen's Bench recognized that some restrictions on the publication of identifying information about child and adolescent victims could be a constitutionally justifiable restraint on freedom of the press.

With youthful offenders, there is a body of published research — albeit American — which indicates that the publication of identifying information may negatively affect their rehabilitation. There are no research studies on the harmful effects on victims of crime of being identified in the media. While concerns about the protection of privacy and the vulnerability of children support a prohibition on the publication of identifying information about child and adolescent victims without the consent of a court or their parents, in the absence of empirical evidence that youth who are victimized suffer from the publication of identifying information, the portion of section 38 of the *YOA* that prohibited this type of publication was held by Agrios J. to be unduly restrictive and, hence, unconstitutional.

Section 111 of the *YCJA* provides for broader exceptions than section 38 of the *YOA* to the restrictions on the publication of identifying information about child and adolescent victims and witnesses. Section 111(2) allows such information to be published with the consent of the parents of a child or young person who is under eighteen years or who has died. A person who has reached adulthood and was a victim or witness while a youth may also consent to the publication of identifying information about his or her involvement in the youth justice system as a victim or witness.

Section 111(3) allows a child or young person who is a victim or witness to apply to a youth justice court to permit the publication of identifying information. This provision is intended to deal with a situation where parents are unwilling or unavailable to consent to the publication of such information. The court is only to permit publication of identifying information if satisfied that this "would not be contrary to his or her best interests or the public interest." The circumstances in which a parent refuses to consent to the disclosure of identifying information that is deemed to be in the best interests of his or her child and the public interest are presumably narrow, but might, for example, arise if a child was victimized by other family members and wants his or her identity revealed. Even in this situation, an aspect of the public interest would require the court to also consider the privacy interests of any young person who has committed, or is alleged to have committed, an offence and who might be identified as a result of the publication.

In comparison to the *YOA*, sections 111(2) and (3) of the *YCJA* modestly expand the scope for publication of identifying information about child and adolescent victims. The decision in *R. v. Thompson*

Canada Ltd. would suggest that section 111(2) and (3) provide a constitutionally adequate balance between the concerns about the protection of the privacy of child and youth victims with freedom of the press.

3) Public Access to the Youth Justice Court: Section 132

Section 132 of the *YCJA* provides that while youth justice court proceedings are generally open to the public, the judge may make an order excluding some or all members of the public if their presence "would be seriously injurious or seriously prejudicial" to a young person accused of an offence or to a child or youth who is a witness. This provision of the *YCJA* essentially replicates section 39 of the *YOA*.

There is a presumption in favour of having youth justice court proceedings open to the public, and there is an onus on the person seeking exclusion of the public to demonstrate some likelihood of harm, perhaps by calling expert evidence. Youth justice court judges will not, for example, exclude the public merely because a youth is facing serious charges in a relatively small community, even though open proceedings may make it likely that his identity will become known within the immediate community.[79] This accords with the public interest in having access to the court system and open trials. In general, people such as friends and neighbours of an alleged victim or the accused as well as members of the public have the right to attend court and see that justice is done.[80]

The youth justice court also has the power under section 132 (1)(b) to exclude members of the public and potential witnesses, other than the accused youth and a parent, from all or part of the proceedings where this "would be in the interest of . . . [the] administration of justice." Under the *YOA*, this provision[81] was generally invoked to exclude persons who will be witnesses prior to their testifying, so that they will not be influenced by what other witnesses may say. It may also, for example, be invoked to exclude members of the media during a *voir dire* into the admissibility of a confession, since the evidence in such a hearing should not be reported even without identifying the youth.[82]

---

79   *R. v. S.(M.)* (November 26, 1984) (Ont. Prov. Ct. (Fam. Div.)) [unreported] [summarized (1984), 13 W.C.B. 192].

80   See, for example, *N.S. (A.G.) v. MacIntyre* (1982), 40 N.R. 181 (S.C.C.).

81   *YOA*, above note 3 (1982), s. 39(1)(b).

82   *Southam Inc. v. R.*, above note 72.

Section 132(1)(b) may also be invoked by the judge to exclude members of the public when a child or adolescent witness, including the accused young person, is actually testifying. Children and adolescents may feel intimidated, or at least more reticent, in the presence of a significant number of strangers. In some cases, exclusion of members of the public during the testimony of a child or young person may be necessary for the administration of justice to ensure that this vulnerable witness can fully communicate his or her evidence to the court.[83] A judge may exclude from the court an accused youth who disrupts the proceedings under section 650 of the *Code*. A person who disrupts court proceedings may also be charged with contempt of court.

4) Disclosure of Youth Records

Sections 113 to 129 of the *YCJA* govern the records relating to young offenders kept by the police, youth justice courts, probation offices, and correctional services, as well as records of other agencies to the extent that they are administering sentences or related to the youth justice court process. These provisions restrict access to records and control the disclosure of information contained in those records. They are intended to reflect the principles of "limited accountability" and "protection of the privacy" of youth that are in section 3 of the Act, and thereby to minimize the stigmatization of youths and increase the likelihood of their rehabilitation. The record-keeping and non-disclosure provisions of the *YCJA* are similar to those in the *YOA*, although there have been some changes. Some of the provisions of the original *YOA* that dealt with records and non-disclosure provisions were amended in the late 1980s and 1990s in order to facilitate the sharing of information among professionals.

A host of minor changes have been introduced with the records and non-disclosure provisions of the *YCJA*, some of which may actually serve to increase the protection of the privacy of youth, such as section 119(2)(c), which allows access to records relating to a case that is dismissed without trial for only two months, compared to twelve months under the *YOA*. Most of the changes in the *YCJA*, however, are intended to allow for longer retention of records of serious offenders and to

---

83   For a number of offences involving sexual or physical violence, a youth justice court may also invoke s. 486(2.1) of the *Criminal Code*, above note 1, to allow a child or adolescent witness to testify from behind a screen or through closed-circuit television, if this is considered "necessary to obtain a full and candid account of the acts" alleged to have occurred.

facilitate the sharing of information among professionals who work with adolescents. The *YCJA* expands access to youth records while still recognizing the limited accountability of young persons and affording a second chance to those adolescents found guilty of criminal offences.

Sections 113 to 129 identify and govern a range of records kept by police, Crown prosecutors, youth justice courts, youth probation and corrections services, and other agencies involved in the supervision of young persons being dealt with under the *YCJA*. Access to these records is restricted, and it is an offence punishable under section 138 of the *YCJA* to improperly disclose the records or information contained in them. The Act defines a period during which there can be access to a record by specified persons. After that statutory period, in general there can be no access to the record, and no use can be made of the fact that the youth was convicted of that offence. The access period depends on the nature and disposition of the offence, the type of record and whether there is later offending. The access periods set out in section 119(2) include:

- if extrajudicial sanctions are used, two years from the date that the youth consented to be subject to the sanction (s. 119(2)(a));
- if the youth is acquitted after a trial, two months from the date that the period for filing an appeal expired, and if there is an appeal three months from the completion of all proceedings (s. 119(2)(b));
- if the Crown withdraws the charges, two months from the date of withdrawal, and if the court stays the charges, one year after the stay is entered (ss. 119(2)(c)–(d));
- if the youth is convicted and a reprimand is given, two months from the finding of guilt and if absolute discharge is imposed one year from the finding of guilt (ss. 119(2)(c)–(e));
- if the youth is convicted of a summary offence, then three years after completion of the sentence, and if convicted of an indictable offence then five years from the date of completion of the sentence (ss. 119(2)(g)–(h));
- if the youth is convicted of a presumptive offence, then there are provisions that allow for indefinite retention and use of the records within the justice system (s. 120);
- if the youth receives an adult sentence, then the records related to that offence are treated as adult records (s. 117).

There are limited circumstances in which records can be retained and accessed after the passage of these statutory periods. Sections 119(2)(i)–(j) provide that if a youth is convicted of a further offence in youth justice court, then the original records of conviction may be retained and accessed for a further period of three years for a summary offence and a further five-year period for an indictable offence. Section 119(9) of the *YCJA* provides that, if a youth commits a further offence after becoming an adult — before the period of accessibility of the youth record has expired — then the youth record is to be treated as an adult record and may be retained indefinitely unless there is an adult pardon.

While the *YCJA* provides that, in general, no use can be made of a youth record after the statutory non-disclosure period, there is no requirement that there be a physical destruction or electronic deletion of such records, except where section 128 requires that a youth's record of conviction must be purged after the specified period from the computerized central Canadian Police Information Centre record which is maintained by the RCMP.

After the statutory period for permissible access and use, section 123(1)(a) of the *YCJA* gives a youth justice court judge a narrow jurisdiction to permit the use of documents or records related to a young offender, if satisfied that this is a "valid and substantial interest" in the record and the disclosure is "in the interest of the proper administration of justice." Section 123(2) makes clear that disclosure under section 123(1)(a) is "only for the purpose of investigating [an offence believed to have been] committed against a young person" while the young person was serving a sentence. This provision is limited and is intended to be used in situations where there is an investigation of possible abuse by staff in a correctional facility.[84] Section 123(1)(b) also allows a youth justice court to permit disclosure of youth justice court

---

84 In *R. v. McKay*, [1996] B.C.J. No. 1019 (C.A.) (QL), Prowse J.A. ruled that it was permissible for a judge sentencing an offender in adult court to take account of a prior youth court record that was more than five years old (then the relevant statutory period under the *YOA*, above note 9), and upheld a ruling of a youth court judge to permit disclosure of the record under s. 45.1(1) of that Act, which also permitted disclosure where it is in the "interest of the proper administration of justice." She was concerned that the prior record, which related to a serious offence, should not be ignored, and noted that 1995 amendments to the Act record provisions "reflected Parliament's intention to readjust the balance between the rights and interests of young persons and the interests of society by favouring more disclosure, albeit in limited circumstances." Justice Southin, in dissent, argued that allowing disclosure after the expiry of the statutory period rendered s. 45(4) virtually meaningless; this approach seems more consistent with the principles of the *YOA*. Ss. 123(1)(a) and (2)of the *YCJA*, above note 1, is consistent with the dissenting approach of Southin J.A., narrowly restricting the use of a youth record after the expiry of the statutory crime-free period.

records or other records relating to young offenders if this is considered "desirable in the public interest for research or statistical purposes."

The *YCJA* prohibits disclosure of information in records related to the investigation of offences believed to have been committed by youths, to youth justice court records, and to records related to young offenders. These provisions in general prohibit the disclosure of records or information to members of the public and to professionals not involved in the justice system. There are a significant number of exceptions to these rules which are intended to facilitate the administration of justice, meet the needs of victims, recognize the interests of victims, and protect public safety, as well as for purposes of research and gathering statistics. During the period of permitted use, there are a number of provisions in the *YCJA* to allow sharing of information and disclosure of records by professionals. Unless permitted by the Act, however, disclosure of a youth record or sharing of information in such a record is an offence under section 138 of the Act.

Police officers have significant authority to release information in the course of their duties. Section 125(1) of the *YCJA* allows for the disclosure of information by police concerning a young person before the courts if such information is "necessary to disclose in the conduct of the investigation of an offence." Section 125(4) allows a police officer to disclose information concerning a crime believed to have been committed by a youth to the representative of an insurance company that is investigating a claim arising out of the offence. Crown prosecutors are permitted under section 125(2) to disclose information in court records or police files concerning a young person to a co-accused or the lawyer for a co-accused. A prosecutor may also disclose information about a suspected or convicted young offender to an accused person if that youth is going to be a witness against that accused. (See also s. 119(1)(q).) Consistent with the *Charter*, section 125(2) gives priority to ensuring a fair trial for accused persons over concerns over the protection of the privacy of youth.

Section 119 allows a range of judicial and government officials working in the youth justice and corrections systems to have access to information to allow them to deal effectively with a young person. This section also permits disclosure of information about a young person to individuals who are participating in a conference or in the administration of extrajudicial measures for the youth. There are also provisions to allow youths, and their parents and lawyers, as well as victims to have access to records and to obtain disclosure of information.[85]

---

85   *YCJA*, above note 1, ss. 119(1)(a), (b), (d), & (e), and 124.

Section 125(6) allows a Crown prosecutor, a police officer, a provincial director, or a youth worker to disclose information, without prior court approval, about a young person being dealt with in the youth justice system to a "professional or any other person engaged in the supervision or care of a young person" including representatives of a school board or other educational or training institution if the disclosure is considered necessary:

- to ensure compliance by the youth with an order of the youth justice court, such as the term of judicial interim release or probation, or with the terms of a reintegration leave under section 91;
- to ensure the safety of staff, students or other persons; or
- to facilitate the rehabilitation of the young person.

Section 127(7) provides that information released to a school board or other agency under section 125(6) must be kept confidential within the institution, including the requirement that the information about youth offending is to be kept separate from other information, such as the student's academic record, and that the records are actually to be destroyed when "no longer required for the purpose for which it was disclosed." Thus, for example, if information is sent to a school so that the principal can report on a probation term that required school attendance, then any records at the school related to the youth justice court sentence would have to be destroyed once the sentence is completed. School officials are also required to ensure that the information is only released to employees who need this "for the purposes for which it was disclosed."

In Re F.N.,[86] the Supreme Court of Canada held that section 38(1.13) of the YOA, which is virtually identical to section 125(6) of the YCJA, was not broad enough to permit the circulation to a school board of the youth court dockets that provide information about all young persons in the community involved in the youth justice system. Justice Binnie recognized that, in some cases, schools will be involved under what is now section 125(6)(a) with ensuring compliance with a court order, acknowledging that:

> School boards do have a legitimate interest in knowing of members of its student body that could present a danger to themselves or others. The schools may well desire the information for their own purposes. . . . timely information from the Youth Court has in the past assisted schools . . . to address legitimate safety concerns, including

---

86   *Re F.N.*, above note 68.

assignment of a student assistant to monitor a student charged with arson to ensure no incidents of arson occurred; preparation of risk assessments in cases where students have been charged with serious violent offences; placement of a student in another school after an attack on a classmate to reduce the risk of further assault or confrontation; and restriction of a student's movement within a school so as to reduce the safety risk to other students.[87]

On the other hand, Justice Binnie also acknowledged that there are many non-violent offences for which there may be no issue of ensuring "compliance" with a court order and for which there are no safety concerns to justify disclosure of information to schools: "With respect to safety . . . young persons charged with offences such as shoplifting, which ordinarily would not raise safety concerns at all, should be . . . excluded from the general distribution to school boards linking specific accused with specific offences."[88]

Because of the similarity of the *YCJA* record provisions to those of the *YOA*, the Supreme Court ruling in *Re F.N.* will be highly persuasive in interpreting the *YCJA*. The judgment allows for the implementation of a notification procedure tailored to safety issues but not for blanket distribution to a school about information about all of its students involved in the youth justice system.

Section 127(1) of the *YCJA* allows for the police, a Crown prosecutor or a provincial director to apply to a youth justice court to permit the disclosure of information about a young offender who is in the community if the court is satisfied that this is necessary and the court is satisfied that:

- the youth has been found guilty of an offence involving "serious personal injury;"
- the youth poses "a risk of serious harm" to other persons; and
- the disclosure of the information is "relevant to the avoidance of that risk."

Section 127(1) allows for the disclosure of information about a specific young offender to members of the community, so that those who are informed about the youth and the record of offending might take steps to reduce the likelihood of further offending or victimization. This provision is based on a 1995 amendment to the *YOA* that was intended to address the criticisms of politicians and members of the public that arose after one highly publicized case in British Columbia,

---

87   *Ibid.* at paras. 35 and 53.
88   *Ibid.* at para. 51.

in which a young sex offender who had been released into the community from custody on probation sexually assaulted and killed a neighbourhood child.[89] There has, however, been no reported use of this provision of the YOA.[90] The lack of use of this provision may reflect how difficult it is to establish that there is a "risk of serious harm" *and* that notifying a specific individual or group of individuals would be "relevant to the avoidance of that risk."

While professionals who are counselling or working with youths who have a history of violence should have adequate access to information about them, it may be difficult to establish that public safety will actually be increased if more information about specific young offenders is made available in the community. Such public release of information can lead to more negative stereotyping and to labelling of young offenders within their communities, making rehabilitation more difficult as a result. Once neighbours or fellow students are warned about a particular youth, meaningful reintegration into the community may be much more difficult. Young offenders who are ostracized by neighbours may feel compelled to move away from their community and family supports, and to seek anonymity in large urban centres, making rehabilitation much more difficult to achieve. The American experience with these types of "public warning" provisions suggests that they may often be counterproductive in terms of producing safer communities.[91]

Section 119(1)(s)(ii) allows for an application to be made to a youth justice court to permit disclosure of information to "any person or member of a class of persons," if the judge is satisfied that access to the record is "desirable in the interest of the proper administration of justice." Given the broad prohibitions on the disclosure of information and the extensive enumerated list of exceptions, it is submitted that this provision should be interpreted narrowly. Although not explicitly

---

89   See, for example, "Tracking Young Sex Predators," *Vancouver Province*, March 31, 1994.

90   *YOA*, above note 9 (1995), s. 38(1.5).

91   See, for example, P. Davis, "The Sex Offender Next Door," *New York Times Magazine*, July 28, 1996: 20 and "Whitman Latest to Urge Laws on Notices of Sex Offenders," *New York Times*, August 6, 1994: 24, reporting on the Washington State notification scheme for adult sex offenders, which has three levels of community notification depending on the offender's record and the likelihood of recurrence of an offence, and the judgment of experts. In one case in Washington, the home of a sex offender was set on fire after the community was notified. There are concerns that the Washington scheme is "just creating a class of people that are moving from community to community."

required in the statute, if the application relates to a specific young person, that youth should be notified of the application and given an opportunity to oppose the application.

Section 119(1)(s)(i) allows an application to be made to a youth justice court to permit access to youth justice court or other records related to young offenders for "research or statistical purposes." Given the need for better information and understanding about young offenders, permission for access to this information should be given, provided that it is *bona fide* research that has passed an ethics review and there are assurances that there will be no disclosure of identifying information. The decision by a youth justice court judge to allow, or not allow, access to records under the discretionary provisions of section 119 is not subject to appeal or review by a higher court.[92]

While during the specified statutory period significant use can be made of youth justice court records within the justice system (e.g., for purposes of sentencing for a later offence), section 82 of the YCJA provides restrictions on the use that can be made of a youth justice court record outside of the justice system. It states that except for specified justice system purposes, once a youth sentence has been completed, a youth shall be deemed not to have been convicted of the offence. Section 82(3) of the YCJA provides that employers governed by federal law are prohibited from asking a potential employee whether he or she has ever been charged or found guilty of an offence prosecuted pursuant to the YCJA or the YOA, unless that person is still subject to a youth sentence. This provision recognizes the limited accountability of young persons and is intended to afford a second chance to those adolescents found guilty of an offence while a youth. However, a youth who is applying for a position with an employer that is not under federal employment law,[93] such as a private employer or a municipality or provincial agency, may be required to submit to a security clearance that may include a check of youth justice court records kept by the police.[94]

---

92   *R. v. C.(S.)* (2002), 58 O.R. (2d) 332 (Sup. Ct.) appellate review (*mandamus*) not available to review exercise of discretion under *YOA* s. 44.1(1)(k).

93   Federal employment law governs about 10 percent of the labour force and includes direct employees of the federal government, such as the RCMP and the armed forces, as well as those enterprises that are subject to federal regulation, such as banks and airlines.

94   *O.(Y.)* v. *Belleville (City) Chief of Police* (1993), 12 O.R. (3d) 618 (Div. Ct.), rev'g (1991), 3 O.R. (3d) 261 (Gen. Div.).

FURTHER READINGS

DELISLE, R.J., & D. STUART, *Learning Canadian Criminal Procedure*, 6th ed. (Toronto: Carswell, 2000) cc. 2 and 3

PLATT, P., *Young Offenders Law in Canada*, 2d ed. (Toronto: Butterworths, 1995) cc. 12, 13, 16, 17, 18, 21, and 22

QUIGLEY, T., *Procedure in Canadian Criminal Law* (Toronto: Carswell, 1997) cc. 12, 13, 16–19, 21, 22, and 24

SCOTT, S., M. WONG, & B. WEAGANT, *Defending Young Offender Cases*, 2d ed. (Toronto: Carswell, 1997) cc. 5, 6, and 7

CHAPTER 8

SENTENCING UNDER THE *YOUTH CRIMINAL JUSTICE ACT*

A. STRUCTURING THE EXERCISE OF SENTENCING DISCRETION

Under the *Youth Criminal Justice Act*[1] adolescents are generally subject to the same substantive criminal laws as adults, with the same offence provisions and the same available defences.[2] Section 50 of the Act, however, makes clear that the principles and provisions of the *Criminal Code* that apply to the sentencing of adults generally do not apply to young offenders (with the exception of the most serious offences for which adult sentence can be imposed on young offenders, a topic more

---

1   *Youth Criminal Justice Act*, S.C. 2002, c. 1 (royal assent February 19, 2002, to come into force April 1, 2003), often referred to in this book as the *YCJA*.

2   There are a number of quasi-criminal provincial laws that create age-based offences, such as those which set minimum ages for drinking or driving that may be prosecuted in youth justice court. Some situations in which an adolescent may have a defence to a criminal charge based on age include certain sexual offences for which s. 150.1 of the *Criminal Code*, R.S.C. 1985, c. C-46, allows a person under the age of sixteen years to raise the defence of the consent of the complainant if the accused is not more than two years older than a complainant who is under the age of fourteen. These provisions (sometimes referred to in the United States as "statutory rape") make it an offence for an adult or older adolescent to have sexual relations with a child under fourteen years of age, even if there is apparent consent, but allow for age-appropriate consensual sexual relationships.

fully discussed in Chapter 9). Like the *Young Offenders Act*,[3] the *YCJA* has extensive provisions governing the sentencing of young offenders, and these provisions are central to the youth justice system. The fundamental purpose of juvenile justice legislation such as the *YCJA* is to ensure that those adolescents who are guilty of criminal behaviour are dealt with by a different set of principles than those which apply to adults, that they are provided with age-appropriate rehabilitative services, and that they are separated from adult offenders who might exploit or further corrupt them.

The *YCJA* sentencing regime provides more guidance to judges than the *Young Offenders Act*, but the new Act is also more complex. Part IV of the new Act sets out the principles and process for sentencing, and regulates the various sentencing options, while Part V deals in greater detail with custodial sentences for young offenders. The *YCJA* provides a more explicit set of sentencing principles and guidelines than the *YOA*. The new Act places a clearer emphasis on accountability and proportionality, has greater restrictions on the use of custody, and encourages community-based sentences. Reflecting the limited maturity and accountability of adolescents, the Act also makes clear that sentences imposed on young offenders are not to be as severe as those sanctions imposed on adults who have committed similar offences. While rehabilitation remains an important concern for the youth justice system under the *YCJA*, rehabilitative or child welfare concerns cannot be invoked to justify a sentence that could not be justified on the basis of accountability principles.

Under the *YOA*, while the Canadian youth justice system was marked by great interprovincial variation in disposition patterns, the country as a whole had one of the highest rates in the world of use of custody for adolescent offenders.[4] The Preamble to the *YCJA* makes clear that the Act is intended to address the concern about the overuse of custody, proclaiming that a prime purpose in enacting the new legislation is to have a youth criminal justice system "that commands

---

3   *Young Offenders Act*, R.S.C 1985, c. Y-1, enacted as S.C. 1980–81–82–83, c. 110. The Act was also amended in 1985 through *An Act to amend the Young Offenders Act, the Criminal Code, the Penitentiary Act, and the Prisons and Reformatories Act*, R.S.C. 1985 (2d Supp.), c. 24, in force September 1, 1986 and November 1, 1986, and in 1995 through *An Act to amend the Young Offenders Act and the Criminal Code*, S.C. 1995, c. 19.

4   The *YOA*, above note 3, used the euphemistic term "disposition" to refer to a sanction imposed by a youth court, to contrast with a sentence imposed on an adult offender under the *Criminal Code*, above note 2. Reflecting its accountability approach, the *YCJA*, above note 1, uses the term "sentence."

respect, takes into account the interests of victims, fosters responsibility and ensures *accountability through meaningful consequences* and effective rehabilitation and reintegration, and that *reserves its most serious intervention for the most serious crimes and reduces the over-reliance on incarceration for non-violent young persons*" [emphases added].

The *YOA* had no explicit sentencing principles, with that Act's Declaration of Principle (section 3) offering only general guidance and resulting in different judges adopting differing sentencing philosophies and practices. For example, the Alberta Court of Appeal held that general deterrence, the imposition of a punishment on one youth for the purpose of deterring — or warning — other youths, should have no role in the sentencing of young offenders under the *YOA* since it was not explicitly mentioned in section 3 of that Act.[5] On the other hand, the Quebec Court of Appeal held that general deterrence was an appropriate factor to consider, as an aspect of the protection of society.[6] Despite the fact that theoretically the Alberta courts took no account of general deterrence while those in Quebec should have been using this factor to impose more severe custodial sentences, Alberta had a much higher rate of use of custody under the *YOA* than did Quebec. This suggests that judicial statements of principle in regard to the sentencing of young offenders have only limited significance.

The Declaration of Principle and the sentencing principles provisions of the *YCJA* articulate explicit principles that are intended to guide the sentencing decisions of judges in the youth justice courts. The Declaration of Principle (also section 3) makes clear that "fair and proportionate accountability" is the central principle for the sentencing of young offenders. Section 38 offers a more detailed set of sentencing principles, while section 39 places restrictions on the use of custodial sentences. None of these provisions make any mention of deterrence as a sentencing factor. It is submitted that, in sentencing young offenders under the *YCJA*, judges should not make deterrence a specific objective of sentencing. However, the fact that youths are held accountable in the youth justice system should serve a deterrent function.

5   *R. v. G.(K.)* (1986), 73 A.R. 376 (C.A.).

6   *R. v. L.(S.)* (1990), 75 C.R. (3d) 94 (Que. C.A.). To some extent, this controversy was resolved by *R. v. M.(J.J.)*, [1993] 2 S.C.R. 421, where the Supreme Court of Canada held that under the *YOA*, above note 3, general deterrence could be a factor in the sentencing of young offenders, albeit one that is less important than for adults.

The *YOA* section 20(1) states that the court shall "consider any . . . relevant factors [and] make one of the following dispositions." This provision gave judges a broad discretion to select the factors that they considered important. By way of contrast, section 38(1) of the *YCJA* states that a youth justice court shall impose "just sanctions . . . thereby contributing to . . . long term protection" and further specifying in section 38(2) that any sentence "must be proportionate" to the offence. The *YCJA* adopts a clearer, more focused sentencing philosophy.

While section 24 of the *YOA* provided that a young offender should be held accountable through non-custodial dispositions *"whenever appropriate,"* the restrictions on the use of custody in section 39(1) of the *YCJA* are mandatory. Although the drafters of the *YOA* intended to restrict the use of custody, they sent judges mixed messages and gave them very significant discretion. By way of contrast, unless one of the conditions of section 39(1) of the *YCJA* is satisfied, a custodial sentence shall not be imposed. Further, the *YCJA* makes clear that a custodial sentence that is more severe than warranted by accountability principles should not be imposed to achieve rehabilitative objectives or to address such social concerns as a lack of housing or an abusive home environment. By having a clearer set of sentencing principles, the *YCJA* is intended to reduce the disparities in the sentencing of young offenders by different judges and to reduce the number of youths in custody, especially for non-violent offences.

Even though the new Act gives clearer guidance for sentencing decisions than the *YOA*, the *YCJA* will continue to give individual youth justice court judges significant discretion. It is not only judges who continue to have discretion. Police and Crown prosecutors have a broad discretion about whether a youth should be charged or referred to extrajudicial measures, and Crown prosecutors will have significant discretion in the types of sentences that they may seek. Provincial directors, probation officers, and correctional officials are given significant discretion in how to deal with young offenders placed under their care or supervision. The *YCJA* gives provincial governments an even wider discretion than that accorded under the *YOA* for the establishment and control of community-based dispositions and custodial facilities. Given the variation in approach of different provincial governments to policies, programs and facilities for young offenders, and the discretion conferred upon a range of justice system professionals, significant variation in the treatment of individual young offenders who have committed the same offence in similar circumstances will likely continue.

B. SENTENCING PRINCIPLES

The Declaration of Principle in section 3 of the *YCJA* has numerous provisions that are relevant to the sentencing of young offenders and the administration of the youth corrections system. Section 3(1)(a)–(b) is primarily directed at those responsible for the administration of the youth justice system and for the operation of correctional programs and facilities within that system. Some statements in section 3(1)(b), however, are directly relevant for the sentencing of individual young offenders, especially the principle in section 3(1)(b)(ii) of limited accountability in comparison to adults to reflect the reduced maturity of young offenders. Section 3(1) provides:

> 3. (1) The following principles apply in this Act:
>
> (*a*)   the youth criminal justice system is intended to
>   (*i*)   prevent crime by addressing the circumstances underlying a young person's offending behaviour,
>   (*ii*) rehabilitate young persons who commit offences and reintegrate them into society, and
>   (*iii*) ensure that a young person is subject to meaningful consequences for his or her offence in order to promote the long-term protection of the public . . .
>
> (*b*)   the criminal justice system for young persons must be separate from that of adults and emphasize the following:
>   (*i*)   rehabilitation and reintegration,
>   (*ii*) fair and proportionate accountability that is consistent with the greater dependency of young persons and their reduced level of maturity,
>   (*iii*) enhanced procedural protection to ensure that young persons are treated fairly and that their rights, including their right to privacy, are protected.

Section 3(1)(c) is the most relevant section for the sentencing of individual young offenders, emphasizing that the sentencing of young offenders is to be based on "fair and proportionate accountability." Respect for societal values, repair of harm to victims, rehabilitation, and recognition of the special requirements of individual youth are also to be taken into account. Section 3(1)(c)(ii) and 3(1)(d)(ii)–(iii) emphasizes the importance of involving victims in the sentencing process and in offenders "repairing the harm" that they have done. Thus principles of "restorative justice" are important for the sentencing of young offenders. Section 3(1)(c) provides:

3. (1)(c) within the limits of fair and proportionate accountability, the measures taken against young persons who commit offences should

(*i*)   reinforce respect for societal values,

(*ii*) encourage the repair of harm done to victims and the community,

(*iii*) be meaningful for the individual young person given his or her needs and level of development and, where appropriate, involve the parents, the extended family, the community and social or other agencies in the young person's rehabilitation and reintegration, and

(*iv*) respect gender, ethnic, cultural and linguistic differences and respond to the needs of aboriginal young persons and of young persons with special requirements

Section 3(1)(d) offers some guidance for the *process* of sentencing, emphasizing that young persons, victims and parents of young offenders all have the right to participate in the sentencing process:

3(1)(*d*) special considerations apply in respect of proceedings against young persons and, in particular . . .

(*i*)   young persons have rights and freedoms in their own right, such as a right to be heard in the course of and to participate in the processes . . . that lead to decisions that affect them.

(*ii*) victims should be treated with courtesy, compassion and respect for their dignity and privacy and should suffer the minimum degree of inconvenience as a result of their involvement with the youth criminal justice system,

(*iii*) victims should be provided with information about the proceedings and given an opportunity to participate and be heard, and

(*iv*) parents should be informed of measures or proceedings involving their children and encouraged to support them in addressing their offending behaviour.

Section 3 articulates general principles that are intended to guide the sentencing of young offenders, while section 38 offers a more explicit and directive set of principles. Section 38 emphasizes that the central principle of sentencing for youth justice court is to hold a young person "accountable . . . through the imposition of just sanctions."

Section 38 amplifies and explains the general principle of section 3(1)(b)(ii) that sentencing of young offenders is to be premised on "fair and proportionate accountability." Section 38(2)(e) makes clear that any sentence must be the least restrictive sentence that is capable of achieving the objectives of accountability and rehabilitation. Section 38(1) of the *YCJA* makes clear that rehabilitation is viewed as a means of achieving the long-term protection of the public. This approach may be contrasted with some provisions of the *YOA*, most notably section 16(1.1) which dealt with the imposition of adult sanctions and, at least in that context, treated the protection of the public and the rehabilitation of young persons as competing objectives that needed to be "reconciled" or balanced against each other. Section 38(2)(a) provides that the sentence imposed on a young offender is not to result in a punishment that is more severe than would be imposed on an adult convicted of the same offence in similar circumstances. This provision was enacted because, under the *YOA*, notwithstanding that Act's principle of limited accountability, some young offenders, especially non-violent offenders, were actually receiving longer sentences than adults in similar circumstances because the youth courts wanted to achieve rehabilitative or social objectives, or because of a perceived need to deter youth crime.

Section 38(2)(b) requires that the sentence imposed on a young offender is to be similar to the sentence imposed on other young persons "in the region" who have been convicted of the same offence committed in similar circumstances. Section 38(2)(a)–(b) requires judges to have knowledge about how young offenders "in the region" are being sentenced, as well as to be aware of sentencing patterns for adults. It is submitted that "region," a term not statutorily defined, refers to the local region in which there is access to the same types of programs and resources as are available to the youth before the court. Crown or defence counsel may have to make submissions at the sentencing hearing for a young offender about sentencing practices of other youth justice court judges in the region, as well as about the sentencing of adults in similar cases. Section 38 provides:

> 38. (1) The purpose of sentencing under section 42 (youth sentences) is to contribute to the protection of society by holding a young person accountable for an offence through the imposition of just sanctions that have meaningful consequences for the young person and that promote his or her rehabilitation and reintegration into society.
>
> (2) A youth justice court that imposes a youth sentence on a young person shall determine the sentence in accordance with the principles set out in section 3 and the following principles:
>
> (a) the sentence must not result in a punishment that is greater than the punishment that would be appropriate for an adult who has been convicted of the same offence committed in similar circumstances;

(b) the sentence must be similar to the sentences imposed in the region on similar young persons found guilty of the same offence committed in similar circumstances;

(c) the sentence must be proportionate to the seriousness of the offence and the degree of responsibility of the young person for that offence; and

(d) all available sanctions other than custody that are reasonable in the circumstances should be considered for all offenders, with particular attention to the circumstances of aboriginal offenders.

(e) subject to paragraph (c), the sentence must

    (i) be the least restrictive sentence that is capable of achieving the purpose set out in section (1),

    (ii) be the one that is most likely to rehabilitate the young person and reintegrate him or her into society, and

    (iii) promote a sense of responsibility in the young person, and an acknowledgement of the harm done to victims and the community.

(3) In determining a youth sentence, the youth justice court shall take into account

(a) the degree of participation by the young person in the commission of the offence;

(b) the harm done to victims and whether it was intentional or reasonably foreseeable;

(c) any reparation made by the young person to the victim or the community;

(d) the time spent in detention by the young person as a result of the offence;

(e) the previous findings of guilt of the young person; and

(f) any other aggravating and mitigating circumstances related to the young person or the offence that are relevant to the purpose and principles set out in this section.

Concerns about the rehabilitation of a youth may justify the imposition of a community-based sentence with a focus on treatment in a case that might otherwise warrant a custodial sentence, but neither rehabilitation nor the welfare of an offender can be used to justify a custodial sentence if it would not be justified on accountability-based principles or which seems disproportionate to the offence. The emphasis in the *YCJA* on using community-based sentences is consistent with a significant body of research that reveals that for most young offenders a community-based sentence is more likely to effect rehabilitation than a custodial sentence. Appropriate services and supervision that are provided to youths in the context of their family and community are more likely to reduce the risk of reoffending than removing youths from their community and placing them in custody. Although treatment and rehabilitative services are usually offered to youths in custody, the negative influences of other youths with a history of offending and the fact that the youth's problems cannot be addressed in the context in which they occur, result in it being more difficult to rehabilitate youths in custody than in community-based programs.[7]

Section 38 of the YCJA sets out a sentencing philosophy for young offenders that is quite different from that applicable to adults. In particular, section 718(b) of the *Criminal Code* provides that one of the objectives in sentencing adults is to "deter the offender and other persons from committing offences." Although some opposition members of the Parliamentary Committee studying the YCJA prior to its enactment advocated the inclusion of deterrence as an explicit consideration, the drafters of the Act deliberately omitted deterrence as a youth sentencing factor. As a matter of principle, it was felt that one youth should not be sanctioned more severely in order to deter others from committing the same offence, nor should individual youths be subjected to ever-increasing sanctions to deter them from reoffending. This is consistent with research that reveals that increasing the severity of sentences does not deter youth offending. Adolescents, especially those likely to commit offences, generally have less foresight and judgment than adults. They are not considering the possibility of being apprehended, let alone the consequences of apprehension, when they are offending. As a result, there is no deterrent effect from increasing the severity of youth sentences. While improved policing — increasing the likelihood of getting caught — can have some deterrent effect on youth crime, increasing the severity of youth sentences — increasing the consequences of getting caught — has no impact on youth crime.[8]

The expectation that youths who commit offences will be held accountable and face meaningful sanctions related to the harm done undoubtedly serves to deter crime. However, the YCJA does not permit judges to take added account of deterrence as a factor to *increase the*

---

7   See, for example, M. Lipsey, "What do we learn from 400 research studies on the effectiveness of treatment with juvenile delinquents," in J. MacGuire, ed., *What Works: Reducing Offending* (Chichester, UK: John Wiley and Sons, 1995) .

8   See, for example, A.N. Doob, V. Marinos, and K.N. Varma, *Youth Crime and the Youth Justice System in Canada: A Research Perspective* (Toronto: University of Toronto, Centre of Criminology, 1995) at 56–71.

severity of a sentence for a young offender. For example, the fact that a particular offence, such as mischief arising from vandalism from painting graffiti on buildings, has been an increasing problem in a community should not in itself result in a more severe sanction for a youth who happens to be apprehended and sentenced by a youth justice court than a youth who may have committed the same offence in another community or at a time when there was less concern about this particular offence. Thus, while the youth justice system as a whole may serve to deter youth crime by holding youths accountable, the sentence imposed on a specific youth should not be made more severe than proportionality requires to serve a deterrent function.

Section 38(2)(e)(ii) requires that the sentencing judge impose a sentence that is "most likely to rehabilitate the young person." Appropriate correctional services have the potential to reduce the risk of reoffending; research reveals that appropriate intervention, especially community-based intervention, will result in a reduction in the *risk* of reoffending. However, there is no assurance that any *particular* youth who is before the court can be rehabilitated and will not reoffend. Thus, rehabilitative concerns are not to be used as a justification of a more onerous sanction than could be justified on proportionality principles.

If the parents of a youth appear supportive and express a willingness to work with probation authorities by providing their child with support and control, this may favour a non-custodial sentence with a rehabilitation orientation.[9] If the parents or other adult relatives are concerned and actively involved, there may be a greater likelihood of rehabilitation with a community-based sentence and there may a greater likelihood of effective supervision in the community. Although in practice this may tend to favour adolescents from middle-class families, there are many families of very limited means in which parents are actively concerned and engaged in the youth justice process. The attitude of a young offender may also be an important factor in determining the effectiveness of any intervention; at least at some point in their lives, some adolescents may be quite resistant to any type of intervention, and may have a high risk of reoffending no matter what type of service or programming is offered.

While some types of services are more effective in dealing with youth with particular problems, and an effort should be made to ensure that an individual youth receives the most appropriate services avail-

---

9   *R. v. F.(A.)*, [1995] O.J. No. 2323 (Prov. Ct.) (QL) (twenty-four months probation for several property-related offences involving breach of trust and $50,000 in losses).

able, no program can provide an assurance that none of the youth who participate will reoffend This lack of certainty about the efficacy of rehabilitation is reflected in section 38(2)(e)(ii) which only requires that, after ensuring that sentence is "proportionate to the offence" and holds a youth accountable for his or her acts, the judge shall impose the sentence that is "*most likely* to rehabilitate the young person and reintegrate him or her into society" [emphasis added].

In addition to the principles of accountability and rehabilitation of section 38(2), under section 38(3) the youth justice court is reminded that it is required to take into account factors that are typically considered aspects of accountability, relating to the offence, the offender, and the harm done by the offence. While the offence, the youth's degree of participation in the offence, and the youth's prior record are the most important factors, other factors can be legitimately considered. Section 3(1)(b)(ii) of the YCJA, for example, allows courts to take account of the age and maturity of youths, reflecting the practice under the YOA, where youth courts were especially reluctant to impose custodial sentences on younger adolescents.[10] Section 38(3)(c) allows a youth justice court to take account of the attitude of a young offender. A young person who appears to have appreciated the harm done by his or her offending and genuinely expresses remorse, may have a sentence mitigated from what would otherwise be imposed, but a perfunctory expression of remorse after a long record of offending may appear insincere and might not affect the sentence imposed.

Under the YOA, youth courts clearly indicated that, for gang-related offences, especially those involving violence, deterrence was more important and more severe sentences would be imposed. The goal — to deter other gang members — reflects the fact that such offences often have a "premeditated" or "cowardly" element.[11] Similarly, offences involving violence or bullying in schools received a more severe sanction because of concerns about deterrence and maintaining order as well as the protection of victims who may again be confronted by the young offender.[12] While the principles of the YCJA do *not* allow youth justice

---

10   R. v. W.(B.) (1995), 61 B.C.A.C. 136 (C.A.) (one month in custody followed by probation for serious assault by twelve-year-old).

11   R. v. E.(R.K.) (1996), 107 Man. R. (2d) 200 (C.A.) (twenty-four months secure custody for robbery by youth without prior record).

12   R. v. B.(L.) (1993), 62 O.A.C. 112 (C.A.)(six weeks open custody for fifteen-year-old for assault causing bodily harm to a fellow student); see also R. v. *Justin McK.* (24 September 2001) (Ont. C.A.) Docket #c32241 (charges arising from a fight between teenage boys near a schoolyard).

court judges to take direct account of deterrence as a factor in sentencing, they may legitimately take account of the fact that an offence is gang-related or involves bullying or other forms of intimidation.

As section 3(1)(c) of the *YCJA* recognizes, youth justice courts should "reinforce respect for societal values." Offences that involve intimidation and groups of offenders may cause greater harm as not only the victim but the entire school or community may be affected, and section 38(2)(e)(iii) requires that sentences "promote a sense of responsibility in the young person, and an acknowledgment of the harm done to victims and the community."

Section 38(3)(b) requires the court to consider the "harm done to victims and whether it was intentional or reasonably foreseeable." In cases where an offence involves a death, such as criminal negligence causing death, a custodial sentence may be appropriate even if there was no intent to cause death and there are no concerns about reoffending.[13] In cases involving intentional killing, such as manslaughter and murder, courts are likely to impose sentences near the maximum allowed "even though they may not be the worst possible kinds of cases."

Section 39 is intended to provide explicit guidance to judges who are considering the imposition of a custodial sentence on a young offender and, as stated in the Preamble to the *YCJA*, is intended to reduce Canada's "over-reliance on the incarceration of non-violent young persons." While a custodial sentence may be imposed for a violent offence, section 39(1) places restrictions on the use of custody for non-violent offences, requiring a history of failing to comply with non-custodial sentences, a pattern of non-violent offending, or exceptional circumstances. Section 39 is more fully discussed later in this chapter.

In summary, sections 3 and 38 require the court to begin the sentencing process by considering accountability and proportionality, assessing factors related to the offence and the record of the offender, the types of factors listed in section 38(3). Section 38(2) provides that the sentence that is imposed cannot be more severe than the punishment imposed on an adult in similar circumstances and should be comparable to the sentences imposed on other youths in the region. Before a custodial sentence can be imposed, at least one of the conditions of section 39(1) must be satisfied, and the balance of section 39 must also be considered. The court should then determine whether there are rehabilitative concerns and services available that would justify changing the nature and mitigating the severity of a sentence that would oth-

---

13   *R. v. M.(E.)* (1992), 10 O.R. (3d) 481 (C.A.) (ninety days secure custody for criminal negligence causing death arising out of a motor vehicle accident).

erwise be imposed. Rehabilitative or child welfare concerns should not result in a more severe or intrusive sentence than an accountability-based sentence would warrant.

1) Pre-sentence Detention

If there has been a finding of guilt, the court may order the youth to be detained pending sentencing. This should not be done as a form of immediate punishment but should only be used if there are grounds for detention under section 515 of the *Criminal Code*. Under the *YCJA*, a judge who has just found a youth guilty should *not* order the youth to be detained pending sentencing as a means of giving the youth a "short sharp shock." Further, section 29 provides that a youth justice court judge "shall not detain" a youth prior to sentencing as a substitute for child protection, mental health or other social measures, and that such detention is presumed to be unnecessary unless one the conditions of section 39(1)(a)–(c) would allow committal to custody.

While more explicit under the new Act, it was also clear under the *YOA* that a judge was not to order pre-sentence detention as a means of punishment. For example, in one Saskatchewan case decided under the *YOA*, an appeal court reversed a youth court judge's decision to detain the youth immediately after making a finding of guilt. The appellate judge observed that prior to sentencing, a youth court judge can order detention of the youth only "for either of the purposes referred to in section 515(10): namely, to ensure his attendance in court, or for the purpose of protecting the public. . . . [The trial judge] in remanding [the youth] . . . in custody . . . without sentencing him . . . did so because he was not certain what sentence he wished to impose, and he also apparently wished to provide . . . a 'wake up' call. Neither of these 'purposes' would qualify a person for detention under s. 515(10)."[14]

Under the *YOA*, youth courts usually took account of any period of pre-disposition detention to reduce any sentence that would otherwise be imposed, crediting the youth with this time against the appropriate sentence, although sentencing judges were not obliged to do so and some did not.[15] Section 39(3)(d) of the *YCJA* makes clear that a judge "shall" take into account time spent in detention by the youth before

---

14 *R. v. Y.(D.H.)* (1995), 132 Sask. R. 107 at 111 (Q.B.). See also *R. v. G.(C.)*(1993), 79 C.C.C. (3d) 446 (Ont. C.A.). For a fuller discussion of s. 515(10) of the *Criminal Code*, above note 2, and pre-sentence detention, see Chapter 4.

15 *R. v. W.(S.B.)*, [1995] A.J. No. 686 (C.A.) (QL).

sentencing. Adult offenders usually get extra credit for pre-sentencing detention; indeed with adults it is common to receive two-for-one or double credit, since they are not eligible for parole or statutory sentence remission for this pre-trial detention time, and since there is generally less access to educational, vocational, and rehabilitative programming in detention facilities.[16]

Under the *YOA*, it was held that since there was no statutory sentence remission for young offenders, there should be no greater credit for pre-sentence detention.[17] However, since the *YCJA* has presumptive community supervision for all custodial sentences, it is submitted that ordinarily a young offender detained before sentencing should, like an adult, receive extra credit for pre-trial detention, especially if detention was in a facility that lacked the level of educational, recreational or counselling programming that is available in longer-term custody facilities for young offenders.

2) Reports for a Sentencing Hearing

For relatively minor offences, a youth justice court may have a sentencing hearing immediately after there is finding of guilt, whether based on a guilty plea or after a trial, asking for submissions from the Crown prosecutor and the accused before imposing a sentence. In more serious situations, however, the court will normally adjourn to allow for the preparation of reports to assist the court in making an appropriate sentencing decision, as well as to give counsel time to prepare for a sentence hearing. Before a youth is sentenced, section 40 of the *YCJA* allows a youth justice court judge to order that a provincial director "shall cause [a] pre-sentence report"[18] (or social history) to be prepared and submitted to the court. These reports are usually prepared by a professional employed by the government, referred to as a probation officer or youth worker; these professionals usually have a range of responsibilities with regard to the preparation of reports and supervision of young offenders in the community.

---

16   See A. Manson, *The Law of Sentencing* (Toronto: Irwin Law, 2001) 109–14; and
     R. v. Wust (2000), 143 C.C.C. (3d) 129 (S.C.C.).

17   Adults usually get extra credit for pre-sentencing detention since they do not get
     statutory sentence remission for this pre-trial detention time. Since there was no
     statutory sentence remission for young offenders under the *YOA*, above note 3,
     there was no greater credit for pre-sentence detention; *R. v. O.(S.J.)* (1992), 83
     Alta. L.R. (2d) 413 (C.A.).

18   A pre-sentence report is also known as a PSR. Under the *YOA* the equivalent
     pre-disposition report was often referred to as a PDR.

The order for the preparation of a pre-sentence report must be made by the court, although often there is a request from the Crown prosecutor or defence counsel to the judge that results in the ordering of a report. In some cases defence counsel will argue against the court making an order for a pre-sentence report, as this will delay sentencing and defence counsel may feel that he or she has obtained sufficient evidence to present to the court. If the Crown will be seeking a custodial sentence, a pre-sentence report must be prepared, since section 39(6) of the YCJA requires that before imposing a custodial sentence, a youth justice court "*shall* consider a pre-sentence report" [emphasis added].

Section 39(7) provides an exception to the requirement that a pre-sentence report shall be prepared before a custody sentence can be imposed, but only if the prosecutor *and* counsel for the youth waive this requirement *and* when the judge considers that the preparation of the report is "not necessary." A judge should be reluctant to dispense with preparation of a report before imposing a custodial sentence unless there is a relatively recent report about the youth that had been prepared for use in a previous sentencing hearing.[19] In some cases, if the lawyers have entered into a pre-trial plea bargain and are making a joint submission as to sentence, the court may dispense with the preparation of a report before imposing a custodial sentence despite the absence of a recent report. Even in a situation where there is a joint submission as to sentence, the judge is bound by the sentencing principles of sections 38 and 39, and in particular may not impose a custodial sentence if the conditions of section 39 are not satisfied; accordingly a judge may decide to order a pre-sentence report despite the joint submission.

The youth worker preparing a pre-sentence report will interview the youth and other significant individuals for the youth, such as parents and teachers. The person preparing the report is also expected to contact, "where appropriate and reasonably possible," members of the youth's extended family, to determine whether they can exert "control and influence" on the youth;[20] this type of information is especially relevant for Aboriginal youth, and it may allow for more community-based sentences involving members of the extended family. The report will provide a summary of the youth's family background, school record, and history of offending and involvement in the justice system, as well as about the youth's attitude to the offence and any plans that

---

19   See, for example, *R. v. R.(R.A.)* (1987), 64 Sask. R. 31 (C.A.).

20   See *YCJA*, above note 1, s. 40(2). See the 1995 amendments to the *YOA*, above note 3, ss. 14(2)(c)(v)–(vi).

the youth has for changing his or her conduct. The report will also generally include the youth's record of prior participation in extrajudicial sanctions.

A pre-sentence report may also provide information about the "results of an interview with the victim . . . if reasonably possible."[21] Although information about the impact of the offence on the victim should be available to the court in any case in which there is an identifiable victim, in some cases this will be better provided by a victim impact statement prepared by the victim, or by having the victim testify in court or participate in a conference.

The pre-sentence report should also include information about the "availability and appropriateness of community services . . . and the willingness [of the youth to] avail himself or herself" of those services.[22] While there was an identical provision in the *YOA*, the need for a pre-sentence report to canvass community sentencing options is heightened under the *YCJA*, as the Act emphasizes the duty on the court to canvass all reasonable alternatives before imposing a custodial sentence, and the report is expressly required to address the question of "whether there is an alternative to custody."[23] If a custodial sentence is a possibility, the report will usually provide some information about the custodial facilities that are suitable and have space available. Since the *YCJA* does not allow for a judge to order placement in any specific facility, however, there is no explicit statement in the Act that this type of information about custody is to be provided.

In 1995 the *YOA* was amended to specify that the author of a pre-disposition report could include a recommendation about an appropriate disposition. Even before the enactment of that provision, it was a common but not universal practice for reports to offer recommendations, and section 40(2)(f) of the *YCJA* also provides that a pre-sentence report may include "any recommendation" that the provincial director considers appropriate. This clearly allows for the inclusion of a recommendation about a sentence or range of sentences, but the Act does not require it. Despite the enactment of the provision in the *YOA* allowing for the inclusion of a recommendation, some youth court workers were reluctant to do this, especially if the judge for whom the report was prepared had a reputation for having expressed a concern that providing such a recommendation is "usurping the role of the

---

21   *YCJA*, above note 1, s. 40(2)(b).

22   *Ibid.*, s. 40(2)(d)(v).

23   *Ibid.*, s. 40(2)(e).

court." The extent to which recommendations are made in pre-sentence reports will likely continue to vary.

In more serious cases, or cases where there is particular concern about a young person, the court may make an order under section 34 of the YCJA for a psychiatric, medical, or psychological assessment to assist in arriving at an appropriate sentence. Such assessments are more time-consuming to prepare, though providing more detailed information about the youth. Such a report may be prepared with the consent of the youth and the prosecutor. Section 34 also allows the court to order a report on its own motion or at the request of the prosecutor *or* the youth, and if there is a "pattern of repeated findings of guilt," *or* a "serious violent offence," *or* if the youth appears to be suffering from a psychological disorder, emotional disturbance, or learning disability.[24] A section 34 report may be appropriate when the circumstances of the youth or of the nature of the offence suggest that more information is needed to enable the court to make a sentence which is responsive to the youth's "special requirements."

Section 34 assessment reports, paid for by government, are prepared by professionals in private practice, hospitals or clinics. Although detention is presumed unnecessary, under sections 34(3)–(4) of the YCJA, a youth can be detained for up to thirty days if this is considered "necessary to conduct an assessment" or if the youth consents to detention, for example, in a mental health facility where such an assessment might be done. Some commentators expressed a concern that under the YOA youth courts ordered psychological and medical assessment reports too rarely.[25] Such critics argued that the orientation of the YOA caused the lawyers involved to focus on the offence and disregard the needs and condition of the specific youth. It is apparent that some defence counsel have been reluctant to request assessment reports, since the information about the mental or emotionally troubled youth could result in a more intrusive sentence being imposed under the YOA. Further, the assessment reports generally take longer to prepare than a

---

24   In 1995 Parliament amended the YOA to have a similar provision, making clear that an assessment could be ordered by the court acting on its own motion. The YOA, above note 1, s. 13(1)(b), enacted by the 1995 amendment, s. 4(1).

25   Assessment reports were ordered under s.13 of the YOA, above note 3; see A. Leschied, "The Sentencing and Rehabilitative Principles of the Y.C.J.A. ss. 38 & 39: Providing a Context from the Literature on Effective Youth Justice Programs" (Sept. 2002) National Judicial Institute Youth Justice Education Program; and A.W. Leschied and P.G. Jaffe, "Impact of the YOA on Court Sentences: A Comparative Analysis" (1987) 29 Can. J. Crim. 421.

section 40 pre-sentence report, and the delay that this may cause for a youth may also lead defence counsel to oppose the ordering of an assessment, especially if the youth is either in pre-sentence detention or is likely to be placed in custody for the duration of the assessment.

A large proportion of persistent young offenders have learning disabilities or suffer from such conditions as fetal-alcohol syndrome. Appropriate diagnosis and treatment could do much to reduce offending, but too often these conditions are undiagnosed or ignored by the legal system. Use of section 34 reports, as well as greater awareness by youth justice professionals about these conditions, is essential for developing appropriate intervention strategies. Governments must also ensure that there are suitable programs and facilities for dealing with young offenders suffering from these conditions.[26]

The new Act requires the court to impose a sentence which will be "most likely to rehabilitate the youth," in the context of a sentence that is a proportionate response to the offending. A more intrusive sentence than the offence warrants cannot be justified in order to meet rehabilitative needs, although rehabilitative needs might be used to justify a modification or mitigation of the sentence that pure accountability principles might demand. This change in legislative approach may tend to reduce the opposition of defence counsel to the preparation of assessment reports, but given the nature of the sentencing process, assessments will not be regularly ordered under the *YCJA*.

There are provisions in the *YCJA* to encourage the youth to co-operate with the author of a section 34 or 40 report. Statements made by the youth in the course of preparation of such a report are generally to be used only for the purpose of a sentence or sentence review hearing and are not otherwise admissible against the youth.[27] Most youths are willing to participate in the preparation of reports and often try to put themselves in the best possible light with the person preparing a report. While a youth cannot be compelled to co-operate with the person preparing the report, if the youth is unwilling to assist in the process, it may be difficult for defence counsel to object to any recommendations.[28]

---

26 As many as three-quarters of young offenders in custody have some form of learning disability, a rate five times higher than in the general school-age population. See Y. Henteleff, *Position Paper on the Proposed Amendments to the Young Offenders Act* (Ottawa: Learning Disabilities Association of Canada, 1996); and Canada, Federal–Provincial/Territorial Task Force on Youth Justice, *A Review of the Young Offenders Act* (Ottawa: Ministry of Supply and Services, 1996) at 625.

27 *YCJA*, above note 1, ss. 40(10) and 147.

28 *R. v. R.(A.L.)* (1987), 77 N.S.R. (2d) 338 (C.A.)

A copy of a section 40 pre-sentence report is to be given to the youth, defence counsel, and the Crown prosecutor[29] prior to the sentencing hearing to allow them to prepare for the hearing, as well as given to the judge and any parent in attendance at the hearing. The judge may also direct that a copy of a pre-sentence report is to be sent to a parent who is not in attendance but who is "taking an active interest in the proceedings." If requested, the judge may also authorize the disclosure of the report to other persons who "in the opinion of the court [have a] valid interest" in the proceedings, such as a family doctor.[30] A section 34 assessment must also be provided to the Crown prosecutor and defence counsel before the sentencing hearing to allow them to prepare and decide whether to have the author of the report available for cross-examination. A section 34 report, however, may contain highly personal or sensitive information obtained from the youth, parents or others. A judge may direct that portions or all of an assessment report are to be withheld from the youth or the parents if disclosure would "seriously impair" the treatment or recovery of the youth, or if disclosure would "be likely to endanger the life or safety" of another person or cause "serious psychological harm" to another person. Despite the concerns about potential harm, the court shall not withhold a section 34 report from a parent or youth if "the interests of justice make disclosure essential."[31]

C. SENTENCING HEARINGS

Before imposing a sentence, the judge will consider any reports that have been prepared for the court. Further, the Crown and young person have the right to introduce evidence and to make submissions (or arguments) about the appropriate sentence. The rules of evidence that apply to trials are relaxed at a sentencing hearing. Hearsay and opinion evidence about a youth and about different correctional programs that would be inadmissible at a trial may be introduced through letters or other docu-

---

29 If there is a private prosecution, s. 40(7) of the *YCJA*, above note 1, allows for a judge to withhold a portion or all of a pre-sentence report from the private prosecutor if disclosure may be "prejudicial" to the youth and not "necessary" for the prosecution of the case. See also s. 34(9) concerning non-disclosure of an assessment report to a private prosecutor.

30 *YCJA*, above note 1, s. 40(5) and (8).

31 *Ibid.*, ss. 34(9)–(11); see discussion in Chapter 6.

ments.[32] However, if the young person challenges a factual assertion made by the Crown or in a report, it must be proven beyond a doubt or it should be disregarded by the sentencing judge.[33] In the Supreme Court of Canada decision in *R. v. Gardiner*, Dickson J. observed:

> One of the hardest tasks confronting a trial judge is sentencing. The stakes are high for society and for the individual. Sentencing is the critical stage of the criminal justice system, and it is manifest that the judge should not be denied an opportunity to obtain relevant information by the imposition of all the restrictive evidential rules common to a trial. Yet the obtaining and weighing of such evidence should be fair. A substantial liberty interest of the offender is involved and the information obtained should be accurate and reliable.
>
> It is a commonplace that the strict rules which govern at trial do not apply at a sentencing hearing and it would be undesirable to have the formalities and technicalities characteristic of the normal adversary proceeding prevail. The hearsay rule does not govern the sentencing hearing. Hearsay evidence may be accepted where found to be credible and trustworthy. The judge traditionally has had wide latitude as to the sources and types of evidence upon which to base his sentence. He must have the fullest possible information concerning the background of the accused if he is to fit the sentence to the offender rather than to the crime.[34]

Recommendations in a pre-sentence report or section 34 assessment are not binding on the court. Nonetheless, recommendations in such reports were often influential under the *YOA*. If there were no objections, a report might simply be filed with the court. Crown prosecutors rarely challenged a recommendation in a pre-sentence report; more frequently, it was counsel for the youth who would disagree. As under the old Act, either lawyer has the right to challenge the report under the *YCJA* and may cross-examine the author, as well as introducing independent evidence at the sentence hearing. Defence counsel sometimes introduce character evidence about the youth or other evidence about

---

32 Procedural and evidentiary rules for an adult sentencing hearing are in s. 723 of the *Criminal Code*, above note 2. Although technically this provision does not apply to sentencing in youth justice court because of s. 50 of the *YCJA*, above note 1, as a matter of practice it is likely to provide guidance to youth justice court judges. In practice, under the *YOA*, above note 3, s. 723 was largely followed, although also not technically binding, as it largely codifies the principles articulated by decisions such as *R. v. Gardiner*, below note 34.

33 *R. v. E.(R.K.)* (1996), 107 Man. R. (2d) 200 (C.A.).

34 *R. v. Gardiner*, [1982] 2 S.C.R. 368 at 414.

an appropriate sentence. Parents also have the right to make submissions prior to sentence. In practice, however, in many sentencing hearings, the pre-sentence report is likely to be the only significant source of information about the youth and correctional resources for the judge.

Although counsel have the right to introduce evidence and cross-examine witnesses, in practice, lawyers often play a limited role in youth justice court sentence hearings; they have been criticized for their relatively passive role at this critical stage of the youth justice court process. (See Chapter 6.) There should be an important role for defence counsel to play in challenging the plans put forward by agents of the state and in putting forward independent plans for sentencing alternatives. Defence counsel may also contact the authors of any reports before they are prepared, to ensure that the youth's position is adequately understood. A common judicial response to the low level of involvement of lawyers in the sentencing process has been for judges to adopt more of an inquisitorial role than they do at the trial stage, relying on their understanding of adolescent development and the knowledge of community and correctional resources as much as on any evidence adduced at the hearing.[35]

Section 3(1)(d)(ii) and (iii) of the *YCJA* requires that the victim should be given "an opportunity to participate and to be heard" and should be "provided with information about the proceedings." The involvement of a victim at the sentencing stage may be arranged in a number of different ways, including through the filing of a victim impact statement, the pre-sentence report, or a conference. If the victim is present at the sentencing hearing, the judge should make a special effort to ensure that the victim understands what sentence has been imposed and why it was imposed.

An interview with the victim can be conducted as part of the preparation of a pre-sentencing report, with the results presented to the youth justice court as part of that report. Section 50 of the *YCJA* also adopts sections 722, 722.1 and 722.2 of the *Criminal Code*, allowing for a victim impact statement to be prepared by the victim and presented to the youth justice court as part of the sentencing process. The preparation of victim impact statements, which describe the harm or loss caused by the offence, is usually arranged by the police or a probation officer, but the statements themselves are actually written by victims or, sometimes, by family members of victims. The reference to victim impact statements

---

35 For a discussion of some of the dilemmas faced by judges, see S.K. MacAskill and H.T.G. Andrews, "The Role of the Judge at the Sentence Hearing" (1985), 47 C.R. (3d) 60.

in the *YCJA* and the more general principles in section 3(1)(d) of the *YCJA* are intended to encourage the use of these statements. Although the views of victims should not determine the sentence, it is often important for victims that their views and experiences are communicated to the court. Further, the use of victim impact statements, or testimony by victims at the time of sentencing, can provide young offenders with a greater appreciation of the injury they have caused.

Judges invariably ask the youth and parents if they have anything to say before sentence is imposed. Typically the parents and youth feel intimidated by the court setting and are likely to say nothing. Further, defence counsel will sometimes advise the youth to say nothing, for fear that the youth may make statements that could indicate a lack of remorse or an anti-social attitude. While there is considerable variation in judicial approach, some judges feel that it is important to try to engage the youth and parents in dialogue and will ask more probing questions to learn what they think about the circumstances of the youth, the offence, and an appropriate sentence. There is some controversy about how actively the judge should attempt to engage the young person in the court process, especially at the sentencing stage.

A more active judicial role, attempting to engage the youth in a meaningful dialogue as part of the sentencing process, is encouraged by an approach to the legal process known as "therapeutic jurisprudence," the study of the impact of the law and legal process on the emotional life and on the psychological well-being of those who are appearing before the courts. American law professor David Wexler, a leading advocate of therapeutic jurisprudence, notes that one of the more effective types of rehabilitative program for young offenders, is one which is based on cognitive behavioural treatments:

> One type of these cognitive behavioral treatments encourages offenders to think through the chain of events that lead to criminality and then tries to get the offenders to stop and think in advance. This will enable an offender to figure out two things: (1) what are the high risk situations, in my case, for criminality or juvenile delinquency; and (2) how can the high risk situations be avoided, or how can the situations be coped with if they arise?
>
> These situations may be things such as realizing you are very much at risk on Friday nights after having partied with such and such person. The offender may decide that he or she shouldn't go out Friday nights. This determination is a way of avoiding high risk behaviors. Instead of going out on Friday night with Joe and getting into trouble, the offender may choose to stay home. But what hap-

pens the next night when Joe calls or what happens when Joe knocks on the offender's door?

Therapists have developed approaches of working with these issues, and of having offenders prepare relapse prevention plans. There are also certain programs, like "reasoning and rehabilitation" type programs, that teach offenders cognitive self change, to stop and think and figure out consequences, to anticipate high risk situations, and to learn to avoid and cope with them.

These programs seem to be reasonably successful. One of the issues that I am interested in now, from a therapeutic jurisprudence standpoint, is how this might be brought into the law.[36]

Professor Wexler suggests that one obvious way to make use of cognitive-behavioural programming is to make participation in such a program a term of probation. He goes on to argue that it may also affect the way in which judges sentence in court:

A more subtle way of thinking about this in therapeutic jurisprudence terms, however, is to ask how reasoning and rehabilitation can be made part of the legal process itself. The suggestion here is that if a judge . . . becomes familiar with these techniques and is about to consider someone for probation, the judge might say, "I'm going to consider you but I want you to come up with a type of preliminary plan that we will use as a basis of discussion. I want you to figure out why I should grant you probation and why I should be comfortable that you're going to succeed. In order for me to feel comfortable, I need to know what you regard to be high risk situations and how you're going to avoid them or cope with them." If that approach is followed, courts will be promoting cognitive self-change as part and parcel of the sentencing process itself. The process may operate this way: "I realize that I mess up on Friday nights; therefore, I propose that I will stay home Friday nights." Suddenly, it is not a judge imposing something on you. It's something you are coming up with so you should think it is fair. You have a voice in it, and presumably your compliance with this condition will also be better.

---

36   D. Wexler, "Therapeutic Jurisprudence: An Overview" (2000) 17 Thomas Cooley L. Rev. 1: online <www.therapeuticjurisprudence.org>. See also D. Wexler, P. Stolle & B. Winick, Practicing Therapeutic Jurisprudence: Law as a Helping Profession (Durham, NC: Carolina Academic Press, 2000) and P.D. Gould & P.H. Murrell, "Therapeutic Jurisprudence and Cognitive Complexity: An Overview" (2002) 29 Fordham Urb. L. J. 2117.

There is no rigorous empirical research to support the proposition that a "therapeutic jurisprudence" approach to the sentencing of adolescents is more effective at reducing recidivism, or that it has a real impact on the understanding of youths about the role of the justice system. However, an approach to sentencing that engages a youth has considerable intuitive appeal, and seems consistent with the YCJA. Section 3(1)(c)(iii) of the *YCJA*, which requires that consequences of offending behaviour for youth are to be "meaningful," speaks to the manner in which the consequences are imposed as well as to their nature. This provision in the Declaration of Principle supports a judicial approach to the sentencing process in which an attempt is made to engage the youth in dialogue to ensure that the sentence imposed is meaningful to the youth. At a minimum, this requires that the youth receive an explanation both of what sanction is being imposed and why this particular sentence is the appropriate response to the youth's offending behaviour. A discussion *before* sentencing with the youth, parents, and victim about what sentence would be "meaningful" would be even more desirable. There are, of course, real limits in terms of judicial temperament and time that will constrain individual youth court judges in engaging in this type of discussion in court.

Judges should be careful not to penalize youth who may be uncomfortable in verbalising their thoughts and feelings in court, by imposing a harsher sentence for youths who do not "engage" in the "therapeutic" process. There are also real concerns that if judges engage too heavily in a "therapeutic" approach, the justice system may become more intrusive.[37] Judges must ensure that resistance to participation in discussions about the offence or in therapy itself does not result in a more severe sanction than the offence would warrant.

1) Circle Sentencing

Some Canadian judges attempt to achieve restorative justice in some cases, especially those dealing with Aboriginal offenders, by using a "sentencing circle" (or "healing circle") that tries to more actively engage either adult or youth offenders, their families, victims, and their

---

37   See, for example, M.B. Hoffman, "Therapeutic Jurisprudence, Neo-Rehabilitation, and Judicial Collectivism: The Least Dangerous Branch Becomes the Most Dangerous: (2002) 29 Fordham Urb. L.J. 2063, where an American judge argues that therapeutic jurisprudence is "both ineffective and dangerous," especially in contexts like "drug courts," where the failure to engage in therapy may result in more severe sentences than the offence would merit.

community in the sentencing process. Although there are different methods of circle sentencing, typically, the judge asks the Crown, police or probation officer to arrange for the offender, members of the offender's family, the victim and any supporters, and community members to come to court to express their views of the offence and the offender, and to discuss an appropriate response to the offence. The Crown prosecutor and defence counsel, as well as any police or probation officers who have been involved in the case, will also be participants. Often everyone involved, including the judge and the lawyers, will sit in an open circle, although this is not necessary. The circle is a traditional shape of Aboriginal gatherings, in which everyone in the circle has an equal opportunity to participate. In a courtroom circle, after some opening words from the judge or another person, everyone who is invited is given an opportunity to speak. In some Aboriginal communities it is a common practice to pass an eagle feather or talking stick around the circle: only the person holding the feather or stick is permitted to speak, although participants may speak more than once.

At a sentencing circle offenders can hear directly from the victims, as well as from members of their own family, about the impact that their criminal behaviour has had. As a result of the exchanges, it is possible that a consensus will emerge about an appropriate sentencing plan that will address the needs of the victim and the offender, while holding the offender accountable.[38] Although the court is not obliged to adopt the recommendation of a sentencing circle, if a consensus is reached and has the apparent concurrence of the victim, this will often be very influential with the court. Even if there is no consensus about an appropriate sentence, the judge may use the session to inform his or her own decision about the sentence. This makes it especially important that the victim is properly supported throughout the conference process, and not coerced or pressured into supporting a position put forward by friends or relatives of the offender.

Circle sentencing is more time-consuming than an ordinary sentencing process, not only because more people are involved but because a broader range of issues may be explored than is usually the case in a sentencing hearing. A sentencing circle is used if there is some hope that there may be a degree of reconciliation between the victim and the offender, and some acceptance by the community of the

---

38   See Heino Lilles, "Youth Justice Initiatives in the Yukon" (2000) 24(2) Prov. Judges J. 18; J.V. Roberts and C. LaPrairie, "Sentencing Circles: Some Unanswered Questions" (1997) 39 Crim. L.Q. 69; and Allan Manson, *The Law of Sentencing* (Toronto: Irwin Law, 2001) 371–5.

offender. A restorative approach is more likely to be appropriate if the accused has pleaded guilty and is willing to accept responsibility and is seeking some form of reconciliation, or at least understanding, from the victim and community. Even if there is a guilty plea, it may not be possible to achieve restorative objectives.

Although there is no provision in the *Criminal Code* for use of sentencing circles for adult offenders, Canadian appeal courts have accepted that trial judges have a discretion to use this method of providing advice for sentencing, especially with Aboriginal offenders. The appeal judgments, however, emphasize that the circle is to provide advice about a sentence and should not in any way be involved in fact finding about the offence. There should be an agreed statement of facts or a judicial finding, not only about the legal issue of guilt but also in regard to any aggravating circumstances related to the offence, before the circle is convened.[39]

2) Conferences

The *YCJA* encourages the use of sentencing circles and similar methods of sentencing that have restorative justice objectives, through the statutory recognition of the sentencing conference. Section 41 provides that, after a finding of guilt, a youth justice court judge may directly convene a "conference" to advise the court about an appropriate sentence or may refer the case to another person so that a conference can be convened to make a recommendation about an appropriate sentence that will be communicated to the court. The concept of a conference includes circle sentencing, although the conference is a broader and more flexible institution. The judge who decides that a conference should be held may specify who is to attend or may delegate this responsibility to a police officer, a probation officer, or another professional or community member. Appropriate support and training is needed for any staff who are asked to arrange or convene a conference. Although not explicitly stated in the Act, it is expected that conferences will typically include the youth and parents, members of the community, and where appropriate, the victim. The community members might be volunteers, respected Elders in an Aboriginal community, or might include such professionals as teachers or social workers who are familiar with the youth. If the community is being involved, an effort must be made to ensure that there is "fair representation" from the community, and that the meeting is not overwhelmed with supporters of either the offender or the victim.

39　*R. v. B.L.*, [2002] A.J. No. 215 (C.A.).

If a youth justice court judge convenes and presides over a conference under section 41, it will be held as part of the sentencing process. In this situation, the participants in the conference are technically not witnesses who are subject to cross-examination by counsel, although there may be a dialogue involving the judge, lawyers, and members of the conference. If a conference is attended by the judge, a record of the proceedings should be kept and may be used by the judge for the purposes of making decisions about the youth. The judicially convened conference is intended to bring the community and the court closer together and requires trust and co-operation between members of the community and the judiciary. While the case law about sentencing circles and section 41 of the YCJA makes clear that the recommendation of a conference is not binding on the court, in practice, judges are likely to follow the recommendation of a conference, since this recommendation reflects a consensus of the victim, and members of the community.

D. SENTENCING OPTIONS

If a youth justice court judge finds a young person guilty of an offence, the judge shall impose one or more of the sentences provided for in section 42(2) of the YCJA:

(a) a reprimand;
(b) an absolute discharge;
(c) a conditional discharge;
(d) a fine of up to $1000;
(e) monetary restitution to a victim for damage to property or personal injury;
(f) restitution of property to a victim;
(g) financial compensation to the innocent purchaser of stolen property if that person is required to return the property to its rightful owner;
(h) performance of personal services for a victim;
(i) up to 240 hours of community service work;
(j) an order of prohibition, as allowed in the Criminal Code, such as an order prohibiting driving of an automobile or possession of a firearm for a stated period;
(k) probation for up to two years;
(l) participation in a community-based program of intensive community supervision and support: this sentence can only be imposed with the consent of a provincial director;

(m) attendance at a community-based non-residential program (an attendance centre) for up to 240 hours: this sentence can only be imposed with the consent of a provincial director;

(n) custody and community supervision for up to two years, and up to three years for some more serious offences, with the last third presumptively served in the community;

(o) for a youth convicted of attempted murder, manslaughter, or aggravated sexual assault, a sentence of a total of up to three years of custody and conditional supervision;

(p) for a youth who has *not* been found guilty of a "serious violent offence," a sentence of up to six months of *deferred* custody and supervision may be imposed: under this sentence a youth continues to reside in the community subject to conditions, with the provision that breach of a condition can result in serving the balance of the sentence in custody;

(q) for a youth convicted of murder, the maximum sentence is ten years of custody and conditional supervision in the community, with the initial sentence to be no more than six years in custody and the balance under supervision in the community;

(r) for youth convicted of a third "serious violent offence" or one of the most serious "presumptive offences," a sentence of intensive rehabilitative custody and supervision may be imposed; and

(s) any other reasonable and ancillary conditions.

As under the *YOA*, subsection 42(2) of the *YCJA* allows for the imposition of "any one or more" of the sentences "that are not inconsistent with one another." It is, for example, possible for a judge to order that a young offender shall provide restitution to a victim and perform community service. Under the *YOA*, it was not uncommon for judges to impose a short custodial sentence followed by a relatively long probation term, in order to allow for a long period of supervision in the community after release from custody. The *YCJA* clearly allows for the combination of custodial and non-custodial sentences, although the fact that all custody sentences include a period of community supervision is likely to make this combination of sentences less common than under the *YOA*.

Subsection 42(14) provides that for most offences, the maximum combined duration of sentences is two years, unless it is one of the serious offences for which an adult could receive a life sentence, in which case the maximum custodial sentence in youth justice court is three years, and the maximum combined sentence is also three years. Section 42(15) of the *YCJA* provides that if a youth is being sentenced for more than one offence, the maximum duration of any combination of youth justice court sentences is three years,[40] unless the one of the offences is murder, in which case the maximum total continuous combined sentences are ten years, if one of the offences is first-degree murder and seven years if it is second-degree murder.

The list of sentencing options in section 42(2) of the *YCJA* is considerably longer and more complex than the dispositions found in section 20(1) of the *YOA*. The new youth sentences are: a reprimand; an intensive support and supervision program order; a program attendance order; a deferred custody and supervision order; and an intensive rehabilitative custody and supervision order.[41] These new options are intended to allow for more use of community-based and rehabilitative sentences. The possibility of imposing one of these new sentences, however, is largely dependent on the establishment of programs by the provincial government and the approval of a provincial director for the imposition of such a sentence.

The *YCJA* appears to support a degree of judicial creativity in sentencing, especially in the shaping of community-based sentences. If there is not sufficient flexibility in the specific provisions, section 42(2)(s) allows for judges to "impose on the young person any other reasonable and ancillary conditions that the court considers appropriate." Section 42(2)(s) might, for example, be invoked to require a young offender to write a letter of apology or make a donation to charity, or even to attend counselling without being placed on probation. This provision, however, like all of the sentences in the *YCJA*, is subject to section 42(8), which provides that "nothing in this section derogates from the rights of a young person regarding consent to physical or mental-health treatment." Section 42(8) means that unless a young person is found to be mentally incompetent, there can be no involuntary medical treatment, such as drug therapy.

While there is considerable statutory flexibility for a judge to shape sentences, especially community-based sentences, that make use of existing community resources and programs, the most significant constraint on judicial creativity in sentencing is likely to arise from the limitations of these resources. The jurisprudence under the *YOA* made clear that a youth court judge does *not* have the jurisdiction to order the government to provide specific treatment, counselling, or program-

---

40   See *YCJA*, above note 1, s. 42(16) for maximum sentence if a youth who is already under a sentence is convicted of another offence before the completion of the first sentence.

41   *YCJA*, above note 1, ss. 42(2)(a), (l), (m), (p), and (r).

ming to a young offender who is being sentenced, even if it is clear that these resources would be most likely to address the youth's offending behaviour and reduce the likelihood of reoffending.

The Alberta Court of Appeal ruled that very specific statutory language would be needed for youth justice legislation to be construed as giving the judiciary the authority to order governments to provide or pay for specific programs. There is no such language in either the *YOA* or the *YCJA*. In the absence of a clear statutory power or a violation of the *Charter*,[42] it is inconsistent with the generally accepted judicial role in Canada for a judge to assume the authority to require the government to pay for or provide specific services. The Alberta Appeal Court commented on the role of the sentencing judge in youth court: "If judges were empowered to order the government to make specific additional expenditures, they too would have their hand in taxpayers' pockets, for ultimately governments would have to raise taxes to pay the extra costs. The government has wide latitude in discharging its duties under the *YOA*. The judiciary 'need not and should not tell the government . . . what specific delivery systems should [be] employed'."[43]

Similarly, in *R. v. L.E.K.* the Saskatchewan Court of Appeal observed: "The youth court's jurisdiction is limited not only by the terms of the statute which created it but also by fundamental constitutional principles relating to the separation of powers between the judiciary, whose role it is to impose sanctions, and the executive, whose role it is to administer the sanctions."[44]

While the Preamble and sections 3, 38 and 39 of the *YCJA* recognize the importance of having sentences that address the underlying causes of youth crime and that attempt to rehabilitate young offenders, there is nothing in the Act to allow a youth justice court to order that any particular type of program or service should be provided to a young offender as part of a sentence imposed by the court. While a youth justice court judge can, within limits, impose a sentence that requires a youth to attend available counselling or a treatment program, or that requires the youth to be confined to a place of custody where such services are expected to be provided, the judge cannot require that the government provide specific services to the youth. The judge may recommend that particular rehabilitative services should be

---

42   *Canadian Charter of Rights and Freedoms*, enacted as Part I of the *Constitution Act, 1982*, being Schedule B to the *Canada Act, 1982* (U.K.), 1982, c. 11 (subsequently referred to as the *Charter*).

43   *R. v. R.J.H.*, [2000] A.J. No. 396 (QL), at paras. 35–6; see also discussion in Chapter 2.

44   *R. v. L.E.K.*, [2000] S.J. No. 844 (Sask C.A.), para. 20.

provided, but it is the responsibility of provincial correctional authorities to decide what services will actually be provided to a youth under a sentence imposed by the court.

It is understandable that youth justice court judges want to ensure that appropriate rehabilitative services are provided to the young offenders whom they are sentencing, but it is clear that the YCJA does not allow a judge to order that specific services are to be provided to an individual young offender. However, if a sentence is imposed in the expectation that particular services will be provided and they are not provided, this may be the ground for the review of the original sentence. If, for example, as a result of information in a pre-sentence report, at the time of sentencing the court indicates that it expects that a youth will be placed in a particular custody facility with specific rehabilitative services available and the youth ends up in a facility without these services, this might be the basis for seeking a judicial review of the sentence and early release from custody under section 96.

Custody and supervision sentences present the court with complex options. Under the Act, if a court imposes a custodial sentence, in most cases the sentence is made under section 42(2)(n), and must be one with the first two-thirds to be served in custody and the last third in the community under supervision. There are provisions for earlier release and for a court order to keep a youth in custody to serve the last portion of the sentence. For most offences the maximum sentence is two years in custody and supervision, although, if an adult could be sentenced to life imprisonment for an offence, a young person may receive a maximum sentence of three years' custody and supervision.

There are also special sentencing provisions in section 42(2)(o),(q), and (r) for youths sentenced for the most serious violent offences.

For manslaughter, attempted murder, or aggravated sexual assault, the maximum sentence under section 42(2)(o) is a total of three years of custody and conditional supervision in the community. The sentencing judge has the authority to specify the periods in custody and under supervision in the community. Subject to certain requirements for pre-trial notice and a jury trial being satisfied, the Crown may also seek an adult sentence for a youth convicted of manslaughter, attempted murder, or aggravated sexual assault, in which case the maximum sentence is life imprisonment.

Under section 42(2)(q), for a youth convicted of first degree murder, the maximum sentence is a total of ten years of custody and conditional supervision in the community, with the initial sentence to be no more than six years in custody and the balance under conditional supervision. Subject to certain requirements for pre-trial notice and a jury trial being satisfied, the Crown may also seek an adult sentence for a youth convicted of murder, in which the maximum sentence is life imprisonment.

The sentence of intensive rehabilitative custody and supervision under section 42(2)(r) is only to be imposed if the youth is "suffering from a mental illness or disorder, a psychological disturbance or an emotional disorder."[45] This sentence can only be imposed on a youth convicted of one of the very serious "presumptive offences," or a third "serious violent offence." It will result in a youth being placed in a facility where there is a greater access to rehabilitative and mental health services than in ordinary custody, but the *YCJA* does not allow for involuntary drug or other medical treatment being imposed on a young offender. The maximum length of a sentence of intensive rehabilitative custody and supervision is the same as the maximum for ordinary custody and supervision, and is determined by the offence in question, ranging from two years for some offences to ten years for first-degree murder. This sentence can only be imposed with the consent of a provincial/territorial director.

1) Community-Based Sentences

A reprimand and an absolute discharge are the least serious sentences that can be imposed under the *YCJA*. Neither involves any sanction beyond the appearance in court for a sentence to be imposed; they will generally be used only for relatively minor first offences. A reprimand is a new sentencing option in the *YCJA* and is similar to an absolute discharge, but the record of a reprimand can only be used for two months after it is imposed, while the record of an absolute discharge may be used for one year.[46] Thus, a reprimand is an even less severe sanction than an absolute discharge, and it is the mildest sanction that can be imposed in response to a finding of guilt.

A judge who imposes a reprimand is expected to discuss the offence with the youth and express disapproval of the offence and the expectation that the youth will not offend again. Some judges who are imposing a reprimand will engage the youth and perhaps the parents in a meaningful discussion, which would generally be desirable. With some judges, especially in a busy court, the reprimand is likely to be a fairly perfunctory process. A reprimand will generally only be appropriate for the least serious offences; it may also be imposed in a situation in which

---

45   *YCJA*, above note 1, s. 42(7).
46   *YCJA*, above note 1, ss. 119(2)(c)–(e).

a judge feels that the case was inappropriately the subject of a formal charge and should have been dealt with by means of some form of extrajudicial measure. An absolute discharge is similar to a reprimand, in that it should involve some discussion of the offence by the judge with the youth, with the youth then being discharged without a conviction being entered and with no official sanction other than having a "record of a discharge." Section 42(2)(b) provides that an absolute discharge may be imposed if the court considers "it to be in the best interests of the young person and not contrary to the public interest." This sentence is usually reserved for minor first offenders.

When imposing a reprimand or absolute discharge, the judge is likely to caution the youth that reoffending will result in a more severe sanction and that this is a "last warning." Under the YOA, since most youths committing less serious offences were sent to alternative measures at least once before being sentenced by a youth court judge, an absolute discharge was relatively rarely used by youth courts, being imposed in only 2 percent of cases.[47]

As originally enacted in 1984, the YOA had no provision for a conditional discharge. The failure to provide for a conditional discharge was premised on the view that the various non-disclosure provisions meant that all youths who did not reoffend were in effect conditionally discharged. Judges and other youth justice system professionals, however, expressed a desire to have an explicit conditional discharge option. Subsection 45(1)(d.3) was added to the YOA in 1995 to provide for a conditional discharge.

There is also provision for a conditional discharge in the YCJA section 42(2)(c), which allows a youth justice court judge to give a youth receiving a sanction a message that, if the terms of the sentence are complied with and the youth does not reoffend, the youth will have the "record wiped clean;" the youth will then not be viewed as an offender, although the record of the discharge can be used for three years after a finding of guilt in the event that there is a subsequent conviction. Section 42(2)(c) allows a court to order that a "young person be discharged on such conditions as the court considers appropriate."

Conditions for a discharge might include making a donation to a charity, undergoing counselling, doing community service work, making restitution to a victim or reporting to a probation officer. If the youth obeys the conditions and commits no further offences during the stipulated period, the sentence will be deemed to be "discharged." Under section 42(11) a conditional discharge cannot be combined with

47   Statistics Canada, "Youth Court Statistics 2000–2001" (2002) 22:3 Juristat.

a sentence of probation (section 42(2)(k)), an order for intensive community rehabilitation and support (section 42(2)(l)), or an attendance order (section 42(2(m)). However, at least some of the terms that would normally be associated with a probation order, such as keeping the peace and being of good behaviour or meeting regularly with a probation officer, can be terms of a conditional discharge. If there is a further offence within three years after the finding of guilt, the court sentencing for that offence may consider the prior record of a conditional discharge. The fact that a discharge was imposed is viewed as less stigmatizing than a regular sentence, which may help the youth if there is a potential that the record may be considered for immigration or employment purposes.

Judges dealing with young offenders have usually been reluctant to impose a fine on a youth, since this is a purely punitive sanction. While serving an accountability function, and perhaps reminding the youth that the offence has caused some harm to the community, the imposition of a fine serves little or no rehabilitative purpose. Further, many youths have little or no income of their own, and may be unable to pay a fine from their own income or funds. In higher-income families, a parent may end up paying the fine, an outcome that sends a bad message to a young offender. In lower-income families, a fine may create a substantial burden for the youth or family. A fine could even lead a youth to commit another offence to raise funds to pay the fine. Section 54(1) requires that a judge shall take account of the "present and future means of the young person to pay" a fine before imposing this sentence. In some cases a youth will have employment and a fine may be an appropriate sentence. Fines were used either alone or in combination with another sentence in about 6 percent of cases under the *YOA*, with most fines in the range of $100 to $500.[48] As under the *YOA*, the maximum fine under the *YCJA* is $1000.

Section 53(1) of the *YCJA* allows for the provincial government to set aside a portion of any fines paid to a victim assistance fund. If the province has not established a program to automatically direct a portion of every fine to such a fund, section 53(2) permits a sentencing judge to add a surcharge of up to 15 percent on any fines paid to be directed to a victim assistance fund. Under section 54(2) of the *YCJA*, a provincial government may establish a "fine option" program to allow youths to "work off" their fines by performing some form of community service work instead of making monetary payments. However, not many fine option programs were established under the *YOA*. If it seems

---

48   Statistics Canada, above note 47.

unlikely that a youth will be able to pay a fine, it is more common for judges to directly impose a community service order.

Because of its restorative and symbolic value for youths and their communities, judges often impose some type of reparative sanction. Such sanctions include restitution or compensation to a victim, or a community service order. This type of sanction has the advantage of making clear to the youth the damage caused by the offence, while compensating in some way for the victim's loss, and promotes the objective found in section 3(1)(c)(iv) of the *YCJA* of having sentences that "repair the harm done to victims and the community." Under section 42(2)(e)–(h), a youth justice court judge may also order that a young offender provide some form of monetary compensation or do some type of work for a victim. Before ordering any form of compensation or restitution to be given to a victim, the youth justice court shall consider the representations of the victim about whether compensation is being sought and what was the amount of the loss.

Section 42(2)(e) is a broad provision that allows a youth justice court to order that a young person provide financial compensation to any victim for damage to property, loss of income or other verifiable expenses (or "special damages") caused by an offence. If the amount of the loss is readily ascertainable and the offender has the financial means to pay compensation, it is very appropriate to make a compensation order. If the amount of damage caused by a young offender is difficult to determine or beyond the means of the young offender to pay, the focus of sentencing should be on holding the young person accountable to society. In cases of significant financial loss, a victim may have to seek compensation from insurers or provincial compensation for victims of crime programs. A judge who orders a young offender to pay some form of compensation or a fine should be satisfied that payment can be made from the savings or earnings of the youth, and not by the parents.

As discussed in Chapter 2, in some cases parents of a young offender who have failed to adequately supervise their children may have civil liability imposed, but a youth justice court should not, as a part of a sentence, make a compensation order that in effect requires the parents to provide the money to satisfy the order. Section 54(6) makes clear that the court shall not order that a young offender perform services as means of compensating a victim without the consent of the victim. While some victims may be willing to have a youth who has caused them damage perform services for them, such as having an offender shovelling snow for an elderly neighbour whose property was intentionally damaged by the youth, some victims will not want an offender to be in contact with them.

With a community service order, the court orders the youth to perform a certain a number of hours of work to be performed, up to a maximum of 240 hours. The youth justice court sets the number of hours of work to be done but the specific type of community service work is generally arranged by a youth probation officer or through a community agency. These orders are intended to remind youths that they have done an act that has harmed the whole community, and that the community is entitled to some form of compensation through the youth's service. Sometimes the community service work can be related to the offence, so that, for example, a youth who has vandalized public property might be required to do some maintenance work for the municipality. In some cases the damages suffered may be extensive and compensation, or full compensation, may not be realistic.

Section 54(1) requires a youth justice court to have regard to a youth's ability to pay any amount in a compensatory order before it is made, while section 54(7)(b) requires that a court not order a youth to perform community service work or provide services to a victim unless satisfied that doing so would not interfere with the normal hours of employment or schooling of the youth. Section 54(7)(a) requires that before making an order that a young offender is to provide services to a victim or the community, the judge should be satisfied that the youth is a "suitable candidate." The judge should be satisfied that the youth is reasonably well motivated and likely to do this work in a responsible fashion. With both community service orders and orders that work should be done for a victim, there is a potential for problems in supervision of the work; some young offenders may require substantial supervision to ensure that the work is properly done.

The *YCJA* has two new community-based sentences that are intended to provide young offenders with significant support and supervision in the community, while having therapeutic elements that may reduce the likelihood of reoffending. Section 42(2)(m) allows a youth justice court to order a young offender "to attend a non-residential program" for up to 240 hours. Section 42(2)(l) allows a youth justice court to order a young offender "into an intensive support and supervision program." An order can only be made under these provisions if the specific program is approved by the provincial director, who indicates that there is a place available for the youth who is being sentenced.[49] While various therapeutic services may be provided to a

---

49   *YCJA*, above note 1, s. 42(3).

youth who is subject to either of these sentences, section 42(8) makes clear that the mere fact that a youth is subject to a youth justice court sentence does not derogate from the right of a young person who is not mentally incompetent to consent or refuse to consent to specific medical treatments, such as undergoing drug treatment.

While the YOA did not explicitly allow for these two types of community-based sentences, in some cases probation orders were made under the Act that may have been similar in effect to orders made under section 42(2)(l)–(m) of the YCJA. The enactment of these provisions is intended to encourage provincial governments to establish community-based sentencing programs, although section 42(3) makes clear that a judge may only impose one of these sentences if a provincial director "has determined that a program to enforce the order is available" for the youth who is being sentenced.

The attendance order requires that governments or other agencies establish programs that young offenders can attend in the community where they will be provided with guidance and support in order to help them not reoffend. Community-based programs may give youths an opportunity to meet with counsellors individually or in groups with other young offenders to discuss problems, values, and behaviours. These programs might deal with such issues as: the effects of crime on victims and the community; anger management; dealing with antisocial peers; substance abuse; or developing employment skills.

In addition to the requirement under section 42(3) that the provincial director specify that a program is available, section 54(7) requires that a court not order a youth to attend such a program unless satisfied that the youth is a "suitable candidate" and that participation will not interfere with the normal hours of work or education of the youth. The maximum duration of an attendance order under section 42(2)(m) is 240 hours. By way of contrast, an order for intensive support and supervision under section 42(2)(l) may be in effect for up to two years,[50] and contemplates a longer and more intensive level of support and control over the youth in the community. It is expected that a youth who is subject to an order of intensive support and supervision will, in effect, be on probation, and a youth justice court may order that a youth who is subject to an attendance order will also be placed on probation.

Section 55(1) provides that a youth who is subject to a section 42(2)(l) intensive support and supervision order shall "keep the peace and be of good behaviour" and appear in youth justice court as required, while section 55(2) permits a court to add any of the terms

---

50   YCJA, above note 1, s. 42(14).

that can be made as part of a probation order. A youth who violates any of these conditions may be prosecuted under section 137 of the *YCJA*.

The orders for intensive support and supervision require community-based programs that will provide a higher level of service and control than is ordinarily offered by probation services. In some provinces, this type of supervision and support will be provided by regular probation officers with a smaller case-load, while in other provinces the responsibilities may be contracted to community agencies. A major focus should be on the provision of support for youth in dealing with their behavioural problems. The community-based multi-systemic treatment program, which has been tried on an experimental basis in some Ontario communities, is an example of a program that might qualify as "intensive support and supervision."[51]

The provision of mental health services, counselling, and behaviour management direction may be central components of this type of program. However, given the restrictions in the *YCJA* that are placed on the use of custodial sentences, including intensive rehabilitative custody and support under section 42(2)(r), it seems clear that a youth cannot be confined to a mental health facility or other place under an order for intensive support and supervision; orders under section 42(2)(l) are expected to constrain the behaviour of youth and provide services, but they are not to be removed from the community under this type of order. The provisions for attendance centre orders and intensive community support and supervision have significant potential for offering youth justice courts effective community-based sentencing options, but they can only be used if provincial governments are ready to approve and fund appropriate programs.

Section 42(2)(j) of the *YCJA* gives a youth justice court judge the authority to make a prohibition or forfeiture order that may be imposed under any other Act. This type of order is almost always imposed in addition to some other sentence and is intended to reduce the risk of reoffending when certain types of offences have been committed. The two most commonly imposed orders are a prohibition on driving, and a prohibition on the possession of weapons, which under section 51 may

---

51   Multi-systemic treatment is discussed more fully in Chapter 10. See also, for example, C.M. Borduin, *et al.*, "Multi-systemic Treatment of Serious Juvenile Offenders: Long-Term Prevention of Criminality and Violence" (1995) 63 J. of Consulting and Clinical Psychology 569; S.W. Henggeler, "Treating Serious Antisocial Behavior in Youth: The MST Approach" (May 1997) Office of Juvenile Justice and Delinquency Prevention Juvenile Justice Bulletin 1 at 3; and London Family Court Clinic online at <www.lfcc.on.ca>.

be mandatory for certain offences. It is also possible to impose a prohibition under section 446(5) of the *Criminal Code* on the ownership or
care of animals if a person has been convicted of an offence involving
cruelty to animals. Section 42(2)(j), however, states that a youth justice
court cannot impose a prohibition order on being in school or otherwise
associating with persons under fourteen pursuant to section 161 of the
Criminal Code; this type of order is commonly made against sexual
offenders, but is considered inappropriate for young offenders, who will
often be associating with adolescents or children, and some of whom
may be under fourteen years of age themselves.

If an adult is convicted of an offence involving consumption of
alcohol and operation of a motor vehicle, in addition to any other sanction under the *Criminal Code*,[52] there is a mandatory prohibition on
driving as well as the possibility of suspension of a driver's licence
under provincial licensing laws. A person who drives in violation of a
prohibition order commits a *Criminal Code* offence which the courts
view very seriously, even if it does not result in an accident. For young
offenders convicted of an impaired driving offence, the youth justice
court may impose a prohibition on driving, but in keeping with the
philosophy of individualized justice for adolescents, unlike with adults
this type of prohibition order is not mandatory for this type of offence.

For adults convicted of offences involving the use of firearms or
other weapons, section 109 of the *Criminal Code* provides that a prohibition on the possession of weapons will usually be mandatory, subject
to certain exceptions under section 113, if it can, for example, be
shown that the person needs to use a weapon to sustain him- or herself through hunting. Under section 110 of the *Code*, there is also the
possibility of a weapons prohibition order against an adult convicted of
an offence involving violence but without the use of weapons. Under
the *YOA*, it was held that the mandatory weapons prohibition of section 109 did not apply to young offenders,[53] although judges could
choose to impose such a prohibition in appropriate cases; the courts
were more reluctant to impose such a prohibition for youths living in
rural or remote areas. Because of the increased concern about youth
violence, section 51 of the *YCJA* provides that if a youth is convicted of
an offence involving weapons, in addition to any other sentence, youth
justice court presumptively shall impose a minimum two-year prohibition on the possession of weapons. As for adults, if a young person
requires the use of a weapon to hunt to sustain the youth or the youth's

52   *Criminal Code*, above note 2, s. 259.
53   *R. v. C.F.B.* (1987), 33 C.C.C. (3d) 95 (N.W.T. C.A.).

family, or use of a weapon is needed for employment and there are no other prospects for employment, section 113 of the *Code* allows for the court to not impose a weapons prohibition. Under section 52 of the *YCJA*, there is also provision for weapons prohibitions in other cases where a violent offence has been committed that did not involve the use of a weapon.

Section 59 of the *YCJA* is essentially identical to section 32 of the *YOA*, providing for review of non-custodial youth sentences by the youth justice court. The review can be initiated by the young person, a parent, the Crown prosecutor, or the provincial director. This sentence-review mechanism enables the courts to revisit a sentence imposed on a young person and to consider whether it was still appropriate in the circumstances, allowing for it to be varied or even terminated. For example, such a hearing can be held if a young person is unable to pay a fine and wants to request a reduction in the amount, or if there is a need to review the terms of a probation order because of a change in a youth's circumstances or in the availability of community-based programs.

2) Probation

The most frequently imposed disposition under the *YOA* was probation, with about half of youths subject to *YOA* dispositions receiving probation, sometimes in combination with some other sanction, such as a requirement for community service.[54] Probation will likely continue to be the most commonly imposed sentence under the *YCJA*. Under both the *YOA* and the *YCJA*, the judge ordering probation has significant discretion to impose conditions that are considered "appropriate in the circumstances." In some cases the conditions of a probation order may be very minimal, while in other cases a probation order may be very intrusive, determining where a youth will reside, what type of schooling, employment, or other activities the youth will engage in, and requiring the youth to participate in counselling or other treatment. While probation orders commonly require that a youth meet regularly with a probation officer for counselling or supervision, this is not an essential part of a probation order. A probation order may include conditions that a youth keep a curfew, attend school, reside with parents, or even complete a wilderness program.[55]

---

54   See Statistics Canada, above note 47 reporting that in 48 percent of youth court cases the most serious disposition was probation.

55   *R. v. B.(J.P.)* (1993), 31 B.C.A.C. 81 (C.A.).

Judges should impose only probation conditions that are a proportionate and appropriate response to the offence, and should avoid imposing conditions that do not address offending behaviour. Imposing conditions that are not related to offending but may be breached can result in an escalating spiral of involvement in the legal system and, ultimately, in an inappropriate custodial sentence. A judge might, for example, think that it would be desirable for a seventeen-year-old who has dropped out of school to return to classes; however, if the youth has a long history of school difficulties and non-attendance, this may be "setting up the youth for failure." Under the *YOA*, offences involving breach of probation terms were among those offences most likely to result in a custody sentence. Because imposing probation terms can result in a breach and in further escalating charges and involvement in the youth justice system, judges should be satisfied that any probation terms are truly responsive to offending behaviour and proportionate to the offence.

At a minimum each probation order requires that a youth "shall keep the peace and be of good behaviour," and appear before the youth justice court when required to do so.[56] Some judges exercise the power to have a youth return to the court so that his or her progress can be monitored. However, these terms generally have limited practical significance, since youth on probation are usually required to return to court only if they are charged with a breach of probation or for a completely new offence. Youths may be charged with an offence under section 137 of the *YCJA* as a result of breach of a specific term of a probation order, such as a failure to attend school if required to do so by the probation order. A youth may also be required to return to court if there is an application under section 59 to review the probation order to make the terms less restrictive.

Sometimes a judge will set out the nature of the terms of probation but delegate to another person the responsibility to specify the details. For example, a judge may order that a youth shall keep a curfew set by a parent or attend counselling as directed by a probation officer. These orders are quite commonly made and allow for flexibility. Some judges, however, have ruled that it is not permissible for a judge to delegate sentencing powers in this way, holding that a youth who fails to abide by specific terms imposed by a parent or probation officer cannot be convicted of breach of probation. Judges have accepted that they must determine the nature of the terms of a probation order, but that they may

---

56   *YCJA*, above note 1, s. 55(1).

delegate the details of implementation to a probation officer. Thus it was held under the *YOA* that a judge can validly delegate to a probation officer the authority to set specific times for a curfew, provided that the judge has made clear that the probation officer has this responsibility.[57]

Allowing a probation officer some authority to specify details within parameters set by the judge provides flexibility, which is required to meet changing circumstances. It may also allow for specific terms to set about matters for which there may be an absence of information at the time of sentence, such as providing the name of a specific drug counsellor whom the youth is to meet with. However, a probation officer should not be given the authority to determine the conditions on which a youth will reside in the community. Further, giving parents the authority to establish the details of a probation order can be very problematic and may place parents in a difficult position in the event of breach.[58]

Section 55(2)(g) of the *YCJA* specifically allows a judge to include in a probation order that a youth shall "reside in such place as the provincial director may specify." These types of residence orders were quite frequently made under the *YOA* and allow a judge to provide that young offenders may be placed outside their homes if parental care is inadequate or unavailable, without requiring that a youth receive a custodial sentence. A residency term may result in a youth residing with a relative, or being required to complete a wilderness program, or being placed in a child welfare facility or group home,[59] and allow for government financial support for these types of placements.

Under the *YOA*, some judges went so far as to hold that a provincial director may direct a youth to reside in an open-custody facility pursuant to a probation order.[60] Legitimate concerns have been raised about such use of probation orders as a back door to custodial sentences. The better interpretation of the *YCJA* is that, in light of the statutory restrictions on the use of custody by judges and the provisions of the Act that are intended to reduce the use of custody, it would not be appropriate to allow the provincial director to be able in effect

---

57   *R.* v. *James G.*(1994), 23 W.C.B. (2d) 49 (Ont. Prov. Ct.), per Hardman J.

58   See, for example, *R.* v. *F.(P.D.)* (1987), 57 C.R. (3d) 22 (Ont. Prov. Ct.), Nasmith Prov. J. (probation term: "Live with mother and obey rules and curfew" unenforceable); but see *contra*, *R.* v. *G.(J.)* (26 October 1993), (Ont. Prov. Ct.) [unreported] [summarized 23 W.C.B. (2d) 49] and *R.* v. *R.(B.J.)* (13 January 1986), (Ont. C.A.) [unreported] [summarized Y.O.S. 86–026].

59   *R.* v. *M.(A.D.)* (30 October 1984), (Man. C.A.) [unreported] [summarized [1985] W.D.F.L. 130].

60   *R.* v. *J.(M.K.)* (1994), 137 N.S.R. (2d) 260 (C.A.).

to impose a custodial sentence on a youth who has been sentenced by a court to probation.[61]

When a probation order is made, the youth justice court shall "cause the order to be read . . . and explained to the young person . . . and confirm that the young person understands it."[62] This may be done by the judge or a court clerk and is often done by a probation officer. A copy of the probation order is to be given to the youth and to any parent in attendance at the court. After the explanation is given, the youth is expected to sign an acknowledgment that the purpose and effect of the order has been explained and that a copy of the order was provided to the youth. The judge may also direct that a copy of the probation order is to be given to a parent who is not in court at the time of sentencing but who seems to have been taking an active interest in the proceedings, an interest that is most likely to have been demonstrated by having attended court at an earlier occasion or by communicating with the court through the youth worker who prepared a pre-sentence report.

If a youth is to be convicted of breach of probation under section 137 of the *YCJA*, it must be proven that the youth was given an adequate explanation of the probation order, so that it can be established that the youth was aware of the significance of failure to follow the terms of the order.[63] This will usually be done by producing the signed acknowledgement of the young person, although it is also possible to call as a witness the probation officer who gave the youth the explanation.

Under the *YOA*, there were cases in which the courts held that the failure of the Crown to prove that a copy of the probation order was given to the parents and the youth's lawyer would prevent the youth from being convicted for breach of the probation order, as it was necessary to prove that these adults were aware of the terms of the order and able to advise the youth about the need to comply with the order.[64] Even under the *YOA*, some judges held that, if it could be proven that a youth was aware of the terms of a probation order, the youth should not be acquitted on a breach charge on the basis that there was an administrative error and the youth's parents or lawyer were not given a copy of the order.[65]

---

61   *R. v. E.(S.M.)* (7 July 1989), (Ont. C.A.) [unreported] [summarized (1989), 7 W.C.B. (2d) 317].

62   *YCJA*, above note 1, s. 56(1).

63   *R. v. C.H.*, [2000] A.J. 1222.

64   *R. v. M.(L.A.)* (1994), 92 C.C.C. (3d) 562 (Ont. C.A.); *R. v. H. (J.)*, [2002] O.J. 268 (C.A.).

65   *R. v. A. (D.C.)* (2000), 143 C.C.C. 302 (Alta. C.A.), leave to appeal to S.C.C. dismissed 147 C.C.C. (3d) vi; and *R. v. H. (J.)*, [2002] O.J. 268 (C.A.), per Doherty J.A. dissenting.

Section 56(4) of the *YCJA* makes clear that the failure of a parent to receive a copy of a probation order or of the youth to have signed an acknowledgment of having received a copy of the order does not affect the validity of the order, while section 48 of the Act makes clear that a lawyer for a young person is only to receive a copy of the probation order or other sentence if the lawyer specifically requests it.

If a young offender who has been placed on probation "wilfully fails or refuses to comply" with a term of the order, the youth may be subject to prosecution of a summary conviction offence under section 137 of the *YCJA*. In practice, probation officers have a significant degree of discretion in deciding whether to have a charge laid for breach of probation and will generally be reluctant to have a charge laid unless there is a significant or persistent breach, or a new offence is believed to have been committed. Probation officers appreciate that sometimes the threat of laying a charge may be more effective in securing compliance with a probation order and changing the behaviour and attitudes of a youth, than actually taking the matter back to court. The probation officer is aware that proceeding with a new charge can be a slow process, especially if the youth pleads not guilty to the charge, typically resulting in delay until the youth can retain legal counsel and a trial date can be set.

The *YCJA* is intended to help ensure that there is not a rapid escalation of responses to a breach of probation, with section 39(1) providing that a custodial sentence should only be considered if there has been a failure to "comply with non-custodial sentenc*es*" [emphasis added]. This indicates that a first breach of probation charge should generally only result in another community-based sentence, perhaps a longer term of probation, or a requirement to participate in the program of an attendance centre if one is available. Even a second breach of probation order should not automatically result in a custodial sentence, as the restrictions on the use of custody in sections 38 and 39 continue to apply. In dealing with breach of probation, a youth justice court judge should attempt to understand the reasons for the youth's non-compliance. In some cases, the terms of the original order may have proven to be unnecessarily restrictive and some modification in the terms of a probation order may be appropriate. Section 59 of the *YCJA* allows for the review of any non-custodial order if, for example, a youth is experiencing "serious difficulty in complying" with the terms of a probation order and modification seems appropriate.

Unfortunately, however, many of the youths who breach probation orders are unwilling or unable to accept reasonable restrictions on their behaviour and, at some point, a custodial sentence will be an appropriate way to hold the youth accountable and uphold the integrity of the probation system. If a person who was sentenced to a probation order under the YCJA breaches a term of that order when past the age of eighteen, then this is a summary conviction offence contrary to section 137 of the YCJA, but that person is to be charged as an adult and is subject to sentencing under the *Criminal Code*.[66]

3) Responding to the Over-Reliance on Custody

The YOA, as enacted in 1984, created a discretionary sentencing regime which resulted in great differences in sentencing practices among provinces and even among individual judges in the same city.[67] During the time the YOA was in force there was a substantial increase in the number of custodial sentences for young persons who had violated the criminal law.[68] The average daily population of young offenders in custody in Canada increased by 24 percent between 1986 and 1994, although on average, youths sentenced to custody under the YOA served shorter periods of time in custody than those sent to training school under the *Juvenile Delinquents Act*.[69] In 2000–2001, more than three-quarters of youth custody sentences were for less than three months, and only 6 percent were for longer than six months,[70] although only a minority of youths who received custodial dispositions were convicted of violent offences. While Canada has had a relatively extensive rate of use of youth custody, studies indicated that at least half of those young offenders who were placed in custody reoffended and returned to an adult or youth custody facility.[71]

The increase in the use of custody under the YOA in comparison to the *Juvenile Delinquents Act* can, in part, be attributed to the sentencing decisions which, when balancing the principles articulated in Section 3 of the YOA, emphasized the protection of society and responsibility over *limited* accountability and addressing special needs. There was, for

---

66   See, for example, *R. v. A.A.E.* (1991), 14 W.C.B. (2d) 356 (Nfld. S.C.).

67   *YOA*, note 3. See A.N. Doob and L.A. Beaulieu, "Variation in the Exercise of Judicial Discretion with Young Offenders" (1992) 34 Can. J. Crim. 35.

68   See A. Markwart, "Custodial Sanctions under the *YOA*" in R.R. Corrado, *et al.*, eds., *Juvenile Justice in Canada: A Theoretical and Analytical Assessment* (Toronto: Butterworths, 1992) 229.

69   *Juvenile Delinquents Act*, R.S.C. 1970, c. J-3.

70   Statistics Canada, above note 46.

71   S. Moyer, *A Profile of the Juvenile Justice System in Canada*, Federal–Provincial/Territorial Task Force on Youth Justice (Ottawa: Ministry of Supply and Services, 1996).

example, a very significant increase in the use of short sentences (that is, under three months) under the YOA. Such sentences, although unlikely to have therapeutic or rehabilitative value and in some cases harmful to a youth's development, were regarded as serving accountability or deterrent functions. The best rehabilitation programs in custody facilities for adolescents with serious problems require twelve to fifteen months to have a lasting rehabilitative impact.

Arguably, some of the increase in the use of custody may be attributed to changing patterns of criminality — or, at least, police charging practices — and in particular to an increase in charges for violent crime by young persons in the late 1980s and early 1990s. However, only about twenty percent of youths sentenced to custody under the YOA had committed violent offences. It is disturbing to note that as many as one-third of all young persons receiving custodial dispositions were found guilty of administration of justice offences, such as failing to attend court or complying with the terms of a probation order. This indicates that many youths are placed in custody because of a failure of community supervision, rather than because their offending behaviour represented a direct threat to society.

In some cases, some judges under the YOA were imposing custodial dispositions to address social needs or child welfare concerns of youths. Some custodial dispositions were a disproportionate response to the offence and could not be justified on accountability principles, but were justified on the basis that they were intended to meet the needs of the youth and effect rehabilitation.[72] Prior to the enactment of the YOA, youths who were sentenced under the *Juvenile Delinquents Act* and who needed assistance could be placed by the juvenile court judge directly into facilities administered by child welfare authorities. This type of disposition was not possible under the YOA.

In several provinces, the enactment of the YOA was accompanied by a shift in resources and adolescents from the child welfare and mental health systems toward the juvenile justice system. In most Canadian jurisdictions, after the coming into force of the YOA in 1984, child welfare agencies were increasingly reluctant to assist adolescents who engage in offending behaviour — even though such behaviour is common among those who have been victims of parental abuse during childhood, the very adolescents whom the child welfare system should be trying to help. While the YOA did not require this type of shift, with the fiscal cuts of the 1980s, child welfare agencies increasingly focused their resources on pre-adolescent children who were victims or abuse

---

72 See, for example, *R. v. M.(J.J.)*, [1993] 2 S.C.R. 421.

and neglect, giving lower priority to the difficult-to-serve adolescent population. Community professionals who worked with youths under the YOA might have wanted to use resources outside the youth justice system. All too often, the only available programming and care for troubled adolescents was in youth custody facilities and so these professionals may have recommended custody for troubled adolescents who committed relatively minor offences. This combination of factors resulted in Canada under the YOA having one of the highest rates in the world of use of youth custody for adolescent offending.

Custody is a socially and financially expensive response to youth offending. While custody is clearly needed for some young offenders, in most cases young offenders are more likely to be rehabilitated in a community-based program. There is a growing body of research that indicates that treatment programs for chronic young offenders are most likely to be effective in reducing recidivism if they address the underlying problems that youths are experiencing in their families, communities, and schools, and if the treatment is undertaken in the context of working with the youth and family in their community.[73] If use is made of custody, a crucial element of rehabilitation must be supportive reintegration into the community at the completion of the custodial portion of the sentence.

When less serious adolescent offenders are placed in custody, they can be negatively influenced by the attitudes and ideas of more serious offenders. Rather than serving to prevent further offending, a custodial sentence may enhance a youth's reputation in the community as a "tough kid" and lead to further offending in the future. In amending the YOA in 1995, the Liberal government hoped to give a clearer message to youth court judges about the principles for sentencing of young offenders.[74] The intent was to reduce the disparity between judges in their sentencing practices and to encourage the use of more effective

---

73   See, for example, A. Leschied, "The Sentencing and Rehabilitative Principles of the Y.C.J.A. ss. 38 & 39: Providing a Context from the Literature on Effective Youth Justice Programs" (2002) National Judicial Institute Youth Justice Education Program; P. Gendreau and R.R. Ross, "Revivification of Rehabilitation: Evidence from the 1980s" (1987) 4 Justice 349–408; A.N. Doob, V. Marinas, and K.N. Varma, Youth Crime and the Youth Justice System in Canada: A Research Perspective (Toronto: University of Toronto, Centre of Criminology, 1995) at 14 and 87; and Centre for the Study of Youth Policy, Home-Based Services for Serious and Violent Young Offenders (Philadelphia: University of Pennsylvania, Centre for the Study of Youth Policy, School of Social Work, 1994).

74   See YOA, ss. 3(1)(a) and 24, as enacted by the 1995 amendment, above note 3. See N. Bala, "The 1995 Young Offenders Act Amendments: Compromise or Confusion?" (1994) 26 Ottawa L.Rev. 643.

and less intrusive community-based sentences for youths who did not pose a serious risk of harm to their communities. These amendments, however, continued to give significant discretion to youth court judges and had little effect on sentencing patterns.

The Preamble, Declaration of Principle, and sentencing provisions of the *YCJA* are intended to send a clearer message to judges, lawyers, probation officers, and others about reducing the use of custody for adolescent offenders. As stated in the Preamble, the new Act is intended to address Canada's over-reliance on incarceration of young offenders and to reserve the "most serious interventions for the most serious crimes." While there are cases in which the seriousness of the offence or threat to community safety requires a custodial sentence, section 39 is intended to ensure that this most serious and intrusive response to youth offending is only used in serious cases.

In contrast to section 24 of the *YOA*, which allowed a discretionary balancing of factors when judges were deciding whether to impose a custodial disposition, section 39 of the *YCJA* imposes clear preconditions which must be satisfied before a custodial sentence can be imposed. Section 39 provides:

> 39. (1) A youth justice court shall **not** commit a young person to custody under section 42 (youth sentences) **unless**
>
> (a) the young person has committed a violent offence;
> (b) the young person has failed to comply with non-custodial sentences;
> (c) the young person has committed an indictable offence for which an adult would be liable to imprisonment for a term of more than two years and has a history that indicates a pattern of findings of guilt under this Act or the *YOA*. . . .; **or**
> (d) in exceptional cases where the young person has committed an indictable offence, the aggravating circumstances of the offence are such that the imposition of a non-custodial sentence would be inconsistent with the purpose and principles set out in section 38. [emphasis added]

Section 39(1) establishes criteria, at least one of which must be satisfied before a custodial sentence can be imposed, although it does not require a youth justice court judge to impose a custodial sentence if any of the criteria are satisfied. Indeed, sections 39(2)–(3) make clear that, even if the conditions in section 39(1)(a)–(c) are satisfied, a custodial sentence is only to be imposed if the court has considered all the alternatives to custody and concluded that there is not a reasonably available alternative to custody that would satisfy the sentencing principles of section 38.

The criterion in section 39(1)(a) is if the youth has committed a "violent offence." The term "violent offence" is not defined in either the *Criminal Code* or the *YCJA*, but in section 2(1) of the Act, there is a definition of "serious violent offence" which suggests that the young person must either have caused bodily harm or have had the intent to cause bodily harm for an offence to be violent. However, a spoken threat to do physical harm is the offence of "uttering threats" contrary to section 264.1 of the *Criminal Code* and is also likely to be regarded as a violent offence, even if there is no proof of intent to cause actual physical injury.[75] Thus, a bomb threat phoned into a school may be a violent offence, even if there is no actual intent to plant a bomb. An offence which might endanger public safety but which did not cause bodily harm and was not intended to cause harm to another, such as impaired driving, would not appear to be a "violent offence." However, the definition of "serious violent offence" suggests that a "violent offence" would be committed if bodily harm or death resulted, even if there was no intent to cause the harm, such as if there was an impaired driving offence arising from an accident.[76]

The criterion for a custodial sentence under section 39(1)(b) of the *YCJA* is if the young person has failed to comply with previously imposed "non-custodial sentences" [emphasis added]. This provision clearly requires that there must have been at least two prior non-custodial sentences which the youth did not comply with. This may, for example, occur if the youth failed to comply with a probation term requiring reporting to a probation officer, violating section 137. The commission of an offence while on probation would also be a breach of the requirement "to keep the peace and be of good behaviour" and hence constitute a failure to comply. To satisfy section 39(1)(b), it is

---

75   In *R. v. McGraw*, [1991] 3 S.C.R. 72, Cory J. held that the offence of "uttering threats," contrary to what is now s. 264.1 of the *Criminal Code*, above note 2, was committed if the accused threatened to rape a woman, even if there was no evidence that he would carry it out. The threat to cause "serious bodily harm" occurs if even if the threat does not involve physical injury as the phrase refers to "any hurt or injury that interferes in a grave or substantial way with the physical integrity or well-being of the complainant" (at para. 21).

76   Under the *YOA* courts have made clear that a custody sentence is usually appropriate when a young offender is guilty of driving a motor vehicle while impaired and a death results. Even if the youth has no prior record and did not intend to cause injury, accountability for such a serious offence justifies a custodial sentence: *R. v. Elizabeth M.* (1992), 76 C.C.C.(3d) 159 (Ont. C.A.).

technically not necessary for there to have been convictions for the failures to comply with previous community-based sentences. However, if there are not convictions for a the previous failures to comply and the youth does not admit these failures to comply, the Crown must prove beyond a reasonable doubt that they occurred. Section 39(1)(b) allows the court to respond to situations where the youth has clearly failed to comply with community-based sentences and a custodial sentence is required to meet concerns about accountability, the protection of the community, or the integrity of the youth justice system. However, if the previous failures to comply with terms of community-based sentences were not recent or involved relatively minor breaches, it may not be appropriate to escalate to a custodial sentence.

The criterion for a custodial sentence under section 39(1)(c) is if the youth has committed an indictable offence for which an adult could receive a sentence of more than two years and the youth has a "history that indicates a pattern of findings of guilt." Section 39(1)(c) is intended to allow a youth justice court to respond with a custodial sentence to a case where a youth has a history of non-violent offending. Clearly, the use of the plural "findings" requires that there must be at least two prior convictions. Indeed, in contrast to section 39(1)(b), the use of the words "history" and "pattern," and the plural "findings" in section 39(1)(c) suggests that there must be at least three prior offences. This interpretation is supported by the French words of section 39(1)(c), "plusieurs déclarations de culpabilité" [several prior findings of guilt].

While the prior offences need not be violent or serious, section 39(1)(c) is only to be invoked if the current conviction is for an offence that is an indictable offence for which an adult could receive a sentence of more than two years. Thus, for this provision to be invoked in regard to a hybrid offence, the Crown should have elected before plea that it intends to treat this as an indictable offence.[77] Further, under section 39(1)(c), the offence for which a youth is being sentenced cannot be the breach of a non-custodial sentence contrary to section 137 of the *YCJA*, since this is a summary conviction offence.

---

77 Many offences in the *Criminal Code*, above note 2, are "hybrid offences" with the Crown having an election to treat them as summary or indictable. In youth justice court, the consequences of a Crown election may be less significant than in an adult proceeding, but the Crown election will affect such issues as the length of time that records may be kept and the appeal process, as well as certain sentencing issues, such as the applicability of s. 39(1)(c). As discussed in Chapter 7, the Crown must ordinarily make an election about a hybrid offence before the youth enters a plea.

Section 39(1)(d) gives a youth justice court judge a narrow discretion to impose a custodial sentence even if none of the conditions of section 39(1)(a)–(c) are satisfied, but it is clearly intended to be exercised only in "exceptional circumstances." This provision gives a judge the power to impose a custodial sentence for a non-violent offence — even if there is not a prior history of offending or a failure to comply with non-custodial sentences — but only if there are "aggravating circumstances" such that the imposition of a non-custodial sentence would be inconsistent with the principles articulated in section 38, which adopts the principles of section 3 of the YCJA. This narrow provision might, for example, be invoked if a seventeen-year-old youth commits a hate crime such as the burning of a cross on the lawn of a black family, an act which is an assault on fundamental societal values and which would cause widespread psychological harm among many Canadians, as well as fear in the immediate victims. Even with this type of hate-related property crime, the age, maturity, and motive of the youth would be relevant to sentencing, and consideration would have to be taken of the effect of a custodial sentence on the rehabilitation of the young person. The same hateful act committed by a misguided twelve-year-old might not merit a custodial sentence.

If one of the conditions of section 39(1) is satisfied, before deciding whether to impose a custodial sentence, pursuant to section 39(2)–(3), the judge must consider whether a non-custodial sentence would be a "reasonable alternative" to satisfy the sentencing principles of section 38. The need for a youth justice court judge to consider community-based alternatives to custody is also emphasized by section 39(9), which requires a youth justice court judge who imposes a custodial sentence on a young offender to "state the reasons" why a non-custodial sentence is not adequate to achieve the purposes of sentencing set out in section 38(1). Sections 39(2) and (3) provide:

> 39. (2) If any of paragraphs (1)(a) to (c) apply, a youth justice court shall not impose a custodial sentence under section 42 (youth sentences) unless the court has considered all alternatives to custody raised at the sentencing hearing that are reasonable in the circumstances, and determined that there is not a reasonable alternative, or combination of alternatives, that is in accordance with the purpose and principles set out in section 38.
>
> (3) In determining whether there is a reasonable alternative to custody, a youth justice court shall consider submissions relating to
>
> (a) the alternatives to custody that are available;

(b) the likelihood that the young person will comply with a non-custodial sentence, taking into account his or her compliance with previous non-custodial sentences; and

(c) the alternatives to custody that have been used in respect of young persons for similar offences committed in similar circumstances.

An analysis by criminologists of the patterns of sentencing under the *YOA* reveals that the history of prior sentences that a young offender received was more important than the prior history of offending in determining what type of sentence was imposed on a young offender.[78] That is, judges tended to operate on a step principle, with each sentence being at least as severe as the prior sentence, even if the offence for which a sentence was being imposed was not more serious than the prior offence. Judges very rarely de-escalated from a prior youth court sentence, even if a new offence was less serious than a prior offence. Section 39(4) is intended to emphasize to judges that there is no expectation that sentences imposed on young offenders will escalate in severity: "The previous imposition of a particular non-custodial sentence on a young person does not preclude a youth justice court from imposing the same or any other non-custodial sentence for another offence." In particular, even if there is a history of prior offending, a judge should only impose a custodial sentence if the criteria of sections 39(1)–(3) are satisfied.

A controversial sentencing issue under the *YOA* was the extent to which social welfare concerns could be considered in imposing custodial dispositions on young offenders. Interpreting that Act in 1986, the Nova Scotia Court of Appeal held that the special needs of youths could be taken into account to impose relatively long custodial sentences, especially in open custody, for adolescents requiring "strict controls and constant supervision."[79] A year later, the Ontario Court of Appeal rejected this approach, stating that the "sentence [must be] responsive to the offence" and held that a long custody sentence should not be imposed on a youth who committed a minor offence but who had "a personality problem and needed a place to go."[80] Rather, such a youth should be dealt with through the child welfare or mental health systems.

---

78 A. Matarazzo, P. Carrington, and R. Hiscott, "The Effect of Prior Youth Court Dispositions on Current Disposition: An Application of the Societal-Reaction Theory" (2001) 17 J. Quantitative Crim. 169–200.

79 *R. v. R.(R.)* (18 June 1986), (N.S.C.A.) [unreported] [summarized (1986), 17 W.C.B. 109].

80 *R. v. B.(M.)* (1987), 36 C.C.C. (3d) 573 (Ont. C.A.).

The Supreme Court of Canada dealt with some of the controversies around *YOA* dispositions in its 1993 decision in *R. v. M.(J.J.)*.[81] The Court affirmed a sentence of two years in open custody for an Aboriginal youth convicted of three counts of break and enter and one of breach of probation. He came from an abusive home environment, which the Court characterized as "intolerable," and therefore child welfare concerns justified the relatively long sentence. Justice Cory wrote: "The situation in the home of a young offender should neither be ignored nor made the predominant factor in sentencing. Nonetheless, it is a factor that can properly be taken into account in fashioning the sentence."[82] In *R. v. M.(J.J.)*, the Supreme Court recognized that, for a variety of reasons, including inadequate funding, child welfare services may not always be available for troubled youths. However, the decision in *R. v. M.(J.J.)* was problematic, as it opened the door to youths receiving more severe sentences because of their disadvantaged family backgrounds. In a dissenting opinion at the Manitoba Court of Appeal level, Madam Justice Helper felt that a sentence of one year in custody was appropriate as a "fit sentence" for the offences that this particular youth had committed, arguing that the "criminal justice system ought not to be used to supplement the lack of resources that exist in the child welfare system."[83] The youth had actually sought assistance from child welfare workers before the offences were committed but failed to receive it.

The *YCJA* rejects the approach of the Supreme Court of Canada in *R. v. M.(J.J.)* and makes clear that social or child welfare concerns are not to be grounds for youth custodial sentences. The youth justice system is not be a replacement for having similar services provided by child welfare or other social agencies, which focus on the best interests of youth: concerns about punishment and promotion of welfare are not to be confused. In particular, section 39(5) of the *YCJA* prohibits the use of custody in order to promote the interests of a youth in a case where it is not justified on an accountability basis: "A youth justice court shall not use custody as a substitute for appropriate child protection, mental health or other social measures."

If a young person has committed an offence that does not merit a custodial sentence based on accountability principles but is engaging

---

81   *R. v. M.(J.J.)*, above note 72.

82   *Ibid.* at para. 25.

83   *R. v. M.(J.J.)* (1991), 75 Man. R. (2d) 296 (C.A.), at 297.

in self-destructive behaviour, such as drug abuse or juvenile prostitution, or if the youth is homeless or suicidal, a youth justice court judge may consider making a referral to a child welfare agency under section 35 of the *YCJA*, or in appropriate cases may consider invoking mental health legislation to commit a youth to a mental health facility. A youth justice court judge might also refer a case to a conference under section 19 in order to ascertain whether the family or community are willing and able to develop a plan to help the youth. It is, however, unfair and often counterproductive to impose a sanction on a youth that is not a proportionate response to an offence but that is being imposed with the intent of helping the youth.

While some custody facilities have good programs that can help the young offenders who are confined in them to deal with psychological, behavioural, and educational problems, rarely would these programs be more effective at addressing the problems of a youth than appropriate programs in the community, or in child welfare or mental health facilities. Confinement in a youth custody facility can result in the stigmatization of an adolescent and, even if the staff and programming in a custody facility have a supportive orientation, the influences of other young offenders can have a negative effect on youths who are placed there. Further, the youth justice court judge who is imposing a custodial sentence does not have the authority to determine which facility a youth will be placed in: some facilities have quite extensive services and support, but others do not. While there may be the expectation that a troubled adolescent being sentenced to custody will receive needed services in a particular custody facility, it is far from certain that it will occur.

The decision in *R. v. M.(J.J.)* represented an effort by judges to make the best of a situation where the only available resources for a particular troubled adolescent were in the youth corrections system. While sections 39 and 35 reject this approach, they do not resolve the problems that face troubled adolescents who are not receiving appropriate services. Although section 35 of the *YCJA* allows the judge at any stage of a youth justice court proceeding to refer a young person to a child welfare agency for an assessment to determine whether the youth is in need of child welfare services, it is for that agency to decide what type of help or care, if any, will be provided. Youth justice court judges cannot make an order under section 35 that appropriate services are to be provided. This recognizes that child welfare agencies may face legal and financial constraints on their ability to provide services for troubled adolescents, especially those who are unwilling to seek their help or remain in care.

In most provinces, child welfare laws restrict the situations in which youths who are not willing to stay in care (often called "runners") can be detained; in some provinces, legislation focuses the child welfare agency mandate on youths under the age of sixteen. While it may be intensely frustrating for youth justice court judges dealing with troubled youth who may be engaging in self-destructive behaviour, the *YCJA* reflects the belief that the role of the youth justice system is limited to responding to offending. Although rehabilitative services should be provided as an aspect of custodial or other sentences, the desire to provide services or care cannot be used to justify a more intrusive response than the offence-related circumstances would warrant. It is to be hoped that the *YCJA* will result in more effective and less extensive use of custody than that under the *YOA*. However, if new legislation is introduced without also increasing the availability of community-based sentencing alternatives and resources, it may have a limited impact on sentencing patterns.

E. SENTENCES FOR CUSTODY AND SUPERVISION

Under the *Juvenile Delinquents Act*, judges could commit a delinquent youth to an industrial school for an indefinite period, with release occurring only when correctional officials felt that the youth was ready for release or when the youth reached the age of twenty-one.[84] Since the philosophy of the *Juvenile Delinquents Act* was, at least in theory, exclusively rehabilitation-oriented, the juvenile was to be returned to the community only if it was believed that rehabilitation had occurred. With more emphasis on accountability and due process, the *YOA* eliminated indefinite committals to custody, providing for custodial dispositions of a definite term, although allowing for disposition review and early release from custody under some form of supervision in the community if considered appropriate. Under the *YOA*, however, the process of review of custodial dispositions was cumbersome, and many youths served their full custody terms and were then released into the community without any supervision or support.

Section 42(2)(n) of the *YCJA* governs custodial sentences for most offences, with section 42(2)(o) and (q) dealing with custodial sentences for the most serious presumptive offences, including murder. If

---

84   *Juvenile Delinquents Act*, above note 69, ss. 20(1)(g) and 21.

the conditions of section 39 are satisfied and a custodial sentence is considered appropriate, a youth justice court judge may, under section 42(2)(n), make an order for "custody and supervision" for a stated period. Except for in cases involving the murder and the other presumptive offences sentenced under section 42(2)(o) and (q) (discussed below), a sentencing judge who is imposing a custodial sentence must impose a total sentence with the first two-thirds to be served in custody and the last third to be served under supervision in the community. However, as discussed below, once the sentence is being served, there are provisions in the *YCJA* that provide some flexibility to permit early or late release into the community, or that can be invoked to return a youth to custody after release on supervision.

Section 42(2)(n) specifies that for most offences the maximum sentence of custody and supervision is two years.[85] For an offence for which an adult can be punished by life imprisonment, however, a youth may receive a sentence of up to three years of custody and supervision. For murder, the maximum youth sentence under section 42(2)(q) is ten years, although there is also the possibility of a longer adult sentence if, after a finding of guilt, a determination is made under section 62 of the *YCJA* that the youth should be sentenced as an adult. If a youth who is already subject to one sentence of custody and supervision receives another such sentence before the first is completed, the courts must ensure that the sentences are served in a fashion that all custodial portions of the sentence are completed before any community supervision commences; sections 43 to 46 deal with these potentially complex sentence calculation issues.

By comparison to the *Juvenile Delinquents Act*, judges imposed many more custodial sentences under the *YOA*, although the average length of time that youths spent in a custodial facility declined. Under the *YOA*, extensive use was made of short custodial sentences. For example, in 2000–2001, 34 percent of all custodial dispositions were for less than one month, 44 percent were from one month to three months, 15 percent from four to six months, and only 6 percent were over six months. Critics have argued that relatively short sentences (i.e., three months or less) are highly disruptive to the lives of adolescents but are too short to allow any meaningful rehabilitation. They are, in effect, purely punitive and, because of their disruptive and

---

85 Under the *YCJA*, above note 1, s. 38(2), no sentence imposed on a young offender shall exceed that which is applicable to an adult for the same offence. For summary offences, the maximum custodial sentence for a youth or an adult is six to eighteen months.

labelling effects, tend to make rehabilitation more difficult.[86] The intent of sections 38 and 39 of the *YCJA* is to reduce the use of custodial sentences, especially the relatively short sentences for non-violent offenders, by encouraging more use of community-based sentences. However, since limited accountability and proportionality are central to the *YCJA* sentencing scheme, there will likely continue to be a significant degree of use of relatively short custodial sentences under the Act.

A major concern about the use of custody under the *YOA* was the failure to provide adequate community follow-up and supervision following release from youth custody. Under the *YOA* a youth court judge could attempt to provide some community support by ordering a custodial sentence followed by a period of probation. That Act also allowed for a discretionary review of custodial sentences and early release on probation. Despite the existence of these options under the *YOA* and, unlike with adult offenders — who are almost all released on parole with some level of supervision — a common occurrence under the *YOA* was for young offenders to serve their full sentence and be released into the community without any supervision or support. This was problematic since young offenders are especially prone to reoffending in the period following release from custody.

The process of readjustment from custody to living in the community can be very difficult, whether youths are again residing with their families or seeking other living arrangements. A youth released from custody will often have difficulty in reintegrating into the community, and in securing employment or getting into an educational program; the youth may associate with other youth who have been in custody, and their negative influences may also increase the risk of reoffending. The *YCJA* addresses the concern about inadequate support and supervision following release from custody by providing that a mandatory portion of each custodial sentence is to be served in the community under supervision. Section 39(8) specifies that in imposing a custodial sentence, the youth justice court judge shall not take into consideration the fact that the last third of the sentence is to be served in the community, or that there is the possibility for review of a custodial sentence leading to a earlier release on community supervision under section 94.

Section 88 of the *YCJA*, which articulates the principles and purposes of custody, specifies that one of the purposes of youth custody is to facilitate the reintegration of young offenders into the community.

---

86   V. Marinos, "What's Intermediate About Intermediate Sanctions? The Case of Young Offender Dispositions In Canada" (1998) 40 Can. J. Crim. 355–75.

Section 90 requires an individualized "reintegration plan" to be developed for each youth who is released from custody into the community, including plans for preparation of the youth while in custody and for effective programming after release. Issues related to review of custodial sentences and release into the community are more fully discussed below, suffice to note that as with so many questions related to young offenders, the ultimate value of community supervision and support will depend on the resources that provincial governments devote to this critical stage of a youth sentence, as well as on the skill of individual youth workers.

1) Deferred Custody

As part of the effort to reduce the use of custody, the *YCJA* provides for a new type of youth sentence. Under section 42(2)(p) a judge may sentence a young offender to "deferred custody and supervision," which allows the youth to serve what would otherwise be a custodial sentence in the community but subject to strict conditions and with the possibility of immediate apprehension and placement in a custody facility if the youth is believed to "have breached or to be about to breach" any of the conditions. This provision is in some respects similar to the adult "conditional sentence of imprisonment" — sometimes colloquially called "house arrest" — although there are also some significant differences.[87] Section 42(5) specifies that a sentence of deferred custody and supervision is only to be imposed if a youth has been found guilty of an offence that is "*not* a serious violent offence." Further, the imposition of such a sentence must be "consistent with the principles and purposes" of section 38, and the conditions for imposition of a custodial sentence in section 39 must be satisfied. While section 42(5) makes clear that deferred custody can be used for a offence that involved violence, albeit not "serious violence," it is most appropriate in cases where the risk of reoffending and to the community seem relatively low. Deferred custody is an alternative to a sentence of custody and supervision, and might be used, for example, to allow for the imposition of community-based conditions that would promote rehabilitation. It should not, however, be used to impose a strict regime of community supervision in a case in which custody is not appropriate.

In one of the leading Supreme Court of Canada decisions on adult conditional sentences, *R. v. Proulx*, Lamer C.J.C. noted that, because this type of sentence is "served in the community, it will generally be

---

87   *Criminal Code*, above note 2, ss. 742–742.7.

more effective than incarceration at achieving the restorative objectives of rehabilitation, reparations to the victim and community, and the promotion of a sense of responsibility in the offender." He went on to point out that where "punitive objectives such as denunciation and deterrence are particularly pressing, such as in cases where there are aggravating circumstances, incarceration will generally be the preferable sanction."[88] This type of analysis has, for example, effectively precluded the use of conditional sentences for adults in cases involving sexual assaults or resulting in death, even if the death is a result of negligence.

While it is clearly appropriate for a youth justice court to consider the "harm done to the victim and the community" in deciding whether a deferred custody and supervision sentence is appropriate, deterrence is not mentioned as a sentencing principle under the YCJA, which suggests that the case law dealing with conditional sentences may be of limited value for dealing with the question of whether to impose deferred custody. There may be cases in which a youth might receive deferred custody but an adult might not be eligible for a conditional sentence, as deterrence is not a factor in youth sentencing.

In light of section 3(1)(c)(iv) of the YCJA deferred custody may be particularly appropriate to consider as an alternative to custody for an Aboriginal offender, especially if there are available community-based resources that will help the offender deal with his or her offending behaviour.[89] If counsel for a youth is proposing a deferred custody sentence, it will be important to adduce evidence both about the resources and support in the community for the youth, and about the youth's willingness to comply with the proposed conditions and engage in a rehabilitative process. Even if counsel does not adduce this type of evidence (e.g., if an offender is unrepresented), it is incumbent on the judge, especially when dealing with an Aboriginal youth, to acquire information about community services and supports that might allow this type of sentence to be imposed.[90]

Under section 42(2)(p) the maximum length of a sentence of deferred custody and supervision is six months, in comparison to the maximum of two years less a day for the adult conditional sentence. The shorter maximum duration under the YCJA reflects the lesser accountability of adolescent offenders as well as their different perception of time. It may be argued, however, that, in some cases, youth justice court judges will be unwilling to impose a deferred custody sentence on a

---

88   R. v. Proulx, [2000] 1 S.C.R. 61 at 82 and 120.
89   See, for example, R. v. Wells, [2000] 1 S.C.R. 207.
90   R. v. Gladue, [1999] 1 S.C.R. 688.

youth in a situation in which an adult might receive a conditional sentence, since the youth judge might consider that a six-months deferred custody sentence is not long enough. This could give rise to an argument under the *Charter*,[91] based on a claim of discrimination against a youth based on age. It is, however, to be expected that in situations in which a judge considered that a conditional sentence would be appropriate for an adult, albeit with a longer duration, the youth justice court would also impose a deferred custody sentence on the youth, even if the sentence is shorter. The shorter youth sentence of deferred custody may be followed by probation. Indeed, since the sentencing principles of section 38 emphasize the lesser accountability of youth and do not include deterrence as a sentencing principle, there may well be cases in which a youth would receive deferred custody while an adult in a similar case might not have a conditional sentence.

Section 42(2)(p) specifies that a youth who is subject to a sentence of deferred custody and supervision is subject to conditional supervision in the community under the mandatory terms of section 105(2) and that, at the time of sentencing, the court may impose other conditions under section 105(3). The conditions of section 105(2) require that the youth "keep the peace and be of good behaviour"; report to a probation officer (provincial director), including an obligation to inform immediately the probation officer of any questioning or arrest by the police; not possess weapons; and comply "with any reasonable instructions that the provincial director considers . . . necessary to prevent a breach of a condition or to protect society." The youth justice court may also impose conditions on residency, attendance at school or employment, abstention from consumption of drugs or alcohol, and any other conditions that may promote rehabilitation. The terms of conditional supervision may be stricter than those of probation. Further, under section 106 the provincial director may issue a warrant for the apprehension of a youth on conditional supervision if it is believed that the youth "has breached or is about to breach a condition." Although this is subject to later youth justice court review, the provincial director's power of apprehension is broader than the power under section 102 for dealing with a youth on ordinary community supervision.

If a youth justice court judge is satisfied "on reasonable grounds" that a young person subject to deferred custody "has breached or was about to breach" a condition of the community supervision, under section 109(2)(c), the judge may order that the young person serve the remainder of the sentence as an order of custody and supervision under

---

91 *Canadian Charter of Rights and Freedoms*, above note 42, s. 15.

section 42(2)(n). As section 106 requires only "reasonable grounds" for the belief that a condition has been breached, which is the standard in the *Criminal Code* for the laying of an information to commence criminal proceedings, it is clear that a court may consider hearsay evidence in deciding whether this low standard of proof has been satisfied. This allows the suspension of the deferral of custody if there are reasonable grounds to believe that a condition of the supervision in the community has been breached, facilitating supervision in the community.

2) Intermittent Custody and Supervision

In an effort to mitigate the disruptive effects of a custodial sentence and facilitate reintegration into society, the *YCJA* allows for a youth justice court judge to impose a sentence of intermittent custody and supervision, provided the provincial government has established custody facilities that allow for this. A sentence of intermittent custody and supervision is intended to allow a young offender to serve the custodial portion of a sentence for intermittent periods, such as on weekends. This type of sentence might permit a youth to continue to attend his or her school or continue to maintain employment.

Under section 47(2), a youth justice court judge may order intermittent custody only if the total sentence is less than ninety days (i.e., the custodial portion is less than sixty days), while section 47(3) provides that this type of sentence can only be imposed if the provincial director indicates that a youth custody facility with this type of program is available. Under the *YOA*, provincial governments gave priority to the establishment of intermittent custody programs for adults, who are more likely to have employment and family responsibilities, and there were few opportunities for youths to have this type of sentence. Intermittent custody is generally more expensive for governments to provide than continuous custody, and it is difficult to arrange suitable rehabilitative programming for young offenders serving this type of custodial sentence. As a result, intermittent custody is not expected to be widely available under the *YCJA*.

3) The Nature and Levels of Custody

Under the *YOA*, every custodial disposition was to be served in open or secure custody. Under section 24.1 of the *YOA*, provinces and territories were permitted to have the initial decision about the level of custody made by the provincial director, and the youth was to have the right to appeal the decision about the level of custody to a youth court.

Under that Act, all provincial and territorial governments decided that it was more efficient and fairer to allow youth court judges to make a decision about the level of custody at the same time as they made a custodial disposition. Section 24.1 of the *YOA* defined an open custody facility as a "community residential centre, group home, child care institution, or forest or wilderness camp, or . . . any other like place or facility designated . . . as a place of open custody" by the government, and a secure custody facility as a place "for the secure containment or restraint [of young persons] designated [as] secure custody" by the government.

The courts held that section 24.1 gave provincial and territorial governments significant discretion to determine whether a facility was "open" or "secure," since a key part of the definition was the power of "designation." In some cases, a custody facility that might be designated "secure" at one time could be redesignated as "open" without significantly changing its nature.[92] However, if a provincial or territorial government designated as "open custody" a facility with a physical environment, programming, and staffing arrangements that were clearly inconsistent with the meaning of "open custody," the courts were prepared to declare a designation invalid and to order that no youth sentenced to open custody could be placed there. This happened, for example, in one case where the government of Nova Scotia designated a former adult jail as a place of both open and secure custody, with youths in "open custody" having unlocked cells. The court observed: "Parliament has stated that open custody would be something other than the previous traditional form of incarceration."[93]

In a case in Alberta, a female young offender subject to an open custody sentence was placed in a facility that was designated as both as open and secure custody, with the girl on the open custody sentence subject to the same conditions and routines as girls being held in secure custody within the same unit. Her application for a writ of *habeas corpus* was successful, and the court ordered that she was to be either held in a truly open custody facility or released. This case illustrates the benefit that judicial scrutiny of levels of custody could have for protecting those youths in custody with special needs, particularly girls, who make up only a small minority of the population of youths in custody. There are special concerns about whether the rehabilitative needs of girls are appropriately addressed in the juvenile corrections system, as there are relatively few of them and most programming is geared to

---

92   *F.(C.) v. R.* (1985), 30 Man. R. (2d) 297 (C.A.).

93   *Re B.(D.)* (1986), 72 N.S.R. (2d) 354 (T.D.).

male offenders. These concerns may be heightened under the *YCJA*, as there is less scope for judicial control over the placement process.

Under the *YOA* there was also a judicial expectation that open custody facilities would have a rehabilitative focus, and this was taken into account when sentencing a youth. In *R. v. M.(J.J.)* the Supreme Court of Canada upheld a two-year open custody sentence for an Aboriginal youth with a very difficult family situation whose offence and record clearly did not merit such a lengthy sentence. Justice Cory commented on open custody facilities: "[T]hose facilities are not simply to be jails for young people. Rather they are facilities dedicated to the long-term welfare and reformation of the young offender. Open custody facilities do not and should not resemble penitentiaries."[94] While under the *YOA*, the provinces and territories had significant discretion about the designation of facilities as "open" or "secure," the secure custody facilities tended to be larger institutions, with more emphasis on security. Open custody facilities tended to be group homes, wilderness camps, or farms, with young offenders who were likely to be attending school in the community. In some jurisdictions open custody facilities might have both young offenders and adolescents in the care of child welfare authorities.

Section 85(1) of the *YCJA* specifies that each province and territory must have "at least two levels of custody . . . distinguished by the degree of restraint of the young persons in them." This provision is likely to be applied by most provinces in a way that will continue the *YOA* regime of open and secure custody, although a jurisdiction might adopt the three-level adult classification of "minimum, medium and maximum security." Unlike the *YOA*, there is no definition of "open" or "minimum security" in the *YCJA*. Thus, while the new Act requires at least two levels of custody, it may be more difficult than under the *YOA* for a young person who is sentenced to "open custody" — or whatever new term is used to describe the lowest level of restraint — to challenge a provincial or territorial designation of a facility as "open," because there is no requirement for openness or a low level of restraint; instead, there is only to be some distinction based on the "degree of restraint." However, a youth subject to a sentence at the lowest level of restraint and placed in a facility with youths sentenced to a higher level of security might be able to mount a successful challenge to this under the *YCJA*.

Section 85(3) of the *YCJA* allows a province or territory to have the option of having the determination about the level of custody for a

---

94   *R. v. M.(J.J.)*, above note 72, at 430–31.

young offender made by the provincial director after a sentence is imposed, provided that the "due process rights of the young person are protected" and the youth has an "opportunity to be heard before a decision" is made about the level of custody and to seek review of the decision before an independent review board.[95] Concerns have been expressed that provincial directors could be influenced by budgetary and institutional pressures in making decisions about the level of custody. Given these concerns, and recognizing the potential complexity of any review process, most provinces and territories are continuing the practice under the *YOA* of having youth justice court judges make the initial decision about the level of custody at the time that a sentence is imposed, as permitted under section 88 of the new Act.

As originally enacted, the *YOA* had statutory rules to restrict the use of secure custody, permitting its use only if a youth committed a more serious offence or had a record of not complying with *YOA* sentences; there were tighter restrictions for the use of secure custody for youths under fourteen.[96] Amendments in 1995 removed the offence, record, and age-based statutory criteria for the use of secure custody. Thus, section 24.1(4) of that Act gave judges a broader discretion to make decisions about young offenders that would meet the needs of individual youths, while still attempting to restrict the use of secure custody. Under the *YCJA*, the decision about the level of custody, whether made by a provincial director or a youth justice court judge, is to be guided by section 85(5), which is very similar to section 24.1(4) of the *YOA*. Section 85(5) of the new Act provides:

> 85 (5)(a) that the appropriate level of custody for the young person is the one that is the least restrictive to the young person, having regard to
>> (i) the seriousness of the offence in respect of which the young person was committed to custody and the circumstances in which that offence was committed,
>> (ii) the needs and circumstances of the young person, including proximity to family, school, employment and support services,
>> (iii) the safety of other young persons in custody, and
>> (iv) the interests of society;
> (b) that the level of custody should allow for the best possible match of programs to the young person's needs and behaviour, having

---

95　*YCJA*, above note 1, ss. 86–87.

96　*YOA*, ss. 24.1(3) and (4), as amended in 1995, above note 3, by s. 17.

regard to the findings of any assessment in respect of the young person; and

(c) the likelihood of escape.

Section 85(5) governs the decision about the level of custody to which a youth is sentenced, and reflects the general sentencing principle of section 38(2)(e)(i) that courts are to impose the sentence which is the "least restrictive alternative."

Under the *YOA* judges were reluctant to impose a secure custody sentence on a youth who had not already been sentenced to open custody, although the courts held that, even a first offence by a youth which involved a significant degree of violence might warrant secure custody to "act as a sufficient general deterrent and to reflect society's abhorrence of this kind of violence."[97] While deterrence is not explicitly recognized as a sentencing principle under the *YCJA*, the sentencing principle of proportionality and section 85(5)(a)(i) clearly direct that the seriousness of the offence is to be a factor in deciding the level of custody, while the safety concerns of section 85(5)a)(iii) also require a secure custody sentence for offenders who pose safety risks.

Section 85(5)(b) requires that a decision about the level of custody is to take consideration of the "best possible match" of the programs available in each level of custody to meet the needs and behaviour of the young person. However, even if a province gives the youth justice court judge the authority to make the section 85(5) decision about the level of custody, under section 85(6), the provincial director will make the decision about which specific facility within that level of custody the youth will be placed in. There may be only one or a very small number of available facilities with a particular level of custody in a region, and the sentencing judge may have a very good idea of where the youth will be placed. Further, at the time of sentencing, the youth justice court may hear evidence about programs available at specific facilities to meet the needs of a particular young offender and the judge may make a recommendation about placement in a specific facility. A judicial recommendation about a specific facility is not, however, binding on the provincial director. The decision of a provincial director under section 85(6) about initial placement within a specific facility within a level of custody or transfer between facilities within a level of custody is not subject to any type of review process. In some cases, however, an argument that the particular facility in which a youth is placed may not meet the needs of a youth may be the basis for seeking a sentence review under section 94 of the *YCJA*. Section 84 of the Act

---

97   R. v. H.(S.R.) (1990), 56 C.C.C. (3d) 46 at 51 (Ont. C.A.), Galligan J.A.

requires that, with some defined exceptions, those who are committed to custody as young offenders under the Act are to be held "separate and apart from any adult . . . in custody." This is similar to section 24.2(4) of the *YOA*, which was applied in different ways throughout Canada. In some places, youths were merely kept in separate sections of adult facilities, although most youth custody facilities are completely separate from adult correctional facilities.

In general, youth in custody have access to educational programming; in some facilities the educational programming is quite sophisticated, with special efforts to identify and address the needs of adolescents with learning disabilities. Most youth custody facilities have some type of behaviour modification program, with young offenders receiving increased privileges for good behaviour, and some type of sanctions for non-compliance. The more severe types of misconduct may be criminal offences that could result in further charges. Some custody facilities have intensive rehabilitative programs with psychological and other rehabilitation services, while in others, which have little in the way of programming or rehabilitative services, youths spend much of their time watching television. While some facilities, especially open custody, have staff who have appropriate educational qualifications as well as an interest in working with youth, in other facilities, particularly secure ones, the staff focus more exclusively on security issues. Some facilities have programming to deal with certain age groups or types of offenders, such as violent offenders. Other facilities deal with all offenders in a geographical area and have little in the way of therapeutic services.

It is now clear that many adolescents in custody facilities operating under the *Juvenile Delinquents Act* were subjected to physical, sexual, and emotional abuse. With increased awareness of these abuses and greater access by youths to advocates, the level of abuse of young offenders by staff has fallen, although institutional abuse remains a serious concern. Significant evidence shows that some staff continue to abuse some youth in custody and may, for example, use such restraints as handcuffs inappropriately or excessively. Abuse and exploitation of some young inmates by other inmates remains a major problem, and it is apparent that in some cases this occurs with the awareness,[98] if not

---

98 For example, see "Inquiry Sought in Jail Death of Teen," *Globe and Mail*, September 10, 1996, reporting that a sixteen-year-old boy was beaten to death by another youth while in a secure youth custody facility. There were allegations of staff incompetence in failing to protect the victim. The Ontario government announced more specialized training for youth corrections workers in the wake of a coroner's inquest: Ontario Ministry of Correctional Services, "Youth Custody

the tacit encouragement of some staff.[99] There are concerns in all present facilities that youths who are more vulnerable or sensitive may be subject to negative influences from more aggressive offenders, as well as experiencing feelings of isolation in an institutional environment. Many youths, however, report relatively positively experiences in custody and treatment by staff.[100]

After the *YOA* came into force, secure custody facilities were almost all operated by governments, while some open custody facilities were operated by private operators or non-profit organizations under contract with a provincial government. There has been an increasing tendency for both open and secure facilities to be operated by non-government agencies, a development that has caused concerns with some critics.[101] While there have been incidents of abuse by staff at government-operated youth custody facilities in Canada,[102] the American experience suggests that "the worst abuses happen at privately run juvenile prisons"[103] Cases of severe abuse and even death of inmates in the United States raise questions about whether for profit corporations can run youth facilities without reducing expenditures on staff training or youth programs. Problems with high staff turnover, low morale, and inadequate training are recurring themes in allegations of abuse at privately run correctional facilities.[104]

System Strengthened with Implementation of Inquest Jury Recommendations" (June 30, 2000) (available online at time of writing at <www.corrections.mcs.gov.on.ca>).

99 M. Peterson-Badali and C.J. Koegl, "Juvenile Offenders' Experiences" (2002) 30 J. of Crim. Justice 41–9; and C. Cesaroni, "The Case for Standards for Youth Custody in Canada" (2001) 20 Can. J. Community Mental Health 107–22.

100 B. Bidgood and S.M. Pancer, "An Evaluation of Residential Treatment Programs for Young Offenders in the Waterloo Region" (2001) 20. Can. J. Comm. Mental Health 125–44.

101 For example, Ontario's Camp Turnaround, a strict-discipline or boot camp is operated by a for-profit corporation, although it is a secure youth custody facility. See also T. Blackwell, "Review Finds Problems at Youth Facilities" *National Post*, September 27, 2000.

102 For example, "Youths Win Settlement in Jail Assaults," *National Post*, September 21, 2002, on the financial settlement given to 12 youths as a result of abuse by staff. See also Zareski, "Handling of Teens Appalls Judge," *Star Phoenix*, April 20, 1999, where abuses at a Saskatchewan custody facility are alleged.

103 "Louisiana Settles Suit, Abandoning Private Youth Prisons," *New York Times*, September 8, 2000.

104 See for example, "Ontario Youth Jail Denies Abuse Allegations," *National Post*, April 4, 2001, discussing allegations of abuse at a privately operated secure youth custody facility in London, Ontario, where a mattress was used to pin a

4) Custody Innovations

About one-third to half of all youths sent to youth custody facilities reoffend. Professionals who work with young offenders have tried to develop various alternatives to the usual custody-based programs with the aim of reducing recidivism. Two significant innovations have been wilderness programs and boot camps.

a) Wilderness Programs

In the 1970s in Canada, the first wilderness programs for young offenders were established. Adolescent offenders are placed in a wilderness setting where co-operation and self-reliance can be developed in a program involving physical challenge. These programs are intended to give participants the opportunity to test themselves in a series of challenges to build self-confidence, self-esteem, and a more internalized locus of self-control. Some research studies report that, while wilderness programs do improve self-esteem, and offending behaviour may decline immediately after release, these positive effects erode within six months after youths return to their communities; long-term recidivism may not be reduced as a result of participation.[105] However, other research is more positive and suggests that, on average, wilderness challenge programs do reduce recidivism, especially if the programs include a therapeutic component as well as physical challenges.[106] Culturally appropriate wilderness custodial programs may be most appropriate for youths from Aboriginal communities who may be able to apply more easily some of the attitudes and skills that they develop on their return to their communities: Aboriginal youth may find it easier to communicate with community Elders who may mentor them after they have participated in a culturally appropriate wilderness program.

b) Boot Camps

Another recent custodial innovation has been boot camps, a concept in youth corrections that was first developed in the United States in the

---

fourteen-year-old young offender to the ground. Guards who were interviewed complained of poor funding and high staff turnover.

105 J. Winterdyk and R. Roesch, "A Wilderness Experiential Program as an Alternative for Probationers: An Evaluation" (1982) 24 Can. J. Crim. 39.

106 See S. Wilson and M. Lipsey, "Wilderness Challenge Programs for Delinquent Youth: A Meta-analysis of Outcome Evaluations" (2000) 23 Evaluation and Program Planning 1, reporting that based on an analysis on twenty-two studies, the wilderness programs reduced the recidivism rate to 29 percent from 37 percent for comparison subjects.

1980s. While there are different types of boot camps, they are all based on some form of strict discipline regime that adopts some features of camps for military recruits, with youths (almost always males) in uniform and subject to a physically demanding regime and strict supervision. Some of the American boot camps actually use former military personnel as staff. This type of regime, which is popular with conservative politicians, is premised on notions that young offenders need discipline and that, as offenders are more likely to feel punished in this type of environment, they may be deterred from committing further offences. It is also based on the somewhat romanticized idea that a quasi-military experience can "turn boys into men." The American experience with these programs reveals that discipline during a custodial sentence, in itself, has no effect on recidivism after release. Fred Mathews, a Toronto psychologist with extensive experience in working with young offenders, comments:

> The assumption of a boot camp is that it is only the absence of strict discipline that got these kids into trouble in the first place, which is so far down the list of difficulties they've had to deal with in their lives. It's not the absence of strict discipline that got these kids into trouble. It's being beaten up and abused; it's living in poverty; it's living in neighborhoods that are under-resourced and poorly supported; it's cutting services and support for families far earlier in their lives than adolescence.[107]

Indeed, the success that some boot camps have had seems to be dependent largely on the therapeutic programs offered within those boot camps. These therapeutic programs can also be offered in other custodial settings. The John Howard Society has pointed out that military camps were designed to train soldiers to obey orders and, if necessary, to kill; as such, they are "not designed to make citizens better able to deal with life in the community outside of the military."[108]

American research on boot camps reveals that those facilities which are closest to military models, emphasizing discipline and physical activity, are no better than ordinary custody programs at reducing the recidivism of adolescent offenders. The American boot camps that are successful have significant educational, counselling, and life-skills programs for youth in custody, and provide substantial supervision and

---

107 Quoted from J. Coyle, "Boot Camps Tough, But Where is the Love?" *Kingston Whig-Standard*, February 13, 1997.

108 John Howard Society of Ontario, *Boot Camps for Young Offenders* (Toronto: 1996).

support after release.[109] Despite the research indicating that the military regimen of boot camps has little or no effect on reducing recidivism, variations of boot camps and strict discipline programs have been established in some of Canada's more conservative provinces, such as Ontario, Manitoba, and Alberta. These secure-custody facilities emphasize strict discipline and a controlled, busy schedule with a significant component of physical activity.[110] Drawing on American experience,[111] these facilities also have significant rehabilitative and educational components, as well as post-release community follow-up. Some critics of boot camps have questioned whether the discipline and regimentation are crucial to the success of these programs, arguing that the rehabilitative and educational services in custody and the community follow-up are the keys to reducing recidivism.[112]

The Ontario government has claimed that its research indicated that strict discipline programs, such as "Project Turnaround" (a secure-custody facility), were more successful than the usual youth custody facilities in reducing recidivism.[113] A careful review of this research by respected Canadian criminologist Anthony Doob raised questions about the conclusions of the government's research.[114] This criticism

---

109 D.L. MacKenzie, *et al.*, "Boot Camp Prisons and Recidivism in Eight States" (1995) 33 Criminology 327.

110 Task Force on Strict Discipline for Young Offenders, "Recommendations from the Task Force on Strict Discipline for Young Offenders" (Toronto: Ontario Solicitor General and Minister of Correctional Services, 1996).

111 Ontario, Solicitor General, *Recommendations from the Task Force on Strict Discipline for Young Offenders* (Toronto: Queen's Printer, 1996); J. Rusk, "Old prison farm to be used as boot camp, Runciman says," *Globe and Mail*, February 12, 1997: A6.

112 John Howard Society of Ontario, above note 108; and Blair B. Bourque, *et al.*, *Boot Camps for Young Offenders: An Implementation Evaluation of Three Demonstration Projects* (Ottawa: National Institute of Justice, 1996).

113 T3 Associates Training and Consulting, *Project Turnaround Outcome Evaluation — Final Report* (Toronto: Ontario Ministry of Corrections, 2001). This government-sponsored research did report that young offenders who were placed in the strict discipline program had a lower recidivism rate than a "comparison group" placed in regular secure custody. However, the difference in rates did not reach a statistically significant level. Further, while the offences and records of the two groups were matched, psychological testing before placement of those who were selected for the strict discipline program revealed that they were more likely to have a positive attitude toward their own rehabilitation.

114 See Anthony Doob, *Criminological Highlights* (Toronto: University of Toronto, Centre of Criminology, 2001) 4:1. See also Alan Leschied, "The Sentencing and Rehabilitative Principles of the *Y.C.J.A.* ss. 38 & 39: Providing a Context from the Literature on Effective Youth Justice Programs," *National Judicial Institute Youth Justice Education Program* (2002)

led the Ontario corrections minister to concede that there might be problems with the government-sponsored research, but also to argue that, even if the recidivism rates are the same, the advantage of boot camps is that they are "cheaper [and] a better deal for the taxpayers."[115]

It should be noted that some young offenders have expressed a preference for the boot camp experience, as it may be more challenging or interesting than ordinary custody, and the degree of supervision may reduce the opportunities for abusive conduct by incarcerated youth towards one another. While there is no single program or type of facility that can solve the problems of all young offenders, some types of programs will work better than others for youths with particular needs and problems. Courts and correctional officials need to assess the situation and needs of individual young offenders and match them with programs that meet their particular circumstances. For some youth, wilderness programs or even boot camps may be effective, but for many youths these programs will not be effective in preventing recidivism. While secure facilities are needed to supervise relatively small numbers of young offenders, within these institutions there should be individualized assessment and treatment for youths. If no such assessment and treatment is available, their needs will not be met, making it more likely that they will reoffend after release. For those youths who are placed in custody, community-based after-care programs to guide re-entry into the school system, family, and labour force are critical to efforts to reduce recidivism.[116]

5) Youth Confinement and Transfer Between Facilities

Part 5 of the *YCJA* governs the confinement of young offenders in custody, and their release into the community on supervision. Section 83 begins this part of the Act, setting out the purpose of the youth custody system and the principles that are to guide the courts and juvenile correctional officials. Section 83 provides:

> 83. (1) The purpose of the youth custody and supervision system is to contribute to the protection of society by
>
> (a) carrying out sentences imposed by courts through the safe, fair and humane custody and supervision of young persons; and

---

115 Ontario Minister of Corrections, Rob Sampson, quoted in "Expert Calls Boot Camp Success Rate 'Nonsense'," *National Post*, February 4, 2002.

116 R.A. Silverman and J.H. Creechan, *Delinquency Treatment and Intervention* (Ottawa: Justice Canada, 1995).

(*b*) assisting young persons to be rehabilitated and reintegrated into the community as law-abiding citizens, by providing effective programs to young persons in custody and while under supervision in the community.

(2) In addition to the principles set out in section 3, the following principles are to be used in achieving that purpose:

(*a*) that the least restrictive measures consistent with the protection of the public, of personnel working with young persons and of young persons be used;

(*b*) that young persons sentenced to custody retain the rights of other young persons, except the rights that are necessarily removed or restricted as a consequence of a sentence under this Act or another Act of Parliament;

(*c*) that the youth custody and supervision system facilitate the involvement of the families of young persons and members of the public;

(*d*) that custody and supervision decisions be made in a forthright, fair and timely manner, and that young persons have access to an effective review procedure.

As well as the more general statements in the Preamble and Section 3 of the *YCJA*, section 83 makes clear that the primary focus of the youth corrections system is the rehabilitation of young offenders, the preparation for their release, and the supervision of their reintegration into the community. However, the protection of the public and the safety of staff and other young offenders are also important. To achieve and balance these concerns, youth corrections officials have considerable discretion, although this is subject to some supervision by the courts.

Section 85(6) of the Act makes clear that while a sentencing judge can make a recommendation about placement of a young offender in a particular facility, youth corrections officials will select the facility in which a youth will be placed within the level of custody that a youth has been sentenced to. Further, correctional officials can transfer youths between facilities within a level of custody without any judicial or administrative right of review.

Transfers from a less secure level of custody (i.e., open custody) to a more secure facility (i.e., secure custody) may be justified, for example, if the youth poses a risk to others or there are concerns that the youth will escape from the less secure facility. This type of transfer, however, imposes a greater degree of restraint than imposed by the original sentence and can only be done if there is a possibility for an independent review of the decision. Under section 87, a provincial government may decide to give correctional officials the authority to transfer a youth to a more secure facility, subject to the youth having a right to seek a review hearing before an independent review board. While the youth must have an opportunity to call and challenge evidence at the hearing, the review board may consider evidence not heard by the youth if considered "strictly necessary in order to protect . . . safety or security." Instead of allowing for a review by an independent board, a provincial government may decide under section 88 that the review of transfer decisions from a less secure to a more secure level of custody is to be subject to review by a youth justice court.[117]

Section 92 allows for the transfer of a young offender who has reached the age of eighteen from a youth-custody facility, although, if the youth has not reached the age of twenty, this is only to be after a youth justice court hearing and with the authorization of the court. Under section 93, there is a presumption that a person who was sentenced as a young offender and who is still in youth custody at the age of twenty will be transferred into an adult correctional facility; with the permission of a youth justice court such a person may be transferred to a federal penitentiary. The provisions to allow transfer of a person sentenced as a young offender into an adult correctional facility are further discussed in Chapter 9.

6) Release into the Community

Under section 90, the provincial director is required to designate a youth worker "without delay" after a custodial sentence is imposed to work with each young offender placed in custody to prepare a "reintegration plan" that identifies the programs available in custody to maximize the youth's "chances for reintegration." Once the youth is released into the community, a youth worker (probation officer) is responsible to assist the youth by implementing the plan, as well as monitoring any conditions of the release. There is ample evidence that the period following release from custody is vitally important for the long-term rehabilitation of young offenders who have been placed in custody. Youths who receive support and direction and are able to successfully reintegrate into their communities and families, and the edu-

---

117 A provincial government may decide, under *YCJA*, above note 1, s. 88, that the provisions of the *YOA*, above note 3, which govern transfer from one level of custody to another (ss. 24.1–24.3; as well as ss. 28–31), including allowing for youth justice court review, will continue to apply under the *YCJA*.

cation system or employment, are much less likely to reoffend than those released without meaningful support.[118]

Section 91 of the *YCJA* authorizes a provincial director to allow a youth to leave custody for a period of up to thirty days to permit the youth to seek educational, rehabilitative, or employment opportunities, or for compassionate reasons, such as to attend a funeral. Such a "reintegration leave" may be for a specified number of hours each day, for example, to attend school, or for a specified period of days to allow a visit home to facilitate reintegration into the community after release. The release may be with an escort, which may be appropriate if there is a release to attend a funeral, or without an escort, which may be appropriate if there is a release to allow school attendance. The *YCJA* makes clear that correctional officials may grant back-to-back reintegration leave passes after conducting a reassessment of whether this is justifiable. At any time, the director may revoke authorization for reintegration leave. The section 91 reintegration leave allows for a youth to be released into the community before completion of the custodial portion of a sentence without the need for any review by a court. A youth who is on leave may be arrested without a warrant if the youth fails to comply with any condition of the leave or if the leave is revoked by the director. There is no process for a youth to seek a review or appeal of the decision of the director not to grant or to revoke a reintegration leave.

Under section 96 the provincial director may make a recommendation to the youth justice court for early release of a young offender from custody on conditional supervision. The director will send a recommendation and supporting documents to the youth, the parents, and the Crown prosecutor; any of them can notify the court of an objection and a hearing must be held before the youth is released. If no notice of objection is filed, the youth justice court judge may release the youth on conditions without holding a hearing. Usually, if no objection is filed, the youth justice court will act on the recommendation of the director and authorize the release on the terms recommended, although the judge is not obliged to do so. Where a review hearing is held, the provincial director can explain why early release is being sought.

As under the *YOA*, the *YCJA* gives the youth justice court a continuing authority to review sentences to ensure that they continue to meet the changing needs and circumstances of a young offender. A youth justice court review cannot increase the severity of the original sentence. Under section 98, a youth justice court may decide that a youth

---

118 See, for example, R. Silverman and J. Creechan, *Delinquency Treatment and Intervention* (Ottawa: Department of Justice, 1995).

must remain in custody on the scheduled release date to serve the full sentence of custody and supervision in custody, but as discussed below, the test is quite narrow. Further, if a youth commits a new offence while subject to a prior sentence, the court may impose an additional sentence for the new offence.[119]

Section 94(1)–(2) of the *YCJA* require that if a youth is in custody, there must be an annual review hearing by a youth justice court to determine whether the youth should continue to serve the original sentence or be released under supervision into the community before the scheduled release date. Section 94(3) allows the provincial director, the young person, a parent, or the Crown prosecutor to apply for a youth justice court review of any custodial sentence of longer than ninety days. If the sentence is for longer than one year, an optional review under section 94(3) can be sought six months after the last court hearing for sentence or a sentence review hearing. If the custodial sentence is for less than a year, at least one-third of the sentence must have been served before an optional review can be sought. Prior to a section 94 review hearing, the provincial director must have a progress report prepared for the court dealing with the youth's performance in custody; this report may include information on the youth's "family history and present environment."[120]

At the review hearing, the youth, his or her parents, and the Crown prosecutor are to be given an opportunity to present evidence and make submissions. The provincial director will also participate in the hearing, and may support or oppose the early release of a youth from custody onto conditional supervision. Under the *YOA*, in the absence of the support of the provincial director, many judges were quite reluctant to release a youth before the end of the original sentence. There was effectively an onus on the youth to justify a variation in the original sentence. Section 94(6) of the *YCJA* also suggests that for a sentence to be varied, the onus is on the youth to establish that he or she has made "sufficient progress to justify a change in the youth sentence"; or that the opportunity for rehabilitation in the community is greater, perhaps owing to a change in the family or other circumstances; or that new programs are available in the community. If the correctional authorities do not support a youth's release, it is important for the youth to present a basis for a review, and counsel for the youth

---

119 *YCJA*, above note 1, ss. 43–46, deals with the complex issues that arise if a person is sentenced for an offence while already subject to a prior custodial sentence; the youth justice court may impose a consecutive sentence so that the total sentence may exceed three years.

120 *YCJA*, above note 1, ss. 94(9)–(12).

can have a critical role to play in helping to develop a plan and present evidence to the court to support a review.

The review provisions are intended to give youths in custody an incentive to "mend their ways" by participating in rehabilitative programs while in custody, and by changing their behaviour and attitudes. In one case decided under the *YOA*, the judge characterized the sentence review provisions as a "wonderfully malleable" tool and a "humane" provision.[121] In some localities, under the *YOA* review hearings were usually conducted by the same youth court judge who imposed the original sentence, as that judge was likely to have a better understanding of the youth and the expectations for the sentence. Neither the *YOA* nor the *YCJA* require this, however, and in some places it was and is impractical to do this. Further, the review hearing may, with the consent of the youth and Crown, be held at a court near where the custody facility is located, which may be far from the original court. This variation in practice is likely to continue under the *YCJA*. Under the *YOA*, delays in conducting review hearings commonly occurred, and there will continue to be concerns that under the *YCJA* this type of hearing may not have a priority in the scheduling of court.

Under the *YOA*, some judges showed considerable flexibility in applying the review provisions, ruling that factors related to the offence and concerns about deterrence are less important at the review than at the original sentencing, while the progress and circumstances of the youth are more important.[122] It has also been recognized that the failure to reduce the sentence of a youth who has made good progress in custody may discourage that youth and imperil efforts at rehabilitation, as well as have a negative impact on other youths in custody.[123] Other judges, however, seemed reluctant to reduce the original sentence.

In 1995, amendments were made to the *YOA* providing that a youth who is released from custody into the community before the scheduled release is to be on "conditional supervision."[124] The addition of the concept of conditional supervision was intended to increase control over youths who are released from custody into the community and thereby encourage judges to be more flexible about approving early release. The *YCJA* continues to provide that early release at a review hearing is to be on "conditional supervision" for a period not exceeding the remainder of the original total sentence. If a youth is

121 *R. v. T.(K.)* (1994), 125 Sask. R. 260 at 266 (C.A.), Bayda C.J.S.
122 *R. v. T.(M.)*, [1995] Y.J. No. 6 (Terr. Ct.) (QL), Lilles Terr. J.
123 *R. v. R.(R.)*, [1996] O.J. No. 1101 (Prov. Ct.) (QL), Renaud Prov. J.
124 *YOA*, above note 3, s. 28(17)(c)(ii), enacted by the *Young Offenders Act*, 1995, above note 3, s. 21(3).

released under section 94 or 96 before the release date scheduled at the time of sentencing, this is to be on a conditional supervision order under section 105. A youth on conditional supervision may be subject to similar conditions to a youth released on community supervision at the scheduled supervision release date under section 97, but there is a significantly wider authority for probation staff to control the youth who has been released on conditional supervision.

The conditions that a court may impose on an early release are governed by section 105 of the YCJA. The conditions must include reporting to a probation supervisor, and may require the youth to live with parents or at a place specified by the provincial director. The conditions may include any terms that are aimed at securing the youth's "good conduct" and preventing the youth from committing further offences; this might include a requirement for counselling or participation in community programs. School attendance may also be required. Section 106 provides that if the provincial director has "reasonable grounds" to believe that a young person on conditional supervision "has breached or is about to breach" a condition of release, the director may suspend the conditional supervision and require the arrest of the youth.

Under section 109, this suspension of the conditional supervision is to be subject "without delay" to a review hearing by a youth justice court judge. The court will consider evidence about the youth's conduct since release. The youth justice court only needs to be satisfied that there are reasonable grounds to believe that the youth "has breached or was about to breach" a condition of the release to confirm the suspension of the release and to order that the balance of the sentence will be served in custody. This low standard of proof indicates that the judge may consider hearsay and other evidence that might not be admissible at an ordinary criminal trial. This low standard of proof is intended to facilitate the return to custody of a young offender in circumstances where there are concerns about the youth's conduct in the community, even if there is not proof that would ordinarily satisfy a court that there is criminal conduct or even the breach of a condition of release. In practice, this should tend to give the probation officers a considerable degree of control over a youth being supervised on conditional supervision, provided that the officer has the time to monitor the youth. As discussed more fully below, the provisions for the return to custody of a youth on community supervision, after release on the scheduled release date, give a youth a somewhat broader set of rights than a youth who is released early on conditional supervision.

Sections 98 to 104 of the YCJA govern the release or continuation in custody of a youth on the date scheduled for release at the time of the original sentence. There were no equivalents to these provisions in the *YOA*, which allowed for an application to be made for review and early release but did not create a presumption of release at any particular date. As a consequence, youths sentenced under the *YOA* often served their full custodial dispositions, while adults were usually released on parole, sometimes after serving just a third of their sentences and usually after serving two-thirds to three-quarters of their sentence. The release provisions for youths sentenced to custody and supervision under section 42(2)(n) of the *YCJA* are in some ways loosely similar to those that apply to adults seeking release on parole. As discussed above, there is the possibility of a sentence review and an early youth justice court-ordered release under section 94 after one-third of the total sentence has been served. After two-thirds of the total sentence of custody and supervision has been served, there is the presumption of release on conditions into the community, although under section 98 the youth justice court may order that the full sentence is to be served in custody (i.e., the equivalent of the "gating" of an adult offender[125]). These provisions of the *YCJA* create a strong presumption that a youth will be released after serving two-thirds of the total sentence to serve the remainder of the sentence in the community.

Section 98 provides that before the expiry of the custodial portion of a sentence of custody and supervision, the provincial director or Crown prosecutor *may* apply to the youth justice court for an order that the youth is to remain in custody until the completion of the total original sentence. If no application is made under section 98, the youth must be released to serve the last portion of the sentence under community supervision, with the conditions to be set by the provincial director. If a youth is released on community supervision, section 97(1) sets out some mandatory terms that are to be in all community supervision orders and are to be in effect for the period that the youth is subject to community supervision. These terms include that the youth:

- shall keep the peace and be of good behaviour;
- shall report to the provincial director and be under the supervision of the director, and may be required to report regularly to the police or a probation officer;
- shall immediately inform the probation officer on being arrested or questioned by the police;

---

125 See *Corrections and Conditional Release Act*, S.C. 1992, c. 20, s. 127, which allows the Parole Board to order that an adult inmate is to be incarcerated past the statutory release date and required to serve the full sentence.

- shall advise the probation officer of any change in residence, family situation, and employment or schooling; and
- shall not possess any weapon, unless authorized in writing by the provincial director.

The provincial director is authorized under section 97(2) to set additional conditions to address the needs of a young person, to promote reintegration into the community, and to "offer adequate protection to the public from the risk that the young person might otherwise present." These conditions might include requirements that a youth reside with parents or in another place specified by the director, attend school, or obtain counselling.

While there are significant powers for the apprehension and return to custody of a youth who is on community supervision, a youth who is released under section 97 or 98 at the scheduled date of release has more legal protection for remaining in the community than a youth who is released early on conditional supervision under section 94 or 96. Section 102 provides that, if the provincial director has reasonable grounds to believe that a young person on community supervision has "breached or is about to breach" a condition of release, the provincial director may suspend the community supervision and require the arrest of the youth. However, the director is only to have the youth arrested if satisfied that the breach is "a serious one that increases the risk to public safety." If the breach does not reach this level of concern, the director may add additional conditions. If the youth is charged with committing an offence while on community supervision, this is an aggravating factor that may affect the decision about whether to detain the youth before trial, as well as any sentencing decision. It may also be a ground for revoking the community supervision, although a subsequent charge does not result in automatic suspension.

If the youth who has been released on community supervision is returned to custody by the provincial director for a serious breach of the terms of the community supervision order, a youth justice court hearing shall be held "without delay" under section 103. The youth justice court shall consider whether it is satisfied on reasonable grounds that the youth "has breached or was about to breach" a condition of the community supervision. This low standard of proof indicates that the judge may consider hearsay and other evidence that might not be admissible at an ordinary criminal trial. This low standard of proof is intended to facilitate the return to the court for reconsideration of the situation. If the judge is not satisfied that there are reasonable grounds, that the youth has breached a condition or is about to breach a condition, the judge must order the youth to be returned to the community under supervision, although the court may vary the conditions of the order. If the youth justice court is satisfied on reasonable grounds that there was a breach that was serious, the court shall order that the youth is to serve the remainder of the sentence in custody. If the breach is not found to be serious, the court may vary or impose new conditions but shall release the youth. Those who are responsible for supervising and monitoring youth who are released from custody into the community may expect some relapses in behaviour, especially if the youth has an extensive record of prior offending. However, as long as the youth is making progress, has appropriate community supports, and is not endangering the community, the courts and probation supervisors should not be quick to return a youth to custody for a breach of one of the conditions of release.[126]

Under section 98 the Crown prosecutor or provincial director may apply, "within a reasonable time before the expiry of the custodial portion" of a sentence of custody and supervision, to the youth justice court for an order that the youth is to remain in custody until the completion of the total original sentence. If the section 98 hearing cannot be completed before the scheduled release date, the youth is only to be detained in custody pending completion of the hearing, if the court is satisfied that the application was made in a reasonable time before the release date and there are "compelling reasons for keeping the youth in custody." The young person and the parents are to be given at least five days' notice of a section 98 hearing, and are entitled to participate in the hearing. Section 99 requires that a report is to be prepared by correctional officials about the youth's progress in custody; the report may include information about a youth's history or propensity for violence and about any mental illnesses or psychological disorders.

Under section 98 a youth justice court is only to order that a youth is to stay in custody for the remainder of the sentence if the court is satisfied that there are reasonable grounds to believe that the youth is "likely to commit a serious violent offence before the expiry" of the sentence *and* any conditions that would be imposed on the youth would be "not be adequate to prevent the commission of the offence."

---

126 M. Ungar, E. Teram, and J. Picketts, "Young Offenders and Their Communities: Reframing the Institution as an Extension of the Community" (2001) 20 Can J. Comm. Mental Health 29.

Section 98(4) lists some of the factors that the court may consider, including:

- the prior record of offending;
- whether any of the prior offences involved "brutal behaviour" or the youth seemed "indifferent" to the consequences of his or her behaviour to others;
- psychological or psychiatric evidence about physical or mental illness or disorder;
- and "reliable information" about the youth "planning to commit" a serious violent offence before the expiry of the sentence.

The court may also consider the resources available in the community and whether the youth "is more likely to reoffend if he or she serves [the entire youth sentence in custody] without the benefits of community supervision." While the standard of proof for an order under section 98 directing that the youth remain in custody only requires a finding that the court is to be satisfied based on reasonable grounds, a low standard of proof, there must be evidence of a high propensity for serious violence in the period following release from custody onto supervision.

Section 98 creates a strong presumption that a youth will be released into the community on supervision and will serve the balance of the original sentence in the community. It is recognized that, generally, a youth ought to have the benefit of a period of support and supervision in the community after release. During this period, the youth's activities are monitored and the youth may have access to services paid for by the government. If the youth is detained until the end of the entire sentence of custody and supervision, there will be no possibility for this support, counselling, and supervision.

Section 37(11) makes clear that there is no right to appeal any sentence review decision of a youth justice court concerning the issue of whether or not to allow the early release of a youth under section 96. Sentence review is intended to be an expeditious process and it is likely that a youth would have an opportunity for a further youth court review hearing before an appeal could be heard. Under section 101, however, the youth has a right to seek review by the provincial Court of Appeal of a decision under section 98(3) of a youth justice court whether to continue to hold a young offender past his or her scheduled date for release onto community supervision. Sections 104(5) and 109(8) also allow for review by the Court of Appeal of the decisions of a youth justice court concerning the revocation and return to custody of a youth on community or conditional supervision.

7) Sentences for Murder and Other Presumptive Offences

Murder is the youth offence that has most captured public attention and political scrutiny. Relatively few youths in Canada — twenty-five to sixty per year — are charged with this offence. Many youths who are charged with murder are ultimately convicted only of manslaughter, since often the Crown cannot establish the requisite mental intent for murder. These adolescent killings often seem to be unpredictable and senseless acts. Murder sentencing is an important, controversial issue in youth justice law, one that has undergone substantial change since the *YOA* came into force in 1984. That Act, as originally enacted, provided for a maximum sentence for a conviction for murder in youth court of three years in custody; youths could, however, be transferred to adult court, where they would face the full adult sanction of life imprisonment. In 1992, the *YOA* was amended to increase the maximum custodial sentence that a youth court could impose for murder to five years less a day,[127] while still allowing for the possibility of transfer and longer adult sentences. Under the 1995 amendments, the maximum sentence for first degree murder in youth court was further increased to ten years, with a presumption that no more than six years would be served in custody and the balance on conditional supervision in the community.[128] For second degree murder, the maximum youth court sentence was seven years, with the first four years in custody and the balance on conditional supervision.

The 1992 and 1995 increases in maximum youth court sentences for murder were not a response to evidence that there was a danger to the community from having a maximum of five years less a day. Rather, the increases were clearly political, an attempt to satisfy concerns that the *YOA* was "too soft" on crime. As stated by Allan Rock, Justice Minister at the time of the 1995 amendments, the government believed that the maximum youth court penalty for murder of five years less a

---

127 In 1992 five years less a day was selected as the maximum youth court sentence for murder because the *Canadian Charter of Rights and Freedoms*, above note 42, s. 11(f), provides that a person is entitled to a jury trial if the maximum sentence is five years or longer. Jury trials are not easily accommodated in youth court, though. As discussed in Chapters 7 and 9, youths facing murder charges in youth justice court are now entitled to jury trials. Such trials, however, are presided over by superior court judges, albeit in proceedings governed by the *YCJA*, above note 1.

128 *YOA*, above note 3, ss. 20(1)(k.1) and 20(4), enacted by the 1995 amendment, s. 13(3)–(4).

day was "simply wrong . . . as a matter of principle."[129] That is, the issue of accountability was the dominant concern in the increase in the maximum youth court sanction to ten years, although the effect of having a longer maximum youth sentence may also make it somewhat less likely that an adult sanction will be imposed.

The YCJA follows the same basic model as the 1995 YOA amendments for sentencing for murder. Under section 42(2)(q) of the YCJA, the maximum youth sentence in cases of first degree murder is custody and supervision for up to ten years, with a continuous custodial period of up to six years, followed by conditional supervision in the community.[130] For second degree murder, youths are liable for sentences of custody and supervision for up to seven years, with a continuous custodial period of up to four years, followed by conditional supervision in the community.[131] Section 42(2)(o) of the Act provides for special sentences for presumptive offences other than murder: attempted murder, manslaughter, and aggravated sexual assault.[132] For these three offences, the maximum sentence is three years of custody and supervision, with the youth justice court having a discretion about how to divide the sentence between custody and supervision. Further, the supervision portion of a sentence under section 42(2)(o) is to be on conditional supervision, as compared to a sentence for other offences under section 42(2)(n) which is for a period in custody followed by community supervision.

Section 105 requires that, at least one month prior to the expiry of the custodial portion of a sentence imposed under section 42(2)(o) or (q), the provincial director will arrange for a youth justice court hearing to set the terms of the youth's conditional release into the community. Alternatively, the Crown prosecutor may make an application to the youth justice court under section 104 for an order that the young offender should continue to remain in custody for a period not exceeding the remainder of the total original sentence. For either a hearing

---

129 *Minutes of Proceedings and Evidence of the Standing Committee on Justice and Legal Affairs* (22 June 1994) 34:19. See similar comments by Val Meredith, Reform Party critic: "If [youth] murders are down [without changing the law], that's great. But that doesn't mean that those who commit these kinds of crimes shouldn't be dealt with in a different fashion" Canadian Press, February 1, 1995.

130 YCJA, above note 1, s. 42(2)(q)(i).

131 YCJA, above note 1, s. 42(2)(q)(ii).

132 Murder, attempted murder, manslaughter and aggravated sexual assault are referred to as "presumptive offences" because there is a presumption that an adult sentence will be imposed. A third "serious violent offence" also has a presumptive adult sentence; see YCJA, above note 1, s. 2(1).

under section 104 or 105, the provincial director is required to prepare a report for the court about the youth's history and information about the period in custody, including the youth's conduct and response to any services or treatment provided. There may also be a psychological or psychiatric assessment prepared, under section 34.

At a hearing under section 104, the Crown has the onus of satisfying the court that there are "reasonable grounds to believe that the young person is likely to commit an offence causing death or serious bodily harm to another person before the expiry of the youth sentence." Further, the court must be satisfied that any conditions that would be imposed on the youth would "not be adequate to prevent the commission" of a serious violent offence before the expiry of the sentence. Section 104(3) lists some of the factors that the court may consider, including:

- the prior record of offending;
- whether any of the prior offences involved "brutal behaviour" or the youth seemed "indifferent" to the consequences of his or her behaviour to others;
- psychological or psychiatric evidence about physical or mental illness or disorder;
- "reliable information" about the youth "planning to commit" an offence causing the death or serious harm to another person before the expiry of the sentence; and
- the resources available in the community that would "offer adequate protection to the public from the risk that the young person might otherwise present until the expiry of the youth sentence."

At the conclusion of a section 104 hearing, the judge may either order that the youth remain in custody for a period not exceeding the remainder of the original youth sentence, or may decide to release the youth on conditional supervision under section 105.

A youth who is released into the community on conditional supervision will be subject to conditions set out under section 105. These terms will include reporting to a probation officer, and a prohibition on the possession of weapons unless authorized by the court. There are also likely to be conditions on residency and behaviour, such as requiring participation in therapy or drug counselling, attendance at school or seeking employment, prohibition on the use of drugs or alcohol, and restrictions on association with any known offenders.

Section 106 provides that if the provincial director has reasonable grounds to believe that a young person in the community on conditional supervision "has breached or is about to breach" a condition of release, the provincial director may require the arrest of the youth. Under section 109, this suspension of the conditional supervision is "without delay" to be the subject of a review hearing by a youth justice court judge. The court will consider evidence about the youth's conduct since release. The youth justice court only needs to be satisfied that there are reasonable grounds to believe that the youth has breached or was about to breach a condition of the release in order to confirm the suspension of the release, and order that the balance of the sentence will be served in custody. This low standard of proof indicates that the judge may consider hearsay and other evidence that might not be admissible at an ordinary criminal trial. This low standard of proof is intended to facilitate the return to custody of a young offender in circumstances where there are concerns about the youth's conduct in the community, even if there is not proof that would ordinarily satisfy a court that there is criminal conduct or even the breach of a condition of release. This is intended to give the probation officers who are supervising youths who have committed the most serious offences a greater degree of control than in cases where a youth is released on community supervision for a less serious offence.

Youths who are in custody under section 42(2)(o) or (q) have the right under section 94 to an annual review hearing before a youth justice court judge, which may result in early release from custody into the community on conditional supervision. Youths who are serving a sentence for murder or another presumptive offence are also eligible for release on conditional supervision on the recommendation of a provincial director under section 96, and for reintegration leave under section 91.

For youths who are fourteen years of age or older at the time of commission of any of these most serious offences, there is a presumption that an adult sentence will be imposed. Under the YCJA, this does not involve a pre-adjudication transfer of the case to adult court, but rather the possibility of the imposition of an adult sentence upon a finding of guilt. (This change in procedure is discussed in more detail in Chapter 9.) Another option provided by the YCJA, as an alternative to youth or adult custody sentence, is the sentence of intensive rehabilitative custody and supervision under section 42(2)(r) (discussed below). Such a sentence, which would be subject to the same maximum periods for each offence as a custody and supervision youth sentence,[133] provides a more individualized response for treatment to meet the rehabilitative needs of a youth who is suffering from a "mental illness . . . a psychological disorder or an emotional disturbance."

---

133 *YCJA*, above note 1, ss. 42(2)(r)(ii) and (iii).

Once a young person who has been convicted of an offence in youth justice court and placed in custody reaches eighteen, correctional officials can apply under sections 92 of the *YCJA* to a youth justice court judge for an order to transfer the youth to an adult provincial correctional facility[134] to serve the balance of the sentence. If a person is still in youth custody at the age of twenty, the provincial director may transfer that person to an adult provincial correctional facility without a court order, and may apply to the youth justice court for permission to transfer that person to an adult federal penitentiary, where adults serving sentences of two years or longer are confined. If this custodial transfer under section 92 or 93 occurs, the person becomes subject to the legislation governing other prisoners in those facilities.[135] The court is to make this order only if it is considered in the "best interests of the young person or in the public interest."[136] These custodial transfers are most likely to be made only for those serving longer sentences under section 42(2) (o) or (q), or if they have been disruptive in a youth facility. The imposition of adult sentences for murder and other presumptive offences is further discussed in Chapter 9.

8) Intensive Rehabilitative Custody and Supervision: Section 42(2)(r)

An order for "intensive rehabilitative custody and supervision" may be imposed under section 42(2)(r) of the *YCJA*. It is intended to provide an alternative for the most serious offences to ordinary custody and conditional supervision in cases where a youth has mental health problems, providing a secure placement for treatment followed by a high level of supervision and support in the community. This is a relatively

---

134 Adult correctional facilities for those serving sentences of less than two years are operated by the provincial and territorial governments, while adults with sentences of two years or longer are placed in penitentiaries, prisons operated by the federal government. In general there is a more hardened group of offenders and a more brutal atmosphere in the federal prisons, although federal prisons are divided into levels of security — minimum, medium, and maximum — with the most dangerous and abusive offenders being placed in maximum security.

135 *YCJA*, above note 1, ss. 92(3) and 93(3): in the case of a provincial correctional facility, the *Prisons and Reformatories Act*, R.S.C. 1985, c. P-20 and, the case of a federal penitentiary, the *Corrections and Conditional Release Act*, S.C. 1992, c. 20; a "young person" subject to correctional transfer to an adult facility retains the protections of Part 6 of the *YCJA*, which governs such matters as access to youth records and non-publication of identifying information.

136 *YCJA*, above note 1, s. 30(4).

expensive and intrusive sentencing option, and there are significant statutory limits on when it can be ordered.

Intensive rehabilitative custody and supervision is a new sentencing alternative for some of the most serious and disturbed youthful offenders. There are similarities between this sentencing alternative and the "treatment order" provision that was in the YOA as it originally came into force in 1984. Section 20(1)(i) of the YOA allowed a youth court judge to make a treatment order to have a young offender "detained for treatment" in a psychiatric hospital or other "treatment facility" instead of being placed in a custodial facility. Treatment orders under the YOA were controversial for a number of reasons. Mental health professionals criticized the requirement in the YOA that a youth had to consent to the making of a treatment order, arguing that "youth, especially those involved in offending, may not be in the best position to make ultimate decisions regarding the value of mental-health intervention."[137]

For many young offenders, their mental or emotional disturbance both contributes to their criminal behaviour and affects their capacity to appreciate their problems. As a result, some mental health professionals advocated removal of the requirement in the YOA for a youth's consent to a treatment order. Although these mental health advocates acknowledged that "the efficacy of compulsory treatment for young offenders is an area laden with considerable debate," they believed that once emotionally disturbed adolescents are placed in a treatment facility, they are willing to participate in treatment even though they are unwilling to consent to it formally when asked in a courtroom. Treatment orders were very rarely made under the YOA. This reflected both difficulties in securing the consent of young offenders to the making of such orders, as well as the concerns of mental health facilities about their legal position if a youth consented to the making of an order but withdrew the consent on arrival at the facility.[138] As a result of the controversy over the consent provision and the lack of use of treatment orders, this disposition option was removed from the YOA in 1995.

There is no requirement under the YCJA that a youth consent to the making of an order for intensive rehabilitative custody and supervision (referred to as IRCS). Further, section 42(8) provides that nothing in section 42 of the Act "abrogates or derogates from the rights of a young

---

137 A.W. Leschied and P. Gendreau, "Doing Justice in Canada: YOA Policies That Can Promote Community Safety" (1994) 36 Can. J. Crim. 291 at 293.

138 R. v. A.(L.), [1996] A.J. 957 (Prov. Ct.).

person regarding consent to physical or mental health treatment or care." Therefore, a youth who is subject to a sentence for intensive custody and supervision can be placed in a mental health facility or other treatment facility; while he or she can be expected to attend individual or group counselling sessions, a young offender cannot be required to have drug treatment or other medical treatment unless he or she consents. A youth may be subject to involuntary treatment if lacking in the capacity to consent under provincial child welfare or mental health legislation, or if there is no provincial legislation under the common law, but these are narrow circumstances.

While there is no requirement for the consent of a youth to the making of an order for intensive custody and supervision, a youth justice court judge should only make such an order if there is an indication that the young offender will participate in the treatment program being offered. If the youth is clearly unwilling to participate, there is little point in sending a youth to a treatment facility. If a young offender who is under an intensive custody order is unresponsive to treatment or refuses to participate in the treatment program of the facility where he or she has been placed, the provincial director may apply to the youth justice court under section 94(19) to have the sentence converted into a ordinary sentence of custody and supervision, with the total custody and community portions of the sentence being in accord with the original sentence.

Section 42(7) of the Act provides that orders for intensive custody and supervision can only be made if four conditions are satisfied:

(a) the youth has been found guilty of one of the most serious offences: murder, attempted murder, manslaughter, aggravated sexual assault or a third "serious violent offence;"

(b) the young offender is "suffering from a mental illness or disorder, a psychological disorder or an emotional disturbance." Although not explicitly stated, a finding that a youth suffers from such a condition will inevitably require a report from a psychologist or psychiatrist, which could be a result of an assessment carried out under section 34, or other involvement with the youth;

(c) a plan of treatment has been developed for the youth, and there are "reasonable grounds to believe that the plan might reduce the risk of the young person repeating the offence or committing a serious violent offence." This provision would appear to require appropriate evidence from a mental health professional about the plan and its likelihood of success, although this may be provided through a section 34 report or other report; and

(d) the provincial director has determined that a program of intensive rehabilitative custody and supervision is available and the
youth's participation is "appropriate."

Section 42(7)(a)(i) allows a sentence of intensive custody and
supervision to be imposed if the youth is convicted of murder, attempted murder, manslaughter or aggravated sexual assault. Section 42(7)(a)
(ii) also allows such a sentence to be imposed if a young person is
found guilty of a "serious violent offence for which an adult is liable to
imprisonment for a term of more than two years and the young person
has been found guilty at least twice of a serious violent offence." For a
sentence of intensive custody and supervision to be imposed for a serious violent offence, there clearly must be a judicial determination
under section 42(9) that the offence for which a sentence is being
imposed is a "serious violent offence" (a process more fully discussed
below). The requirement that there must be two previous convictions
for serious violent offences may be satisfied if there was a determination
at the time that those previous convictions occurred; in this situation,
intensive custody and supervision would be available as a sentencing
option for a "presumptive offence," with the Crown having given notice
that an adult sentence might be imposed and intensive custody and
supervision are being considered as an alternative to an adult sentence.

The wording of section 42(7)(a)(ii) also allows for a judge who
determines that a serious violent offence has been committed to decide
that two previous convictions were also for serious violent offences,
even if there was not a determination under section 42(9) at the time
when those convictions were made. This is different from the situation
where the Crown is seeking an adult sentence for a third serious violent
offence, in which case it is clear that there must have been two prior
determinations at the time those convictions occurred and the youth
must receive pre-trial notice that an adult sentence may be sought. This
difference derives from the fact that section 42(7)(a) does not refer to
the "presumptive offence" definition of section 2(1), which is used for
the adult sentencing provisions and clearly requires that there be prior
determinations under section 42(9) at the time the convictions
occurred. This difference may be especially significant in the period
after the initial coming into force of the YCJA, since convictions that
occurred before the Act came into force cannot be used as the basis of a
presumption of an adult sentence. Such convictions, however, might be
used as the basis for an order for intensive custody and supervision
under section 42(7)(a)(ii). Unlike the adult sentence for a presumptive
offence, which can only be imposed on a youth who is fourteen years of

age or older at the time of the offence, a sentence of intensive custody and supervision can be ordered for a youth who is twelve or thirteen.

The maximum length of a sentence of intensive custody and supervision is the same as the maximum length of custody and supervision and, hence, can be two, three, seven, or ten years, depending on the offence of which an accused has been found guilty. For most offences, a judge who is imposing such a sentence has a discretion to set the length of the custody and community supervision portions of the sentence; the provision for two-thirds custody and one-third community supervision that applies to ordinary custody does not apply to intensive custody and supervision. The absence of statutory direction reflects the fact that intensive custody and supervision is to be an individually tailored sentence. For murder, however, section 42(2)(r)(ii)–(iii) provides the same limits as with a regular custody order, namely that for first-degree murder there is to be a maximum sentence of no more than ten years, with no more than six years in intensive custody and, for second-degree murder, there is a maximum youth sentence of no more than seven years, with no more than four years in intensive custody.

Section 104 of the *YCJA* allows for an application to be made to a youth justice court to keep the young person in intensive custody and supervision past the community release date on the basis that the youth is likely to commit an offence causing death or serious harm to another person. There is no basis for keeping a person in intensive custody and supervision past the end of the original sentence; in some cases, if the person is suffering from a mental illness and poses a serious risk to him or herself or to others, provincial mental health legislation might be invoked, subject to court review, to confine that person to a mental health facility. Just as for the release from ordinary custody for a youth who is subject to a sentence for a presumptive offence under section 42(2)(o) or (q), young persons who are subject to a sentence for intensive custody and supervision and released into the community are released on conditional supervision under section 105. A youth justice court must set the conditions of this release. There are also wider powers for a provincial director to apprehend and return the youth to custody under sections 106 and 107 than for a release under an ordinary custody and community supervision order. It is not necessary for a youth to breach a condition: it is sufficient to believe that a young person "has breached or is about to breach a condition," although the apprehension is subject to later youth justice court review.

In considering the legitimacy and appropriateness of orders for intensive custody and supervision or other sentences, it should be appreciated that non-invasive rehabilitative services can be provided in custody facilities without such court orders. However, provincial laws generally require that young persons in custody like adults, consent or at least acquiesce to the provision of mental health or other medical services. Further, without their consent, young offenders are sometimes placed on probation with a requirement that they attend counselling or participate in a treatment program (e.g., for drug or alcohol abuse, or for adolescent sexual offenders). In addition to the sentencing option for intensive custody and supervision in the YCJA, in cases involving severely disturbed youths, the mental disorder provisions of the *Criminal Code* or provincial mental legislation can still be invoked (as discussed in Chapter 7). Invocation of these provisions could require a youth suffering from a mental disorder to be involuntarily confined in a mental health facility. Some youths who commit relatively minor offences can be diverted in order to receive assistance in the community for their specific needs through the mental health, education, or child protection systems.

The most effective means of successfully engaging a young offender who is in custody, therapy, or counselling will usually involve offering the possibility of early review and release from custody as an incentive to participation. This type of inducement can serve to secure the youth's co-operation, and it makes sense to offer early release to a youth who has successfully undergone treatment. Youth who are subject to a sentence for intensive rehabilitative custody and supervision are eligible for early release under sections 94 or 96, as well as for rehabilitation leaves, which may provide an incentive for active engagement in any treatment programs that are offered. Despite the provision for new sentencing options such as intensive custody and supervision, some of the biggest difficulties in providing rehabilitative services and counselling to young offenders, both in custody and in the community on probation, arise from the failure of provinces to provide an adequate level of funding and service, not from any legal concerns.

F. DETERMINATION OF "SERIOUS VIOLENT OFFENCE"

The YCJA has special provisions for those youths found guilty of a serious violent offence, especially if it is a third such offence. The term "serious violent offence" and the process for determining whether an offence is a serious violent offence had no equivalent under the YOA. Section 2 of the YCJA defines the term "serious violent offence" to mean "an offence in the commission of which a young person causes or attempts to cause serious bodily harm." The third conviction for such an offence is clearly indicative of a pattern of serious violent offending. It is, however, important that there has been a proper determination that each offence was a "serious violent offence," and not merely a "violent offence."

Section 42(9) of the *YCJA* makes the process of determining whether an offence is a "serious violent offence" an important part of sentencing. If a youth justice court determines that a youth has committed a third "serious violent offence," the youth may presumptively be sentenced as an adult. In the alternative, a youth convicted of a third serious violent offence may be liable under section 42(2)(r) to a sentence of intensive rehabilitative custody and supervision. On the other hand, section 42(5) provides that a youth cannot receive a sentence of deferred custody and supervision for any serious violent offence. Section 2 of the Act provides that, for purposes of an adult sentence, a presumptive offence includes, in addition to murder, attempted murder, manslaughter, and aggravated sexual assault, a third serious violent offence: specifically, it includes "serious violent offences for which an adult is liable to imprisonment for a term of more than two years."[139]

Significantly, while a youth must be fourteen years or older at the time of the commission of the offence to be sentenced as an adult, the *YCJA* permits a determination to be made that a youth aged twelve or thirteen has committed a serious violent offence. Thus, initial determinations of the commission of a serious violent offence may be made for youths under the age of fourteen years, for possible use to establish that an offence committed after the age of fourteen is the third such offence and, hence, a presumptive offence. This determination may also allow a sentence of intensive rehabilitative custody and supervision to be imposed on a youth under the age of fourteen.

Recent public demands have been expressed for a more severe response from the youth justice system to the problem of youth violence. As a result of changes in attitudes and policies, judges may find themselves under pressure to determine a broad range of offences to be "serious violent offences." It is, however, submitted that the definition

---

139 A provincial government may decide that the age for presumptive sentencing as an adult is only to start when a youth is 16 years of age or older on the date of the alleged offence; see s. 61 of the *YCJA*, above note 1, and discussion in Chapter 9.

in section 2 of the *YCJA* is intended to be relatively narrow, with the serious violent offence being distinguished from the ordinary violent offence. The impact of such a determination on the life of a youth may be profound and, consequently, the discretion to make such determinations should be exercised with caution. There will, however, be cases in which such a determination is appropriate both to allow for the possibility of a more severe sanction and to send a message to a youth who may pose a serious risk of reoffending.

A "serious violent offence" will usually involve a significant physical injury to the complainant, or an attempt to cause injury. A sexual assault involving significant psychological injury will also be a "serious violent offence." The definition of "serious violent offence" relies on the concept of "serious bodily harm" which is not defined in either the *YCJA* or the *Criminal Code*. In *R. v. McGraw*, the Supreme Court of Canada held that the phrase refers to "any hurt or injury that interferes in a grave or substantial way with the physical integrity or well-being of the complainant,"[140] and includes a rape even if there is no physical injury.

The definition of "serious violent offence" in the *YCJA* enacted by Parliament in 2002 is narrower than the definition in the 1999–2000 version of the Act (Bill C-3), which was not enacted.[141] Section 2 of Bill C-3 provided that "serious violent offence means an offence that causes or creates a substantial risk of causing serious bodily harm." For an offence that did not actually result in serious bodily harm, that definition focused on the degree of risk of harm, rather than the youth's state of mind at the time of the offence. This definition would likely have included such offences as impaired driving, in the commission of which the accused may have endangered public safety without intending to do so and without actually having caused serious bodily harm.

In contrast, to fall within the definition of "serious violent offence" in the enacted version of the Act, a youth must either have actually caused serious bodily harm, or have attempted to commit an offence that was intended to cause serious bodily harm but did not do so.

If the offence actually results in serious bodily harm, then the state of mind of the youth may not be relevant, so that criminal negligence causing death would be within the definition. However, if serious bodily harm did not result, there must have been an intent to have caused serious bodily harm, in which case the psychological state of the youth

---

140 *R. v. McGraw*, [1991] 3 S.C.R. 72 per Cory J. at para. 21.
141 See Bill C-3, Second Session, Thirty-sixth Parliament, 1999.

would be relevant. Factors which may also be important to determining whether an act constitutes a "serious violent offence" include: the extent of injury caused; the extent of deliberation and planning; whether there was unusual cruelty or callousness; and an assessment of the mental state or intent of the youth.

The offence of impaired driving would likely have been within the definition of serious violent offence in Bill C-3, since it is an offence that "creates a risk of serious bodily harm." On the other hand, impaired driving does not appear to be a serious violent offence in the *YCJA* as enacted, as there is no intent to cause harm. If an accident and serious injury result from impaired driving, this could be a serious violent offence, given the reckless disregard for public safety that is involved in impaired driving combining with the actual injury to merit this designation.

Section 42(9) of the *YCJA* is discretionary: the youth justice court is empowered to determine that an offence is a serious violent offence, but it need not do so. This determination is to be made only on application of the Crown, which must give notice to the youth of the application. The youth justice court must hold a hearing before making a determination. The procedural and evidentiary rules that govern a sentencing hearing should apply to a court making this determination with, for example, the court permitted to rely on hearsay evidence. It is likely that most determinations will be based on submissions, with the judicial finding of guilt and the evidence from the sentencing hearing used as the basis for such a determination. Section 42(10) of the *YCJA* allows for an appeal of the determination that a criminal act was or was not a serious violent offence in the same way as a sentence appeal.

The judicial discretion to determine that an act is a serious violent offence is more limited than the discretion held by judges for most sentencing issues. This is because such a determination can only be made on application by the Crown. This limit is important when, for example, joint submissions are made by Crown and defence counsel as a result of plea negotiations. Where an application to have a determination that an offence is a serious violent offence is made by the Crown and conceded in a joint submission, the judge is not necessarily bound by this submission. Notwithstanding such a submission, the judge may decline to determine that the crime was a serious violent offence. However, if, as a result of making a joint submission, the Crown does *not* make such an application under section 42(9), the judge cannot make a determination that the offence constituted a serious violent offence.

Procedurally, the determination of whether an offence is a serious violent offence is to be made only after a finding of guilt. It is submitted that the time for making such a determination is as a part of the sentencing stage for a particular offence, as the judge will then have full information about the offence. It might be argued that the language used in section 42(9) is sufficiently broad as to allow the Crown to raise the issue of having a determination made at some time after sentencing that an offence is a serious violent offence. For example, a Crown prosecutor might seek to do so if another serious violent offence has been subsequently committed by the youth.

Although the wording of section 42(9) does not explicitly preclude a later determination that a prior offence is a serious violent offence, when read purposively and contextually, the *YCJA* would not appear to permit this. This interpretation is reinforced by the doctrine of *functus officio*, which provides that once a final decision is made by a judge, in the absence of explicit legislative provision, the judge has no further jurisdiction to deal with the case.[142] The doctrine of *functus officio* has been applied in a wide range of legal contexts. In the criminal context, Martin, J.A. of the Ontario Court of Appeal held that a judge who renders a finding of guilt is only *functus* after the judge has imposed a sentence.[143] However, once the sentence is imposed, the judge is *functus* and the determination of guilt or sentence can only be changed by the statutory appeal process. This inclusion of section 42(9) in the sentencing provision of the *YCJA*, together with the common law doctrine of *functus officio*, indicates that a determination whether an offence is a serious violent offence must be done as part of the sentencing process by the judge who has knowledge of the circumstances of the offence and who is imposing the sentence.[144]

---

142 Justice L'Heureux-Dubé in *Chandler* v. *Association of Architects Alberta*, [1989] 2 S.C.R. 848, summarized the doctrine of *functus officio*: "an adjudicator . . . once it has reached its decision cannot afterwards alter its award except to correct clerical mistakes or errors arising from an accidental slip or omission" (at para. 40).

143 See *R. v. Lessard*, [1972] 2 O.R. 329 (C.A.).

144 The concept of *functus* would not apply to the situation where a judge, after making a finding of guilt, was unable by reason of illness or death to impose a sentence and make a determination under s. 42(9). In this situation, s.131 of the *YCJA*, above note 1, adopts s. 669.2(1) of the *Criminal Code*, above note 2, and allows for another judge to impose sentence and make the determination of whether it is a "serious violent offence."

Although the determination that an act constitutes a serious violent offence is made only after a finding of guilt has been made, the process for trying a youth will be different if that young person is *alleged* to have committed a third such offence. After two convictions for serious violent offences, a charge for a third offence which may later be deemed a serious violent offence opens the possibility of adult liability to the youth and so makes available such adult procedures as the right to a jury trial. This clearly requires that the latest time at which a determination can be made that an offence is a first or second serious violent offence is before the youth is required to enter a plea for what might be a third serious violent offence.

G. DNA SAMPLES UNDER THE *CRIMINAL CODE*

Since 1998 section 487.05 of the *Criminal Code* has allowed the Crown to obtain a warrant from a court for the collection of a sample of DNA from a person reasonably believed to have been a party to a "designated offence," in order to assist in the investigation of the suspected offence. This may be especially useful to help identify the perpetrator of a sexual offence if, for example, the police have obtained a semen sample from the body of a complainant. A DNA sample from a suspect may be used to help establish whether he is the perpetrator. Typically the DNA sample is obtained from the suspect by taking a few individual hairs or a saliva swab from the mouth, although it can also be done by taking a small sample of blood by pricking the skin surface of the suspect with a sterile lancet, which involves minimal discomfort. A comparison of DNA collected at a crime scene with the DNA sample of a suspect may conclusively establish that the suspect could not have committed the offence, or may be establish a very high probability that a particular person was the perpetrator.[145] (The taking of DNA samples for investigative purposes is discussed in Chapter 4.)

---

145 The likelihood that any two individuals will have identical DNA is very very small (except for identical twins, who have identical DNA). There are, however, cases in which it can be difficult to do a clear DNA match between a suspect and a crime scene if, for example, there is only a very small blood or tissue sample at the crime scene, or there has been a mixing of blood from several individuals at the crime scene or through contamination of collected suspect samples.

Section 487.05 allows an investigative DNA warrant to be obtained whether the suspect is an adult or a young person.[146] Although most likely to be useful for the investigation of a "primary designated offence" — a sexual offence or an offence involving serious violence or death — the police may obtain an order for a DNA sample for the investigation of "secondary designated offences," which includes a range of other offences involving violence or risk of injury to others, such as assault, robbery, or arson. If a person is eliminated as a suspect, or acquitted at trial, a DNA sample obtained under section 487.05 must be removed from the national DNA data bank. But, if there is a conviction, a sample may be retained.[147]

If a DNA sample has not been taken under the *Code* for investigative purposes, section 487.052 allows for a court order to be made at the time of sentencing for the gathering of DNA samples from persons, whether adult or youth offenders, convicted of either primary or secondary designated offences for inclusion in the national DNA data bank for possible use in the investigation of other offences. The sentencing court has a discretion to refuse to make an order for the provision of a DNA sample by a convicted person, taking account of the convicted person's privacy, the nature, and circumstances of the offence, and the protection of society. There is a very strong presumption that, in the event of a conviction for a sexual offence or an offence involving serious violence, a DNA order will be made. The courts have indicated that, even if an offence does not involve significant injury and relates to property, such as break and enter, "given an adult offender's diminished expectation of privacy following conviction, it will usually be in the best interests of the administration of justice" for an order to be made.[148] The fact that an offender's DNA sample is in the national DNA data bank may help facilitate future investigations, as well as deterring future offending by that person.

It is submitted, however, that the courts should be more cautious about making an order under section 457.052 for a DNA sample to be provided by a young offender as opposed to an adult offender, especially those youths convicted of less serious offences and without a signif-

---

146 The *Criminal Code*, above note 2, s. 487.07(4), requires police who are executing a warrant to obtain a DNA sample for an investigation to give a young person the opportunity to consult with a parent and counsel before the warrant is executed, and to have that person present while the warrant is executed. This reflects the special legal protections for adolescents in the *YOA*, above note 3, and *YCJA*, above note 1.

147   *DNA Identification Act*, S.C. 1998, c. 37, s. 9(2).

148   *R. v. P.R.F.*, [2001] O.J. 5084, 57 O.R. (3d) 475 (C.A.).

icant record of prior offending.[149] While the physical taking of a DNA sample is not intrusive, the collection of DNA by a government agency does constitute a significant intrusion into the privacy of individuals. Once this type of data is collected, it can be used to track an individual. Although it is contrary to federal government policy, there is nothing in the legislation to prevent a government in the future from using the data acquired for other purposes than merely identification of offenders. The government might, for example, start to use the DNA samples it has gathered to predict medical, physical, or mental characteristics of offenders, or, for example, want to use predictive information based on a DNA analysis in sentencing hearings.

Given the potentially sensitive nature of DNA samples, sections 187–89 of the *YCJA* modify the provisions of the *DNA Identification Act*, which govern the retention of DNA samples taken from a young offender.[150] In general, reflecting the principle of limited accountability of young offenders, DNA samples taken from young offenders and records relating can be retained for shorter periods than those taken from adults. For young offenders convicted of a summary conviction offence, the DNA sample must be destroyed three years after the completion of any sentence; for most indictable offences, the retention period is five years from the completion of the sentence. For those youth convicted of the most serious presumptive offences for which there may be an adult sentence imposed, the DNA sample of a young offender may be retained for ten years or longer from the completion of any sentence imposed.

---

149 But see *R. v. B.K.G.* (2001), 291 A.R. 344 (Prov. Ct.), where Wenden Prov. J. observed that there is no provision in s. 487.05 of the *Criminal Code*, above note 2, which would indicate that Parliament intended to give special rights or protections to young persons at this stage of the process, in contrast to s. 487.07(4) which imposes special obligations on the police when executing an investigative DNA warrant against a young person. The judge stated that in regard to ss. 487.051 and 487.052: "No distinction is made between adult offenders and young persons." This decision actually dealt with an application by the Crown for an order under s. 487.052 for a 22-year-old person convicted of assault, and the central issue was what weight should be placed on the lengthy prior youth court record, including convictions for sexual assault and robbery. Insofar as if a person is convicted of an offence while an adult, for the purposes of s. 487.051, it seems clear that there should be no discounting of a prior youth record (unless s. 119(2) of the *YCJA*, above note 1, applies in which case no use can be made of that record). However, if the person was a young person when the offence was committed for which a s. 487.051 order is being sought, it is submitted that the age of the person should be a mitigating factor.

150 *DNA Identification Act*, S.C. 1998, c. 37, ss. 9 & 10; See *YCJA* ss. 188–89.

H. THE IMPORTANCE AND LIMITATIONS OF SENTENCING

The sentencing process and the sentences imposed on young offenders lie at the heart of the youth justice system. The *YCJA* makes significant changes to the law governing the sentencing of young offenders and the treatment of adolescents in the youth corrections systems. While judges will continue to play a central role in the sentencing process, the new Act provides more structure for the exercise of judicial discretion, with a greater focus on accountability and proportionality of sentences. An understanding of the social context of a youth and rehabilitative concerns may be important factors in the shaping of a sentence, but they cannot be used to justify a more onerous sentence than accountability principles would allow. While sentences are to be a just response to the circumstances of the offence and the record of the offender, it remains clear that young offenders, owing to their immaturity, are to receive less onerous sentences than adults in similar circumstances.

The *YCJA* places greater restrictions on the use of custody and is clearly intended to reduce Canada's over-reliance on incarceration for non-violent offenders. The new Act has a number of provisions intended to discourage the use of custody and encourage the use of community based sentences. Ultimately, however, the new Act continues the Canadian tradition of judges having a significant but limited role in the sentencing and rehabilitation of young offenders. While the new Act encourages judges to consider community based sentencing alternatives, it clearly does not allow judges to require that governments provide community based programs or services.

The sentencing process may, in some cases, help to change the attitude of a young offender, a factor that may be critical to the youth's rehabilitation. Active engagement of a youth in the sentencing process may help to change the attitude of a young offender. Use of conferencing and allowing young offenders to directly hear from their victims may cause some adolescents to change their attitudes and behaviour. Further, those providing information and making submissions to the youth justice court must be cognizant that the judges are obliged to impose a sentence that is most likely to rehabilitate the young person and reintegrate him or her into society. Ultimately, however, it is not judges, lawyers, and those involved in the sentencing process who are likely to rehabilitate a young offender who has significant problems. Probation officers, therapists, corrections workers, and other professionals and volunteers who work with youths after they are sentenced are in the best position to help a youth and his or her family address the circumstances underlying the young person's offending behaviour. There are significant resource constraints that can make it very difficult for those who work in the youth corrections system to be as effective as they would like to be. It must also be appreciated that despite the best efforts of professionals, volunteers, and families, at least at some points in their lives, there are some young offenders who are not ready to participate in their own rehabilitation and are destined to reoffend.

FURTHER READINGS

BEGIN, P., *Boot Camps: Issues for Consideration* (Ottawa: Library of Parliament Research Branch, 1996)

CANADA, FEDERAL–PROVINCIAL/TERRITORIAL TASK FORCE ON YOUTH JUSTICE, *A Review of the Young Offenders Act and the Youth Justice System in Canada* (Ottawa: Ministry of Supply and Services, 1996) cc. 6, 7, and 8

MANSON, A., *The Law of Sentencing* (Toronto: Irwin Law, 2001)

MARRON, K., *Apprenticed in Crime: Young Offenders, the Law, and Crime in Canada* (Toronto: McClelland-Bantam, 1992) cc. 8 and 9

PLATT, P., *Young Offenders Law in Canada*, 2d ed. (Toronto: Butterworths, 1995) cc. 19 and 20

QUIGLEY, T., *Procedure in Canadian Criminal Law* (Toronto: Carswell, 1997) c. 23.

SCOTT, S., M. WONG, & B. WEAGANT, *Defending Young Offender Cases*, 2d ed. (Toronto: Carswell, 1997) cc. 7, 9, and 10

CHAPTER 9

ADULT SENTENCING FOR YOUTHS

A. ADULT SANCTIONS FOR YOUNG OFFENDERS

1) Purpose of Adult Sanctions

All juvenile justice systems have provisions that allow for the most serious of offenders to receive sentences that are similar or identical to those imposed on adults. The statutory provisions that allow for adult sanctions to be imposed on adolescents are significant not only for the youths directly involved but for the entire juvenile justice system, since they set an outer boundary for that system and help to define its nature. There is a recognition that some youths have committed offences that are so serious, and pose such a great risk to the public that it would be inappropriate to subject them to the limited sentences that are available under juvenile justice laws. However, countries vary greatly in the legislative provisions which allow for adult sanctions to be imposed on adolescents. In most American states, for example, the decision about whether to seek an adult sentence is made by the prosecutor before trial and any trial in such a case is likely to be fully publicized. Thousands of juveniles are serving sentences in adult prisons in the United States; in some states, capital punishment is even possible for juveniles who commit murder. However, in some other countries, such as New Zealand, only one or two juveniles per year are likely to face an adult sanction.

In Canada, the process for imposing adult sentences is judicially controlled. Under the *Young Offenders Act*,[1] this process generally resulted in under 100 youth a year receiving an adult sentence (i.e., about 1 in 1000 youth court cases). Although cases involving adult sentences for youths occur relatively rarely in Canada, these cases involve serious, often brutal offences. They are challenging cases for the justice system and are among the most highly publicized young offender cases. Laws allowing for imposition of an adult sanction have been controversial and, as a result, these provisions have been changed more frequently than any other parts of Canada's youth justice legislation over the past two decades. The provisions of the *Youth Criminal Justice Act*[2] that allow for adult sanctions to be imposed on a youth are intended to deal with those relatively rare cases where the ordinary youth justice sentencing regime is considered inadequate to hold a young offender accountable for a particularly serious offence.

Adolescents who are Aboriginal or members of visible minorities are much more likely than Caucasian youth to be sentenced as adults. While this pattern is better documented in the United States, where juvenile offending data records the race of the youth, the available Canadian data as well as reported case law reveal the similar disturbing trends in this country.[3] The vast majority of youths who are subject to adult sanction are male.[4]

The provisions for adult sentencing have been characterized as a form of "safety valve" for those relatively rare circumstances where the provisions of the *YCJA* — in particular the limits on the maximum length of

---

1   *Young Offenders Act*, R.S.C 1985, c. Y-1,enacted as S.C. 1980–81–82–83, c. 110. The Act was also amended in 1985 through *An Act to amend the Young Offenders Act, the Criminal Code, the Penitentiary Act, and the Prisons and Reformatories Act*, R.S.C. 1985 (2d Supp.), c. 24, in force September 1, 1986 and November 1, 1986, S.C. 1992, c.11, and in 1995 through *An Act to amend the Young Offenders Act and the Criminal Code*, S.C. 1995, c. 19.

2   *Youth Criminal Justice Act*, S.C. 2002, c. 1 (royal assent February 19, 2002, to come into force April 1, 2003), often referred to in this book as the *YCJA*.

3   See, for example, the Correctional Investigator, *Annual Report of the Correctional Investigator* (Ottawa: 1999–2000); that report stated that eight of the nine youths in Canada in 2000 under eighteen years who were placed in federal adult penitentiaries were Aboriginal or members of visible minorities. For American data, see J. Fagan, *The Changing Borders of Juvenile Justice* (Chicago, IL: University of Chicago Press, 2000).

4   In 1999, under the *YOA*, above note 1, 52 youth were transferred, of whom 47 youths transferred were males and 5 females: Statistics Canada, CANSIM II. In 2000–2001, eighty-six cases were transferred to adult court, of which 57 percent involved seventeen-year-olds: Statistics Canada, *Youth Court Statistics 2000–01* (2002) 22:3 Juristat.

sentence — are considered to be insufficient for holding a young person accountable. A judge who determines that a youth ought to be subject to adult sanction is, in essence, deciding that the *YCJA* — its sentencing principles and the resources established pursuant to it — represent an inadequate response to the offence committed by a young person. Youths could be subjected to adult sentences under both the *YOA* and its precursor, the *Juvenile Delinquents Act*.[5] The procedure and the test for sanctioning adolescents as adults are substantially changed by the *YCJA*.

2) Transfer Under the *Juvenile Delinquents Act*

Under the *Juvenile Delinquents Act* there was a relatively informal process for transfer of juveniles into adult court for trial and possible sentence. This process could occur before or after trial in juvenile court, or even after part of the juvenile sentence was served. The transfer process under the *Juvenile Delinquents Act* could be initiated by a juvenile court judge without the request of counsel, though it was usually commenced as a result of an application by the Crown prosecutor. Under the *Juvenile Delinquents Act*, a juvenile who was transferred into adult court for trial could immediately be detained in an adult prison pending adult trial and, if convicted of murder, faced the prospect of capital punishment.[6]

3) Transfer Under the *Young Offenders Act*

The determination whether to transfer a young person to the jurisdiction of adult court under the *YOA* was complex. The transfer hearing was held before trial, and was to determine whether a youth would be tried in adult court. If convicted in adult court, the youth would be subjected to an adult sentence. In dealing with transfer, the youth court judge was to consider a broad range of evidence, much of which was inadmissible in a criminal trial, to determine which court and corrections system and which legal regime was preferable for dealing with the young person. In making such a decision, the youth court was to be guided by the specific provisions of section 16 of the *YOA*, as well as the more general Declaration of Principle in section 3 of that Act.

---

5   *Juvenile Delinquents Act*, enacted as S.C. 1908, c. 40; subject to minor amendments over the years, finally as *Juvenile Delinquents Act*, R.S.C. 1970, c. J-3.

6   See, for example, *R. v. Truscott*, [1959] O.W.N. 320 (sub. nom. S.M.T., Re.) 31 C.R. 76, 125 C.C.C. 100 (H.C.J.). See also Isabel Lebourdais, *The Trial of Steven Truscott* (London: Gollancz, 1966); and Julian Sher, *Until You are Dead: Steven Truscott's Long Ride into History* (Toronto: Knopf Canada, 2001).

The application of that Act's statutory principles to specific cases was often exceedingly difficult. In one transfer, the Alberta Court of Appeal commented:

> Transfer orders present a difficult adjudicative challenge. . . . The statutory imperatives that are supposed to guide the court are couched in terms of inconvenient vagueness. . . . The facts offered to the court during applications for transfer are unusually pliable. . . . Opinion, inference, evidence of character, good and bad, are all received. . . . Such an inquiry — one commencing with sentence to be followed by judgment — is no longer the private precinct of Alice and the Queen of Hearts.[7]

The *YOA* provided that youths who were fourteen or older (as of the date of the alleged offence) and charged with a serious offence could be subject to a pre-adjudication transfer hearing, typically brought as a result of an application by the Crown. The pre-adjudicative transfer hearings under the *YOA* could be unfair to youths, as youth court judges had to make decisions about the "seriousness and circumstances" of an offence without hearing all of the evidence at trial. Not infrequently a youth court judge would decide to transfer a youth on a very serious charge, such as first-degree murder, but at the later trial, after all of the evidence was heard, the youth was only convicted of the less serious offences of manslaughter or being an accessory to a murder. However, since the youth had already been transferred into adult court, the youth was still subject to an adult sentence.

In addition to consideration of the seriousness of the offence, under the *YOA* youth courts would consider the age, character, and prior record of offending of the youth in making a transfer determination. Typically, psychologists or psychiatrists provided critical testimony about the likelihood of rehabilitation and future offending. While portions of the test for deciding whether to transfer a youth to adult court under the *YOA* were changed over the years, one constant feature of the test was that the youth court was required to balance the protection of the public against the rehabilitation of the youth. There was significant variation in how the youth courts in different provinces interpreted the transfer provisions, and some provinces consistently had much higher transfer rates than other provinces. If a youth court decided a charge against a young person should be transferred, the trial was held in adult (or "ordinary") court with the adult rules allowing for publication of identifying information. Since the charges were usu-

---

7   *R. v. M (G.J.)* (1993), 135 A.R. 204, at 206–08 (C.A.).

ally very serious, the youth was likely to have a jury trial. If a youth was convicted in adult court, an adult sentence would be imposed on him or her under the *Criminal Code*. For most offences, the adult court judge who was sentencing a young offender might take account of the age of the youth as a mitigating factor in sentencing. However, the statutory provisions of the *YOA* that limited maximum dispositions did not apply to youth who were transferred.

If a youth was sentenced as an adult, the court had discretion to allow a portion of his or her sentence to be served in a youth custody facility. There was a presumption that the youth would be placed in a youth custody facility until the age of eighteen and would then be placed in an adult correctional facility. If sentenced as an adult, a youth was generally subject to adult rules governing parole and release, although provisions of the *Criminal Code* provided that, if convicted of murder, for which there is a mandatory life sentence, a person who was a youth at the time of the offence would be eligible to be considered for release by the parole board earlier than an adult convicted of the same offence.[8]

Under the *YOA* a youth could be subjected to an adult sentence only if the proceedings were transferred to the adult criminal justice system prior to adjudication. This requirement that transfer hearings were to be held before trial was problematic. A central issue in many transfer hearings was the seriousness of the offence. However, since there had not yet been a trial, the youth court did not know what in fact had occurred. Generally, the court made its decision on the basis of the factual allegations of the Crown and relied on hearsay and opinion evidence about the alleged offence from the investigating police officers.[9] Although in theory a youth could testify at the transfer hearing and the *YOA* prevented any direct use of testimony given by the youth in a later trial,[10] defence counsel were understandably reluctant to have their clients take the stand at this pre-trial stage and be subjected to cross-examination by the Crown. It was quite common under the *YOA* for a youth who was charged with first-degree murder to be transferred to adult court for this charge based on the police allegations but only be convicted after trial in adult court of manslaughter or some lesser offence. The young person may well have had some involvement in the offence, but a full trial revealed that the youth's role in the killing was

---

8   *Criminal Code*, R.S.C. 1985, c. C-46 ss. 745.1, 745.3 & 745.5.

9   See *R. v. H.(A.B.)* (1992), 10 O.R. (2d) 683 (Gen. Div.), Garton J., aff'd (1993), 12 O.R. (3d) 634 (C.A.).

10   *YOA*, above note 1, s. 16(12).

less culpable than alleged at the transfer hearing. Thus, conducting *YOA* transfer hearings on a pre-trial basis often produced unfair results. Further, holding the transfer hearing before trial complicated and delayed the legal process. In some cases, there was a lengthy transfer hearing and then the youth was acquitted at trial.

Substantial variation in how courts in different provinces applied the transfer provisions persisted in the face of amendments to the transfer provisions of the *YOA* in 1992 and 1995. The courts in Manitoba and Alberta consistently took interpretative approaches that resulted in those two provinces having transfer rates that were the highest in the country.[11] Judges in these provinces tended to give primary importance to the interests of society. The courts taking this approach emphasized that societal interests in accountability, deterrence, and incapacitation all favoured transfer for youths facing serious charges, especially homicides. In comparison to courts in other jurisdictions, the courts in these provinces also placed less emphasis on the potentially harmful effects on youths of transfer into adult correctional facilities and on the typically better prospects for rehabilitation in the youth system. The approach of the Manitoba and Alberta courts differed from the more restrictive approach to transfer apparent in the Quebec, Ontario, and Saskatchewan courts.

Appellate judges in Ontario, Quebec, and Saskatchewan emphasized their concerns about the enormous potential harm to young persons from serving long sentences in adult correctional facilities. They argued that neither the youth nor society is served if the young person is irreparably harmed by a sentence in an adult facility,[12] at least if there are reasonable prospects of rehabilitation within the youth system. These courts were unwilling to transfer youths who might have been transferred if the allegations had arisen in Alberta or Manitoba. Some of the variation in transfer rates among provinces may have reflected differences in judicial perceptions of the adequacy and security of the youth corrections system in different jurisdictions. It is also apparent that there was significant disagreement about the appropriate interpretation of section 16. The significant legislative changes in the transfer provisions of the *YOA* in 1992 and 1995 had little impact on transfer rates and the differing approaches to the issue of adult sanctions for young offenders.

---

11   There are a number of explanations for the high transfer rates in Manitoba and Alberta, but it cannot be ignored that these two provinces have a conservative political climate, and were, for example, the first two provinces to establish strict-discipline (boot camp) custody facilities.

12   See, for example, *R. v. S.(W.)* (1989), 69 C.R. (3d) 168 (Ont. C.A.).

4) Adult Sentencing Under the *Youth Criminal Justice Act*

The provisions of the *YCJA* that deal with the imposition of an adult sentence on a person who was a youth at the time of the commission of an offence differ substantially from those in effect under the *YOA*, although Canada has retained a model of judicial control over this process. While the *YCJA* introduces very significant procedural and substantive changes, as under the previous statute, only the most serious offenders will be considered for an adult sentence and the rate of imposition of adult sentences on youth is likely to remain relatively low in comparison to the United States. One of the most significant changes in the adult sentencing provisions is procedural.

Under the new Act the decision about whether to impose an adult sanction is only to be made after the youth is convicted of an offence, when all relevant facts about that offence are known. This should reduce delays that arose in the adult sentencing process under the *YOA*, as well as ensuring that the court has better information when making such an important decision. If an adult sanction might be imposed, the youth must generally be notified before trial, and in most cases will be able to choose to have a jury trial. Because the adult sentencing determination is made only after conviction under the *YCJA*, it is not the unique type of transfer proceeding as under the *YOA*, but is really part of the sentencing process.

Under the *YCJA*, as with the previous Act, an adult sentence may only be considered if the youth was fourteen or older at the time of commission of the offence. For some of the most serious offences there is a presumption that youth will be sentenced as adults, though this presumption may be overcome. In addition to cases of murder, attempted murder, manslaughter, or aggravated sexual assault, the category of "presumptive offences" under the *YCJA* includes a third conviction for a "serious violent offence." The test for deciding whether an adult sentence is appropriate is whether the court considers that a sentence imposed under the *YCJA* would be of "sufficient length to hold a young person accountable for his or her offending behaviour."

As under the *YOA*, there are provisions in the *YCJA* to allow a court to impose an adult-length sentence, but with a portion to be served in a youth custody facility. Most adolescents who will be subject to an adult sentence will remain in youth custody facilities until reaching adulthood, and during that time will continue to have access to age-appropriate rehabilitative services and will be less likely to be subject to exploitation by adult offenders.

Under the *YCJA*, as under the *YOA*, a youth who is sentenced as an adult is generally subject to adult rules governing parole and release. However, provisions of the *Criminal Code* continue to provide that if convicted of murder, for which there is a mandatory life sentence, a person who was a youth at the time of the offence will be eligible to be considered for release by the parole board earlier than an adult convicted of murder.

Publication of identifying information is prohibited until after the youth is convicted. If an adult sentence is imposed, the *YCJA* allows the media to publish identifying information about the youth. Further, for the category of very serious presumptive offences for which an adult sentence will presumptively be imposed — even if the youth justice court decides against imposing an adult sanction — the court may allow identifying information to be publicized.

As under the *YOA*, there are provisions in the *YCJA* that allow for correctional transfer. The courts may allow a young person who was sentenced under the *YCJA* but is over the age of eighteen to be transferred from the youth corrections system into an adult correctional facility. There is a presumption that a young person who is in youth custody at the age of twenty (e.g., as a result of having a long *YCJA* murder sentence) will be placed in an adult correctional facility.

B. OFFENCES SUBJECT TO ADULT SENTENCE

It seems likely that under the *YCJA*, as under the *YOA*, courts will generally be asked to consider the imposition of an adult sentence only for youths who have committed the most serious offences. However, in theory, the *YCJA* continues to allow for the possibility for an adult sentence to be imposed on a young offender for a broad range of offences, both violent and non-violent.

Under the *YOA*, a youth could be transferred to adult court for a broad range of offences, including property offences where the value exceeded $5000. The *YOA* permitted a youth court to transfer to adult court a youth who was fourteen years of age or older at the time of an alleged offence and charged with any "indictable offence[s] *other than* an offence referred to in section 553 of the *Criminal Code*." Section 553 of the Code sets out a number of less serious offences for which a provincial court judge has absolute jurisdiction, including: property offences where the value of damaged or stolen property does not exceed $5000, such as theft; obtaining money or property by false pretenses; and possession of stolen property and mischief, as well as a number of other less serious offences. There were cases under the *YOA* involving young persons who were over eighteen by the time they appeared in youth court — and perhaps also facing other charges in adult court for subsequent offences — and were transferred to adult court to face property-related charges. These older youths typically requested or agreed to be transferred on these charges, expecting that any sentence that the adult court would impose would be relatively short, and they were likely to actually serve less time in adult jail under adult parole rules than they would serve in a youth custody with its relatively cumbersome process for review of sentences. Further, some of these older young offenders preferred to be in adult jail, sometimes for such reasons as the relatively tolerant attitude to activities such as smoking in the adult system in comparison to the youth system.

While some youths were transferred to adult court for property offences under the *YOA*, almost all contentious cases involved charges for serious violent offences for which a much longer sentence would likely be imposed in adult court than under the *YOA*.[13] Section 62 of the *YCJA* provides that any youth fourteen years or older at the time of an offence may be subjected to an adult sentence for the commission "of an indictable offence for which an adult is liable to imprisonment for a term of more than two years." This permits an adult sentence to be imposed for a broad range of offences, including theft where the property is worth more than $5000. In practice, however, it seems likely that the Crown will generally only seek an adult sentence for serious violent offences, or in cases where the person may have committed an offence while a young offender but was charged only after reaching the age of eighteen.

1) Presumptive Offences

An important feature of the 1995 amendments to the *YOA* was the introduction of a category of charges for which a sixteen- or seventeen-year-old youth would be dealt with in adult court unless the young person successfully applied under section 16(1.01) to a youth court judge

---

13   In 2000–2001, under the *YOA*, above note 1, there were 86 cases transferred to adult court; 48 for violent crimes including 18 out of the 84 charges in Canada for murder, manslaughter and attempted murder (Statistics Canada, *Juristat*, above note 4). In 1999, 52 youths were transferred, of whom 47 youths transferred were males and 5 females; 31 of 47 transfers were for violent offences (Statistics Canada CANSIM II, above note 4).

to have the case dealt with in youth court.[14] For sixteen- and seventeen-year-old youths charged with murder, attempted murder, manslaughter, and aggravated sexual assault, the youth had the onus to show why the case should not be dealt with in adult court. For all other offences for older youths, and for fourteen- and fifteen-year-old youths charged with any offence, including the presumptive offences, there was an onus under the *YOA* on the Crown to satisfy the court that the case should be transferred. There is often real difficulty in determining how a youth will respond to the rehabilitative services provided in custody and how great a future danger a youth may pose to society. Accordingly, the onus under the *YOA* could be very important for determining the outcome of transfer proceedings.[15]

The *YCJA* continues having different onuses of proof in different situations. The Act, however, expands the range of presumptive offences, albeit in the context of a post-adjudication model of decision-making about whether to impose an adult sanction on a young offender. Section 2(1) of the *YCJA* defines a "presumptive offence" as:

- first or second degree murder;
- attempted murder;
- manslaughter;
- aggravated sexual assault; or
- a third serious violent offence.

While youths aged fourteen or over were subject to transfer under the *YOA*, it was only sixteen- and seventeen-year-olds who were presumed liable to an adult sentence for the most serious offences. The *YCJA* provides that youths fourteen or older at the time of conviction of a presumptive offence will face an adult sentence,[16] although section 61 of the Act does allow a provincial government to set the age of fifteen or sixteen as the minimum age at which the presumption of adult sanction applies. Section 61 allows a province to continue the age categories for the presumptive regime of the *YOA*, with different presumptions based on age. Even if a province chooses to invoke section 61, it will still be possible for fourteen- and fifteen-year-old youths in that jurisdiction to receive an adult sentence, but the onus will be on the Crown to justify this sentence. At the time of writing no decisions have been announced about the ages that will be selected. However, it seems likely that

---

14   In theory, the Crown could also make an application under s. 16(1.01) of the *YOA* to have charges against a sixteen- or seventeen-year-old for a presumptive offence murder to be "transferred down" into the youth court for trial.

15   *R. v. H.(H.A.)* (2000), 51 O.R. (3d) 321 (C.A.).

16   *YCJA*, above note 2, s. 2(1).

Quebec will decide to keep sixteen as the age for presumptive adult sanction for the most serious offences, while other jurisdictions are likely to adopt the age of fourteen. Under the YCJA, a youth who is charged with or convicted of a presumptive offence may decide not to request a youth sentence. In such cases, an adult sentence will be imposed without any hearing to determine whether this is appropriate.

2) Serious Violent Offences

The YCJA adds a new category of offences for which there is a presumption that a youth will be sentenced as an adult, the third serious violent offence. Under section 42(9) of the Act, a youth justice court that has found a young person guilty of an offence may, on the application of the prosecution and after hearing both parties, determine that the offence is a serious violent offence and endorse the information accordingly. The determination of a serious violent offence must be made by the judge who convicts the youth as part of the sentencing process. A "serious violent offence" is defined in section 2 of the Act as "an offence in the commission of which a young person causes or attempts to cause serious bodily harm."

If there have been two prior determinations that a youth has committed a serious violent offence, and the youth is charged with a third offence which might be considered by the court to be a serious violent offence, before the trial the Crown may give notice to the youth that, if there is a conviction, an application will be made to have an adult sentence imposed.[17] The YCJA provides that a youth who has received this notice is entitled to elect to have a preliminary inquiry and a jury trial.[18] This provision was enacted because section 11(f) of the Charter of Rights[19] guarantees the right to a jury trial for an accused facing a possible sentence of five years or longer. If the youth justice court convicts the youth and determines that this is a serious violent offence, a youth

---

17   YCJA, above note 2, s. 64(2). Since the YOA had no provision for making a determination that an offence is a "serious violent offence," these prior determinations will have to be made in cases in which a youth was sentenced after the YCJA came into force; see YCJA s. 161.

18   YCJA, above note 2, s. 67.

19   Canadian Charter of Rights and Freedoms, enacted as Part I of the Constitution Act, 1982, being Schedule B to the Canada Act, 1982 (U.K.), 1982, c. 11 (subsequently referred to as the Charter).

20   As discussed above, instead of the age of fourteen, under s. 1 of the YCJA, above note 2, a provincial or territorial government may set fifteen or sixteen years of age as the minimum age for presumptive offences, including a third serious violent offence.

who is at least fourteen years of age at the time of the commission of the third such offence[20] is presumptively subject to an adult sentence. The onus is then on the youth to satisfy the court that a sentence under the *YCJA* is sufficient to hold the youth accountable.

This provision in the *YCJA* for dealing with a third serious violent offence in a more punitive fashion is modelled on the American sentencing laws — sometimes characterized as "three strikes and you're out"[21] — and responds to public fears in Canada about violent youth offending. This provision will in theory expand the range of situations for which youths will be subject to adult sanction, although relatively few youths have this type of record of serious violent youth offending. It should be noted that each determination of whether an offence is a serious violent offence, including the third, is discretionary. Even if there are three such findings that a serious violent offence has been committed, the youth justice court has the discretion to decide whether an adult sanction should be imposed. Under section 42(7)(a)(ii) a youth who is convicted of a third serious violent offence may receive a sentence of intensive rehabilitative custody instead of having an adult sentence imposed. In some cases, the alternative of a relatively long youth sentence in a secure, treatment-oriented setting may be preferable to the imposition of an adult sentence, which is likely to be served in a facility where there is less access to appropriate rehabilitative services. (Serious violent offences and the intensive rehabilitative custody sentence are more fully discussed in Chapter 8 on sentencing.)

3) Crown Not Seeking Adult Sentence for Presumptive Offence: Section 65

Section 65 allows the Crown to give a notice to a youth charged with one of the listed presumptive offences, namely murder, attempted murder, manslaughter, or aggravated assault, that it will not seek an adult sentence. Such a notice can be given before or after a conviction. If such a notice is given, the court is to order a ban on the publication of identifying information about the youth. If the youth has not elected a mode of trial before a notice is given under section 65, the youth will not have the election of having a preliminary inquiry and jury trial and will be tried by a youth justice court judge. An exception arises if the youth is charged with first or second degree murder,[22] in which case, the prospect of a maximum ten-year youth sentence entitles the youth to

---

21   See J. Fagan, above note 3.
22   *YCJA*, above note 2, s. 66.

elect to have a preliminary inquiry and jury trial even if the Crown has given a notice under section 65 that it will not seek an adult sentence.

One situation in which the Crown might give a notice before plea that it will not seek an adult sentence for a presumptive offence is if the Crown wishes to avoid the possibility of having a preliminary inquiry and jury trial. These are time-consuming and expensive proceedings, and may be especially daunting for victims. Another situation in which the Crown might give a section 65 notice is as part of a plea bargain arrangement, demonstrating the commitment not to seek an adult sentence. There may also be provincial governments, most notably Quebec, which may establish policies that certain types of serious cases are not suitable for adult sentences.

C. TRIAL PROCEDURES

If a young person faces the possibility of an adult sentence or is charged with first or second degree murder, section 67 requires that before the youth enters a plea, the youth is to be put to an election or choice as to mode of trial. Essentially these provisions give youths facing the possibility of a sentence of five years or longer the opportunity to have the same rights in regard to the manner of trial as an adult, and in particular have the right to a jury trial as guaranteed by the *Charter*. The youth will have an election to be tried by:

- a youth justice court judge;
- a preliminary inquiry before a youth justice court judge and then a trial before a superior court judge sitting without a jury; or
- a preliminary inquiry before a youth justice court judge and then a trial before a superior court judge sitting with a jury.[23]

Section 67(7) and (8) provide that if a youth elects to have a preliminary inquiry, it will be conducted in the youth justice court, with the procedure governed by Part XVIII of the *Criminal Code*. At the preliminary inquiry, the Crown must introduce sufficient evidence of the youth's guilt to establish that the case should go to trial.[24] A preliminary inquiry can serve a useful role for defence counsel by facilitating trial preparation. It is very rare, however, for such an inquiry to conclude

---

23   *YCJA*, above note 2, s. 67(6), allows the Crown prosecutor to require a trial by superior court judge and jury for a youth facing a murder charge or the possibility of an adult sentence, regardless of the youth's election.

24   *Criminal Code*, above note 8, s. 548.

that there is insufficient evidence to have the case proceed to trial. The powers of the judge at a preliminary inquiry are limited. At this stage, for example, the judge cannot deal with alleged breaches of the rights of an accused youth under the *Charter*.[25]

If there is a trial in superior court, whether with or without a jury, the general trial procedure is governed by Part XIX of the *Criminal Code*, though the restrictions on publication and protection of the privacy of the youth continue to apply to the trial.[26] Also, the provisions of the *YCJA* regarding the admissibility of statements made to the police apply at the trial. If there is a conviction, the superior court judge who convicted the youth will sentence him or her, whether or not the judge has decided that the adult sentencing provisions or that the provisions of the *YCJA* will apply.

1) Superior Court Judges Sitting in Youth Justice Court

There is some concern that superior court judges may be less familiar with the *YCJA* and less understanding of the needs and capacities of adolescents than judges who ordinarily deal with youth justice matters. Beyond becoming familiar with some of the procedural and evidentiary features of the *YCJA*, superior court judges will be required to deal with issues that require some understanding of adolescent development, for example when dealing with the admissibility of statements. These judges will also have to apply the test set out in section 72, which requires an understanding of the sentencing principles of the *YCJA*. Sentencing of a young offender, especially if a decision is made not to impose an adult sentence, will also be an unfamiliar exercise to many superior court judges.

It would also be helpful for sentencing judges to have some knowledge of adolescent development issues and of the resources available in the youth justice system as well as the sentencing principles of the Act. Some superior court judges have had extensive professional experience as lawyers in dealing with youth justice issues but many have not. Cause for concern about lack of familiarity of superior court judges with issues related to adolescents and the *YCJA* may be reduced by counsel providing careful guidance and information to the court. In some cases it may also be useful for counsel to call expert evidence about issues related to adolescent development or youth corrections.

---

25   *R. v. Hynes*, 2001 SCC 82.
26   *YCJA*, above note 2, ss. 13(2)–(3). Section 13(2) provides that in Quebec a youth electing for a trial by judge alone after a preliminary inquiry will be tried

2) Pre-hearing Disclosure

A youth court dealing with a *YOA* transfer application would generally receive evidence about the circumstances of the alleged offence as
well as about such matters as the character and previous conduct of the
young person. Quite possibly, the court would also hear evidence about
the adequacy of the facilities available in the different correctional systems to meet the youth's needs. In *R. v. Stinchcombe*,[27] the Supreme
Court of Canada emphasized the importance of the constitutional right
of an accused prior to entering a plea to full disclosure from the Crown
of all of the evidence in its possession. The courts held that this duty
of Crown disclosure also applied to a transfer hearing under the *YOA*,
as the liberty of an accused was clearly affected by such a hearing.[28] A
sixteen- or seventeen-year-old youth charged with a serious offence
and having an onus under section 16(1.01) of the *YOA* to apply for
"transfer down" for trial in youth court also had the right to disclosure
from the Crown before deciding whether to make this application.

With the post-adjudicative timing for determining whether to subject a young person to adult sanction, the *YCJA* resolves many concerns
about Crown disclosure. Most issues related to disclosure are likely to
be dealt with before plea, with the relevant evidence in the possession
of police or the Crown disclosed at that stage as part of the ordinary
trial process. However, if the Crown intends to rely on evidence or
reports that were not previously disclosed to justify an adult sentence,
the Crown must disclose this prior to the hearing to determine whether
an adult sentence should be imposed. An example of such material
might be evidence establishing that the youth who committed a crime
was a member of a gang. Disclosure will allow counsel and the youth
to adequately prepare for the hearing. Prior to the hearing, a young
person and counsel are also generally entitled to a copy of any pre-sentence report and medical or psychiatric report prepared for the hearing.[29] This will allow adequate preparation for the hearing. The author
of any such report is also subject to cross-examination.

---

by a judge of the Court of Quebec (provincially appointed), except for murder
(s. 469 of the *Code*), which must be tried by a superior court judge.

27   *R. v. Stinchcombe*, [1991] 3 S.C.R. 326.

28   *R. v. F.(T.)*, [1992] O.J. No. 494 (Gen. Div.) (QL).

29   As discussed more fully in Chapter 8, there is a limited power in s. 34(9) of the
YCJA for the youth justice court to withhold part of a medical or psychological
report from a young person where disclosure "might be prejudicial to the youth"
and in the opinion of the judge disclosure is not "essential in the interests of
justice."

3) Involvement of Parents

Section 71 of the *YCJA* provides that "both parties and the parents of the young person shall be given an opportunity to be heard" at the hearing. This is virtually identical to the provision in section 16(1) of the *YOA* that the parents of a youth were to be given "an opportunity to be heard" before an application for transfer was decided.

While there are a number of provisions of the *YCJA* that specifically require parents to be notified of certain types of hearings,[30] there is no explicit statutory requirement for parents to be notified of the fact that an application has been made to have an adult sentence imposed on their child. It would, however, be appropriate for counsel involved in making such an application to ensure that the parents are notified. This would allow for parents to attend proceedings and provide support for their child, as well as being available to provide information to the court. Even so, defence counsel should obtain permission from their youthful client before contacting his or her parents.

4) Conduct of Section 71 Hearing on Adult Sentencing

The hearing about whether to impose an adult sentence — whether or not it is a presumptive offence — is a part of the sentencing rather than the adjudicative stage of the court process. As such, the youth justice court judge "enjoys a wide discretion" in regard to the conduct of the hearing.[31] Courts dealing with sentencing issues[32] (and transfer under the *YOA*) have, for example, accepted that a judge may admit "credible

---

30 See, for example, *YCJA*, above note 2, s. 85(7), which requires a parent to be notified about a hearing to be held to determine the level of youth custody.

31 See, for example, *R. v. N.B.* (1985), 21 C.C.C. (3d) 374 (Que C.A.), a case dealing with conduct of a transfer hearing under the *YOA*, above note 1.

32 See, for example, *R. v. Gardiner*, [1982] 2 S.C.R. 368, where Dickson J. observed:

> Sentencing is the critical stage of the criminal justice system, and it is manifest that the judge should not be denied an opportunity to obtain relevant information by the imposition of all the restrictive evidential rules common to a trial. Yet the obtaining and weighing of such evidence should be fair. A substantial liberty interest of the offender is involved and the information obtained should be accurate and reliable.
>
> It is a commonplace that the strict rules which govern at trial do not apply at a sentencing hearing and it would be undesirable to have the formalities and technicalities characteristic of the normal adversary proceeding prevail (at 414).

These comments are undoubtedly also highly relevant for the stage of the sentencing process under s. 71 of *YCJA*, above note 2, where the court decides whether a youth or adult sentence will be imposed.

and trustworthy" hearsay evidence at this type of hearing which would not be admissible at trial,[33] and the youth justice courts will undoubtedly take this approach for the section 71 hearings that determine whether to impose an adult sentence. A judge has the authority to control the presentation of evidence at this stage, and a judge may even decide to call certain witnesses (identified by counsel) as the court's witnesses to give both counsel an opportunity of cross-examination.[34]

Fairness may require the court to require the Crown to call its evidence first.[35] It is submitted that even for presumptive offences where the onus is on the youth to satisfy the court that an adult sentence should not be imposed, it will usually be fair for the judge to require the Crown to present its evidence and argument first, giving the youth an opportunity to respond. Such a procedure may also ensure a more logical flow of testimony and is consistent with *Charter* cases, where the persuasive onus is also on the accused applicant to exclude evidence, but the judge often requires the Crown to present its evidence first in order to ensure a fair process.

Case law from adult sentencing hearings makes clear that the sentencing judge is "bound by the express and implied factual implications of the jury's verdict."[36] Thus, for example, if a youth is charged with murder but the jury only convicts the young offender of the lesser and included offence of manslaughter, it is not open to the judge to make a decision to impose an adult sentence based on the premise that it was a planned and deliberate murder. Such a decision would require a conviction for murder. On the other hand, if there are matters that there were the subject of evidence at trial, but which were not essential for the jury's verdict, "the trial judge [is] entitled to make up his own mind on disputed questions of fact which are relevant to the sentence "based on the evidence presented at trial."[37] Therefore, the judge may rely on the evidence presented at trial to make determinations about the "circumstances and seriousness of the offence."

5) Reports

Section 72(3) of the *YCJA* requires a youth justice court that is holding a hearing to determine whether to impose an adult sentence to order and consider a pre-sentence report. Such reports are prepared by a

---

33   See, for example, *R. v. William Y.* (1988), 4 W.C.B. (2d) 267 (B.C.C.A.).
34   *R. v. N.B.* (1985), 21 C.C.C. (3d) 374 (Que C.A.).
35   See D. Stuart, "Annotation to *Kutynec*" (1991), 12 C.R. (4th) 153.
36   *R. v. Brown*, [1991] 2 S.C.R. 518 at 523.
37   *R. v. Templelaar*, [1995] 1 S.C.R. 760.

youth court worker or probation officer. The *YOA* similarly required that a youth court dealing with a transfer application consider a pre-disposition report.[38] Given the serious nature of the decision which the youth court faced, reports prepared under that provision of the *YOA* were typically more thorough than those prepared for a disposition hearing. These reports might, for example, include information relating to incidents of misbehaviour and violence by the youth that did not result in criminal charges and sometimes cited incidents which took place as far back as far as junior kindergarten.[39] This type of complete behavioural history was often important, since youths with a lengthy history of escalating violence are generally considered more likely to pose a risk of future offending than those who commit a single, serious act of violence.

It was also common at a transfer hearing under the *YOA* to have an assessment report prepared by a psychiatrist or psychologist under section 13 of that statute. Under the *YOA*, a central issue in transfer decisions was a youth's amenability to rehabilitation in the youth justice system. Evidence from a psychiatrist or psychologist was often highly relevant, so these reports were commonly ordered for transfer hearings. Section 34 of the *YCJA* also allows for the youth justice court to order a medical or psychological report for a hearing that will determine whether an adult sentence is to be imposed. However, since the primary focus under the new Act is on the issue of accountability, these reports are likely to be less significant than under the *YOA* in regard to the issue of whether an adult sentence should be imposed.

Provisions of the *YOA* prevented the direct use of statements made by a youth for the purposes of such a report for other legal purposes. However, there were situations in which defence counsel was concerned that information disclosed could restrict the conduct of the defence at a subsequent trial or might indirectly lead the police to new evidence that might be used against the youth.[40] Accordingly, when reports were prepared for transfer hearings under the *YOA*, defence

---

38   *YOA*, above note 1, s. 16(3).

39   See, for example, the *YOA*, above note 1, ss. 13.1 and 14(10); see also *R. v. O.(D.)*, [1996] O.J. No. 2703 (Prov. Ct.) (QL).

40   While the *YCJA*, above note 2, section 147, restricts the direct subsequent use of statements made to an assessor, the statements may, for example, be used to challenge the youth's credibility at a later trial. Because a youth is not obliged to co-operate with a person preparing a pre-sentencing report, it has been held that ordering such a report for a transfer hearing did not violate the prohibitions against self-incrimination under the *Charter*, above note 18, s. 11(c). See *R. v. H.(A.B.)*, above note 9.

counsel frequently advised their clients not to discuss the circumstances of the offence with the professional preparing the report or even not to meet with the professional at all. Section 40(10) of the YCJA restricts subsequent use that may be made of statements by a youth to a person preparing any pre-sentence report. Similarly section 147 restricts the use of statements made by a young person in the course of preparation of a section 34 medical or psychological report.

The use of statements made by a youth to the person preparing such a report is limited to hearings regarding the imposition of an adult sentence or the imposition of youth justice court sentence, or at a hearing to review a youth justice court sentence. Therefore, if a youth admits involvement in criminal acts that have not resulted in charges to the person preparing a report, those admissions cannot be used in other proceedings. They might, however, be considered as factors related to the youth's character and hence affect the sentencing decision.

Disclosure of information for the report should result in a more complete report being prepared.[41] In some cases, this may assist the youth. However, a young person cannot be compelled to cooperate with any person preparing a report for the court. Even if a youth fails to cooperate with a person preparing a report, the report can still be used in the sentencing proceeding. The defence may also retain its own mental health professional to provide an independent assessment of the youth. This occurred frequently in transfer cases under the YOA involving serious offences. However, cuts to legal-aid funding are making it more difficult for defence counsel to obtain such assessments. Further, information about a youth's character, mental state, and amenability to rehabilitation may be less relevant to a hearing under the YCJA to decide whether an adult sentence should be imposed than to a transfer hearing under the YOA.

6) Presumptions, Burden, and Onus of Proof

Section 62(a) of the YCJA provides that youths who are convicted of a presumptive offence are to be subject to an adult sentence, unless an application is made to have a youth sentence imposed. A youth's application for a youth sentence despite his or her conviction for a presumptive offence is made under section 63. The application by the young

---

41   See, for example, R. v. P.(L.), [1992] O.J. No. 871 (Prov. Div.) (QL), where several mental health professionals prepared reports for a transfer hearing under the YOA, above note 1. The judge gave greatest weight to the views of the one psychiatrist, retained by defence counsel, who spoke to the youth in question about the circumstances of the offence.

person is generally likely to be made by the youth only after conviction and before a sentence is imposed. To protect young offenders, there is an obligation on the youth justice court judge to specifically ask a youth who has been convicted of a presumptive offence whether he or she wants to make an application under section 63. A judge is to do so before receiving any evidence or submissions about sentence.

If a youth makes an application to be sentenced as a youth for a presumptive offence, section 63(2) allows the Crown to give notice to the youth justice court that it does not oppose the youth's application. In such a case, the judge will not hold a hearing on this issue but shall make an order that an adult sentence is not to be imposed.[42] It is likely that in most cases the youth's application for a youth sentence will only be made if there is a conviction. However, the youth has the right to make the application under section 63 at any time, including before trial. If the Crown consents to a youth's pre-trial application, the Crown may seek an order before trial that no adult sentence may be imposed. Such a pre-trial order might, for example, be the result of a plea bargain, or reflect the agreement of the youth and Crown prosecutor that there will be a trial in youth justice court without a preliminary inquiry or jury. If the Crown does not consent to the youth's application, then after any conviction and before sentencing, a hearing will be held to determine whether to impose an adult sentence. Under section 72(2) in this situation the onus is on the youth to satisfy the court that a sentence under the *YCJA* is "of sufficient length to hold the young offender accountable"; otherwise an adult sentence will be imposed.

Under section 62(b), if a youth is convicted of an indictable offence (other than a presumptive offence) for which an adult could receive a sentence of two years or more, and the youth was fourteen years of age or older at the time of the offence, the Crown may apply to have an adult sentence imposed. This application is made after conviction and before a sentence is imposed. In these cases the onus is on the Crown to satisfy the youth justice court that a sentence under the *YCJA* is inadequate to hold a young offender accountable. These applications are likely to be rare. Such an application might, for example, be made if a person is charged in youth justice court with an offence that occurred while the youth was seventeen, and before that case is resolved there are further adult charges; if there are convictions in both youth justice and adult court, it might then be appropriate to have an application under section 62(b) and have a single sentencing hearing with all sentences imposed under the adult provisions of the *Criminal Code*.

---

42   *YCJA*, above note 2, s. 63(2).

Under section 64(2) if the Crown intends to make an application under section 62(b) for an adult sentence for a non-presumptive offence, the Crown must ordinarily give the youth notice before a plea is entered. If the Crown gives such notice of the intent to seek an adult sentence for a non-presumptive offence, the youth will have the right to elect to have a preliminary inquiry and jury trial. The fact that such notice is given may affect how a youth pleads to the charge, as well as choices about the mode of trial, so the Crown should usually give notice of the intent to seek an adult sentence for a non-presumptive offence before plea. However, under section 64(2) the Crown may seek the leave, or permission, of the youth justice court judge to give this notice after plea and before trial. The judge might take account of how close the case is to trial before deciding whether to grant leave. It would not be appropriate to allow the Crown to give notice after the youth has entered a guilty plea without allowing the plea to be struck.

Although the terminology and structure of decision-making in the *YOA* were different, that Act also distinguished between a relatively narrow range of very serious offences and a broader category of offences. For the very serious offences, there was a presumption that a youth who was sixteen or seventeen years of age would be treated as an adult. For other offences, the Crown had the onus to establish that treatment as an adult was appropriate. As Brownlee Prov. J. stated with reference to the *YOA* provision dealing with situations where there is a presumption of adult treatment,[43] technically this should not be described as a "reverse onus" provision but rather as a provision that places a tactical or procedural burden on the applicant.[44]

One of the first reported Ontario decisions under the 1995 *YOA* provisions was *R. v. O.(D.)* The case involved a youth just under sixteen at the time of an alleged first degree murder. There was no clear explanation offered for the killing but at the transfer hearing the judge accepted that the "most probable" explanation seemed to be that the youth felt that he had been "dissed" (i.e., disrespected) by the deceased. Expert evidence and testimony about the youth's background revealed a history of behavioural problems and school difficulties but no prior criminal record. The youth had no clearly identified mental health problems or personality disorder. As a consequence of having no diagnosis of mental or psychological disorder, medical experts were

---

43   *YOA*, above note 1, s. 16(1.1).
44   *R. v. C.(R.)*, [1996] A.J. No. 909 (Prov. Ct.). In this case, the judge stated that, "as the onus rests upon the young person," the youth was required to call his witnesses first (at para. 4).

unable to offer a clear prognosis about the length of time that would be required to rehabilitate the youth. Judge Cole refused the Crown's transfer application, concluding: "In summary, I cannot say with any certainty that the interest of society and the rehabilitation of the respondent cannot be reconciled by the respondent remaining within the youth court system. Mindful of the need for restraint in the invocation and application of the criminal law process, in the absence of clear evidence, I feel it is only right to revert to the 'default' position."[45] The question of onus for establishing whether or not to transfer this youth to adult court under the *YOA* was crucial to the outcome for this fifteen-year-old youth.

The lowering of the age for presumptive offences in section 61 of the *YCJA* is likely to result in more fourteen- and fifteen-year-olds being sentenced as adults. However, the statutory test and issues relevant to deciding whether to subject a young person to an adult sanction are quite different under the *YCJA*. Case law under the transfer provisions of the *YOA* will be of limited relevance for cases decided under the new Act. Under the new Act, the onus on the young offender seeking a youth sentence under section 63 in a presumptive offence situation has procedural, tactical, and persuasive elements. The onus is procedural in the sense that the youth must make an application to prevent the imposition of an adult sentence. It is tactical in the sense that there is an onus on the youth to adduce some evidence about why a youth sentence is appropriate, though the youth is not obliged to testify, and as discussed above, the court may still require the Crown to lead its evidence first. Further, section 72(2) provides that "the onus of satisfying the youth justice court" as to the matters referred to in section 72(1) is on the applicant. This places a "persuasive" burden on the youth to satisfy the youth justice court that a youth sentence would be of "sufficient length to hold the young person accountable for his or her offending behaviour." As in cases where there is an onus on the accused to satisfy the court of certain issues under the *Charter* or *Criminal Code*, it would seem that the standard of proof that the youth faces for factual matters that are a part of his or her case in a section 63 application should be the ordinary civil standard of proof, proof on the balance of probabilities.

Conversely, for non-presumptive offences, the combined effect of sections 62 and 72(2) is to place a procedural, tactical and persuasive onus on the Crown. The Crown must make the application to have an

---

45   *R. v. O.(D.)*, [1996] O.J. No. 2703, at para. 171.

adult sentence imposed and present evidence to satisfy the court that an adult sentence is needed to hold a young person "accountable." Whether the application is made under section 63 or section 64 , there may be factual matters that are in dispute in regard to the Crown's case at a hearing to determine whether to impose an adult sentence, such as, for example, whether the youth was a member of a gang. It is submitted that the common law and the *Charter* require that, even at the sentencing stage, the Crown must prove any disputed facts that are a part of its case beyond a reasonable doubt. In regard to an adult sentencing hearing, this point was made by Lamer C.J.C in *R. v. Pearson*:

> The interaction of s. 7 and s. 11(d) [of the *Charter*] is also nicely illustrated at the sentencing stage of the criminal process. The presumption of innocence as set out in s. 11(d) arguably has no application at the sentencing stage of the trial. However, it is clear law that where the Crown advances aggravating facts in sentencing which are contested, the Crown must establish those facts beyond reasonable doubt. . . . The [Supreme] Court in *Gardiner* cited with approval . . . the following passage from J.A. Olah, *Sentencing: The Last Frontier of the Criminal Law* (1980) . . . : "because the sentencing process poses the ultimate jeopardy to an individual . . . in the criminal process, it is just and reasonable that he be granted the protection of the reasonable doubt rule at this vital juncture of the process."[46]

Although *Gardiner* was not a *Charter* case, the problem it confronted can readily be restated in terms of sections 7 and 11(d) of the *Charter*. While the presumption of innocence as specifically articulated in section 11(d) of the *Charter* may not cover the question of the standard of proof of contested aggravating facts at sentencing, the broader substantive principle in section 7 almost certainly would.

This general approach should be applicable to cases involving young offenders, whether the dispute over a factual matter arises at the sentencing hearing itself, or at the earlier hearing to determine whether an adult sentence is appropriate. Both types of hearings are a fundamental threat to the liberty of the young person and accordingly must comply with section 7 of the *Charter* and this ruling in *Pearson*.[47] In the absence of explicit statutory provision, factual assertions that are an

---

46   *R. v. Pearson*, [1992] 3 S.C.R. 665.

47   The *Criminal Code*, above note 8, s. 724(3), enacted in 1996, requires that at an adult sentencing hearing, the Crown must prove aggravating facts "beyond a reasonable doubt," while the accused only has to prove mitigating facts on the "balance of probabilities." This provision is not directly applicable to the sen-

aspect of the Crown's case in a section 72 hearing should be proven beyond a reasonable doubt. There may be different factual issues in the section 72 hearing with different persuasive and evidentiary burdens. This adds to the complexity of this type of hearing. However, similar complexity arises in the adult sentencing process due to section 724(3) of the *Criminal Code*, where there are different burdens and onuses of proof for different issues.[48]

Section 72(2) of the *YCJA* makes clear that the ultimate persuasive burden, of satisfying the court that a youth sentence is or is not "of sufficient length to hold a youth accountable" rests on the applicant. In the case of a presumptive offence the ultimate persuasive burden is on the youth; in other cases the ultimate persuasive burden is on the Crown.

D. THE TEST FOR IMPOSING AN ADULT SENTENCE: SECTION 72

Under section 16(1.01) of the *YOA*, a young person was only to be transferred into adult court for trial if a youth court judge was satisfied that the "objectives of affording protection to the public and rehabilitation of the young person [could not] be reconciled" in the youth system. If the court was satisfied that it was likely that these two objectives could be reconciled within the dispositional provisions and youth corrections programming available for the youth, then the youth was to be dealt with in the youth court. Otherwise, the youth was to be transferred. The *YOA* required an assessment of the youth's amenability to rehabilitation in the youth system, balanced against the risk posed to society by the youth. It required an individualized assessment by the youth court, with expert evidence about the future dangerousness and amenability to rehabilitation to be considered by the court. In considering these issues, the youth court was required to consider the seriousness and circumstances of the alleged offence, and the youth's age, character, and background. The court was also to compare the adequacy of the legislative provisions and resources in the adult and youth correctional systems.

---

tencing of a youth unless an order is made that an adult sentence will be imposed. However, it is submitted that this general distinction applies to the section 71 hearing under the *YCJA*, above note 2, to determine whether an adult sentence should be imposed, owing to the combination of *Pearson*, *ibid.*, and the *YCJA*, s. 72(2).

48 See A. Manson, *The Law of Sentencing* (Toronto: Irwin Law, 2001) at 172–83. See also the discussion there about use in the sentencing process of evidence from the trial.

The *YCJA* has a different test for deciding whether an adult sentence should be imposed on an adolescent offender. The central issue in section 72 is whether the judge considers the maximum sentence that could be imposed under the *YCJA* to be of "sufficient length to hold the young person accountable for his or her offending behaviour." Section 72 of the *YCJA* provides:

> 72. (1) In making its decision on an application heard in accordance with section 71, the youth justice court shall consider the seriousness and circumstances of the offence, and the age, maturity, character, background and previous record of the young person and any other factors that the court considers relevant, and
>
> (a) if it is of the opinion that a youth sentence imposed in accordance with the purpose and principles set out in subparagraph 3(1)(b)(ii) and in section 38 would be of sufficient length to hold the young person accountable for his or her offending behaviour, it shall order that the young person is not liable to an adult sentence and that a youth sentence must be imposed; and
>
> (b) if it is of the opinion that a youth sentence imposed in accordance with the purpose and principles set out subparagraph 3(1)(b)(ii) and in section 38 would not be adequate to hold the young person accountable for his or her offending behaviour, it shall order that an adult sentence be imposed.

The primary focus of the section 72 test is on the adequacy of the *YCJA* to hold the youth "accountable." However, this assessment of the adequacy of the Act's accountability regime must be undertaken in accordance with the purposes and principles for sentencing young offenders as set out in section 3(1)(b)(ii) of the Declaration of Principle and section 38, which sets out the general principles of youth sentencing. That is, all of the principles that govern youth sentencing are to be considered in deciding whether to hold a youth accountable as an adult.

In particular, in deciding whether to impose an adult sentence the court should be guided by the principle that accountability of adolescent offenders is limited, in comparison to adults. This principle is articulated in section 3(1)(b)(ii), which is specifically referred to in section 72, and states: "the criminal justice system for young persons must be separate from that of adults and emphasize . . . fair and proportionate accountability that is consistent with the greater dependency of young persons and their reduced level of maturity." The limited maturity, judgment, and experience of adolescents means that they should not be held as accountable as an adult who may have committed the same crime. In general, the younger the offender at the time of the offence, the less accountability he or she will have for the crime.

Section 38 of the *YCJA* is also specifically incorporated into the section 72 test and requires that in determining whether to impose an adult sanction, the court should impose a sentence on a youth that is a "just sanction [with] meaningful consequences *and* that promote[s] his or her rehabilitation and reintegration into society, thereby contributing to the long term protection of society." Section 38 provides:

> 38. (1) The purpose of sentencing . . . is to contribute to the protection of society by holding a young person accountable for an offence through the imposition of just sanctions that have meaningful consequences for the young person and that promote his or her rehabilitation and reintegration into society.
>
> (2) A youth justice court that imposes a youth sentence on a young person shall determine the sentence in accordance with the principles set out in section 3 and the following principles. . . .
> (b) the sentence must be similar to the sentences imposed in the region on similar young persons found guilty of the same offence committed in similar circumstances;
> (c) the sentence must be proportionate to the seriousness of the offence and the degree of responsibility of the young person for that offence; and
> (d) subject to paragraph (c), the sentence must
> (i) be the least restrictive sentence that is capable of achieving the purpose set out in section (1),
> (ii) be the one that is most likely to rehabilitate the young person and reintegrate him or her into society, and
> (iii) promote a sense of responsibility in the young person, and an acknowledgement of the harm done to victims and the community.
>
> (3) In determining a youth sentence, the youth justice court shall take into account
> (a) the degree of participation by the young person in the commission of the offence;
> (b) the harm done to victims and whether it was intentional or reasonably foreseeable. . . .
> (d) the time spent in detention by the young person as a result of the offence;
> (e) the previous findings of guilt of the young person; and

(f) any other aggravating and mitigating circumstances related to the young person or the offence that are relevant to the purpose and principles set out in this section.

The articulated focus of the inquiry under section 72 is on the question of whether the sanctions that can be imposed under the Act are sufficient to hold the youth accountable. However, by specifically incorporating the purpose and principles of sections 3(1)(b)(ii) and 38 into the section 72 test, Parliament is requiring the youth justice court to engage in the same type of weighing of factors as occurs when sentencing any other young offender. In comparison to the *YOA*, both the general sentencing principles and the test for whether adult sanctions will be imposed in the new Act focus more on a proportionate response to the offence and on accountability. In comparison to dealing with adult offenders, however, the *YCJA* requires that youth justice courts recognize the limited accountability of adolescent offenders and the importance of their rehabilitation.

While the limited responsibility of youth and rehabilitation are factors in determining whether to impose an adult sentence, the focus on accountability in section 72 suggests that there may be an increase in the number of young offenders receiving adult sanctions under the *YCJA* in comparison to the *YOA*. This is especially the case for the presumptive offences, which are the most serious violent offences. The test of section 72, however, remains sufficiently indeterminate as to continue to give individual judges significant discretion in deciding whether to impose an adult sentence.

Under the *YOA*, despite significant changes in the statutory formulation for whether to transfer a youth, rates of transfer remained relatively constant and the patterns of regional variation remained relatively stable. This suggests that judicial attitudes to the imposition of adult sanctions on adolescent offenders may be more important than the precise words of the statute that is being applied.

The policies of provincial governments and attitudes of prosecutors are also likely to have a significant effect on the number of youths sentenced as adults. In some situations, such as those involving a serious sexual assault, there will be significant police or prosecutorial discretion about whether to lay a charge with a presumption of adult sentencing. If a lesser charge is laid, such as sexual assault causing bodily harm, the onus remains on the Crown to satisfy the court of the need to impose an adult sanction, but if the charge is for aggravated sexual assault and the youth is fourteen or older, it will be a presumptive offence. In some respects, the *YCJA* may increase the discretionary role of prosecutors in the adult sentencing process by creating the vaguely defined power to seek a judicial ruling that an offence is a serious violent offence. There may be significant variation in how prosecutors exercise this authority.

1) Section 72 Factors for the Court to Consider

Section 72(1) of the *YCJA* specifies that a youth court "*shall* consider the seriousness and circumstances of the offence, and the age, maturity, character, background and previous record of the young person and any other factors that the court considers relevant to consider" in deciding whether to impose an adult sentence. The list is intended only to serve as a guide to judges and not a mandatory checklist. Persuasive precedent under the *YOA* makes clear that the factors listed in section 72 are not necessarily all significant in every case. Rather, the judge is to determine which are the most relevant, while the "any other factors" clause gives the court a discretion to consider factors that are not specifically named.[49] Despite this flexibility, in most cases the factors listed will be the most significant.

2) Of Sufficient Length: Comparing Sentences

Section 16(2)(c) of the *YOA* specified that in making a transfer decision, the court was to consider the adequacy of the *YOA* in comparison to the *Criminal Code* "to meet the circumstances of the case." If the judge felt that a sentence of longer than the three year maximum (or ten years for first degree murder) was required, then a transfer to the adult system might be considered appropriate. On the other hand, if there was no need to provide for incarceration or treatment beyond the three-year maximum disposition (or ten years for first-degree murder), there was no need to transfer the youth. Comparison of maximum sentence length will undoubtedly be central to the decision-making under the *YCJA*; the principal question is whether the sentence imposed would be of "sufficient length to hold the young person accountable."

When comparing the adequacy of a *YCJA* sentence to an adult criminal sentence, it should be appreciated that a youth who is subject to an adult sentence will generally be eligible for parole after serving one-third to half of the adult prison sentence. Early release under the *YOA* was judicially controlled and occurred less frequently than the early release of adult offenders. In most transfer cases under the *YOA*,

---

49   See, for example, *R. v. M (A.J.)* (1986), 73 A.R. 52 (Q.B.).

judges compared the real time likely to be served in each system, as opposed to the "paper time," the sentence the courts imposed.[50] In other words, outside of situations where a life sentence is imposed, the actual sentence that would be served by a young person who was transferred into adult court might well have been less than the time served under the YOA. The YCJA does not preclude judges from engaging in this type of real-time comparison, but the early release and community supervision provisions make it less likely that a youth sentence will be served entirely in custody under the YCJA, making this a less significant factor than it was under the YOA.

In most provinces judges dealing with transfer under the YOA emphasized the potential harm to a young person placed in an adult facility and the superior rehabilitative resources of the youth system. In 1989 the Ontario Court of Appeal refused to transfer six youths charged with a brutal sexual assault, emphasizing the potential risks to young offenders in the adult system, including the risk of physical attack, of becoming involved in involuntary homosexual activities, and of having to accept the internal codes of behaviour in an adult facility.[51]

---

50   See, for example, *R. v. C.(T.P.)*, [1993] O.J. No. 719 (Prov. Ct.) (QL).

51   *R. v. S.(W.)* (1989), 69 C.R. (3d) 168, 47 C.C.C. (3d) 72 (Ont. C.A.). There is relatively little rigorous Canadian empirical research on the long-term effects of imprisonment on adolescents, in particular on those who are adolescents or young adults at the time that a sentence is commenced; see J. Bonta and P. Gendreau, "Reexamining the Cruel and Unusual Punishment of Prison Life" (1990) 14 Law & Human Behaviour 347. However, it is believed by those who work with offenders that such sentences are psychologically destructive. See John Howard Society of Ontario, "Jailing Kids in Adult Prisons" (Toronto, March 1990), which describes many of the concerns about placing youths in adult facilities. The Society writes: "We think the admission of young people into adult institutions is absolutely abhorrent and unnecessary. Young offenders are recognized as not having the degree of maturity which would warrant that they be handled as adults. Every day we see adults in our prison system who are barely able to survive in the hostility and fear which predominates in these places. The prospect of placing a young person, who has already demonstrated his/her immaturity and lack of responsibility, into such a damaging environment is terribly short-sighted." The Society quotes a penitentiary inmate: " 'Terrible crimes will always shock us, but the truth of youth in prison would shock us more than the most terrible of crimes. Young people know what it is to die each day in prison. . . . How would a child with an unformed body and undeveloped mind know better? Rather than condemn them to share the ultimate adult horror, we should help them by seeing them at the very least remain in places designed for the young. No society should allow its children to be raped, tortured and murdered as punishment. If we are to change the youthful offenders' act, then let's never confine them in adult facilities or consider punishing them as adults.' "

The *YOA* explicitly required judges to compare the availability and adequacy of the treatment and correctional resources in the adult and youth justice systems when making a transfer decision.[52] This was an especially important factor prior to the 1992 amendments, when the consequence of a transfer order was that a young person was required to serve any sentence in the relatively harsh environment of an adult custodial facility and denied any possibility of access to the rehabilitative programs that might be afforded in the youth system. The educational and rehabilitative resources for adolescents available in the youth system are generally regarded as better suited to serve the needs of youth. Further, placing a young person with adult offenders has been recognized as posing significant psychological and physical risks for the youth.

It may be that for some offenders, especially older adolescent sexual offenders, there may actually be better treatment programs in the adult system. Judges, however, have recognized that even if the rehabilitative programs and services in the federal system seem more suited to the conduct of a particular young offender, the negative effect of the adult environment, including the increased risk of exposure to drugs, alcohol, and inmate abuse, weighs against holding adolescents in adult facilities.[53]

The 1992 *YOA* amendments and the *YCJA* allowed for young offenders sentenced as adults to serve a portion, or even all, of their sentences in the youth correctional system. After the 1992 *YOA* amendments, it was possible for a youth to be transferred to adult court for trial while the courts were given the jurisdiction to decide whether the youth would be detained and serve a portion of any sentence in a youth facility.[54] The 1992 amendments to the *YOA* substantially diminished the significance of a comparison of the youth and adult correctional systems.

Even after 1992, expert witnesses, including both correctional and mental health professionals, would be called to help assess the amenability of the young person to treatment in each system, as well as to explain the effects on the youth of placement in an adult correctional facility. However, this type of evidence was clearly less significant after judges were given the authority under the 1992 *YOA* amendments to keep young offenders in youth custody facilities after transfer.[55] In *R. v. M.(G.J.)*, the Alberta Court of Appeal discussed the 1992 amendments and commented: "[T]he statutory machinery available for the appropriate placement of a young person who has been transferred to

---

52   *YOA*, above note 1, s. 16(2)(d).
53   *R. v. L.(R.A.)*, [1995] B.C.J. No. 2459 (C.A.) (QL).
54   *YOA*, above note 1, ss. 16.1 and 16.2.
55   See, for example, *R. v. Darryl C.* (1993), 85 C.C.C.(3d) 547 (Ont. C.A.).

the adult system has been usefully widened by the amending provisions."[56] This flexibility meant that judges were less reluctant to make a decision that imposed an adult sentence, since the youths who were transferred might not be placed in adult facilities until after reaching adulthood.

In some *YOA* cases, the court indicated that if youth had "exhausted all the resources" in the youth system, this was a reason for transfer. The court considered whther the youth had been sentenced by the youth court on previous occasions, and what effect a period(s) in youth custody had on further offending. Even under the *YOA*, it was not necessary for the Crown in a transfer application to prove that all resources in the youth system had been tried and failed,[57] but such an exhaustion of resources clearly supported transfer.

Difficult issues arise when a judge believes that the youth system should have resources available to help a youth but does not. In the 1987 *YOA* case of *R. v. M.(C.R.)*, a young person charged with first-degree murder was transferred, in part because "the facilities of the youth court system are not adequate to treat the youth for his severe alcohol problems."[58] It could be argued that making adult sentencing orders in such circumstances only helps ensure that these programs, often badly needed in the youth system, will never be developed in the future. In *Re E.(N.G.)*, Kimelman A.J.C.M. commented: "I think there is responsibility on the part of the provincial government to arrange for adequate programs for the likes of this boy and its failure to do so should not be a good reason for transferring a 15 year old boy to the adult system for the purpose of enabling him to be sent to the penitentiary."[59]

The *YCJA* does not explicitly require a comparison of youth and adult facilities, and evidence on this issue is less significant under the accountability test of the new Act than it was under the *YOA*. A comparison of likely treatment in adult and youth facilities is not, however, totally immaterial under the *YCJA*, since a youth who is subjected

---

56 *R. v. M.(G.J.)* (1993), 135 A.R. 204 at 206–8 (C.A.).

57 See *R. v. M.(D.)* (1990), 61 C.C.C. (3d) 129 (Ont. C.A.).

58 *R. v. M.(C.R.)* (1987), 46 Man. R. (2d) 315 (C.A.), aff'g (1986), 46 Man. R. (2d) 317 (Q.B.). Some American courts have accepted that juveniles should not be penalized by the "realities" of the youth correctional system. In the United States some judges have responded to this type of situation by refusing to transfer youths or ordering that adequate facilities be provided. See *J.E.C. v. Minnesota*, 225 N.W. 2d 245 (1975).

59 *Re. E.(N.G.)* (8 August 1986), (Man. Prov. Ct. (Fam. Div.)) [unreported] [summarized [1986] W.D.F.L. 2096].

to an adult sentence is *more likely* to spend at least part of the sentence in an adult facility, while one sentenced in youth justice court is *more likely* to serve all of the sentence in youth custody facilities.

3) Seriousness and Circumstances of Offence

Most reported *YOA* transfer decisions involved the most serious offences such as murder, manslaughter, robbery, and aggravated sexual assault, although there were cases involving less serious offences such as escaping custody or multiple charges of break and enter. Some decisions under the *YOA* appeared to suggest that, for very serious offences, most notably murder, it is almost axiomatic that it is in the interest of society to have proceedings result in an adult sentence. However, unlike the situation in some American states, it is clear from the Canadian legislation that there is no offence for which an adult sentence is automatic. The seriousness of the offence is only one factor, albeit an important one, in assessing the "interest of society" in an adult sentencing hearing. In *R. v. H.(E.E.)*, Sherstobitoff J.A. of the Saskatchewan Court of Appeal refused to order the transfer under the *YOA* of three youths charged with second degree murder, stating: "The facts of the alleged murder in this case, given that all murders can be said to be brutal and vicious, do not by themselves require transfer to adult court."[60] The seriousness of the offence was an important factor in the transfer decision under section 16 of the *YOA*. It is an even more important factor, although not in itself determinative, under section 72 of the *YCJA*, with its focus on accountability.

A significant question when assessing the circumstances and seriousness of the offence is the youth's role and degree of participation in the alleged offence. Therefore, a court will be less likely to impose an adult sentence on a youth who is a party to a murder as a result of having acted as a lookout but who did not have a significant role in carrying out the physical acts of violence. As observed in a *YOA* transfer case by Goodman J.A.: "[I]t is self-evident that a young person who delivers the death blows to a victim is more likely to be a threat to the safety of the public than one who is an aider or abetter, and perhaps a somewhat reluctant one, to a murder."[61]

Section 38(3)(a) of the *YCJA*, which is incorporated into section 72, reinforces this approach, since it explicitly requires the court to

---

60   *R. v. H.(E.E.)* (1987), 54 Sask. R. 304 at 309 (C.A.).

61   *R. v. S.(G.)*, (1991) 5 O.R. (3d) 97 at 108.

consider the degree of participation by the youth in the commission of the offence. Conversely, there will be a greater tendency to impose an adult sentence where a youth has a role as an instigator or principal participant, or where a homicide seems particularly brutal[62] or deliberately executed, as opposed to more spontaneous.[63] A premeditated murder, especially one that appears to be recreational or to be motivated purely by greed, seems more reprehensible. Rehabilitation of such offenders is likely to be more difficult and concerns about accountability would weigh strongly in favour of imposing an adult sentence.[64] If a young person commits a serious offence while already in youth custody, this may be an aggravating factor, since it indicates that the youth corrections system may not be adequate to protect society. Concern with such cases also reflects the desire to protect staff and youth in custody facilities.[65]

It is likely that judges will be more apt to impose an adult sentence on a youth who is charged with acts of violence, especially murder, that are committed against strangers. This is particularly the case if the violence occurs in the course of commission of a robbery or rape.[66] Conversely, there may be a more sympathetic approach in cases where a youth commits an act of violence against a family member, such as a parent, especially if the act is reflective of an emotionally difficult family life. Familial circumstances do not justify an offence, but they may mitigate against full societal accountability and offer a somewhat better prognosis for rehabilitation.[67]

---

62   As noted in R. v. K.(C.J.), [1994] M.J. No. 74 (C.A.) (QL) by Helper J.A., in a case where a youth charged with second-degree murder was not transferred: "All murders are violent, brutal and shocking. I make no attempt to minimize the violence involved in this offence. However, I have no hesitation in stating that some murders are more violent and more brutal and more shocking than others."

63   See, for example, R. v. R.(S.) (1991), 1 O.R. (3d) 785 (C.A.).

64   See, for example, R. v. P.(L.), [1992] O.J. No. 871 (Prov. Div.) (QL), where three youths were transferred on murder charges arising out of the alleged planned, "recreational" killing of a friend; and, for example, R. v. F.(D.M.), [1992] B.C.J. No. 705 (C.A.) (QL), where two youths were transferred for involvement in an alleged "contract killing" arranged to secure an inheritance.

65   R. v. W.(R.), [1995] O.J. No. 3627 (Prov. Div.) (QL) (youth transferred for attempted murder charge based on an attack on a staff member at an open-custody facility).

66   See, for example, R. v. I.(J.), [1993] O.J. No. 3123 (C.A.) (QL).

67   See, for example, R. v. C.(D.) (1993), 14 O.R. (3d) 705 (C.A.) (youth charged with murder of his mother and attempted murder of his father not transferred). See also J. Toupin, "Adolescent Murders — Validity of Typology and Study of Their Recidivism" in A.V. Wilson, ed., Homicide: The Victim-Offender Connection (Cincinnati: Anderson, 1993).

4) Age, Maturity, Background, and Previous Record

Many *YOA* decisions considered the age of the youth and, in particular, his or her closeness to eighteen, as an important factor in transfer proceedings. In considering age, courts generally[68] focus on the date of the alleged offence, not the date of the hearing.[69] In *R. v. M.(C. R.)*, the Manitoba Court of Appeal dealt with the transfer of a young person who was one week away from the age of eighteen at the time of the alleged offence.[70] The age of the youth was an important consideration in deciding to transfer the case. The trial court noted that the youth was not "a person of tender years." Similarly, in *R. v. S.(G.)*, the Ontario Court of Appeal ordered a youth facing a murder charge transferred, noting that it was "influenced . . . by his age, as he is now nineteen years old and for all other purposes an adult."[71] However, age is not always decisive, as in *R. v. H.(S.J.)*, where the young person was one month short of his eighteenth birthday and was charged with the first degree murder of his mother but was not transferred. Glube C.J.T.D. stated: "It is my view that, although the current age of the person may be beyond the age of 16, the person is looked at as a young person for purposes of the transfer and for other considerations namely, the interest of society and the needs of the young person."[72]

Maturity was considered in *R. v. H.(D.P.)*, where a youth was charged with indecent assault, gross indecency, sexual assault, and buggery. The judge granted the transfer application, in part because of the youth's maturity and sophistication, stating:

---

68   However, in cases where charges are not laid until the accused "youth" is well into adulthood, an adult sentence may be more appropriate. See *R. v. J.(W.W.)*, [1992] Y.J. No. 232 (Terr. Ct.) (QL), where a twenty-six year-old was transferred for various sexual offences alleged to have occurred more than a decade earlier.

69   See *R. v. Z.(D.A.)*, [1992] 2 S.C.R. 1025, where Lamer C.J. remarked: "It would be unjust to subject a person to a higher standard of accountability merely because of his or her age at the time of the trial. . . . It is the age of an accused at the time of the offence which must determine the appropriate measure of accountability and not his or her age at the time of being charged or tried" (at 1048–49).

70   *R. v. M.(C.R.)* (1987), 46 Man. R. (2d) 315 (C.A.), aff'g (1986), 46 Man. R. (2d) 317 (Q.B.). See *contra R. v. C.(D.)* (1986), 43 Man. R. (2d) 246 (C.A.), where the same court refused to transfer a young person charged with second-degree murder who was just a few weeks short of his eighteenth birthday at the date of the alleged offence.

71   *R. v. S.(G.)* (12 December 1989), (Ont. C.A.) [unreported] [summarized] (1989), 9 W.C.B. (2d) 222].

72   *R. v. H.(S.J.)* (1986), 76 N.S.R. (2d) 163 at 170 (T.D.).

The accused has been living independently at a Bible College in the State of Iowa [for five months] . . . and he intends to return there to complete his program. He has no prior record of offences. He has a Grade 12 education, has been involved in school sports, and apparently is not involved in the consumption of alcohol and drugs. As a result of this background, I have concluded that he has a considerable degree of adult maturity.[73]

It may seem ironic that the youth's lack of record and his stable background should be considered as maturity for the purposes of transfer and, in effect, held against the youth. However, other cases have also suggested that "the gravity of the alleged offence is greatly increased by the young person's good background, high level of intelligence [and] lack of psychiatric or psychological illness."[74] These circumstances may make an adult sentence more appropriate since a youth from an advantaged background should be more accountable for his or her acts. While some reported decisions under the YOA seemed to place little weight on the age of the young person, there was a much greater reluctance to transfer youths who were fourteen or fifteen years of age at the time of the alleged offence.

Section 72 of the YCJA explicitly mentions age as a factor in making a decision about an adult sentence. Further, section 3(1)(b)(ii) makes clear that a reason for holding youth less accountable than adults is their "reduced level of maturity." The implication of this is that there should be a greater prospect for adult accountability for those youths who commit serious offences and are closer to the age of eighteen. Section 72 of the YCJA also makes clear that the "previous record" of a young offender may be an important factor in deciding whether an adult sanction should be imposed. This is consistent with section 38(3)(e) and general principles of assessing accountability.

Although not always determinative, a longer and more serious record of prior offences greatly increased the likelihood of transfer under the YOA, especially if the record involved violent offences. This same reasoning will almost certainly apply under the YCJA. When assessing the character of a youth, and especially whether there has been a history of violence that may make adult sanction more appropriate, courts may consider not only the history of convictions but also

---

73   *R. v. H.(D.P.)*, (19 January 1987), (Man. Prov. Ct.) [unreported] [summarized 2 W.C.B. (2d) 39].

74   See *R. v. M.(D.M.)*, [1992] B.C.J. No. 705 (C.A.) (QL).

other evidence of violence which did not result in charges being laid.[75] A longer history of violence, especially of acts of increasing seriousness, will make adult sanction more likely. Conversely, a shorter history of violence or misconduct that starts later in adolescence suggests a youth sentence will be sufficient to hold an adolescent accountable for his or her criminal behaviour. However, in dealing with a preadjudication transfer under the *YOA*, the courts took a relaxed approach to the rules of evidence and issues of burden of proof. As discussed above, in a hearing under section 71 of the *YCJA*, if there is a factual dispute about an aggravating factor, such as a history of violent behaviour that is not reflected in the record of prior convictions, the onus should be on the Crown to prove this matter beyond a reasonable doubt.[76]

In assessing the character and amenability to rehabilitation of a youth, good conduct and response to treatment while in detention pending trial may be important factors in convincing a court not to impose an adult sentence.[77] In contrast, a youth who is disruptive in a detention facility, engages in abusive behaviour toward other youths or does not seem motivated toward rehabilitation was much more likely to be transferred under the *YOA*,[78] and seems more likely to be subject to adult sentencing under the *YCJA*.

5) Any Other Factors Considered Relevant

Section 72(1) of the *YCJA* provides that the court can consider "any other relevant factors" in making a decision whether to impose an adult sentence on a youth. This broad language accords a wide discretion. A number of transfer decisions under the *YOA* held that gang-related offences should also be viewed more seriously, as denunciation and general deterrence weigh in favour of transfer, especially if the case involves the death of a victim.[79] While general deterrence should not be a factor in dealing with a young offender under the *YCJA*, involvement in a gang may also support an argument that a youth has adopted a set of values and attitudes that will make rehabilitation more

---

75 See, for example, *R. v. O.(D.)*, [1996] O.J. No. 2703, where the court considered conduct as far back as kindergarten. Since this was a transfer case under the *YOA*, above note 1, the standard of proof for the history of violence was not proof beyond a reasonable doubt.

76 See discussion above about onus of proof and *R. v. Pearson*, [1992] 3 S.C.R. 665.

77 *R. v. W.(A.C.)* (1993), 121 N.S.R. (2d) 300 at 307 (C.A.).

78 *R. v. M.(G.J.)* (1993), 135 A.R. 204 at 206-8 (C.A.).

79 *R. v. P.(K.N.) (No. 2)*, [1996] M.J. No. 224 (Prov. Ct.) (QL).

difficult. It may also be argued that involvement in a gang raises broader concerns about the harm done to the community by an offence, which is a legitimate accountability factor.

6) Co-accused Young Offenders

The treatment of co-accused individuals was a factor in *YOA* transfer decisions, though it was never determinative. In particular, courts would consider the involvement of adults who were charged with the same offence and would face trial in adult court. In *R. v. M.(D.)*, a seventeen-year-old youth was transferred on nine charges, including three counts of attempted murder, where there were several adult co-accuseds. The Ontario Court of Appeal cited with approval the comment: "While not determinative in and of itself, in the interests of avoiding multiplicity of proceedings as well as inconsistent verdicts and uneven sentencing the presence of adult co-accused in this case clearly weighs in favour of transfer."[80] When young persons were co-accused facing very serious charges, it was common under the *YOA* to have a joint transfer hearing. While a desire for fair treatment often suggested that both should be treated in the same fashion, the courts made clear that each youth was to be considered as an individual.

In *R. v. R.(E.S.)* and *R.(W.J.)*, the Manitoba Court of Appeal dealt with two co-accused youths charged with attempted murder. Hall J.A. stated: "Each accused must be viewed separately. Both should be treated the same if the circumstances warrant but it does not have to be the case. . . . It is only one factor to be taken into account."[81] The court in that case emphasized that one youth was older and had a more serious previous record and worse prospects for rehabilitation; he was transferred but the other youth was not transferred.

Since the *YCJA* process for determining whether to impose an adult sentence is done on a post-adjudication basis as part of the sentencing process, the fact that there are joint accused is less significant. However, if there are two or more youths who are convicted of a joint offence in a situation where there is to be a hearing to determine whether to impose an adult sentence, it may be appropriate for the judge to receive evidence and submissions about each before rendering a decision. There may be good reasons for treating the two youths differently, for example, the nature of their involvement in the offence may have differed and they may have different prior records. However,

---

80   *R. v. M.(D.)* (1990), 61 C.C.C. (3d) 129 at 130 (Ont. C.A.).
81   *R. v. R.(E.S.)* and *R.(W.J.)* (1985), 49 C.R.(3d) 88, 36 Man. R. (2d) 276 (C.A.).

before treating co-accuseds differently, judges should ensure there are good reasons to do so.

7) Position of the Youth

Under the *YOA* a young person could make an application to be tried in adult court. This might be done, for example, if the youth wanted a jury trial.[82] In some cases young persons either close to or over eighteen years of age may have wanted to have an adult sentence because they had friends or fellow gang members in adult prison. Or they may have preferred some of the rules of adult facilities, such as those regarding smoking or conjugal visits. Further, in cases involving offences that were less serious, parole eligibility rules applicable to those sentenced as adults might have resulted in a youth serving less time in custody if sentenced as an adult than if he or she received a disposition under the *YOA*. With such youth dispositions, release would be possible only pursuant to a disposition review under the *YOA*.

Under the *YCJA*, a youth who is charged with or convicted of a presumptive offence may indicate that he or she does not wish to make an application to have a youth sentence. In such a case, an adult sentence shall be imposed without any hearing to determine whether this is appropriate.[83] For offences which are not presumptive, a judge may only impose an adult sentence if the Crown gives pre-adjudication notice that such a sentence will be sought and makes an application under section 64(1) after conviction. In cases where the youth gives notice to the court that he or she does not oppose the application for an adult sentence, if the youth is convicted of the offence an adult sentence shall be imposed without a hearing.[84]

E. APPEALS: SECTION 72(5)

Most of the provisions of the *YCJA* that govern appeals of youth justice court decisions are similar to those contained in the *YOA*.[85] However, the new Act alters the appeal process for adult sentencing decisions.

---

82   If a youth was charged with murder under the *YOA*, above note 1, there was the right to a jury trial even if the youth was not transferred.

83   *YCJA*, above note 2, s. 70(2).

84   *YCJA*, above note 2, s. 64(5).

85   See *YOA*, above note 1, ss. 10(4), 27, and 47(6); and *YCJA*, above note 2, ss. 37 and 42(10).

Section 16(9) of the *YOA* provided for the "review" by a provincial Court of Appeal of the decision of a youth court on a transfer application. Under section 72(5) of the *YCJA*, the decision about whether to impose an adult sentence is subject to an "appeal," which will also be to the provincial Court of Appeal, with the possibility for a further appeal to the Supreme Court of Canada. The 1989 decision of the Supreme Court of Canada in *R. v. M.(S.H.)* made clear that the scope for a review of a *YOA* transfer decision was broader in scope than an appeal. McLachlin J. concluded:

> Section 16(9) and (10) [of the *YOA*], by conferring on the reviewing court the "discretion" to confirm or reverse, establish different rules for the review than normally apply on appeals, where the court is limited to correction of error. The reviewing body's function must be to "review" the decision, and then, "in its discretion", confirm or reverse it. This involves evaluation, not only of whether the court below made an error of law or jurisdiction, but of whether its conclusions are correct based on the factors set out in the Act. *In short, the reviewing tribunal can go into the merits of the application.* If this review leads to the conclusion that the decision below was wrong for any of these reasons, the reviewing court in the exercise of its discretion may substitute its own view for that of the judge below. . . .
>
> In summary, it is my conclusion that the review court . . . is *not confined to asking whether the youth court judge has erred, but should make an independent evaluation on the basis of the facts found by the Youth Court judge.* [Emphases added.][86]

This passage was widely cited by appellate courts as giving a broad scope for review of a transfer under the *YOA*. Such a broad approach allowed for fairly extensive review proceedings by a higher court in transfer cases.

Under the *YCJA*, there is no separate review or appeal of an adult sentencing decision. Rather the appeal of the decision to impose or not impose an adult sentence under section 72(5) is to be combined with any appeal of the conviction and of the sentence imposed. Since the word "appeal" is used in section 72(5), it is clear that the role of the appellate court is narrower than in a "review" under section 16(9) of the *YOA*. Under the *YCJA*, the appeal court must be satisfied that there was a clear error.

---

86   *R. v. M.(S.H.)*, [1989] 2 S.C.R. 446 at 465–66.

F. ADULT SENTENCING FOR YOUNG OFFENDERS

If a young person is subject to an adult sentence, then section 74 of the *YCJA* requires the court to apply the procedural and substantive sentencing provisions of the *Criminal Code*, except to the extent that there is an express contrary provision in the Act. The adult sentencing principles of sections 718–718.2 of the *Criminal Code* apply, so that the court will consider deterrence of others as well as denunciation and accountability. The degree of deliberation and participation in the offence, any genuine expressions of remorse, and amenability to rehabilitation will all be important mitigating factors.[87] The age of the offender is also a mitigating factor. In imposing an adult sentence on a young person, the court is still obliged to consider the age of the offender, both because immaturity at the time of the offence lessens moral accountability and because relative youth increases the burden of a sentence, especially one that may be served in an adult facility.[88] This is reflected in sections 745.1 and 745.3 of the *Code*, which require earlier parole eligibility for those sentenced as adults to life imprisonment for a murder committed under the age of eighteen. It should also be reflected in sentencing decisions for less serous offences. The *YCJA* further provides that, even if a young person is subject to an adult sentence, this does not automatically mean that he or she will spend all of the sentence in an adult correctional facility. It is, however, likely that a young person will be placed in an adult correctional facility sometime after he or she reaches the age of eighteen.

The law governing the treatment of adolescents who are subject to adult sanction has evolved significantly over the past quarter century. Under the *Juvenile Delinquents Act*, adolescents subject to transfer into adult court were confined in an adult prison, even before trial, and, if convicted faced adult sentences, including the death penalty until that was abolished in 1976. Under the *YOA* as originally enacted, as soon as a transfer order was made, a youth in pre-trial detention was placed in an adult prison, and if a youth was convicted in adult court, the ordinary adult sentencing provisions applied. The 1992 amendments to the *YOA* created a presumption that after transfer a youth under eighteen years of age would continue to be detained in a youth custody facility

---

87 See, for example, *R. v. Socobasin* (1995), 147 N.S.R. (2d) 225 (S.C.); and *R. v. Bishop* (1994), 162 A.R. 190 (Alta. C.A.).

88 See Manson, above note 48, at 103–106.

and, if convicted in adult court, permitted the judge to allow the youth to serve a portion, or even all, of the sentence in a youth custody facility.[89]

Under the YCJA, if an adult sentence is imposed on a "young person," there must still be a judicial hearing to determine whether the youth will be placed in a youth custody facility or in an adult correctional facility. Section 76(2)(a) creates a presumption that youths subject to adult sentences who are under the age of eighteen at the time of sentencing are to be placed in a youth custody facility. The sentencing judge may, however, order that a youth under the age of eighteen is to be placed in an adult correctional facility if the court is satisfied that holding him or her in a youth facility "would not be in the best interests of the young person or would jeopardize the safety of others."[90] If the sentence is longer than two years, the court may allow placement in a federal penitentiary, with adult offenders serving sentences of that length,[91] although this will rarely be appropriate for an adolescent, since these are the facilities in which the most serious adult offenders are placed. If the sentence is less than two years, the adult facility must be a provincial correctional facility for adults, which is where adults with shorter sentences are imprisoned.

Section 76(2)(b) creates a presumption that young persons who have attained the age of eighteen at the time of sentencing and are subject to an adult sentence will be placed in an adult correctional facility. However, the sentencing court may order that such a young person shall be placed in a youth custody facility if satisfied that placing that person in an adult facility "would not be in the best interests of the young person" and that placement in a youth facility would not "jeopardize the safety of others."

Only a limited amount of case law reports how the courts interpreted section 16.2 of the YOA, which is similar to section 76 of the YCJA, allowing for placement of young persons in youth custody despite being subject to adult sentences. The reported case law emphasizes that, despite an adult sentence for an offence such as murder, in making a placement decision the court should take account of the rehabilitation and needs of the youth. Normally, these considerations favour placement in the youth system if the young person is under eighteen at

---

89 *YOA*, above note 1, ss. 16.1 and 16.2.

90 Placing young persons under the age of eighteen in an adult correctional facility is a violation of Article 37 of the *United Nations Convention on the Rights of the Child* (discussed in Chapter 2), which provides that child and adolescent offenders are to be held separate and apart from adults. However, Canada has filed a reservation to this provision to indicate that it is not bound by it.

91 *YCJA*, above note 2, s. 76(1).

the time of sentencing. Judges recognize that the adult corrections system has a relatively harsh and exploitative environment.

Adolescents placed in an adult correctional facility are likely to be victimized or exploited, and they may themselves become even more violent or enmeshed in an inmate gang subculture.[92] Judges are also aware that the youth system is comparatively well resourced and has programs suitable for adolescents. Youths under eighteen years of age in federal prisons are not infrequently placed in segregation for their protection, which is psychologically debilitating and does nothing for their rehabilitation.[93] Despite the lack of reported judgments in which the court has ordered youths under eighteen to be placed in adult facilities, Corrections Canada reports that under the *YOA* there were up to a dozen youths at a time under the age of eighteen in federal penitentiaries.[94] Presumably these are youths who would pose a risk to other adolescents in the youth system or clearly not benefit from its resources. The initial placement orders made under section 76(2) at the time of sentencing are subject to review by the court, after a hearing, if the "circumstances that resulted in the original order being made have changed materially."

There is a statutory presumption that, at the age of twenty, the young person subject to an adult sentence and initially placed in a youth custody facility will be placed in an adult facility; the court, however, has a discretion to allow that person to remain in a youth facility, if satisfied that "this would be in the best interests of the youth and would not jeopardize the safety of others" in the youth facility.[95]

A young person who is subject to an adult sentence is generally subject to the adult rules about parole, whether the youth is placed in an adult or youth correctional facility.[96] The *Criminal Code* section 745.1 creates an important exception to the rule that adult parole laws apply

---

92 See discussion in J. Fagan, "This Will Hurt Me More than it Hurts You: Social and Legal Consequences of Criminalizing Delinquency" (2002) 16 Notre Dame J L Ethics & Public Policy 101, especially at 130–136.

93 *R. v. Rahman* (1993), 18 W.C.B. (2d) 554 (Ont. Prov Ct.) (court orders youth sentenced to eleven years for manslaughter placed in youth system to age of twenty-one); *R. v. T.M.* 2000 SKQB 287 (court orders youth aged seventeen at time of sentencing for second-degree murder to remain in youth custody to nineteenth birthday); and *R. v. B.T.* (1997), 118 Man. R. (2d) 256 (C.A.) (court orders youth convicted of attempted murder and robbery who was sixteen at time of offence and seventeen at sentence to be transferred from segregation unit in federal penitentiary into youth custody).

94 The Correctional Investigator, above note 3.

95 *YCJA*, above note 2, s. 76(9).

96 *YCJA*, above note 2, ss. 77 and 78.

to young persons sentenced as adults, for youths convicted of murder and sentenced as adults. A young person convicted of first or second degree murder and subject to adult sanction will receive a life sentence, the same as an adult. However, reflecting their lesser maturity and accountability, there is earlier parole eligibility. For youths who are fourteen or fifteen when they commit a murder and are sentenced as an adult, the sentencing judge shall set a parole eligibility date of five to seven years. The jury will be asked to make a recommendation for a parole eligibility date of between five and seven years. However, the judge will decide the parole eligibility date, taking account of such factors as the jury's recommendation, the youth's age and prior record, and the youth's degree of involvement in the offence, as well as the nature of the offence.[97] A longer period of parole ineligibility may be appropriate if the crime was deliberate and there is an absence of genuine remorse.[98]

For youths who are sixteen or seventeen years of age when they commit second degree murder, the parole eligibility date is seven years. If the offence is first degree murder, then a sixteen- or seventeen-year-old youth will be eligible for parole in ten years. A youth sentenced for murder as an adult will thus be eligible for parole in five to ten years, while an adult will have a parole eligibility date of ten to twenty-five years.[99] For those sentenced to life imprisonment, there is the right to a parole hearing at the time of the parole eligibility date. Also, earlier temporary release on day parole by the National Parole Board is possible. However, such release is not automatic and will be decided based on the offender's progress in custody and on an assessment of future dangerousness.

For those youths who are sentenced as adults, the provisions of the YCJA that are intended to protect privacy and to reflect limited accountability generally do not apply. Hence, the adults rules about access to and non-disclosure of records apply, rather than the more protective rules of the YCJA.[100] At least in theory, a youth who is subject to an adult sentence could be the subject of an application by the Crown to be identified as a dangerous or long-term offender.[101] Such an application could result in an indeterminate adult sentence. However,

---

97 *Criminal Code*, above note 8, ss. 743.3 and 745.5.

98 See, for example, *R. v. David Michael M.* (1993), Y.O.S. 93-096 (B.C.CA.); and *R. v. Socobasin*, above note 87.

99 *Criminal Code*, above note 8, s. 746, provides that for the purposes of determining the parole eligibility date, the period in custody begins on the date on which pretrial detention begins.

100 YCJA, above note 2, s. 117.

101 YCJA, above note 2, s. 74(1).

the criteria for a successful Crown application of this sort are quite strict,[102] and it seems unlikely that a significant number of adolescent offenders will be subject to this type of application.

1) Adult Incarceration for Those Sentenced as Youths

Sections 89, 92, and 93 of the *YCJA* deal with situations that arise when young persons who have a youth custody sentence reach adulthood. For young persons who have relatively long sentences imposed under the *YCJA* and have reached the age of eighteen while in youth custody, it may be appropriate owing to program, security, or social concerns to have that person placed in an adult correctional facility. If so, the provincial director may apply pursuant to section 92 to the youth justice court to have the youth transferred to an adult correctional facility. The youth justice court is required to hold a hearing before allowing a transfer to an adult facility. After giving correctional officials from the youth and adult systems and the young person an opportunity to present evidence and make submissions, the judge may authorize the transfer to the adult correctional system.

Case law under a similar provision of the *YOA* held that this type of hearing is not a criminal trial.[103] Although the rules of natural justice apply, the court may receive hearsay evidence, including records from the correctional facility. Since guilt or innocence is not at issue, statements made by the young person to correctional officials in the course of his confinement were admissible without the kind of cautioning necessary for the admission of a statement to a person in authority at a trial. The youth justice court must be satisfied that placement in an adult facility is "in the best interests of the youth or in the public interest."[104] Such a transfer may be appropriate if there is more suitable programming available for the young person in the adult correctional system, or if the older young person is being disruptive or a security threat in a youth custody facility.

A person in custody under the *YCJA* may be transferred by correctional authorities to an adult provincial correctional facility without a court hearing after he or she reaches the age of twenty.[105]

Adults who commit less serious offences are placed in provincial correctional facilities, while only those adult offenders who have com-

---

102 See Part XXIV of the *Criminal Code*, above note 8; and A. Manson, *The Law of Sentencing* (Toronto: Irwin Law, 2001) at 320–44.

103 *R. v. A.D.G.* (2001), 290 A.R. 304 (Prov. Ct.), per Franklin P.C.J.

104 *YCJA*, above note 2, s. 92(1).

105 *YCJA*, above note 2, s. 93.

mitted serious offences and have sentences of longer than two years are placed in federal penitentiaries. A provincial director for youth may apply to the youth justice court to have a young person over the age of twenty (i.e., someone sentenced under the *YCJA* for an offence committed before the age of eighteen who is over the age of twenty and still in the youth correctional system) to be transferred to a federal penitentiary, provided that more than two years are left to serve in the sentence.

If a person is over twenty years old when a youth sentence is imposed, that sentence shall be served in a adult correctional facility.[106] This might occur, for example, if the person sexually abused a child who delayed disclosure and reported the offence to the police after the offender had reached adulthood.

For a person who is sentenced as a young offender under the *YCJA* and is placed in or transferred to an adult correctional facility after reaching the age of eighteen under sections 89, 92 or 93, adult laws and procedures governing parole and sentence remission will apply. However, restrictions on publication of identifying information and disclosure of information in the *YCJA* will continue to apply.[107]

2) Murder Sentencing in Youth Justice Court

Relatively few youths are charged with murder: twenty-five to sixty per year. The majority of them are ultimately convicted of manslaughter since, often, the Crown cannot prove that the unpredictable and senseless acts were deliberate homicides. By the end of the 1980s, judges and correctional experts, as well as politicians and members of the public, recognized the inadequacies of the original *YOA* transfer provisions as they applied to cases of murder. Under that Act as originally enacted, in a case involving first-degree murder, a judge in a transfer hearing was faced with the stark choice between the three-year maximum disposition or the possibility of life imprisonment in the adult system with no opportunity for parole for at least twenty-five years.[108] In many cases, neither extreme was appropriate; one was too short and the other too long.

---

106 *YCJA*, above note 2, s. 89(1).

107 *YCJA*, above note 2, ss. 89(3), 92(3), and 93(3).

108 Under s. 742 of the *Criminal Code*, above note 8, for a second-degree murder the parole eligibility date is set at the time of sentencing from ten to twenty-five years. Section 745 of the Code — the so-called faint-hope provision — allows for an adult inmate serving a sentence for first- or second-degree murder to seek a jury review after fifteen years for early parole eligibility. Only about a third of

The *YOA* was amended in 1992 and again in 1995 so that the maximum length of sentence that a youth court could impose on a youth convicted of murder was increased to ten years. The possibility of a longer sentence for murder in the youth court under the *YOA* lessened the need for judges to transfer youths charged with this most serious offence. Other amendments to the *Criminal Code* provided that for young persons transferred to adult court and convicted there, the sentence for murder was still life imprisonment, but parole eligibility was no longer that set out in the adult provisions at ten to twenty-five years, but rather was to be set at five to ten years.

Under the *YCJA* for youths not sentenced as adults, the maximum sentence that a court may impose is the same in the 1995 amendments to the *YOA*. The maximum sentence is ten years for first degree murder, with a continuous custodial period of up to six years, followed by conditional supervision in the community.[109] In cases of second degree murder, youth sentences have a maximum of custody and supervision for up to seven years, with a custodial period of up to four years, followed by conditional supervision in the community.[110] These are maximum custodial sentences and, in appropriate cases, youth justice courts can impose shorter sentences or release youths earlier on review. These relatively long youth justice court sentences for murder require custodial arrangements for young offenders who may ultimately be in their mid-twenties. Some of these offenders will be released on community supervision before reaching the age of twenty. Other will be transferred into adult correctional facilities under sections 92 or 93 of the *YCJA* sometime after reaching their eighteenth birthday.

G. PUBLICATION OF IDENTIFYING INFORMATION

One of the major public criticisms of the *YOA* was that it denied the public the right to know the identity of violent young offenders who might pose a risk to their community. At least in part this concern may have been fed by media that felt constrained by the restrictions on the publication of certain types of information. It is far from clear that

---

those eligible apply for jury review, and only about one-quarter of those are eventually paroled. See H. Hess, "Early Parole Appeals Draw Diverse Rulings," *Globe and Mail*, May 27, 1997.

109 *YCJA*, above note 2, s. 42(2)(q)(i). See discussion in Chapter 8.

110 *YCJA*, above note 2, s. 42(2)(q)(ii).

allowing the media to publicize the identity of young offenders actually does anything to promote community safety. Indeed to the extent that publicizing the identity of young offenders and their resulting stigmatization may make rehabilitation and reintegration into society more difficult, more reporting may actually increase the risk to the public. In response to public and political pressure, however, the *YCJA* provides for publication of identifying information about adolescents who are convicted of serious violent offences in more instances. Such publication may be possible even if they are not subject to adult sentences.

If a young offender has an adult sentence imposed, the provisions of the *YCJA* that prevent the publication of identifying information about a young offender do not apply. Section 110(2)(a) of the *YCJA* permits publication of information about young persons once an adult sentence has been imposed. Under the *YOA*, publication of identifying information about a young person was permitted as soon as the youth was the subject of a transfer order, and hence the trial of a young person in adult court could be publicized, even if the youth was acquitted.[111] Under the *YCJA*, the publication of identifying information is allowed only after an adult sentence is imposed. If a young person is convicted of a presumptive offence but not subject to an adult sentence, section 110(2)(b) of the new Act allows the media to publish identifying information after a sentence is imposed, unless either: "a youth justice court has made an order under section 75(3) prohibiting publication of identifying information; or the Attorney General has given notice under section 65 that an adult sentence will not be sought."

Section 110(2)(b) thus presumptively allows for publication of identifying information after conviction about young persons fourteen years of age or older on the date of the offence and convicted of: murder, attempted murder, manslaughter, or aggravated assault, or convicted of a third serious violent offence, provided that the Crown gave notice that an adult sentence might be sought.

Section 65 allows the Crown to give notice that it will not seek an adult sentence for a youth charged with one of the listed presumptive offences (i.e., murder, attempted murder, manslaughter, or aggravated assault). If this notice is given, the youth justice court shall make an order prohibiting the publication of any identifying information about the

---

111 *YOA*, above note 1, s. 38(1)(a). Section 17 of the Act also provided that an order prohibiting publication of any information revealed at a transfer hearing had to be made if requested by the Crown prosecutor or by defence counsel, as there was typically significant evidence introduced at a transfer hearing that would not be admissible at trial, and its public release could prejudice a fair trial.

youth even after conviction. If the Crown determines that it is not appropriate to even consider an adult sentence, publication of identifying information is not appropriate. If a section 65 notice has not been given by the Crown, after conviction for a presumptive offence, the youth justice court may determine after a section 72 hearing that an adult sentence should not be imposed. If this occurs, before proceeding to impose a *YCJA* sentence, the judge is required to ask whether the youth or Crown wish to make an application for a ban on the publication of identifying information.[112] If the Crown or youth make the application, a hearing will be held to decide whether to impose a publication ban. Under section 75(3) the youth justice court may order a ban if "the court considers this appropriate in the circumstances, taking into account the importance of rehabilitating the young person and the public interest."

There is no statutory requirement that media organizations need to be given notice of the request for a publication ban under section 75(3). However, the constitutionally guaranteed right of freedom of the press has been recognized by the Supreme Court of Canada to have "superordinate importance" when it concerns public access, including media access, to the courts. In some communities there is a judicial practice of notifying the media of requests for any publication bans to allow the media to appear and make representations.[113]

The *YCJA* does not give a great deal of direction about how judges are to balance the interests in a youth's rehabilitation against the public interest, nor does it explain what is meant by the "public interest" in a section 75(3) hearing. Clearly the public has an interest in media access to the courts, but the *YCJA* also recognizes the importance to society of rehabilitation of youth and reintegrating them into society.[114] Although there is not as much research or case law as one might desire on the subject, available empirical research suggests that publication of identifying information about a young offender makes rehabilitation more difficult.[115] Canadian case law has clearly recognized the importance of

---

112 *YCJA*, above note 2, s. 75(1).

113 On the importance of media access to the courts, see, for example, *Dagenais v. Canadian Broadcasting Corporation*, [1994] 3 S.C.R. 835 (S.C.C.); for a case (not involving a young person) in which the media was notified of the request for a publication ban, see *R. v. Prosper*, [2001] N.S.J. 508 (Prov. Ct.), per Curran Prov. Ct. J.

114 *YCJA*, above note 2, s. 3(1)(a)(ii).

115 See, for example, O.C. Howard, J.T. Grisso, and R. Nearns, "Publicity and Juvenile Court Proceedings" (1977) 11 Clearinghouse Review 203; and K.M. Laubenstein, "Media Access to Juvenile Justice: Should Freedom of the Press Be Limited to Promote Rehabilitation of Young Offenders?" (1995) 68 Temple L. Rev. 1897.

restricting the right of the media to publicize the names of young offenders, as doing so might hinder their rehabilitation.[116]

In 2001, the court in *R. v. Prosper* declined to make an order banning publication of identifying information about a twenty-year-old Aboriginal woman who was seeking to challenge the constitutionality of legislation creating the offence of communicating for the purpose of prostitution. In the course of his judgment, Curran Prov. Ct. J. observed:

> In upholding bans on distribution of records containing the identity of young persons charged under the *Young Offenders Act*, the Supreme Court of Canada has described the identity of young persons as only a "sliver of information": *N.(F.), Re.* (2000), 35 C.R. (5th) 1, at para. 12. It must be borne in mind, however, that the rehabilitation of the young person is the overriding goal of the *Young Offenders Act* and publicly identifying the young person is likely to limit the possibility of rehabilitation. Rehabilitation is one of the goals of sentencing under the *Criminal Code*, but it is not the only one, and identifying the accused is not inconsistent with the other goals. In fact, identifying the accused could be particularly important for the goals of deterring the accused person from committing further offences and denouncing the crime.
>
> Altogether apart from the consequences of sentencing, which of course merit limited consideration in the case of someone merely accused of a crime and having the presumption of innocence, there is a public right to know about pending criminal charges so that other members of the public can adjust their own way of living. For example, a parent might well want to know whether persons associating with their children are subject to criminal charges.[117]

The *YCJA* continues to place more emphasis on the goals of rehabilitation and reintegration into society for young offenders than is the case for adults. General deterrence is not a principle of sentencing under the *YCJA*. Thus, the analysis of Curran Prov. Ct. J. would suggest that those youth convicted of presumptive offences but not subject to adult sentences should continue to expect that the court will not allow the publication of identifying information. Publication might be appropriate if the youth is already over eighteen at the time of the hearing, or if there is a particular concern in the community about the identity of

---

116 *Southam Inc. v. R.* (1984), 48 O.R. (2d) 678 (H.C.J.), aff'd (1986), 53 O.R. (2d) 663 (C.A.).

117 *R. v. Prosper*, above note 1123, at paras. 7–8.

the perpetrator. There is, however, no empirical evidence that allowing the identity of a young offender to be publicized increases safety in the community, and some research suggests that rehabilitation may be more difficult.

H. CHALLENGES UNDER THE *CHARTER*

Defence counsel have argued that the "reverse onus" created in the 1995 *YOA* amendments for presumptive offences was unconstitutional. Such arguments were not accepted by the courts in challenges to the validity of section 16(1.01) of the *YOA*. The challenges were principally based on claims of age discrimination, in violation of section 15 of the *Charter*, since sixteen- and seventeen-year-olds charged with the listed offences faced a burden not placed on youths age fourteen and fifteen. In *R. v. C.(R.)*,[118] the Alberta Youth Court rejected a Charter challenge to the "reverse onus" transfer provisions of the *YOA*. Brownlee Prov. Ct. J. focused on the procedural nature of the provisions, and observed that the transfer provisions of 1984 and 1992 also created age-based differences (i.e., between twelve- and thirteen-year-olds and older young persons) and had been held constitutionally valid. Similarly, in *R. v. P.(M.G.)*, Davies J. concluded that these provisions of the *YOA* did not affect the presumption of innocence. In rejecting a section 15 *Charter* argument, the judge noted that sixteen- and seventeen-year-olds do not constitute a "discrete and insular" minority who could claim to be "historical" victims of discrimination. Even if the *Charter* were violated, Davies J. ruled that section 1 of the *Charter* could be invoked, since these provisions were justifiable to protect the public.

Because under the *YCJA* the adult sentence hearing is held only if there is a conviction and the presumptive offence provision in the *YCJA* is similar to that in the *YOA*, the precedents under the former statute which rejected Charter challenges are likely to be highly persuasive under the new Act. The transfer provisions of the *YOA* treated youths fourteen and over differently from those under fourteen who could not be transferred, and the courts consistently rejected arguments that this difference in treatment violated the *Charter*.[119]

---

118 *R. v. C.(R.)*, [1996] A.J. No. 909 (Prov. Ct.).
119 See, for example, *R. v. H.(A.B.)*, above note 9.

I. THE CHALLENGE OF ADULT SANCTIONING

Cases that raise the question of the possibility of adult sentencing are the most challenging for the youth justice system and those who work in it. These cases usually involve very significant injury or death to the victim, and in many cases no sentence can ever be truly restorative or even just. Not infrequently the crimes will seem especially senseless and callous. At least at the time of their arrest, many immature adolescent offenders will seem to be lacking in remorse or understanding of the devastation that they have caused. Nevertheless, given the amenability to rehabilitation and limited maturity of adolescent offenders, even for these most serious and often tragic crimes, young offenders should in general not be held as accountable as adults who may have committed the same crime. Even for a brutal crime, incarceration of an adolescent in an adult prison is unlikely to be an appropriate or socially useful response. Laws governing the imposition of adult sanctions on juvenile offenders have undergone significant change. The *YCJA* replaces the *YOA* pre-adjudication model of transfer hearing with a fairer and more expeditious procedure that requires the decision about whether to impose an adult sentence to be made only after the youth is convicted.[120]

The *YOA* required an explicit balancing of the protection of the public against the rehabilitation of the youth when deciding whether to allow an adult sentence to be imposed. The *YCJA* offers a less balanced approach, with the focus only on the question of whether a youth sentence is "of sufficient length to hold the young person accountable." Very significantly, however, this question is to be decided in the context of the principle of limited accountability of adolescent offenders and of the general principles for sentencing of youthful offenders, with their focus on rehabilitation. Very serious cases that may raise the possibility of an adult sanction are inevitably the most highly publicized cases, and the provisions of the *YOA* that dealt with transfer to adult court were among the most contentious in the Act.

Some of the political rhetoric, from both opposition and government members, at the time when the *YCJA* was introduced in Parliament, suggested that these provisions were part of a "get-tough" approach to serious violent youth offending, leaving the impression that more of these youths would be subjected to adult sanction. It is, however, not clear that there will be a significant increase in the num-

---

120 See Canada, House of Commons Committee on Justice and Legal Affairs, *Reviewing Youth Justice* (1997), 63–65, which endorses this recommendation except for cases within s. 16(1.01).

bers of adolescents subject to adult sanction under the *YCJA*. Indeed, a close reading of the text suggests that Parliament intended to give judges discretion to make individual decisions about youth sentencing, with a general presumption that youth should not be held as accountable as adults for their crimes. The new Act continues an approach based on individualized judicial decision-making, which contrasts with the approach in many American states. In the United States, the decision about whether to impose an adult sanction is usually made by the prosecutor or police, without allowing for judicial decision-making about this critical issue. Further, there is a presumption in Canada that adolescents who receive adult sentences will not be placed in adult correctional facilities until reaching the age of eighteen.

The transfer provisions of the *YOA* were substantially amended in 1992 and 1995, each time with political rhetoric suggesting that politicians intended to "get tough" with serious youth crime, but also with the use of an evolving test that gave judges significant discretion to make individual decisions. It is revealing that, while there were significant procedural and substantive changes in the *YOA* transfer test in 1992 and 1995, transfer rates remained relatively constant after the changes. While there were significant interprovincial variations, with some provinces (e.g., Manitoba) having relatively high transfer rates throughout the period when the *YOA* was in effect, and other provinces (e.g., Saskatchewan) maintaining a relatively low rate, the change in the statutory test had little effect on the relative rates.

A comparison of the relevant provisions of the *YCJA* and *YOA* suggests that it is likely that more young offenders will receive adult sentences under the new statutory regime owing to the lower age and the broader offence range for presumptive offences, and the focus on accountability. However, the total number of youth who commit the presumptive offences that will receive these adult sentences is likely to remain relatively small. Further, the experience with the *YOA* amendments would suggest that provincial policies and programs, and the attitudes of prosecutors and judges, may have more effect on the rate at which adolescents are subject to adult sanction than the words of the relevant statute. Some argue that changes expanding the scope of adult sentencing are necessary to increase social protection.[121] However, available social science research suggests that increasing the number of youths subject to adult sentences does not have any deterrent effect on

---

121 D.M. Bishop, C.E. Frazier, and L.K. Lonn, "The Transfer of Juveniles to Criminal Court: Does It Make a Difference?" (1996) 42 Crime & Delinquency 171.

other offenders or enhance the protection of society. Indeed, there is evidence that adolescents who are placed in adult prison are more likely to reoffend on release than adolescents who have committed the same offences and have the same prior records but are kept in youth custody facilities.[122] This is not surprising when one considers the relative rehabilitative value and inmate subculture in the different types of custody facilities.

FURTHER READINGS

BALA, N., "The 1995 *Young Offenders Act* Amendments: Compromise or Confusion?" (1995) 26 Ottawa L.Rev. 643

CANADA, FEDERAL–PROVINCIAL/TERRITORIAL TASK FORCE ON YOUTH JUSTICE, *A Review of the Young Offenders Act and the Youth Justice System in Canada* (Ottawa: Ministry of Supply and Services, 1996) c. 8

FAGAN, J., ed., *The Changing Borders of Juvenile Justice* (Chicago, IL: University of Chicago Press, 2000)

MANSON, A., *The Law of Sentencing* (Toronto: Irwin Law, 2001)

PLATT, P., *Young Offenders Law in Canada*, 2d ed. (Toronto: Butterworths, 1995) c. 14

SCOTT, S., M. WONG, & B. WEAGANT, *Defending Young Offender Cases*, 2d ed. (Toronto: Carswell, 1997) c. 8

---

122 There is a significant amount of American research that indicates that increasing the transfer rate in a jurisdiction does not produce any reduction in youth offending. Indeed recidivism rates are higher for adolescents who are transferred than for those who remain in the youth system, taking account of the nature of the offence and the prior record. See J. Fagan, above note 92.

CANADIAN YOUTH CRIME IN CONTEXT

by Sanjeev Anand and Nicholas Bala

A. APPROACHES TO YOUTH JUSTICE: CANADA IN AN INTERNATIONAL CONTEXT

Concerns about adolescent irresponsibility, rebellion, and offending date back through history to Roman times and are common in all modern societies.[1] Patterns of offending, however, are not the same in all societies. While some level of youthful deviance is an inevitable part of the adolescent stage of development, a host of complex social, economic, political, cultural, and legal factors interact to influence the nature and extent of youthful offending. Canada is currently going through a period of rapid and profound social change, which is influencing adolescent behaviour as well as societal perceptions of and reactions to that behaviour. Canada has a serious youth crime problem, but contrary to the perceptions of many members of the public, it is not a problem that is spiralling out of control. While the reported number of cases in youth court increased substantially in the decade or so after

---

1 K. Onstad, "What are we Afraid of? The Myth of Youth Crime" (1997) 112:2 Saturday Night 46. See also B. Schissel, *Social Dimensions of Youth Justice* (Toronto: Oxford University Press, 1993) at 10.

the *Young Offenders Act* came into force in 1984,[2] official reports of youth crime seemed to fall slowly fall or at least stabilize in the 1990s. Further, there is still controversy over whether the increase in juvenile crime reports in the late 1980s reflected a change in youth behaviour or police charging practices. It is clear that in the 1990s there was a dramatic increase in media coverage of youth crime in Canada, and politicians gave unprecedented attention to the issue of youth offending and to public demands for tougher laws for young offenders.

Canada has higher rates of youthful violence than many Commonwealth and European countries but also has a much lower rate of serious youth violence than does the United States, especially if the comparison focuses on youth homicide rates. Canada has also come to rely on a formal youth justice system response and youth custody to a greater extent than other countries. This type of response is an expensive and often ineffective way to combat youth crime; its inability to reduce levels of offending seems to create demands for ever more punitive responses, while its expense creates a growing justice-corrections industry that can lobby for ever more resources. While the youth justice and corrections systems have an important role in responding to crimes that have occurred, they play only a small part in making Canada a safer nation.

B. CRIME PREVENTION THROUGH SOCIAL DEVELOPMENT

This book has examined the manner in which youths who have committed offences, or who are suspected of having committed offences, are dealt with under the *Youth Criminal Justice Act*.[3] Although those youths old enough to be brought within the ambit of the Act can often be directed away from further offending if there are appropriate interventions and sufficient resources directed toward them, the most effective youth crime prevention strategies target younger children and their

---

2   *Young Offenders Act*, R.S.C 1985, c. Y-1,enacted as S.C. 1980–81–82–83, c. 110. The Act was also amended in 1985 through *An Act to amend the Young Offenders Act, the Criminal Code, the Penitentiary Act, and the Prisons and Reformatories Act*, R.S.C. 1985 (2d Supp.), c. 24, in force September 1, 1986 and November 1, 1986, and in 1995 through *An Act to amend the Young Offenders Act and the Criminal Code*, S.C. 1995, c. 19.

3   *Youth Criminal Justice Act*, S.C. 2002, c. 1 (royal assent February 19, 2002, to come into force April 1, 2003), often referred to in this book as the *YCJA*.

families. In 2001, the Surgeon General of the United States released a report documenting the magnitude, causes, and prevention of youth violence.[4] The report documented that youths who become violent before age thirteen generally commit a larger number of offences over a longer period of time and their offences tend to be more severe than those of young people whose violent tendencies first manifest themselves later in life. This finding underscores the need for youth crime prevention initiatives that target young children. Some offences, however, are committed by youths who did not display inappropriate behaviour in early childhood, or who are not from high-risk backgrounds. A complete youth crime prevention strategy must address the needs of both children and adolescents. Fortunately, one of the principal conclusions of the U.S. Surgeon General's report was that the window for effective interventions opens early and rarely, if ever, closes.

One effective type of early intervention program is home visitation for families with infants and young children. Home visitation programs involve a visitor coming into the family home to observe the parent-child dynamic and teach child-rearing skills to the parents or provide counselling services to family members. The visitor may be a professional, such as a public health nurse or social worker, or may be a trained member of the community. The Perry Pre-school Program and the Syracuse University Family Development Research Program are American home visitation programs that have demonstrated great promise in achieving long-term reductions of youth crime. The Perry Pre-school Program involves teachers visiting the homes of high-risk children of African-American heritage between the ages of three and five on a weekly basis for two to three years. Children are identified as high-risk if family members have a record of involvement with the criminal justice system or if the family has a history of child welfare intervention.

Similarly, the Syracuse University Family Development Program utilizes social workers who visit the homes of high-risk children of African-American heritage aged newborn to five years on a weekly basis for five years. Researchers found that children who participated in either of these two programs experienced a 75-percent reduction in later arrests compared to a group of comparable high-risk children who

---

4   B.B. Potter, *et al.*, *Youth Violence: A Report of the Surgeon General* (Washington D.C.: Surgeon General of the United States, 2001) (available online at the time of writing at <http://www.surgeongeneral>).

were not enrolled in home visitation programs.[5] Researchers have also analyzed the monetary costs associated with the Perry Pre-school Program. They found that a program expenditure of about US$5,000 per child produced an average savings in criminal justice, social welfare, and other costs of US$29,000 by the time the child reached the age of twenty-seven.[6] Because of the positive results garnered by home visitation programs in the United States, research into such early intervention programs is being conducted in Canada.[7]

Based on the results of the American home visitation studies, it is clear that a social-development response to youth crime has great human and financial advantages. Unfortunately, it is a long-term strategy. Resources invested today will only produce a return over the lifetimes of the children and adolescents who are helped. When Canadian politicians, who face re-election every four or five years, are making resource decisions, the time horizon for a return on a social-development approach to crime prevention may seem too far away to make the investment attractive. Indeed, in times of fiscal restraint, prevention and early intervention programs are among the first to be cut, and resources tend to be concentrated on responding to those who have already committed crimes. Only through public education and political support will society adopt a preventive approach.

Dr. Fraser Mustard, one of Canada's most eminent scholars and social commentators, has warned of the social and economic costs of not focusing resources on children at risk, in particular those children growing up in poverty:

---

5   See J.R. Berreuta-Clement, *et al.*, *Changed Lives: The Effects of the Perry Pre-school Program on Youths Through Age 19* (Ypsilanti, MI: High/Scope Press, 1985) and J.R. Lally, P.L. Mangione, and A.S. Honig, "The Syracuse University Family Development Research Project: Long-Range Impact of an Early Intervention with Low-Income Children and their Families" in D.R. Powell, ed., *Annual Advances in Applied Developmental Psychology: Parent Education as Early Childhood Intervention — Emerging Directions in Theory, Research, and Practice* (Norwood, NJ: Ablex, 1988) vol. 3 at 183.

6   L.J. Schweinhart, *et al.*, *Significant Benefits: The High/Scope Perry Pre-school Study Through Age 27* (Ypsilanti, MI: High/Scope Press, 1993).

7   See R. Peters and C. Russell, "Promoting Development and Preventing Disorder: The Better Beginnings, Better Futures Project" in R. Peters and R. McMahon, eds., *Preventing Childhood Disorders, Substance Abuse and Delinquency* (Thousand Oaks, CA: Sage, 1996) at 19-47 and R. Peters, *et al.*, *Developing Capacity and Competence in the Better Beginnings, Better Futures Communities: Short-Term Findings Report* (Kingston, ON: Better Beginnings, Better Futures Research Coordination Unit Technical Report, 2000).

The higher the degree of income inequality, the harder it is to get economic growth because your society is becoming destabilized. You just can't build an economy with an unstable society because you put too many people in prison and lock them up and shift too many resources into policing and all kinds of things. . . . It's probably how you were handled before the age of three and certainly before the age of six that basically sets your rhythm for adult life. To build a new economy you actually need a high quantity of well educated population. If you degrade children then they're going to be handicapped as adults and it is going to be very difficult to build a new economy and it also leads to juvenile crime and delinquency problems.[8]

Dr. Mustard's message is persuasive. Indeed, while many Canadians are concerned about youth crime and may express frustration with the youth justice system, public opinion polls reveal that a majority of Canadians believe that preventive programs are the most effective deterrent against youth crime.[9]

Roy McMurtry, the Chief Justice of Ontario and a former politician, at the opening of the courts in 2002 recognized the "challenges and tragedies represented by young people at risk in the sense that their environments have the potential to encourage serious criminal activity."[10] Citing a social environment in which school drop-out rates and problems with literacy are increasing, and resources for children are decreasing, as contributing to the rise in the number of cases in the youth courts, McMurtry observed that "the courts, unfortunately, have a relatively little role to play" in reducing levels of youth crime.

Canadian politicians have also shown that they are willing to provide at least symbolic support for a social-development strategy of youth crime prevention. For instance, the first two paragraphs of the Preamble to the YCJA read:

---

8 J. Hall, "Rough Waters Ahead," *Toronto Star*, September 1, 1996: E1 at E2. His views about the importance of societal investment in the early years of childhood are detailed in: M. McCain and F. Mustard, *Reversing the Real Brain Drain, Early Years Study: Final Report* (Toronto, ON: Ministry of Education and Training, 1999).

9 C. Cobb, "Canadians against Police Crackdowns" *Ottawa Citizen*, March 12, 2001: A3.

10 Reported in "Youth Issues Dominate Opening of Courts," *Law Times*, January 14, 2002 at 3 and at the time of writing was available online at <http://www.ontariocourts.on.ca/>

WHEREAS members of society share a responsibility to address the developmental challenges and the needs of young persons and to guide them into adulthood;

WHEREAS communities, families, parents and others concerned with the development of young persons should, through multi-disciplinary approaches, take reasonable steps to prevent youth crime by addressing its underlying causes, to respond to the needs of young persons, and to provide guidance and support to those at risk of committing crimes.

Futher, as was discussed in Chapter 2, the *YCJA* contains a Declaration of Principle that states, "the youth criminal justice system is intended to . . . prevent crime by addressing the circumstances underlying a young person's offending behaviour."[11] Yet, the Act simply recognizes the importance of a strategy that prevents youth crime through social development; it does not compel governments to allocate more resources to such endeavours.

Appeal courts consistently held that the Declaration of Principle of the *YOA* — in particular the statements declaring the importance of youth crime prevention and rehabilitation — did not empower youth court judges to order provincial or territorial governments to pay for specific treatment programs for young offenders.[12] The courts ruled that very specific language must be used before legislation will be construed so as to give the judiciary the power to order governments to pay for specific programs. Because the provisions in the *YCJA* are no more specific than the provisions of the *YOA* concerning the power of youth justice court judges to order government to pay for young offender treatment programs, it seems likely that the case law decided under the old juvenile justice legislative regime will continue to be persuasive under the new legislation.

Although there is no legal requirement to provide preventive programs, the rhetorical statements in the Declaration of Principle and the

---

11   Section 3(1)(a)(i) of the *YCJA*, above note 3. This section of the *YCJA*'s Declaration of Principle and the quoted portions of the Act's Preamble are similar to s. 3(1)(a) of the *YOA*, enacted in 1995, above note 2, s. 1, which stated that "crime prevention is essential to the long-term protection of society and requires addressing the underlying causes of crime by young persons and developing multi-disciplinary approaches to identifying and effectively responding to children and young persons at risk of committing offending behaviour in the future[.]"

12   *R. v. R.J.H.*, [2000] A.J. No. 396 (Alta. C.A.) (QL); and *R. v. L.E.K.*, [2000] S.J. No. 844 (Sask. C.A.) (QL). These cases are more fully discussed in Chapters 2 and 8.

Preamble of the *YCJA* about the importance of addressing the social conditions that contribute to youth crime reflect a political commitment to take action. After the aggressive cuts to government spending in the 1990s, Canadian governments have taken some steps to bolster social-development programming for children and adolescents at risk and their families.

In September 2000, the provincial premiers agreed with the federal government to improve and expand early childhood development programs and services over time, focusing on four key areas: (1) promoting healthy pregnancies, births and early infancy periods; (2) improving parenting and family supports; (3) strengthening early childhood development, learning and care; and (4) strengthening community supports to meet the needs of children and families. In support of this agreement, the federal government committed $2.2 billion over five years for early childhood development programming. This money will be turned over to the provinces under the Canada Health and Social Transfer (the block funding mechanism used to transfer funds from the federal government to the provinces for health, post-secondary education, and social welfare purposes). Nothing, however, compels the provinces to spend the increased transfer payments in a particular manner. While the federal support of early child development programming is laudable, Ottawa's $2.2 billion infusion must be seen in the context of the massive cutbacks in federal transfer payments to the provinces over the previous decade. In many respects, the increase in federal payments for social-development programming is simply returning the provinces to the funding levels they experienced before the cut-backs began.

Intensive early intervention programs cannot eliminate such problems as youth offending, but they do reduce them significantly and produce substantial economic and social returns. Failure to direct sufficient resources to these programs will seriously erode the prospects for a safer, more prosperous Canadian society. The importance of crime prevention and rehabilitation were recognized in reports of the Justice Committee of the House of Commons in 1993 and 1997, and are recognized, at least rhetorically, in the Preamble of the *YCJA*.[13] However, without the expenditure of resources, the articulation of these goals may not be significant. Ontario Provincial Court Judge Ormston,

---

13   Canada, House of Commons, *Twelfth Report of the Standing Committee on Justice and the Solicitor General: Crime Prevention in Canada: Toward a National Strategy* (Ottawa: Ministry of Supply and Services, 1993); Canada, House of Commons, *Thirteenth Report of the Standing Committee on Justice and Legal Affairs: Renewing Youth Justice* (Ottawa: Ministry of Supply and Services, 1997).

speaking at the Convention of Canadian Provincial Court Judges, stated that "if you really want to reduce crime, take the money from one superjail and put it into an early childhood development centre."[14]

C. COMMUNITY ACTION AND POLICING

While a social-development strategy premised on early intervention with children at risk can produce a social environment in which fewer adolescents are committing fewer crimes, there are also more direct steps that communities can take to reduce levels of youth crime. Some of these measures engage schools, families, and adolescents in programs that make it less likely that youth will commit crimes. Other strategies are aimed at improved policing and other security measures that deter criminal behaviour.

Starting in the mid-1990s the federal government began to develop and fund a new national crime prevention program, which is now administered by the National Crime Prevention Centre. Under this program, federal funding of community-based crime prevention initiatives has increased to $30 million per year, including some money directed specifically at the prevention of youth crime.[15] This money is intended to fund demonstration projects, research, and dissemination of information about crime prevention. Increased federal spending on youth crime prevention programming is welcome, but the money allocated pales in comparison to the amount spent by the federal and provincial governments on policing, youth justice courts, and custodial institutions for young offenders.[16] The types of projects that will be funded by the national crime prevention program have significant potential for reducing youth crime.

When then Justice Canada Minister Anne McLellan announced the national crime prevention strategy in June 1998, she did so at the Ottawa-Carleton Police Youth Centre. This centre is a community-based recre-

---

14 K. Makin, "Judges Chafe at Social Worker Role," Globe and Mail, September 21, 2000.

15 S.S. Anand, "Preventing Youth Crime: What Works, What Doesn't, and What It All Means for Canadian Juvenile Justice Policy" (1999) 25 Queen's L.J. 177 at 209–211.

16 In June 1998, the federal government announced that $3.75 million per year would be directed specifically to youth crime prevention, while in 1994–95 federal and provincial spending on youth custody and community service was estimated at $526 million (Canadian Centre for Justice Statistics, Justice Spending in Canada (Ottawa: Statistics Canada 1997) at 6; also Juristat 17:3).

ation program, which the minister described as the kind of pilot program the federal government will be funding in other locales.[17] The centre is a place for adolescents to meet and participate in sporting and other recreational activities. Many people support the establishment of new community-based recreation programs for youth because, in the words of one editorial: "[C]hildren need places to go and things to do. . . . [T]he best way to prevent the majority of juvenile crime . . . is to provide kids with suitable outlets for their energy[.]"[18] Indeed, a number of empirical studies demonstrate that establishing community recreation and cultural programs in high-crime areas does reduce youth crime in those areas.[19] Despite the success of such programs, it must be appreciated that the adolescents who are at the highest risk of serious repeat offending are often the most difficult youths to engage in voluntary recreational programs. In fact, it is futile to attempt to reduce a young offender's recidivism by directly and solely focusing on the youth. For this reason, it is often beneficial to take a broader approach in youth crime prevention by focusing on the social environment and families of youth.

Crime prevention programs established in schools have the potential to significantly increase community safety. From the age of six, children spend a considerable portion of their lives in the school environment. This is also a setting in which offending behaviour is prevalent. The most frequent victims of youth crime are other adolescents and children, with offences frequently occurring at school.[20] Research has linked weak academic performance and poor school attendance with school misbehaviour and later juvenile crime.[21] School-based interventions have the

---

17   J. Tibbetts, "Ottawa to Dole out Crime Prevention Money to Communities," *Canadian Press Wire Service*, June 2, 1998.

18   Editorial, "Crime Prevention, a Home Issue," *Globe and Mail*, June 4, 1998 at A18.

19   See M.B. Jones and D.R. Offord, "Reduction of Anti-social Behaviour in Poor Children by Nonschool Skill Development" (1989) 30 J. Child Psychology and Psychiatry and Allied Disciplines 737; and S.P. Schinke, M.A. Orlandi, and K.C. Cole, "Boys and Girls Clubs in Public Housing Developments: Prevention Services for Youth at Risk" (1992) OSAP Special Issue Journal of Community Psychology 118.

20   See, for example, J. Gomes, *et al.*, *The Extent of Youth Victimization, Crime and Delinquency* (Calgary, AB: Canadian Research Institute for Law and the Family, 2000), reporting that 54 percent of the students in an Alberta study reported being victimized in the past year while at school.

21   See, for example, D.C. Gottfredson, M.D. Sealock, and C.S. Koper, "Delinquency" in R. DiClemente, W. Hansen, and L. Ponton, eds., *Handbook of Adolescent Health Risk Behavior* (New York: Plenum Publishing Corp., 1996) at 34; and J.C. Howell, *et al.*, *A Sourcebook on Serious, Violent, and Chronic Juvenile Offenders* (Newbury Park, CA: Sage Publications, 1995).

potential to be effective in dealing with many of the precursors to youth criminality and ultimately reduce youth crime. Programs that clarify school rules and ensure consistent enforcement of these rules have been shown to reduce youth crime and known risk factors for youth crime.[22] In addition, moving high-risk students into smaller groups within schools has shown promise as a youth crime prevention measure, possibly because these small groups allow for more teacher-student interaction or because they instill a sense of community in the students.[23]

Substance abuse, a known risk factor for delinquency, has been successfully combatted through substance-abuse education programs delivered as part of the curriculum for secondary schools. Researchers have discovered that such programs that employ resistance skills training to teach students about the social influences that encourage substance use and how to effectively resist these pressures are more effective than programs that simply teach students about the risks associated with drug use.[24]

Concerns about crime prevention should be a factor in any decisions about policies and programs for adolescents. Unfortunately, while some governments have adopted policies that are likely to reduce youth crime, others have not. Some provinces, such as Ontario, are moving toward a policy of "zero tolerance" for violence in schools.[25] Such policies are a response to the fact that many Canadians perceive that violence in schools has increased over the past five years and that schools are too lenient in dealing with the problem — although it is far from clear that there is more violence in Canadian schools than there was five or ten years ago.[26] While it is not clear that there is more violence in schools than in the past, steps must be taken to protect students and teachers in school, and it may be necessary to remove some disruptive or violent students from regular school settings. However,

---

22   See, for example, D. Olweus, "Bullying Among Schoolchildren: Intervention and Prevention" in R.D. Peters, R.J. McMahon, and V.L. Quinsey, eds., *Aggression and Violence Throughout the Life Span* (Newbury Park: Sage Publications, 1992) at 100.

23   See D.C. Gottfredson, "Changing School Structures to Benefit High-Risk Youths" in P.E. Leone, ed., *Understanding Troubled and Troubling Youth* (Newbury Park: Sage Publications, 1990) at 246.

24   L.W. Sherman, *et al.*, *Preventing Crime: What Works, What Doesn't, What's Promising* (Washington, D.C.: Office of Justice Programs, U.S. Department of Justice, 1997) at 5–28.

25   V. Galt, "Ontario to Force Schoolchildren to Sing Anthem, Pledge Allegiance to Queen," *Globe and Mail*, April 27, 2000 at A3.

26   R. Mackie, "Schools are More Violent: Poll," *Globe and Mail*, September 8, 1998 at A7.

the students who are engaging in offending behaviour are also those with the greatest need for assistance from the education system. If they are not placed in alternative educational settings where they receive substantial supervision, direction, and support, they are very likely to commit more serious offences in the future.

There is also a nexus between youth unemployment and crime. Those youth who commit crimes tend to be out of the labour force or unemployed; areas in which crime is heavily concentrated tend to have persistently high rates of joblessness.[27] This suggests that youth crime prevention programs should include initiatives aimed at increasing youth employment. In the United States, intensive voluntary residential programs which provide a year-long extensive skills training and general education course to young people who have dropped out of high school coupled with job-placement services after graduation have shown considerable promise at reducing juvenile crime.[28] These types of programs may deliver enough remedial skills training to make up for the educational deficits of the enrolled youth. Moreover, the residential aspect of these programs may serve to re-socialize youth by breaking antisocial group ties, presenting pro-social role models and reducing illegal earnings opportunities.

One community-based program that shows considerable promise for reducing reoffending by high-risk youth with a history of offending is multi-systemic treatment, an intervention focusing on the family and community.[29] The model of multi-systemic treatment that is being tested in Ontario is not imposed by court order but may be made available on a voluntary basis to youth involved in the justice system or considered at high risk of (re)offending by police or probation workers; this type of program could also be imposed by a court order. The premise underlying multi-systemic treatment is that criminal conduct has multiple causes and must be understood as related to characteristics of the individual youth, his or her family, and the community. As a result, although multi-systemic treatment requires that a youth have at least one person who will act as a parent or surrogate, it focuses on more than just the parent-child relationship. Multi-systemic treatment addresses the multiple sources of criminogenic influence, including those in the youth's school, peer group, and neighbourhood.

27 Sherman, et al., above note 24, at 6-1 and 6-5 to 6-6.
28 See C. Mallar, et al., *Third Follow-Up Report of the Evaluation of the Economic Impact of Job Corps* (Princeton, NJ: Mathematica Policy Research Inc., 1982).
29 See, for example, C.M. Borduin, et al., "Multi-systemic Treatment of Serious Juvenile Offenders: Long-Term Prevention of Criminality and Violence" (1995) 63 J. Consulting and Clinical Psychology 569.

Multi-systemic treatment differs from conventional therapy in some important respects. It is a highly individualized, flexible intervention tailored to each situation. Multi-systemic treatment therapists operate in the community (i.e., home, school, etc.) rather than in an office and are available twenty-four hours a day if needed.[30] The average case load is only four to six families per worker, and while the initial multi-systemic treatment involvement may be intense, perhaps requiring daily contact with the therapist, the ultimate goal is to empower the family to take responsibility for making and maintaining gains. Multi-systemic treatment service duration ranges from three to five months, with the average duration of treatment being approximately sixty hours of contact over four months, with the final two to three weeks consisting of less intensive contact to monitor the maintenance of therapeutic gains.

The multi-systemic treatment process necessitates a number of steps. The first step is the identification of problematic behaviours of the youth (e.g., truancy, violence, drug or alcohol-dependency). The parents of the youth are critical to identifying the treatment targets for the multi-systemic treatment intervention. The next step involves an assessment of the factors in the youth's environment that support the continuation of the problem behaviours and the factors that operate as obstacles to their elimination. To perform this assessment, the therapist has to spend time with the youth's peer group, extended family, and teachers. Therapists sometimes find such factors as poor discipline skills on the part of the parents and teachers, peer reinforcement of problem behaviours, and neighbourhood cultures that condone violence or other antisocial behaviour. Finally, the multi-systemic treatment therapist attempts to find positive aspects of the youth and his or her environment that would tend to promote positive change in the young person. With all of this information, the multi-systemic treatment therapist is able to develop a strategy to produce observable results in the youth's problematic behaviour.

To better understand the multi-systemic treatment process it is useful to review an actual case of multi-systemic treatment intervention.[31] One case involved a sixteen-year-old male who had recently returned

---

30   S.W. Henggeler, "Treating Serious Anti-Social Behavior in Youth: The Multi-systemic Therapy Approach" (May 1997) Office of Juvenile Justice and Delinquency Prevention Juvenile Justice Bulletin 1 at 3.

31   This case is taken from the files of the London Family Court Clinic. Full particulars of the case, except for the subject family's name, was found on April 4, 2002 online at <http://www.lfcc.on.ca>.

home from serving his second custodial sentence. The youth entered multi-systemic treatment with the following background: (1) his prior criminal record consisted of numerous property-related offences, one breach of probation, and one robbery offence; (2) he consistently failed to meet his curfew and was very threatening to his mother, with whom he lived; (3) he lived in a neighbourhood where drug and alcohol use was rampant; and (4) he had a poor academic and school attendance record which resulted in his previous school refusing to have him back. Initially, the multi-systemic treatment therapist saw this family three to four times per week with a fair amount of telephone contact. Visits eventually decreased to twice weekly, and for the last month of the four-month intervention the visits were reduced to once a week with reduced telephone contact. The therapist began the intervention by assessing the problem behaviours of the youth and the systemic barriers to changing them. She found that the youth was disrespectful of authority figures, non-compliant, truant, and had substance abuse issues. The youth's mother minimized his academic needs and overestimated his abilities. She frequently gave in to her son's demands and enforced house rules sporadically. The youth was easily influenced by his peers, who also had substance abuse issues. Despite these negative features of the youth and his environment, positive characteristics were also identified; the youth wanted to get a job, and his best friend was a positive influence who did well in school and had not been in conflict with the law.

Using this information, the therapist articulated some targeted goals pertaining to family, school, and peers. The objectives of intervention were for the youth to: (1) follow the rules at home and in the community as evidenced by self-reports, parent observations, and no further police contact; (2) to find a school placement that could meet his academic and behaviour needs as evidenced by regular daily attendance, passing grades, and completed assignments; and (3) increase his association with pro-social peers as evidenced by efforts to obtain a job, completion of outstanding court-ordered community service hours, and a decrease in drug and alcohol use. To attain these objectives, the therapist began working with the mother. To ensure that the mother made time to learn the required parenting skills and was motivated to do so, the therapist provided time-saving services to the mother (e.g., driving the mother to do errands). The mother acquired the tools she needed to discipline her son effectively and enforce house rules. She posted clear house rules and the consequences for breaking them; she engaged in active listening and made use of time-outs. As a result, the youth stopped breaking his curfew and threatening his mother. As well, the mother and the therapist found an appropriate school place-ment to meet the boy's academic and behaviour needs. The mother's weekly calling of her son's new school and regular monitoring of his homework completion led to an improvement in the youth's atten-dance record and grades. The mother also actively encouraged the youth to obtain a part-time job, to refrain from committing further criminal acts, and to complete his outstanding community service hours, which he did. The youth's mother began to give clear and con-sistent messages of non-acceptance concerning the youth's drug and alcohol use. Consequently, the youth reduced his intake of these sub-stances. Finally, to monitor and curtail her son's negative peer associa-tions, the mother kept a telephone list of all of her son's friends and contacted their parents when necessary. The multi-systemic treatment intervention was terminated without the therapist establishing a sub-stantial therapeutic relationship with the youth because the objectives of the intervention were reached through empowering his mother.

Aside from generating positive social outcomes for youths and their families, multi-systemic treatment would appear to be a cost-effective response to actual or potential youth offending. A recent study by the Washington State Institute for Public Policy found that, after subtracting the cost of the intervention itself, multi-systemic treatment saved taxpayers, on average, over US$20,000 per youth in reduced cor-rectional and victims-of-crime costs.[32] The government of Ontario has established a pilot project to evaluate the effectiveness of multi-sys-temic treatment programs in four communities. It is to be hoped that, if this type of multi-systemic community-based approach proves effec-tive in a Canadian context, it will be replicated elsewhere.[33]

The research discussed in Chapter 8 makes clear that a deterrence-based model of youth sentencing will not increase social protection: that is, lengthening the time that youths spend in custody or increas-ing the number of youths dealt with as adult offenders does not reduce levels of offending. Moreover, making custodial institutions more puni-tive does not result in less youth crime. Adolescents who are likely to offend are not giving any thought to getting caught, let alone to the penalties that might be imposed by the justice system. While tougher

---

32   Washington State Institute for Public Policy, "Watching the Bottom Line: Cost-Effective Interventions for Reducing Crime in Washington" (January 1998) 3162 Seminar 5.

33   A description of the project evaluation was online at the time of publication at <www.lfcc.on.ca/>.

sentencing will not reduce youth crime, improved and more visible policing efforts in communities where there are serious youth crime problems can have some effect. Although some adolescents will not be affected by increased police presence, others will be deterred because increased police visibility serves as a reminder of the likelihood of apprehension. Further, an increased police presence can change the social atmosphere in high-crime areas by giving potential victims a greater sense of security and by encouraging positive social values. Commentators believe that much of the decline in American youth homicide rates in the mid-1990s was attributable to increased policing in high-crime areas, although improvements in the economy and other factors may also have played a role.[34]

Canadian police forces are similarly moving toward "community policing" and focusing more attention on preventing youth violence by having an increased presence and involvement with schools and community agencies.[35] For police to be successfully engaged in youth crime prevention and detection, specialized education and training is needed. Many police forces identify officers with the personality and temperament for this type of work, and have specialized youth bureaus or designated officers to do it. Such officers need to have good working relationships with a range of social agencies and the schools.

As discussed in several places in this book, Canada makes more use of a court-based response to juvenile offending than other countries, but there is very substantial variation in provincial charging rates and use of custody. Most of the responsibility for initial charging and entry into the court system rests with the police. Police need to appreciate the limitations of the traditional court-based response, and they also require training and policies that will encourage them to make increased use of alternatives to the formal court process for youth. As discussed in Chapter 5, the *YCJA* places a greater emphasis on the police role in screening and diversion to extrajudicial sanctions programs.

---

34 "New York's Gift to Clinton: A Lower National Crime Rate," *New York Times*, September 1, 1996 at E5.

35 See, for example, *Police Reference Manual on Youth & Violence* (Ottawa, Solicitor General of Canada, 1994). Prompted by a survey of Alberta youth, in which 42 percent of grade nine students admitted to slapping, punching, or kicking someone during the past school year, the Calgary police chief, Christine Silverberg, called for more policing in junior high schools, which cover grades seven, eight, and nine in Alberta (C. Harrington, "Alberta to Beef up Security at Schools to Halt Violence," *Globe and Mail*, May 9, 2000 at A6).

D. RESPONDING THROUGH THE YOUTH JUSTICE SYSTEM

Efforts at prevention have significant potential to reduce levels of youth crime, but there will always be some role for a youth justice system response with the objectives of providing accountability and a sense of justice for victims of crime, as well as a need to provide rehabilitative services. For most young offenders, a formal court-based response is not required and is too intrusive and expensive. The *YCJA* recognizes the need to make more use of expeditious, informal, community-based responses to youthful offending, such as police cautioning and restorative justice approaches that involve community members and victims, as well as offenders and their parents. Because the length of a youth's prior criminal record is the most influential factor in determining whether he or she will receive a custodial or non-custodial disposition,[36] the increased use of extrajudicial measures can play a vital role in reducing Canada's high custodial disposition rates for youth. Through a more robust implementation of extrajudicial measures for young people, their records will contain fewer judicial findings of guilt and youth incarceration rates will likely drop.

Although the *YCJA* carefully specifies that it does not create the legal right to diversion, sections 4 and 5 are intended to encourage police and prosecutors to divert more youth from the formal court-based justice system. Sections 6 to 9 of the *YCJA* do explicitly recognize such options as police and Crown cautioning and family group conferencing. At the same time, the *YCJA* retains the provisions of the *YOA* dealing with alternative measures programs, simply renaming them programs of "extrajudicial sanctions." Further, sections 19 and 35 encourage youth justice court judges to use court-based family group conferencing and, where appropriate, to refer youths to the child welfare system rather than having them dealt with in the youth justice system.

The problem under the *YOA* was that, in many places in Canada, especially outside of Quebec, diversion initiatives were not being used as much as would have been desirable. A combination of restrictive provincial policies and lack of local support resulted only in the limited use of diversion. More community justice and diversionary programs with wider mandates need to be established. Many youth dealt with by the courts under the *YOA* posed little risk to their communities

---

36   P.J. Carrington and S. Moyer, "Factors Affecting Custodial Dispositions under the *YOA*" (1995) 37 Can. J. Crim. 127.

and could have been better dealt with outside the formal youth court system.[37] A response that involves the community has especially great potential for Aboriginal offenders.

The *YCJA's* explicit recognition of different types of diversion programs is intended to increase the use of these programs. However, some of the provinces may be reluctant to establish additional extrajudicial programs unless the federal government provides adequate financial support to assist in their implementation.[38] Even with federal support, each province retains responsibility under the *Constitution Act, 1867,* for the administration of justice and will determine how extensively to make use of extrajudicial measures. The experience under the *YOA* suggests that there will be significant variation among provinces in levels of government support for extrajudicial measures under the *YCJA,* and even within provinces there will be differing levels of community support and use of these alternatives to the court-based youth justice system.

Some young offenders have serious problems that relate to their offending, or they have committed serious offences, for which an informal response is not appropriate. These youth require a more intrusive response and should be identified and targeted for intervention. In Canadian society, an intrusive criminally based response gives rise to the need for respect of legal rights and access to a formal court-based system.

There is clearly a need to research and monitor what types of programs, facilities, and responses are most effective for serious offenders

---

37   Recent research has found that legal sanctions imposed on youths predict further increases in delinquency and decreases in the quality of parenting given to these youths. As a result, the researchers concluded that programs that minimize youth exposure to the formal criminal justice system may ultimately end up reducing recidivism. See E. Stewart, *et al.,* "Beyond the Interactional Relationship between Delinquency and Parenting Practices: The Contribution of Legal Sanctions"(2002) 39 J. of Research in Crime and Delinquency 36 at 52.

38   The federal government initially reimbursed the provinces for fifty percent of the programs and services that were established or expanded as a result of the coming into force of the *YOA* in 1984, above note 2, but federal funding for youth justice and corrections was frozen in 1989 while costs continued to increase. Consequently, the overall federal share of spending on youth justice, including diversion programs, fell to less than one-third of eligible provincial costs. In 1998, when the federal government first introduced the *YCJA,* above note 2, in Parliament, it announced that an extra $400 million would be transferred over the next five to six years to the provinces to help implement the new youth justice regime: Canada, Department of Justice, *A Strategy for the Renewal of Youth Justice* (Ottawa: 1998) at 10. These increased transfer payments still bring the total federal share to less than half the cost of programming for the youth justice system.

or those who do not respond to informal intervention.[39] While there is a need for more knowledge, much is already known. A purely custodial response based on deterrence of the individual youth or other adolescents will not provide social protection. Responses must be individualized to meet specific needs that are relevant to offending. Most serious young offenders have problems that can be ameliorated by working with their family and community. Even those young offenders who have genetic, physiological, or neurological conditions related to their offending behaviour (e.g., fetal alcohol syndrome or a learning disability) will usually benefit from an appropriate response that meets their criminogenic needs. For many young offenders, the most effective dispositions are community-based or at least include a community-based component. As discussed earlier in this chapter, for most young offenders the interventions that are most likely to reduce the risk of reoffending have a significant link to their community, families,[40] schools, and employment opportunities. The ultimate aim of youth justice interventions is for youth to live in their communities without offending, and youth justice court sentences should always be imposed with this objective in mind.

Some new non-custodial sentencing options are available under the *YCJA* that were not under the *YOA*, such as orders compelling young people to attend intensive community support and supervision programs. Further, custodial sentences will include a presumptive period of supervision in the community to monitor and support a youth's reintegration into the community. These are significant changes that should encourage more use of community-based sentences. However, the extent to which community-based sentencing options are available to judges, and the degree to which supervision and support in the community will be meaningful, will depend on the willingness of provincial governments to provide adequate resources. This may be a significant barrier to fully realizing the potential of community-based responses to youth crime under the *YCJA*. Community-based sentences should be

---

39   Much of the research about juvenile corrections programs is lacking in methodological rigor, often failing to utilize such standard research procedures as randomization and control groups. See J. Latimer, "A Meta-Analytic Examination of Youth Delinquency, Family Treatment, and Recidivism" (2001) 43 Can. J. Crim 237–53.

40   Programs that include family intervention are most effective in reducing recidivism for youths under fifteen. See J. Latimer, *ibid*.

designed to hold a young offender accountable, but if a youth has serious problems that are related to the offending, there must also be measures that will address these areas of concern. For a youth justice court to be able to identify and address problems, judges must have adequate information about the youth; this will often require an assessment prepared by a competent professional. Judges also need to have access to appropriate resources for intervention with young offenders.

While too many youths are in custody in Canada, some youths' offending behaviour and related troubles are sufficiently severe that removal from the community is required. However, unless the underlying problems of the individual young offender are identified and addressed in custody, the custodial placement is likely to be an expensive but ineffective exercise. Custody facilities that are relatively small, close to the offender's home, culturally appropriate, and properly resourced have the best chance of effecting positive change in a youth. If a period in custody is required, close supervision and support after a return to the family and community are critical to reduce chances of recidivism.

Some Canadian provinces, including Alberta and Ontario, have started to make use of boot camps or strict-discipline custody facilities. These facilities have a very structured daily program, with elements of military-style discipline. The first boot-camp style youth corrections facilities were instituted in the United States. Their establishment in both Canada and America has been more politically driven rather than based on research pertaining to crime reduction effectiveness. The political motivation for boot camps reflects a get-tough approach, responding to a sense among many members of the public and politicians that the young offenders (and perhaps young people in general) of today require more discipline, and a belief that this type of program will deter youth crime. The research on the success of boot camp programs at reducing recidivism is at best mixed. It is apparent that merely sending youths to a custodial facility with a strict military style of program does not reduce recidivism. However, when a boot-camp style program has substantial educational and counselling components and includes significant community support and monitoring after release, it may have the potential to reduce recidivism, and certainly appears to be no worse than traditional custodial programs.

The age, offending record, physical and emotional condition, and other characteristics of an individual young offender all affect the youth's responsiveness to different types of corrections programs. There is clearly a need for more research into what type of custodial programs are most effective with which types of young offenders.[41] There is also a need for better education and training for lawyers and judges who work in youth justice courts. All professionals who work with adolescent offenders should have at least basic knowledge about adolescent behaviours and needs, as well as training to improve communication with these troubled youths.

E. RECOGNIZING THE LIMITS OF THE LAW

The youth justice system and such legislation as the *YCJA* clearly play an important role in the societal response to youth crime, but the limitations of the legal response must be appreciated. No piece of legislation can, by itself, produce safer communities. Further, no single type of program will by itself have a significant impact on levels of youth offending. To reduce youth crime, a range of different types of strategies, programs and facilities are needed. While additional and more rigorous research in prevention and treatment are required, existing studies already demonstrate that the most effective long-term strategy for reducing levels of youth offending, and for producing adults who are generally mature, law abiding, and productive members of society, requires a long-term investment in social infrastructure and family support, with a particular emphasis on the early childhood and pre-adolescent stages of life.

For adolescents who are at high risk of serious or repeat offending, community-based programs that involve families and schools can also play an important role in diverting youths away from criminal behaviour, while custodial-based rehabilitation is necessary for a relatively small minority of adolescent offenders. A response that emphasizes social investment in children and adolescents, without ignoring the role of the justice system for serious or repeat offenders, is dominant in western European countries. These countries have lower youth crime rates than Canada and there is every reason to believe that such an approach would have similar results here.

Certain types of policing strategies and improvements to community security measures can also help reduce offending behaviour. It is, however, clear that a punitive model of juvenile justice, one that focuses on longer sentences or treating more young offenders as adults, is

---

41   Boot camps, wilderness programs, and other correctional innovations are more fully discussed in Chapter 8.

not the answer. The United States has tried this deterrence-based model of social protection and it has not achieved its objectives. A punitive response may serve the political function of appearing to do something about crime, but it does not lead to a safer society.

The limitations of present Canadian approaches were recognized by the Manitoba Court of Appeal in *R. v. T.(B.)*,[42] a case decided under the *YOA*. The Court upheld a decision to transfer a fifteen-year-old youth charged with armed robbery and attempted murder to the adult justice system. The youth, from a Laotian immigrant family, had a difficult background but was described as "very manageable" while in detention at the Manitoba Youth Centre. A psychologist testified that he was amenable to treatment and that it could be completed in two to three years. Unfortunately, there were no youth custody facilities in Manitoba that had treatment programs that lasted more than a few months, and the court concluded that the youth therefore had to be transferred to adult court. Justice Monnin deeply regretted this result and wrote:

> There is a crying need for a facility which would offer long-term intensive psychotherapy or psychological intervention. . . . That such a facility is not available is no doubt for the oft-cited reason of lack of funds. That is a shortsighted approach to the problems which society is facing today. . . . [The] authorities may wish to consider the desirability of improving the resources available for young people. This is surely the best approach to long term public protection.[43]

Focusing on social development as a primary strategy for reducing youthful offending does not mean that there is no role for the youth justice system. Social development takes a long time and will never be completely successful in eliminating serious youth crime. The law has an important role in terms of social symbolism, support for victims, and the protection of the public. The public rightly expects the legal system to provide justice. Justice requires fair treatment and due process for those charged with offences, but it also includes an important element of accountability to victims and society for those who are found guilty, while recognizing that for adolescents this level of accountability should be lower than for adults. As well, there is a small minority of adolescents who commit such serious offences and who pose such a threat to society that long-term incarceration is justifiable.

---

42   *R. v. T.(B.)*, [1997] M.J. No. 97 (C.A.) (QL).
43   *Ibid.* at paras. 31–32.

When considering issues pertaining to the reform of the youth justice system, it is always important to realistically assess the function and likely effect of any changes. Changes that make the youth justice system more punitive may serve political and symbolic functions for their advocates, but they will be very expensive and not produce a safer society. Reforms most likely to result in increased social protection are those that hold adolescents accountable for their behaviour without disregarding their special needs, development, and capacities for personal change.

It must be recognized that not all young offenders can be rehabilitated or directed away from crime. In some cases a youth will, at least at some points in time, be totally resistant to change. In addition, the prospects for understanding or responding adequately to the complex problems of an individual youth are sometimes low. In some cases, what may have seemed to be an appropriate intervention strategy is tried and fails. However, too often it is not a lack of knowledge or adolescent resistance that results in an inappropriate or unsuccessful response to youth crime; rather, it is a lack of commitment of necessary resources. Canada can certainly do more to help adolescent offenders overcome their problems and become productive law-abiding adults.

FURTHER READINGS

ANAND, S.S., "Preventing Youth Crime: What Works, What Doesn't, and What It All Means for Canadian Juvenile Justice Policy" (1999) 25 Queen's L.J. 177

BALA, N., J.P. HORNICK, M.L. MCCALL, & M.E. CLARKE, *State Responses to Youth Crime: A Consideration of Principles* (Ottawa, ON: Department of Justice, 1994)

CANADA, HOUSE OF COMMONS, *Thirteenth Report of the Standing Committee on Justice and Legal Affairs: Renewing Youth Justice* (Ottawa, ON: Ministry of Supply and Services,1997)

HORNICK, J.P., N. BALA, & J. HUDSON, *The Response to Juvenile Crime in the United States: A Canadian Perspective* (Calgary, AB: Canadian Research Institute for Law and the Family, 1995)

HORNICK, J.P. & S. RODAL, *The Use of Alternatives to Traditional Youth Court: An International Comparison* (Calgary, Canadian Research Institute for Law and the Family, 1995)

NATIONAL CRIME PREVENTION COUNCIL, *Money Well Spent: Investing in Crime Prevention* (Ottawa: 1996)

POTTER, B.B., *et al.*, *Youth Violence: A Report of the Surgeon General* (Washington, D.C.: Surgeon General , 2001)

SCHISSEL, B., *Blaming Children: Youth Crime, Moral Panics, and the Politics of Hate* (Halifax, NS: Fernwood Publishing, 1997)

SHERMAN, L.W., *et al.*, *Preventing Crime: What Works, What Doesn't, What's Promising* (Washington, D.C.: Office of Justice Programs, U.S. Department of Justice, 1997)

SILVERMAN, R.A. & J. CREECHAN, *Delinquency Treatment and Intervention* (Ottawa, ON: Department of Justice, 1995)

VENNARD, J., D. SUGG, & C. HEDDERMAN, *Changing Offenders' Attitudes and Behaviour: What Works?* (London, UK: Home Office Research and Statistics Directorate, 1997)

WADDELL, C.J., J.D. LOMAS, D. OFFORD, & M. GIACOMINI, "Doing Better with 'Bad Kids:' Explaining the Policy-Research Gap with Conduct Disorder in Canada" (2001) 20 Can. J. Community Mental Health 59

GLOSSARY

accountability: the principle of intervention and sentencing that considers the responsibility of offenders for their acts and calls for a response that is proportional to the offence. Section 3(1)(b) of the *YCJA* declares that youths should be held accountable, but generally not to the same extent as adults.

adult: a person eighteen years of age or older. Within the justice system, age is generally established as of the date of the alleged offence.

adult sentence: a youth fourteen years or older who has committed a very serious offence may have an adult sentence imposed. If the Crown wishes to have the youth justice court impose an adult sentence, the youth must receive notice before trial and will have the right to a jury trial. An adult sentence can only be imposed after a youth justice court determines under s. 72 of the *YCJA* that a youth sentence would "not be adequate to hold the young person accountable." If the youth justice court determines that an adult-length sentence is appropriate, it may still decide that a youth will serve a portion of the sentence in a youth custody facility.

adversarial: a system of justice premised on each party having an obligation to present evidence and argument to support its position, though there are special obligations of fairness for the Crown prosecutor. A hallmark of Canada's adversarial system is that the judge, a neutral figure, remains relatively passive during a trial; in the inquisitorial model of justice used in some European countries, judges play a more active role in investigation of the alleged offence and questioning witnesses.

aid and abet: an act by a party to assist or encourage another person in carrying out a crime; *see also* party.

alternative measures: the term used under the *Young Offenders Act* for what is referred to as "extrajudicial sanctions" under the *YCJA*; a program to deal with youth outside the formal court system.

attendance order: a sentence imposed under s. 42(2)(m) of the *YCJA* requiring a youth to attend a particular facility that offers some form of rehabilitative or counselling program, for example, after school.

bail hearing: a court hearing, usually held soon after the initial arrest, at which it is determined whether the accused will be detained in a custody facility pending trial, or released, often with some conditions imposed (e.g., refraining from contacting the complainant). Technically in the *Criminal Code*, a bail hearing is referred to as a "judicial interim release hearing." It is also called a "show cause hearing," since the onus is generally on the Crown to show why the accused should not be released pending trial. "Detention before sentencing" is largely governed by the provisions of Part XVI of the *Criminal Code* which determine whether an accused person should be detained, modified by provisions of ss. 28 to 31 of the *YCJA* which encourage release of youths, allow for release under parental supervision, and require detention separate from adults.

Canadian Charter of Rights and Freedoms: the part of the *Constitution Act, 1982*, that guarantees fundamental rights and freedoms of individuals in their relationship to the government and its agents. The *Charter* can be invoked by a judge to exclude evidence that was obtained by the police in violation of guaranteed rights if its admission in court proceedings "would bring the administration of justice into disrepute." In some cases a *Charter* violation may result in a judicial stay of proceedings. The *Charter* is occasionally used to nullify pieces of legislation, as for example happened to abortion provisions of the *Criminal Code* in 1988.

caution: a form of extrajudicial measure that involves a police officer or a prosecutor meeting with the youth, and often the parents, to warn the youth against further offending, and perhaps make a voluntary referral for counselling or support from some agency. A record is kept of the caution, as a future charge may be dealt with more formally, but record of a caution cannot be used in youth justice court proceedings. There is no technical distinction between a "warning" and a "caution," but the term "warning" refers to an informal caution, given by the investigating officer at the time of apprehension of a youth.

child: for the purposes of the *YCJA* refers to a person under twelve years of age who cannot be charged with a criminal offence. The term "child" is sometimes used more broadly, for example in the *United Nations Convention on the Rights of the Child,* to refer to anyone under eighteen (i.e., not an adult).

circle sentencing (sometimes called a "healing circle"):   a method of sentencing that is sometimes used with Aboriginal offenders (and occasionally with other offenders). Typically the judge, lawyers, police, offender, and parents, victim, and other community members and professionals sit in a circle. Everyone has an opportunity to express their feelings about the offence and offender, and their views about an appropriate sentence. If a consensus emerges about an appropriate sentence, the judge will usually impose this sentence, though the judge is not obliged to do so. There is a body of jurisprudence dealing with the appropriateness of circle sentencing for adults, and section 41 of the *YCJA* recognizes the judicially convened "conference," which includes the possibility of circle sentencing.

complainant: the term used in the *Criminal Code* to refer to the alleged victim of an alleged offence. Although complainants often report to the police, they are not legally obliged to do so. Sometimes allegations of an offence are reported by someone other than the complainant.

community service: This involves the youth doing work for a community agency, municipality, or non-profit organization for a specified number of hours. It may be a sentence imposed by a court or a sanction imposed as extrajudicial measures. If imposed by a youth justice court as a sentence under s. 42(2)(i) of the *YCJA*, it is subject to conditions in s. 54, such as a maximum of 240 hours, and performance is not to interfere with education.

community supervision: When a youth justice court imposes a sentence of "custody and supervision" under s. 42(2)(n) of the *YCJA*, the first two-thirds of the sentence is the "custodial portion," while the last one-third is to be served in the community under a supervision order. The period of supervision is subject to mandatory conditions regarding reporting set out in s. 97(1) of the *YCJA*, and the provincial director may impose other conditions to "promote reintegration of the youth" into the community or "protection of the public." There is an expectation that the youth will have a level of supervision and support from youth workers while living in the community. If there is a "serious" breach of the conditions, the youth may be returned to custody subject to court review under s. 103. Before expiry of the custodial portion of a sentence, a provincial director may apply to a youth justice court under s. 98 for an order that the youth remain in custody rather than being released under community supervision.

conditional sentence: *see* deferred custody and supervision.

conditional supervision: When a youth is sentenced to a period of custody for murder, manslaughter, attempted murder, or aggravated sexual assault under s. 42(2)(o) or s. 42(2)(q) of the *YCJA*, or sentenced for a serious offence to "intensive rehabilitative custody" under s. 42(2)(r), the last portion is to be served under "conditional supervision" in the community. A youth on "conditional supervision" is subject to stricter legal controls than a youth on "community supervision." Prior to the date scheduled for release under conditional supervision, a youth justice court hearing is to be held under s. 105 to determine the conditions of release, or decide that the last portion of the sentence is to be served in custody. Subject to later court review, a provincial director may return a youth on conditional supervision to custody if there are reasonable grounds to believe that a youth has breached or is about to breach a condition of release.

conference: a conference is a group of persons who meet to provide advice for dealing with a youth who has committed an offence. The concept is very flexible, but normally the youth, parents of the youth, community representatives and the victim will be invited to participate. A police officer, a youth justice court judge or the provincial director convenes a conference. A conference may give advice on appropriate extrajudicial measures, conditions for release from pre-trial detention or custody, sentence or sentence review. The conference concept is intended to allow a more restorative and community-based response to be taken to youth offending.

Crown: refers to the government or state, or prosecution team, including the police, in the *YCJA* or adult criminal cases. In some contexts, the term "Crown" refers to the lawyer who represents the Crown in court; this person may also be referred to as the Crown attorney or Crown prosecutor. Occasionally if the Crown is unwilling to prosecute, cases are prosecuted "privately," typically by the victim or a lawyer acting on the victim's behalf, but this is rare in youth justice court as s. 24 of the *YCJA* requires the consent of the Attorney General to a private prosecution.

custody (or custody and supervision):   the most severe sentence that can be imposed by a youth justice court under the *YCJA* is to place a youth in "custody," which requires that the youth reside in a facility. Youth custody facilities must not have any adult offenders confined with youths. Under s. 85 of the *YCJA* provinces must establish at least two different levels of custody; under the *YOA* there were two levels of custody: "open" and "secure." Depending on the province, the provincial director or the youth justice court judge who imposes the sentence determines the level of custody. In all provinces, the provincial director determines the specific facility that a youth will be placed in, and may move the youth from one facility to another within the designated level. There is significant variation in the size and nature of custody facilities both between and within jurisdictions. Youth custody facilities range from separate parts of an adult jail to small treatment-oriented group homes.

deferred custody and supervision: if a youth is convicted of a non-violent offence, instead of placing a youth in custody, a court may impose a sentence that places the youth in the community subject to various conditions, with the provision that if any of the conditions are breached the youth may serve the remainder of the sentence as a custody order. A sentence of "deferred custody and supervision" under s. 42(2)(p) of the *YCJA* is similar to a "conditional sentence" for adults under the *Criminal Code*. The conditions may result in a youth being under "house arrest" in the community, or the conditions may give a youth the freedom to attend school, have employment, obtain counselling, or engage in other activities.

delinquent: the term (juvenile) delinquent was developed in the nineteenth century to distinguish youthful offenders from adult criminals. Delinquents were to be treated in a fashion that promoted their welfare, as reflected in the *Juvenile Delinquents Act*, in force from 1908 to 1984. The term "delinquent" is sometimes used to refer to any youthful offender.

determinate: for a specified period. The *YCJA* and the *YOA* have determinate custodial dispositions, while the *Juvenile Delinquents Act* allowed for indeterminate committal to training school.

deterrence: a principle of sentencing that punishing offenders is intended to cause a reduction in future offending because of a desire to avoid punishment. "Specific deterrence" is concerned with punishment to inhibit reoffending by the person being sentenced, and "general deterrence" uses the punishment of one offender as a warning to other potential offenders of the consequences of offending. Under the *Criminal Code*, s. 718(b) courts may consider both specific and general deterrence in sentencing an adult. There is, however, no mention of deterrence as a sentencing factor in the *YCJA*, and it seems inappropriate for deterrence to be a direct consideration for sentencing a young offender.

disposition: the term used under the *YOA* to refer to a sentence imposed by a youth justice court on a youth who was found guilty of an offence. The *YCJA* uses the term "sentence," which is the same as the term used for adults. The change to the term "sentence" reflects the greater emphasis on accountability in the *YCJA* .

diversion: refers to the idea that some youths who have committed offences should not be dealt with by formal youth court processes, but rather should be diverted from the youth justice system and dealt with informally. Extrajudicial measures, including police and Crown screening as well as extrajudicial sanction programs, give effect to the concept of diversion.

due process: refers to the idea that the legal rights of a person in the criminal or youth justice system are protected, in particular the expectation that an accused person will have access to legal representation and a fair hearing. The trend toward adoption of a due process model of justice in Canada was reflected and reinforced by the adoption of the *Canadian Charter of Rights and Freedoms* in 1982. The *Juvenile Delinquents Act* placed much less emphasis on due process than the YOA. The *YCJA* also maintains a due process model of juvenile justice, although in some respects there is less protection for due process rights under the *YCJA* than there was under the *YOA*.

duty counsel: a lawyer paid by the provincial or territorial legal aid plan who is available to consult and assist those with an immediate need for legal assistance, but who generally does not provide legal representation at a trial. Duty counsel may be at youth justice court; in many places, duty counsel is available to assist those individuals who are at the police station being questioned by police. Most duty counsel schemes involve lawyers from private practice, paid on an hourly basis, although in some places legal aid staff lawyers act as duty counsel.

expert evidence: evidence presented by a person who is accepted by the court as an expert, based on his or her educational qualifications and experience, and who is permitted to express an opinion about technical or complex issues. In youth justice court proceedings, the most commonly admitted expert evidence deals with mental health issues and the likelihood of rehabilitation or future offending. Expert evidence may also be introduced to deal with such forensic issues as DNA evidence. Expert evidence may involve testimony by a witness, or, if not contested, can be presented to the court by a written report.

extrajudicial measures: measures other than judicial proceedings to deal with a youth who is believed to have committed an offence. Extrajudicial measures are encouraged under ss. 4 and 5 of the *YCJA* as an appropriate response for youth who have committed less serious offences. Extrajudicial measures include programs for extrajudicial sanctions, as well as decisions made by police or prosecutors to screen cases and police decisions to informally warn a youth and not charge the youth.

extrajudicial sanctions: a program to deal with youth who have committed offences outside the formal court system established under s. 10 of the YCJA. Some extrajudicial sanction programs operate pre-charge and accept police referrals of youth believed to have committed offences but who are not charged, while other programs are post-charge and accept referrals from the police or Crown of youth who have been charged.

family group conference: a type of "conference" that involves members of the family of the offender, as well as the offender, the victim, and perhaps a few members of the community. The family group conference was first developed as a possible legal response to youth offending in New Zealand.

forensic: to do with the court or investigation. For example, a forensic assessment of a youth may be conducted by a psychiatrist pursuant to s. 34 of the *YCJA* to assist the court in determining whether the youth is mentally competent to stand trial. Forensic investigation by the police covers a range of scientific techniques to apprehend criminals, such as fingerprinting and DNA analysis.

healing circle: *see* circle sentencing

hearsay evidence: a statement made by a person who is not a witness that is repeated by a witness in court in order to establish the truth of a statement. In general, a witness in a criminal trial cannot give "hearsay testimony," that is, testify about something that another person (i.e., the declarant) told the witness. There are a number of exceptions to the hearsay rule, and it is generally not applied at bail or sentencing hearings.

hybrid offence: *see* summary offence.

indeterminate: without specified length. Under the *Juvenile Delinquents Act*, committal to training school was usually indeterminate, with release occurring when correctional officials believed that the delinquent was rehabilitated or had reached adulthood at the age of twenty-one. The *YOA* and *YCJA* have determinate dispositions or sentences of a specified length, subject to early termination through a review process.

indictable offence: *see* summary offence.

information: the sworn statement that a person (usually a police officer) makes before a justice of the peace to commence a criminal prosecution.

intensive support and supervision: a sentence of intensive support and supervision may be imposed under s. 42(2)(l) of the *YCJA*. Although not defined under the Act, this order contemplates a higher level of support and supervision than ordinary probation, while allowing the youth to continue to reside with his or her family. The youth might, for example, be required by the provincial director to attend a particular educational or treatment program every day. A youth justice court may make an order for intensive support and supervision only if the provincial director consents. The maximum duration is two years.

intensive rehabilitative custody and supervision: a sentence of intensive rehabilitative custody and supervision may be imposed under s. 42(2)(r) of the *YCJA* for a youth found guilty of one of the more serious presumptive offences, if the youth is suffering from a mental or emotional disturbance. The youth is placed in a facility that has more rehabilitative resources than an ordinary custody facility, which may be a mental health facility. A youth justice court may make an order for intensive rehabilitative custody only if a "plan of treatment and intensive community supervision" has been developed and the provincial director consents. The sentence includes a period of conditional supervision in the community, which is subject to stricter legal controls than for a youth released on community supervision following the custodial portion of an ordinary order of custody and supervision.

joint submission: *see* plea bargain.

judicial interim release hearing: *see* bail hearing.

judicial notice: a legal doctrine that allows a judge to make a decision based on "common knowledge" without receiving testimony or other evidence on the matter.

justice of the peace: the lowest level of judicial officer, usually not legally trained. Responsibilities are limited in criminal proceedings, especially under the *YCJA*, though a justice of the peace may conduct bail hearings. They have broader responsibilities, especially for adults, under provincial/territorial offence statutes (e.g., the *Highway Traffic Act*) including trials and sentencing.

Juvenile Delinquents Act: legislation enacted in 1908, which placed much less emphasis on legal rights, and had a child welfare-oriented or *parens patriae* philosophy. It was in force until 1984 when replaced by the *YOA*.

non-violent offence: not defined in the Act, but based on the definition of "serious violent offence," it is an offence in the commission of which a young person does not cause or attempt to cause bodily harm. This would typically be a property or drug-related offence. Arguably, a minor assault that results from a scuffle between youths might not be a violent offence, but if there is any bruising or other injury, it would be a "violent offence." There is a presumption for non-violent offences that youths without a prior record will receive extrajudicial measures, and that youths with a prior record will receive a non-custodial sentence.

obiter dicta: [Latin for "things said by the way."] In an appellate court judgment, the *ratio decidendi* (the reason for the decision) is binding on lower courts, but the judicial comments that are *obiter dicta* , which are not necessary for the judgment, are only "persuasive" for future cases.

opinion evidence: it is a general rule of law that witnesses can only testify about what they observed, but an expert witness can express an opinion or draw a conclusion. There are certain matters about which even a lay person can express an opinion in court, such as whether another person was intoxicated or seemed tired.

parens patriae: [Latin for "parent of the country"] refers to the child welfare-oriented philosophy reflected in the *Juvenile Delinquents Act*, with the judge acting as a stern but wise parent.

parent: defined in s. 2(1) of the *YCJA* to include, in respect of a young person, "any person who is under a legal duty to provide for the young person or any person who has, in law or in fact, the custody or control of the young person, but does not include a person who has the custody . . . of the young person by reason only of proceedings" under the *YCJA*. It may include a biological parent, a legal guardian, or a child-protection agency for youths who have been made an agency ward.

party: a person who helps (i.e., aids or abets) another person who is the principal offender to commit an offence. A person is only guilty as a party if he or she has done some act to assist or encourage the principal and has a degree of knowledge or common intention related to the offence. A party is guilty of the same offence as the principal, although the sentence imposed on a party may be influenced by the degree of participation. See *Criminal Code* s. 21.

plea: a declaration by an accused person to the court of "guilty" (i.e., admitting the charge) or "not guilty" (which requires the prosecution to attempt to prove guilt). There are other pleas that are occasionally made, such as guilty but not criminally responsible owing to mental disorder. *Autrefois acquit* or *autrefois convict* refer to pleas that can be made if the accused asserts that he or she cannot be tried for this offence as there was already a trial for the same offence that resulted in acquittal or conviction.

plea bargain: an agreement about the resolution of charges. Usually made between the Crown prosecutor and defence counsel, that the accused will plead guilty to one or more charges if the Crown drops other charges or agrees to make "joint submissions" (i.e., with the defence counsel) about an appropriate sentence. While the judge is not bound to follow a joint submission or plea bargain about a sentence, it is usually adopted by the court. The term "plea resolution discussion" is sometimes used in more formal contexts instead of "plea bargain," to emphasize that the court is not bound by the outcome of these discussions.

preliminary inquiry: a hearing held to determine whether there is sufficient evidence to require an accused person to stand trial for an alleged offence. Adults facing indictable charges under the *Criminal Code* generally have the right to a preliminary inquiry. Generally, youths do not have the right to a preliminary inquiry. However, young persons charged with murder or other very serious offences and may be subject to an adult sentence if convicted, have the right to a preliminary inquiry and jury trial.

pre-sentence report: a report on the personal and family history and present environment of a young person prepared in accordance with s. 40 of the *YCJA* for use at a sentencing hearing. A pre-sentence report (often referred to as a PSR) is prepared by a youth worker or probation officer. A pre-sentence report is usually prepared for a sentencing hearing, but can also be prepared for use at a hearing to determine whether to impose an adult sentence. Under the *YOA*, this type of report was referred to as a pre-disposition report (PDR).

presumptive offence: defined in s. 2(1) of the *YCJA* as murder, attempted murder, manslaughter, or aggravated sexual assault. A presumptive offence also includes a serious violent offence if there have been two previous judicial determinations at earlier *YCJA* proceedings that the youth committed a serious violent offence. If a youth fourteen or older is charged with one of the serious presumptive offences, there is a presumption that there will be an adult sentence imposed if the youth is convicted. Youths facing a charge for a presumptive offence and the possibility of an adult sentence normally have a right to a preliminary inquiry and a jury trial.

private prosecution: *see* Crown.

progress report: a report on the performance of a young offender since the sentence was imposed, prepared for a youth justice court sentence review hearing under s. 94 of the *YCJA*.

probation officer: often colloquially referred to as "P.O." *See* youth worker.

provincial director: a person designated by the provincial or territorial government to carry out a range of duties in connection with the *YCJA*, especially in regard to supervision of young offenders. Each jurisdiction has a significant number of individuals with this designation.

R.: abbreviation for the Latin terms *Regina* (queen) or *Rex* (king) to refer to the prosecution, which in Canada is, in theory, brought in the name of the sovereign. The "R." appears in the style of cause or name of a criminal case, as in *R. v. Boucher* or *R. v. B. (A.)*. The "v." is the abbreviation for "versus" (or against). For adults, the last name of the accused is used in the style of cause. For young persons, because of the prohibition on publication of identity in s. 110 of the *YCJA*, law reports use the first initial of the last name, generally followed in brackets by the first and other initials.

recidivism: refers to repeat offending after being processed by the youth justice system for an earlier offence.

restitution: a court order or extrajudicial measure that requires the offender to compensate the victim of the crime for the loss or injury. It may be a sum of money, or an order that the offender perform some services for the victim, if this is acceptable to the victim.

restorative justice: an approach to justice issues that focuses on reconciliation and repair of harm as opposed to conventional retributive approaches. In *R. v. Gladue*, [1999] 1 S.C.R. 688, Cory and Iacobucci J.J. wrote: "In general terms, restorative justice may be described as an approach to remedying crime in which it is understood that all things are interrelated and that crime disrupts the harmony which existed prior to its occurrence, or at least which it is felt should exist. The appropriateness of a particular sanction is largely determined by the needs of the victims, and the community, as well as the offender. The focus is on the human beings closely affected by the crime" (at 726).

sentencing hearing: the stage of the youth justice court process after a finding of guilt when the judge imposes the sentence. In less serious cases, the sentence may be imposed immediately after a finding of guilt, but in more serious cases the proceedings will be adjourned to allow for the preparation of reports and other evidence for the sentencing hearing.

sentence review: a review of a youth justice court sentence under the *YCJA* ss. 59 or 94, which may result in a reduction in the severity of a sentence. While there can be a youth justice court hearing, if all parties agree, there may simply be a "paper" review by a judge without a formal hearing.

serious violent offence: as defined in *YCJA* s. 2(1) means an offence "in the commission of which a young person causes or attempts to cause serious bodily harm." If two previous serious violent offences have been committed, a youth who commits a third such offence faces the presumption of an adult sentence. An offence is only considered to be a "serious violent offence" if at the time of sentencing a judge makes a judicial determination under s. 42(9) of the *YCJA* that it is a "serious violent offence."

show-cause hearing: so-called because of the onus on the Crown to show cause or reasons why a youth should be detained pending trial. See bail hearing.

status offence: an offence that is only a crime for a person under a particular age, that is having a particular status, namely being a "child" or "juvenile." A number of status offences were created by the *Juvenile Delinquents Act*, such as the vaguely worded "engaging in sexual immorality." The *YOA* and *YCJA* eliminated status offences, although some provinces retain the status offence of truancy, the failure of a child under a specified age, usually sixteen, to attend school without lawful excuse.

stay of proceedings: a suspension of court proceedings without resolution of guilt or innocence. A judge may, for example, stay proceedings if there has been an abuse of process. The Crown sometimes enters a stay, for example, if a youth is referred to extrajudicial sanctions. A proceeding stayed by the Crown may be recommenced within one year (*Criminal Code* s. 579). Sometimes a violation of the *Charter* may result in a judicially ordered stay of proceedings.

summary offence: one of three categories of offences under the *Criminal Code*, the other two being indictable and hybrid. A relatively small number of the least serious offences are summary offences; adults charged with these offences must be tried by a summary process without a jury. Indictable offences are the more serious offences, including robbery and homicide, for which adults may face longer sentences and generally have the right to a preliminary inquiry and a jury trial. Many offences, such as sexual assault and theft, are hybrid, with the Crown having an "election" (or choice) to proceed summarily or by indictment. For adults, if the Crown elects to proceed summarily, the maximum penalty is less, but the accused loses the opportunity to have a preliminary inquiry and jury trial.

By virtue of s. 142 of the *YCJA*, proceedings against young persons in youth justice court generally have a summary process (no jury or preliminary inquiry), although the offences retain their character as summary, hybrid, or indictable for such purposes as arrest. At the time of arrest, a hybrid offence, even for a young person, is regarded as indictable (*Interpretation Act* s. 34(1)(a)). The Crown will often elect in youth justice court to treat a hybrid offence as indictable, for such purposes as having a longer records retention period, as well as the longer maximum sentence (generally six months is the maximum sentence for summary or hybrid offences treated as summary, whereas for hybrid offences treated as indictable under the *YCJA* the maximum is two or three years in custody).

training school: the term most often used when the *Juvenile Delinquents Act* was in force to describe facilities that would today be secure custody. Training schools were also called industrial schools or reformatories.

violent offence: not directly defined in the Act, but based on the definition of "serious violent offence," a violent offence is an offence in the commission of which a young person causes or attempts to cause bodily harm. It is possible for a youth who has committed a violent offence that has not caused serious injury to be dealt with by extrajudicial sanctions or receive a non-custodial sentence.

voir dire: an inquiry in a trial to determine whether a particular piece of evidence, such as a confession of the accused to the police, is admissible in evidence. In a jury trial, the jury will be excluded during a *voir dire*, while, if the judge is sitting alone, as is normally the case in youth justice court, the judge must not consider any evidence heard at the *voir dire* if it is ruled inadmissible. The expression is derived from *vrai dire* (to speak the truth) in Norman French, the language used in mediaeval English courts.

warning: *see* caution.

Young Offenders Act (YOA):   the federal legislation in effect from 1984 to 2003 that established the legal regime for dealing with youths aged twelve through seventeen, who were alleged to have committed criminal offences or who have been convicted of an offence. The YOA replaced the *Juvenile Delinquents Act*, and was in turn replaced by the *Youth Criminal Justice Act*.

young offender: a young person (twelve through seventeen as of the date of the alleged offence) who has been found guilty of an offence.

young person: a person who is or, in the absence of evidence to the contrary, appears to be twelve years of age or older but under eighteen years of age. Section 2(1) of the *YCJA* specifies that "if the context requires [young person] includes any person who is charged . . . with having committed an offence while he was a young person or is found guilty of an offence under this Act." That is, even if a person has passed his or her eighteenth birthday, for most purposes, the person alleged to have committed an offence while a young person will continue to be treated under the *YCJA* for purposes of prosecution, sentencing, and sentence review.

Youth Criminal Justice Act (YCJA):   the federal statute that is replacing the *Young Offenders Act*. It deals with youths aged twelve through seventeen who are alleged to have committed criminal offences or who have been convicted of an offence.

youth justice court: the court designated by the provincial or territorial government as having jurisdiction over cases prosecuted pursuant to the *YCJA*. In most jurisdictions the youth justice court is at the provincial or territorial court level. If a youth is charged with murder or is facing an adult sentence, the "youth justice court" may be presided over by a Superior Court judge, sitting with or without a jury. The *YOA* used the term "youth court," and the term is likely to remain in colloquial use.

youth worker: a person appointed by the provincial or territorial government to perform a range of functions in relation to the youth justice system, including preparation of s. 40 pre-sentence reports, supervision of youths on probation, and working with youths after release from custody on community or conditional supervision. In some jurisdictions, youth workers (also called probation officers) have case-loads of only youths; in others, they may work with both adult and youth offenders. In some places, youth workers also do social work with non-offender populations.

TABLE OF CASES

INDEX

ABOUT THE AUTHOR

Nicholas Bala is a Professor at the Faculty of Law at Queen's University and one of Canada's leading experts in the field of family law and children's law. He has published extensively on such topics as legal issues related to child witnesses and child abuse, young offenders, custody and access following divorce, child support, the legal definition of the family and leagl responses to family violence. His work is often cited by the courts, including the Supreme Court of Canada. He has done considerable consulting on law reform issues in the family law field for federal and provincial governments as well as for aboriginal organizations, and has appeared as a witness at a number of Parliamentary hearings. He is also the author of *Young Offenders Law* (1997) in Irwin Law's Essentials of Canadian Law series.